# Fact and Method

*Explanation, Confirmation and*
*Reality in the Natural*
*and the Social Sciences*

R I C H A R D   W.   M I L L E R

PRINCETON UNIVERSITY PRESS

Copyright © 1987 by Princeton University Press
Published by Princeton University Press, 41 William Street,
Princeton, New Jersey 08540
In the United Kingdom: Princeton University Press,
Guildford, Surrey

*All Rights Reserved*
Library of Congress Cataloging in Publication Data will be
found on the last printed page of this book

ISBN 0-691-07318-X  (cloth)
          02045-0  (pbk.)

This book has been composed in Linotron Baskerville

Clothbound editions of Princeton University Press books
are printed on acid-free paper, and binding materials are
chosen for strength and durability.
Paperbacks, although satisfactory for personal collections,
are not usually suitable for library rebinding

Printed in the United States of America
by Princeton University Press,
Princeton, New Jersey

# FACT AND METHOD

*For Steve*

# CONTENTS

# PART TWO: Confirmation

# PART THREE: Realism

## ACKNOWLEDGMENTS

A Rockefeller Foundation Humanities Fellowship (1979-80), a National Endowment for the Humanities Summer Stipend (1984) and a National Endowment for the Humanities Fellowship (1984) helped me in writing this book. My thanks to Peggy for years of patient support.

# FACT AND METHOD

# Replacing Positivism

FEW people, these days, call themselves "positivists." In fact, I have never met a self-proclaimed positivist. Yet in a broad sense of the term, positivism remains the dominant philosophy of science. And the most urgent task in the philosophy of science is to develop a replacement for positivism that provides the guidance, philosophical and practical, that positivism promised. Describing, defending, and starting to use such an alternative is the goal of this book.

In the broad sense, positivism is the assumption that the most important methodological notions—for example, explanation, confirmation and the identification of one kind of entity with another—can each be applied according to rules that are the same for all sciences and historical periods, that are valid a priori, and that only require knowledge of the internal content of the propositions involved for their effective application. Positivism, in this sense, is an expression of the worship of generality that has dominated philosophy at least since Kant: the idea that absolutely general, a priori rules determine what is reasonable. If this worship has distorted our view of science, as I will argue, it may have distorted our views of ethics, principled social choice and much else besides.

In the first half of this century, when Russell, Schlick, Hempel, Carnap and many others made positivism a source of major innovations, the general, a priori rules of method were supposed to be concerned with logical form. Thus, one great question of methodology—"When does a set of hypotheses, if true, explain why something happened?"—was supposed to be resolved by analyzing the hypotheses and the event statement to see whether the former consisted of empirical general laws and statements of initial conditions, together entailing the latter. The other dominant question in the philosophy of science—"When does a body of data confirm a given hypothesis?"—was to be answered by providing general rules, valid in every field, describing appropriate patterns of entailment connecting hypothesis with data.

Difficulties of this classical positivism, which often centered on vivid and recalcitrant counter-examples, have recently produced new versions of positivism, adding to the raw material of concepts and theories that the rules of method use. In addition to the categories and theories of deductive logic, counterfactual conditionals and the theory of probability are now commonly employed. These devices were sometimes introduced by important critics of classical, "logical positivism." Yet the underlying approach is still entirely positivist in the broad sense, concerned to resolve methodological questions through a priori rules, valid in all fields and at all times. I will be arguing that the newer styles of positivism are as wrong as the old style, and in the same ways. My strategy will be to begin by describing in detail the content and the rationale of the best-hedged, best-defended versions of classical positivism. The omissions and distortions that turn out to be most fundamental, in those older views, will reappear, precisely, in the new versions. That classical positivism was often attacked by throwing isolated counter-examples at inferior versions of it, not by criticizing the rationale for the best version, is one cause of the long survival of positivism in the broad sense.

## A QUANDARY FOR NON-POSITIVISTS

At least as a working hypothesis, positivism is the most common philosophical outlook on science. Yet there are current alternatives to it with extremely broad appeal. Often, they remove beyond the bounds of rational criticism options that a positivist would judge and find wanting, using methodological rules.

In present-day philosophy of science, anti-realists, i.e., those who reject claims to objective truth for scientific theories, often challenge positivist accounts of confirmation. For typical anti-realists today, the acceptance of theories is always relative to a framework of beliefs, and the actual shared framework of current theoretical science is no more reasonable as a guide to truth than rival frameworks, dictating contrary conclusions. Not only were positivists wrong to suppose that general a priori rules single out a theory as the one most likely to be true, in light of the data. Disbelief in the entities theories describe is always one reasonable option.

For the practice of scientific inquiry, the debate over positivism has been most urgent in the social sciences, where hypotheses are most apt to be judged on purely methodological grounds. Here, another major alternative to positivism has broad appeal. While many social scientists have hoped that positivist rules would give their work the certainty and clarity they think they see in the natural sciences, many others have been frustrated by the continual tendency of those rules to exclude interesting and plausible hypotheses as pseudo-explanations not subject to real scientific tests. The result has been the continued vitality of hermeneutic approaches, basing the study of human conduct on distinctive forms of explanation and justification, immune from criticism by the standards dominating the natural sciences. For example, in Habermas' critical theory, positivist rules properly govern the natural sciences, but would subvert the human sciences, where we should use distinctive capacities for empathy and "self-reflection" to pursue distinctive goals of communication and enlightenment.

Of the many who find positivism intolerably restrictive, many, if not most, find these alternatives to it unbelievable. Even if the bounds of reason in the natural sciences are not described by general, a priori rules, agnosticism about molecules and electrons no longer seems a reasonable option. Even if many interesting social hypotheses deserve to be defended against positivist criticism, social science in the hermeneutic style often seems to be little more than the self-expression, interesting or dull, of the investigator. Whether certain feelings of empathy or enlightenment are real sources of insight seems a subject for scientific argument, not an unquestionable premise for inquiries utterly different from natural-scientific investigations. Similarly, the hermeneutic assumption that social processes are governed by the subjective factors that empathy and introspection might reveal seems an appropriate topic for scientific inquiry, not a defining principle of a special logic of inquiry.

In short, many people are in a quandary, seeking to give scientific justification and criticism something like the scope they have in positivism, but also rejecting the constraints of positivist rules of method. In the abstract, there is no difficulty in this view of scientific reason. Justification and criticism in thoughtful, explicit science seem to employ the same tactics as honest lawyers' arguments, mutually respectful political arguments or intelligent everyday disputes of any kind. And these less technical arguments do not appear to be governed by positivist rules of method. Still, in practice, only a definite alternative account of scientific reasoning will end the worry that everything (or, at least, anti-realist and hermeneutic things) is permitted, if methodological questions cannot be resolved by the effective application of general, a priori rules.

## EXPLANATION

I will develop alternatives to positivist accounts of explanation and of confirmation, and then use these replacements to describe and justify a new assessment of scientific realism. The slogan version of my alternative approach to explanation is: an explanation is an adequate description of the underlying causes bringing about a phenomenon. Adequacy, here, is determined by rules that are specific to particular fields at particular times. The specificity of the rules is not just a feature of adequacy for given special purposes, but characterizes all adequacy that is relevant to scientific explanation. The rules are judged by their efficacy for the respective fields at the respective times—which makes adequacy far more contingent, pragmatic and field-specific than positivists allowed, but no less rationally determinable.

As for causation itself, it has no informative and general analysis. Even recent counterfactual analyses of causation only fit a narrow class of simplified causal systems; this class is not significant for most tasks of explanation, and it can only be described by using the notion of a cause. The concept of a cause, like the concept of a number or of a work of art, centers on a diverse but stable core of cases: impact's causing motion, pain's causing crying, and so on through the paradigmatically banal examples (compare counting and measuring numbers, as the core for the concept of a number, or representational easel paintings and statues, as part of the core for "work of art"). Further development from the core outward is governed by science, not by a general analysis. The basic repertoire of causes is properly expanded when a phenomenon ought to have some cause but ascription from the old repertoire has become unreasonable (compare the expansion of the repertoire of numbers when a task of calculation, resembling old ones, cannot be accomplished by old means). In this way, standards of what could be a cause, and, with them, standards of what could be an explanation, evolve as science evolves. Whether something could be a cause, so that its description could explain, is established, in the final analysis, by specific empirical arguments over proposed extensions from the elementary core.

Finally, explanatory causes must be underlying, must not be too superficial to explain. As I develop it, this requirement of causal depth marks off one of several ways that positivist methodology is less restrictive than it should be, despite its excessive strictness elsewhere.

After defending this causal model of explanation, my main concern will be to apply it to the standard problems in the philosophy of the social sciences: value freedom, methodological individualism, the status of functional explanation, and the relation between natural-scientific inquiry and inquiry into human conduct. While positivism took its paradigms of reason from the physical sciences, it has real power, above all, in the social sciences, supporting the dismissal of many intriguing hypotheses as pseudo-explanations, unworthy of empirical investigation.

## CONFIRMATION

The theory of confirmation that I will develop is causal, comparative and historical. Confirmation, on this view, is fair causal comparison: a hypothesis is confirmed if there is a fair argument that its approximate truth, and the basic falsehood of current rivals, is entailed by the best causal account of the history of data-gathering and theorizing so far. The relevant notion of a causal account is that specified in the theory of explanation in the first third of this book. Otherwise, a positivist account of explanation might reduce this proposal about confirmation to a variant of traditional positivist views. Which account of the data is best is determined by a framework of substantive background principles, more specific, causal and contingent than positivists suppose. The requirement of fair comparison is, above all, the requirement that a rival not be dismissed using a principle absent from the framework of its partisans. In fact, there are usually enough shared principles, the levers of comparison, for confirmation to take place. As usual, the deep theory of scientific method that I defend duplicates superficial appearances of actual scientific practice. After all, actual empirical justifications in science look like efforts to show, with all fairness to rival approaches, that a favored hypothesis does better than its rivals at explaining why relevant facts are as they are. To beg the question by simply assuming that partisans of a rival hypothesis rely on false background beliefs is to do too little. To try to vindicate a hypothesis from the perspective of every possible approach to a field, regardless of whether anyone actually takes it, is to attempt more than anyone does in practice. So far as confirmation is concerned, this limitation on relevant alternatives is valid in the final analysis, not just for practical purposes.

The dependence on actual rivalries and frameworks, and on the actual pattern of the evolution of hypotheses and data makes the existence of confirmation a historical matter in ways that classical positivists denied. The further requirement that confirmation be comparative and causal is another one of the constraints that classical positivists, for all their strictness, failed to impose. Many current revisions of positivism appear to account for the relevant phenomena of scientific comparison by employing Bayes' Theorem, a general, a priori principle derived from probability theory. I will argue that this appearance is an illusion. Granted, most empirical arguments can be paraphrased in talk of what is likely on the evidence or on a hypothesis in question. But good empirical reasoning is blocked, or fallacies are endorsed, when this talk of likelihoods is regulated by an interpretation and extension of the probability calculus.

## REALISM

The most important dispute among philosophers of science, right now, is over scientific realism, roughly speaking, the claim that scientific theories are often approximately true descriptions of actual unobservable entities. Both leading realists and leading anti-realists are among the most influential critics of positivist theories of explanation and confirmation. Yet the latest stage in the realism dispute is haunted by positivism, haunted from its start in the 1960s to its present non-conclusion. For this reason, the anti-positivist accounts of confirmation and explanation, in the first two-thirds of this book, will play an important role in the final chapters, which attempt to clarify and to settle the current issue of realism.

Any version of the question of scientific realism that is worthy of the label must be concerned with whether we are in a position to claim that descriptions of unobservables are approximately true. Since this is a question about justification, it is not surprising that different versions of this question turn out to be at issue as the consensus about the nature of scientific justification changes. Thus, in the golden age of classical positivism, deductivist theories of confirmation, in which testing was a matter of entailing observations, constantly suggested a strong form of anti-realism, even to philosophers who wished such conclusions were wrong. This anti-realist implication was that a hypothesis is confirmable only to the extent that it is a statement about actual or possible contents of observations. Every attempt to avoid this conclusion within a classical positivist theory of confirmation opened the floodgates, and admitted countless absurdities as confirmed. Thus, the anti-realism to which Russell and Carnap were, at times, attracted was a construal of empirical justification as solely supporting claims as to actual or possible observations, and a corresponding interpretation of well-established sciences as really, in the final analysis, hypotheses that if certain kinds of observations occurred certain others would follow.

This cannot be the issue in the current dispute over realism and anti-realism, at least not if the dispute is worth taking seriously. These days, leading anti-realists do not appeal to any definite theory of confirmation. Indeed, van Fraassen, Putnam and Feyerabend are at once, leading anti-realists and important critics of the classical positivist approach to confirmation. Certainly, anti-realists now reject efforts to interpret all scientific propositions as about observables. Electron theory, in their view, is about electrons in the final analysis. So what is there to dispute?

I will use the theory of confirmation as fair causal comparison to clarify the current issue, and to start to resolve it. Confirmation (I will have tried to show) is the establishment of a certain kind of causal account as best, in an argument that is fair to all current frameworks of background hypotheses; such an argument need not be fair to all possible frameworks. But even if the question of confirmation is restricted to actual disputes, a further question can be asked: when a hypothesis about unobservables is justified in all frameworks that are actually employed, is there always a possible alternative framework, composed of principles which it would be reasonable to believe in the face of current data, supporting the conclusion that the standard statement about unobservables is not even approximately true? To answer "yes" is to be an anti-realist. More precisely, this is the one version of anti-realism that has any rational appeal once positivist theories of confirmation are rejected. And it is, on a close reading, the basic position of most present-day anti-realists.

This anti-realist philosophy of tolerance is hard to accept. Indeed, for many of us it is incredible. Can disbelief in molecules be a reasonable option in the late twentieth century? On the other hand, realists have not yet vindicated any standard belief about unobservables as the only reasonable option at present, or so I shall argue. The realism debate has stalled. The barrier to progress is the tendency of both sides to be guided, at crucial junctures, by the positivist tradition they explicitly reject.

When anti-realists argue for tolerance in questions of truth, they usually assume that positivist rules of method are adequate standards for reasonable theory choice. They point to the fact that these rules only make choice determinate by appealing to simplicity or similar virtues. And they note, quite properly, that these virtues need not be taken to be signs of truth. It will be important to my arguments against anti-realism that the initial assumption is too kind: positivism fails as an account of rational theory choice (truth to one side), if the middle chapters of this book are right.

When the most important and creative realists try to show that some standard beliefs about unobservables are the only reasonable alternatives at present, they are influenced in a different but related way by the positivist worship of generality. The vindication of theoretical science is expected to come from an inference based on a general principle according to which it is unreasonable not to accept the best explanation of a certain general pattern of success. When a science displays this general pattern of successful use of theories (for example, the uses of intra-theoretic plausibility that Boyd describes with great sophistication and force), a failure to believe in the approximate truth of the theories is supposed to be an unreasonable acceptance of miracles or cosmic coincidences. I will argue that this residual faith in the power of general principles of inference is undeserved. In all of the current defenses of realism, either the principle of inference is wrong, i.e., it is reasonable to reject the realist explanation of the pattern of success in question; the principle is vacuous, i.e., the use of theories does not make the contribution that the realist seeks to explain.

So far, anti-realism is unbelievable (for many of us) while realism is unsupported. However, the theory of confirmation as causal comparison, and the account of causal explanation it presupposes, suggest a very different strategy for defending realism. It might be that relevantly deviant frameworks would sometimes be unreasonable because an argument for the standard unobservables rests on relatively humble, topic-specific principles, that no one with our actual experiences can deny except on pain of being unreasonable. More precisely, the right sort of argument would combine these well-hedged truisms with the very surprising data that has been so important in the best-established theoretical sciences. So belief is only dictated by reason given the data we have—which is all that modern realists have ever supposed.

Some of the banalities that figure in important arguments for unobservables are these topic-specific principles, describing prima facie reasons and corresponding burdens of proof: if a non-living thing is in constant erratic motion, that is reason to suppose that it is being acted on; if something makes the barely perceptible clear and distinct, it is apt to be revealing what is really present when it makes the invisible visible. After describing in more detail the content of these principles and their role in distinguishing reasonable from unreasonable belief, I will use them to defend realism in the only way now available. The right defense is not a grand argument from a general pattern of success but a series of piecemeal defenses, displaying the power of specific arguments that have actually been compelling for modern scientists, by showing how they rely on appropriate topic-specific truisms as their essential framework. Two important case studies will be the Einstein-Perrin argument for molecules (as opposed to Cannizzaro's earlier, wonderful argument from the best explanation, which made no impact on anti-realism and did not deserve to), and the argument by which Leeuwenhoek, Hooke and others established in a matter of months that a drop of pond water teems with invisible living things.

I will end this book with a defense of a realist interpretation of quantum physics, a field that has a special status in debates about scientific realism and about scientific method in general. Experimental findings and widely used physical principles seem to dictate an interpretation according to which quantum physics solely describes statistics for measurements to occur in various experimental situations. If so, modern physics shows that there is a field in which confirmation does not involve arguments about underlying causes; and (what is much stranger) it shows that the small-scale description of all material processes refers only to observations. To the contrary, I will argue, the enormous achievements of quantum physics can only be preserved through a realist interpretation in which properties of whole systems, described by means that are radically different from those of classical physics, wholly govern the propensities for dynamical events to occur. The feasibility of this interpretation depends on the conceptions of cause and of confirmation that I will develop. These replacements for positivism are supported by their fulfillment of needs of a field that is supposed to be the stronghold of positivism. As for the modern anti-realist's question of whether reason and evidence dictate literal belief in realist quantum physics, that question turns out to have different answers for different micro-entities, all of them usefully posited—just as a topic-specific notion of reason would lead one to expect.

## CHANGING TRADITIONS

By analyzing causation in terms of a central cluster of diverse and specific processes, by connecting hypothesis and data through particular frameworks of causal beliefs and by basing dictates of reason and evidence on topic-specific principles, this book attempts to show that philosophers respect generality too much. At least since Kant, the dominant tendency has been to take rationality to be determined by absolutely general rules, valid a priori. The rational person need only use these rules to interpret observations, intuitions and desires. Positivism is the worship of generality in the philosophy of science.

There is a tradition that criticizes the thirst for the general in philosophy, and emphasizes the regulating role of specific, often quite non-technical beliefs. Wittgenstein, Moore and Austin are among its leading figures. The survival of positivism has been encouraged by the isolation of this so-called "ordinary language" tradition from the main trends in the philosophy of science. Both sides have often been at fault, the one for dogmatic denials that technical science could fundamentally challenge everyday beliefs, the other for supposing that genuine achievements in the philosophy of science must have the formal look of most accomplishments in mathematics or the physical sciences. The gap needs to be bridged. This need is suggested not just by current problems of both styles of philosophy, but by the most fundamental achievements in the natural sciences themselves. From Galileo on, these achievements have combined deep non-formal reflections on the most sensible way out of crises in the sciences with formal ingenuity in devising means to compare a new outlook with the old ones.

THIS book is addressed to the problems of philosophers of science, of natural scientists and social scientists coping with methodological constraints, and of people who wonder what the triumphs of science can tell them about the nature and limits of rationality. As a result, I will sometimes describe in detail what is familiar to some readers, but known to others not at all or in caricature only. The covering-law model of explanation, the derivation of Bayes' Theorem, and Einstein's path to relativity theory are a few examples. I apologize, but not very much. Time and again it turns out that false leads would not have been pursued if more attention had been paid to the kind of question a brash freshman might ask: "Is geology a general theory?" "Why do we need laws in order to predict?" "Aren't we wrong to expect the future to be like the past?" "How can Bayes' Theorem regulate testing when it doesn't say anything about belief revision, or even time?" "Why are all these cases of empirically equivalent theories taken from physics?" Perhaps it is time to go more slowly, in the philosophy of science.

# PART ONE

# Explanation

# CHAPTER ONE

# Explanation: The Covering-Law Model

THE dispute over the nature of explanation is one of the most heated in the philosophy of science. Yet, for all the heat, a certain consensus reigns.

Both the fierceness of the debate and the depth of the consensus are exemplified in the rivalry between the positivist and the hermeneutic accounts, a rivalry which, in essence, has gone on for over a century. In rough outline, the positivist analysis makes explanation, whether in the social sciences or the natural sciences, a matter of subsumption under general laws. A valid explanation of an event must describe general characteristics of the situation leading up to the event and appeal to general empirical laws dictating that when such characteristics are realized, an event of that kind always (or almost always) follows. In the hermeneutic tradition, this so-called covering-law model is accepted as an accurate analysis of natural-scientific explanation. The crucial positivist mistake is said to be its extension of the model to the realm of social explanation. There, a distinctive human capacity to understand the words, acts and symbols of others yields explanations which violate the demand for general laws. For partisans of the covering-law model, proposed explanations which do not seek to fit it are, not just invalid or incomplete, but pseudo-explanations, mysticism unworthy of scientific consideration. For many hermeneutic theorists, this positivist demand is itself a spiritual disease, a worship of natural science that serves a social interest in manipulating people as if they were things.[1]

[1] Here are two characteristic indictments, one from each side. C. G. Hempel, "The Function of General Laws in History" (originally, 1942) in his *Aspects of Scientific Explanation* (New York, 1965), p. 240: "Much of the appeal of the 'method of understanding' seems to be due to the fact that it tends to present the phenomena in question as somehow 'plausible' or 'natural' to us. . . . But the kind of 'understanding' thus conveyed must be clearly separated from scientific understanding. . . . [T]he criterion of its soundness is not whether it appeals to our imagination, . . . or is otherwise made to appear plausible—all this may occur in pseudo-explanations as well—but exclusively whether it rests on empirically well-confirmed assertions concerning initial conditions and general laws." Juergen Habermas, *Knowledge and Human Interests* (Boston, 1971), pp. 308f., 134: "In the *empirical analytic sciences* . . . [t]heories comprise hypothetico-deductive connections of propositions, which permit the deduc-

Broad agreement on fundamental issues underlies this bitter dispute. Apart from explicit agreement on the adequacy of the covering-law model for the natural sciences, this controversy embodies two tacit shared assumptions. In each approach, once we know that a set of propositions are true, we can tell whether they constitute an adequate explanation without committing ourselves to further controversial empirical claims. In the covering-law model, we need only analyze the logical relations between the hypothesis and the statement of what is to be explained. In the hermeneutic approach, we mull the hypothesis over in appropriate ways, to determine whether it satisfies relevant faculties and interests. In addition, both approaches seek to describe extremely general and unchanging standards by which we can judge whether propositions, if true, are explanatory. These standards hold for all scientific explanation (the covering-law model) or correspond to a few vast types under which all explanations fall (hermeneutic theory). Unlike more specific standards, they do not become obsolete as particular sciences change.

Modifications of each approach have often been proposed. But the shared assumptions are left untouched. Thus, the covering-law model has often been reshaped to allow, or require, deductions of a different logical pattern. Lewis' and Mackie's proposals, in which the empirical laws impose necessary and sufficient conditions, and Railton's and Cartwright's probabilistic alternatives are some recent, ingenious examples. In every case, the criterion of adequacy is still general and a priori. In Dray's important modification of traditional hermeneutic theory, explanations describing agents' reasons are valid departures from the covering-law model, even if they are not the product of distinctive capacities for understanding. Like traditional hermeneutics, though, his account still offers two means of determining when hypotheses explain (if true), means that are valid a priori and that jointly embrace all fields.[2]

---

tion of lawlike hypotheses with empirical content. The latter can be interpreted as statements about the covariance of observable events. . . . [T]heories of the empirical sciences disclose reality subject to the constitutive interest in the possible securing and expansion, through information, of feedback-monitored action. This is the cognitive interest in technical control over objectified processes. . . . The *historical hermeneutic sciences* gain knowledge in a different methodological framework. Here the meaning of the validity of propositions is not constituted in the frame of reference of technical control. . . . Access to the facts is provided by the understanding of meaning, not observation." "The interest [in possible technical control, of the natural sciences] . . . when realized, leads not to happiness but to success."

[2] See David Lewis, "Causation" (1973) in Ernest Sosa, ed., *Causation and Condition-*

An even more striking expression of the power of the demand for a comprehensive, a priori standard is its influence on some of the most fundamental attacks on positivism. Scriven's extensive writings on the covering-law model were an early and fertile source of important counterexamples. Yet his own account of valid explanations that violate the model bases them on "truistic" checklists of possible alternative causes, lists whose validity is not subject to live empirical controversy and whose effective application only depends on equally truistic rules about how each alternative must, of necessity, do its work. Similarly, Davidson's "Causal Relations" begins with a pioneering attack on the assumption that a statement of causal connection indicates a general law by means of which one proposition can be derived from another. But in the end, he insists that a statement of causal connection, in any field, is true, only if a general law does exist, connecting cause and effect under some description.[3]

Although I will begin by criticizing the covering-law model, my ultimate target is the larger project of judging what might count as an explanation on the basis of highly general, a priori standards. Nothing like this project has a reasonable chance of success. A fair and detailed criticism of the covering-law model, taking into ac-

---

*als* (London, 1975), esp. p. 189; J. L. Mackie, "Causes and Conditions" (1965) in Sosa, *Causation and Conditionals*; Peter Railton, "A Deductive-Nomological Model of Probabilistic Explanation," *Philosophy of Science* (1978), pp. 206–26; Nancy Cartwright, "Causal Laws and Effective Strategies," *Nous* (1979), esp. pp. 424–26; William Dray, *Laws and Explanation in History* (London, 1957), esp. ch. 5.

Admittedly, it is not entirely clear in every case whether the rule that is developed is supposed to be applicable solely through analyzing the content of the hypothesis that is judged. For example, it might be Railton's view that only empirical investigations, not an analysis of meaning and an application of a priori rules, could determine whether an explanatory hypothesis describes a "physical probability," as he requires, and whether it contains a theoretical account of mechanisms producing the outcome in question. In this and other cases, my argument will be that the new account of explanation imposes restrictions that are arbitrary, in need of a justification that they do not receive, if they are not justified by traditional positivist arguments that would establish the existence of an effective a priori criterion. These restrictions imposed in the new accounts will turn out to be the same as excessive restrictions imposed in the old ones—suggesting that the traditional positivist assumptions retain their force.

[3] See Michael Scriven, "Truisms as the Grounds for Historical Explanations" in Patrick Gardiner, ed., *Theories of History* (New York, 1959), and Scriven, "Causes, Connections and Conditions in History" in William Dray, *Philosophical Analysis and History* (New York, 1966); Donald Davidson, "Causal Relations" (1967) in Sosa, *Causation and Conditionals*, esp. pp. 90–92.

count its flexibility and its rationales, will make it fairly easy to discern similar distortions in the current alternatives to that model.

## THE COVERING-LAW MODEL

Whoever originated the covering-law model (Hume might claim credit), C. G. Hempel has, without any doubt, developed it in the greatest detail, with the greatest clarity and resourcefulness. My criticism of the model will take the form of a criticism of his views.

According to the covering-law model, an adequate explanation of why something happened must approximate to one of two patterns. In the first, "deductive-nomological pattern," empirical general laws and statements of initial conditions are presented which logically entail the statement that the event in question has occurred. Here is Hempel's own, most famous illustration:

> Let the event to be explained consist in the cracking of an automobile radiator during a cold night. The sentences of group (1) [i.e., the "set of statements asserting the occurrence of certain events . . . at certain times"] may state the following initial and boundary conditions: The car was left in the street all night. Its radiator, which consists of iron, was completely filled with water, and the lid was screwed on tightly. The temperature during the night dropped from 39°F, in the evening, to 25°F in the morning; the air pressure was normal. The bursting pressure of the radiator material is so and so much. Group (2) [i.e., the "set of universal hypotheses"] would contain empirical laws such as the following: Below 32°F, under normal atmospheric pressure, water freezes. Below 39.2°F, the pressure of a mass of water increases with decreasing temperature, if the volume remains constant or decreases; when the water freezes, the pressure again increases. Finally, this group would have to include a quantitative law concerning the change of pressure of water as a function of its temperature and volume.
>
> From statements of these two kinds, the conclusion that the radiator cracked during the night can be deduced by logical reasoning; an explanation of the considered event has been established.[4]

The deductive-nomological pattern gets all of its distinctiveness and power from specifications of the demand that covering-laws be general and empirical. The required generality has two important

[4] "The Function of General Laws in History," p. 232.

aspects. Taken together, the laws must entail that when initial conditions of the general kinds described are realized, an event of the kind to be explained *always* occurs. In addition, the laws must only include general terms, referring to general kinds, not to individuals. "[T]he idea suggests itself of permitting a predicate in a fundamental lawlike sentence only if it is purely universal, or, as we shall say, purely qualitative in character; in other words, if a statement of its meaning does not require reference to any particular object or spatio-temporal location. Thus, the terms 'soft,' 'green,' 'warmer than,' 'as long as,' 'liquid,' 'electrically charged,' 'father of,' are purely qualitative predicates, which 'taller than the Eiffel Tower,' 'medieval,' 'lunar,' 'arctic,' 'Ming' are not."[5]

Of course, many good explainers do not seem to rely on qualitative laws. Good geologists seem to be concerned with mountain formation on a particular object, the Earth, without claiming even approximate knowledge of laws of mountain formation holding on all planets. The best historians seem to be quite unconcerned with qualitative laws independent of particular eras, places, and persons. Despite these appearances to the contrary, something like the requirement of qualitativeness must be right, on further analysis, if the covering-law model is to have a use. Otherwise, the most flagrant pseudo-explanations are admitted by the model. The historian who has told us that Napoleon became Emperor because that was his personal identity could now assure us that he was relying on the empirical generality, "Whoever is Napoleon [or: is born on Corsica of such-and-such parents on such-and-such a date] becomes Emperor of France."

Covering-laws in the deductive nomological pattern must be, not just general, but empirical, subject to disconfirmation by observational data. Thus, we cannot be satisfied by appeals to tautologies, even in the familiar format: "Whenever this kind of factor is sufficiently strong to bring about the effect in question, and the countervailing factors are sufficiently weak, the effect takes place." Though, once again, the excluded generalizations may seem to be a stock-in-trade of good science, this appearance must be misleading, if the model is to be a tool of methodological criticism. For the most flagrant pseudo-explanations can find adequate coverage by tautological principles. Why did Napoleon become Emperor? He had an

[5] Hempel and Paul Oppenheim, "Studies in the Logic of Explanation" (1948) in Hempel, *Aspects*, p. 269. Here I remain faithful to the original version of the model, in Hempel's writings of the 1940s. The major modifications will be discussed later on.

ironclad destiny to become one, and whoever has an iron-clad destiny to become Emperor does so. Why did this egg hatch into a chicken? It had a strong, unopposed tendency to do so, and any piece of matter with a strong tendency to become a chicken does so, if countervailing factors do not intervene.

As for the statements of prior conditions, they are all supposed to state that certain general properties are realized at certain times or places or on the part of certain persons or things. (For simplicity's sake, I will sometimes confine myself to assertions of the realization of a general property at a time.) When all is made explicit, only specifications in this form are to be used in deducing the occurrence of an event by means of general laws. Since the statement of the event to be explained must be logically entailed by these statements of conditions, in conjunction with the general laws, what gets explained, the explanandum, is itself a statement of the same logical form. In explaining why an event occurred, the explicit subject of the covering-law model, we are always explaining why a general property or properties were realized at certain times, places or on the part of certain people or things. This format for questions as to why something happened has the innocent air of a mere stylistic preference. As we shall see, it is powerful enough to support the weighty claim that all valid explanation fits the deductive-nomological pattern, a claim even more restrictive than the covering-law model itself.

The other pattern for explanation is "inductive-statistical" or, more gracefully, "probabilistic." It is a weaker variant of the first. The covering-laws entail the high probability that an event of the kind in question occurs when conditions of the kinds asserted obtain. The high probability is understood to apply to the most specific reference-class in which the explanandum falls, or to the total body of relevant evidence. After all, our commitment to the general view that penicillin is very likely to cure sore throats does not lead us to accept a penicillin injection as a cause of a sore throat cure among subjects with penicillin *resistant* throat infections. Many historical explanations are held to be of the second, probabilistic sort.[6] The dominant interpretations of quantum mechanics would force us to accept the probabilistic pattern as an adequate pattern in the final analysis, not just as a sketch of a deductive-nomological derivation.[7] Also, probabilistic explanation is at work in everyday contexts when,

[6] See Hempel, "The Function of General Laws in History," p. 237.
[7] See Hempel, "Aspects of Scientific Explanation," *Aspects*, pp. 391–93.

for example, we explain "You drew a lot of aces, kings, and queens because this is a pinochle deck."

In some ways, the probablistic pattern is an important loosening of deductive-nomological constraints. Indeed, this pattern will turn out to be less demanding than the rationale for the covering-law model actually allows. But it does not bring the model much closer to the superficial appearances of good science. If geologists do not seem to be appealing to qualitative laws describing when mountain chains always occur on any planet, neither do they seem to be appealing to qualitative laws describing when mountain chains are very likely to occur on any planet. If an explanation of why Lee surrendered does not seem to sketch general properties which always lead to surrender, in any military leader, neither does it seem to sketch properties that almost always do.

That the covering-law model does not summarize the obvious appearances of widely accepted scientific practice is not an argument against the model. It would merely show that positivists must accept a burden of proof, namely, to provide theoretical arguments in favor of the model. Still, even this modest worry about the burdens of proof has not been warranted until we understand how closely an explanation must approach the two ideal patterns in order to fit the covering-law model. No one, Hempel least of all, has supposed that good science is often presented, word for word, in either pattern.

For Hempel, "because" statements have real explanatory power if they bear one of three relations to the basic patterns: elliptical, incomplete, or explanation sketching. An explanation is elliptical, but otherwise adequate, if, when we make explicit all that is to be understood, the result falls into one of the two patterns. An explanation is incomplete if (when all is made explicit) it entails part, but not all of what is to be explained. Thus, when John's psychoanalyst purports to explain his dream of the previous night, in which he shook hands with his ex-wife, as a case of wish-fulfillment, the analyst's explanation shows, at most, that some dream of reconciliation was to be expected in that general period of time, not that a dream of reconciliation by handshake was to be expected on that particular night.

In the covering-law model, an elliptical explanation of why an event occurred really does explain it, though suppressed premises must be understood. An incomplete explanation does not explain why the event occurred, though it does explain it in part. The success of the third significant approach to the basic pattern, an explanation sketch, is harder to characterize. Yet explanation sketches are supposed to be pervasive. For example, "what the explanatory analyses of historical events offer is . . . in most cases, . . . an *explanation sketch*."[8]

An explanation sketch "consists of a more or less vague indication of the laws and initial conditions considered as relevant, and it needs 'filling-out' in order to turn into a full-fledged explanation . . . it points in the direction where these statements are to be found."[9] Accordingly, when we offer an explanation sketch, we make three different kinds of claims. We assert that there is a deduction in one of the two basic patterns, connecting initial conditions which we describe to the event to be explained. We describe, in a vague and incomplete way, the contents of such a derivation. And we assert that research pursued in a certain direction would eventually result in the discovery of all of the indicated laws and initial conditions.

Is an explanation sketch indicating why something happened an adequate explanation, though susceptible to much improvement, if these several claims are valid? There is no clear answer to this question in Hempel's writings. The silence is understandable. Once one concedes that all explanation is an effort to find derivations in one of the two patterns, the important thing is to characterize the various ways in which the patterns might be approximated. What counts as "close enough" may be regarded as a matter of taste or tactics. Still, the silence is frustrating for someone wondering whether to accept the covering-law model in the first place. For purposes of criticism, the fairest tactic is to suppose that nothing less than an explanation sketch is enough, for Hempel, while leaving it open whether such sketching is itself explanatory. If the model is not this restrictive, it is useless as a tool for criticizing proposed explanations.

For all the vagueness which explanation-sketchers are allowed, this outer limit on explanation is an enormous constraint, which many apparently good explainers do not seem to respect. Often, when an explanation is offered, the explainer seems to be in a position to explain why something happened, but is clearly in no position to claim that a covering-law exists, has certain general features, and is apt to be fully revealed through research in a certain direction. Suppose your doctor explains your sore throat as due to a streptococcal infection, basing the diagnosis on a throat culture. Because of the immature state of immunology, it may be that no one is able to sketch the empirical laws describing the general conditions

---

[8] Hempel, "The Function of General Laws in History," p. 238.
[9] Ibid.

in which strep infections produce sore throats. (Usually, strep infections do not produce them.)[10] The general features of those laws may be unknown. No one may be in a position to claim that a certain research program will reveal the full-fledged law. It may even be the case that your doctor thinks that immunology is governed by non-deterministic physical processes that sometimes produce improbable effects. She does not even believe that there is a law making your sore throat likely under the circumstances. Failing, on every count, to have an explanation-sketch, she still seems to be in a position to offer an explanation. A likely cause of a sore throat, a streptococcal infection, was present. There are (we may suppose) reasons to believe the other likely causes were absent. And there is evidence that the infection was strong enough under the circumstances to cause soreness. The evidence is that your throat is sore. Of course, a covering principle of sorts is available: when an infection is virulent enough to produce soreness, then, given the absence of countervailing factors sufficient to prevent soreness, soreness results. But that is a tautology, not an empirical law.

Elsewhere, especially in the human sciences, it is even less obvious that the explainer needs to stake a claim even to the first premise of an explanation sketch, that an appropriate covering-law exists. Suppose that a lucky historian finds Robert E. Lee's secret diary. As the entry for April 7, 1865, he reads "Grant's letter proposing that I surrender has led me to reflect: Sherman has reached Savannah, cutting the Confederacy in two; Richmond has just fallen, our last rallying-point and stronghold. I despair of our cause. Surrender I will." It seems that he might now be in a position to explain Lee's surrender as due to despair at Sherman's successful march to the sea and Grant's taking of Richmond. But the historian is in no position to suppose that there is a true empirical covering-law appropriately linking despair with surrender. Even among Confederate generals, others, such as Thomas Hunt Morgan, well aware that their cause was lost, fought on for weeks after Appomatox. Perhaps there are general properties, evidenced in part by the diary entry, which almost always lead to surrender, if possessed by any military leader at any time or place in the universe. But it does not seem that the historian must be in a position to claim that there are such general properties (which an ideal future pyschology might describe), in order to make his modest proposal about why Lee surrendered.

The covering-law model does not merely leave us free to look for

[10] See Richard Feinbloom et al., *Child Health Encyclopedia* (New York, 1975), p. 395.

empirical general laws, as the explanatory tools of every science. It requires us at least to sketch such covering-laws, whenever we explain. Apparently good explainers often seem to violate this obligation.

## GOALS FOR THE MODEL

Here and there, I have referred to the larger goals toward which the covering-law model is directed. To conclude this exposition, a formal list will be helpful. After all, unless we know what the model is supposed to do, we cannot distinguish mere revisions from admissions of defeat.

At least in its original version, the covering-law model was supposed to achieve four main goals. First, it was supposed to provide a complete explication of what it is to explain why something happened. On this view, "the assertion that a set of events . . . [has] caused the event to be explained amounts to," "the scientific explanation of the event in question consists of,"[11] furnishing, at least elliptically or via a sketch, a deduction in one of the two basic patterns. To fulfill this goal, the covering-law model must describe necessary and sufficient conditions for explaining why something happened. In the second place, conformity to the covering-law model is a requirement that any genuine explanation must meet. Satisfaction of this requirement "distinguishes genuine from pseudo-explanations."[12] A pseudo-explanation is an attempt to explain that can be dismissed without the need for empirical investigation. Some alleged examples are: the explanation of biological phenomena by appeal to entelechies, i.e., inherent biological tendencies of matter which are only definable in terms of their effects; "the explanation of the achievement of an individual in terms of his mission in history";[13] and many Marxist explanations of cultural life on the basis of economic conditions.[14] In Hempel's writings of the 1960s, when he abandons the first goal, of analyzing the concept of explaining an event, he still maintains the second claim, that the covering-law model provides necessary conditions, useful as means of criticizing proposed explanations. Third, the covering-law model provides us with a highly abstract but informative account of how to test an explanation. By establishing what the required laws and initial condi-

[11] Hempel, "The Function of General Laws in History," p. 232.
[12] Ibid., p. 234.
[13] Ibid., p. 234.
[14] Ibid., p. 239.

tions are, we establish a checklist of what must be verified for an explanatory proposal to be confirmed, what can be falsified as a means of defeating it.[15] Finally, the covering-law model tells us what the goals of science are, apart from practical utility and the mere accumulation of facts. The further, non-utilitarian, non-descriptive goal, all agree, is the explanation of phenomena. The covering-law model describes the general features of this goal, and tells us that they are the same everywhere, whether in the natural sciences, or the social sciences, including history. In all of his writings on explanation except "Aspects of Scientific Explanation," this claim is the one that Hempel most strongly emphasizes at the outset. I will be arguing that the goals of all sciences do have an abstract unity, but not the one described by the covering-law model.

Hempel further defines all these goals in a way that puts the importance of all in doubt. They are solely concerned with non-pragmatic aspects of explanation, indeed, with "explanation" in the non-pragmatic "sense." The pragmatic, here, extends far beyond concern with a practical pay-off. Explanatory adequacy is pragmatic so long as it is relative to a particular person or group of people, whether it is relative to their practical interests or to their purely scientific concerns or scientific beliefs.[16]

Since Hempel admits that explanatory adequacy has a pragmatic dimension, his exclusion of the pragmatic from the scope of the covering-law model often sounds like a stipulation. The covering-law model, it might seem, is meant to be a theory of explanatory adequacy insofar as such adequacy does not depend on the beliefs or concerns of inquirers. If so, another account of explanation, including the one I will defend, which claims that adequacy is relative to concerns or beliefs in the background, is not a rival theory, but a theory of something else.

This interpretation would make the covering-law model extremely disappointing. According to many current accounts, Kuhn's, van Fraassen's and Rorty's, for example, every standard of explanatory adequacy applied in the course of real scientific inquiry implicitly refers to beliefs and concerns of a contemporary individual or group. This constraint *seems* to undermine covering-law requirements. For example, concerns which are held to determine the adequacy of an explanation might be satisfied by something less than an explanation sketch. It would be very disappointing to be

[15] Ibid., p. 234.
[16] "Aspects of Scientific Explanation," pp. 425f.

told that the covering-law model is, nonetheless, intact, since it is a theory of another kind of explanation, though perhaps one which is never pursued. Nor would this interpretation fit Hempel's characterization of the model as an attempt "to indicate in reasonably precise terms the logical structure and the rationale of various ways in which empirical science answers explanation-seeking why questions."[17] Here, demands for explanation which actual scientists actually make are surely at issue.

Taking a cue from the quoted passage, we should understand the subject of the covering-law model to be certain demands for explanatory adequacy that all of us make, whatever our philosophical allegiances. All of us accept the coherence, in some cases, of denying that an explanation is adequate while asserting that it is adequate for legitimate purposes. "Filth causes disease" may be an adequate explanation for many purposes of sanitary engineering, but it is not an adequate explanation. The remark, "Resistance leads to heat," may explain why a circuit keeps shorting out, if made by one engineer in a work team in conversation with another. Philosophical theories to one side, we would all accept that this statement, though it is an adequate explanation for those people at that time, is not, strictly speaking, an adequate explanation.

The subject-matter of the covering-law model is yielded by this pre-theoretical distinction. It is strict and literal adequacy, not just adequacy for certain purposes and among certain people. This *is* a stipulation about the scope of the model. In addition, the model makes a substantive claim, which might be confused with the stipulation. The standards governing strict and literal adequacy are non-pragmatic. This is highly controversial. For example, it is not at all obvious that every explanation which violates the covering-law model and which is adequate only relative to the common theoretical concerns of all the most advanced scientists of the time should be labelled "good enough for certain purposes, but strictly and literally inadequate."

## THE STAKES ARE HIGH

That the covering-law model seems to conflict with the best-established practices of explanation challenges positivists, fortifies their enemies, but has relatively little effect on the practice of most natural sciences. After all, positivists do not want to change geology or

---

[17] Ibid., p. 412.

medical diagnosis, only to show that geological and medical success, when fully analysed, fit their model. Elsewhere, however, the practical stakes are high when the covering-law model is assessed. This is especially true in the social sciences, where whole styles of explanation are favored by some, but are rejected by others on positivist grounds.

For one thing, the many proposals to explain institutions or practices in terms of their social functions do not fit the model. Those who have argued that such-and-such an institution has certain features because these features serve a certain crucial social function have not supposed that every institution serving that function must have those features. They have not claimed even a vague grasp of general conditions in which what serves that function almost always has those features. Thus, if the covering-law model is a valid requirement, we should dismiss their explanatory claims a priori, once we have understood them. For example, when Malinowski claimed that Melanesians' ritual voyages of exchange in pursuit of decorative shells were a feature of their society because those voyages held it together, dispersed as it was among small and distant islands, he certainly did not believe that cohesion could only have been guaranteed through those voyages.[18] If the covering-law model must be suited, the empirical and theoretical debate over his claim, a paradigmatic dispute in economic anthropology for sixty years, is a mistake. Malinowski's explanation should have been dismissed on purely methodological grounds. Indeed, such methodological dismissal is advocated by practicing social scientists.[19]

In addition, a covering-law requirement can be and has been used to dismiss most attempts to explain particular historical phenomena as due to underlying social forces. The forces allegedly producing the phenomenon often have had a different sequel in other situations. Usually, the proponents of the explanation do not claim to have even a sketchy notion of general conditions in which a social situation of the kind in question always or almost always has an effect of the kind in question. For example, those who explain the Nazi regime as part of a response to economic crisis of German industrial, banking, and military elites readily admit that other coun-

---

[18] See Bronislaw Malinowski, *Argonauts of the Western Pacific* (London, 1922).

[19] Hempel argues that functionalist approaches in the social sciences are not a source of actual explanations, but a suggestion for further research, in "The Logic of Functional Analysis" (1959) in *Aspects*. For similar doubts from a sociologist, see George Homans, "Bringing Men Back In," *American Sociological Review* (1964), pp. 809–18.

tries, which they take to have been dominated by such elites, have endured industrial crises without a fascist regime. They offer no sketch of general conditions distinguishing all or almost all countries in which the response is fascist from those in which it is not. If the covering-law model is a valid requirement, the long debate over Marxist explanations of fascism should have been ended at the start by remarks like those of the historian, Henry Turner: "Only a few capitalist states have produced phenomena comparable to Nazism; on the other hand, the latter shares its capitalist parentage with every other political movement that has emerged from modern Europe, including liberal democracy and communism."[20]

In addition to discouraging certain investigations, the covering-law model has encouraged research programs emphasizing the discovery of general laws in the social sciences. The pioneers of modern academic sociology, anthropology and economics, Weber, Durkheim, Radcliffe-Brown, Malinowski, Menger, Jevons and Walras, all regarded subsumption under general laws as essential to scientific explanation, and took the discovery of such laws to be the means for making the social sciences truly scientific. Commitment to the covering-law model has kept such goals alive in the face of continual disappointment. For example, when social anthropologists discovered that their fieldwork yielded few interesting general laws involving relatively concrete phenomena, such as motherhood or farming, they did not abandon the pursuit of general laws. Many responded by seeking such general relationships among more abstract structural characteristics, such as "binary opposition." Many economists elaborate the internal logic of some general model, serenely accepting that their work makes no appreciable contribution to explaining specific episodes of inflation or unemployment, or specific international economic relations. The intellectual justification is, basically, that the elaboration of general models is the most promising route to the discovery of general laws, an essential aspect, in turn, of explanations.[21]

[20] "Big Business and the Rise of Hitler" in Henry Turner, ed., *Nazism and the Third Reich* (New York, 1972), p. 99.

[21] The prevalence of the covering-law model in primers of research design is, at once, a measure and a cause of its influence on the practice of the social sciences. For example, in his generally open-minded and perspicuous text, *The Craft of Political Research* (Englewood Cliffs, N.J., 1980), Phillips Shively tells the student, "Social research is an attempt by social scientists to develop and sharpen theories. . . . A theory takes a set of similar things that happen—say, the development of party-systems, in democracies—and finds a common pattern among them that allows us to treat each of these different occurrences as a repeated example of the same thing" (pp. 3f.). A

In the natural sciences, the main effect of the covering-law model is its influence on the interpretation of outstanding scientific achievements. One such example is the philosophical interpretation of quantum mechanics. Given certain plausible constraints on how forces operate (above all, no action-at-a-distance), there are no laws, discovered or undiscovered, from which the subsequent mass-and-motion history of a particle can be deduced in light of its present situation. Indeed, given those constraints, the totality of physical laws admits, even requires, occasional improbable sequences. This conclusion is an important collective achievement of Heisenberg, von Neumann and others. If the covering-law model is right, we are led to a particular interpretation of this achievement: the behavior of matter is, at least sometimes, inexplicable and uncaused. Other investigations, in biochemistry, physiology and genetics, have suggested that life processes have physical (largely, chemical) explanations. Again, the covering-law model creates great pressure toward a certain interpretation: statements about the nature and behavior of living things should be translatable into conclusions that can be deduced from general laws together with particular statements in the language of physics and chemistry.

In short, the covering-law model does not just make philosophy look different. It casts a distinctive light on the whole of science.

## The Metaphysical Argument

The usual strategy for criticizing the covering-law model is to attack it with counter-examples, cases of explanations that seem to be adequate without fitting the model, or that seem to fit the model but fail to explain. The tactic is so dominant that aficionados of the covering-law debate can refer to favorite examples by name, "measles," "paresis," "barometer" or "flagpole."

Such strong emphasis on counter-examples is neither productive

---

good theory is said to be a simple set of generalities providing a basis for accurate predictions (pp. 15f.). The assertion of causal relationships, if something more than the assertion of a correlational covering-law, is "quite subjective" (p. 85). The careful student will be disturbed by the occasional shrewd warnings in which Shively notes that statistical techniques which he takes to be the quite objective means of establishing general correlations presuppose the causal independence of repeated trials (apparently, a subjective characteristic, in his view), require that all causal influences except the ones under investigation be known, assume the absence of hidden causes producing "false correlations," or require prior knowledge both of which factors are causally dependent and of the algebraic degree of their causal influence (pp. 95f., 111f., 149, 151f., 169–72).

nor fair. Thus, the most important controversy has been as to whether adequate explanations have to fit the model. Here, the most that counter-examples show is that what every non-philosopher would call an adequate explanation sometimes escapes the covering-law constraints. *And no positivist would want to deny this.* Such clashes with normal usage are no more severe than unalarming clashes of every working mathematician's usage of "adequate proof" with the standards of adequacy laid down in proof theory or everyone's usage of "pure water" outside of chemistry with chemistry's specification of the term. Positivists need philosophical justifications of their stricter standards. In light of those rationales they can easily concede that loose and non-literal usages of "adequate explanation" may be appropriate to current purposes. And they have offered those rationales. The neglect of these underlying arguments in attacks of the covering-law model has had an even higher cost than unfairness. For an understanding of why the arguments are wrong provides important clues to a superior account of explanation.

The requirement that explanations fit the covering-law model receives much of its support from an argument based on the principle, "Same cause, same effect." I will call it "the metaphysical argument," since Descartes or Leibniz would have felt at home with it, whatever their ultimate verdict. Here is a concise statement of it by Hempel:

> When an individual event b is said to have been caused by another individual event a, then surely the claim is implied that whenever "the same cause" is realized, "the same effect" will occur. But this claim cannot be taken to mean that whenever a recurs then so does b; for a and b are individual events in particular spatio-temporal locations and thus occur only once. Rather a and b must be viewed as events of certain *kinds* (such as heating or cooling of a gas, expansion or shrinking of a gas) of which there may be further instances. And the law tacitly implied by the assertion that b, as an event of kind B, was caused by a as an event of kind A is a general statement of causal connection to the effect that, under suitable circumstances, an instance of A is invariably accompanied by an instance of B. In most causal explanations, the relevant conditions are not fully stated. . . . When the relevant conditions or laws remain largely indefinite, a statement of causal connection is rather in the nature of a program, or of a sketch. . . .[22]

[22] "Aspects of Scientific Explanation," pp. 349f.

The metaphysical argument rests on two distinct ideas. On the one hand, Hempel thinks that every valid explanation either makes or sketches a claim that some cluster of general properties G is realized at some time $t'$ because some other, logically independent cluster of general properties F is realized at some appropriately related time $t'$. (Cf. "b, as an event of kind B, was caused by a, as an event of kind A.") On the other hand, he assumes that it is inconsistent to make such a claim while accepting that there may be some other sequence in which F is realized at another time $t_1$ but G is not realized at $t'_1$. "G was realized because F was realized, but at some other time, G did not follow F" is, if a complete and explicit statement, an absurd one, simultaneously claiming victory and admitting defeat. Thus, a general law is "tacitly implied" in every explanatory claim.

The metaphysical argument has one striking consequence, immediate but unnoticed. Though presented as an argument for the covering-law model, it rules out the probabilistic basic pattern. This argument for "Same cause, same effect" is in no way an argument permitting "Same cause, almost but not quite always same effect." A pattern of explanation which seems to underlie quantum mechanics and much informal explanation as well must be dismissed.

As for the argument itself, the weak point is the first, more innocent-sounding claim about the logic of explanation. If it is valid, so that every explanation (ellipsis and sketchiness to one side) claims that a general property G was realized at $t'$ because a general property F was realized at $t$, then the rest of the argument does follow. It is absurd to claim "One property, temperature increase, occurred there solely because another property, compression, occurred. But elsewhere, under identical general conditions, there is compression without increase of temperature."

In fact, a sound demand for an explanation need not ask why a general property was realized at a certain time. Often, we are asking why an event occurred, but not why a property was realized. An appropriate answer consists of a description of an event that caused it. (As we shall see, the description must fit further structural and pragmatic constraints. But they are not remotely described by the covering-law model.) Suppose I believe the lore that Aeschylus died because an eagle dropped a tortoise on his head. Then I believe that one event, the eagle's dropping the tortoise on Aeschylus' head, caused another, Aeschylus' death. I need not believe, however, that at every other time when an eagle's dropping a tortoise on a person's head occurs, death follows. Nor need I be committed to the existence, much less a sketch of a general law relating death to tortoise impacts when further general properties are realized. If I had claimed that death occurred, on Aeschylus' part and at a certain time and place, because an eagle's dropping a tortoise on a head was realized for him shortly before, there is an implication of commitment to such a generalization. This difference in implications is one piece of evidence that the two explanatory claims are themselves different.

Another piece of evidence is the existence of why-questions which are genuinely ambiguous between two readings, one involving property realization, the other event occurrence. Why was the chief of Allied forces in Europe elected President in 1952? This might be a question asking why military success and political success were combined on a certain occasion. As such, it demands an answer referring to ways in which military success contributes to political success. It might also be a question simply asking why Eisenhower was elected President, referring to Eisenhower by a certain description. Then, though talk of military qualities is invited, it is not required. An answer discussing Eisenhower's special ties with the Eastern Establishment, and their shrewd tactics in outmaneuvering Robert Taft's forces would not beg the question.

It might seem that explanations of why an event took place can only be distinguished from explanations of why a property was realized at the cost of giving bare times and places a troubling causal power. If $a$ could cause $b$, at time $t$, without a general law's covering the connection, then the properties realized in $a$ might occur at some other time without the occurrence of the properties in $b$. Wouldn't this mean that times as such have causal power? This is, presumably, Hempel's basis for his leap from the observation that $a$ and $b$ are "individual events in particular spatiotemporal locations" to the conclusion that "Same cause, same effect" must ascribe causal power to something general, not just to $a$. If the general properties of $a$ could occur without producing anything with the general properties of $b$, then, his words suggest, something beyond the general properties of the former must once have produced something with the general properties of the latter, namely, $b$ itself. But, beyond the general properties, all that is available to do the extra causal work is bare spatio-temporal location.

The first thing to be said about reflections on the powerlessness of bare spatio-temporal location is that they only support much weaker principles than the covering-law requirement, since to demand that $a$ have causally sufficient general properties is not to require that an explainer be able to sketch those properties. The prime example of such a weaker principle is the one Davidson proposed and analyzed toward the end of "Causal Relations": if a causes b, then there must be some set of general properties describing a such that whenever they are realized, some general properties describing b must be realized, as a matter of general law.[23] Apart from Davidson's non-Hempelian ideas about the logical form of the laws, there is an enormous difference in the role Davidson's principle can play in the assessment of explanations. There is no need whatever for the properties to be indicated, even in a sketchy way, by a proposed explanation. For example, one could accept a psychological explanation offered without covering laws on whatever grounds one otherwise would. One would simply rely on general materialist arguments for supposing that a mental event, under a complex and unknown physical description, dictates something else that it causes, perhaps under a similarly complex and unknown description, on the basis of physical laws. The Davidsonian principle could not and is not meant to be an important tool for criticizing particular explanatory proposals.

Though Davidson's principle has seemed to many the kernel of truth in the covering-law requirement, the argument about bare times does not really establish even this conclusion. The denial that the same general properties must have the same general effect only ascribes causal power to bare times if an exceptionally strong form of the principle of sufficient reason is accepted: if a factor has one effect on one occasion, another effect on another, some additional factors must cause the difference. This is hardly obvious, even if one believes that every particular *event* has a cause. Given the distinction between particular events and property realizations, that every particular event has a cause need not entail that every difference between events has one. And there are definite empirical grounds for rejecting the strong principle. Suppose a gram of the radioactive element radon is enclosed in a steel box and loses half its mass in the statistically abnormal period of 3.5 days. Another gram of radon is enclosed in a steel box and loses half its mass in the more normal 3.82 days. We know that the first sample lost half its mass in 3.5 days through the radioactive decay that occurred, since the box was sealed all the time, permitting no other cause of losing mass. Correspondingly for the second. We can explain the loss in mass of radon in each sample, and yet, according to the dominant interpreta-

[23] See "Causal Relations," pp. 90–92.

tion of quantum mechanics, there is no cause of the first's decaying more quickly than the second.

Non-technical explanations point to the same conclusion, that good explainers need not claim Davidsonian coverage any more than they must claim to have a sketch of a Hempelian covering-law. Surely, people are not unreasonable to identify a particular episode of jealousy as the cause of a particular episode of violence, just because they deny that redescriptions, presumably neurological, link the two events as a matter of exceptionless law. It is ironic that a distinction between an event and the fact that a property was realized makes Davidson's demand for a law look excessive. For "Causal Relations" was, itself, the pioneering effort to use such distinctions against the traditional emphasis on appeals to covering-laws as the essence of causal claims.

The criticism of the first rationale for the covering-law model suggests a positive moral. An explanation of why something happened may say why an event occurred, not why a general property was realized, and may do so by describing events, not general properties, that caused it. Yet, in the view of many, this suggestion should not be followed. Notions of lawlike regularity, on this view, are clear enough to be the basis for an analysis of explanation, but notions of causes are not, unless they are analyzed as appeals to underlying lawlike regularities. Even if the metaphysical argument does not work, the covering-law model might still be attractive as an analysis of what we mean when we say one event happened because of another, provided our meaning is clear. We must turn, then, to this, the most ambitious goal of the positivist theory of explanation.

## Unanalyzed Causation

Causal explanation is not analyzed by the covering-law model. Here, counter-examples really are sufficient. A derivation fitting one of the two basic patterns often fails to explain. When a barometer falls, a change for the worse in the weather is very likely to follow. The high probability is dictated by laws of meteorology. But the weather does not change because the barometer falls. In conjunction with basic and utterly general laws of physics and chemistry, the shift toward the red of spectral lines in spectra from more distant stars entails that the observed universe is expanding. The red shift does not explain why the universe is expanding.

Because these examples fit the covering-law model so well (the red shift example is especially impressive) and because the failure to explain is so obvious, they are overwhelming. Unlike challenges to the necessity of covering-law constraints, these challenges to their sufficiency cannot be explained away on the grounds that adequacy for present purposes, not adequacy *simpliciter*, is in question. No special present purposes prevent us from declaring the red shift an adequate explanation of the expanding universe. Indeed, practical concerns would support, not discourage, our labelling these cases "adequate," since reliable symptoms are presented.[24]

These problems are familiar to anyone who has followed the covering-law debate. The usual response in the literature is to modify or enrich the positivist approach to explanation and causality. Deductions in a different logical pattern are proposed, new kinds of derivations based on probabilistic reasoning are introduced, or the apparatus of traditional logical theory is enriched with counter-factual conditionals and allied reflections on similarity among possible worlds. The barometer, the red shift (the flagpole, Koflik spots, and so forth through the standard catalogue) are taken to be signs that different means from Hempel's should be used in pursuit of Hempel's goal of analyzing the concept of explanation without reliance on inherently causal notions.

In fact, the familiar counter-examples are more plausibly taken as a sign that explanation cannot be analyzed without talk of causation. Clearly, this is one way of looking at the familiar counter-examples. A natural account of their failure to explain, more convincing than any suggested by the positivist revisions, is that they identify prior symptoms of an event—not causes, as an explanation must. That this need to rely on causal notions in distinguishing explanation from non-explanation really is indispensable is suggested by the great variety of other cases in which causal distinctions are needed to discriminate covering-law derivations that explain from those that don't. These distinctions are so diverse, so important and so commonly presupposed in sympathetic expositions of the covering-law model that one would be tempted to see the latter as a preliminary to *defending* the ineliminable role of causal notions—were it not, explicitly, an effort to analyze talk of causes as talk of subsumption under general propositions of a certain logical form. The effort to dispense with all the needed causal distinctions is a bad bet.

[24] In 1964, these examples and others led Hempel to accept it as an open question whether conformity to the covering-law model guarantees explanatory status. See "Aspects of Scientific Explanation," pp. 367, 376. Accordingly, he presents the model as a series of requirements, necessary but not jointly sufficient, in his most recent general exposition, *Philosophy of Natural Science* (Englewood Cliffs, N.J., 1966), ch. 5.

The generalities that figure in covering-law derivations are said to be laws. But what is a law? The basic answer is supposed to be: a proposition stating, in purely qualitative terms, an association that always or almost holds. If this is all "law" means, covering-law derivations can clearly fail to explain. After a few minutes spent with German statistics for 1933, I can state, with reasonable confidence, that in any country with such-and-such a percentage of blondes, such-and-such a percentage of automobile-owning families and such-and-such a percentage of cigar smokers a fascist takeover soon occurs. Yet this covering generalization is not qualified to yield an explanation. The Nazis didn't seize power because they functioned in a country with a certain percentage of blondes, and so forth. The defect is that the covering generalization is not a real law. But what is missing from it? The generalization has just the right logical form. One obvious answer is superior to any the covering-law model itself suggests: percentages of blondness, car ownership, and cigar smoking do not cause fascist seizures of power. Tell a science fiction story in which they do, and you tell a story in which the covering-law derivation might be a genuine explanation.

Another, different problem of relevance calls for a similar causal solution. Not every premise in a covering-law derivation is part of an explanation of the explanandum. Otherwise, any true proposition would be part of a valid explanation of every explicable phenomenon. Just add the proposition, say, "Blackbeard was a pirate," as an additional premise, to a valid explanation of the phenomenon, say, Newton's explanation of the shape of planetary orbits in the *Principia*. The expanded version will fit the covering-law model as well as the original.

It might seem that the problem could be solved by a simple amendment, well within the general framework of a philosophy of science emphasizing questions of logical form. The premises of a covering-law derivation must be minimal in that any reduction in their content would make the proposed derivation invalid. Actually, this proposal is too weak in one way, too strong in another. It is too weak because it can be evaded through logical tricks. Take the universal law of gravitation out of Newton's famous derivation and insert two premises: "Either the universal law of gravitation is true or Blackbeard is not a pirate"; "Blackbeard is a pirate." Now, "Blackbeard is a pirate" is an essential part of a covering-law derivation of the planetary orbits. But surely, that Blackbeard is a pirate is not part of an explanation of why the planetary orbits are elliptical.

The narrowness of the proposed requirement that premises be minimal is even more important. For it reflects a problem, the proper relation of theories to observational consequences, which is notoriously resistant to treatment through analyses of logical form. Suppose we want to explain why the pressure exerted by a gas of constant volume increased. After appealing to an increase in its temperature, we may complete the explanation in two ways. In the first format, we simply appeal to the empirical regularities linking pressure and temperature. Alternatively, we might offer an explanation based on the molecular theory of gases and the kinetic theory of temperature: an increase in temperature is an increase in the average energy of translational motion of the molecules; so molecular bouncing against the walls of the constant containing surface is on the average more energetic, exerting higher pressure. This more theoretical explanation is surely acceptable, and may even be preferable in some contexts. But its premises have much excessive content. When fully spelled out, they entail the gas law connecting pressure and temperature, all that is needed to derive the explanandum, together with much else besides. If we required that explanations be stripped down to their minimal core, we would have to eliminate the deeper explanation in favor of the shallower one.[25]

Although considerations of logical form do not seem to discriminate relevant from irrelevant parts of explanations, causal considerations do. Blackbeard's being a pirate is not even part of a cause of the shape of planetary orbits. Gravitational attraction is. The molecular theory of gases describes causal mechanisms contributing to the rise in the pressure of the gas. So do the gas laws, though on a more superficial level. If problems of irrelevance do not immediately occur to us when we encounter the covering-law model, that is because we only think of causally relevant laws and conditions. The moral seems to be that an explanation is a causal description of an appropriate kind.

One further problem of relevance concerns probabilities which are relevant material for the premises in a probabilistic derivation. These probabilities, we saw, must be high relative to the most spe-

---

[25] Compare Hempel's own pessimism in "Empiricist Criteria of Cognitive Significance" (1950, 1951) in *Aspects*. There, he tries to analyze the requirement that a proposition be empirically confirmable in terms of required logical relations between observational propositions and those whose confirmability is in question. Though the explicit subject-matter is different, the problems of eliminating excess content are essentially the same. And this is as it should be: being empirically confirmable ought to be equivalent to being a real part of a potential explanation of an observed phenomenon. By the end of the essay, in the face of problems like those I have sketched, Hempel has dismissed all current logical criteria for empirical confirmability.

cific reference class. Otherwise, an argument for the high probability that penicillin cures streptococcal infections would directly yield an explanation of why an infection disappeared when penicillin was administered, even if the streptococcus was, in fact, penicillin-resistant. No doubt, the derivations excluded by this requirement ought to be excluded, at least in typical cases. But what is missing from these derivations that makes them fail to explain? Suppose I do not know, and have no basis for believing, that the streptococcus infection is penicillin-resistant. Observing that it goes away after penicillin is administered, I reason: "Penicillin is very likely to cure a strep infection; penicillin was administered; so the probability of cure was very high. That explains the cure." My probabilistic premise expresses a rational degree of belief based on a corresponding relative frequency. I have provided a derivation, from valid premises, of the high probability of the explanandum. Of course, the state of my evidence is not ideal, and I lack knowledge which would make another reference class, viz., penicillin-resistant strep infections, salient. But the question of when propositions, if true, explain, is very different from the question of when one has an ideal basis for choosing an explanatory hypothesis. In sum, the requirement of specificity lacks a rationale within the covering-law model.

When we appreciate the causal force of explanations, the maxim of specificity has a justification, though it becomes a maxim of a rather different kind. An explanation must describe a causal factor strong enough, under the circumstances, to bring about the event to be explained. That full awareness of the situation would lead to the attribution of a low probability to a penicillin cure makes it likely that the propensity to cure was not strong enough in this case. The "requirement" of maximum specificity is best taken as a warning to avoid explanatory appeals to a certain causal factor where the total data would make it improbable that the factor is strong enough to do its job in the case at hand.

If the requirement is justified in this way, it is not a strict requirement, just an important rule, all else being equal, in assessing explanatory hypotheses. After all, the improbable does happen, sometimes, if not usually. A factor that is usually inadequate in circumstances of a certain kind is sometimes strong enough even in such circumstances. Thus, penicillin-resistance is not absolute. Suppose that penicillin is administered and a penicillin-resistant strain disappears. Even if we cannot sketch laws making it probable that penicillin would cure in circumstances of that kind (even if there are no such laws to be sketched), we might be in a position to claim that the unlikely has happened. Perhaps no other curative process can be discovered, despite much search, that is as likely as this unlikely one to have been effective, and spontaneous remission is even more unlikely than the unusual penicillin cure. A causal understanding appropriately hedges the demand for maximum specificity, as well as justifying the hedged demand.

Finally, a covering-law derivation may fail to explain, not because it does not describe causes, but because what it describes lacks adequate causal depth. Even though causally sufficient links in the actual chain of events are described, they are simply the means by which the deeper, explanatory causes happened to do their work. Since the complex topic of causal depth will be a main theme of the next chapter, a brief illustration will do, for now.

There may be a failure to explain, out of shallowness, when the phenomenon to be explained would have occurred anyway, in the absence of the causal factor described. The firing of two shots is supposed to have caused the Berlin workers' uprising of March 1848. The firing of the shots led to rumors that troops had fired on a crowd, that led, in turn, to demonstrations, street barricades and widespread confrontations. Suppose that the occurrence of an uprising is entailed by the occurrence of those shots and initial psychological states of relevant Berliners on that day, taken with empirical regularities about response to provocation and anxiety. Still, it might have been the case (and probably was) that a workers' uprising would have occurred anyway in Berlin in 1848, if the shots had not been fired. Given the structure and intensity of social tensions and political controversy in Berlin in 1848, some other incident would have ignited the tinder, if the shots were not fired. In that case, the firing of the shots is not part of an explanation of why rebellion broke out in Berlin in 1848.

The requirement of depth is a further example of the role of causal distinctions in explanatory adequacy. It also suggests a further maxim, which will constantly be of use in replacing positivism. The judgment that an explanatory hypothesis is adequate is, in part, a comparative judgment of rivalries among causal accounts, and this is not just true in practice, but as part of the logic of explanation and justification.

## New Models

Of course, that the covering-law model neglects a variety of important causal distinctions does not show that some revision of the model could not succeed. It only shows that success will be hard to achieve at best. Refutations of the amended versions are needed, tailored to the particular amendments. In such refutations, the survey of causal distinctions implicit in explanation can play an important role. It suggests an effective strategy for criticizing new models of explanation that still have derivation from empirical laws as their core. If the revisionist is trying to avoid ultimate reliance on causal notions, the revision, one always discovers, bears no promise of coping with some of the distinctions just surveyed. On the other hand, if he or she is relying on causal notions, without the hope that they can be analyzed away, the required derivations turn out to be excess baggage; reference to causal processes can do all the explanatory work in the absence of the required empirical laws.

In recent years, greater reliance on probabilistic considerations has been one of the two main sources of revised accounts of explanation or causality, still positivist in the broad sense. (I will discuss the other source, the use of counterfactual conditionals, at length in the next chapter.) Railton's revision of the covering-law model is at once a straightforward and especially thoughtful proposal, in this trend. According to Railton, an adequate probabilistic explanation does three things. It provides probabilistic laws and initial conditions assigning some probability to the explanandum, which may be quite small; it asserts the occurrence of the explanandum; and it derives the probabilistic laws from a "theoretical account of the mechanism at work" producing phenomena such as the explanandum.[26] In effect, deductive-nomological explanation is taken to be an extreme case in which the probability assigned is one.

The requirement of derivation from a theoretical account of mechanisms is essential. It is adopted to distinguish explanations from descriptions of prior symptoms. It also works to exclude such low-probability howlers as the claim to have *explained* a Florida snowstorm by saying, "Snowstorms occur only rarely in southern latitudes." How is this requirement of an underlying theoretical account of mechanisms to be understood? Perhaps it is meant as part of an analysis in which the notion of a causal mechanism can ultimately be analyzed away in favor of formal descriptions of the location of the relevant probabilistic regularities among the entailments of a theory. This seems an unreasonable hope, however. One would have to analyze away talk of causes, while insisting on the distinction between a genuine theoretical account of the mechanisms

---

[26] "A Deductive-Nomological Model of Probabilistic Explanation," p. 214.

at work in the probabilistic principle and a mere deduction of the principle from true premises. After all, the howler about Florida snowstorms would not be adequate just because it is deduced from "It rarely snows in Florida or Blackbeard was not a pirate. And Blackbeard was a pirate." But positivists have never found a satisfactory substitute for the explicitly causal understanding of this distinction. Similarly, Railton's schema has to be restricted to "physical" as against "statistical" probabilities. Otherwise, the silly proposal to explain the Nazi seizure of power on the basis of blondeness and automobiles is vindicated once an appropriate probabilistic law is accounted for in terms of (admittedly indirect) theoretical mechanisms. But the problem of distinguishing laws of physical probability from mere statements of statistical regularity is just a new form of the old recalcitrant problem, of distinguishing laws, even when exceptionless, from mere general truths.

Suppose, then, that causal notions are given an independent role, not analyzed away. Then, the demand for probabilistic laws and for derivation from a theoretical account is pure excess. Worse yet, the excess is pernicious, excluding valid explanations. In the diary example, we can explain Lee's surrender. Once unanalyzed causal notions are admitted, there is no good reason to criticize either the explanation or the argument for it as tentative or vague. But we may be unable to assign any probability to Lee's surrender based on probabilistic laws and associated properties of Lee. Who knows how many military leaders shared the antecedent properties—some of them tenth-century Japanese overlords, some Watusi nobles, some warriors in forgotten Stone Age cultures—and yet would not have surrendered? Even if we did know that the likelihood of a humane general's surrendering in their situation has a certain magnitude, we have no reason to suppose this likelihood is derived from a "theoretical account" of despair and of countervailing factors. If the notion of cause has been independently admitted, we can say what needs to be said, without referring to laws and theoretical derivations: Lee's despair over the fall of Richmond and Sherman's March caused his surrender.

It might seem that causation must, nonetheless, be associated with a law-governed assignment of physical probability in theoretical physics, where the laws explicitly describe all relevant factors and their causal influence, and do so in general terms. In fact, even in classical physics, this is an illusion.

As a first step toward grasping the radical indeterminacy of classical physics, consider the milder indeterminacy that has been evident from the beginning of the field. Actual descriptions of the initial state of a mechanical system have only finite accuracy. Many physically important systems, i.e., ones that would be common in nature if classical physics were true, magnify small differences in initial conditions into gross ultimate differences, rather as a pinball machine defeats the efforts of the most expert player to duplicate the trajectory the ball had on the previous play. One such system is a kind of infinite pinball machine, the universe of hard spheres that came to epitomize the outlook of Newtonian physics. In the causal investigation of the difference-amplifying systems, there are always outcomes that can be traced back to initial events, but that cannot be deduced, even in gross features, from the finitely accurate descriptions of initial conditions together with physical laws. Admitting deductions of mere probabilities as explanatory will not help here. The laws are not probabilistic and the initial conditions can only be made probabilistic through the liberal use of a principle of indifference that leads to outright contradictions (as we shall see in Chapter Six). As Railton is well aware, objective propensities dictated by natural law are the right material for ascriptions of causation, and they are missing here. Still, though the probabilistic deductions are missing, here, they can be sketched, in Hempel's sense, in any given case. In effect, the design of more accurate measuring devices is the relevant research program. The obvious, mild indeterminacy simply condemns us to have no better than an explanation sketch for some trajectories, because precision is finite and small differences are eventually amplified into grossly different outcomes.

The radical indeterminacy begins to emerge when classical mechanics describes certain oscillating systems, treating these systems with the utmost precision. One relevant type of system consists of a subsystem that would oscillate regularly and deterministically if left to itself (i.e., any given state of motion would determine all future states), together with a periodic external force (also deterministic in isolation) which changes the parameters of the subsystem. One example is a swinging pendulum whose point of support is lifted up and down by a piston. Such combined oscillations would be extremely important in nature if classical physics were true, since among internally moving systems, only oscillating ones display stable patterns. In many of the perturbed systems just described, more than one grossly different motion is a possible result of precisely the same state of the system. One striking feature of the technical argument is that it depends on a demand for precise description, in particular, on a refusal to accept so-called second-order approximations in the basic energy equations.[27] Again, any derivation of probabilities for outcomes would depend on an intolerably broad principle of indifference.

Admittedly, these indeterminacies only arise in special cases, in which certain relations exist between the oscillations that each coupled subsystem would undergo, if swinging in isolation from the other. However, further arguments in classical mechanics, technically arcane but uncontroversial, make indeterminacy much more common. There are physically important systems in which any finite range of values for the initial state includes values dictating grossly different motions, as different as a plumb bob's swinging to and fro and its swinging around in a circle. As precision grows and the finite range of values for initial conditions is shrunk, there is no tendency for questions about subsequent trajectories to be settled. The initial indeterminacy persists relative to the smaller interval. This is very different from the familiar, milder indeterminacy, in which greater precision pushes the limits of definite entailment into the future, and trajectory deductions can always at least be sketched. The deductions cannot be sketched, since the project of filling in gaps in the premises now available to provide an eventual basis for deducing the approximate trajectory is doomed, demonstrably and in principle. The needed laws are available—indeed, routine and familiar. But they can be shown to dictate the unavailability of needed statements of initial conditions. Here, a probability-assignment to an outcome, whether an assignment of 1 or of less than 1, cannot be made *and* cannot be sketched. And yet the trajectory that actually unfolds can be traced back to a cause, say, to a perturbing event that actually caused the rotation that might instead have been a swinging.[28]

## CAUSALITY AND RELEVANCE

At this point, it might seem that probabilistic covering-laws are the basis for explanation, not because they can be derived in appropriate ways and assign particular probabilities, but because they can

---

[27] For a concise though somewhat technical account see L. Landau and E. Lifshitz, *Mechanics* (Oxford, 1976), pp. 80–93.

[28] For concise statements of these findings see Ilya Prigogine and Isabelle Stengers, *Order Out of Chaos* (New York, 1984), pp. 261–72, and, in a more technical format, Prigogine, *From Being to Becoming* (New York, 1980), pp. 38–45. A more detailed account, by a leader in the field, is Juergen Moser, *Stable and Random Motions in Dynamical Systems* (Princeton, 1974).

combine with initial conditions to entail changes in probabilities. More precisely, any adequate explanation might be taken to appeal to antecedent circumstances together with empirical, general laws entailing an increase or, in any case, a change in the probability of the phenomenon to be explained given the presence of those antecedents. But Cartwright has shown that this demand is wrong, and that the right principle about changes in probability depends on substantial causal constraints. It is a tribute to the power of the covering-law model, much like the unintended tribute at the end of Davidson's "Causal Relations," that Cartwright, nonetheless, takes herself to have vindicated Hempel's basic claim, that explanatory connections must be covered by laws. In fact, an extension of her argument undermines any effort to rely on probabilities to vindicate Hempel's basic program.

Cartwright's objection to the general demand that causes increase probabilities is that a factor that frequently causes a certain kind of phenomenon may reduce its frequency, on balance, or have no effect on its frequency, because it tends to be associated with another, countervailing factor. She notes, for example, that smoking might be a cause of heart attacks even if smokers were so attentive to their special risks that they had a special tendency to exercise well, reducing the smokers' heart attack rate to that of non-smokers.

Cartwright proposes the following principle as the strongest one that links causes and probabilities. A factor is a cause of a phenomenon only if the presence of the former makes the latter more common in all "test situations," i.e., all situations which are causally the same apart from the factor in question. If populations of smokers had healthy hearts on account of exercise, populations of exercisers who did not smoke would be healthier, yet.[29]

An adequate understanding of causal sameness, here, depends on a variety of robustly causal notions. Once their role is established, any requirement of a covering-law affecting probabilities in a prescribed way turns out to be excessive. And this includes Cartwright's own ultimate proposal of a modified covering-law model.

The features controlled for in test situations must include phenomena subsequent to the onset of the factor in question, for example, subsequent to taking up smoking. That is how such countervailing effects as exercise resulting from learning of health risks are screened out. But a requirement that a test situation be the same in all features, or all causally significant features, other than the presence or absence of the factor in question would be far too un-

[29] See Nancy Cartwright, "Causal Laws and Effective Strategies," p. 423.

discriminating. If we compare smokers with otherwise identical non-smokers, then the smokers who have heart attacks, and have a certain vascular history up until the occurrence of the heart attacks, must be compared with non-smokers with the same kinds of vascular physiologies. Obviously, the heart attack rate will be the same for both groups. Just as much unfairness to the smoking hypothesis results if we try to screen out the intermediate factors by requiring that smoking increase the frequency of the heart attack sequel regardless of the presence or absence of smoking's other effects or of intermediate links in the causal chain actually producing the sequel. Presumably, smoking does not increase heart attacks when it does not produce certain conditions in the circulatory system.

Evidently, the construction of an ideal test situation would depend on the identification of all of the actual particular causal scenarios with the outcome in question. For, in the absence of a more abstract rule defining relevant causal sameness, the general connection between frequency and causation comes to no more than this: the set of actual causal scenarios producing the outcome without a causal contribution from the factor in question must be smaller than the set of scenarios producing the outcome. So the sequel is more frequent because of the causal chains involving the factor. In itself, this connection between frequency and cause is an utterly trivial conclusion. It tells us, in effect, that if smoking is a cause of heart attacks there will be true stories of heart attack production that involve smoking, in addition to any that don't. What is important is that this is the strongest general claim that can be made about the link between causation and changed probability. By keeping this fact in mind, one can often avoid bad inferences from statistics and experiments.

Cartwright takes the connection between increased frequency, test situations and causes to vindicate the most basic aspects of the covering-law model. An explanation, in her view, should indicate how an increased frequency in relevant kinds of phenomena is entailed by general laws, when appropriate kinds of antecedents are present, and frequencies are compared in test situations.[30] It has turned out, however, that an adequate analysis of "test situation" must rely on the notion of a causal connection between particular

[30] See ibid., pp. 424–26. I do not mean to suggest that she offers a full-fledged model of explanation, or that she regards Hempel's as wholly unaffected by her discussion of causation; see her note 6, p. 437. For her more recent views, see *How the Laws of Physics Lie* (Oxford, 1983), esp. essay 2.

events. No alternative analysis of such connections as entailments via certain kinds of general laws seems to single out the right test situations. So far, the bearing of Cartwright's main argument is to undermine an important support for any demand that a covering-law exist. Notions of causing an event, bringing something about and the like are not dispensable in favor of notions of correlation and logical entailment, in any analysis of causation, including probabilistic ones. Rather, the notion of a particular causal connection is required to make it clear when correlations are relevant to causal claims.

Still, it might be true that a reasonable causal claim fits a covering-law model modified in light of Cartwright's article, when test situations are identified as shrewd investigators actually do in practice. It might then be a good bet to pursue the otherwise unpromising task of defining test situations without reliance on prior identification of causal connections. One would be searching for the implicit logic of investigations which do, in practice, uncover connections between cause and effect. In fact, though, the new probabilistic covering-law model does not fit the practice of good explainers.

In one large and important class of cases, X is known to be due to Y, although Y is as likely as not to have an opposite effect. Here, one type of phenomenon is causally sensitive to another, but only the actual outcome reveals which of the alternative sequels is actually produced. The fossil record may show that an ecological disaster led to a certain dramatic change through adaptation, even though there is no general law saying when a disaster of that general kind leads to evolutionary triumph rather than extinction. The historical record shows that early medieval Ireland responded to isolation and barbaric invasion with a rich and original elaboration of indigenous arts. No general principle assigns a likelihood to this outcome as against a dark age. In these and similar cases, we would, of course, accept that an outcome of the kind in question—adaptation or indigenous flourishing—is more likely to occur when the antecedent is present, given that background conditions are facilitating. But that an outcome is apt to occur under circumstances that make an antecedent apt to produce it is a tautology, not a general, empirical law. Belief that we are investigating a facilitating situation is sometimes empirically justified, but on the basis of the actual outcome, *not* by seeing how general properties combine with general laws affecting probabilities.

People who first encounter the covering-law model often think it implies an ironclad, oversimplified determinism. The beginners are literally wrong, since positivists do not suppose that everything is explainable and do admit probabilistic explanations. But they are basically right. The covering-law model, its probabilistic revisions and, as we shall see, its counterfactual revisions as well, cannot do justice to possibilities that the study of non-deterministic systems reveals.

## TESTING, PREDICTION AND PSEUDO-EXPLANATION

Positivists seem to offer a number of other arguments for the covering-law model, for example, an argument from the symmetry of explanation and prediction and an appeal to the need to exclude certain pseudo-explanations. But really, there is just one remaining argument, on which all the rest depend, an analysis of the conditions for testability. As Hempel puts it in his 1940 essay, "Any explanation of scientific character is amenable to objective checks; these include (a) an empirical test of the sentences that state the determining conditions; (b) an empirical test of the universal hypotheses on which the explanation rests; (c) an investigation of whether the explanation is logically conclusive in the sense that the sentence describing the events to be expected logically follows from . . . [these] statements."[31]

To see why the several remaining arguments are really just one, it is helpful to have a synoptic view of departures from the covering-law model. Proposed explanations which do not fit the covering-law mold deviate in one of two ways. When we uncover implicit hypotheses, it may be that the closest we come to an empirical general law is a tautology to the effect that if a certain kind of factor is strong enough (or: a certain process is rapid enough or pervasive enough) and countervailing factors weak enough, an effect of the kind in question results. The explanations of the sore throat and of Lee's surrender were cases in point. In the remaining departures from the model, the closest we come to an empirical general law is a generalization referring to particular times, places, objects, or people. Geology is one apparent example. Historians' explanations relying on principles limited to a particular period and region seem to be others.

Hempel sometimes offers an argument from the symmetry of explanation and prediction as if it were the master argument for the covering-law model. It depends on the requirement, "Any rationally acceptable answer to the question 'Why did X occur?' must offer

---

[31] "The Function of General Laws in History," p. 234.

information which shows that X was to be expected—if not definitely, as in the case of D-N explanation, then at least with reasonable probability."[32] In this sense, any explanation must potentially serve as the basis for a prediction—perhaps a "prediction" of a past event on the basis of yet earlier circumstances. A proposed explanation (the argument goes) can only meet this prediction requirement if it conforms to the covering-law model.[33]

In fact, the prediction requirement is quite compatible with either type of departure from the model. If I know that Lee's despair was great enough and countervailing forces weak enough to produce his surrender, I have excellent grounds for believing that he did in fact surrender, even though the appropriate covering principle is a tautology. Moreover, I might have acquired this ground for "prediction" not on the basis of knowledge that Lee surrendered but by my reading of Lee's diary. Similarly, generalizations restricted in scope to particular times and places can be the basis for predictions, throughout the scope of the restrictions. Indeed, the notion of prediction is so receptive to these departures, that one might take Hempel's doctrine of the "symmetry of prediction and explanation" as part of a powerful argument *against* the covering-law model. "[W]hatever will be said . . . concerning the logical character of explanation or prediction will be applicable to either."[34] A prediction involving knowledge of the conditions leading up to an event may rely on covering principles which are, irreducibly, tautologous or restricted to particular times or places. Therefore, explanations need not fit the covering-law format.

When the prediction requirement is supplemented to exclude these deviant tactics, the result is not an argument about the prediction-explanation symmetry but the argument from testability with which this section began. As the first supplement, the phenomenon predicted must be required to be logically independent of the predictive premises, excluding mere coverage by tautologies. As the second, the explainer must be required to explain away any departure elsewhere from a tendency to which he appeals, by describing a distinguishing general feature of the case at hand which makes the sequel in question predictable here, even if it does not occur in the

[32] "Aspects of Scientific Explanation," p. 369.

[33] See "Aspects of Scientific Explanation," p. 368; "Reasons and Covering Laws in Historical Explanation" (1963) in Patrick Gardiner, *The Philosophy of History* (London, 1974), pp. 93ff.; "The Function of General Laws in History," p. 234; "Studies in the Logic of Explanation," p. 249.

[34] "Studies in the Logic of Explanation," p. 249.

other circumstances; so there is no ultimate reliance on scope restrictions that do not refer to general properties. However, these
constraints are not at all plausible as conditions for prediction in
general. Rather, they might be taken to prescribe the particular
kind of prediction by which a genuine explanatory hypothesis
could, in principle, have been *tested*. It is tempting to suppose that
the test of an explanatory hypothesis must have the form of a prediction deduced from general laws and independent statements of
antecedents which are part of the hypothesis itself. Here, the supplementary conditions might seem to exclude tactics by which failure can always be explained away, making testing impossible. They
rule out ultimate reliance on such dodges as "The factor in question
was too weak in that other case, although I can't say why."

Similarly, in arguments from the distinction between real and
pseudo-explanation, an underlying view of testing is doing all the
work. The covering-law model is often justified as accounting for
the exclusion of various proposals from science. Good explainers
feel free to reject out of hand explanations of Napoleon's career in
terms of his personal destiny, and explanations of chicken embryol-
ogy as due to the inherent tendency of chicken-egg matter to yield
chickens. The covering-law model can account for these dismissals
since the covering principles are, at best, tautologies: those with an
ironclad destiny to lead, do so; what has a strong enough chick-pro-
ducing tendency yields a chick.

In fact, it is not at all obvious that these rightly dismissed hypotheses are to be dismissed on the basis of their logical form. One
of Aristophanes' comic heros believes that a rainshower is caused by
Zeus' pissing through a sieve. Present-day meteorologists would not
bother to investigate this hypothesis. But it is dismissed, not because
its logical form is inappropriate, but because dismissal of this kind
of hypothesis has produced progress, has created no problems, and
is a rejection of what has become obviously false. Indeed, science-
fiction worlds can be imagined in which personal destinies and entelechies do seem worth taking seriously. Bullets fired at Napoleon
swerve from their course. Speakers in the Directoire rise to call for
his dismissal and all are silenced by apoplexy. Some hens lay albu-
men eggs, others sodium ones, others silicon ones, all of the most
diverse chemical structure. Chickens always result. At the very least,
an argument is needed to show that the familiar pseudo-explanations, unlike Aristophanes' extravagantly false explanation, are dis-
qualified by logical form. Again, the only argument offered is the
argument from testability. Because they depart from the covering-

law model, the pseudo-explanations are held not "even roughly to indicate the type of investigation . . . that might lead to evidence either confirming or infirming the suggested explanation."[35]

Now the whole weight of the covering-law requirement is supported by the following argument: an explanation of why an event occurred asserts something more than the occurrence, at appropriately related times, of two logically independent events; the truth of this something more is only subject to empirical test if it consists of the existence of an empirical general law, connecting the two events according to one of the covering-law formats. This central argument rests on a radically impoverished conception of testing, in which auxiliary principles and comparisons among rival hypotheses are denied their essential and ultimate roles.

By an "auxiliary principle," I mean a principle supporting the claim that data of the kind at hand confirm explanatory hypotheses of the kind in question, a principle which is not itself a part of the explanatory hypothesis. One simple example is the principle on which the imagined Civil War historian implicitly relied: the entries in the secret diary of an intelligent, successful public figure are apt accurately to state the rationales producing his or her major strategic actions. Another example is Galileo's principle that telescope images approximately correspond to gross features of celestial objects. This functions as a crucial auxiliary principle in Galileo's arguments for explanations of the phases of Venus. The diary principle is not part of an explanation of why Lee surrendered, any more than the principle that telescopes approximately reveal celestial reality is part of the explanation of why Venus is "horned." Auxiliary principles are not covering-laws, in the explanations they help to evaluate. But knowledge of such principles, together with appropriate data, can put an explainer in a position to offer an explanation, when he or she cannot even sketch a covering-law. This is just what happened to the lucky Civil War historian.

The comparison of rival hypotheses is an aspect of testing that can also provide an empirical warrant for explanations in the absence of covering-laws. Sometimes, an investigator has reason to believe that one or another of a limited group of factors is more likely than not to have caused a phenomenon, if a phenomenon of that kind occurs in the population in question. This list of likely causes may be available, even if none of those factors is likely to have that sequel, as an effect. A sore throat is apt to be caused either by a viral infection, a

---

[35] Hempel, "The Function of General Laws in History," p. 238.

bacterial infection, or by prolonged exposure to an irritant. But none of these factors produces a sore throat more often than not. Sometimes, an investigator can use auxiliary principles to compare these alternatives in light of the data. He or she may be in a position to conclude that one of the factors is the most likely cause of what actually happened, but not in a position even to sketch a covering-law.[36]

If we rely on auxiliary principles, then we can confirm the non-covering-law explanations by arguments from data. (Checklists for causal comparison are a special kind of auxiliary principle.) Conversely, if confirmation were solely regulated by a priori principles concerned with logical form, the covering-law requirement would follow, quite directly. The crucial aspect of testing, here, is the assessment of evidence with the logical form of a counter-example. Suppose that an explanatory hypothesis, when stripped of tautological hedges and particularist restrictions of scope, yields a certain law-like statement as its Hempelian core, say, of the form "Whenever F, G." If the previous way of cataloguing non-covering-law explanations, as either tautologous or particularist, is right, such a core will always exist. If there are no counter-instances, cases of $F$ but not $G$, then the explanation already contained a valid covering-law. Suppose there are counterinstances to the core. Every reasonable investigator accepts that such data sometimes are potentially lethal counter-examples, i.e., phenomena that must be explained away by pointing to a relevant distinguishing feature of the original case. But if whatever has the logical form of a counter-example, i.e., is a counter-instance to a core, *is* a potentially lethal counter-example, then asserting an explanation means maintaining that it sketches a covering-law. The law that must be sketched is the one that would explain away all the potentially lethal counterexamples.

There is only one way out. What has the form of a counter-example is not a genuine, potentially lethal counter-example, unless a further substantive auxiliary principle gives it that status. Such an auxiliary principle would imply that similar causes are apt to have similar effects both in the original circumstance and in the new situation that threatens the explanatory proposal. And this is just how good investigators work with counter-examples. Tilly, for example, explains the counter-revolutionary uprising in the Vendée, a dis-

[36] Scriven, "Causes, Connections and Conditions in History," is an original and influential account of the role of such eliminative reasoning in justifying historians' explanations. See especially pp. 246–50.

trict in western France, in 1793 as based on the monopoly the Vendean clergy had over the peasantry's access to the larger world.[37] If there was a region in eastern France in the eighteenth century or in England in the seventeenth century where the same kind of situation gave no political leadership to the clergy, that would be a relevant counter-example, because of the known similarities in the dominant social processes. On the other hand, Tilly, presumably, has no confidence in his capacity to explain away processes in which an enraged clergy had a monopoly over access to the larger world but could not mobilize the peasantry in tenth-century Japan or neolithic Britain. And no working historian would take this as an admission of defeat, in the dispute over the Vendean uprising.

The pervasive reliance on auxiliary principles is a reassuring sign that non-covering-law explanations can be confirmed. Yet an important source of the argument from testability was the worry that the deviant explanations could not be *dis*confirmed. If apparent evidence to the contrary can always be dismissed on the grounds that the causal factor was not strong enough in the alleged test, or that the case presented was too different, albeit in unknown ways, how can the most obvious nonsense be falsified? It is some help, here, to consider that auxiliary principles could dictate that the evidence is similar enough to disconfirm. But an adequate response would have to account for the frequent inclination of investigators to take it as an admission of weakness when an explanation is defended by appeal to tautologous hedges or particularist restrictions. Surely, investigators are diffident about such remarks as "That situation is too far removed to be relevant, though I can't say just why," on some occasions when they are not influenced by a philosophical commitment to the covering-law model.

Here, the role of comparison in the testing of hypotheses comes into its own. Typically, if not always, an explanation is defeated by an argument that some rival is superior. Such arguments need not be a straightforward matter of identifying one item on a causal checklist as present, another as absent. Often, the rival triumphs because of other virtues that are desirable in explanations. For example, if two rival hypotheses fit all the data equally well, and explain the phenomena immediately in question, one may be preferred, all else being equal, because it conveys more explanatory information. In other words, it furnishes non-tautologous answers to more explanatory questions, which the defeated hypothesis cannot answer. This maxim of superiority results from causal reasoning about the

[37] See Charles Tilly, *The Vendée* (Cambridge, Mass., 1964).

evolution of the hypotheses and the data. If it is false, the more informative kind of hypothesis is easier to defeat, so, if it fares as well, its success is more apt to be a matter of truth, not luck (all else being equal).

The troubling defenses purchase continued good fit with the data at the cost of reduced explanatory informativeness, so that the hedged hypothesis is more liable to defeat, by an informative rival that fits the data just as well. In this way, the familiar examples of "pseudo-explanations" are specially vulnerable. For, by their very nature, they cannot give non-tautologous explanations of departures from the tendency they posit. Rival hypotheses, if empirically accurate, are almost bound to be more informative. Entelechies, by definition, are inherent tendencies for an embryo to develop in a certain way that has no further explanation on the basis of the physical characteristics of the embryo. So, while entelechy theorists were well aware that certain chemical interventions had a tendency to produce certain departures from the developmental norm, they could not explain the departures, except by positing that the entelechy was relevantly weakened. To explain otherwise would have been to abandon entelechy theory, at least in part. Similarly, to appeal to personal destiny is to ascribe an inherent tendency to have a life of a certain kind, a tendency that has no further explanation on the basis of psychology, personal situation or the larger social setting. So personal destiny explanations are, by their nature, vulnerable to defeat by psychological or social explanations, which offer a means of explaining why some people, superficially like the hero, had a different fate.

If this account of the perils of departure from the covering-law model is right, then the familiar examples of "pseudo-explanation" could, in principle, be justified, although they are always specially vulnerable to defeat. This makes it much easier to account for the fact that they have the same logical form (tautologous at the level of general principles) as countless explanations in biology, pathology, psychology, geology, history and elsewhere that seem perfectly legitimate. It also fits the facts of the history of explanation, where "pseudo-explanations" of today were once the province of thoughtful and creative investigators, who seem methodologically acute. For example, in the nineteenth century, the opponents of spontaneous generation, heroes in the history of experimental design, were specially receptive to vitalistic explanations and entelechies.[38]

[38] In particular, people in Pasteur's intellectual circle often took belief in spontaneous generation to be sustained by a false assumption that life-processes were due

Talk of national destiny was once the province of creative and thoughtful historians impressed by the tendency of national cultures to preserve their identities and even to flourish in the face of material obstacles. Even the hypothesis of personal destiny was once an effort to do justice to a perceived tendency of leaders to appear and, unintentionally, to advance national development in accordance with an underlying pattern.

The covering-law model has turned out to rest in large part on a conception of hypothesis-testing as a lonely drama, in which hypothesis and data encounter each other in isolation, with no essential role, in the final analysis, for auxiliary principles or comparison. Of course, positivism produced philosophical theories of confirmation that fit precisely this conception, theories in which a hypothesis is confirmed by data in virtue of its logical relations to the latter. Such theories will be a main subject of the middle section of this book. For now, it is enough to note that this arid conception of testing incessantly conflicts with the appearances of good empirical argument, and that here, much more than in the case of explanation, positivists offer little reason to suppose that reality differs from these appearances. Thus Hempel says, in a characteristic passage, "[I]t seems reasonable to require that the criteria of empirical confirmation, besides being objective in character, should contain no reference to the specific subject-matter of the hypothesis or of the evidence in question; it ought to be possible, one feels, to set up purely formal criteria of confirmation in a manner similar to that in which deductive logic provides purely formal criteria for the validity of inductive inference."[39] Ironically, these appeals to what "seems reasonable" and what "one feels" immediately follow a warning that "a feeling of conviction . . . is often deceptive and can certainly serve

---

to chemical interactions. Though the assumption they took to be false later turned out to be true, the defeat of spontaneous-generation theories was a defeat for contemporary mechanistic theories of life-processes. The great pioneers of organic chemistry, including Berzelius, Mitscherlich and Liebig, overestimated the simplicity of the chemical structure of life processes and, accordingly, were quite receptive to hypotheses of spontaneous generation. Pasteur's ally, de Careil, was rude but not wholly wrong when he told a scientific congress that the doctrine of spontaneous generation of microbes was "a philosophical monstrosity, the leading error of anti-christian physiology, a product of ignorant impiety, an unhealthy theory defended by those who are the children of the eighteenth century, lost in the nineteenth"; see William Bulloch, *The History of Bacteriology* (New York, 1979), p. 103. For a calmer vitalist criticism of support for spontaneous generation, see the remarks by Pasteur's coworker, Duclaux, ibid., p. 52.

[39] "Studies in the Logic of Confirmation" (1945) in *Aspects*, p. 10.

neither as a necessary nor as a sufficient condition for the soundness of a given assertion."

Because the covering-law model is, as philosophical theories go, so powerful and flexible—especially in Hempel's hands—the criticism of the model has yielded clues about its possible replacement. Explanation seems to identify the particular producers of particular events. The basic distinctions between explanation and non-explanation seem to require causal notions, which cannot be analyzed away in favor of non-causal ones. Explanation, together with the justified choice of an explanation, seems to be intrinsically comparative. It is time to use these clues. But first, at least by way of appendix, justice should be done to the recent history of the covering-law model.

## THE FATE OF QUALITATIVENESS: AN APPENDIX

In the 1960s, Hempel abandoned the requirement that covering-laws contain only qualitative predicates. Along with the concession that the covering-law model may not describe a sufficient condition, this is his major revision of the model, in forty years of controversy. Since he has offered alternatives to the old requirement in an extremely tentative spirit, this survey of them will be brief. It will, however, add to the case for the unavoidability of causal notions in the analysis of explanation.

Hempel dropped the requirement of qualitativeness in the face of counterexamples from the practice of scientific explanation. Kepler's laws refer to specific objects, the Sun and the planets. Galileo's law of free fall refers to the Earth. Kepler and Galileo used those laws in explanations of trajectories, and properly so. Yet neither could derive his eponymous law on the basis of other, qualitative principles.[40]

The requirement of qualitativeness must be dropped. Yet many true generalizations restricted to particular times, places or things do seem incapable of supporting explanations. That every coin in my pocket is made of copper does not explain why the dirty coin in my pocket is made of copper. Moreover, if all departures from qualitativeness are allowed, we can trivialize the covering-law model. Faced with a demand for a law to cover the explanation "Y happened because X did," we could submit, with a high degree of confidence: "Whenever an event just like X occurs, one just like Y fol-

---

[40] See "Aspects of Scientific Explanation," p. 342.

lows." If the demand for qualitativeness is abandoned, it needs to be replaced with a restriction playing a similar role.

Using unanalyzed causal notions, we can distinguish between appropriate and inappropriate generalizations. A generalization is an appropriate basis for an explanation if it is correctly held to be made true by causal mechanisms, which inhibit the occurrence of counterinstances. Galileo and Kepler correctly believed that their laws had this status, even though they did not know what the mechanisms were. But, of course, I do not believe that there is a mechanism making all the coins in my pocket copper, and preventing non-cuprous coins from occupying this region. If, however, someone convinced me that there was magical copper-making cloth and that my pocket was made of it, I might very well explain why a coin was copper by appealing to the generalization, "All coins in my pocket are made of copper." The generalization would describe a genuine causal tendency, produced by a mechanism that is not mentioned explicitly. It is a law of my pocket, as Galileo's generalization is a law of our planet.

As usual, Hempel avoids reliance on causal notions in his own analysis, and wisely so. Such notions, once admitted, threaten to do all the work of explicating "explanation." He insists that the covering generalization be law-like and entertains three different ways of defining law-likeness without reference to causality. Each fails, because it is only a partial and crude reflection of the causal distinctions actually at work.

In "Aspects," Hempel expresses the hope that an adequate restriction might be based on the notion of an entrenched predicate.[41] An entrenched predicate is one which has been used in the past in generalizations which are "projected," i.e., held to obtain throughout their scope on the basis of observed instances. But, if we give due credit to the force of novel hypotheses, such a restriction will prove too weak.

In the explanation of new or perplexing data, scientists often use predicates which have not been projected before. That is a mark of sound but novel science. At the very least we must admit that an acceptable predicate for an explanatory law may be, though not itself entrenched, a conjunction of entrenched ones, or may refer to a new value of a magnitude, another value of which has been entrenched. After all, the first scientist to investigate the law, "Whatever is sodium chloride and is placed in benzene dissolves" could

[41] Ibid., pp. 341f.

take it to be a projectible generalization, even if the joint condition in the antecedent had not been involved in projection, before. Similarly, when new data led scientists to assign new values to the gravitational constant, the question of the projectibility of the universal law of gravitation was not reopened.

In principle, we can almost always redescribe a particular time, place, object or person by permissible construction out of entrenched predicates. If a physical object is in question, its precise weight, color, chemical composition, and shape are likely to be enough. Suppose that I find such a predicate, P, singling out my pocket, through such magnitude-fixing and compounding of entrenched predicates. Any acceptable requirement of entrenchment will admit the generalization "Whatever is P is copper." Yet such a generalization would be too accidental in just the way we want to clarify. This pseudo-law is just as accidental as "All coins in my pocket are copper."

As a rule, when we project we take the observed instances as resulting from mechanisms making the general hypothesis true. Accordingly, we might use the hypothesis to explain. But this is hardly a step toward the defense of the covering-law model. It suggests that explanatory potential and projectibility may go together only because both involve the ascription of causes. In Chapter Four, I will argue that this suggestion is right, and, also, that projectibility does not depend on considerations of entrenchment.

More recently, Hempel has noted that generalizations that do not support explanations do not support counterfactual conditionals, either. He has suggested that this might be the basis for a new criterion.[42] For example, science fiction to one side, I would not say of a dime that it would be made of copper if it were in my pocket, even if all the coins in my pocket are.

What counterfactuals must an acceptable generalization support, and how? It would be too much to require that a generalization support all counterfactuals of some standard form dictated by its own internal content. Galileo did not suppose that any non-terrestrial object, if it had been near the Earth, would have covered distances in free-fall according to his equation. He did not believe that the Moon, Jupiter, or the Sun would do so. He had no general description of the appropriate further qualification.

However, if we merely require that a generalization support *some* counterfactual, the criterion is too weak. Propositions can support

[42] See *Philosophy of Natural Science*, p. 56.

counterfactuals in ways that are irrelevant to explanation, because this support does not reflect the presence of causal mechanisms. For example, the past has a special role in the assessment of counterfactuals. Suppose that yesterday, anything that happened while Jones was in his shop happened by 5:00 P.M. On this basis, I can tell Smith, "You were lucky to arrive at 5 sharp. If you had gotten there one minute later, Jones would have been out." Yet surely, the generalization about Jones' day is not, by that token, a covering-law. Jones was not in the shop at 4:30 because he was in the shop until 5:00.

Indeed, in some appropriate contexts for the assessment of counterfactuals, the accidental regularity, all coins in my pocket are made of copper, supports a conditional of appropriate form. Suppose I am assessing the probability that a proposition is the case, on the basis of limited but relevant knowledge. The proposition is that one of the coins once in a friend's collection is now in my pocket. I ask him whether his was a specialized collection, and he tells me all his coins were silver. I note, "All coins in my pocket are copper. If one of your coins were in my pocket, it would be copper. And you have told me none is."

Of course, when we assess generalizations for explanatory potential, we are not supposed to assess the relevant counterfactuals in a context in which the past has a special status, or in which the construction of probabilities on the basis of partial knowledge is the goal. Rather, we should accept the counterfactuals in question if they describe facts which would be produced by the causal mechanisms reflected in the generalization, if different antecedent conditions were to arise. Thus, the demand that a potential covering-law support counterfactuals is an oversimplified and potentially misleading approximation to the genuine criterion: an acceptable generalization should reflect the operation of causal mechanisms bringing the regularity about and inhibiting departures from it. (I discuss other problems of the counterfactual account in the next chapter, in connection with David Lewis' analysis of causation.)

Hempel's remaining, highly tentative suggestion is that an appropriate relation to theories may be the mark of generalizations that can explain. Though no coin in my pocket is other than copper, metallurgy does not rule out such possibilities. Perhaps a generalization is only capable of explaining if a theory rules out all possible exceptions to it.[43]

This proposal would be disappointing, even if literally adequate.

---

[43] See ibid., pp. 57f.

It presupposes the distinction between genuine theories and mere general truths, too accidental to rule out possibilities which did not happen to arise. This sounds suspiciously like the very distinction between laws and accidental regularities which was to be explained. In any case, the proposal fails in just those cases which motivated the search for an alternative to qualitativeness. Kepler's and Galileo's laws were compelling counter-examples to the original requirement because they could be used to explain in the absence of a theory from which they were derived.

In the development of the covering-law model, each attempt to explain what makes a generalization a law has described some frequent accompaniment of belief in the existence of an underlying causal factor, without actually employing that notion itself. All have failed, as a consequence. Rather than avoiding such causal notions in a theory of explanation, we should use them to construct the most informative and accurate theory we can.

# CHAPTER TWO

# The Nature of Explanation

AN explanation is an adequate description of underlying causes helping to bring about the phenomenon to be explained. This is my account of explanation in broadest outline. Of course, any real progress depends on filling in the outline, by clarifying the concepts employed and showing that they are not to be analyzed in a way that yields a positivist criterion of explanation. After all, the usual positivist objection to causal accounts of methodological concepts is, not that they are false, but that they are unclear[1] or "unscientific,"[2] in need of further analysis in a positivist style. Also, there is a legitimate concern that a robustly causal model such as I have sketched will be truistic but useless, unable to help solve specific methodological problems. These uses of my causal model will be the subject of the next chapter.

## THE AUTONOMY OF CAUSATION

What sort of antecedent or concomitant counts as a cause of something's happening? One answer to this question, all agree, is provided and constantly revised by scientific inquiry. In addition, many believe, there is a second answer philosophy provides, an analysis that is valid a priori, and informative enough to resolve questions of whether a hypothesis, if accurate, describes a cause. My basic proposal is that no such second kind of answer is even approximately right. Like the concept of number and the concept of a work of art, the concept of a cause centers on a diverse array of banal but paradigmatic examples and extends beyond them through diverse and unpredictable paths that further inquiry lays down.

Before arguing that the remaining analyses are wrong and then developing this non-analytic conception of causes, some warnings and elaborations may make clearer the way in which "cause" is to be taken in the proposed theory of explanation. For one thing, while our usual lists of causes tend to favor episodes triggering an event

[1] See Hempel, "Aspects of Scientific Explanation," p. 343.
[2] See Nelson Goodman, *Fact, Fiction and Forecast* (1954; Cambridge, Mass., 1983), p. 20.

as against conditions necessary for the triggering, this favoritism is out of place for present purposes. Sometimes, a mere condition would be on everyone's list of causes of an event—for example, if it is crucial but unusual. "The presence of oxygen" looks strange in a list of causes of an ordinary earth-bound fire, but not in an account of why a fire broke out in an unmanned spaceship. And there have been whole fields, for example, quantum mechanics, traditional geology and classical electrodynamics in which the bias is, if anything, toward explanations appealing to conditions. In a causal theory of explanation, it seems best to let anything that helps to bring about something count as a cause, basing further preferences on standards that might assess true causal statements as inadequate to explain, or on other, more pragmatic considerations. Certainly, our normal failure to name the presence of oxygen as a cause of a fire can be based on our awareness that it is a cause that doesn't need to be named, to anyone for whom the naming would otherwise have a point.

Together with the everyday implication that a cause is a trigger, there is a philosophical assumption that needs to be cancelled—that if something causes an event, then it made the event inevitable under the actual circumstances; given the cause and its actual background, the sequel could not have been otherwise. This assumption that all causes are deterministic was never part of everyday causal analysis, where the turn of the honest croupier's hand causes red to come up on a roulette wheel that stops at red by chance. That turn of the hand caused the trajectory ending at red, but it could just as well have led to black. Also, this determinist assumption is no longer part of physics, where a dynamical event is typically attributed to an antecedent total state that need not have had the event as its sequel. And, as we have seen, the philosophical assumption is not a background assumption of any other scientific field—not even of classical mechanics in the most modern formulations. Aside from philosophical rationales that have the flaws of Hempel's "Same cause, same effect" argument, the requirement that causes be deterministic seems to rest on a historical circumstance. The great debates about determinism were debates about free will among people who shared either a belief in an omnipotent God or a belief that causal processes are deterministic in ways that classical physics seemed to reveal. In the theological context, what God causes He utterly controls. In the context of the debate over the metaphysical implications of science, what is outside the realm of deterministic natural laws was taken to be noumenal, i.e., outside the realm of causes or, in any case, causes that we can investigate. No one would want to rest a philosophy of science on either background assumption, now. So it is disappointing that the determinism of causes, in the sense described above, is so freely used as a working assumption, in the analysis of causes today.

Because non-deterministic conditions can be causes, there is no contradiction between the causal theory of explanation and the non-deterministic explanations that are routinely offered in quantum physics. In those explanations, events are attributed to causes: the final location of an electron is attributed to its scattering by an atom; the polarization of a photon leaving a tourmaline crystal is attributed to its having passed through the crystal; and so forth. Yet, typically, a definite physical event is not attributed to a cause that could not have had any contrary sequel. In these non-deterministic situations, the claim that quantum theory could be used to exclude every alternative but one would contradict basic premises and procedures of the theory itself. Because they were reared in classical physics, which required fully adequate causal explanations to be deterministic, the pioneers of quantum physics sometimes identified the denial of determinism with the denial of causality itself. But despite this occasional anachronism in their usage, they, like all subsequent physicists, routinely attributed events to causes in their explanations. Thus, the paper in which Born introduced the probabilistic interpretation is an effort to use Schroedinger's equations to explain scatterings as due to prior collisions. Born's nominal denial of causality, in this paper, is surrounded by clear indications that he is not really denying that prior processes cause events:

> Schrödinger's quantum mechanics therefore gives a definite answer to the question of the *effect* of the collision; but there is no question of any causal description. One gets no answer to the question, "what is the state after the collision," but only to the question, "how probable is a specified *outcome of the collision*" (where naturally the quantum mechanical energy relation must be fulfilled).[3]

Similarly, von Neumann, in introducing his influential notion that the act of measurement is a non-deterministic intervention, distinct from the deterministic evolution of unmeasured quantum states, makes it clear that both types of phenomena are causal: "The two

[3] "On the Quantum Mechanics of Collisions" (1926) in J. Wheeler and W. Zurek, eds., *Quantum Theory and Measurement* (Princeton, 1983). Italics added.

interventions . . . are causal . . . indeed . . . it is not surprising that each change, even if it is statistical, effects a causal change of the probabilities and the expectation values. . . . On the other hand, it is important that 2. [the process described by deterministic laws governing pure states] transforms states into states . . . while 1. [the act of measurement] can transform states into mixtures." He immediately adds, "In this sense, therefore, the development of a state according to 1. is statistical, while according to 2. it is causal." It could hardly be clearer that von Neumann is only denying that the act of measurement is causal in a special, nonliteral usage, encouraged by classical physics, in which only deterministic causes are awarded the title "cause."[4]

It might seem, however, that the connection between event explanation and causality really is broken in special situations such as that described in Einstein, Podolsky and Rosen's famous critique of quantum physics, "Can Quantum-Mechanical Description of Physical Reality Be Considered Complete?" Einstein and his co-authors describe a situation in which an accurate and precise measurement of the momentum of one particle would, as a consequence of fundamental principles of quantum mechanics, instantly make something impossible that would otherwise have been possible at a distant locale, viz., the accurate and precise measurement, at that time, of the position of another particle. Since relativity theory prohibits action at a distance, one might think that the occurrence of the former measurement could not have caused the indefiniteness elsewhere. Yet the quantum-mechanical derivation of indefiniteness here from definiteness there certainly seems to explain why the device for measuring position yields no precise and accurate value. So it is tempting to interpret Einstein's thought-experiment as implying that quantum mechanics would have to include non-causal explanations of events, if it is a complete theory of individual microphysical events. Because such thought-experiments ("EPR-type experiments," as they are called in the trade) pervade the literature on philosophical problems of quantum mechanics, this tempting re-

[4] See von Neumann, *Mathematical Foundations of Quantum Mechanics* (1932; Princeton, 1955), p. 357. For similar reasons, London and Bauer, in their classic monograph on measurement, are careful to use scare quotes when they distinguish " 'causal' transformations" characteristic of the evolution of isolated systems from "transformations . . . which one might . . . call 'acausal' " in which one system "makes physical contact with" another; see "The Theory of Observation in Quantum Mechanics" (1939) in Wheeler and Zurek, eds., *Quantum Theory and Measurement*, pp. 248ff.

sponse often leads people to suppose that the pioneers' loose statements that quantum physics is noncausal should be accepted as literally true. The cost is the paradoxical claim that an event can be explained as due to a change that had no effect on it.

In fact, the aspect of quantum physics that is revealed by EPR-type experiments is, not the denial of (nondeterministic) causality, but the rejection of an assumption, characteristic of classical physics, that change is due to the effect of one part of a system on other, separable parts. Relativistic restrictions on speed of influence are restrictions on speed of energy transfer. They restrict the timing of effects due to energy transfer. They do not restrict the timing of effects due to changes in properties of whole systems that entail instantaneous correlations between distant parts. More concretely, I do not disprove relativity theory when, by jumping, I instantaneously change the center of gravity of the Earth-Miller system, even though that center of gravity is thousands of miles distant from my jumping. Nor did the Franklin National Bank, on Long Island, disprove relativity theory when its failure instantaneously made worthless checks in Milan. If quantum mechanics is complete (indeed, as later analysis of EPR-type experiments revealed, if quantum mechanics is true as far as it goes), then the relevant causal factor in Einstein's thought experiment must be, irreducibly, a property of the relevant dynamical system.

I will have to postpone a completion of this rough outline until the last chapter of this book. For present purposes, the important conclusion is much more general: far from being overthrown in quantum physics, the causal theory of explanation becomes an especially important research tool for investigating consequences of quantum physics. Hypotheses about what exists according to quantum physics are sustained by showing that they reconcile quantum-theoretical ascriptions of causes with experimental findings and with general constraints on the operation of causes.[5]

## CAUSATION AND COUNTERFACTUALS

If and *only* if we are concerned with certain simplified kinds of causal systems, something more can be said. X caused Y just in case Y would not have occurred, under the actual circumstances, unless X had occurred. The relevant simplifications are these.

---

[5] That separability was at issue in the Einstein-Podolsky-Rosen argument was immediately evident in Bohr's reply. Wheeler and Zurek, ibid., contains both the Einstein, Podolsky, Rosen paper and Bohr's response.

(1) The system of causes would not produce a substitute causal chain leading to the given effect, Y, if the chain of events beginning with X actually producing the effect were absent. The literature has focussed on pre-emptive causation, where one causal chain beats another to the punch, so that the latter would have been effective in the absence of the former. We might rule out this complication by stipulating that the relevant causal inquiries are concerned with what made an event happen precisely when it did. But, though this would rule out much, it will turn out not to rule out enough. Other systems, ubiquitous in nature and society, which I will soon describe, have a capacity to introduce substitute chains without time lags.

(2) The causes are deterministic. Given all events occurring at one time in the system, the characteristics of all subsequent events are inevitable.

(3) The connection between a reliable symptom and an event it indicates is always less fundamental than the connection between that event and its causes. In other words, in the systems in question the consequences of suspending the indicator connections are always less bizarre than those of suspending the causal connections.

The world history of mass and motion events as portrayed in the classic eighteenth-century summaries of Newtonian mechanics has the first two characteristics. Even this system, however, lacks the third feature. For example, that orbits whose periods are as the 3/2 power of their distance from a common center are governed by a force varying with the square of the distance from the center is as fundamental as any cause-effect relation, even though the periods of the orbits do not cause the attractive force. In the real world, there is no important system of causal interactions that seems to obey even the first two features. Still, the three simplifications do correspond to certain simplified conceptions adopted for practical purposes, for example, the working billiard player's conception of what happens on the billiard table. Moreover, important philosophical morals can be drawn, once causation in the special, simple situations is associated with counterfactual dependence. Thus, even in such simple situations, causal ascription need not sketch a covering-law. That Y would not have happened without X does not mean that something like Y must happen when something like X does. It does not imply this even under the assumption of determinism, since what determines is X together with accompanying circumstances, whose relevant features may be unknown, even in broad outline. That Lincoln would not have been assassinated that night at Ford's

Theater if Booth had not shot him does not remotely suggest a set of general conditions making Lincoln's death inevitable.

Largely as a result of David Lewis' influential writings, the counterfactual approach, in which a cause is (roughly) an event without which a sequel would not have occurred, is the main current attempt to analyze the notion of cause. And it is the only promising approach that remains, if covering-law and probabilistic analyses are rejected for the reasons given in Chapter One.[6] I have proposed that the counterfactual account be restricted to special kinds of systems of causal interactions, rarely if ever found in reality. This is to reject it twice over, as a philosophical answer to the question of what can count as a cause. The restricted account is not general, and the description of its scope requires explicitly causal talk. So it is important to see why, outside of each restriction, causality frequently violates the counterfactual rule, in important ways.

*Causal Substitution*

In the literature on the counterfactual analysis, causal substitution is discussed in the special form of causal pre-emption. If we consider relatively simple causal inquiries, where descriptions of the chains of individual, deterministic events leading to the effect are all that is causally relevant, this is the way in which causal substitution will threaten the analysis. As Lewis forthrightly acknowledged toward the end of his original article, when one cause intervenes before another runs its course it seems that the effect would still have taken place, without the actual, pre-empting cause, since the pre-empted cause would then come into play.[7]

Suppose a victim has been given a (potentially) lethal dose of arsenic. If he lives an hour longer, the arsenic will produce heart fibrillations which will immediately produce death. But just before his heart would have begun to fibrillate, a shot to the head from a second villain produces massive cerebral hemorrhaging, which immediately kills him. The shot was a cause of his death. But in the absence of the shot, he would have died anyway.

In his brief and general discussion of causal pre-emption, Lewis relies on a detail of his counterfactual analysis of causation that was not brought out in my broader statement. His analysis directly applies to successive events, telling us that one is causally dependent

---

[6] I will subsequently discuss the only other main option, the "pragmatic" analysis of von Wright, Gasking and others. But, on the face of it, this approach is too causal to yield a non-circular analysis.

[7] See "Causation," p. 191.

on another just in case one would not occur if the other didn't. An event causes another if they are joined by a chain of causally dependent events. According to Lewis, the tempting verdict that a pre-empted cause would have worked in the absence of the preempting one results from a failure to appreciate this refinement. He asks us to consider, not just the preempting cause, $c_1$, the pre-empted cause, $c_2$, and the effect, e, but also d, a causal link between $c_1$ and e which would have been absent if $c_1$ had not been a cause. "I . . . claim that if d had been absent, $c_1$ would somehow have failed to cause d. But $c_1$ would still have been there to interfere with $c_2$, so e would not have occurred."[8] No alternative chain would connect with e, if the original one were broken. The existence of the broken chain, $c_1$ without d, would interfere with the processes normally completing a chain from $c_2$ to e.

This possibility is fairly easy to describe in the abstract. But basic causal knowledge rules it out in many cases. If a shot in the head does not cause massive cerebral hemorrhaging and consequent immediate death, it does not prevent a huge dose of arsenic from causing heart fibrillations and consequent immediate death. Our knowledge of physiology tells us that the trauma process and the poisoning process are sufficiently independent that the former can only interfere with the latter by killing the victim first. Whatever grounds for frustration the victim's friends may have, they do not include the thought, "He would have lived, that huge dose of arsenic would not have taken effect, if only there had not been hemorrhaging after the bullet pierced his temple." To deny this is to stipulate that obvious inferences from causal beliefs to counterfactuals are to be suspended simply because they would conflict with an analysis of causation. But then, it is wrong to propose that the concept of causation is what is being analyzed.

Of course, if the victim had not been shot, he would not have died when he did, but an instant later. In general, we can ignore preempted causes left waiting in the wings, if we restrict ourselves to causal questions as to why particular events happened just when they did. Although Lewis does not propose this restriction, it naturally emerges from his conception of causal attribution as, basically, the construction of causal chains with individual events as the links. Yet, if imposed, this restriction would enormously reduce the scope of any counterfactual analysis, so much that it would not remotely be an analysis of causation. The analysis could not deal with ques-

[8] Ibid.

tions as straightforward as "What caused Socrates to die on the day he did?" much less "What caused Socrates' death?", "What caused the Great Crash of 1929?", or "What causes heat to diffuse to a uniform distribution?" Plato tells us that Socrates hastened his own death, as a kindness to the jailer, by walking around his cell. This caused him to die just when he did, and he would not have so died if he hadn't so moved. But walking was not a cause of Socrates' dying sometime on that day.

At any rate, causal pre-emption is just one special case of the general phenomenon of causal substitution. Many systems contain causal processes that substitute one causal chain when another is absent. And frequently the substitution involves no time lag, so that the gap in the counterfactual analysis does not depend on the difference between causing something to happen and causing it to happen just when it did.

In biology, thermodynamics, geology, economics and elsewhere, it often happens that causal efficacy depends on relations between competing factors, so that the initiator of the actual causal chain has the most of something but has, as a potential substitute, at the same time, another factor that would have the most in its absence. Consider the wondrous slime molds, the Acrasiales amoebas. They sometimes exist in a unicellular phase, sometimes in an aggregated phase in which they become functionally organized into a group animal. The change of phase occurs as a population of unicellular amoebas start to exhaust their resources, leading each toward a net diffusion of a metabolic product, cAMP, to the outside of the cell membrane. Aggregation occurs when the gradient of concentration of two cAMP products is steep enough and appropriately oriented toward a center of maximum concentration. The output of the peak cell and its neighbors causes aggregation. But, quite typically, if that cell had not been a peak producer, aggregation would have occurred at the same time around the next highest producer, perhaps one outside the actually effective subgroup.[9] Or consider gradients and aggregations on the New York Stock Exchange. The panic on "Black Friday" in 1929 was started by some individual low offer to sell. Very likely, some other panicky trader was offering to sell low, at the same time, but was overshadowed by the actual panic starter, who was louder, more flamboyant or better-known on the floor. This situation would have started the panic at the same time

[9] See G. Gerisch, "Cell Aggregation and Differentiation in *Dictyostelium*" in A. Moscona and A. Monroy, eds., *Current Topics in Developmental Biology*, 3 (New York, 1968).

through the less attention-getting trader, if his competitor had not been there. In general, in the many "competitive" systems in which differences of degree determine the actual chain of causes, a competing chain would often have been effective if the actual winner had not been present, causing the sequel.

*Determinism*

Suppose one of the common situations has arisen which may produce a certain effect in a variety of ways, none of which inevitably occurs and all of which might be absent (so that the effect itself is not inevitable). Within the next ten seconds, it is even odds whether our enriching of the uranium lights up the screen with an alpha particle, lights up the screen with a beta particle, lights up the screen with a gamma particle, or doesn't light up the screen. Similarly, the insulted Samurai may cause injury in response to the insult with a cutting sword, or flashing hands, or cutting words, or may not respond at all. Next, suppose the creation of the situation does set off a process producing the effect. Would the effect have happened in the absence of this process, its immediate cause? At least if the probability of each alternative intermediate process is neither close to 1 nor close to 0, we are not inclined to subscribe to either the positive or the negative conditional. Though there is a significant chance that a beta particle would have lighted up the screen if the alpha particle had not, we are not inclined to say that one would have or that it would not have, if the probability is in the usual middle range. So, though the alpha particle caused the lighting up, it seems not to be true (or false) that there would have been no lighting up, in the absence of the alpha decay.

However, there is a more detailed analysis of counterfactuals that suggests that this initial judgment is glib. Lewis, essentially following Stalnaker, takes "if p were the case, then q would be" to mean that in the possible world most like the actual one in which p is the case, q is. And, to cope with a variety of objections against both this analysis of counterfactuals and his counterfactual analysis of causes, he proposes that precise similarity of spatiotemporal regions ranks very high in comparisons between worlds, only subordinate to the avoidance of widespread violations of fundamental laws of nature.[10] So, if there was no actual beta- or gamma-decay in those ten seconds, then, in the world most like ours in which there is no alpha-decay, there is also no beta- or gamma-decay and the screen does

[10] "Counterfactual Dependence and Time's Arrow," *Nous* (1979), p. 472.

not light up. Though Lewis himself explicitly restricts both his theory of causation and his theory of counterfactuals to systems of deterministic causes,[11] it might seem natural to extend his possible-worlds analysis to non-deterministic systems, and thus to preserve the counterfactual analysis of causes in such systems: alpha decay caused the screen to light up, and, on deeper analysis, the screen would not have lit up otherwise.

So far, the reflections on possible worlds are a plausible means of revising initial judgments that are not very strong, in any case. But in general, the combination of the possible-worlds analysis of counterfactuals and the counterfactual analysis of causes misrepresents non-deterministic causation. It has an unreasonable bias toward stability. Whenever something that could function as a non-deterministic cause of intermediate processes is *not* brought into play, we must say that reality would not have been changed if it were brought into play. To adapt a thought-experiment of Feynman's, suppose a detonator is connected to a geiger counter, so that it will or won't operate, depending on a random radioactive process. More specifically, villainous gamblers set it up to blow up a train crossing a bridge if the last digit on the cumulative record of clicks is seven or higher when the train reaches the bridge. As the train approaches, a surge of conscience hits, and they disconnect the apparatus. Would the train have safely passed over the bridge if the apparatus had remained connected? That this is not something that can be asserted is as sure as any judgment of counterfactuals in light of causal knowledge. We cannot say what would have happened, since detonation would be unlikely but perfectly possible. Yet, if the possible-worlds analysis is extended to non-deterministic systems, our knowledge of what would happen is secure. The safe passage of the possible train maximizes the precisely parallel spatio-temporal regions, without any gross violations of laws. Indeed, by Lewis' criteria of similarity, we know that the train would have been safe, even if the detonator had been set to make the odds nine-to-one for explosion. Such an unlikelihood hardly constitutes the "big, widespread violations of law"[12] which permit departures from the actual sequence of events.

Lewis claims, "Our best reason to believe in indeterminism is the success of quantum mechanics," and adds, "but that reason is none too good until quantum mechanics succeeds in giving a satisfactory

[11] "Causation," p. 183; "Counterfactual Dependence and Time's Arrow," p. 460.
[12] "Counterfactual Dependence and Time's Arrow," p. 472.

account of processes of measurement."[13] Surely, though, we have a better reason for believing in indeterminism. Though investigators would always prefer to have descriptions of causes in light of which only the actual outcome could have taken place, there is not a single field in which this demand has been met, even as a constraint on explanation sketches. Classical physics is the only field which seemed to ascribe an important range of phenomena to deterministic causes. Whatever question might be raised about quantum physics, there is no question that classical physics is false. And in any case, recent analyses of unstable systems within the framework of classical physics have revealed indeterminism in classical physics itself. The basic reason for disbelief in determinism is the basic reason for disbelief in unicorns: the beast is unlike anything we have ever seen, and it was not found despite much looking.

In any case, the problem of measurement in quantum mechanics is not a good reason for doubting that quantum mechanics speaks truly in asserting that definite physical events typically arise from conditions that might have turned out otherwise. That a generally successful theory has a problem does not show that the theory is pervasively false. No theory, as we shall see, has ever lived up to this counsel of perfection, or has needed to. And, in the words of its most distinguished critic, "Probably never before has a theory been evolved which has given a key to the interpretation and calculation of such a heterogeneous group of phenomena of experience as has the quantum theory."[14] To provide support for determinism, the problems of measurement would have to include good reasons to suppose that quantum mechanics is, specifically, wrong in its anti-determinist claims. They have no such specific implications. On the other hand, the rejection of determinism has turned out to be the best-established philosophically interesting claim in quantum mechanics. First, Bell showed that fundamental principles of invariance require that any deterministic theory in which separable antecedents are the causes of dynamical events has empirical consequences contradicting those of quantum physics. (Admittedly, causation by irreducible properties of whole systems was not contrasted with quantum physical laws. But the only properties of that kind that are known to modern physics are indeterministic in their influence on individual events.) Then, a series of experiments cul-

[13] Ibid., p. 460.

[14] A. Einstein, "Physics and Reality" (1936) in his *Essays in Physics* (New York, 1950), p. 44.

minating in those of Aspect and his colleagues bore out the quantum mechanical expectations. As a matter of empirical science, the denial that physical causes are always deterministic is as secure as experiment and theorizing can make a philosophically interesting view. As a matter of a priori argument, the requirement that causes be deterministic rests on nothing stronger than the positivist arguments criticized in the previous chapter.[15]

*Symptoms and Causes*

Sometimes, an indicator of a phenomenon is so reliable, on the basis of such fundamental laws of nature, that our basis for denying that it causes the phenomenon is just that the connections are of an indicating rather than a causing sort. Such cases eventually led Hempel to admit that the covering-law model did not describe sufficient conditions for causality. The most telling examples work as well against the new, counterfactual account.

The red shift in spectra of more distant stars does not cause the expansion of the universe. Yet if there were no red shift, there would be no expansion. This conclusion is strengthened, not weakened by reflection on the possible-worlds analysis of counterfactuals. That red shift is accompanied by expansion is dictated by laws of optics and physical chemistry as fundamental as the laws of relativity theory and nuclear physics involved in the genuinely causal attributions basing the expansion on the Big Bang. The departures from actuality involved in expansion without the Big Bang are no greater than those involved in a suspension of the optical and chemical principles producing the red shift.

The only remotely appealing reason to take expansion without a red shift as less bizarre than expansion without a Big Bang (and it is not very appealing) is this: in any given context, the breaking of a cause-effect connection is a more serious matter than the breaking of any indicator-indicated connection, in judgments of similarities

[15] See J. S. Bell, "On the Einstein-Podolsky-Rosen Paradox" (1964) in Wheeler and Zurek, eds., *Quantum Theory and Measurement*. A. Aspect and P. Grangier, "Experiments on Einstein-Podolsky-Rosen-Type Correlations with Pairs of Visible Photons," in S. Kamefuchi, *Foundations of Quantum Mechanics in the Light of New Technology* (Tokyo, 1984), is an illuminating presentation of the recent experiments. The more conclusive findings in favor of quantum physics appeared after Lewis' paper.

For further arguments for indeterministic causation see G.E.M. Anscombe, "Causality and Determination" (1971) in Ernest Sosa, ed., *Causation and Conditionals* (London, 1975). I am sure that this essay influenced me in working out the alternative conception of causation that I will present, through Anscombe's insistence on the indispensability of what I will call "elementary varieties" of causation. See ibid., p. 68.

among possible worlds. And that would hardly save the counterfactual analysis. Rather, counterfactual judgments would turn out to depend on the very distinction they were to explain.[16]

The standard response of the philosophically naive seems to be right: all the analyses of causation are unrealistic, and importantly so. In the real world, causes often (albeit *relatively* infrequently) have unlikely effects; correlations of the utmost regularity do not describe a cause; alternative causes do not neatly correspond to causally independent chains of events, as against pre-empting or substituting chains; symptoms are not always more superficial than causes. None of the analyses of causation fits this unruly world, on account of related and sometimes identical problems. Rather than continuing the quest for a general a priori criterion of causality, it seems more promising to ask whether the concept of cause might have a structure that precludes such an analysis, while permitting the rational discovery of causes to proceed.

## THE CORE CONCEPTION

That usage is guided by a general a priori rule would be one way to account for three features of the concept of a cause which might,

---

[16] Though Lewis does not discuss the red shift, he does address himself to the general problem of distinguishing mere symptoms, i.e., epiphenomena, from causes. "Suppose that e is an epiphenomenal effect of a genuine cause c of an effect f. . . . The proper solution [to the problem that f, it seems, would not have occurred if e, the non-cause hadn't] . . . is flatly to deny the counterfactuals that cause the trouble. If e had been absent, it is not that c would have been absent (and with it f . . .) Rather, c would have occurred just as it did but would have failed to cause e. It is less of a departure from actuality to get rid of e by holding c fixed, and giving up some or other of the laws and circumstances in virtue of which c could not have failed to cause e . . . (. . . [I]t would of course be pointless not to hold f fixed along with c)"; "Causation," p. 190. When only local violations of relatively unimportant causal mechanisms are required, the possible-worlds analysis does make Lewis' favored counterfactuals plausible. Though it seems at first that there would have been no storm if there had been no falling barometer, the small, local anomaly of a misleading falling barometer would have been avoided at a huge cost in departure from actuality: either the violation of the basic meterological principles connecting low-pressure systems with storms or the non-existence of the low-pressure system there actually was, the storm that actually followed, and all the further departures consequent on basic meterology. But in the case of red shift without expansion, the violated laws are fundamental and their consequences pervasive. Similarly, that a flagpole's having no shadow at solar noon does not cause it to be vertical is another standard counterexample to the covering-law model that is also a counter-example to the counterfactual analysis, since the connection between symptom and what is indicated mimics causal connectedness in its intimacy, its strength, and the pervasive consequences of breaking it.

together, be called the integrity of the concept. In the first place, though instances of causation are extremely diverse—as different as a sting's causing pain, fear's causing flight and wind's causing leaves to rustle—the use of "cause" in all these instances is the expression of a single notion, not of different ones as when we say, "I was sitting on the bank when I should have been cashing a check at the bank." Apart from this internal unity, there is general agreement in the application of the concept. At any given time, people usually agree as to what kinds of things are causes, even though they disagree as to which causes are operating in particular cases. Finally, when there is disagreement as to whether a kind of thing (process, phenomenon, connection, relation, condition, state, event) could be a cause, reasonable dispute is possible and often leads to resolution, as in the disputes following Newton over action-at-a-distance or the attribution of a causal role to velocity that distinguished Galileo from his predecessors. If we were tacitly guided by a positivist rule, its abstract, non-field-specific character would make for unity-in-diversity; its general possession would make for general agreement, since reasonable people would generally use it well; and it would be the rational standard for resolving disagreements, when people are accused of a basic misstep in their cataloguing of causes. But there seems to be no such rule. Is there any other structure that the concept of cause could have, compatible with its integrity?

The most attractive clue, at this point, is the existence of concepts such as that of a number and of a work of art, which have the same integrity, and are not described by a positivist rule. Rather, each is based on a diverse core of elementary varieties, extended to further cases by rational but unpredictable processes of discovery and criticism.

Integers and fractions are the elementary varieties of number, in the following sense. To have the concept, someone must be able to recognize some instances of one of these varieties, and be prepared to take instances of both varieties as deserving the same label, on sufficient experience. Someone lacks the concept of a number if: he can't count; he counts but sees no point in grouping the numbers he does use as instances of a kind (and, thus, is not a philosophical sophisticate who sees the usual motivations but has special arguments to the contrary); he counts, but if he learns the relation between a pint and a quart, an inch and a foot, and the like, he thinks it as bizarre to group these relations with counting numbers, as we would think it bizarre to label water a number. Similarly, a representational but non–trompe l'oeil easel painting, made for contemplation, and a statue of a person, slightly stylized but not enormously so, and made for contemplation are elementary varieties of works of art. People who deny the title to Pollock drip paintings but give it to Vermeers are philistine or ill-informed, but have the concept. Someone who grants the title to a Pollock but, without visual flaw or critical argument, asks, "Why does anyone call *that* a work of art?" faced with a Vermeer, has a potentially interesting but rather different concept from that of a work of art.

As these last examples show, the scope of each concept extends far beyond the elementary core. The process of extension is roughly this. In grasping the concept, we understand that the elementary instances are supposed to serve certain purposes through certain activities. If we encounter new contexts in which the old purposes, or very similar ones, are served in similar ways by new varieties, the latter are included as instances of the concept. (Or perhaps one should say that it is then reasonable to include them, and that if most experts take advantage of this permission they are included.) Thus, the old purposes of measuring and calculation motivated the further inclusion of the square root of 2. At a certain point in the calculations of area and perimeter, the old numbers proved insufficient. Roger Fry and others showed that Cézanne was doing many of the things that Rembrandt was doing, despite superficial differences. Once new varieties are included and become established, they can be part of a core, in the sense that new candidates are vindicated by relevant resemblance to them, even if there is insufficient resemblance to the elementary varieties. The ancient Egyptians would have been justified in denying the square root of minus two the status of a number, just as the medieval connoisseur, Abbot Suger of Saint Denis, would have been justified in denying a drip painting the status of a work of art. In both examples, the same kind of barrier is at work, the absence of intermediate cases that in fact arose later on.

Because the process of incorporation is piecemeal, there is general agreement at any given time, along with limited disagreement. And the question of whether the old purposes are similarly served by the new candidate is subject to rational dispute. In particular, exclusionary arguments are perfectly possible. If Berkeley had been right, he would have shown there are no infinitesimal numbers. The resemblance to the established core would be illusory, since infinitesimals could not be subjected to the operations that would make them similar to the standard numbers, without generating contradictions. If Michael Fried is right, most "conceptual art" is not similar enough to the core in methods and goals to be a work of art. According to Fried, conceptual art seems to engage our interest in contemplation or visual exploration, but really just startles us by mimicking confrontations with people or with the disturbing banality of the urban landscape.[17]

What is striking, in the case of both concepts, is that conceptual integrity does not require guidance by a general rule. While the study of numbers is the paradigm of precision, mathematicians are not bothered at all by the absence of an informative general statement of necessary and sufficient conditions for being a number of any kind. Of course, at any given time, someone could construct a list of the kinds of numbers there are. But there is no abstract rule describing the features in virtue of which anything belongs on the list, a rule that would effectively determine whether mathematicians should accept proposed new kinds of numbers. Similarly, though aesthetics was dominated until the middle of this century by the pursuit of a general description of necessary and sufficient conditions for being a work of art, few people today think one exists and no one thinks such a rule must exist for there to be a concept of a work of art.

The concept of a number and the concept of a work of art are examples of what I will call a "core concept." Something is a core concept just in case anyone's having the concept involves the following features.

(1) *The core.* The core consists of diverse elementary varieties. These are kinds of things falling under the concept. They are different kinds, and they do not qualify as varieties of the kind expressed by the concept in virtue of satisfying a general rule describing the properties on account of which anything falls under the concept. To have the concept, someone must be able to recognize things as instances of some elementary varieties, and be inclined, on sufficient experience, to take instances of all the elementary varieties to be instances of a single kind. How much recognition capacity is required for a grasp of the concept is a vague matter, as it is for all concepts. In general, someone needs to have an extensive ability to recognize instances of at least a large proportion of important elementary varieties, and must be reasonably well-prepared, as people go, to acquire the ability to recognize instances of the others.

(2) *The extension procedure.* There are varieties falling under the concept that are not elementary. Someone who takes something

[17] See Michael Fried, "Art and Objecthood," *Artforum* (June 1967), pp. 12-23.

other than an elementary variety as falling under the concept possesses the concept if he or she can support the inclusion using the appropriate extension procedure (or if he or she can appeal to experts, who can do so). The extension procedure describes relations to elementary varieties in virtue of which something qualifies as a non-elementary variety.

(3) *Intermediate cases*. The extension procedure must permit inclusion on the basis of appropriate relations to intermediate cases, i.e., to non-elementary varieties having the same relation, in turn, to elementary ones (or to other non-elementary ones, so related to elementary ones, and so forth). The extension procedure is recursive, as mathematicians would put it. So whether inclusion of one non-elementary variety is coherent may depend on the actual existence of other non-elementary varieties. The extension procedure, along with this proviso as to the role of intermediate cases, describes the conditions in which inclusion of a non-elementary variety is consistent with an adequate grasp of a core concept.

This schema is not preliminary to a declaration that core concepts are the important concepts in science. Many important concepts are specifiable using general rules laying down necessary and sufficient conditions, for example, the concepts "rational number" and "kinetic energy." Concepts expressed in natural kind terms, "gold" and "water" for example, are probably best specified in terms of paradigms of a single kind and an inclusion rule relating all instances directly to the paradigms, say, as having the same chemical composition. In contexts in which paradigms are counted as different in kind, it is best not to regard the term as referring to a single natural kind; still, a core concept is not expressed if inclusion is solely governed by direct identification with paradigms. Thus, gold is best regarded as a variety of kinds of stuff when isotopic differences are important. Minerologists are not wrong to regard jade as two different kinds of minerals. No doubt, there are other types of concepts, beyond those mentioned. The modern biologist's concept of a species does not obviously fit any of these molds. Nor does the pathologist's concept of health.

It may even be that core concepts are not commonly used in the practice of scientific argument, description and explanation. (Mathematicians make claims about rational numbers, but rarely about numbers in general.) However, in the philosophy of that practice, the philosophy of science, core concepts are extremely important. Here is a case in point: the concept of a cause is a core concept.

The concept of cause has the same structure as the concept of number or of a work of art. The elementary varieties include pushing (for example, the wind's blowing leaves), giving sensations or feelings (for example, a sting's hurting), and motivating action (for example, fear's motivating flight). Someone who does not recognize any of the elementary varieties, or someone who is not lead by growing experience of them to group these varieties under the same label does not have the concept of cause. Of course, someone can learn to group them under the same heading and then come to attack this inclination with philosophical arguments (for example, hermeneutic arguments that motives are not causes). But such philosophical attack is possible for all concepts. So long as the sophisticated arguments are defective, as they turn out to be here, the informed but unskeptical response preserves the integrity of the concept. To observe the required unity by way of contrast, imagine someone who recognizes a push's moving a wagon and fear's motivating flight, yet finds our using "cause," "because" or "bringing about" in both connections as superficial as the use of "bank" for streams and for financial institutions.

The elementary varieties of causation are quite different one from another, so much so that it may seem a troubling question why we should group them under a common label. The pragmatic analysis is extremely helpful here—only not as a genuine analysis of causation. As von Wright states the analysis, "What makes p a cause-factor relative to the effect-factor q is . . . the fact that by *manipulating* p, i.e., by producing changes in it 'at will' as we say, we could bring about changes in q."[18] As an analysis, this would be incomplete, since the appropriate potential means of control does not always exist when p causes q. It does not exist in situations of causal substitution, since q would be caused in another way if we withdrew p. And p is not a potential means of controlling q *at will* when q is its actual but unlikely effect. Also, the pragmatic analysis becomes question-begging, when we have to make distinctions that troubled the other analyses. That the red shift does not cause stellar expansion while the Big Bang and its consequences do, depends on the distinction between causes and symptoms. The "pragmatic" justification of the distinction between the role of the Big Bang and the role of the red shift would rest on the claim that one can imagine controlling expansion by manipulating consequences of the Big Bang, but can't imagine controlling it by manipulating the red shift.

[18] G. H. von Wright, "On the Nature and Epistemology of the Causal Relation" (1973) in Sosa, *Causation and Conditionals*, p. 107.

But this claim surely derives its validity from our prior understanding of what is a cause, not the other way around.

Still, in all elementary varieties of causation, diverse as they are, typical cases are of interest as means of control. By learning about pushes and other elementary mechanical causes, we learn how to change trajectories. By learning about motivations, we acquire our basic means of changing conduct, namely, persuasion. By learning how to give sensations and feelings, we learn how to change the course of others' inner lives. Our interest in changing some process by affecting another gives point to our having a concept of causation, just as our interest in nutrition gives point to having a concept of food—even though plenty of food is not nutritious.

The scope of causation has been extended, step by step, enormously far from the elementary core. Typically and roughly, a new causal process is added to the current repertoire of varieties of cause in the following way. A regularity is encountered. According to the most basic beliefs about the old repertoire of causes, it cannot be an accident. Regularities in the positions of celestial bodies might be a case in point. Within the old repertoire, attempts to describe the causes of this and other regularities repeatedly fail, so repeatedly that it becomes likely that some other kind of cause operates. A causal account of the anomalies is discovered which is only acceptable if the cause at work is distinguished from anything in the old repertoire. An example might be the account of celestial trajectories as due to a force of attraction between all pieces of matter which is neither specifically directed toward a single celestial body nor the product of pushes and pulls of matter in contact with matter. This something else, the distinctive factor causing the crucial regularities, is added to the repertoire of causes. If it becomes entrenched enough, it may become standard in that new kinds of causes may be introduced because of their resemblance to it. Thus, the nineteenth-century theories of electrodynamics that appealed to action-at-a-distance with a regular time delay depend on the existence of a gravitation theory in which simpler, instantaneous action-at-a-distance occurred. Without their use of notions of energy and its conservation that had previously acquired explanatory force in the nineteenth century, quantum-mechanical derivations would be number-worship, not the identification of causes.[19]

[19] Thus, though he was as enamoured of mathematical formalisms as any great physicist has been, Heisenberg sharply distinguished between the "mathematical scheme of quantum mechanics" and its empirical adequacy, on the one hand, and the analogies with classical concepts of position, velocity and energy that give the scheme

Because the argument for inclusion typically depends on the need to explain a regularity, it might seem that such arguments only require, in principle, the application of a general rule of inference according to which coincidences indicate causes. A full response would require several leaps into later chapters on confirmation, probabilistic reasoning and scientific realism. Here is a mere outline. Not every coincidence is evidence of an underlying cause, and the description of the ones that are (for example, the selection of the predicates describing relevant correlations) depends on a background of specific causal beliefs. Among other considerations, this will turn out to be an implication of Goodman's "new riddle of induction." Even when coincidences indicate causes, the weight of such evidence is often light. It will turn out to be too light to counterbalance worries about speculativeness and anomaly that are always appropriate in real science when a new kind of cause is proposed, even in situations where the proposal should be accepted. Finally, the fact that new causes are frequently vindicated by their power to explain regularities will turn out to reflect, not the priority of a general principle of statistical inference, but the power of an indefinite variety of specific principles of causal similarity. These principles, the common property of scientific conservatives and revolutionaries alike, describe certain specific kinds of situations in which similarities in outcomes are apt to be due to similarities in causes. In short, an adequate argument for extending the concept of causation depends on an acute need for an explanation, and no general a priori rule identifies such needs.

The main advantage of this model of core and principled growth is that it gives the best account of the integrity of the concept of a cause. By contrast, positivist accounts have turned out to distort the meaning of the concept, and to be too circular, in the final analysis, to fulfill their promise of describing the criterion by which the concept is applied. There are other advantages, as well.

For one thing, the core conception vindicates a judgment that seems correct on the face of it, namely, that highly sophisticated causal notions cannot be grasped without an understanding of other, elementary varieties. It seems wrong that someone could have the idea of a change in potential at a point in a field causing a wave without grasping any elementary variety of causation, even

its "physical content," on the other. See his first paper on the "uncertainty principle," "The Physical Content of Quantum Kinematics and Mechanics" (1927), in Wheeler and Zurek, eds., *Quantum Theory and Measurement*, esp. pp. 62–68.

that of a push's moving something. Without any grounding in any elementary notion, there seems to be no sense to the distinction between electrodynamic causation and mere correlation. Yet if causation were a matter of covering-laws, probabilistic derivation or counterfactuals, there would be no problem of principle, here. If (to adapt Hume's nice phrase) the first Adam could understand electrodynamic causation first among all causes, that would just be a sign of surprising agility in Adam, like someone's capacity to learn calculus from the axioms of real number theory, without any help from graphs. By contrast, the core conception explains why the sophisticated causal concepts need to be grounded, yet does not reduce them to elementary ones.

The core conception also vindicates the most plausible assessment of actual disputes as to what could be a cause: they are simultaneously methodological *and* empirical. Such disputes are pervasive in the history of science and concern the most diverse candidates for causal status, for example, entelechies, unconscious processes and structures, action at a distance, electromagnetic fields, and momentum treated as a physical factor involved in the causation of balance points and trajectories. On the positivist analyses, these disputes would either be strictly methodological, be strictly empirical, or fluctuate between the two distinct kinds of arguments. Either the disputants are working toward the general rule for causal status, and criticizing the other side for departing from the rule. Or their dispute concerns the data to which the rule is applied, and is no different in kind from routine empirical disagreements. Yet all the disputes to which I have alluded seem methodological and empirical at once. And the core conception makes it clear why this is so. The dispute over an alleged new kind of cause is empirical because the issue is how to cope with the anomalies of the old repertoire. It is methodological because commitment to a repertoire of causes regulates particular investigations, and is not to be given up in the face of a few empirical problems. After all, it is commitment to a repertoire of causes that motivates scientific perseverence, pursuing a cause in the face of initial difficulties rather than simply declaring that a new kind of cause is at work. The old repertoire is only to be abandoned if its failures are so repeated and damaging that the best explanation is the inadequacy of the repertoire, not the inadequacy of the scientists. So commitment to the repertoire is properly expressed in dicta as to what could be a cause.

Finally, the core conception explains why the counterfactual analysis is so appealing, even though it turns out to be quite inadequate.

The appeal of the counterfactual analysis ultimately depends on the grain of truth in the pragmatic analysis. Typical instances of the elementary varieties are our basic levers for change. Our interest in finding means to change reality gives the core conception of cause its point and its unity. So when a causal situation does not fit the pragmatic analysis, it seems peripheral, at first, until we reflect on how common the exceptions are and how important they are in many sciences. Moreover, what doesn't fit the counterfactual analysis doesn't fit the pragmatic analysis. If Y would have happened, even if X had not, then manipulating the presence and absence of X is not a lever for controlling Y.

Apart from the exclusion of positivist analyses, the core conception has an important implication for epistemology. Certain specific, elementary interpretations of events as involving genuine causation, not just correlation, have no justification and need none, where philosophers have sought a further justification appealing to a general rule. Suppose the question is raised of whether the causal processes in the minimal core really exist or are just mimicked by corresponding sequences. Does the wind ever blow leaves about, or does the wind blow, while leaves spontaneously move around? Do people ever drive nails into boards, or is the hammer's meeting the nail just followed by unrelated movement, the spontaneous passage of nail into hammer? Since we lack an analysis of causation in the minimal core, we cannot justify our preference for the causal alternative. More precisely, though we can rebut specific counter-proposals appealing to alternative causes, and though we can respond philosophically to skeptical arguments, we cannot justify our taking the elementary developments as causal, except in response to a special counter-argument. That an ordinary sequence of movement, contact, and movement of what is contacted is, prima facie, a case of impact's causing motion stands in need of no justification and has none.

Note that nothing has been lost which we otherwise possess. When epistemologies claim to provide us with a priori principles to justify causal attribution, those principles are always rules for passing from past and present observations to an appropriate covering-law, either general or probabilistic. But these days, even people who have faith in a positivist analysis of the meaning of causal claims rarely rely on such rules for justifying inferences to those claims. All proposed rules are widely believed to be defeated by Hume's original problem of induction, Goodman's new problem, or both. At any rate, in the section on confirmation, I will present a variety of arguments that such despair over general and a priori principles of inference to causality is richly deserved.

## EXCLUDING AND INCLUDING

When they first encounter the covering-law model, many people suspect that it will exclude causal claims that really are legitimate. The core conception ought to stimulate the contrary suspicion, "Here, anything goes." So it is essential to consider how proposed extensions beyond the core could be judged—above all, how they could be judged and found wanting. How does one decide whether a kind of phenomenon could be a cause?

Here is an example of justified exclusion. We now are justified in rejecting any proposed kind of cause which would make it possible to transfer energy instantaneously from one part of space to a remote one. It is not just that we have not encountered instances of such a cause, or that none actually exists. None could exist. It is impossible for there to be a causal process such as Laplace admitted in his theory of gravitation, a process in which a collision between asteroids instantaneously changes the location of Sirius. If someone, call him Professor Vendome, were to propose adding a form of action-at-a-distance to the current list of physical causes, informed physicists would know how to judge this proposal. They would remind Vendome that current theories of what spatial remoteness is entail the impossibility of signals travelling faster than the speed of light.

Here, Vendome is taken to be a normal scientist, accepting current basic theories, relativity theory in particular, but needing to be reminded of their consequences. If he did not accept relativity theory, there would be a need to rehearse the usual arguments from experimental findings and classical electrodynamics that establish relativity theory. If he wasn't in possession of relevant findings or theories, they would have to be supplied to show that action-at-a-distance could not be a cause. If he even rejects the truisms implicit in a grasp of the elementary varieties, there is nothing to worry about. The apparent disagreement about causation was merely apparent, since he lacks such concepts as cause and action. (The more radical forms of deviance deserve more attention and will receive it, in the chapters on scientific realism. What is most needed at present is a reconstruction of normal scientific controversies as to what could be a cause.)

This argument that a proposed kind of cause could not be a cause relies on specific, substantive principles about how causes work, not on an a priori rule describing general conditions that any cause must satisfy. The relevant principles are themselves sustained by empirical findings and further specific principles, not by an analysis of the concept of cause in general. The classical positivists were well aware that scientists sometimes argue in this way as to what could be a cause. But they took the issue settled in this way to be an issue of mere physical possibility, of secondary interest to philosophy. The philosophically interesting questions were to be questions of logical possibility, settled by determining whether a hypothesis had the right logical form to be causal. (Sometimes, by combining rules of logical form with analyses of meaning, the classical positivists tried to expand the empire of logical analysis, arguing, say, that relativistic constraints on causality could be sustained by a logical analysis of causal ascriptions in physics.) From the standpoint of the core conception there are no interesting questions as to whether it is logically possible that a proposal should describe a cause. The extension procedure involves ordinary scientific argument. Logic will establish only trivial constraints, useless in the practice of criticizing actual proposals, such as the impossibility of a cause that is logically incompatible with the occurrence of its alleged effect.

In one respect, the Vendome affair is misleading. It might suggest the moral that a proposed new kind of cause should be accepted whenever we have encountered a phenomenon for which we have no explanation based on the current causal repertoire *and* we have no reason to suppose that the new kind of cause could *not* exist. In fact, the burden of proof is always on the innovators. They need to show that the absence of an explanation is due to the incompleteness of the current causal list, not to the incompletenesss of our knowledge and abilities when we apply this list to current problems. This is a difficult task, a difficulty reflected in our inclination to label changed verdicts as to what kind of thing could be a cause "scientific revolutions." It is not an impossible task, as we will see in several case studies in confirmation and in scientific realism. For example, Newtonians were able to show that phenomena that stood in need of explanation in all pre-Newtonian frameworks could not be explained from any pre-Newtonian causal repertoire, given observational findings together with constraints on causes that the other frameworks shared. Not to recognize the burden of proof on someone proposing a new kind of cause is a failure to grasp the extension procedure and, hence, a failure to grasp the concept of cause. Think of someone who responds to the first difficulty in finding his eyeglasses by proposing that there is a force in the universe making eyeglasses disappear.

The question of how to justify including or excluding an alleged kind of cause is not the same as the question of what kinds of things are varieties of cause. After all, Laplace was fully justified in including action-at-a-distance, even though there is no such variety of causation. Still, there is a specially intimate relation between justification and actual extension, here. What could be a cause is what would be connected to the elementary varieties by valid arguments for extension when all the facts are in. To forestall possible misunderstandings: this is not meant as a special instance of any interesting general claim that truth is justification at the ideal limit. The latter claim is interesting only if ideal justifiability has a general description in terms of virtues other than truth. In Chapter Eight, I will argue that no such description exists. The relation between extension and ideal arguments is unavoidable, where causation is concerned, on account of the special structure of core concepts.

Presumably, Professor Vendome means what we do by "cause" and is simply wrong in his proposal that a form of action-at-a-distance could be a cause. What about M. Laplace, though? Is there any sense in which the meaning of causation changed from his time to ours?

Laplace, presumably, had the same core of elementary varieties and the same extension procedure. So he expressed the same concept by "*cause*" as we do by "cause." Yet it has always seemed misleading to say, without qualification, that the meaning of "cause" does not change in scientific revolutions. The core conception shows why. Laplace made fully reasonable judgments as to what could be a cause that are different from ours. Indeed, because of the role of intermediate cases he would, with reason, have made different judgments of a variety of proposals, for example, proposals as to what electrodynamic causes there could be. That people disagree as to whether something *is* an X is not usually a sign that they use the term with different meanings. That they disagree as to whether what has certain properties *could be* an X *is*, typically, a sign that different meanings are involved. After all, the disagreements we assess are normally disagreements among contemporaries, and reasonable contemporaries, in a position to have opinions as to what could be an X, will usually have access to the same (or equally good) evidence. So if we say that Laplace and Richard Feynman have the same concept of a cause, and stop there, what we say is misleading.

The usual concomitant, agreement as to what could fall under the concept, fails to obtain.

It is not literally true that the concept of cause has changed. But there is a large grain of truth in this false idea. It might be expressed in the statement that standards of causality, justified descriptions of what could be a cause, have changed in the course of history.

## ADEQUATE CAUSAL DESCRIPTION

When is a description of causes helping to bring about something informative and thorough enough to explain its occurrence? No general answer seems right—and this is the first step toward the right answer.

To require a list of causes that were jointly sufficient to bring about the effect is, in general, to demand too much (assuming that the requirement is not met by describing a cause as strong enough given the presence of unspecified causal factors). In his typical historical explanation, Tilly could appeal to the social situation and consequent political power of the Vendean clergy, and stop causal description at that point—without, of course, proposing that this was the only causal factor that played a crucial role in the uprising. Symptoms have long been properly explained as due to infections, by doctors who were well aware that other unknown aspects of the suffering organism play a causal role. On the other hand, it is often too little to require that an explanation list causal factors sufficient to bring about the effect in the circumstances in which the latter actually arose. Through an immunological fluke, the British politician, Hugh Gaitskell, died from a common cold virus. But "Gaitskell died because he caught a cold" is not an adequate explanation, though it lists a factor sufficient in the case at hand. In the circumstances at hand, a wave of selling in the stock market in 1929 produced the Great Depression. But no economic historian supposes that the Great Depression is explained by that wave of selling. The task of explaining why the Great Depression occurred largely consists of offering an informative specification of the circumstances in which a stockmarket crash would trigger a general economic collapse.

In some cases, a standard requiring a list of causes sufficient under the circumstances is too weak. But in other cases, a standard requiring a list of causes sufficient in themselves is too strong. We need a compromise, in between these two extremes. Yet it is hard to see how any one compromise can be generally binding, or binding no matter what the empirical facts concerning specific enterprises of explanation.

The question of what causal lists are adequate to explain is, I would propose, an empirical question, whose answer varies from field to field. It is always a pragmatic question, in Hempel's sense. Hempel to the contrary, explanation has an essentially pragmatic element. Real adequacy, as against mere satisfaction of current interests, is governed by facts about the actual state of the field in question. On the other hand, not every interest which might make it desirable to choose an explanation yields an acceptable standard of adequacy. The relation of scientists' interests to explanatory adequacy is not an all or nothing matter.

By way of preliminary sketch, an adequate description of causal factors must have two features. First, it must list causal factors which *were* present in the circumstances in which the explanandum actually arose and which *were* jointly sufficient in those circumstances to bring about the explanandum, under those circumstances. Second, it must conform to an appropriate "standard causal pattern." By a standard causal pattern, I mean a rule that says: in this field, an adequate explanation of such-and-such phenomena may describe causal factors of these kinds in these ways, attributing the phenomenon in question to the operation of those factors in the circumstances at hand. A standard causal pattern, in part, prescribes the permissible division of labor between explicit description of kinds of factors at work and allusion to unspecified actual circumstances in which the explanandum arose. It presents a repertoire for causal analysis and prescribes a degree of freedom to break off the work of causal analysis with the remark that the factors described were sufficient under the actual circumstances. To borrow a phrase from statistics, a standard causal pattern is a stopping rule.

A standard causal pattern is appropriate for a certain field in a certain period if conformity to it best advances the pursuit of accurate causal descriptions in that field and period. An accurate list of causes conforming to an appropriate standard causal pattern is an adequate explanation. Of course, it may be desirable for some investigators to go further, seeking to specify the circumstances which help those causes achieve their effect. But the project of finding an explanation can be broken off, at the point described, without that end constituting a defeat. An explanation has been found, meriting the rating "adequate," though perhaps not the rating "perfect" or "perfectly complete."

This sketch needs much filling in. But first of all, it cries out for

illustration. Here is a survey of some outstanding cases of the operation of standard causal patterns in a variety of fields: physics, disease theory and history.

As physics has evolved, successive theories of motion have
brought with them shifting standard causal patterns.[20] In Aristotelian physics, explanations of motion were adequate if they fit one of
two patterns. In the first, the composition of an object is analyzed
into its elements. Its motion is attributed to the balance of the inherent tendencies of those elements, weighted according to their proportions. Thus, the fact that a stone moves straight down is explained by pointing to the fact that it is composed of earth, since it is
the inherent tendency of earth to move straight to the center of the
Earth. If there is a deviation from the trajectory dictated by inherent tendencies, it is explained according to a second pattern. The
trajectory is attributed to the inherent tendencies together with in-
terfering episodes of push, pull, or impact. Provided all the particular episodes of interference are singled out, in the description of
causal factors, the explanation is adequate. Unlike explanations in
the first pattern, explanations in the second need not describe factors dictating the explanandum, as against every conceivable variation. In these cases, where "the course of nature is interfered with,"
such detailed analysis is unnecessary and unavailable.

In the seventeenth century, a new physics arose in which an adequate explanation of a trajectory ascribes it to pushes, squeezes, and
impacts of matter in contact with matter, which dictate that precise
trajectory according to general laws. Or, in any case, this was the initial mechanistic program, in Descartes' physics, for example. Aristotelian physics was condemned not just because its premises were
false, but because its explanations did not function as explanations
should. An appeal to a tendency in a kind of stuff was held not to
explain unless that tendency is grounded in further causes. Aristotelian explanations of departures from the course of nature were
regarded as self-condemned, on account of their admitted intrinsic
imprecision.

The mechanistic model gradually broke down in the course of the
next two centuries. It soon developed that the appeal to at least one
inherent tendency, the inherent gravitation attraction of matter to
matter, must be allowed. However, for many physicists forces of this
kind, varying with distance, remained the sole loophole in the

[20] See Thomas Kuhn, "Concepts of Cause in the Development of Physics" in his *The Essential Tension* (Chicago, 1977).

mechanistic program. Almost a century of debate over mechanical models of electromagnetic fields finally produced a new revision of the standard pattern, in which derivations from field equations were accepted as adequate even when unsupported by appeals to mechanical force.

Finally, with quantum theory, new and, in some ways, weaker standards of explanation were adopted. For example, phenomena of motion are explained by deriving their probability using probabilistic equations, even though the derivation does not exclude the occurrence of alternative phenomena.

These shifting standards are quite different and have important effects on the judgment of proposed explanations. The willingness of theoretical physicists today to admit that their theory of collisions cannot reduce all arrival points after a collision to a single one would be an admission of explanatory defeat for previous generations. Appeals to gravitational attraction as explaining Kepler's laws would be, for Descartes, a sign of the inability to explain those laws. It is hard to believe that these shifting explanatory standards can all be based on the logical analysis of the concept of explanation in general.

The history of disease theory includes another shift in standard patterns, a vivid illustration of the possibility that greater laxity can be the way of progress, as much as greater strictness. In many Greek and Renaissance theories of disease, disease is an imbalance among bodily fluids. An explanation of symptoms describes the increase or diminution of fluids. The description includes all relevant circumstances, i.e., all relevant changes in ratios of fluids. In these theories causal factors must be described which are bound to produce the symptoms in all circumstances. Later, in the germ theory of the late nineteenth century, many symptoms are ascribed to the invasion of microorganisms. Appropriate circumstances are required for infection to produce disease. But a description of those circumstances is not required in general. In this period, scientific progress typically requires willingness to break off the task of explanation when the infectious agent has been identified. Otherwise, the pursuit of explanations would bog down in the first attempt to connect infection with symptoms. Immunology is not ripe, yet. ———

Somewhat more precisely, the new standard causal patterns for infectious disease are these. If the symptoms have the infection as a cause in normal members of the species in question, the identification of the infectious agent is adequate. So "he sniffles because he is infected by a cold virus" will do. If the outbreak of symptoms requires abnormality, the necessary departure from normality, sufficient in conjunction with the infection, should be described. But the description may be vague, and the total causal list may entail the occurrence of the effect. "Gaitskell died because he was infected by a cold virus" does not explain. "Gaitskell died because he was infected by a cold virus and his immunological system was abnormally weak, unable to defend against the virus" will do.

In the social sciences, standard causal patterns also regulate the acceptance of explanations. For example, many political historians operate in a framework in which adequate explanations may simply describe actions of political leaders which were sufficient to bring about the event to be explained in the circumstances at hand. Thus, the downfall of the French Bourbons can be attributed to the blunders of individual kings and ministers. But other historians employ frameworks which require, in addition, the description of the social conditions which gave individual actions their power to produce large-scale effects. For them, an explanation of the downfall of the Bourbons as due to a series of mistakes is inadequate, since it does not describe the social conditions which made those blunders lethal for a whole system.

In addition to such controversial standard patterns, uncontroversial ones exist in the social sciences. In the political history of postmedieval Europe, for example, it is acceptable to explain a large-scale political phenomenon as due to causal factors sufficient to bring it about anywhere in the nation-state in question in the period in question. So Tilly's explanation is valid, if its premises are true. But, unless further special arguments are available, an appeal to unspecified circumstances in a subregion of a nation-state is not acceptable. An explanation of the Vendée uprising as due to factors sufficient in western France, but known to have been insufficient in contemporary eastern France, fails to explain.

In light of these illustrations, explanatory adequacy seems on the face of it to be determined by field-specific standards. In each field, we do encounter proposed explanations which are adequate choices for certain investigators, given their concerns, but not adequate explanations. These causal descriptions, however, seem utterly different in status from the ones which are licensed by the various *standard* causal patterns. Thus, for Gaitskell's doctors, it might have been good enough to identify his critical condition as due to a cold virus. They had no time to pursue a more thorough causal account, and a more thorough one would probably have added nothing to their therapeutic abilities. Philosophical theories to one side, we still sharply distinguish "He is dying because he caught a cold," which may be adequate for immediate practical purposes, from "He is dying because he caught a cold and has a peculiar immunological deficiency with respect to this cold virus," which is an adequate explanation, though not an ideally specific one.

Discussions of the pragmatics of explanation often identify explanatory adequacy with the satisfaction of demands posed as contrastive questions, "Why did X occur, as against such-and-such alternatives?"[21] In one way, the theory of standard causal patterns can be made to parallel such discussions. The stopping rule in a standard causal pattern can be formulated as a requirement that the causes which are specified be sufficient by themselves to cause the outcome in question rather than certain others, e.g., to bring it about that a normal organism developed symptoms rather than remaining free of those symptoms. But unlike these discussions, the theory of standard causal patterns does not imply that an accurate causal list is adequate, provided it responds to whatever contrastive question the investigator has in mind. "Gaitskell died because he caught cold" is not an adequate explanation of why Gaitskell died. If the investigator who announces this "explanation" tells us, "I am only interested in why a sequel occurred in one organism rather than in ones with just the same physiology, no matter how abnormal that physiology is," that is an interesting autobiographical remark, but it does not make the explanation adequate. "The Great Depression occurred because of an episode of precipitous selling on the Stock Market" is not an adequate explanation. Again, it does not become adequate just because the investigator clearly and sincerely assures us, "When I pursue explanations of historical phenomenon, I only pursue causes of their beginning when they did, as against their non-occurrence at those precise moments."

A standard causal pattern is appropriate to a given field in a given period if it satisfies the two, jointly sufficient criteria that I sketched very briefly, above. On the one hand, the causal factors singled out for description must actually exist and must be causally sufficient in typical cases in question. This relatively non-pragmatic criterion is especially prominent in the natural sciences, where standard causal

---

[21] See, for example, Scriven, "Causes, Connections and Conditions in History," pp. 254–58; Fred Dretske, "Contrastive Statements," *Philosophical Review* (1973), pp. 411–37; Alan Garfinkel, *Forms of Explanation* (New Haven, 1981), ch. 1; Bas van Fraassen, *The Scientific Image* (Oxford, 1980), pp. 127f. I am indebted to Garfinkel for his illuminating description of the pragmatics of causation and his discussion of phenomena that I will group under the heading "necessity as depth."

patterns are usually overthrown in disputes concerning this dimension of adequacy. However, in most fields, whether in the social or the natural sciences, the first criterion does not dictate the choice of a standard pattern. For most subject-matters, causality is complex enough that accurate causal accounts can be more or less thorough. And the question of adequate thoroughness is resolved by the other criterion: choose a pattern if conformity to it would most improve the pursuit of accurate causal descriptions in the subject-matter and period in question. By "conformity" I mean a situation in which the standard pattern is an accepted stopping rule, so that the typical investigator typically ends his or her investigation when the pattern is met, along with the other constraints on explanation. Thus, in early twentieth-century disease theory, a standard pattern is suited if someone's symptoms are found to be caused by an infectious agent which is a normal cause of such symptoms. To require more, as a general rule, would stall disease theory. At this point in time, investigators are so far from specific knowledge of how the state of the organism determines whether infection will be symptomatic that the pursuit of the explanation of a single set of symptoms would have to continue indefinitely, for success to be declared. To require less is to require too little. Accessible diagnoses will be missed. Inaccurate diagnoses, unconnected with infection, will be encouraged. New kinds of infectious processes, potentially yielding many new explanations of particular symptoms, are much less apt to be discovered. For scientific purposes, the actual standard pattern aims neither too high nor too low. Similarly, it would be too much to require that explanations of political phenomena describe factors which would create similar phenomena anywhere in the world. The pursuit of relevant causal factors would grind to a halt. On the other hand, to require only a list of causes adequate to produce a political event in the particular locality and time where it arose is to require too little. Many accessible causes would be missed. The repertoire of possible causes is much less apt to be expanded beyond immediate and superficial causal triggers, if investigation is governed by this charitable stopping rule. For it will rarely require that the political historian say why this provocation or that official blunder had its effects in the case at hand.

This description of the validity of standard causal pattern presupposes that research is a social process requiring organization by socially accepted rules. The proposed account of explanatory adequacy applies to a world of science in which different people engage in different research projects; projects are not willingly ended before success is achieved; research projects depend on the results of prior projects; these results typically include explanatory hypotheses that have been vindicated, not just a stream of raw data. The classical positivists were certainly aware that science has this social structure. But they thought it could be neglected in an account of what makes a hypothesis simply and literally an adequate explanation. In their view, the right philosophical account of adequacy would also fit a world of science in which empirical findings consisted of the random recording of events by a single observer in a mere observational diary, or "protocol" as some logical positivists put it, while hypotheses emerged spontaneously in a single theorist's mind. In such a world, the only relevant concept of adequacy probably is the one described by the covering-law model. In the previous chapter, that concept turned out not to correspond to the difference between adequate and inadequate explanation. So it is fortunate for those interested in replacing positivism with a substantial alternative that the "protocol sentence" world of science is not the real one. Of course, someone might knowingly construct an analysis of a notion of adequacy that no one actually employs, that no one needs to employ, and that sheds light on no notion that is employed. But that would be a philosophical joke, very far from the classical positivists' serious intentions.

So far, the benefits relevant to justifying a pattern have been purely scientific, the encouragement of causal insight in the subject matter in question. In some cases, though, we might rank the effects of a stopping rule as better or worse on extra-scientific grounds. Consider this example, adapted from E. H. Carr.[22] Jones, a smoker, runs out of cigarettes late at night. He drives along a mountain road, toward Kelly's grocery, the nearest source of cigarettes that late at night. Coming around a turn, he encounters drunken Robinson, coming from the other direction, careening into his lane. Jones dies instantly. A variety of explanations of the fatal crash might be acceptable. It occurred because Robinson was drunk, because he was in the wrong lane, because he was careening down the road, and, perhaps, because Jones was not paying enough attention driving on a mountain road late at night. But the statement that the fatal crash occurred because Jones was a smoker is not an adequate explanation. It is not adequate, even though the crash would not have occurred, had Jones not been a smoker.

There is a rationale for accepting drunkenness and insufficient

[22] See Carr, *What Is History?* (New York, 1961), pp. 137f.

attention as explanations of car crashes, but not accepting being a smoker, when that was merely the motive for an unlucky errand. This rationale is practical. We can better pursue our practical concern about car crashes, viz., reducing their number, if we know more about the role of drunkenness and inattention in causing them. For example, we can make a more informed decision about penalties for drunk driving. We can decide to drive with more care on certain kinds of roads. But knowledge of the errands which led individuals to be at the wrong place at the wrong time does not help us to pursue this interest. Had Jones known that yielding to his craving for tobacco would have led to the accident, he would not have yielded. But he could not know this, and his death is past. No one's effort to avoid vehicular death is supported by knowledge that Jones would not have been killed if he had not smoked.

In the organized scientific pursuit of explanation, practical concerns may also dictate choice of a standard causal pattern. In the early nineteenth century, many investigators had come to explain the prevalence of certain diseases in certain places as due to filth and overcrowding. For example, the prevalence of tuberculosis in urban slums was understood in this way. In these explanations, the microbial agent was not, of course described. But the causal factors mentioned were actual causes of the prevalence of some of those diseases. If Manchester had not been filthy and overcrowded, tuberculosis would not have been prevalent. On the purely scientific dimension, acceptance of accurate environmental explanations probably did not encourage as many causal ascriptions as would a standard requiring explanation of why some victims of filth and overcrowding became tubercular, some not. Those who pressed the latter question were to lead the great advances of the germ theory. But in a practical way, the environmental explanations did a superior job, encouraging more important causal accounts. Guided by those accounts, sanitary measures produced dramatic reductions in tuberculosis and other diseases, more dramatic, in fact, than the germ theory has yielded. A perspicacious investigator might have argued, "We know that some specific and varied accompaniment of filth and overcrowding is crucial, since not every child in the Manchester slums is tubercular. But we should accept explanations of the prevalence of a disease which appeal to living conditions. For they accurately, if vaguely, describe relevant causal factors, and give us the means to control the prevalence of disease."

At times, both practical and scientific concerns seem to be at work. In political history, acceptance of causes sufficient in the current circumstances of the nation in question partly reflects the relative availability of such accounts. But it also reflects the fact that the nation-state is the most important unit in policy-making. When sources of political control are more local, as in Swiss cantons or nineteenth-century American cities, more localized causal standards seem more appropriate, as well.

This account of the role and rationale for standard causal patterns departs from positivist philosophy of science in three general ways. In the first place, explanatory adequacy is essentially pragmatic and field-specific. Standard causal patterns change from field to field and time to time, depending on the strategies of investigation and their consequences under the circumstances; and yet they help to determine what is an adequate explanation, not just what is presently acceptable. Also, standard causal patterns need not require even a sketch of any of the positivist ideals for explanation. Finally, so far as standard causal patterns are involved, the judgment of particular explanations proceeds at a different level of comprehensiveness than positivists suppose. In positivist philosophy of science, once we understand a particular explanatory hypothesis, i.e., what is said to be a cause, what the causal connection is said to be, and what is supposed to be explained, we can judge whether the hypothesis explains, if it accurately describes, by applying a priori principles. So no empirical commitments are made when an explanation is chosen except those latent in the explanation itself. But in the present approach, the adequacy of a particular explanation may depend on whether a causal pattern is best for the relevant field. That a pattern would be the best means of gaining insight into the particular explanandum at hand may be unknown, indeterminate or even false, when it is best for the field and, hence, appropriate. Perhaps pressing the question of whether the situation of the peasantry, the clergy and the bourgeoisie in the Vendée would have led to a Vendée-type uprising at any time or place would quickly yield an informative covering-law explanation of the Vendée uprising. Then it is too bad that Tilly did not so expand his horizons. But his concentration on the nation-state yields an adequate explanation, because of its appropriateness to modern political history, as a whole.

Because explanations are assessed at a variety of levels, there is a danger that investigators will talk past each other, when they disagree, misidentifying the issues that divide them. Here, the theory of standard causal patterns is of practical use, eliminating irrelevant arguments without implausible declarations that the disagreement is just a matter of taste. For example, in disputes over such great political events as the French Revolution, the United States Civil War and the Nazi seizure of power, there seems to be a substantive disagreement between historians who emphasize the decisions, motives and resources of leading individuals and those who emphasize large-scale social processes. Yet when these historians confront one another, the results are often disappointing. Either there is much defense, to no effect, of the existence of each side's favored causal linkages, say, more arguments by narrative historians that these politicians were hot-headed, this president was naive. Or there are methodological skirmishes based on one aspect or another of the covering-law model, as when individual narratives are criticized on the ground that a certain political action would have had no result if the surrounding circumstances were very different. Reflecting on these disheartening controversies, critics are apt to declare that issues of taste are being elevated to the status of substantive differences—which makes it strange that there are so many intelligent but stubborn disputants on both sides. In fact, the disagreement is often over policy for the field (when it is not a disagreement about causal depth, the subject of the next section). The narrative historian is relying on a standard causal pattern according to which a description of the actions producing change, and the rationales behind them, is adequate if those actions and reasons were sufficient under the circumstances. His implicit justification might be that his pattern leads to the discovery of causes which would otherwise be ignored and, as a stopping rule, discourages the pursuit of a "deeper cause" in the many cases in which none exists. The social forces historian believes that the individualistic pattern will discourage the potentially fruitful pursuit of new causal factors, outside the repertoire of individual psychology. He is committed to a pattern requiring informative description of social forces determining the success or failure of major individual political initiatives. This is a substantive dispute about the consequences of different stopping rules for the practice of modern political history, to be resolved if possible at that intermediate level, in between particular historical controversies and absolutely general rules for explanation.

An appreciation of how practical interests can regulate standard causal patterns is also useful, in clarifying controversies. Perhaps because of a widely shared view that it is unprofessional to emphasize controversies over policy in theoretical matters, connections between interests and causal choices are often repressed in the social sciences, even when the theoretical controversies are especially

heated because the practical stakes are so high. For example, one recurrent style in the study of racial prejudice is the psychological
mode epitomized by Allport's book, *The Nature of Prejudice*.[23] Allport
attempts to explain the prevalence of racial prejudice in the United
States by describing the defects of personality that lead people to become prejudiced. The need to construct a firm self-identity by plac-
ing others in outcast groups is a typical example of a defect he describes. Allport's data are, on the whole, small-group experiments
or surveys of isolated episodes, for example, scenarios of "race
riots." Suppose that Allport has described the individual psychological processes that typically result in racial prejudice in the United
States. Has he explained the prevalence of racial prejudice in the
United States? Many social scientists want to say "no." But when they
justify their denial they usually appeal to some excessive, positivist
constraint, in particular, a demand based on general and a priori
principles that Allport describe the kinds of circumstances in which
those seeking to stigmatize a group would chose groups that are racial.

The real issue becomes much clearer when one considers how alternative standard causal patterns might be assessed in light of the
overriding practical interest that both sides share, the reduction of
racial prejudice. It may be that prejudices characteristic of a society
are maintained by a limited repertoire of psychological mechanisms
such as Allport describes. It may also be the case that these mechanisms are prevalent, effective, and directed against particular
groups because of facts which the empirical investigation of personality structure will *not* reveal, for example: the objective interests,
power, and social situation of different social groups; or patterns of
migration, occupational structure, and economic change. Even so,
whether the explanation of prejudice needs to be pushed beyond
the psychological depends on a further question: what knowledge
would be an adequate basis for reducing prejudice? If it were feasible and effective to reduce prejudice through widespread propaganda revealing the psychological distortions which create it, that is
a basis for choosing the psychological pattern which Allport adopts.
In this way, his book reflects the hopes of the period, shortly after
World War II, in which it was written. Suppose, on the other hand,
that such a campaign will not occur or will not be effective unless the
social circumstances are changed. An economic and political elite

[23] Gordon W. Allport, *The Nature of Prejudice* (Boston, 1954).

has too great an interest in the tendency of racial divisions to preserve status quo.[24] Or, to cite a very different hypothesis, whites, in
the present economic context, have too great an interest in preserving a "white skin privilege." Then a causal pattern requiring the description of social factors is to be preferred—on the same kinds of
grounds as determine our judgment in Carr's example. To neglect
the pragmatic dimension of adequacy, here, is to prevent a relevant
and fully scientific stage in the controversy—namely, the justification of a stopping-rule for the pursuit of adequate explanations—
through a premature judgment that investigators are dogmatic, are
separated by non-rational tastes in explanation, or are guilty of elementary methodological blunders.

## CAUSAL DEPTH

Suppose a list of causes fits an appropriate standard causal pattern and accurately describes factors sufficient under the circumstances to bring about the effect in question. It may still fail to explain because those causes lack sufficient depth. Roughly speaking,
a cause is too shallow to explain why something occurred if it is just
one of the ways in which another cause, as intimately connected with
the effect, produced the latter. In the slogan version of the causal
theory of explanation, such causes are excluded by the requirement
that "underlying" causes be described. Actually, "not underlain"
would be the more accurate, but absolutely ugly term, since the
question is whether one cause is undermined by another.

More specifically, a cause, X, helping to bring about Y, is too shallow to explain why Y occurred if a cause, Z, of Y undermines X in
one of two ways: (a) If X had not occurred, Y would have happened
anyway; Z would have produced some causal substitute for X,
bringing Y about in some other way. I will label the depth that X
lacks, and Z may have here, "depth as necessity." (b) Z is a condition
in which Y arose that caused Y, and caused it, in part, by causing X;
Z is causally prior to X yet, also, too intimately related to Y to be
bracketed as a remote cause. I will refer to his aspect of depth using
the label "depth as priority."

### Depth as Necessity

Disputes as to whether the actions of famous people explain historical events are sometimes good illustrations of the role of depth as

[24] See, for example, Michael Reich, *Racial Inequality* (Princeton, 1981).

necessity. Consider the role of individual leaders of the German establishment in the Nazi seizure of power. Hindenburg's invitation to Hitler to become Chancellor is sometimes portrayed as a senile blunder, involving a stupid underestimate of Hitler's political ability. Suppose this was the case. Hindenburg's mistaken estimate of Hitler's capacities would be a cause of the Nazi seizure of power. Moreover, in the actual circumstances, which included Hindenburg's great prestige and Hitler's shrewdness and ruthlessness, this mistake was sufficient to bring about the Nazi seizure of power. Still, it may be, as some historians, most prominently Franz Neumann, have argued, that the political needs and powers of German big business and of the military would have led to state power for the Nazis, even if Hindenburg had been brighter. On their view, a Nazi government was worth the real attendant risks, from the standpoint of the German establishment, given the Nazis' unique ability, if installed in power, to repress domestic discontent while mobilizing for war. Had Hindenburg been less naive, he or his successor would have come to appreciate these facts, and would have installed a Nazi government anyway. In that case, Hindenburg's mistake and other causal links in familiar narrative histories do not explain why the Nazis came to power. Rather, the needs and powers of big business and the military are the underlying cause. The individual decisions do explain why the Nazis came to power in January 1933, rather than a bit sooner or later. But that question of precise timing is much less interesting. Its resolution by appeals to social forces has never been at issue.[25]

For certain historical questions, the existence of the undermining, deeper cause is fairly obvious, and the inference from depth as ne-

[25] See Franz Neumann, *Behemoth* (New York, 1944), especially the historical "Introduction." Rupert Palme-Dutt, *Fascism and Social Revolution* (New York, 1936), contains useful arguments and elaborations in support of an account similar to Neumann's, along with extraneous conspiratorial speculations. A number of recent studies offer evidence, tending to support Neumann's account, concerning the nature of support for and opposition to the Nazis and the relation between social trends in the Weimar Republic and under Hitler's regime. These data are the more impressive in light of the investigators' general hostility toward Neumann, Palme-Dutt and their political strategies. See David Schoenbaum, *Hitler's Social Revolution* (New York, 1966) for statistics on the continuity between Weimar- and Hitler-period trends; William S. Allen, *The Nazi Seizure of Power* (Chicago, 1965), on the role of the Social Democratic party and other established alternatives to the Nazis; and Richard Hamilton, *Who Voted for Hitler?* (Princeton, 1982), on the social origins of support for the Nazis. F. L. Carsten, *The Rise of Fascism* (Berkeley, 1971), chs. 3 and 4, is at once a good example of traditional narrative explanations and an extremely useful chronology of the basic events.

cessity is commonly drawn. The United States Civil War would have lasted longer had Grant or Sherman not been such brilliant and ruthless generals. But virtually every military historian accepts that, in the absence of their generalship, the North would have won anyway. The industrial superiority of the North, its superior railroad network, and its vast numerical superiority in committed fighters would have produced Northern victory through some other route, including more intermediate Northern defeats. Thus, the generalship of Grant and Sherman does not explain why the North won, even though their generalship was a cause of the North's winning.[26]

I have used the label "necessity as depth" for the first kind of undermining depth. In relevant disputes over explanations, appeals to this requirement of depth often involve such phrases as "It was bound to happen anyway." While these expressions are not inaccurate, it is important to keep in mind two implicit limitations of the sort of necessity which is claimed.

In the first place, the necessity required is relative to conditions in the background of the phenomenon to be explained. Although Y would have happened anyway in the absence of X, its occurrence would have depended on the operation of other factors, which happened to be present, which would have produced a substitute for X. If Neumann proposes that the Nazis were bound to come to power, even if Hindenburg had been less naive, he is not committing himself to some metaphysical thesis that the Nazi seizure of power was fated from the beginning of time.

The necessity pursued is weak in another respect. It might be true that the phenomenon in question would have occurred anyway, in the absence of the shallow cause X, even though there is a small but significant probability that this phenomenon might not have occurred under the other circumstances obtaining at the time. Those who believe that the Nazis would have come to power anyway, in the absence of the particular chain of decisions leading to Hitler's chancellorship, may be right or wrong, but they are not refuted by the following consideration: if Hitler had not been made chancellor when he was, he, Goebbels and Goering would have been crossing

---

[26] A die-hard counterfactualist might be inclined to say, here, that Grant's generalship was not a cause of the North's winning, but only of the North's winning in the spring of 1865. But by the same token, no other capacity or episode restricted to the battlefield would be a cause. So along with the odd-sounding claim that Grant's brilliance was not a cause of the Northern victory, we would be committed to the more metaphysical absurdity that the North's military victory had no causes among battlefield events.

different street corners at different times and just might have been killed in simultaneous accidents, a blow from which the Nazis would not have recovered. As the possible-worlds analysis of counterfactuals entails, the "inevitabilists" are actually claiming that late-Weimar circumstances would have brought about the Nazi seizure of power in some way, if not through the individual episodes that actually caused it, provided nothing *extraordinary*, of a sort that never did occur, prevented the seizure of power. This is surely the force of analogous counterfactuals in ordinary usage. When I say, in a bridge *post mortem*, "Jones would have won, even if the finesse had not worked. He could have gotten to the board in the next round and established his spades," I mean that something extraordinary, for example, a lapse of memory remarkable in a player such as Jones, would have been required to prevent victory through the alternative strategy.

Evidently, the assessment of explanations is governed by judgments of what is normal or extraordinary and, so, is no more determinate than those relatively vague notions. This helps to account for the indeterminacy of many of our judgments of explanatory proposals. Did Carter defeat Ford because of Ford's blunders and appearance of stupidity; because the Ford administration was tainted by Watergate; or is it that only the two factors combined explain? Any unhedged choice seems unwise, here, even though the facts of the case are by no means obscure. And vagueness about what is normal corresponds to this indeterminacy about which explanation or explanations are right. We have no standards of the normal level of presidential competence and public tolerance definite enough to determine whether Carter would have defeated an incumbent who was a normal, but non-extraordinary performer, otherwise the same as Ford.

Among philosophical theories of explanation, depth-as-necessity rules out both the covering-law analysis and some of its most influential rivals. The covering-law analysis cannot be complete, since a covering-law derivation is no guarantee of depth-as-necessity (or depth-as-priority). Perhaps generalship such as Grant's and Sherman's is bound to produce victory in their kind of situation. Still, the victory of the North has not been explained.

In the social sciences, the hermeneutic approach is the most important alternative to the covering-law model. According to hermeneutic theorists, a phenomenon is explained when it is rendered intelligible by describing the motives of the participants. But, as we have seen, an accurate description of the motives of the participants in the Nazis' coming to power might fail to explain, on account of shallowness. Finally, consider Scriven's influential alternative to the covering-law requirement: an explanation of why something happened describes a phenomenon sufficient under the circumstances to bring it about, without which the explanandum would not have occurred, unless some alternative had played the role of substitute cause.[27] Hindenburg's blunder might, in these ways, have been necessary and sufficient under the circumstances for the Nazis' seizure of power. Yet it might still have failed to explain.

*Depth as Priority*

The other kind of explanatory depth involves a form of causal priority. Suppose a causal factor is sufficient under the circumstances to bring about a phenomenon, and necessary in the sense that the phenomenon would not have arisen eventually, by some alternative route, in the absence of that factor. What is more, suppose that a description of that factor fits an appropriate standard causal pattern. Still, the description might fail to explain because a prior cause is present. The shallow causal factor is itself the result of this cause, which is no less immediately connected with the phenomenon to be explained.

When rival explanations both appeal to large-scale social processes, they often conflict because of the requirement that a causal description possess depth-as-priority. Among explanations of the Nazi seizure of power that appeal to broad social forces, some explain the Nazi regime as a revolt of the middle classes, a product of the radical rightward drift of German middle class opinion during the Great Depression. This was the initial explanation offered by the leaders of the German Social Democratic party. Others, left-wing Social Democrats such as Neumann and Communists such as Palme Dutt, argued that the rightward turn of middle-class opinion was itself a result of the ideological and political power of German big business, a power that resulted in the Nazi seizure of power in the conditions of the Great Depression. Both sides in this furious debate (which still continues) accept that the more Marxist explanation is not just a supplement to the "revolt of the middle classes" explanation, but a rival. If the revolt of the middle classes was just one of the means by which big business domination of Germany produced a fascist response to German economic crisis, then the Nazi seizure of power cannot be explained as due to the rightward

---

[27] "Causes, Connections and Conditions in History," p. 249.

turn of the middle class. Yet both sides accept that the Nazis could not have come to power without the broad support they had, primarily from the middle classes. In the absence of this causal factor, the phenomenon to be explained would *not* have happened anyway. In addition, no independent disagreement over standard causal patterns is at issue. In this particular debate, both sides reject explanations appealing solely to the decisions of individual political leaders. The social circumstances which made such decisions either effective or ineffective are themselves to be described.

In other, less controversial cases, virtually everyone would agree that a proposal fails to meet the requirement of depth-as-priority. This is often the case with extremely one-sided explanations. Perhaps an expert on the history of printing tells us that the use of moveable type explains the Industrial Revolution. It is plausible that moveable type was a necessary factor, since the rapid dissemination of technological advances requires it. Perhaps, this printing phenomenon was sufficient under the actual circumstances. It is not obvious how an appropriate standard pattern would rule out this reliance on unspecified reference to circumstances. Yet depth-as-priority seems lacking. Moveable-type printing required no great intellectual innovation. Its currency was due to contemporary social factors, which stimulated industrialization in this and other ways. Where these factors were absent, as in the Orient, moveable-type printing remained a mere curiosity, not widely used. The explanation worth considering does not just mention the use of moveable type, but specifies the deeper causes.

The major problem in explicating depth-as-priority is to describe the relation that the deeper cause must have to the phenomenon to be explained. This relation must be intimate. It is absurd to deny that a cause of a phenomenon explains just because a more remote cause produced the cause in question. The fact that the polite form of address in German is the third person plural is usually explained by noting that usages in the Hapsburg court in Madrid were once the epitomes of politeness for Germans, and that the Hapsburg Emperor was addressed in the third-person plural, by courtiers in Madrid, to acknowledge his multiple titles as Holy Roman Emperor, King of Aragon and Castile, Emperor of the Seas, and so forth. It would be obsessive madness to reject this explanation on the grounds that political history gives further causes, omitted in the linguists' explanation, of the Hapsburgs' becoming Holy Roman Emperors, Kings of Aragon and Castile, and so on.

To exclude irrelevant types of priority, I have required that the deeper cause itself cause the phenomenon to be explained, and be as intimately connected with it as the shallower cause. A more precise depiction of this intimacy might refer to the circumstances in which the shallow cause is supposed to be sufficient. Suppose that the circumstances in which X is sufficient to bring about Y must include Z, which itself causes X. Then Z has depth-as-priority and X is too shallow to explain. Thus, the circumstances in which the rightward drift of the middle classes is sufficient to produce the Nazi seizure of power might have to include the dominance of the German elites, which is responsible for that rightwards drift. Had that trend occurred, while the German establishment did not support the Nazi seizure of power, there would have been no Nazi triumph. Or so Neumann and Palme Dutt argue. On the other hand, the circumstances in which Spanish usage influenced German standards of etiquette did not include Columbus' voyage and the other prior conditions which brought about those circumstances connecting usage in Madrid and usage in Germany.

Both depth-as-priority and depth-as-necessity add a crucial comparative dimension to explanation. A causal factor may fail to explain simply because another factor has superior causal status. The most accurate knowledge of the links tying a factor to the explanandum may fail to tell us what the explanation is, because a deeper cause underlies the linkage.

## THE UNITY OF EXPLANATION

Explanation, on the present account, has several dimensions, each fairly complicated. Why, then, does characterizing something as an explanation play such an important role in our lives? We can see the overall unity and utility of this complex activity of explanation, if we view it as the kind of description which is most fundamentally a basis for coping with reality, i.e., for promoting or preventing change. Such description will be description of causes, for all means of control are causes, even if the converse is not true. Describing causes is a social activity with a long history of interconnected episodes. So, if it is to aid in coping, adequacy will be governed by standards fitting the scientific needs of the time. But, even when guided by these standards, the description of causes would often fail to aid in coping, unless the requirement of depth is imposed.

Without the requirement of depth, we could not expect explanation generally to direct us toward a crucial point at which to intervene in order to change reality. When depth as necessity is lacking, it will be a waste of time to try to prevent phenomena like the explanandum, in similar cases, by preventing the shallow cause. The sequel will simply arrive by another route. Also, in similar circumstances, when the shallow cause is missing, *encouraging* a phenomenon like the explanandum by encouraging the shallow cause will often be an unnecessary waste of time. Where the shallow cause might have worked, a substitute will often be doing the same work. Similarly, when a cause lacks the needed priority, it is probably a bad point at which to intervene. In similar circumstances, trying to produce something like the explanandum by producing something like the shallow cause will be a waste of effort. If the prior cause is absent, the shallow one will be ineffective. If the prior cause is present, the intervention is unnecessary, since the prior cause produces the shallow one. Moreover, although the shallow cause is necessary, if we are trying to *prevent* something like the explanandum our efforts are very likely to be misdirected if we try to do so by preventing the shallow cause, in ignorance of the prior one. The prior cause is likely to be powerful enough to defeat our efforts, unless we consciously direct our efforts at it. This practical interest in the strategic point at which to prevent phenomena is, of course, the basis for the passion of debates over depth-as-priority in explanations of the triumph of fascist movements and the outbreak of undesired wars. In sum, the requirement of depth makes the possession of an explanation a helpful guide in general to changing reality. If the requirement is not met, it is reasonable to expect no useful lesson to be derived from a causal description.

Explanation directs us toward those parts of the history of the world that are of most use in coping with the world. This singles out the activity of explanation, even though individual successes in explanation may not yield lessons about promoting or preventing change. (The necessary background circumstances may be too unique, for example, or the causes too uncontrollable.) This is the point of the activity as a whole. So an adequate account of explanation should describe an activity uniquely fitted to play this role. The different aspects of the causal theory of explanation are united as means of fulfilling this requirement.

CHAPTER THREE

# Applications

A THEORY of explanation should be not just true but fruitful. Since explanation is a central goal of science, perhaps the central one, a theory of explanation should make a difference in current debates throughout the philosophy of science, including many that lie outside the topic of explanation, narrowly construed. Such fruitfulness is especially important for a robustly causal theory of explanation. For many people avoid such theories not out of a fear that they are bound to be false, but out of a fear that they are bound to yield nothing but truisms given the refusal to analyze causation. In this chapter, I will describe some of the distinctive answers and arguments that the present causal theory contributes to standard debates in the philosophy of science. The topics will be value-freedom, methodological individualism, functional explanation, the distinctiveness of the human sciences, and the logical structure of theories.

## VALUE-FREEDOM

That the pursuit of scientific explanations, in the social as well as the natural sciences, should be value-free is a dogma in the English-speaking academic world. As with all dogmas, there are heretics. They accept (often proudly) the status of a less than respectable minority. Also, as with all dogmas, value-freedom is usually understood by orthodox and heterodox alike as a cruder doctrine than it was when it originated, as a heresy.

The prophet, all agree, was Max Weber. (Originally, his brother Alfred, together with Werner Sombart were his only allies.) The bitter debate over value-freedom that Weber provoked at the first meeting of the German Sociological Association, in 1910, is said to be a major reason why there was no second meeting until after the World War.[1] Most of the hundreds of pages that Weber devoted to

[1] For more on Weber's writings and activities in the original value-freedom controversy, see my "Reason and Commitment in the Social Sciences," *Philosophy and Public Affairs* (1979), pp. 241–66; David Frisby's introduction to the English translation of T. Adorno, ed., *The Positivist Dispute in German Sociology* (New York, 1976); and the records of Weber's advocacy of his doctrine within the Verein fuer Sozialpolitik—for

this topic develop sensitive qualifications of the maxims of value-freedom. The issue is the extent to which social scientists are reasonably governed by their value commitments, i.e., their beliefs as to what ought to be, when they pursue explanations of phenomena. With characteristic subtlety, Weber frequently notes that investigators must, of course, be governed by their value commitments in choosing which explanatory question to answer. The reasonable choice is the choice of the most important question, and importance is reasonably assessed in terms of values, including extra-scientific ones. However, when a question has been chosen (often in a prolonged process of clarification and assessment from an initially vague starting point), rational inquiry is value-free, in two ways. The inquirer should be as non-partisan as possible, trying to free himself from the influence of all value commitments, except the "inherent norm" of science, that valid explanations should be pursued.[2] Also, the answer to the explanatory question should not make a value judgment. "[A] value judgment is absolutely not a causal explanation."[3] Of course, without making a value judgment, an explanation might appeal to people's value judgments as playing a causal role. Weber is excluding explanations of the English Civil War as due to Stuart injustice, not explanations of the War as due to the widespread belief that the Stuarts were unjust. In fact, such appeals to the influence of value judgments are especially prominent in Weber's own practice.

Though much more satisfying than crude pronouncements that values should be kept out of scientific research as such, Weber's account of value-freedom is implausible or underargued in important ways. And yet, once the claims are hedged further and the inadequate arguments withdrawn, a certain hard core of truth seems to remain. The role of the causal theory of explanation will be to penetrate this core.

On reflection, the general maxim of non-partisanship is quite implausible, even as a rule for achieving purely scientific goals. Surely,

---

example, his contributions to the discussions on productivity and on cooperative enterprises in *Schriften der Verein fuer Sozialpolitik*, vol. 132, and the memorandum to his fellow members, "Gutachten zur Werturteilsdiskussion" in *Max Weber: Werk und Person*, ed., Baumgarten (Tuebingen, 1964).

[2] "The Meaning of 'Ethical Neutrality' in Sociology and Economics" in Weber, *The Methodology of the Social Sciences*, tr. Shils and Finch (New York, 1949), p. 5. See also "Objectivity in Social Science and Social Policy" in ibid., pp. 54f.

[3] "Critical Studies in the Logic of the Social Sciences" in *Methodology of the Social Sciences*, p. 123. See also "Ethical Neutrality," p. 33.

there are some contexts for research in which truth-distorting social forces are best resisted through commitment to certain extra-scientific values. For example, Franz Boas and other pioneers of anthropology had to create new research tools, engage in physically excruciating fieldwork and put their careers in jeopardy to challenge the universal academic opinion that non-white non-literate peoples had no culture worthy of the name. In their discovery of the truth, they were helped in crucial ways by their extra-scientific commitments, such as Boas' desire to be "a member of humanity as a whole" working for "the ideals of the Revolution of 1848."[4] It is by no means obvious that his further, purely scientific commitment to find the truth would, by itself, have been an adequate inoculation against pervasive truth-distorting factors. A more recent example might be Leon Kamin's perseverance, out of anti-racist motives quite unconnected with his own work in animal psychology, through the years of tedious investigation in which he unmasked Cyril Burt, a universally respected founder of modern psychology, as a racist fraud.[5] No doubt, extra-scientific motives also have their distinctive dangers, as sources of wishful thinking, self-deception or the neglect of unwelcome data. But to impose a general rule of non-partisanship, without substantial argument, as Weber and his followers do, is simply to express a broadly positivist faith that every peril to rationality has its cure in a general a priori rule.

The other soft spot in the classical account consists of the arguments for the denial that explanations ever evaluate. For all the subtlety of his hedges, Weber's positive arguments, here, are fragmentary and unconvincing. In part, they consist of appeals to the premise that a statement of what ought to be can never be derived from a statement of what is. If this means that evaluative statements are never factual claims, it is question-begging. If it means that non-evaluative factual claims never jointly entail an evaluation, it is useless. Few people now believe that descriptions of behavior ever entail ascriptions of emotions. But non-behaviorists still coherently insist that science, indeed a single science of psychology, discusses both, and often explains the former by appeals to the latter. Elsewhere, Weber makes an epistemological argument: if a statement is scientific, then reason and evidence would dictate that every fully informed person accept or reject it; and value judgments do not have this universal status. But if value-freedom is to be the outcome

---

[4] Boas, "An Anthropologist's Credo" in Clifton Fadiman, ed., *I Believe* (New York, 1939), p. 19. See also, George Stocking, *Race, Culture and Evolution* (New York, 1968), ch. 7.

[5] Leon Kamin, *The Science and Politics of I.Q.* (Potomac, Md., 1974).

of this argument, every scientific statement must satisfy the demand for universal demonstrability, while no value judgment does. This stark distinction seems quite implausible, and Weber never supports it. Take, as the value judgment, the wrongness of Caligula's most violent activities and, as the scientific statement, Weber's explanation of the rise of modern capitalism. As with the prohibition of partisanship, a typical worry about particular value judgments has, again, been elevated to a general, a priori rule.

These criticisms affect aspects of value-freedom that have enormous influence. And yet, they leave untouched a hard core of each maxim of value-freedom. What seems to be the grain of truth in non-partisanship is this: whatever influences an investigator should maintain or exclude in the context of research after an explanatory question is chosen, extra-scientific value judgments have no legitimate role to play in *justifying* an answer. In addition, even if Weber's denial that value judgments explain is wrong, in its substance as well as in the rationales just criticized, the dismissal of evaluative explanations might still be basically right. Value judgments always supervene on certain non-evaluative statements of fact: the value judgment is properly maintained in virtue of the latter, and the same evaluation must hold in any situation having the same not intrinsically evaluative characteristics. The same acts as made Caligula a moral monster, performed in the same context, would merit the same judgment. If value judgments ever do explain, there seems always to be an alternative explanation available, namely, an explanation appealing to the supervened facts. And, one might conclude, in a modern revision of Weber's argument from "Is never entails Ought," that, given the availability of the alternative, it should be chosen. Ontological economy is promoted in this way, by excluding a vast new realm of intrinsically moral facts from science.[6] And confusion is avoided, since value judgments are especially apt to have different implications for different investigators. In sum, the hard core of value-freedom is the principle that value judgment plays no legitimate role in justifying a scientific explanation together with the principle that explanations using concepts that are not inherently evaluative are always to be preferred, for scientific purposes, to moralizing explanations. Both principles are quite appealing to logically perspicacious philosophers and social scientists, sensitive to

---

[6] For influential arguments of this kind see Gilbert Harman, *The Nature of Morality* (New York, 1977), chs. 1 and 2; John Mackie, *Ethics: Inventing Right and Wrong* (New York, 1977), ch. 1, esp. pp. 38–42.

the real difficulties of social scientific research. Surely, this is an important reason why Weber is taken to be basically right.

The causal theory of explanation, not just a general doubt about positivism, is essential, now, to distinguish the true from the false in the hard core. If the causal theory is right, extra-scientific values do have a legitimate, if indirect, role to play in the justification of proposed explanations, namely, their role in the justification of the relevant standard causal pattern. The usual scientific question of whether a causal description is adequate to explain may depend, for an answer, on a choice of a standard pattern as part of the most effective strategy for promoting what is desirable, i.e., desirable for extrascientific reasons. The judgment of Allport's theory of prejudice was a case in point.

Does this mean that there is sometimes no objective fact of the matter as to whether a hypothesis explains a phenomenon? In effect, this is the question of whether the relevant judgments as to what is desirable would be the rational judgments of all fully informed people. Since this meta-ethical question is exceptionally difficult, the best course for the philosopher of science is to hedge his or her bet. To use a distasteful but common philosophical figment, if there could be an Ultimate Nazi who rationally holds, as an ultimate belief, retained despite knowledge of relevant evidence, that killing non-Aryans is good, then he might have reasons to reject the assessment of Allport's explanation that would be rational for the rest of us. So questions that are a part of scientific justification and scientific belief, not just its practical sequel, would not be objective, in the way that most concerns Weber and later partisans of value-freedom. But if the wrongness of the Nazis' "Final Solution" and other relevant parts of morality are rationally compelling in light of the facts, explanatory adequacy is objective, though value-governed. To these hedges, I will merely add a conjecture, plausible, I hope, that I have defended elsewhere. Special philosophical outlooks to one side, it seems likely that some value judgments, say, concerning brutality of Caligula's and of Hitler's sort, are rationally determinable, but that many others are not. Anthropology and psychology support this view when combined with the conception of reason and its limits that I will present in later chapters on scientific realism. If rational determinability in relevant value judgments is not an all-or-nothing matter, scientific judgments of whether an accurate causal description explains will sometimes, but not always have a universal warrant.[7]

---

[7] See my "Ways of Moral Learning," *Philosophical Review* (1985). I also discussed

According to the other core principle, moralizing explanations always have non-moralizing alternatives which we should prefer. Since in many areas none but the wildly naive would favor a moralizing explanation, it is best to concentrate on the sort of account that moralizing historians do offer, explanations of shifts in belief as due to moral insight. For example, Dwight Dumond and other historians of the coming of the United States Civil War explain the beginnings of abolitionism as due, in crucial measure, to the acute moral insight of the early abolitionists. They deny that abolitionist belief was initially a natural inference from prior moral beliefs and knowledge of current events. For most early abolitionists had been brought up in the early nineteenth-century consensus, according to which social peace was to be preserved by muting the question of slavery. (Of course, only the white minority among early abolitionists is in question, here.) Certainly, abolitionism was not the result of self-interest, in its beginnings, since many abolitionists faced ostracism, even physical attack.[8] The familiar Whig explanation of the Glorious Revolution of 1688 as due to Stuart injustice and the special moral perceptiveness of English country squires is another moralizing explanation in just the same general pattern. A mere blanket denial that value judgments ever describe facts would be utterly question-begging in the face of these historical claims.

Of course, moralizing explanations may be rejected, from case to case, without rejecting the underlying moral judgment of the situation in question. For example, David Donald has sought to explain the rise of abolitionism as due to the wounded sense of superiority of younger members of the New England mercantile aristocracy, which had entered into decline.[9] But why suppose that moralizing explanations are always and in principle to be avoided? The one general and a priori consideration that remains is the argument from supervenience. Even if abolitionism was not the natural outcome of a prior system of beliefs, it was the result of a chain of individual psychological episodes involving the early abolitionists. This person reads an account of deaths in the slave trade and it produces outrage in her. This person sees a slave beaten and is appalled. The talk of moral perceptiveness supervenes on these chains of events. To avoid admitting novel kinds of facts into science and to reduce the dangers of confusion, social scientists should prefer

---

these meta-ethical issues, now often addressed under the label "moral realism," in "Reason and Commitment," pp. 246–55.

[8] See Dwight Dumond, *The Anti-Slavery Origins of the Civil War* (Ann Arbor, 1939).

[9] David Donald, *Lincoln Reconsidered* (New York, 1956), pp. 21–36.

summaries of the supervened episodes (or so the argument from supervenience concludes).

The causal theory of explanation shows how this general rejection of moralizing explanation violates a more important scientific principle than economy or ease of communication, the principle that causal descriptions fail to explain when they are too shallow. Presumably Dumond thought that the particular chains of events that could in principle be picked out by non-moralizing psychology were too shallow. In the absence of these episodes abolitionism would have accumulated its first recruits in other episodes, so long as there were whites of moral insight and slavery had entered an enduring and specially vicious phase with the invention of the cotton gin. Dispensing with the moralizing explanation in favor of the non-moralizing narrative might have too great a cost in causal depth. It might be the same kind of mistake as the more obvious blunder of deserting all leading explanations of the coming of the Civil War in favor of the description of the states of mind and resources of Lincoln and Davis on the day of the firing on Fort Sumter.

Like the question of whether to avoid partisan influences, the question of whether to avoid moralizing explanations turns out to be empirical and to lack a general answer, once positivist prejudices are removed. As the social sciences have developed, the tendency to replace appeals to moral insight with appeals to interests and cultural beliefs has usually led to improved explanations, more detailed, more fruitful and tying up more explanatory loose ends (for example, questions left open by moralizing explanations as to why certain groups were morally perceptive at certain times). Yet it is by no means clear that this preference for non-moralizing descriptions contributes to the pursuit of explanations in every case. For example, in the many rival histories of the English working class, the principle that people rebel when their human dignity is violated seems to have produced better explanations than explanatory principles of a non-moralizing but one-sided sort, connecting rebellion to lowered wages or increased risks of unemployment. Beyond the truism that relatively vague explanations, such as moralizing explanations are, should be replaced by relatively informative ones, all else being equal, the most one can add in general is that some explanatory improvement seems always to have come (up until now) when the general emphasis in a whole field has shifted away from moralizing explanation. This does not mean, though, that the total elimination of the moral would be an improvement. A minimum may be a prerequisite for causal depth. Nor does it mean that social scientists should adopt a standard causal pattern in which adequate explanation has not been achieved until moralizing descriptions are eliminated.

In the second part of this book, the discussion of confirmation, we will encounter one other appropriate location for moralizing principles, in an area of scientific reasoning whose main features have already been sketched. I will argue that testing is a form of comparison that takes place against a background of substantive, specific principles. The vagueness that is a disadvantage when evaluations are used in ultimate explanations is not nearly as undesirable in the background principles used to chose explanations. Since the phenomenon of human dignity is vague and can be violated in a number of ways, even the most sternly moralizing historian of the English working class would want to supplement moralizing explanations with more specific ones that do not use distinctively moral language. But as a framework principle, the hypothesis that offenses to dignity are a powerful force for rebellion, more so than mere limitations on income and opportunity, may even gain from its vagueness. Being vague, it can describe a very plausible alternative on a causal checklist brought to bear, say, in explaining turmoil. Because it embraces many different kinds of circumstances, the principle about dignity can help to establish the force and relevance of data from other circumstances, as bearing on the circumstances under investigation. Because it is wide-ranging, it is a plausible description of what is normal, and hence, an important tool for "would have happened anyway" measurements of causal depth. Thus, quite apart from the choice of standard causal patterns, value judgments can play an important role in justification—even among investigators who prefer interests, culture and beliefs to moral properties in their actual explanations. This helps to resolve many dilemmas as to who is a moralizing historian. Obviously, the best left-wing historians of working people, from Marx to E. P. Thompson and Rodney Hilton, have tried to replace moralizing with an investigation of the causal role of interests, resources and ideology. And yet value judgments have, clearly, been part of the means they use to sift through explanatory alternatives.

## METHODOLOGICAL INDIVIDUALISM

Apart from value-freedom, Weber's main methodological legacy has been methodological individualism, the principle, roughly put, that social explanations should refer to the psychologies and resources of participants. For example, in his encyclopedic *Economy and Society*, he describes sociology as the science "which attempts the interpretive understanding of social action thereby to arrive at a causal interpretation of its course and effects. In 'action' is included all human behavior when and insofar as the acting individual attaches a subjective meaning to it."[10] In clarifying the notion of subjective meaning, he identifies it with the goals and beliefs that are the agent's reasons for acting, as opposed to other ends which the individual's actions might objectively serve.[11] While such individualism is not pervasive enough to be a dogma of present day Anglo-American social science as a whole, it is widespread and often used to condemn hypotheses to permanent exile from science. Thus, a historian explains that "The Marxist assessment of fascism stands on metaphysical or at least transhistorical grounds" because of its "imputation of a class basis to diverse groups which themselves were usually supraclass in conscious ('subjective') orientation."[12] Two political theorists, important critics as it happens of the academic establishment, ask, "Suppose there appears to be universal acquiescence in the status quo. Is it possible, in such circumstances, to determine whether the consensus is genuine or instead has been enforced by nondecision-making [i.e., the withholding of opportunities for political controversy]? The answer must be negative. Analysis of this problem is beyond the reach of the political analyst and perhaps can only be fruitfully analyzed by a philosopher."[13]

As with value-freedom, methodological individualism is often discussed in versions much cruder than the authentic Weberian doctrine. And even the authentic principle is, in part, implausible when clearly understood, though it has an extremely attractive core.

A definitional version, which would require that social concepts be definable in terms that could apply to a single individual, outside of society, is much too restrictive. No one has succeeded in defining "checking account," much less "government" in this way. Other versions are crude in the opposite direction, triviality. No doubt, social

[10] *Economy and Society*, vol. 1, *Theory of Economic and Social Organization*, tr. Henderson and Parsons (New York, 1947), p. 88.

[11] See "Ueber einige Kategorien der verstehenden Soziologie" in Weber, *Gesammelte Aufsaetze zur Wissenschaftslehre* (Tuebingen, 1968). In *Theory of Economic and Social Organization*, p. 87, Weber cites this article as an especially strict and detailed explication of his basic concepts of meaningful social action.

[12] G. M. Wilson, "A New Look at the Problem of 'Japanese Fascism' " in Henry Turner, ed., *Reappraisals of Fascism* (New York, 1975), p. 202.

[13] Peter Bachrach and Morton Baratz, *Power and Poverty* (New York, 1970), p. 49.

processes and institutions are the result of and are realized in the interactions of individuals with one another and their material environment. But no one denies this. Even Hegel, the arch-holist villain of social science as individualists see it, insisted that the master plan of history is realized in such individual interactions, in the phenomenon he labelled "the cunning of Reason." Also, it must, no doubt, be possible to frame a social explanation in such a way that it appeals to the tendencies and resources of individuals and the nature of their material environments. But, again, this maxim, with its liberal admission of any tendency whatever, is so easy to satisfy that it is useless. Hegel could quickly fulfill it by ascribing to Caesar the tendency—very far, of course, from Caesar's intentions—to raise the idea of freedom to a higher level.

It is a shame that so much of the debate over methodological individualism concerns these crude versions, since Weber and the most reflective philosophical exponents of the idea, for example, J.W.N. Watkins, are proposing a constraint that is neither trivial nor ridiculous. A social explanation, in their view, must appeal to actual or typical participants' resources, environments and *their reasons* for acting as they did. More precisely, this is true of explanations of large-scale, important social processes and institutions. Also, a valid explanation at a certain level might describe a large-scale process in a different mode from the resources-and-reasons one. But it must be possible to explain that process in turn in an individualist way, as a neo-classical economist explains inflation in terms of an upward trend in wages, and the wage trend in terms of (typical) individuals' decision-making in the bargaining process. The issue, then, is how to explain, not how to define, and not what exists. And the constraint is the specific restriction to agents' reasons, exemplified in Weber's definition of sociology as ultimately explaining by appeals to subjective meanings.[14]

The demand that social explanations appeal to agents' reasons is flexible enough to serve as the working hypothesis in an important program in the social sciences. Weber's sociology is a case in point. However, strictly imposed as a general rule for all explanation, it is excessive, though less obviously so than definitional individualism. As everyone with some practical experience has discovered, the rea-

---

[14] In addition to Weber's methodological writings, see J.W.N. Watkins, "Methodological Individualism and Social Tendencies" (1957) in May Brodbeck, ed., *Readings in the Philosophy of the Social Sciences* (New York, 1965); and Karl Popper, *The Open Society*, 2nd ed. (Princeton, 1963). I discuss Watkins' writings in detail in "Methodological Individualism and Social Explanation," *Philosophy of Science* (1978), pp. 387–414.

son why someone acts as he does is not always the same as his reason for so acting. When an unemployed person, in need of credit, tells the neighborhood grocer that she has many sure leads for jobs and is certain to get one soon, her reason for saying this may be that she believes it and believes it on good grounds. Yet, while accepting her sincerity, a moderately insightful grocer will suppose that the reason why she made the firm prediction is her objective need for credit. She was not lying, but she should have known better. Similarly, it is intelligible (whether true or false) that the typical engineer in the nuclear power industry believes that nuclear power is perfectly safe because of his need to regard himself as in a socially useful line of work, even if his reasons for having the belief are the scientific arguments he sincerely offers.

Surely, objective interests that are not agents' reasons have sometimes been among the underlying causes of a large-scale social process. Often, a massive shift in belief is accompanied by no new evidence but by a dramatic change in objective interests. Thus, around 1800, typical leaders of the American South regarded slavery as an unfortunate relic, that should be allowed to die out, though in a gradual way so as to preserve social order. By 1830, slavery was vigorously defended as a positive good. No new evidence for the benefits of slavery was discovered in the meantime. But the cotton gin was discovered, and it created an enormously strong interest in the expansion of slavery. Here, as in similar cases, to insist that people's reasons explain what they believed and did is either hopelessly naive or hopelessly cynical. It would be much too cynical to assume that people were typically lying and hiding their reasons, when they defended the doctrine of the positive good of slavery.

Still, there is a hard core of methodological individualism that remains untouched by such reflections on the varieties of psychological causation. The proposed explanations of what the grocery store customer did, what the nuclear engineer believed, and the plantation owners' change of heart are, after all, psychological. While they do not refer to the agents' reasons they do refer to their motives, i.e., to beliefs, goals or interests that the agents have, whose effect on action characterizes the agents' psychologies. Moreover, when belief and conduct are motiveless, they seem too blind, accidental or rigid to be the typical basis of a large-scale, important social process or institution. So the more plausible core of individualism becomes: important social phenomena are always explainable as due to participants' resources, environments, and their motives. Presumably, attraction to this core principle often stands behind distrust of hypotheses appealing to large-scale structural factors.

Here, again, the causal theory of explanation helps to sort out the true from the false in the most basic doctrine. It does seem to be true that the causes of an important social process or institution are interactions typically governed by agents' motives. Even here, however, the social and large-scale can have a distinctive impact on the psychological and the individual. Psychological causation, like causation in general, is a core conception. The limits of what functions as a motive are established, not by a general criterion, but by extending the concept beyond its core as facts and needs for explanation require. The core consists of the cases in which someone's beliefs and desires are his reasons for doing what he did, and the cases in which belief is due to learning by perceiving or reasoning. But how much further the concept extends may depend on evidence and theorizing concerning large-scale social processes. Thus, Althusser's discussion of people's location in an ideological structure, Foucault's arguments about the role of epistemological fields, and some of Kuhn's remarks about the impact of paradigms add to the repertoire of motives for maintaining beliefs and responding to evidence. But the justifications for their expansions of the psychological basically derive from the need to explain the large-scale pacing and pattern of socially prevalent beliefs.[15]

What is false about the core principle is the assumption that some network of psychological causes will always serve to explain. Often, though the causes existed and were causally sufficient, the description of these psychological causes is too shallow to explain. There are descriptions of military resources, motives and decisions that identify sufficient causes of the North's victory in the Civil War. They are the narratives in the best traditional military histories. And yet, almost certainly, they fail to explain why the North won, since the North would have won anyway, for reasons of superiority in numbers, industry, transport, international support, and because the plantation owners faced a growing internal enemy, among their slaves. These resources would have led to victory had motives and decisions been otherwise. Of course, not just any motives and decisions would do. No sane historian, Hegel included, has ever denied this.

When the relatively structural account is as clearly superior as the

---

[15] See, for example, Louis Althusser, "Ideology and Ideological State Apparatuses" in his *Lenin and Philosophy* (New York, 1971); Michel Foucault, *The Birth of the Clinic* (New York, 1973) and *The Order of Things* (New York, 1973); Thomas Kuhn, *The Structure of Scientific Revolutions* (Chicago, 1970), esp. chs. 5, 9 and 10. I am proposing that these are valid expansions of the repertoire of psychological explanation, not that all their alleged epistemological implications are clear or true.

appeal to the North's advantages in the Civil War, almost every investigator accepts, in practice, that the individualist rival does not explain, despite its causal accuracy. But methodological individualism does have an impact in the many cases in which a non-individualist hypothesis is inferior in some important ways to an individualist causal account. These cases are common in historical controversies. Individualist causal descriptions usually rely on common sense psychological principles that are absolutely indispensable to us, while many non-individualist explanations rely on relatively novel and controversial principles, often in the style of Durkheim or of Marx. In addition, anyone but a hopeless cynic or a philosophical skeptic takes people's endorsing an explanation of their own behavior as important evidence that the explanation is valid. And the endorsed explanations are, almost invariably, concerned with agents' reasons. Thus, Neumann's explanation of the Nazi seizure of power bears a distinctive burden of speculativeness, because he relies on a distinctive, Marxist theory of the political process and because he discerns causes that conflict with the self-explanations that political leaders would have endorsed.

So long as the core principle of the adequacy of psychological explanation goes unchallenged, such burdens will lead to the premature discounting of many non-individualist hypotheses. If the cost in speculativeness is to be supported, it must be for the sake of an important gain. Often, the only commensurate gain would be the capacity to explain a phenomenon that would otherwise go unexplained for want of causal depth. Of course, an argument for this advantage requires an argument for the existence of the deeper cause. But individualists are making a definite claim, as well, when they deny that deeper causes exist. What they cannot do, if they seek to explain, is refuse to involve themselves in speculation about non-individualist causes, "sinister" as against "innocent" ones, in Watkins' words.[16] In short, the core principle of methodological individualism conceals the fact that breaking with the individualist pattern can be worth the risks, in the more controversial cases of non-individualist social explanation.

## FUNCTIONAL EXPLANATION

The worry about explanatory appeals to large-scale structural factors that has methodological individualism as its general expression

[16] Watkins, "Methodological Individualism," p. 274.

tends to be most acutely felt in the face of a particular kind of social explanation: explanations appealing to objective social functions. These explanations of a social phenomenon appeal to its tendency to benefit a larger system in a certain way, without claiming that those benefits operate as people's reasons for creating or maintaining the phenomenon. Thus, social anthropologists often explain why a society has a practice by appealing to the tendency of this practice to enhance social stability, a tendency which is very far from participants' actual reasons for conformity. Left-wing historians and sociologists often explain an institution or a large-scale pattern of government policy as due to the tendency of respectable institutions in a class society to conform to the long-term interests of the economically dominant class. Often, these explainers are not committed to the view that crucial participants make the crucial decisions on the grounds that the economically dominant class is, thereby, served.

Though extremely common, such explanations strike many people as mysterious on at least three different grounds. First, if the covering-law model is accepted, then it seems impossible that these hypotheses could be adequate, in light of obvious facts about the phenomena in question. In the second place, even those who reject the covering-law model often find it hard to imagine how objective social functions could play an appropriate causal role, unless talk of them is really shorthand for talk of more familiar causal links. Modern biologists, in saying that the opposing thumb evolved in humans because of its function in using tools, may be taken to sketch an underlying appeal to differential survival rates and natural selection. It might seem that explanations appealing to social functions are as mysterious as appeals to inherent goals in organic evolution, unless the appeal to the effects of the functions is, similarly, derivative. And yet, an investigator appealing to an objective social function often seems not to have even a sketch of an underlying non-functional explanation. Finally, in addition to questions about how functional explanations could be true, there is the question of how they could be verified. Unless functional explanations are shorthand for non-functional ones, it can seem a mystery how they might be confirmed through empirical argument. The causal theory of explanation helps to solve all these mysteries, while clarifying what is valid in the idea that functional explanations must be grounded on explanations of other kinds.

Consider, by way of illustration, Mary Douglas' explanation of the so-called "bride price" custom of the Lele, a traditional agricultural society in Africa, relatively egalitarian, coordinated by informal councils of elders. A young Lele man cannot, for all practical purposes, separate from his family and set up his own home until he gets married. But marriage requires substantial gifts to the bride's family, which Europeans call the "bride price." The bride price must include certain luxury items which can only be bought after accumulating extraordinary reserves of the traditional currency. Accordingly, the prospective groom must go about among his elders borrowing to accumulate the means to acquire the bride price.

As far as material production is concerned, the requirement of bride price simply promotes wasted effort. The crucial luxury goods serve no important consumption need. Yet, Douglas argues, bride price does play a role which explains its persistence in traditional Lele society. By forcing young Lele to acquire a network of obligations to older, established people, it helps the elders to mediate and coordinate a society in which the system of independent and equal homesteads otherwise tends toward disintegration. Of course, the people involved in the acquisition and giving of bride price do not act as they do because they believe these actions maintain the power of the elders. They are concerned with getting married, acquiring a young protégé, or finding a suitable match for a child.[17]

Douglas' explanation seems plausible, worthy, at least, of further investigation in light of the case she makes. But if the covering-law model is valid, this and most other functional explanations cannot be valid. For no appropriate covering-law seems to be available. In particular, there is no reason to believe that in all or almost all societies sharing relevant general features with the Lele, if bride price would contribute to social coherence in the same general way, bride price exists as an institution. For one thing, very different institutions might play the same cohesive role. No one, including Douglas herself, has even attempted to sketch general properties of situations in which the bride price practice usually occurs, as a matter of empirical law, if it is a way of maintaining social cohesion.[18]

This first barrier to accepting functional explanations can be lifted once the covering-law model is replaced by the causal theory, in which an unanalyzed notion of causation is used to describe how a successful explanation works. A functional explanation succeeds

[17] See Mary Douglas, "Raffia Cloth Distribution in the Lele Economy" (1958) in G. Dalton, ed., *Tribal and Peasant Economies* (Garden City, N.Y., 1967).

[18] Cf. Hempel's arguments for denying that functionalist anthropology is a genuine theory in "The Logic of Functional Analysis."

if the objective social function is an underlying cause of the maintenance of the phenomenon in question (or its creation or its vicissitudes—which one will depend on the specific subject matter of the functional explanation). Moreover, using causal language divorced from appeals to covering-laws, one can do justice to the fact that functional causes operate by means of more immediate causes of the conduct of participants. According to a functional explanation, the function is a cause of preservative causes (assuming, as in the typical anthropological case, that maintenance is the subject matter). More specifically, someone explaining a phenomenon Y as due to an objective function X is making the following claims, in addition to asserting that Y does serve function X. (1) In the situation in question, and in the period in question, there are causal factors, at any given time, sufficient to maintain Y in the face of normal stresses, so long as it serves function X. (2) The fact that Y serves function X causes the preservative causes; subject to conditions such as a counterfactual analysis usually requires (above all, causal pre-emption must not be at work), this means that the Y-preserving factors would not exist or would not operate to preserve Y if Y did not serve function X.[19]

Thus, Douglas is committed to claiming: (1) that there are causal factors in Lele society sufficient to maintain the bride price institution in the face of normal stresses, so long as bride price maintains cohesion, and (2) (with the usual qualifications) that the factors maintaining bride price would not work to that effect if bride price did not serve that function. Suppose, on the other hand, that bride price were just a fashion among the Lele, which will not survive the normal tendency for fashions to succumb to boredom. Or suppose that bride price would survive among the Lele, if it did not enhance cohesion, because the Lele are so traditionalist or because they have such a consuming desire to regulate human conduct through com-

[19] Pre-emption would interfere with the counterfactual analysis if, for example, a neighboring group in which bride price is a basic practice is about to invade, dominate and impose its practices, in any case. If the function of social cohesion is causing the bride price to be maintained, the functional explanation is valid. Yet it is not the case that there would be no bride price if it did not serve this function. In "The Logic of Functional Analysis," Hempel describes certain phenomena of causal preemption and notes how they interfere with counterfactual analyses of the meaning of functional explanations. He takes this interference to be a sign that appeals to objective functions are never really explanations, just vague heuristic indications of where the explanation should be sought. But if explanation is causal description, the phenomena of pre-emption merely indicate the difference in general between causation and counterfactual dependence.

mercial exchange. Then Douglas' explanation is not valid. It is not valid even if bride price does in fact maintain social cohesion among the Lele.

The second worry about functional explanations was that they are mysterious when not reducible to explanations of other kinds. The proposed cause-of-causes schema does justice to the grain of truth in the demand for reduction. The objective social function and the phenomenon it explains are always connected by causal chains of events in a manner that the functional explanation does not itself assert. The schema also helps to show, by contrast, why nothing more should be demanded in the way of reduction.

The functional explainer need not have a sketch of the causal links connecting function and phenomenon explained. Among the Lele, the gerontocratic function might be connected with the bride price custom by any or all of a variety of factors, the means by which the custom might be preserved if it serves its function. They might include: a tendency of prospective in-laws to forbid a daughter a marriage without the bride price; a tendency of the elders to respond to departures from tradition by making life difficult for the deviants; a tendency for households formed without the traditional bride price payment ultimately to break up, when powerful patrons are not available in times of crisis; or a human tendency to act in ways that maintain social relations whose persistence serves one's overall interests. (This last factor would be a specific form of the direct motivation by objective interests that was discussed in the last section.) In offering her explanation, Douglas committed herself to the existence of these or other linkages, since a functional explanation describes a cause of causes of appropriate conduct. But this general consideration still permits her not to sketch which linkages actually operate. Such permissiveness is typical of principles linking different levels of causation, throughout the sciences. Metallurgists are committed to the view that the processes they study are governed by molecules and intermolecular forces. So a metallurgist explaining a fracture as due to crystallization under repeated stress is committed to the existence of molecular interactions, governed by intermolecular forces, connecting stress with crystallization and crystallization with fracture. Still, the metallurgist need have no idea what this molecular story is, and, indeed, until recently, metallurgists had none.[20]

[20] This and related points are well-made in Garfinkel, *Forms of Explanation* (New Haven, 1981).

It would also be very misleading to insist that an objective social function must not be among the linkages in the chains of causes that maintain the phenomenon in question, from moment to moment, i.e., the chains produced by the objective social function itself. For objective social interests can serve directly as participants' motives, even when they are not participants' reasons. Indeed, there is significant evidence that an objective interest in cohesion does serve as an effective motive, but not a reason, in societies similar to the Lele. For example, when ecological changes make cooperation among women more important than cooperation among men, corresponding changes in rules for residence after marriage arise—husbands join wives' families, rather than vice versa—among peoples who always insist that such rules are sanctioned by long tradition, not by considerations of social utility.[21] From the standpoint of the causal theory of explanation, the need to ground functional explanations in causal connections among participants is a matter of differences in level of causal interaction, not necessarily a matter of a difference in the content of the causal connections.

To test the demand for reducibility in one other aspect, suppose we knew that the institution to be explained was maintained through certain chains of events and that the causal linkages in that network did not include the influence of an objective social function. Would a functional explanation be dispensable then, a means of convenient summary like the biologist's teleological talk about the opposing thumb? Not necessarily. It might be that other local causes would substitute for the actual ones, if the stress on the system is not abnormal and the same social function obtains. So the causal description is too shallow to explain. Here, social anthropology is not the best source of examples, since the ethnographies that are the paradigm of functional explanation, there, describe a society at a single point in time. It is functional analyses of industrial societies, especially Marxist analyses, that typically illustrate the capacity for causal substitution. For example, in Neumann's view, German government became fascist because only this kind of regime could serve the interests of the dominant military-industrial-banking elite in the conditions of the Great Depression. As he describes them, the individual causes bringing about this kind of regime largely consist of the efforts of traditional conservative political figures to repress trade-union and left-wing militancy by employing repressive aspects of the Weimar constitution and prerogatives of the judiciary

[21] See Elman Service, *Primitive Social Organization* (New York, 1965), pp. 121f.

and bureaucracy. Presumably, Neumann would claim, nonetheless, that if the typical conservative politician had followed the path of Konrad Adenauer and opposed fascism as a threat to legitimate order, the same objective need would have led to fascism by a more disruptive route. Perhaps mass demonstrations against the established political order, in the manner of Mussolini's March on Rome, would have played a more significant role. A conservative regime might have been violently overthrown, as Dollfuss' was in Austria. In short, Neumann's causal account moves at two levels, and only the functional one is presented as deep enough to explain.

The explanation of causal substitution—whether counterfactual substitution as in Neumann's explanation, or an actual shift, such as the change in residence rules—plays a further role in functional explanation, which the core conception of causation reveals. Objective social functions certainly are not among the elementary varieties in the minimal core. The justification for counting them as causes must be the need to expand a prior repertoire of causes to explain phenomena that ought to have an explanation. Prominent among these phenomena are strikingly similar episodes of dramatic social change. The existence of such a phenomenon needs explanation. It is explained by appeals to social functions that were served. Some examples are: the replacement of democratic by fascist regimes in country after country between the World Wars, as a result of diverse chains of immediate political causes; the rise of parliamentary democracy in country after country in Western Europe in the seventeenth and eighteenth centuries, again as a result of different chains of political events (compare England and Holland, for example);[22] rapid shifts from virilocal to uxorilocal residence, or from egalitarian to headman-dominated social organization in non-literate societies which legitimate practices by appeals to tradition.[23] Thus, while holists have been right to suppose that appeals to objective social function are a change in the concept of causation, they have been wrong to suppose that the shift is a departure from the logic of

[22] These seventeenth- and eighteenth-century shifts seem to have been especially important in the development of Marx's social theory. Among works written from 1845 to 1850, see, for example, *The German Ideology*, pp. 60–62, "The Communist Manifesto," pp. 110f., 137, "The Bourgeoisie and the Counter Revolution." p. 139, all in Marx and Engels, *Selected Works in Three Volumes* (Moscow, n.d.); and "A Review of Guizot's Book, *Why Has the English Revolution Been Successful?*" in Marx and Engels, *Articles on Britain* (Moscow, 1971).

[23] See Service, *Primitive Social Organization*, pp. 121f., Julian Steward's extensive writings, and Edmund Leach's classic account of a society oscillating between egalitarian and hierarchical structures, *Political Systems of Highland Burma* (Boston, 1954).

causal inquiry elsewhere. The justification for positing objective social functions as causes is the normal one for expanding the repertoire, the same in kind as the basis for taking gravitational attraction or perturbations in electromagnetic fields as causes.

Loosening the ties between functional explanation and familiar explanations of individuals' conduct may seem to heighten the final mystery, the empirical basis of functional explanations. How can such explanations be justified empirically in light of the abstractness of their causal claims? Typically, such justification is a matter of comparison, one of the dimensions of scientific argument which the covering-law model must neglect. A functional explanation is adopted because, among current rivals, it provides the best causal account of the shape of the data. For example, virtually every important functional explanation in social anthropology is supported by a case with these outlines: "Here is an enduring pattern of behavior, on the part of intelligent, appropriately informed people. Its existence repeatedly violates these people's individual, immediate interests. No strong state apparatus is mobilized to maintain it. Yet it endures. The best explanation of why it endures is that it serves a long-term, large-scale function of preserving certain features of the society." In such an argument, the functional alternative is defended as against the most likely non-functional bases for the persistence of a pattern of conduct, viz., the conformity of that conduct to individual immediate interests and the tendency of people to stick to old patterns of conduct when those habits have no great costs, or none that they can perceive. The functional explainer is relying on the principle that persistent, complex behavior violating individuals' immediate interests requires an explanation. And he or she is arguing that this explanatory need cannot be satisfied without appealing to objective social functions. Similarly, the thesis that United States foreign policy has been molded, in large measure, by the needs of big business is to be tested by comparison, matching it against competing sources of answers to standard historical questions: "What are the origins of the Spanish American War?" "Why did the United States enter World War I?" "Why were atomic bombs dropped on Hiroshima and Nagasaki?" "Why has the United States supported unpopular, authoritarian regimes in Guatemala, El Salvador, Iran, South Vietnam and elsewhere?" Within these familiar debates, the left-wing functionalist arguments seem coherent and relevant, even if one doubts their ultimate empirical validity. It is when they are removed from the context of specific explanatory rivalries that the left-wing functional hypotheses seem to merit the standard methodological dismissal, "This is either a conspiracy theory or a metaphysical article of faith."

## HUMAN SCIENCE/NATURAL SCIENCE

So far, the causal theory of explanation has been applied to methodological questions within fields that seek explanations of human conduct. Yet the most enduring debate in the philosophy of the human sciences is not so much within these fields as about them. Are the human sciences as a whole fundamentally different from the natural sciences? Dilthey, writing in the middle of the nineteenth century, developed impassioned arguments for basic difference that have continued to be made, and continued to be controversial, to the present day. Collingwood, between the World Wars, Habermas, Dray and Taylor, at present, are other leading figures in the argument for difference. Positivists have led the argument for similarity. Indeed, the basic unity of the human and the natural sciences is the dominant theme of the most influential presentation of the covering-law model, Hempel's "The Function of General Laws in History." In writings on both sides, the central issue is whether history, the oldest of the human sciences, is basically different from the natural sciences. This has remained a useful way to avoid pointless problems of departmental definition. For the newer fields, such as economics, sociology, anthropology, and psychology, happen to have achieved academic respectability in forms that consciously imitated natural scientific models.

From the standpoint of the causal theory of explanation, this perennial controversy is one of those frustrating debates in which one side (Dilthey's, here) adds up the real facts to reach the wrong conclusion, while the other defends a position that is right in broadest outline, on the basis of a profoundly distorted view of the facts. In essence, the partisans of basic difference have argued that history is distinguished from the natural sciences by its fundamental reliance on the identification of agents' reasons, by its use of empathetic understanding, and by its interest in expanding the scope of human sympathy and mutual understanding. No doubt history does differ from natural sciences in all these methods and interests. The problem is that no one has ever doubted this, *or has needed to*. After all, meteorology also differs from non-meteorological natural sciences in its explanatory appeals to high- and low-pressure systems, its reliance on barometers and its interest in coping with bad weather. That history is distinctive in the indicated ways makes it no more different from most natural sciences than meteorology is. Of course, the indicated methods and interests of historians are important to the partisans of basic difference for a specific reason. They think these features of history would be ruled out if history were to adopt rules of method that do unite all the natural sciences, for example, the covering-law model. In this, however, they are too kind to the other side.

If explanations in terms of agents' reasons do not fit the covering-law model, this is because the search for a general covering-law produces tautology as it reaches truth. Someone who wants to accomplish A and believes that B is a means to this end does not always or even almost always do B. Belief in a less costly means, interest in projects other than A, confusion, procrastination, weakness of will, craziness and death are some of the factors that might intervene. No doubt if someone is succeeding in making choices rationally and thinks that a certain course of actions is the best way of achieving his or her ultimate goals on balance, he or she will adopt that course of action. This fails to provide a covering-law because it is a tautology.[24] And it is through the same deviation into tautology that pathologists' explanations appealing to infectious agents fail to fit the covering-law model. Only a shared false theory of natural-scientific explanation supports the inference from the violation of the covering-law model in history to the conclusion that history is more different from any typical natural science than many typical natural sciences are from one another. By the same token, the other side, the positivists are wrong in their assumption that questions of what explains, what confirms and what hypothesis should be preferred are resolved by the same rules in every field, even if they are right to conclude that history, while distinctive in its content, embodies forms of reasoning that are found in the sciences. The methods of history are no more different from the methods of geology than the latter are from the methods of theoretical physics—and that difference is very great.

By contrast with both sides of the traditional debate, the previous criticisms of positivism suggest the following location for history among the sciences. The basic methods and goals of history are no more different from those of most natural sciences than the basic methods and goals of any given natural science. Yet history does have distinctive methods and goals, for example, reliance on em-

[24] Cf. Donald Davidson, "Hempel on Explaining Action," *Erkenntnis* (1976), pp. 239–53.

pathy and a distinctive concern for certain humane purposes which regulate the choices of standard causal patterns. And the distinctive features of history are not just specific versions of universal rules for science. Of course, the distinctive methods and goals of history, if fundamental in this way, are inescapably, distinctively important for all of us, professional interests to one side; for we are the subjects and targets of history.

Apart from the uncontroversial differences in content, it seems unlikely that history will differ from all the natural sciences in the logical form of its explanations. For, on the account I have been defending, the forms displayed by the natural sciences are as various as anyone would want. Admittedly, Dilthey and Collingwood sometimes deny that a historian's identification of reasons for an action is an identification of causes—which would constitute a radical difference. But "cause" turns out to be restricted, in their writings, to connections governed by empirical general laws.[25] Dray's account of what is distinctive in historical explanation is, on the other hand, genuinely non-causal. According to Dray, a historian's explanation of an action may be adequate when all it does is accurately to describe why the action was the reasonable thing to do under the circumstances.[26] But surely this condition for adequacy is too weak. We are only satisfied that the rationalization explains if, in addition, we suppose that the agent was acting reasonably, so that the reasonableness of the act was a cause of the action.

What one *can* say, following the account of "cause" as a core concept, is that reasons are an elementary variety of cause, not a special case satisfying a more general definition. Does this mean that reason-giving explanations do differ from others in form as well as content, after all? The contrast between form and content is simply out of place, here. No specification of the form-content metaphor clarifies any real distinction.

In addition to the reason-giving sort of explanation, history is often said to depend on a sort of justification not found in the natural sciences, namely, reliance on empathetic understanding. That one feels one would do what someone else did out of certain motives when one puts oneself in his or her place is evidence in favor of that

[25] See, for example, Wilhelm Dilthey, *Pattern and Meaning in History*, ed., H. P. Rickman (New York, 1961), pp. 108f.; R. B. Collingwood, *The Idea of History* (New York, 1956), p. 214.

[26] See Dray, *Laws and Explanation in History* (London, 1957), pp. 122–26, and his "The Historical Explanation of Actions Reconsidered" in Patrick Gardiner, ed., *The Philosophy of History* (New York, 1974).

ascription of motives. And (the argument continues) nothing corresponds to this kind of justification in the natural sciences. After all, an astronomer does not justify an explanation of Mercury's orbit by putting himself in Mercury's shoes.

Though positivists have traditionally been wary of reliance on empathy, their reasons for distrust are unclear. On the face of it, that normal humans with no special expertise have a special means of identifying motives is no more surprising than that they have special means of identifying shapes. Of course, empathetic imaginings are not infallible, and, if further experience sometimes extends the scope of the technique, it sometimes reveals limits of culture and temperament beyond which empathetic inferences are foolish. But the same kinds of warnings are appropriate when people discern shapes by looking and touching.

Still, even if empathy has evidential weight, it would not support an interesting claim that history is basically different if reliance on empathy is validated, in turn, by an argument of a kind that is common to all fields of inquiry. Positivists seem on firmer ground when they claim that reliance on empathy is unreasonable unless it is so justified. As a result, reliance on empathy could not be a distinguishing feature of history, if it is a reasonable method. History would be like any field in relying on whatever methods are relevant to its questions and validated by the universal techniques of scientific inference from data.

But in fact, there is no obvious need to justify the elementary sort of reliance on empathy on which all further empathetic understanding is based, namely, our tentative, partial reliance on empathy in everyday encounters with intimates. And people who have tried to construct a justification for this minimal reliance have failed.

If our claims to grasp the motives of others were claims to be able to predict their behavior, then these claims could, perhaps, be tested by standard natural-scientific techniques. However, the two kinds of claims are quite different, even if they are sometimes related. We all know some people whose behavior we can easily predict without having the foggiest idea of what goes on in their minds, other people whose minds we can read like a book though we can predict their behavior only with difficulty, if at all. Extremely disturbed and rigid people are often of the first kind, emotionally thriving and open people of the second. Empathy is a means of gaining insight into motives. But it is not a reliable means of predicting behavior. It does not give greater access to predictions than the mere practice of finding the routine patterns of response characteristic of the various people one encounters. Or in any case, any small contribution that empathy makes in the way of prediction does not support our substantial reliance on it to gain access to motives. How, then, can I tell whether I should give some significant evidential weight to the results of empathetic imagination? If the other person is an ancient Roman author, this is a real question, to be answered by considering whether interests and practices that are superficially like modern ones really are, on further analysis. But if the question is why I should rely on empathy in seeking to understand a close friend, of similar background, whose behavior has not routinely and blatantly conflicted with my empathetic guesses, there seems to be no answer. And why suppose that the belief that empathy gives us some emotional access to those we know and love stands in need of justification?

It might seem that language provides the way to validate routine, tentative reliance on empathy: we have discovered that others have the motives we think by hearing them say they do. But this response assumes that we can tell when others have access to their motives and are being sincere. In such assessments we seem especially dependent on empathetic understanding.

Suppose that a minimal reliance on empathy has no further justification and needs none. Does this make the human sciences fundamentally different from the natural sciences? As usual in the dispute over the distinctiveness of the human sciences, the question about distinctiveness itself seems misdirected. Fundamental reliance on *specific* means of detection is *common* to all fields. If our capacity to identify motives is not justified by a general and a priori method, then the same is true, presumably, of our capacity to tell the approximate shapes of middle-sized objects, seen close-up in moderate sunlight. And without this capacity, there could be no justification in physics. The starting points of historical inquiry do not just consist of general rules of method, and this makes history *like* every natural science.

Finally, traditional defenders of the distinctiveness of history have noted that empathy is not simply a method of inquiry but a goal. We want to broaden our capacity to imagine how others feel and think. That history serves this interest and the natural sciences do not is supposed to be a distinguishing mark of historical explanation. Indeed, it is the central distinction according to Habermas' influential account in *Knowledge and Human Interests*.[27]

[27] Habermas, *Knowledge and Human Interests* (Boston, 1971), p. 176. For an earlier version of this claim, see Dilthey, *Pattern and Meaning*, p. 119.

The causal theory of explanation helps to make it clearer just how important and how distinguishing the goal of empathy is. The status of this goal has always been problematic. Positivists, while accepting that much history has this edifying function, take this to be a use of history, not a criterion for adequate historical explanation. Certainly, they are right to deny that fulfilling this function is enough, by itself. The *Iliad* does a superb job of expanding a modern reader's capacity for empathy, even if it is a tissue of folk tales and Mycenean propaganda.

The interest in empathy is involved in explanatory adequacy, and not just in the uses of explanations, because of its role in justifying standard causal patterns. Many historians in all subfields of history and all in some employ standard causal patterns which admit explanations which merely list people's reasons for acting as they did. Biography, after all, is a part of history. No one supposes that a typical reason-giving explanation in a biography must also describe the features of personality and environment which made these reasons effective for this person, when they were not for others. This would be good, but it is not a criterion of adequacy. One justification for this causal pattern is purely scientific. At least where biography is concerned, the pursuit of explanations would soon stall if a more stringent stopping rule were adopted. But another rationale has independent weight. It might convince a historian who is more optimistic than most of us about the accessibility of empirical general laws covering psychological explanation. Reason-giving explanations ought to be furthered, even if the specification of other necessary conditions for action is somewhat inhibited, because access to the motives of others plays a special role in broadening our sympathies and enriching our experience.

On the other hand, the dimensions of explanatory success besides the satisfaction of standard causal patterns describe constraints that always override the interest in empathy. The requirement of accurate causal description is one. The requirement of causal depth is another, easier to neglect, in practice. The narrative that helps us to imagine what it was like to be part of the Northern victory may do nothing to explain why the North won the Civil War. Though a preference for the empathetic perspective has often been defended as advancing human freedom, the discounting of causal depth can in fact deprive us of guidance we seek in reducing oppression. If empathy is made an overriding goal, the ideal study of fascism will be something like Emil Nolte's *The Three Faces of Fascism*, the ideal study of slavery something like David Brion Davis' *The Problem of Slavery in Western Culture*: detailed accounts of the ideologies used to justify institutions, with little information about the interests and resources which may have sustained the ideologies and the institutions themselves. What expands empathy may be a bad guide to change, including changes that create a more empathetic social environment.[28]

In reformulating the traditional debate over history and the natural sciences, I have constantly relied on the diversity of the natural sciences, the difference of most fields from textbook versions of physics and chemistry. It might seem that a basic question has been avoided as a result. The causal patterns that historians employ are much farther from the covering-law model than physicists' and chemists', even if the difference is not as dramatic when the comparison is with geology, pathology or biology. Why is this so, i.e., why does historical explanation stray so far from the physicists' and the chemists' format of derivation from general laws? The traditional answers are not convincing. Most hermeneutic theorists, from Dilthey to the present, take the departures from covering law derivations to reflect the special human capacity for free choice. But this explanation is at least as problematic as the denial that a free decision can be a typical consequence of certain general factors, even when some or all of them are psychological. Positivists take the departures from the covering-law model as revealing the special immaturity of the human sciences, by comparison with physics and chemistry. Yet it has always been puzzling that an endeavor that seemed reasonably mature by the time of Thucydides is so childish compared with enterprises tracing their maturity to the times of Newton or Lavoisier. Similarly, a common response of conservative social philosophers, that the human mind or human society is just more complex than the non-human world, reflects unjustified pessimism about explaining human interaction, combined with undeserved optimism about explaining non-human processes. The everyday inquiries into motives and conduct from which sophisticated historical investigations developed are at least as successful and complex as the everyday inquiries into motion and physical change from which sophisticated physical investigations developed. There is no reason to suppose that the Book of Nature is simpler for

[28] See Ernst Nolte, *Three Faces of Fascism* (New York, 1969); David B. Davis, *The Problem of Slavery in Western Culture* (Ithaca, N.Y., 1966); and, for a powerful critique of this approach, as epitomized in Davis' work, Moses I. Finley, "The Idea of Slavery: Critique of David Brion Davis' *The Problem of Slavery in Western Culture*" (1967) in L. Foner and E. Genovese, eds., *Slavery in the New World* (Englewood Cliffs, N.J., 1969).

us to read than the Book of Human Life or Society.[29] Still, though the traditional answers are not very good, the traditional question about the enormous difference between historical explanation and physicists' and chemists' derivations demands an answer.

The lesser rigor of historians' standard patterns, as against physicists' and chemists', is largely the result of the greater freedom that physics and chemistry have to emphasize questions expected to yield appropriately rigorous answers. This freedom has at least two different sources, constituting different ways in which we define the proper subject matters of physics and chemistry. In the first place, when an explanatory question cannot be answered with something like a covering-law derivation, although the explanandum is due to a physical or chemical process, we locate that question, not in physics or chemistry, but in some other discipline, say, applied physics, applied chemistry, engineering, geology or biology. For example, the famous New Hampshire cliff, the Old Man of the Mountains, has the shape of an old man's face because of physical processes. Physics and chemistry shed light on the general nature of those processes. But questions about natural features of objects, framed in a non-technical vocabulary, e.g., "Why does the cliff, the Old Man of the Mountains, have the shape of an old man's face?", do not have answers fitting a covering-law pattern. Accordingly, although those features are due to physical and chemical processes, the answers to them are not held to characterize explanation in physics or chemistry. Even if we had a godlike knowledge of every molecular episode in the evolution of the New Hampshire rock, the corresponding causal description would not explain, because it would lack adequate depth. Underlying structural constraints would still have resulted in a rock with the face of an old man if different molecular bumpings had occurred. Those constraints are described in a field called, not "physics," but "geology." In that field, explanations are not expected to conform to the covering-law model, especially when relatively small-scale features are at issue.

By contrast, the explanatory questions about actual events that physicists and chemists are expected to answer are questions about controlled experiments, or natural phenomena chosen in the belief that they have built-in controls. To the greatest possible extent, the

[29] F. A. von Hayek, "The Theory of Complex Phenomena" (1964) in his *Studies in Philosophy, Politics and Economics* (Chicago, 1967), is a concise and clear example of the conservative judgment of relative complexity. Of course, if explanation were potential prediction on the basis of general empirical laws and independent initial conditions, pessimism about explaining human conduct would be well-justified.

experimenter controls the background circumstances so that all the causal work is being done by a few specifiable causal factors. (The presence of only one kind of causal factor, internal to the system, of significance for planetary orbits makes orbital phenomena in the solar system a natural controlled experiment for astronomy.) In an uncontrolled situation, a tennis ball rolling down a sidewalk, as against a ball bearing carefully released at the top of a smooth inclined plane, the use of the best available physics yields explanations which depart very far from the covering-law model. But these explanations are located in "applied physics," if they are located in physics at all.

In the second place, as physics and chemistry develop in the course of history, old questions are sometimes neglected and new ones given a central place, when the shift makes for more rigorous standard patterns within the field. On this basis, in the seventeenth and eighteenth centuries, the central questions of physics ceased to concern a broad array of perceptible qualities of medium-sized objects and came to concern trajectories of point masses. Similarly, the central questions of chemistry in the eighteenth century ceased to involve the colors, textures and smells of substances, and became questions of mass.

In contrast, historians lack the physicist's freedom to choose questions specially susceptible to rigorous answers. When questions about colors and textures and about trajectories encountered in everyday life ceased to be central, physics remained physics. An investigation of human behavior which, in the interests of rigorous and thorough explanation, does not seek to explain wars, revolutions, the acquisition and the loss of national power, or changes in political or economic institutions is not history, but something else. To a much greater extent than physics or chemistry, history is committed to asking questions that are salient because of their practical importance, not because of their susceptibility to rigorous answers. This is not a difference between history and all natural sciences. Disease theory shares this constraint to a large extent, geology to some extent. A science of the earth that said nothing about why earthquakes and volcanic eruptions occur, or why mountains and riverbeds have their shapes would not be geology, even though the shift in subject matter might make its explanations more rigorous. In biology, though practical concerns are not as dominant, the subject matter is closely tied, nonetheless, to a stable array of central questions about speciation and the structure of organs defined by life function.

It is possible in principle that a standard pattern resembling the covering-law model would be appropriate in history or in one of the latter natural-scientific fields. But it would be a lucky and unlikely break, if this were so. For the reasons why the dominant questions dominate have little or nothing to do with their susceptibility to answers suiting rigorous patterns. Trajectories of point masses in controlled settings are of interest in physics partly because they can be derived from specified conditions using general laws. That is not the reason for our interest in revolutions, diseases, earthquakes, or physiology.

The existence of these different strategies of self-definition helps to explain why present-day physics and chemistry involve derivations from precise empirical laws to a much greater extent than present-day work in history. And this explanation undermines one form of physics worship, the lament that the human sciences are defective by comparison with physics. But the different strategies of self-definition do not help to explain why acceptable physics and chemistry has a great deal to say, or why this body of theory has contributed to many successes outside of physics and chemistry, including applied, as against theoretical pursuits. So reflections on self-definitions will not resolve the most heated controversy about the physical sciences at present, the topic of the last chapters of this book: "Should physical theories be believed, as approximately true descriptions of a real world of theoretical entities?" At most, reflections on self-definition will block a naive inclination toward realism based on the prestige of numbers and precision: "If expert physicists and chemists confidently speak with such precision, it is unreasonable to doubt that they describe something real." The avoidance of imprecision, here, is a matter of vocational choice, not knowledge.

## THE STRUCTURE OF THEORIES

The final application of the causal account of explanation concerns a question common to the natural and the social sciences: What is the role and structure of a theory? A theory is whatever explains empirical facts (often, regularities or patterns) of relatively observational kinds, through the description of less directly observable phenomena. Different understandings of what a theory is interpret this neutral formulation in more specific ways. For example, the notion of observability is variously construed and various departures from observability are allowed. Successful theoretical explanation is sometimes connected with simplification, sometimes with the presentation of an intuitively compelling model. Despite these and other differences, a certain assumption is widely shared. The explaining which a theory accomplishes is thought to be entailment, in an appropriate format, of the phenomena explained, when the theory is combined with supplements helping to connect theoretical hypotheses with observable phenomena. The further disagreements concern the pattern of entailment which constitutes theoretical success. The prime examples, in all these deductivist accounts, are triumphs of theoretical physics, such as the derivation of thermodynamic gas laws from the molecular theory of matter (supplement: the interpretation of certain molecular phenomena as temperature) and the derivation of Kepler's laws from Newtonian mechanics (supplement: the enormous mass of the sun as compared with the planets and the absence of external or non-gravitational forces with significant effects on planetary orbits).

In sum, a theory is portrayed as a set of premises for deductions of more directly observable phenomena; whether a theory is acceptable depends on its playing this deductive role in successful explanations. That the dominant views of the nature of theories have this deductivist core should not be surprising. The covering-law model remains the working hypothesis of most philosophy of science. The deductivist assumption is a natural extension of the covering-law requirement from the explanation of events to the explanation of relatively observable phenomena by appeal to relatively unobservable ones. Given the universal acknowledgement that theories are explanatory tools, the deductivist picture of theories results.

As with the explanation of events, the deductivist assumption is distorting and overly restrictive. Indeed, it has helped make certain disputes over actual theories interminable and unproductive for all sides.

As we move beyond textbook presentations of theoretical physics, the deductivist understanding of what a theory is becomes increasingly implausible and artificial. The problem, in general, is this. A theory of a domain of empirical phenomena is whatever explains observed facts in that domain. Correspondingly, we ought to accept theories on account of their power to explain the appropriate facts. But many actual theories are not sufficiently well-connected with our knowledge of background conditions to be accepted as tools for explanation in the *deductive* style. Depending on what supplements are permitted in the crucial derivations, they either do not yield deductions of empirical facts, or do so only in ways that make no contribution to explanatory power and empirical acceptability.

Sometimes, we have so little independent knowledge of crucial initial conditions, or other supplements, that deductions based on the theory we reasonably accept are not of a sort that would justify our acceptance of it. Evolutionary theory is, notoriously, of this kind. Evolutionary theory is supposed to be a means of explaining speciation. But the theory entails no observable fact about speciation unless it is supplemented with premises concerning the differential survival rates of inherited traits in relevant environments, over long periods of time. When we consider the nature of these supplements, evolutionary theory turns out to be incapable of the successes that are the job of a theory, on the deductivist account. In the real world of biology, selective advantages crucial to speciation are not known independent of commitment to evolutionary theory. That the toes of *Eohippus*, the ancestor of the horse, became sufficiently disadvantageous as its native swamps dried up to lead to evolution toward hooves is inferred backward from the transformation to the more hoof-like structure of the successor species' foot. Evolutionary theory supplies its own supplements in the derivations alleged to epitomize its explanatory power. Perhaps susceptibility to ad hoc supplement is a virtue. But it is hardly an important enough virtue to support reasonable biologists' acceptance of evolutionary theory. After all, most half-baked speculations can be supported in this ad hoc way. Small wonder, then, that deductivists are driven to deny that evolutionary theory really is a theory.[30]

In the twentieth century, the feats of laboratory geneticists in mutating *Drosophila* and studying consequent differences in survival have obscured the still insuperable difficulty of directly measuring the long-term selective advantages in natural environments relevant to speciation. In fact, *Drosophila*, specially malleable to begin with, are mutated by artificial means for traits that are usually not functional or so dysfunctional that they would disappear quickly in nature. And the complex, diverse, changing, ecologically structured

[30] Denials that there is a genuine theory of biological evolution are especially vivid in Karl Popper's writings. "There exists no law of evolution, only the historical fact that plants and animals change, or, more precisely, that they have changed. The idea of a law that determines the direction and the character of evolution is a typical 19th-century mistake, arising out of a general tendency to ascribe to the 'Natural Law' the functions traditionally ascribed to God." Popper, "Prediction and Prophecy in the Social Sciences" in Patrick Gardiner, ed., *Theories of History*, p. 280. See also Popper, *The Poverty of Historicism* (New York, 1960), pp. 106–9.

challenges of the natural setting are not remotely represented in the laboratory environment. By contrast, in Lewontin's stark statement, *"To the present moment no one has succeeded in measuring with any accuracy the net fitness of genotypes for any locus in any species in any environment in nature."*[31] By way of explanation, Lewontin describes a variety of systematic difficulties, including the biological fact that the mutations along the road to speciation will, individually, be of very small differential advantage and the elementary statistical fact that the assessment of proportions of surviving offspring, based on samples, is highly susceptible to random error.[32]

If the pursuit of supplementary statements of initial conditions creates some departures from the deductivist model, others result from the anomalies that even good theories encounter. Thus, according to the modern theory of infectious disease, symptoms are caused by a breakdown of the normal equilibrium between the host organism and its flora of microbes. But no general empirical rule for distinguishing normal equilibrium from infection preserves the truth of the theory, when symptoms are observed that would not be expected on the basis of the theory alone. For example, typical microbial populations in a species do not always behave in the normal way. In some very old people, the intestinal bacteria that all humans carry and from which almost all benefit become an infection, penetrating the intestinal lining and producing "blood poisoning." The true general principles yielded by the theory are tautologies that say that the balance between host and flora causes disease when it tilts farther toward the flora than health allows. They add nothing to the statements of initial conditions that would have to "supplement" them in the process of deduction.[33] No observed pattern of infection followed by pathology can be deduced using the germ theory of disease, unless the theory is specified in a way that makes it false.

Similarly, though there seems to be a structural-functional theory of non-literate societies without a state apparatus, no reasonably shrewd theorist would present it in a form that produces useful premises for deductions. No one thinks that every institution that would stabilize such a society exists in it. And no one thinks that every important institutional feature of such a society is shaped by a role in maintaining the effectiveness and stability of the social sys-

---

[31] His emphasis. See *The Genetic Basis of Evolutionary Change* (New York, 1974), p. 236.

[32] See ibid., pp. 234–39, 266–71.

[33] For an especially perspicuous discussion, see R. Feinbloom et al., *Child Health Encyclopedia* (New York, 1975), pp. 385–402.

tem as a whole. Obviously, some important institutions are relics that have lost their functions, while others are means by which subgroups defend special and potentially destabilizing privileges. No one thinks that these exceptions can all be specified in advance. Someone who responds that what passes for structural-functionalism is, therefore, too vague to be a theory will have a hard time making sense of the state of anthropology. For structural-functionalism is constantly treated as a full-fledged competitor of hypotheses whose status as theories is not in doubt.

Apart from problems in specifying what a theory is, the deductivist account provides no satisfying basis for distinguishing the core of a theory from its total content. Even someone with an anti-realist view of theorizing wants to find some way of saying that Dalton's theory of matter, Boltzmann's, and Bohr's had a common core, the atomic theory of matter. For there is surely some sense in which experiment and theorizing have been kinder to the atomic theory of matter than to the phlogiston theory of chemical change or the caloric theory of heat. The core of the former theory, but not of the latter theories survives. Yet if theories are essentially premises for deductions of observations, it seems wrong to say that the core of Dalton's theory survived, while the core of the phlogiston theory did not. Both provide premises that are no longer used, though both resemble current theories in significant ways.

If we understand theoretical explanation on the basis of the causal account, we can see why parts of science that everyone, when not thinking about positivism, calls theories *are* theories, and we can see why these parts of science can be acceptable. We can distinguish the core from the periphery of theories in satisfying ways. Finally, I will try to show, we can rejuvenate the debates over Marx's theory of history and Freud's theory of personality.

Extended from event explanations to theories, the causal account of explanation takes the following form. A theory is a description of underlying causal factors which, in actual circumstances, are sufficient to bring about more directly observable phenomena of the kind studied by the field in question. A theoretical *explanation* is an explanation describing a factor which is an instance of a relatively unobservable factor described in the corresponding theory. An underlying, relatively unobservable factor responsible for a relatively observable fact might be called a causal mechanism. Thus, one might say that a theory is a description of a repertoire of causal mechanisms, a theoretical explanation, an explanation appealing to instances of such a repertoire.

A description of a repertoire of mechanisms can be more or less precise and can supply more or less of the content of theoretical explanations. In principle, a theory could offer a complete list of the mechanisms regulating a general class of phenomena and describe, in general terms, precisely what effects the mechanisms have in every case. That was at least the ideal of eighteenth-century mechanics. But no science has ever achieved it. More often a theory tells us that certain mechanisms cause certain patterns to occur when the latter do occur; or that the mechanisms described have a certain impact on phenomena when the former are strong enough; or that certain mechanisms are typically the cause of the most important features of certain phenomena.

How theories are tested will be a major topic of the next several chapters. One claim that I will be defending sounds, I hope, like scientific common sense. A theory is tested by comparing it with relevant current rivals. Very abstractly put, the question is which theory is a better basis for explaining phenomena. This standard will have to be developed, refined and illustrated at length. But even this broadest statement helps to show how theories departing from the deductivist model can be confirmed, once theories are construed, in general, as descriptions of a causal repertoire. One confirms a theory by showing that the best explanations of relevant phenomena appeal to instances of mechanisms in the repertoire of the theory, rather than relying on rival theories.

In discussions of particular sciences, the most important alleged departure from this conception of a theory as a description of causal mechanisms is, ironically, mechanics itself. For example, in an influential essay of 1912, Russell claimed, "In the motions of mutually gravitating bodies, there is nothing that can be called a cause and nothing that can be called an effect; there is merely a formula. Certain differential equations can be found, which hold at every instant for every particle of the system, and which, given the configuration and velocities at one instant, or the configurations at two instants, render the configuration at any earlier or later instant theoretically calculable. . . . This statement holds throughout physics."[34] That physics describes patterns of variation without describing causes is certainly the impression conveyed by the first chapters of most late twentieth-century textbooks in advanced classical mechanics. The advanced treatment, stemming from the work of Hamilton, Euler, Lagrange and others in the second half of the eighteenth and the

[34] "On the Motion of Cause" in *Mysticism and Logic* (London, 1918), p. 194.

first half of the nineteenth century, presents, as premises for mechanics, partial differential equations and variational principles which link energy, momentum, position and time, no matter what coordinate system is used. Similarly, the most familiar premises for quantum mechanics, the Schroedinger equations, link the quantum-mechanical analogues of those magnitudes in partial differential equations governing the evolution over time of any mechanical system. Aside from the apparent challenge to the proposal that a theory of a subject-matter is a description of causal mechanisms, these formats seem to undermine the claim, in Chapter One, that a covering-law in an explanation must reflect the operation of a causal tendency. For a mechanical explanation is, in advanced treatments, a solution of the equations of motion.

The continuing fundamental status of causal mechanisms is revealed when we, as it were, go beyond the first chapters of mechanics and consider how equations of motion are used to explain actual changes in systems. Whether or not they are expressed in differential equations, Newtonian laws can only be used to explain a mechanical event if forces governing variations in the system are identified; otherwise trajectories are entirely undetermined. In Lagrangian and Hamiltonian formulations, the use of the general equations always depends on expressing energy terms as functions of other magnitudes. And these relationships result from fundamental causal processes at work in the system (or, in the case of a free particle, from their absence.) As principles contributing to explanations, the most general equations of motion are general constraints on the particular causal processes identified in the explanation of events: gravitation or the Coulomb force, say, in nineteenth-century physics; electromagnetic couplings, Fermi couplings and strong interactions, in late twentieth-century physics.[35]

The first principles of mechanics can be stated without reference to any causal mechanism, because of the way in which mechanics has come to be defined. Mechanics consists of the most general statements about the evolution of dynamical magnitudes, statements that are true no matter which of the basic causal mechanisms is responsible. It describes constraints that every item in the causal repertoire obeys. These utterly general constraints add nothing to an

---

[35] See Dirac's distinction between the dynamical hypotheses used to explain the evolution of mechanical systems, hypotheses which require specific physical insights into those systems, and the general theory of quantum states, a mathematical framework in which those hypotheses are stated in *The Principles of Quantum Mechanics* (Oxford, 1981), pp. 84f.

adequate description of all causal mechanisms governing dynamical events together with the remark that the list of mechanisms is complete. They are made true by the existence of this total repertoire. Nonetheless, the general principles, which do not explicitly mention causal mechanisms, may play an essential role in the investigation of the mechanisms. For proposed additions to the causal repertoire are assessed, in part, by determining their conformity to shared features of the current repertoire.[36]

When theories are viewed as descriptions of causal mechanisms, evolutionary theory, structural-functionalist theory, and, as we shall soon see, Marxist and psychoanalytic theory are not misnamed. Evolutionary theory describes causal mechanisms involving mutation and natural selection and claims that *appropriate* mutations, *strong enough* selective pressure, and *adequate* isolation of populations is the basis for adaptive species change, when it occurs. (For reasons of convenience I will put to one side recent controversies over the role and basis of non-adaptive organic change. They raise no new issues of principle in the present context.) When we develop the particular explanations that support the theory, we do not have independent evidence that the factors making for change were strong enough in the cases in question. As a set of premises for derivations the theory provides not covering-laws but covering tautologies (". . . will have this result, if powerful enough to"), adding nothing to the content of the theoretical explanation. But in case after case, the explanations from the Darwinian repertoire are the only ones we have which fit our background knowledge. That is how Darwin is vindicated. Similarly, though Douglas does not use the actual general thesis of structural functionalism in the explanation which supports the theory, she does describe an instance of the causal mechanism specified by the theory. If, in creative and individualized ways, she and other structural-functionalist investigators have drawn from the repertoire to provide superior explanations, that is what vindicates structural-functionalist theory.

Finally, we have a principled basis for the needed distinctions be-

[36] As Wigner puts it, in a closely related context, "if we knew all the laws of nature . . . the invariance properties of these laws would not furnish us new information. They might give us a certain pleasure and perhaps amazement to contemplate, even though they would not furnish new information. Perhaps also, if someone came around to propose a different law of nature, we could more effectively contradict him if his law of nature did not conform with our invariance principle—assuming that we have confidence in the invariance principle." See Wigner *Reflections and Symmetries* (Bloomington, Ind., 1967), p. 17.

tween core and periphery. If a theory is a specification of a repertoire of mechanisms, its core is described when we specify the kind
of things it lists. Of course, it is sometimes hard to distinguish the
kind of thing which is described from what is said about that subject-
matter. But in particular cases, the distinction is clear enough to en-
able us to specify a common core of different theories. Thus, all versions of "the atomic theory" attribute the observable properties of
substances to the nature and interrelations of small bits of matter,
not in direct contact, and not easily dismantled. That is a common
core that is not falsified every few decades. We could describe this
core on the deductivist view, as well. But there would be no reason
to regard it as the central aspect of Dalton's, Boltzmann's and Bohr's
theories. After all, the deductions of Dalton, Boltzmann and Bohr
involve premises as different as caloric theory, classical statistical
mechanics and quantum theory. Yet identifying the common feature as centrally important is crucial to the assessment of the atomic
theory as a whole. We need a way of distinguishing the basic defeat
of phlogiston theory from the basic victory of atomic theory.

In practice, the most important damage done by the deductivist
account of theories has been to introduce distortions and confusions
into both sides of debates over highly controversial theories whose
claims are hard to interpret. More specifically, the deductivist model
has made it virtually impossible to assess the theory of historical
change pioneered by Marx and the psychological theory pioneered
by Freud. Each of these theories can be construed in two ways. It can
be understood as a description of a causal repertoire, and, thus, as a
set of propositions which constrain the explanations of specific observable phenomena, but are not part of the deduction of those
phenomena. Or it can be construed as the most general propositions figuring in such deductions. The deductivist account makes
only the latter a theory worthy of the name. The result has often
been dogmatism for partisans, and, for opponents, empty attacks
unrelated to the practice of those who actually put the theories to
work.

Marx's theory of historical change can, on the one hand, be construed as a set of propositions constraining the explanation of historical changes, but not supplying actual ingredients for their derivation. The core of this theory is a conception of the mechanisms by
which class-divided societies undergo basic change due to internal
causes. In such societies, the political and cultural institutions function to preserve the economic dominance of the main class controlling the surplus product. A radical change in such a society, if due

to processes internal to it, must be based on an ultimately self-destructive tendency of socially accepted processes by which material goods are produced. In such a process of self-transformation, politically or culturally sanctioned processes of an economic kind must ultimately give a subordinate class the will and the ability to destroy the dominance of the old ruling class. This may, for example, be due to the enhanced productivity of means of production controlled by the rising class, combined with constraints on further enhancement, or to enhanced coordination and access to coercion, combined with deepening economic conflict. In either case, one locates the underlying and ultimate causes of basic internal change in the old mode of material production and the interests and resources it creates.

Much more can be said to clarify the terms of this general theory. I have tried to say it, in *Analyzing Marx*, while defending this view of history as theory and as interpretation.[37] Even in a brief and rough statement, though, it should be clear that this theory does guide and constrain explanation in the way theories must. An investigator explaining basic internal changes from this repertoire will not, for example, take the cultural innovations of a charismatic leader and their routinization in processes not based on economic interests and resources as underlying causes. The naive view that an assessment of Marx's theory must, in part, be a comparison of his and Weber's explanations of the rise of capitalism turns out to be perfectly correct. Yet, though the theory provides a testable causal repertoire, it does not provide testable premises for deductions.

The theory of history that I have sketched, the "mode of production theory," as I called it in *Analyzing Marx*, describes causal mechanisms through which basic internal change occurs, when it occurs. But it is no part of this theory to describe general conditions in which basic internal change does, inevitably or usually, occur. In other words, there is no non-tautologous account of when the balance tilts toward change as between the preservative factor, dominance of culture and politics by the main class extracting a surplus product, and the transforming factors, dependent on interests and resources in the process of production. Indeed, while Marx's usual concern is to explain basic internal change, he takes the traditional societies of China and India to have been permanently stabilized, in the absence of intrusions from abroad.[38] Even the question of

[37] *Analyzing Marx* (Princeton, 1984), esp. chs. 5-7.
[38] See Marx, *Grundrisse*, tr. M. Nicolaus (New York, 1973), p. 486; *Capital*, vol. 1 (Moscow, n.d.), pp. 140, 330.

whether basic internal change ever occurs, much less approximately when, is not resolved by the general theory.

It might seem that this theory could be made to fit the deductivist model by making the crucial deductions derivations of a pattern in social change. Whenever basic internal change does occur, it is preceded by conflicts within the mode of production in the indicated way. But, like similar attempts to make other controversial theories fit the model, this one is defeated by the realities of scientific comparison. No one denies that basic internal changes are preceded by changes in the mode of production, of those vaguely indicated kinds. The issue is whether the latter are the basic, underlying causes. Because of the absence of appropriate deductive premises, positivism would make it impossible in principle for Marx's theory to win in this debate.

When one looks at its crucial tests, attempts to use instances of the causal repertoire in the practice of explanation, this theory of history departs from deductivism in another way that is characteristic of many other legitimate theories. From case to case, important terms of the theory are applied or withheld in ways that could not be predicted on the basis of a general rule. One important example out of many is Marx's conception of feudalism, and hence of the time of basic change in his most important single explanation, the account of the rise of capitalism in England at the end of volume one of *Capital*. Marx locates the transition from feudalism to capitalism in a period from the end of the sixteenth to the middle of the seventeenth century. Without such a location, his explanation would not support the general theory. And yet this means calling English society feudal after corvée labor had been replaced by money rents and the independent military power of nobles as against the Crown had ended. Essentially, Marx takes Tudor England to be late-feudal because he takes a society to be feudal if the main process of surplus extraction is from workers who largely control their own means of production and if this process is most directly based on political and military dominance, as against market forces. The local political dominance of the gentry and the economic privileges flowing from the royal court still define the central aspects of economic life in Tudor England. This conception of what was basic does not result from applying any general criterion of what is a basic difference in economic structure. It is justified by its fruitfulness in explaining economic change and political and cultural processes, in the context of Marx's overall social theory. Thus, from a deductivist standpoint, the account of the rise of capitalism that seems to support the theory really pushes it toward a tautology:

the mode of production is an underlying cause of changes that are basic by criteria that make the mode of production an underlying cause of basic changes.

This pattern of choosing the option for specification that makes the theory most effective occurs throughout Marx's writings, affecting the labelling of phenomena as inside the mode of production as against purely political, internal against external, and characteristic of a ruling class as against merely characteristic of well-off people. A similar conceptual flexibility is found in all other writers who are recognizably Marxist and recognizably competent historians, for example, Engels, Lenin, Hill, Hilton, De Sainte Croix and (in their more Marxist moments) Finley, Thompson and Morton Fried.[39] One would have thought that these writings were splendid illustrations of the general theory. So the positivist verdict that they undermine the theory sounds especially unreal.

For a similar case of the partially circular application of concepts in the natural sciences, consider Daltonians' distinctions between processes of true chemical compounding and mere mixtures. A number of extremely stable combinations violate the law of definite proportions and are more completely explained by pre-Daltonian than by Daltonian principles. Usually, Dalton and his followers dismissed them as irrelevant, on the question-begging grounds that only molecular compounding was true compounding.[40] Of course, it is essential, in both the chemical and the historical cases, that uses of the theory not always be so self-supporting. There must be phenomena that stand in need of explanation and that receive a superior one from the contested causal repertoire, superior by standards that are shared by the competing theories. Still, as a premise figuring in all relevant deductions the theory would become tautological, if saved from empirical defeat. For the premise would be hedged with the proviso that it does not apply where the deductions lead to failure.

[39] Among the more recent writers, see, for example, Christopher Hill, *The English Revolution* (London, 1940); Rodney Hilton, *The Decline of Serfdom in England* (New York, 1972); G.E.M. De Sainte Croix, "Karl Marx and the History of Classical Antiquity," *Arethusa* 8 (1975), pp. 7–41; M. I. Finley, "Was Greek Civilization Based on Slavery?" (1959) in his *Economy and Slavery in Ancient Greece* (New York, 1983); E. P. Thompson, *The Making of the English Working Class* (New York, 1966); Morton Fried, *The Evolution of Political Society* (New York, 1967).

[40] See Thomas Kuhn, *The Structure of Scientific Revolutions*, pp. 130–34. Aaron Ihde, in *The Development of Modern Chemistry* (New York, 1964), pp. 98f., describes in more detail the most sustained attack on the law of definite proportions, by the distinguished and innovative chemist Berthollet.

General discussions of Marx's theory of history are largely concerned with very different theories from the one that I have sketched. Whether sympathetic or unsympathetic, interpreters typically assume that Marx's theory is some form of technological determinism, in which economic structures change to adapt to changes in technology.[41] There are a few passages in Marx, very small in size but intriguing in content, that might be taken to endorse such a view. But the degree of emphasis on technological determinism in discussions of Marx's work is both surprising and frustrating. It is surprising because Marx's voluminous historical writings are not at all technological-determinist, and are clearly closer to the mode-of-production theory I previously sketched. In the history of the rise of capitalism there is no suggestion that this social change is to be explained as an adaptation to technological progress. Marx's one extensive discussion of technology, his history of the Industrial Revolution, is notable for its emphasis on class struggle between employers and skilled workers as an independent, causally prior factor in the shaping of technology.[42] If a Marxist theory of history should have an important connection with the histories written by Marx and other Marxist historians, something like the mode of production theory, not technological determinism, should be central to analysis and debate. That the reverse is true is frustrating. The debate over Marx's general theory of history has become virtually useless to historians. Meanwhile a growing body of historical explanation exists that everyone regards as Marxist, but whose common features are hardly ever analyzed by those with an interest in definitions and methods.

In part, this situation has political causes. Technological determinism has played an important role in strategic arguments by Marxists, sometimes for the inevitability of socialism, more often, these days, for the judgment that so-called underdeveloped countries are not ripe for socialism. But the emphasis on theories of history that play so little role in Marxists' writing of history has another cause as well, the pervasive influence of positivism. According to the deductivist model, technological determinism is a theory worthy of the name, while the mode of production theory is not. For, as elaborated by those sympathetic to Marx, technological determinism

---

[41] The major contemporary exposition of this view is Gerald Cohen, *Karl Marx's Theory of History* (Princeton, 1978). G. V. Plekhanov, *The Development of the Monist View of History* (1895; Moscow, 1956), is the best and probably the most influential of the works that originally established this interpretation.

[42] See *Capital*, vol 1, pp. 407f., 410.

says when basic internal change is bound to occur, roughly, when the power-relations in the mode of production discourage the further growth of technology. Thus, a shared deductivist model has led sympathetic, hostile and neutral writers (assuming the latter exist) to devote great ingenuity and passion to a theory of history that has guided no important historian, Marx included.

Psychoanalytic theory has had a similar fate. On the one hand, it can be construed as a description of a repertoire of mechanisms for change, which provides the ingredients for explanations but not deductive premises for explanation. Two central principles would be that the capacity to cope and to be emotionally open are largely determined by unconscious desires and thoughts originating in childhood; and that unconscious desires originating in childhood are the most important source of psychic pain and impulsive or inflexible behavior. A more distinctively Freudian version of psychoanalytic theory would add that sexual drives are the dominant source of unconscious desires and that unconscious conflicts originating in the Oedipal triangle dominate the subsequent emotional outlook of people who can achieve a moderate degree of emotional maturity. Some of these principles are more specific and controversial than others. But none provides a premise for a deduction of the course of someone's emotional life. For one thing, whether pathological symptoms develop is determined by a balance of pathological tendencies and ego strength, for which there is no formula in psychoanalytic theory.

This non-deductive structure is directly evident in most of Freud's writings. For example, "Character and Anal Eroticism," Freud's pioneering effort to trace adult character types to the direction of erotic interest in childhood, ends with the remark: "At any rate, one can give a formula for the formation of the ultimate character from the constituent character-traits: the permanent character-traits are either unchanged perpetuations of the original impulses, sublimations of them, or reaction-formations against them."[43] If the essay were meant to sketch premises for derivations of observable behavior, its promise would have been abruptly withdrawn, here. According to this final formulation, the style of the adult's behavior either expresses the continued presence of certain earlier traits, or pursues a genuinely non-sexual goal with some vague analogies to the original ones, or expresses the rejection of the original ones. From a deductivist point of view, the admission of

---

[43] See Freud, *Character and Culture*, ed. P. Rieff (New York, 1963), p. 33.

this range of diverse sequels is the abandonment of a claim to have a theory of character. However, in the context of his preceding remarks and his general theories, Freud is offering a repertoire of causal mechanisms for use in the explanation of adult character.

On the other hand, if only an ingredient in deductions of phenomena is part of a theory worthy of the name, psychoanalytic theory must consist of claims such as these: difficulties in moderating one's attraction, as an infant, to one's mother, experienced in a climate of sexual taboos, produce self-defeating, rigid or impulsive behavior patterns or medical complaints without organic cause; feminine traits emerge in girls just in case strong penis envy is experienced during the resolution of the Oedipus complex. These generalizations could directly figure in the deduction of empirical regularities correlating psychological phenomena with environmental conditions.

These deductively useful principles certainly are advanced by Freud and others. But they are not the bulk of any important version of psychoanalytic theory. Moreover, they are the least promising material for the core which might be taken to have been verified, in the history of psychoanalysis up until now. Certainly, Freud's own statements of the essence of psychoanalysis are very far from insisting upon deductively useful claims. Here is one characteristic summary, admittedly brief:

> *The Corner-stones of Psychoanalytic Theory.* —The assumption that there are unconscious mental processes, the recognition of the theory of resistance and repression, the appreciation of the importance of sexuality and of the Oedipus complex—these constitute the principal subject-matter of psychoanalysis and the foundations of its theory. No one who cannot accept them all should count himself a psychoanalyst.[44]

The assumption that premises for deductive explanation are what is at stake when a theory is assessed has had a disastrous impact on psychoanalytic theory, among partisans, opponents and those pursuing a balanced judgment. Partisans are often led to insist on a variety of rigid, deductive premises, with warnings that no one who rejects any of *them* "should count himself a psychoanalyst." Critics are satisfied with going through lists of Freud's more rigid and specific claims, without really assessing the bulk of his theory, much less the core. Indeed, they do not face, as something deeply problematic

[44] "Psychoanalysis" in ibid., p. 244.

but unavoidable, the distinction between Freud's being right in all his mature and considered statements and his being basically right. Those of less contentious or more eclectic temperament assess psychoanalysis by making a list of deductively useful psychoanalytic propositions, rating many as true, many as false. The truths are often a series of shrewd insights, but they never add up to a theory in anyone's sense of the term. In sum, the core of psychoanalytic theory is rarely subjected to anyone's systematic scrutiny, on account of a false conception of what a theory must be.[45]

## FREEDOM OF EXPLANATION

As compared with applications of the covering-law model, these applications of the causal account have been highly permissive. Suspicious persons from the covering-law perspective, historians making arguments from empathy, structural-functionalist anthropologists, Marxists, and psychoanalysts, are cleared of the charge that their hypotheses violate a priori constraints on explanation.

If the causal account of explanation is valid, there is probably no attempt to explain ever made by someone in his or her right mind which can be shown to be doomed, just by analyzing its content. Applying the causal account helps us to resolve methodological controversies, to understand the content of explanations, and to see what is at stake when hypotheses are in dispute. It does not help us to exclude hypotheses as intrinsically unworthy of empirical tests.

This liberality in the causal theory of explanation puts a heavy burden on any accompanying theory of confirmation. In positivism, many purported explanations are dismissed as pseudo-explana-

---

[45] For influential sympathetic interpretations of Freud in a deductivist style, see Otto Fenichel, *The Psychoanalytic Theory of Neurosis* (New York, 1945), and Charles Brenner, *An Elementary Textbook of Psychoanalysis* (Garden City, N.Y., 1973), where the reader is told on pp. 1f. that the "proposition that consciousness is an exceptional rather than a regular attribute of psychic processes," and the "principle . . . that in the mind . . . nothing happens by chance," "have received so much confirmation and appear to be so fundamental in their significance that we are inclined to view them as established laws of the mind." The most influential deductivist critique is now Adolf Gruenbaum's vigorous and resourceful book, *The Foundations of Psychoanalysis* (Berkeley, 1984). Gruenbaum's scholarly reliance on Freud's own words makes especially striking the absence of any effort to distinguish the core of psychoanalysis from the various propositions that Freud believed at various times: usually without comment, Gruenbaum routinely moves back and forth among claims that the ever-changing theorist made in different, sometimes widely distant, decades. For an exceptionally evenhanded example of the eclectic approach, see Roger Brown, *Social Psychology* (New York, 1965), ch. 8.

tions, not meriting empirical investigation. In the present approach, all the serious work of sifting hypotheses takes place in the confrontation of hypotheses with data. This process had better be strenuous, and its description detailed. For there are plenty of terrible attempts at explanation richly meriting dismissal.

Some features of a compatible theory of confirmation have already emerged. In this theory, the testing of explanatory hypotheses will often be governed, indispensably, by auxiliary hypotheses. The testing of explanatory hypotheses will often, perhaps always, consist of comparison with a limited number of rival hypotheses. Moreover, if, as seems likely, confirmation is a causal affair, say, because it makes a statement about the causes of the data, then talk of causes cannot be analyzed away in favor of considerations of logical form, or in favor of probabilistic calculations. But these are bare hints, which now must be developed.

# PART TWO

# Confirmation

# CHAPTER FOUR

# Confirmation as Causal Comparison

SCIENTISTS and philosophers of science want to know when a given set of propositions, if true, explain why something happened. They also want to know when a given body of data confirm a proposition, a proposition which might, then, be used to explain. The answer to the second question that I will be developing is causal, comparative and historical. Confirmation, I will argue, is the fair causal comparison of a hypothesis with its current rivals. A hypothesis is confirmed just in case its approximate truth, and the basic falsehood of its rivals, is entailed by the best causal account of the history of data-gathering and theorizing out of which the data arose. (A "causal account," here, means an explanation, as the concept was explicated in the causal theory of explanation.) That an account is best is determined, not just by the data and a priori, general principles, but by a diverse framework of specific and, on the whole, contingent principles. Because partisans of different hypotheses will often be committed to different principles that might figure in the framework, it is essential that the framework for confirmation be fair. Above all, arguments establishing the superiority of a hypothesis must not employ principles that partisans of rival hypotheses reject. So confirmation is triply historical, depending on the rivalries among hypotheses that have actually arisen, the rival framework principles employed by their partisans, and the causal explanation of the history of experiment, observation and theorizing.

If this sounds like a description of any good argument for a hypothesis in which the arguer appeals to empirical facts, that is as it should be. Questions of detail (for example, the insistence on causal depth) to one side, confirming arguments in the natural and the social sciences seem like good arguments in any field where agreement on particular facts is often available, while agreement on some general principles is combined with disagreement on many others. In arguments for hypotheses, as against textbook expositions of findings, the best scientists sound like honest, intelligent lawyers and like principled, mutually respectful people engaged in political controversy. It is understandable that most logical positivists, embattled Social Democrats in central European universities between the World Wars, hoped that scientific argument would be a specialized form of discourse, orderly and definitive as compared with extra-scientific controversy. But this was only a hope. And it has, ironically, led to despair over the role of reason in science, as the apparent gap between scientific arguments and positivist canons has widened.

## AMBIGUITIES OF CONFIRMATION

The question of when a body of data confirms a hypothesis can be understood in a variety of different and legitimate ways. "Confirmation," after all, is a term of art. While there is no point in legislating one meaning for "confirmation," it is important to distinguish the different subjects that a theory of confirmation might have, to make it clear which question is being asked, and when.

One of these distinctions among alternative subject-matters determines the structure of all the rest of this book. Confirmation can be taken to be a goal that scientists commonly pursue when they use data to support a hypothesis. The theory of confirmation, then, is an account of what it takes to reach this goal. Presumably, the kinds of justification such a theory describes will be present, at least implicitly and approximately, in the most important arguments of the most reasonable scientists. The theory of confirmation I will develop and the alternatives I will criticize are of this kind, concerned with a central goal of scientists arguing from data.

However, there is another kind of question that can be raised concerning empirical justification. If positivism is right, then the answers to questions of the first kind will provide answers to questions of this second kind. But the theory of empirical justification need not be so uniform if positivism is wrong.

Suppose that a hypothesis is supported by all available data when the data are assessed using all relevant frameworks, i.e., all frameworks that are relevant to the goal of justification that actual scientists commonly pursue. The latter, actual goal may or may not impose the same ultimate demands as the following goal of justification: to be justified when the total data are assessed using any possible reasonable framework, i.e., any possible framework that a possible person, possessing the data, could employ without being unreasonable. In short, we can also ask whether reason alone ever dictates that the available data be taken to support a hypothesis. This situation might also be described as "confirmation" (though I will not use the label in this way). The classical positivists hoped for an account of scientific reasoning in which the two situations of justification were the same, in the final analysis. When the practice of reasonable scientists was made fully explicit, it was hoped that hypotheses would be connected with data in virtue of appropriate relations of logical form. The rules describing those relations would be a priori canons that everyone must respect, on pain of being unreasonable. So the only ultimate framework used by actual reasonable investigators to assess data as supporting hypotheses would be part of the equipment of every possible reasonable person. Confirmation relevant to the actual goal of science would be justification fulfilling a more metaphysical goal (much as the positivists hated the term), the goal of finding an assessment of a hypothesis depending on reason and evidence alone.

On the other hand, if the frameworks that are relevant to the actual goal of scientists are not, in the final analysis, all possible rational frameworks, then the more metaphysical question is left open, when the first one, involving "confirmation" in my favored sense, is answered. It may or may not be true, in the final analysis, that a given hypothesis which is confirmed by all relevant data would be supported by the data as assessed by any reasonable means. I will be attacking positivist accounts of confirmation. Accordingly, I will leave the more metaphysical questions open—apart from a few vague promises—until the final chapters, when I discuss the issue of scientific realism. There, I will begin by arguing that the more metaphysical question is the only issue that remains under the heading of "scientific realism," once the positivist theory of confirmation is defeated. And I will use the replacement for that theory as a first step in an attempt to resolve the outstanding issue. Because some issues about the status of the scientific consensus will be postponed, my account of confirmation will sometimes seem relativist. In fact, it will eventually be used to set limits on relativism that are true to the real diversity of the sciences and the prevalence of scientific failure, true to the facts of science as contemporary defenses of scientific realism are not.

Even when the nature of confirmation is circumscribed in this way, a variety of further distinctions must be made. To begin with, confirmation can be understood as support for commitments of different strengths. The strongest commitment that is reasonable in the sciences is tentative belief, with openness to revision in the face of further developments in science. But prudent scientists may avoid even this much commitment to a hypothesis that they regard as confirmed by present data. Thus, an astronomer may not believe (or disbelieve) the Big Bang hypothesis, because she takes present-day cosmology to be too speculative, but may still speak of that hypothesis as confirmed by all data now available. As against belief in the basic falsehood of the hypothesis, belief in its approximate truth is more reasonable in light of present data. If one had to choose between the two appraisals, approximate truth would be the more reasonable choice. But noncommitment is at least as reasonable.

This distinction that prudent scientists make is necessary, in any case, to avoid the infamous "paradox of the lottery." Knowledge that a thousand tickets have been issued in a fair lottery in some sense *confirms* the hypothesis that this ticket, that ticket—and so on for any given ticket—will not win. But in some sense, it seems that the conjunction of a set of hypotheses is *confirmed*, if each is. So the senses of the italicized uses had better be different. Otherwise, though the lottery is known to be fair, it is confirmed that no one will win. The solution is that the reasoning from odds made pessimism more reasonable than optimism in each case, but left non-commitment reasonable, as well. The reasoning about conjunction applies only when actual belief has become uniquely reasonable.

The theory of confirmation that I will develop is primarily an account of justification for the more moderate commitment, in which acceptance is taken to be more reasonable than rejection, but suspended judgment is not excluded. In this, it reflects the state of the art. No theory of scientific justification purports to give a general description of when the argument for a hypothesis is strong enough to make (tantative, approximate) acceptance the only reasonable alternative. Still, it is a great advantage if a theory can shed some light on this further question, especially in controversial and important cases. This is the way I will use the present theory in the last chapters of this book, in discussing the reasonableness of agnosticism concerning the unobservable entities posited by successful theoretical hypotheses.

Apart from the different strengths of commitment that might be justified by something worth calling "confirmation," there are different kinds of commitments. In recent years, a form of anti-realism has flourished, according to which reason and evidence do not ever dictate even tentative belief in the approximate truth of theories, although they often dictate acceptance of theories. The kind of acceptance in question is not, and cannot be, mere willingness to use a theory for important purposes. After all, modern anti-realists are trying to describe and justify the attitudes of working scientists, at their best. And modern scientists' acceptance of general relativity, whether realist or anti-realist in tenor, is a very different attitude from their willingness to use Ptolemaic astronomy to construct navigational tables. The specific attitude of acceptance that is the anti-realist's alternative to belief is a willingness to use a theory as a source of explanations, a means of formulating questions and pursuing answers, and a basis for the design of experiments and other tests. When immersed in the practice of science, someone who has this attitude believes, say, that matter is made of molecules no less (and no more) than someone immersed in reading *War and Peace* believes that Pierre Bezhukov is a man of integrity.

My theory of confirmation is not meant to presuppose any assessment of the role of this kind of acceptance, as against literal belief, in rational scientific practice. In part for reasons of convenience, I will usually speak of confirmation as concerned with beliefs about approximate truth. But an anti-realist will always be free to take this as an account of hypothesis choice, i.e., as an account of grounds that make acceptance of theoretical hypotheses more reasonable than rejection, even when literal belief is not made more reasonable than disbelief in what the theory posits. Because of this neutrality in the presuppositions, it will be important if the resulting account of confirmation supports one side or other of the realism dispute. Later, I will try to show that most anti-realists' attitudes toward standard hypothesis-choices are incompatible with their anti-realism, given this theory of the strategy for choice.

Finally, different theories of confirmation will idealize the nature of scientific research in different ways. The idealizations consist of the investigation of situations of belief, doubt and inference more definite, stable or one-sided than any that play an important role in actual science. For example, classical positivist theories are, on the whole, analyses of situations in which a hypothesis is tested in light of given propositions as to what has been observed, propositions to which the investigators are totally committed. These observational beliefs are used in testing but not subject to revision. In reality, no significant scientific argument takes place in this epistemic situation. But the idealization can be rendered harmless, if there are real situations in which those who disagree about a hypothesis actually accept a common body of beliefs about observations for the sake of their arguments. So long as there is this agreement, the analysis of the ideal situation provides tools for criticizing the actual arguments of the real-life disputants. And the criticism of arguments is the real fruit that a theory of confirmation should bear.

Different theories idealize at different points. Thus (to use some jargon which will be translated at length, later on), Bayesians idealize in a different style from classical positivists. They are free to take any distribution of degrees of belief over possibilities as describing the evidence; but, for their theories to be useful, likelihoods must be kept relatively rigid, serving as a given in a similar way to the classical positivists' data. A style of idealization is better only to the extent that the corresponding theory provides better tools of criticism, and is able, in the final analysis, to distinguish dogmatic from non-dogmatic belief.

To make the present theory an effective tool for criticizing arguments, I will sometimes apply it at successive levels of idealization. In other words, I will describe the structure of confirmation in certain situations in which a relatively large body of propositions are taken as given, then consider the further arguments that need to be developed when some of those propositions are in controversy, and can no longer be treated as part of a given framework. It will turn out to be essential to respect differences in level, in the theory of confirmation, since the arguments at each level differ in form, as well as content. More specifically, three levels will be distinguished. At level I, there is a single, complete and unquestioned framework of principles playing the roles required to compare a hypothesis with its rivals. This is a typical situation in judging an explanation of why a particular event occurred. It is less typical, but still quite common when general principles are chosen—say, when constants in an empirical law are measured during a period of tranquility in a natural-scientific field. At level II, many of the principles that could serve to compare hypotheses in light of the data are themselves in controversy; but there is a common body of framework principles that are in fact accepted, though they might well be rejected by other scientific communities at other periods. In the theory of level II, rules for fair comparison in the face of disagreements in background principles are all-important. Procedures for finding implicit agreement on principles of highly abstract but useful kinds are also important. In contrast, the logic of argument at level I is largely supplied by the causal theory of explanation. In the natural sciences, the rules for confirmation at level II are especially important in those disagreements over large theoretical principles that are accompanied by disagreements over how to detect features of nature. In the social sciences, the constraints of fairness and the search for levers of comparison affects both theoretical controversies among rival schools of thought and the rival explanations of great historical events that are the hallmarks of these rival schools.

Finally, even if there is insufficient agreement in shared but debatable scientific principles, there can be an appeal to a further level. Level III consists of truisms that only a crazy person or a philosopher could doubt, such as the truism that normal eyesight usually reveals the approximate shapes of medium-sized objects seen close-up in moderate sunlight. In scientific practice, this level is most important in summarizing and consolidating the case for a radically new theory of an important subject-matter. The inevitable problems of trade-off between successes in some areas and failures elsewhere are resolved, if at all, by an appraisal, based on such truisms, of why the new theory is superior in some ways but inferior in others. With respect to large philosophical issues, level III is crucial in showing when and why it would not be dogmatic to claim that purely hypothetical dissenters from the current scientific consensus would be unreasonable to reject a favored proposition in light of the data at hand. It is at level III that my theory first emphasizes certain claims which, though topic-specific as compared with positivists' general rules, are (in a weak and limited sense) valid a priori. This is true, in particular, of certain assessments of what stands or does not stand in need of justification. In later discussions of scientific realism, I will consider this special kind of truism in more detail, for the light it sheds on the issue of whether data ever rule out all possible rational dissent from a scientific theory. (This is different from the issue in the present chapter of whether actual commitments are non-dogmatic, though the two issues are related.)

When all three levels are taken into account, this theory of confirmation is less idealized, more realistic than its rivals, in the only way a theory of confirmation can be realistic. It can be applied to more actual arguments without distorting the facts of the controversy. In particular, hypothesis, data, and framework are defined by roles, not content, with no requirement that what is taken as a given be stated in a certain vocabulary, be discovered in a certain way, or have a specific logical form or probabilistic structure.

Someone who believes that confirmation is comparison has a special duty to compare his or her theory with current rivals. Apart from piecemeal criticisms, I will postpone until the next three chapters my arguments against the two approaches that sharply conflict with my account of confirmation. But a brief sketch of these alternatives may be useful, at the outset.

One rival approach is characteristic of classical positivism, as it flourished from the 1920s through the 1950s. I will call it deductivism—without confusion, I hope with the deductivist model of theories, which is, in any case, intimately related to it. In deductivism, a given body of data confirms a hypothesis just in case the hypothesis, when appropriately supplemented, entails observations among the data, in deductions of an appropriate logical pattern. The task of confirmation theory is to lay down rules describing what supplements and patterns of entailment are appropriate. These rules are the same for all fields of inquiry, and are valid a priori. As Hempel declares toward the start of "Studies in the Logic of Confirmation," "In fact, it seems reasonable to require that the criteria of empirical confirmation, besides being objective in character, should contain no reference to the specific subject-matter of the hypothesis or of the evidence in question; it ought to be possible, one feels, to set up purely formal criteria of confirmation in a manner similar to that in which deductive logic provides purely formal criteria for the validity of deductive inference."[1] This feeling has been widely shared, even among those—for example, Popper—who give confirmation itself a different status from Hempel or describe it using different rules.

Positivism in the broadest sense requires that confirmation be determined by general, a priori rules, but not that those rules solely describe entailment patterns. In recent years, a new version of positivism has flourished in which the apparatus of deductivism is enriched by devices from probability theory. In this other main alternative to the account that I will develop, the theory of confirmation is based on some interpretation of the mathematical theory of probability under which it governs the rational revision of degrees of belief as new data are encountered. This approach is usually labelled "Bayesian," because Bayes' Theorem, an elementary but powerful consequence of the axioms of probability, plays a central role in any such theory of the dynamics of belief. Especially in the piecemeal criticisms of the present chapter, I will sometimes be attacking aspects of deductivism which Bayesians have broken from, as well. In particular, revision according to Bayes' Theorem is intrinsically comparative and intrinsically concerned with background beliefs, reflected in conditional probabilities. But in subsequent chapters I will try to show that all of the most fundamental problems that defeat deductivism reappear and defeat the new, Bayesian positivism, as well. There is also one other respect in which my theory will seem, at first, more Bayesian than it really is. Vernacular talk of likelihoods

---

[1] Hempel and Paul Oppenheim, "Studies in the Logic of Expansion" (1948) in Hempel, *Aspects of Scientific Explanation* (New York, 1965), p. 10.

will sometimes play a crucial role in the description of scientific inference. However, I will be arguing in Chapter Seven that the crucial maxims of inference are distorted if they are understood as the outcome of any satisfactory interpretation of probability theory. Here as elsewhere, common sense is a better, not just a more familiar basis for scientific method than more technical alternatives.

The theory of confirmation that I will now explore is an example of the causal approach to epistemology, in which terms of epistemic appraisal are explained as abstract descriptions of the causes of subjects' beliefs and experiences. Although I will often emphasize aspects of my account of confirmation that are different from, even contrary to, earlier work of this kind, I have benefited from many insights in Boyd's causal theory of evidence, Goldman's causal theory of knowledge, and Harman's theory of justification as inference from the best explanation.[2]

## THE IDEA OF CAUSAL COMPARISON

In a way, the basic idea that confirmation is causal comparison stands in no need of specific illustration. Choose any instance you will of empirical justification, and it will be easy to put it in the following form, when implicit steps are made explicit and notions of cause and explanation are understood as in Chapter Two: "These are the facts. This is how they are explained assuming the approximate truth of the favored hypothesis. This is why they are not explained as well on the rival hypotheses which are the current competitors." The facts that function as data may be of extremely diverse kinds, for example, observations, experimental findings, testimony, generally accepted regularities, or patterns in a body of observations such as the abstract characterizations used in statistical inference. The propositions used to rate alternative explanations may be virtually anything that is not in controversy. Two obviously important and common bases for comparison are principles validating a procedure or instrument as a reliable means of detection and laws of nature that no acceptable hypothesis should violate when combined with the facts.

Still, many empirical arguments are not explicitly in the causal-comparison format, as many are not explicitly in any of the formats

[2] See Richard N. Boyd, "Realism, Underdetermination, and a Causal Theory of Evidence," *Nous* (1973), pp. 1–12; Alvin I. Goldman, "A Causal Theory of Knowing," *Journal of Philosophy* (1967), pp. 355–72; and Gilbert Harman, "The Inference to the Best Explanation," *Philosophical Review* (1965), pp. 88–95.

described by theories of confirmation. Good arguers are only as explicit as they have to be, given actual dangers of question-begging and confusion. One would expect the underlying nature of confirmation to be most explicit when the dangers of evasion and confusion are at their highest because an investigator is defending a novel hypothesis or seeking to resolve in a novel way an issue that has divided scientists into different schools of thought. In fact, it is at these junctures that the surface facts of argument best illustrate the idea that confirmation is causal comparison.

Darwin's *The Origin of Species* is the greatest natural-scientific argument that is still, on the whole, good science and that is accessible to anyone, no matter how powerful his or her mathematics block may be. A certain argument about bats there, is an especially elegant, but otherwise typical example of Darwin's reasoning from his data:

> I have carefully searched the oldest voyages, but have not finished my search; as yet, I have not found a single instance, free from doubt, of a terrestrial mammal (excluding domesticated animals kept by the natives) inhabiting an island situated above 300 miles from a continent or great continental island; and many islands situated at a much less distance are equally barren. . . . Though terrestrial mammals do not occur on oceanic islands, aerial mammals do occur on almost every island. New Zealand possesses two bats found nowhere else in the world: Norfolk Island, the Viti Archipelago, the Bonin Islands, the Caroline and Marianne Archipelagoes, and Mauritius, all possess their peculiar bats. Why, it may be asked, has the supposed creative force produced bats but no other mammals on remote islands? On my view this question can be easily answered: for no terrestrial mammal can be transported across a wide space of sea, but bats can fly across. [More specifically, bat transport occurs to provide a basis for speciation through natural selection, but occurs so infrequently that variants on remote islands are not overwhelmed by migrants from the more competitive mainland.][3]

Note some particular aspects of the idea of causal comparison that are embodied in this example. Here as throughout the book, Darwin is comparing his favored hypothesis of speciation through natural selection not with the mere supposition of its falsehood but with rival hypotheses about the factors at work in the phenomena.

[3] See *The Origin of Species*, J. W. Burrow (Baltimore, 1968), pp. 382f.

The existence of islands with terrain hospitable to terrestrial mammals lacking such endemic species is important because the main rival is the hypothesis, dominant among the best-informed secular-minded scientists of the time, that species are created, without ancestors, by a force that makes them well-adapted to their environments. Also, Darwin makes his argument on the basis of principles he shares with the other side, for example, the shared principle that offspring are like their parents but subject to small variations, not the tendentiously anti-creationist, though plausible principle that a complex oganism must be the offspring of another. Finally, Darwin is not claiming to have a complete explanation of the phenomena in question, although he certainly thinks that the complete answer would entail the approximate truth of his natural-selection hypothesis. Elsewhere, he makes it clear both that the mechanisms of heredity and variation are mysterious to him and that there is no way of predicting how an observed advantage will affect the actual course of speciation.[4] The issue for him is whether the best available account of the data, however vague or incomplete, entails the superiority of the natural selection hypothesis over its current rivals.

Though it has always seemed that Darwin was choosing among rival causal accounts, this might be thought to be just a rough or metaphorical statement of the methods of more precise sciences than biology, physics in particular. But in fact, when fundamental controversies force great explicitness on physicists, their arguments often seem, on the face of it, to fit the pattern. This is even, indeed *especially* true of the two prime examples of theory confirmation in deductivist accounts, Newton's vindication of his celestial mechanics and the triumph of the molecular-kinetic theory of heat.

Most of the *Principia* is occupied, of course, with the development of means for deriving forces from given motions and motions from given forces, assuming the three laws of motion. It is, almost entirely, in Book Three that Newton is trying to confirm a hypothesis about forces in nature and their effects, namely, the description of how the planets, sun, moon and sea ineract that he calls "the system of the world." The case Newton presents for his system of the world

---

[4] "Our ignorance of the laws of variation is profound. Not in one case out of a hundred can we pretend to assign any reason why this or that part differs, more or less, from the same part in the parents" (ibid., p. 202). "It is good thus to try in our imagination to give any form some advantage over another. Probably in no single instance should we know what to do, so as to succeed. It will convince us of our ignorance on the mutual relations of all organic beings; a conviction as necessary, as it seems to be difficult to acquire" (p. 129).

is, not a mere derivation of data from theory, but a powerful example of confirmation by causal comparison. In general, he is appealing to the absence of any rival explanation of his own success in pursuing the particular strategy announced in the Preface to the *Principia*: "from the phenomena of motions to investigate the forces of nature, and then from these forces to demonstrate the other phenomena. . . . [B]y the propositions mathematically demonstrated in the former Books, in the third I derive from the celestial phenomena the forces of gravity with which bodies tend to the sun and the several planets. Then, from these forces, by other propositions that are also mathematical, I deduce the motions of the planets, the comets, the moon and the sea."[5] The derivations of forces from motions are independent of the derivations of motions from forces. Thus, Newton applies his laws of motion and his rules of reasoning in philosophy (i.e., natural philosophy, physics) to assign forces which vary with the product of masses and the square of distance, basing the derivations on certain observed motions of the planets around the sun, the jovian moons around Jupiter and free fall to the earth. The laws of motion then dictate that the forces have further effects on motion, a consequence which observation might have contradicted, but actually validates. For example, the assignment of forces dictates a variety of facts about planetary orbits (including subtle variations over time), trajectories of comets, and the general characteristics of tides. As Newton frequently emphasizes, his ability to extract a causal account of some data and to use it to account for a variety of other data has no explanation in any alternative system of the world in which rival hypotheses are asserted. His comment on his account of Montenari's comet is typical. "[T]he theory which justly corresponds with a motion so unequable, and through so great a part of the heavens, which observes the same laws with the theory of the planets, and which accurately agrees with accurate astronomical observations, cannot be otherwise than true."[6]

The nature of the particular rivals to his celestial mechanics, namely, Cartesian vortex theories and descriptively plausible geocentric systems such as Brahe's, also explains a variety of details in Newton's argument. For example, he pays enormous attention to

[5] Newton, *Principia*, ed. F. Cajori (Berkeley, 1962), p. xviii.

[6] Ibid., p. 519. In form, Newton's method of argument fits Glymour's "bootstrapping" model far better than other deductivist patterns, and I am indebted to Glymour's discussion of Newton in *Theory and Evidence* (Princeton, 1980), pp. 203–26. I will be criticizing the morals Glymour would derive from this and other case studies, in Chapter Five, below.

comets. Indeed, two-fifths of his summary pamphlet, "The System of the World," is concerned with this topic. Such concern is appropriate because comets are such effective levers of fair causal comparison. The crucial features of their orbits can be derived using principles of geometric optics that everyone shares. Once those orbits are established, they show both that the celestial spheres of Ptolemaic astronomy cannot be real, since otherwise comets would bump against them,[7] and that Cartesian vortices cannot be moving the planets, "for comets are carried . . . through all parts of the heavens indifferently, with a freedom that is incompatible with the notion of a vortex."[8] Newton's emphasis on the fact that Jupiter's moons obey Kepler's third law, revolving in periods in proportion to the 3/2 power of their distances from the center of Jupiter, is another example of his tact in causal comparison. Shared optical principles establish the phenomenon, yet only Newtonian hypotheses explain it.

In contrast, a deductivist version of Newton's arguments is both different from his construals of his method and a weak argument, given the need for auxiliary hypotheses connecting his physical theory with his data. The weakness in brief (to be analyzed in detail later on) is this. The laws of motion and the universal law of gravitation only entail that some observations will follow, given others, if there are additional assumptions, for example: only gravitational force has a significant effect on celestial trajectories; the mass of the sun is much greater than that of the planets; the fixed stars are so far away that their influence on the planets is negligible. But rival theories, for example, Cartesian vortex theory, can entail the same connections among data if ad hoc supplementation with auxiliaries is allowed. Moreover, Newton cannot dispense with tactics of ad hoc defense. Like any important theory, including physical theories of the present day, his has its own empirical anomalies which would defeat it if ad hoc supplement were ruled out, in general.

Admittedly, there is another way of understanding the empirical arguments of the *Principia*, according to which they are inferences based on the "Rules of Reasoning in Philosophy," and those rules are, in turn, precursors of positivism. Certainly, the Rules are meant to summarize a consensus about the methods of physics to which Newton subscribes, and which he hopes to strengthen. They are the methods that are the common property of natural philosophers in

[7] *Principia*, p. 550 (in "The System of the World").
[8] Ibid., p. 543 (in the *Principia* proper).

the Galilean style, whatever their other disagreements. However, in "The System of the World," where Newton is trying to appeal to the broadest audience, he is perfectly capable of arguing his case without appeal to the Rules. And in the *Principia* itself, he argues more resourcefully and extensively for his system of the world than the Rules require. Presumably, this is because the rules do not justify any very high degree of confidence in the hypotheses they favor. To use one of his own examples, Rule III, a generalizing principle, leads us to conclude that all bodies are impenetrable, on the basis of our experience of bodies on the earth. And yet, Newton admits, this argument "concludes" with relatively little "force," since among bodies "in the celestial regions, we have no experiments, nor any manner of observation" of inpenetrability.[9] Since the physics of the *Principia* has its own anomalies, such as the inaccurate assignment of velocity to sound, it is essential for the underlying argument to have more power than the Rules can guarantee.

Similarly, when we consider how the molecular-kinetic theory was actually confirmed, not just how it is presented in textbooks, the case for this paradigm in deductivism looks like an example of causal comparison. Scientists began speaking of an experimental test of the molecular-kinetic theory quite late in the development of that theory. Comfirmation was based, above all, on the investigations of Brownian motion in which Einstein was the main theorist, Perrin the main experimentalist. Einstein's description of how the molecular-kinetic theory might be confirmed is, quite explicitly, an account of possibilities of causal comparison. Thus, he begins his first paper on the subject by noting that osmotic pressure from suspended particles should not exist, strictly speaking, given the causal repertoire of classical thermodynamics, the rival to the molecular theory of heat. Once thermal equilibrium is achieved in the solvent, there would be no energy available to move the particles. "But a different conception is reached from the standpoint of the molecular-kinetic theory of heat. . . . We must assume that the suspended particles perform an irregular movement—even if a very slow one—in the liquid, on account of the molecular movement of the liquid."[10] Both here and in his subsequent elegant calculations of quantitative observable consequences of the molecular theory, Einstein is taking advantage of a framework that is shared between classical and mo-

[9] Ibid., p. 400.
[10] Einstein, "On the Movement of Small Particles Suspended in a Stationary Liquid Demanded by the Molecular-Kinetic Theory of Heat" (1905) in Einstein, *Investigations on the Theory of the Brownian Movement*, ed. R. Fuerth (New York, 1956), pp. 3f.

lecular thermodynamics. If a particle is accelerated, something has moved it; and given thermal equilibrium that something will involve items in the catalog of forces that the two theories share. In both frameworks, certain motions must be caused by little bumps. While the Einstein-Perrin derivations are deductions, a deductivist cannot explain why they had a special power to confirm a hypothesis that had seemed just a deductively useful speculation for over a century.

That confirmation is fair causal comparison is, I hope, beginning to sound like common sense. But, after all, no philosopher of science has ever asserted that this idea is utterly mistaken. Rather, they have been inclined to deny that confirmation operates only on current rivals, that such comparison is sufficient, that it is essential, that the comparison must be causal, in the final analysis, or that rational comparison can go on in the absence of general, a priori rules for rating rival hypotheses. To develop the theory of confirmation further, I will consider each question in turn.

## The Scope of Comparison

Confirmation, on the present theory, is comparison with relevant current rivals, to see which alternative is part of the best causal account of the data. Which alternatives are to be compared is determined by the current frameworks actually employed at the time when confirmation is assessed. By a "framework," I mean a body of beliefs, at least fairly stable, held by an investigator and applied in the identification of causal factors and the rating of causal accounts as better or worse. Thus, Ptolemaic, Copernican and Newtonian investigators employed different frameworks in assessing explanations of celestial observations. A sufficiently rich framework provides a checklist of causes that might be producing the data at hand, and provides means of sifting through the alternative causes, in pursuit of a causal account that is more likely to be correct than any of the rival accounts in the framework. If only one framework is employed in a field, then data confirm a hypothesis if it wins out in this causal sifting. However, the most important scientific arguments occur when more than one framework is being employed. Then, fairness dictates that a hypothesis undergoing empirical test be compared with rivals supplied by all current frameworks, using arguments that do not beg the question by assessing the status of a rival using principles that are absent from the framework of those who would support the rival. Thus, Copernican astronomy was not confirmed by the apparent retrogression of Mars, since Ptolemaic astronomy provided a rival account of the phenomenon, just as good according to shared standards of judgment. That variations in the brightness of planets, when seen through a telescope, were only accounted for on Copernican hypotheses might have been confirming, were it not for the following fact. Variations in brightness in naked eye observations are not Copernican, but Ptolemaic. The brightness of Mars to the naked eye shows little variation, indicating that Mars has an approximately circular orbit around the Earth—perhaps a circle with epicycles. Only through a telescope are the variations large, as one would expect if Earth and Mars revolve with different periods about a common center. And in the Aristotelian framework that Ptolemaic astronomers employed, natural organs of observation were regarded as intrinsically reliable, to be preferred as means of investigating a realm of phenomena in the absence of specific arguments for preferring artificial apparatus. There was such an argument for preferring telescopic findings on the earth, since telescopic observations of the writing on a distant weathervane can be verified by climbing the relevant roof. But Aristotelians had good reason not to project this rating into the heavens, since they took sublunar matter to be a radically different medium from celestial matter.[11] For variations in brightness, each hypothesis was best in its own framework but not in the other, so the data on brightness confirmed nothing. On the other hand, scientists who took Venus to be revolving around the sun could explain the apparent telescopic phases of Venus, and others could not in their respective frameworks. So these data did confirm the heliocentric orbit of that planet.

In short, the rivals that are to be compared are candidates actually being put forward, or implicit in current frameworks; and they are to be assessed in ways that are fair to all current frameworks. This contrasts with the classical positivist assumption that confirmation is a logical relation between the confirmed hypothesis and the confirming data, unaffected by further historical variations in the state of scientific controversy.

Both scientific and everyday usage strongly favor such historicism. Newton's use of astronomic observations is, all agree, a paradigm of confirmation. But, given the limits of accuracy of which he was aware, the data do not discriminate between Newton's celestial mechanics and relativistic celestial mechanics. Nonetheless, the data

[11] For a richly documented discussion of this problem of comparison, see Paul Feyerabend, *Against Method* (London, 1975), pp. 101–19.

did confirm his theory. On the other hand, by the twentieth century, those data no longer vindicated the theory as against all current rivals. And it would surely have been wrong for one of the many Newtonian astronomers circa 1914 to have claimed, "Our theory is the one the data confirm"—even putting to one side the special fit between general relativity and variations in the perihelion of Mercury.

In less technical contexts as well, empirical justification appears and disappears depending on which alternatives are salient. To adapt an example of Goldman's, I am normally justified, having seen the dog, in believing that a spaniel crossed my path in Central Park, if I can tell a spaniel from a dachshund, a terrier, and other common Central Park breeds. But let someone ask if I have seen a Tibetan Lapso Apso ("It looks like a spaniel, but it really is related to a bulldog") and my justification is lost.

## The Sufficiency of Comparison

If a scientific argument showed that the evidence favored a hypothesis over any that might emerge from a framework that any possible rational person might employ, favored it when the causes of the data are judged from a standpoint that is fair to all possible frameworks—then, no doubt, the argument would be sufficient to confirm the hypothesis. But in the real world of science, causal comparison does not usually range over all possible alternatives. Newton's did not defeat an actual future alternative, general relativity. As a result, it might seem unreasonable and dogmatic to take triumph in causal comparison among current rivals as sufficient to confirm. How can a hypothesis be confirmed by comparison, when an indefinitely large number of rivals have not, even implicitly, been judged?

Here, it is essential to distinguish two stages at which alternatives are compared, namely, within a framework and between frameworks. Suppose an investigator has certain beliefs about the world which he or she employs to refine, improve and extend favored hypotheses. This framework expresses his or her present commitments as to which causes might be producing phenomena of certain kinds. Working within the framework, the investigator can often single out one among all *possible* alternatives as the causal process actually at work. Thus, if the investigator is Newton, the three laws of motion and the Rules of Reasoning in Philosophy are a good part of the framework, and, combined with the data, they single out the universal force of gravitation as the source of celestial motions, as compared with all possible alternatives. Causes of motion departing from the three laws are impossible in this framework.

If one has established the superiority of a hypothesis given the data and one's own beliefs as to what causes might be operating, is it dogmatic and unreasonable to take the hypothesis to be confirmed? The question is not rhetorical. In fact, it is dogmatic and, hence, unreasonable to take the data to vindicate the hypothesis when people who dispute it have a rival framework in which the data do not establish superiority. At least implicitly, one ought to have non-question-begging arguments making their continued disbelief unreasonable. Suppose, though, that one has these arguments, as Newton had fair arguments that defeated rival frameworks for describing celestial causes. Is it dogmatic to claim that the hypothesis is confirmed, just because other frameworks might arise, in addition to the actual ones, against which one would be powerless?

Surely not, given the tentative nature of the attitude that confirmation supports. One presently prefers belief in the hypothesis to disbelief, while one is willing to change one's preference should future developments motivate the change. These developments might consist of new data, or of an evolution in scientific thinking that produces a new framework in actual employment. It is hardly dogmatic or unreasonable to take this attitude of present commitment to be supported by the data, when the data are interpreted using the only present framework to survive criticism. One might as well suppose that my recent agonized choice of a Volkswagen Quantum was unreasonable simply because Toyota may someday produce a car that is comfortable for six-footers. What would be unreasonable is to ignore a rival that is part of a causal account made likely by one's own framework, or by a current framework that one cannot criticize effectively.

Note that once one knows which frameworks must be respected, one may have to take seriously the vague rival hypothesis that the data are due to some unknown factor or combination of factors, that cannot as yet be specifically described. Within a framework, such an alternative is rated as more or less likely, in comparison with more definite rivals. And we sometimes have means to access its likelihood, in light of data—for example, using statistical reasoning to assess the likelihood that a correlation is due to chance. But even statistical reasoning relies on an extensive framework of beliefs concerning causal factors and the extent and independence of their variations. What the non-dogmatic investigator need not do is to compare the hypothesis undergoing tests with the bare possibility that a contrary framework for causal assessment is correct.

These reflections suggest that confirmation is inherently social. It depends on the actual nature of controversy within the investigator's scientific community. Admittedly, this verdict has depended on putting a certain question to one side. Are investigators ever in a position to say that anyone accepting the data but departing from the favored hypothesis would be unreasonable, even if he or she were committed to a deviant framework that no actual person shares? When I return to this question, in the discussion of scientific realism, I will argue that the truisms in level III do sometimes support this broader claim. But usually, scientists are content with much less, namely, with showing that their actual preferences are the reasonable ones in the actual state of science.

## THE REQUIREMENT OF COMPARISON

In classical positivism, comparison is neither sufficient nor necessary for confirmation. A hypothesis is confirmed by data just in case it entails data in appropriate ways, when appropriately supplemented. Confirmation is a lonely encounter of hypothesis with evidence.

Here, classical positivism is much more charitable than the practice of reasonably shrewd critics of particular scientific arguments. Consider the following attempt to confirm a hypothesis about difference in psychological capacities.

In an article published under distinguished auspices, "Preference for Delayed Reinforcement: An Experimental Study of a Cultural Observation," Walter Mischel claims to "validate, experimentally, an observation about cultural differences" in Trinidad. The hypothesis is that relative to other ethnic groups "Negroes are impulsive, indulge themselves, settle for next to nothing if they can get it right away, do not work or wait for bigger things in the future but, instead, prefer smaller things immediately." Here, in full, is Mischel's description of the procedure by which he allegedly confirmed this "inability to postpone immediate gratification for the sake of delayed rewards."

### Procedure

The experimenter (E) was introduced as an American interested in gathering information on children in the local schools of the island. To help with this the Ss [i.e., the subjects, 53 children in an integrated elementary school] were asked to fill out the questionnaire. When these were completed, E expressed his wish to thank the group for their cooperation. He displayed the two kinds of reinforcements and said: "I would like to give each of you a piece of candy but I don't have enough of these (indicating the larger, more preferred reinforcement) with me today. So you can either get this one (indicating the smaller, less preferred reinforcement) right now, today, or, if you want to, you can wait for this one (indicating) which I will bring back next Wednesday (one week delay interval)." To insure clarity, these instructions were repeated in rephrased form and both reinforcements were carefully displayed. The fact that getting the (smaller) candy today precluded getting the (larger) one next week, and vice versa, was stressed. Ss were asked to indicate their choice by writing "today" (T) or "next week" (W) on their questionnaires. The response made here was the measure of choice of a larger (or more preferred) delayed reinforcement or a smaller (less preferred) immediate reinforcement. Ss were seated sufficiently far apart from each other to insure reasonably that their choices were made independently in this group setting.

In the investigator's view, the hypothesis was confirmed. Comparison of the black and non-black children's choices "yielded a chi square of 4.17 ($p$ between .05 and .02), a significantly larger proportion of Negro Ss choosing immediate reinforcement."[12]

[12] W. Mischel, "Preference for Delayed Reinforcement: An Experimental Study of a Cultural Observation," *Journal of Abnormal and Social Psychology* (1958), p. 59. The chi square is a technical measure of the difference between the correlations actually observed and the total absence of any observed distinction as between the groups involved. $p$ is the probability that the particular observed departure from total non-difference is wholly due to random factors influencing the sampling from the general populations in question.

Mischel's study has had a brilliant career in the literature. Though it was an investigation of differences between black and ethnically East Indian children in Trinidad, the findings have often been applied to black-white differences in the United States. Thus, Urie Bronfenbrenner, a leading figure among liberal educational psychologists, cited Mischel's "series of ingenious experiments" as evidence that "the most immediate, overwhelming and stubborn obstacles to achieving quality and equality in education now lie as much in the character and way of life of the American Negro as in the indifference and hostility of the white community. . . . [These inadequacies] present problems not only to the Negro child but also to his white companion, who is exposed to the contagion of disorganized and antisocial behavior." Bronfenbrenner, "The Psychological Costs of Quality and Equality in Education," *Child Development* (1967), pp. 909, 910, 916. In Edward Banfield's *The Unheavenly City* (Boston, 1970), Bronfenbrenner's article and others employing Mischel's study are cited

If deductivist theories of confirmation were right, this study really would have confirmed the hypothesis that black children tend to have a lesser ability to postpone gratification. The hypothesis serves in deductions of the observed racial difference, of the same logical pattern as those which are deductivist paradigms of empirical support.

On reflection though, this study stands out as a particularly grisly example of non-confirmation. There is, of course, an alternative explanation for the candy-bar data. The typical experiences of black children give them a greater rational basis for the expectation that promises made by outsiders with official standing will be broken. The black children's tendency to dismiss the future possibility was based on distrust, not animal-like impulsiveness. Because this very natural hypothesis of distrust does at least as good a job of explaining the data as the hypothesis of impulsiveness, the data do not confirm the hypothesis. The empirical argument is invalid, for reasons which are made explicit in the requirement of comparison.

The same moral emerges when we ask what investigators are, in general, pursuing, when they seek to confirm a hypothesis. Every theory of confirmation presently disclaims the intention of describing the basis for outright acceptance of a hypothesis. Confirmation is to mean something less than this. But what is this limited subject-matter? The question is not answered simply by relabelling the subject-matter "partial confirmation," even if such confirmation is said to lie on an interval from 0 to 1, and more or less elaborate formal theories are described, connecting propositions with these numerical values.

In every current way of understanding the goal of confirmation, its achievement requires comparison. In the interpretation that best fits scientific practice, data confirm a hypothesis if they make belief more reasonable than disbelief. If one has to bet on either truth or falsehood, and has to use the data as one's basis for the bet, the bet on truth is more reasonable. This bet is not more reasonable, and

in support of the claim that a fifth to a half of non-whites in urban areas are in a lower class, a member of which "either . . . cannot discipline himself to sacrifice a present for a future satisfaction or . . . has no sense of the future. He is therefore radically improvident: whatever he cannot consume immediately he considers valueless. His bodily needs (especially for sex) and his taste for 'action' take precedence over everything else—certainly over any work routine. . . . [H]uman nature seems loath to accept a style of life that is so radically present-oriented" (pp. 53f., see also pp. 85, 266–68, 280). *The Unheavenly City* was, almost certainly, the most widely assigned text on urban problems in the 1970's. In recent years Bronfenbrenner has reportedly disowned views expressed in his 1967 article.

the data do not confirm, if the data are explained as well on the basis of a rival hypothesis, which fits them as well and is otherwise just as acceptable.

In some approaches, the subject-matter of confirmation theory is a weaker relation, probability-raising. A hypothesis is said to be confirmed by data just in case it is more probable after the data are taken into account than it was before.[13] In fact, this is much less than is claimed when investigators actually assert confirmation. A test does not confirm that a sore throat is due to throat cancer when it raises the probability of the latter from one in a million to one in five hundred, while raising the odds of a streptococcal cause from one in ten to nine in ten. Still, probability-raising might, more plausibly, be equated with giving some evidential support, and the theory of how a body of data confirms a hypothesis might be taken as a description of how this support is added up to see whether belief is more reasonable than disbelief. In my discussion of Bayesianism, I will be arguing that no such adding procedure exists in general. But for present purposes, these doubts can be put to one side. A requirement of comparison emerges, in any case, in the probabilistic account. Whatever probability is, the sum of the probabilities of all possibilities does not change, as research continues. So the probability of a hypothesis is only raised at some cost to rivals.

Of course, taking all alternative possibilities into account is rarely feasible. Indeed, at important junctures in the assignment of probabilities it is impossible (or so I shall argue in Chapter Seven). Still, if we look at most actual processes of assessment, comparison becomes, if anything, more pressing, if the goal is probability-raising. When we assess the impact of data, we usually divide hypotheses into two groups, "natural" hypotheses, which are to be taken seriously, and a residue of "farfetched" hypotheses, only to be taken seriously if all the natural ones have severe difficulties in the case at hand. Here, no encounter with data is a step toward genuine confirmation unless the hypothesis does a better job of coping with the data than some natural rival. That a farfetched hypothesis fits the facts is, in itself, just a curiosity. That a natural hypothesis fits is not, in itself, a step toward confirming it, since bets on its truth are no more reasonable than they were before. It was assumed to fit the facts well. What strengthens a hypothesis, here, is a victory that is, at the same time, a defeat for a plausible rival.

[13] See, for example, Roger Rosenkrantz, "Does the Philosophy of Induction Rest on a Mistake?" *Journal of Philosophy* (1982), p. 80.

So far, I have adopted the normal simplification in which the subject-matter of confirmation is taken to be truth and falsehood, belief and disbelief (or, if one is being anti-realist, acceptance or outright rejection). But in fact, the only important subject-matter for research is approximate truth (basic acceptance). A few banalities to one side (e.g., "If humans ingest nothing they die within six months"), no precise statement of an empirical regularity is ever meant strictly and literally, unless it reflects deep theoretical facts. Yet no theory has survived more than a few generations of scientific criticism unscathed, and there is no reason to believe that the parade of partial defeats has ended. So even with deep theories, approximate truth is the only reasonable hope. This modesty of real science provides a final argument for the necessity of comparison.

What is the *approximate* truth which scientists support through confirmation? Part of it may consist of a good fit with most observations. But this cannot be the whole story. Ptolemaic astronomy fits most observations. But it is not confirmed by the current body of astronomical data. Rather, the approximate truth which scientists seek has, itself, an intrinsically comparative dimension. The claim that the data establish the approximate truth of a hypothesis is, in part, the claim that they establish its superiority to rivals. It is on this comparative dimension that modern data fail to confirm Ptolemaic astronomy. That they fail to establish its strict and literal truth is not interesting, in this context. If we count the history of astronomy among the data of astronomy (as, I shall argue, we must), then the data are not a rational basis for a bet on the strict and literal truth of modern astronomy, either.

## CONFIRMATION AND CAUSALITY

Empirical arguments in science look like cases for an assessment of the causes of the data. Even statistical inference consists of choosing what probabilities to ascribe in characterizations of a "statistical model," an abstract causal structure governing the outcomes in question. Thus, for all his Humean prejudices, DeFinetti made Bayesian reasoning useful by connecting it with a question about the cause of a set of outcomes: if a causal factor is operating with constant intensity in repeated trials of a setup the subsequent operation of which is not changed by prior outcomes, what does the distribution of observed outcomes imply about the actual intensity of the cause? Still, despite the appearance that confirmation claims are causal claims, classical positivist theories of confirmation take the really instructive cases to involve no reference to causes. Confirming an empirical generalization such as "All ravens are black" is regarded as a typical instructive example, and is supposed to depend on nothing more than formal relations between the hypothesis and statements of the data. Thus, in Hempel's account, "All ravens are black" is confirmed by instances of ravenhood and blackness and is confirmed just in virtue of the fact that they are instances. An assessment of the idea that confirmation is causal might fairly begin with an examination of these favorite cases of the other side.

On the causal account, the observation of a black raven does not confirm the generalization (or even provide evidence for it) simply because that datum has the logical form, observation of an instance. Rather, in a fair assessment based on current frameworks, there must be a case for tracing this observation to the fact that the raven species is all black. More precisely, an explanation of the observation in which this species characteristic plays a causal role must be superior to all explanations in which a contrary view of the species is involved. Presumably, the governing framework includes the principle that ravens are, indeed, a species, or, in any case, a natural kind, and, hence, that ravens share causal properties governing many of the traits that our familiar property terms describe. Without requiring some such background principle, we could not admit black raven sightings as confirming "All ravens are black" without also taking them to confirm "Whatever is a raven or a goat is black," a generalization of which blackness in a raven is also an instance. Yet the latter inference seems silly, and would be silly even if goats were very rare. Given our reliance on causal reasoning, it will, strictly speaking, take more than one sighting to provide evidence that all ravens are black, since otherwise the black sighting might just as well be a product of the extreme variability of raven color, or the existence of black as one of several raven colors. Also, it will be essential that hypotheses attributing repeated observations of blackness to the nature of the observation process be inferior to those attributing data to the blackness of the species. In other words, the causal characterization, that the sightings resulted from fair sampling, is crucial as well. Another implication of the causal account is that occasional variations, albinism, for example, would always be admitted, since the fixing of a characteristic in a species is, at most, highly typical, according to relevant framework principles. All of this counts in favor of the causal approach, since it fits the inferential practice of any reasonably shrewd zoologist.

One sign that evidential support does not, in fact, exist when only a formal connection links hypothesis and data is a certain general constraint on the use of data. In general, we are not in a position to use an observed uniformity to support a general hypothesis unless we are in a position to claim that the uniformity is "no accident." And this is a causal claim, that there are causal factors which connect the correlated properties and prevent departures from the correlation. Thus, we would not dream of taking the observations that raven number one weighed 20.1334 grams, raven number two weighed 21.5412 grams, and raven number three weighed 20.1111 grams as confirming the generalization "All ravens weigh either 20.1334 grams or 21.5412 grams or 20.1111 grams." Yet the logical form of the hypothesis is familiar from good science, for example, from descriptions of isotopes of an element. Nor do we suppose that the degree of rational confidence in the three-weights generalization is raised by these sightings, unless we are in the grip of some philosophical theory. The sightings had to instantiate *some* disjunction of this form. It was an accident that they instantiated this one, we suppose. Thus, our degree of credence is not raised.

It is important to distinguish the mere existence of an observed positive instance, which is supposed to confirm but doesn't in this case, from other facts about the observing, that might indeed confirm, but on account of causal connections rather than formal ones. For example, the fact that the observation bore out a hypothesis previously developed in a certain way might be confirming. Suppose someone who knew nothing about how raven observations would subsequently be conducted proposed the three-weights hypothesis, and then ravens were captured, by people with no commitment to the hypothesis, and found to have the three weights. This might be taken to support the hypothesis, since it is hard to explain the hypothesizer's success except as due to insight into ravenhood. That causal relations, not the positive-instance relation, are confirming, here, is shown by a contrasting case. The three weights might first be taken, and someone discovering the record of the weighings might, after the fact, frame the three-weights hypothesis to fit it. It would be absurd to suppose that the hypothesis is confirmed, since the fit can obviously be explained by the guile of the hypothesizer, not the nature of the species. Yet, if only logical form is relevant, confirmation would be just as strong.

Just as the accidental fit of weights with the three-weights hypothesis does not support the latter, color sightings would not support a hypothesis about the color of ravens in general if the distribution of colors in the sightings were taken to be an accident, as against a product of the nature of the species. Of course, we might be rationally committed to the latter connection, between observed color and species nature, when we know very little about what gives a species its nature and how that nature constrains the features of individuals. To take a closely analogous situation, people are quite capable of resolving paternity suits without any knowledge of DNA. The explanation of the sightings that vindicates the color hypothesis must be better than its rivals. It need not be complete.

The view that confirmation is a relation of logical form cannot be helped by noting that "weighs either 20.1334 grams or 21.5412 grams or 20.1111 grams" is a complex bit of language, and declaring that such complexities do not denote real properties, in alleged contrast to "is black." A simpler predicate, "Is threight," can be defined in terms of the three-weights hypothesis, while "is black" necessarily refers to the same property as "is yellow if the Hamilton-Cayley Theorem is false, is brown if the third term in the expansion of pi is nine, otherwise is black." Judgments as to what is a simple, or is "a single real" property sometimes are relevant to the assessment of evidence. But on the face of it, these judgments reflect beliefs about the world that linguistic or logical reflection do not provide. Being jade is not a simple or a single real property, at least not unambiguously so, since jade mines turn out to yield two very different, though similar looking, minerals, jadeite and nephrite. So the weighing of water displaced by a bit of jade is a bad basis for confirming the claim that all jade has the corresponding specific gravity. No one would take the relevant assessment of simplicity to be a discovery of logical analysis.

It would be rash to justify the three-weights hypothesis on the basis of the three-weights data. Much of the literature on confirmation turns on even more serious charges than recklessness, though, namely, charges that standard formalist rules for confirmation produce "paradoxes" or outright contradictions. These difficulties are another sign that experimental reasoning might be causal reasoning, since they are best diagnosed as a consequence of neglecting the causal dimension.

After developing his instantial account of how empirical generalizations are confirmed, Hempel described one such apparent paradox, which he then tried to expose as apparent only. It results when we combine the idea of instantial confirmation with a further, truistic premise: what confirms a proposition in one formulation confirms it in all other logically equivalent formulations. That a pencil is red is an instance of "All non-ravens are non-black." So the

observation of a red pencil ought to confirm the equivalent generalization "All ravens are black."[14]

Many formalist accounts try to dissipate the air of paradox, by
making explicit background assumptions which would lead any reasonable person to take the *degree* of confirmation to be small to the
point of insignificance in the case of a red pencil, significant in the
case of a black raven. In assessing the relation of red pencils to the
hypothesis we rely on the background assumption that the class of
non-black things in indefinitely large, while the class of ravens is
minute, by comparison. If we are told that something is not black,
we know already, on the basis of our assumption, that the odds are
indefinitely small that it will turn out to be a raven. On the other
hand, if we are told that something is a raven, we cannot, reasoning
from our background assumption, dismiss as almost negligible the
odds that it is non-black. It seems paradoxical that "a is a non-black
non-raven" and "a is a raven and black" should be on par as confirming "All ravens are black" since, on the basis of our background
assumptions, they represent the overcoming of risks of enormously
different size, the former almost infinitesimal. In effect, the feeling
of paradox results from our confusing the question of whether confirmation exists at all with the question of whether any significant
degree of confirmation exists, then resolving the latter question in
light of background beliefs.[15]

The appeal to numerical differences as explaining the feeling of
paradox cannot be the whole or the basic story. When we compare
"All mammals lack titanium" with its equivalent "Whatever contains
titanium is not a mammal," we may not be inclined to suppose that
the class of things containing titanium is indefinitely large, compared with the class of mammals. Yet it seems paradoxical to claim
that "This is titanium-containing and an ant" is a confirming instance of "All mammals lack titanium," on a par with "This is a mammal and lacks titanium." Indeed, the air of paradox is the same as
the one surrounding the original ravens example.

Of course, it is only relative to some assumed universe of discourse that "contains titanium" very rarely applies. If there are indefinitely many molecules and every distinct collection of molecules
is a different item in the universe of discourse, then indefinitely
many things contain titanium. But, in fact, generalizations are
understood in relation to some universe of discourse, or some vague

[14] See Hempel, "Studies in the Logic of Confirmation," p. 15.
[15] See ibid., pp. 19f.

cluster of universes. Animals on earth or earthly things of kinds with ordinary names are apt to be the relevant universes, in the case at hand. This is both the usual understanding of generalizations, and the one imposed in the semantics of Hempel's most technical expositions of his theory.[16] What is more important, Hempelian "paradoxes" do emerge, and demand resolution, when restrictions to a universe of discourse are understood. The conclusion that observing a red pencil confirms "All ravens are black" is implied by the logical-instance account and is paradoxical, when the universe of discourse is restricted to ordinary kinds of material things, so that there is no need to worry about confirmation of "All ravens are black" by the existence of non-black members.

If confirmation requires causal superiority, the natural judgment of the red pencil datum is easy to explain, without implausible charges that it rests on a confusion. We have no reason to believe that the best causal account of why a red pencil was observed will refer to a causal factor making it true that all ravens are black. In science fiction worlds, this might not be so. We might know that everything is colored by The Master Painter, that only birds and pencils exist, and that he wants some kinds of things to be red, others black. Then, the observation of a red pencil is best accounted for in a way that supports the blackness of all ravens. But in this world, the observation of a red pencil *would* be evidence that all ravens are black.

Goodman's "new riddle of induction" is an even more serious burden for standard rules of confirmation, since it shows that those rules would always endorse hypotheses differing about all unobserved instances. If confirmation consists of instantiation, the observations of green emeralds that have confirmed "All emeralds are green" equally confirm the contrary hypothesis "All emeralds are grue," where grue is the property of being green if observed up until now, blue if observed hereafter.

Goodman's own response is to supplement classical positivist rules of confirmation with an additional principle referring to actual language use. "Like Hume, we are appealing here to past recurrences, but to recurrences in the explicit use of terms as well as to recurrent features of what is observed."[17] In Goodman's evocative terminol-

---

[16] See, for example, "A Purely Syntactic Definition of Confirmation," *Journal of Symbolic Logic* (1943). The point is somewhat obscured by Hempel's broad and idiosyncratic notion of the logical type of a variable. See "Studies in the Logic of Confirmation," p. 18.

[17] *Fact, Fiction and Forecast* (1954; Cambridge, Mass., 1983), p. 96.

ogy, a hypothesis is only projectible on the basis of the data so far, if there is no conflicting hypothesis fitting the data as well, with predicates that are better entrenched on the basis of actual projections so far. In somewhat more detail (the details are many, but not all are important here): a predicate is entrenched to the extent that it, or a coextensive predicate, has actually been used in general hypotheses accepted on the basis of observed positive instances, general hypotheses of which no negative instances have as yet been observed. A hypothesis is projectible, i.e., may be extrapolated from positive instances, if there is no hypothesis better entrenched in its predicates, fitting the data just as well, but conflicting in what it says about as yet unobserved cases. So "All emeralds are grue" is not projectible, since it is defeated by the existence of the better-entrenched term in the conflicting hypothesis "All emeralds are green."

Goodman's proposal is a definite break from positivism, even in the broad sense of the term. General rules describing when data confirm now refer to the actual history of science, not just the content of the hypothesis and the data. Indeed, Goodman's theory of projectibility was the first systematic effort to show that positivism failed through a neglect of the relevance of actual scientific practice. Yet the way in which the history of science is relevant is quite narrow. It simply produces certain kinds of favoritism in the vocabulary for hypotheses, the favorites varying from time to time. Applying Goodman's general rules concerning entrenchment one can, at any given point in time, construct a ranked word list with ranks reflecting relative entrenchment. Given the ranked word list and general rules of confirmation, one could, for the moment, behave just like a positivist, applying the rules to the content of hypotheses and observations to tell what is confirmed. Here, the role of background knowledge—namely, the extraction of ranked word lists from the record of past projections—is extremely narrow, compared with the theory of confirmation as causal comparison, where causal accounts are assessed in light of the fair use of complex and substantive frameworks.[18]

If confirmation is fair causal comparison, it also follows that "All emeralds are grue" is not confirmed. Either there have or there have not been huge numbers of blue emeralds in the ground up un-

---

[18] Admittedly, Goodmanesque investigators also have to determine whether a predicate is coextensive with an entrenched one. But such judgments are, presumably, justified in light of positivist rules and other rankings of other past projections. In any case, the admission of the judgments of coextensiveness would still be a specific and narrow admission of the relevance of background belief.

til now, so many that they and they alone will be dug up subsequently. If there have been, then it is unexplained, but in urgent need of explanation, why we have only dug up green ones. If there haven't been, and yet all emeralds are grue, then vast numbers of emeralds now in the ground have now changed to blue or have acquired a disposition to change to blue before observation. And these causal changes are at least as miraculous as the previous alternative, our missing the pervasive blue emeralds. There is no causal mechanism in our repertoire remotely capable of creating the needed color switch. Moreover, because of the nature of grue we could not possibly have evidence forcing a switch to a framework more receptive to grue, before the surprising observations of blueness actually occur. This explains why taking the grue hypothesis seriously is not just bad science, but wholly unmotivated bad science.

If this is how projection of grue is excluded, mightn't Goodman's conventionalism simply be transferred from assessments of hypotheses to assessments of frameworks? In the framework we use in confirming hypotheses, we are prejudiced toward color constancy. If something changes color, a cause must intervene (painting, say, or ripening) to produce the change. If the change is definite and dramatic, the cause of change, we assume, is definite and dramatic. So coordinated color changes among vast numbers of independent rocks would require a vast number of coordinated interventions, a coincidence of a kind that should not be posited without good and specific reasons. By contrast, we do not suppose that color constancy requires continual interventions. That observed emeralds are not at present changing from green does not require pervasive, coordinated interventions. This prejudice toward color constancy might seem to be mere prejudice. One can define a "spectrum" of "crulers," standing to colors as grue stands to green. Bleen, for example, would be the property of being blue if observed up through now, green if observed hereafter. Color constancy, then, is cruler change. The emerald that is not now about to change color is about to change from grue to bleen. Does anything except custom and principles giving priority to the customary count against a preference for cruler constancy, i.e., a demand that cruler change be ascribed to an intervention? The latter prejudice, would, of course, sustain a argument that grueness is the best explanation of emerald observations so far.

In fact, someone who has the prejudice for cruler constancy (or better, verbal dispositions corresponding to those prejudices) does not have the concept of something's possessing a color. So he is not advancing the cruler hypotheses Goodman has in mind, hypotheses conflicting with standard color hypotheses. For him to be making a contrary statement to ours, about things he and we have observed, he must share enough of our framework for his projection to be ruled out as depending on an inferior account of the data.

Suppose someone had the relevant prejudice toward cruler constancy. Then it would be normal for him to exclaim in surprise, when the grue-defining time has just passed and the emerald stays green, "What a shock. Something has happened to change what I am observing." The surprise would not be based on belief that the stone was primed to change from green to blue by a specific process, a peculiar sort of ripening, say, that something has overridden. Even in the absence of any special belief about the thing he is looking at, he would think that the absence of a dramatic change in its color stands in need of an explanation.

This person does not have the concept of something's having the color, green (and, hence, does not form the hypothesis about grue that Goodman has in mind). If something's continuing to look green is a sign of a change in its state, then its looking green is not a sign of a state it is actually in. When the grue-defining time is reached, the person who is supposed to have a prejudice toward cruler constancy takes something's continuing to look green to be a sign of something's changing its state; for him, continuing to look green is in itself a sign of change, even in entirely normal causal circumstances. Someone who does not take looking green to be, in itself and in normal circumstances, a sign of something's actual state, does not have the concept of something's being green. A general connection between how something seems and what it is has been broken, a connection involved in all ascriptions of properties to objects. So this particular barrier to justified grue projection provides, as Goodman's riddle requires, analogous objections to the infinity of analogous attempts to project.[19]

[19] That we do not take cruler change to be a sign of change of state may show that we lack the concept of something's having a cruler. This is no surprise, since most readers of Goodman's riddle have always wondered whether grue is a real property. The lack of the concept is not a defect in us, if, as the previous discussion suggests, having a concept requires reasoning in certain ways. We would be defective (i.e., in our reasonings from experience) if we had the concept of something's being grue.

In emphasizing the bad fit between the requirements for having the concept of grue and the background principles necessary for projecting it, I am indebted to Sydney Shoemaker's "On Projecting the Unprojectible" (1975) in his *Identity, Cause and Mind* (Cambridge, 1984). Because of an ambiguity in Goodman's original riddle, he relies on a somewhat different definition of "grue," and, partly for that reason, em-

Another, complimentary reason for excluding the deviant frameworks is suggested by the core conception of causality. That conception suggests that having the concept of a cause requires making certain standard judgments in simple cases. Someone with the prejudice toward cruler constancy sometimes takes an emerald's staying green to require an intervening cause, even though no causally special background circumstances exist. He also takes a change from green to blue to occur without any underlying causal processes. Such a person, the core conception suggests, lacks the concept of a cause. Or, in any case, he fails to grasp causation where color is concerned. So, if confirmation is causal comparison, he lacks the means to confirm a hypothesis. Putting the problems about property possession in the previous paragraph to one side, he may have the capacity to frame general statements about correlations. So one might not perceive his incapacity, if one accepted a covering-law analysis of causation. But anyone who takes Goodman's riddle seriously has reason not to analyze causation in this way. Given the liberal use of predicates that produces the grue hypothesis, anything would be connected to anything else by a well-instantiated covering-law.

So far, the theory that confirmation is causal comparison has turned out to account for the absurdity of grue projection, without appealing, directly or indirectly, to the priority of the entrenched. If, in addition, this answer to Goodman's riddle is superior to his own, the riddle strongly supports the model of causal comparison. And something is wrong with Goodman's answer. In light of rational scientific practice, his emphasis on which projection comes first is too restrictive.

Goodman acknowledges that his emphasis on what actually was projected, not on what could have been, will strike many people as making valid inference depend too much on brute facts about who did what first. In his view, their feelings are based on misplaced philosophical hopes for justifications and guarantees, hopes which Hume combatted when he dissolved his old riddle of induction. Using the extremely artificial examples dominating the literature on "grue," it is hard to challenge Goodman's diagnosis. It does seem strange to suppose that if projection using "grue," "crulers," "emeroses" and other such strange growths had been entrenched, it would be legitimate. But the feeling of strangeness could simply be

---

phasizes somewhat different constraints on meaningful use. Though different, the constraints are analogous to the ones I have proposed.

our reaction to the strangeness of the world history we are asked to imagine.

However, our judgments of the validity of empirical arguments in the actual history of science are usually more secure than a philosophical inclination to accept or to reject Goodman's sort of reliance on bare contingency. And there, it frequently has happened that the less entrenched of two contrary hypotheses has been as reasonable an inference from the data. Frequently, a field has been dominated for decades by two rival frameworks, supporting contrary projections, one of which started before the other. During the period of coexistence, neither outlook can be vindicated by fair argument, and an appeal to the greater entrenchment of the hypothesis that came first is clearly an irrelevancy, to which the shrewd and resourceful arguers in these controversies did not resort. (Perhaps the greatest harm that Whiggish history of science does to philosophy is to expunge the eventual loser from the record, so that rational practice in these contexts is forgotten or restricted to abnormal periods, of scientific revolution.)

Thus, from the scientific revolution of the seventeenth century through the beginning of this century, virtually every physical science was contested in a rivalry between the physics of continuity and the physics of interaction between wholly discontinuous matter.[20] If special massless substances were the burden of the first approach, violations of deep-seated constraints on physical reasoning afflicted the second. Classical electrodynamics is a good example. From the standpoint of continuity, electromagnetic causes produced their effects by inducing stresses in a pervasive, massless substance, the ether. This was the basic standpoint of Maxwell and Faraday. From the standpoint of discontinuity and action at a distance, electrodynamic causes produced remote effects without the need for any intermediate changes. This was the basic outlook for Coulomb, Gauss, Weber and C. F. Neumann, partly shared by Helmholtz. By the middle of the nineteenth century, both frameworks had to take into account phenomena of apparent delayed response. An electrodynamic change at one point, say, a movement of a charge, can cause a change, say, a movement of another charge, at a remove in space *and* time, with the time delay governed by a constant, the speed of light; and often there seems to be no intermediate change as a part

[20] See Enrico Bellone, *A World on Paper* (Cambridge, Mass., 1980), for extensive and detailed illustrations of the persistence of this rivalry, with creative and eminent scientists always aligned on both sides.

of the process. For Maxwell, this appearance of discontinuity was unreal. The first change causes the remote one by creating stress in the ether, propagated in a continuous series of fluctuations finally reaching the second charge. It was a troubling explanatory loose end that independent evidence for the existence of the ether could not be found, especially since phenomena of resistance and refraction suggested that massy matter and ether could interact. For Gauss and most German-speaking physicists, the discontinuity was real. The laws of nature dictate that certain changes act not just at a distance, but with a time delay, even across a literal vacuum. And (though Whiggish histories obscure it), this approach carried its own burden of anomaly. It had been a basic and successful principle of reasoning about physical causes, at least since the time of Galileo, that an inanimate object does not act as if it had a memory, being directly influenced by events that ceased a finite interval before. Thus, all of Galileo's most interesting inferences from inclined-plane phenomena depend on the assumption that motion of the ball, when it leaves the inclined plane, is determined by its state as it leaves the incline, and not, in addition, by its state when it was on top.[21] In the delayed-action account, pairs of charges do have memories. Though obscured by Whiggish histories, this cost of dispensing with the ether should not be surprising. If there was no such cost then Maxwell, perhaps the most creative scientist of his century, was continually the victim of thoughtless metaphysical prejudice.[22]

On a neutral reading of them, Maxwell's equations could be included in both outlooks. They were confirmed by the data. But the two outlooks also produced contrary hypotheses. In an ether theory, a certain kind of motion of a charge produced a certain kind of stress in the ether, at a remove in space and time. There is also a consequent motion in any charge that happens to be there. But even without the latter charge, there is still stress. As an unobserved phenomenon, this ether stress is like future blueness in "grue." In a delayed action theory, the same kind of antecedent creates the same kind of consequent motion in a second charge, but nothing happens at that point and time if the charge isn't there. Since there was no way of resolving the underlying controversy which was fair to both

[21] See, for example, Galileo, *Two New Sciences*, tr. S. Drake (Madison, Wis., 1974), pp. 197–99.

[22] See Maxwell, *A Treatise on Electricity and Magnetism* (New York, 1954), pt. 3, ch. 23; and Kelvin's Preface and Hertz' Introduction (Theoretical) in Hertz, *Electric Waves* (London, 1900).

frameworks, until the dawning of special relativity, neither hypothesis is unreasonable but neither is confirmed by the data.

This is surely the natural assessment of how far confirmation extended in the era of classical electrodynamics, and the one most in accord with the judgments of the best scientists of the time.[23] It is also the outcome of fair causal comparison. No decisive explanation of current data could be vindicated in an argument that was fair to all relevant rival frameworks. And this situation is by no means unique to electrodynamics. In "classical" thermodynamics, which was a physics of continuity, the law of how systems wind down dictated that all motion cease in a closed system in the long run. In molecular-kinetic thermodynamics, what ceases is only structured motion. Where the outlooks supported the same laws, they were confirmed by nineteenth-century observations. Where they conflicted, confirmation and disconfirmation had to wait until studies of Brownian motion and allied phenomena at the start of the twentieth century.

Presumably, someone in one perspective started projecting before anyone in the other. But it seems utterly arbitrary and irrelevant to claim that the relative late-comers were always trying to project the unprojectible, in each case. We might have to say, for example, that all the distinctive ether hypotheses conflicting with delayed-action hypotheses were non-confirmed, simply because delayed-action theory had started up some years before. And having said so, we might be forced to switch to the diametrical opposite by the discovery of some old notebooks in an attic in Manchester, a week from now. Even worse, fairly well-known facts about the history of science would force us to reverse basic judgments of what has been rational in science, if entrenchment is decisive. Newton is known to have thought that universal gravitation could not be true action at a distance, but must operate through an intervening medium.[24] He was the first projector of universal gravitation, and data contrary to his universal law of gravitation were not developed until the triumph of general relativity. So we would have to say that the only gravitational hypotheses that ever were confirmed were descriptions of how forces are propagated through a universal medium. (In general relativity, universal gravitation, on any pre-twen-

---

[23] See Hertz, *Electric Waves*, pp. 24–28.

[24] See the excerpts from Newton's letters in Cajori's notes to the *Principia*, pp. 632–36, 674f.

tieth-century interpretation, is a pseudo-force, like "centrifugal force" in the *Principia*.)

It might seem that Goodman's solution works, in any case, for hypotheses like the ones about green and about grue, that are compounded from observational predicates and are vastly different in entrenchment. But the solution was that a less entrenched rival is not projectible, and this solution ought to work wherever scientists go beyond the data and can rely on a past history of efforts to go beyond the data. In determining whether entrenchment counts as such, we ought to give decisive weight to secure judgments of realistic cases. It should not be surprising if realistic cases of conflicting projections, realistic enough to command some secure assessment, are derived from theoretical enterprises. That is where difficulties of explanation actually lead to the development of alternative concepts, characteristic of different approaches. In any case, the rival hypotheses are sometimes compounded out of observational predicates. This is true, for example, of the different laws of entropy to be found in the two versions of thermodynamics. Admittedly, the laws refer to closed systems, and to tendencies over the indefinitely long run. But if such non-observational hedges put a hypothesis beyond the scope of Goodman's rule, it would have nothing to do with hypotheses in science.

The causal solutions to Hempel's "paradox" and Goodman's riddle help to make it clear why confirmation by positive instances is such an attractive principle, even though it leads to bad instances and contradictory conclusions when taken too seriously. The proposal that generalizations are confirmed by observing positive instances has a grain of truth. That what is F is, at least typically, G is confirmed by a body of data containing observations of positive instances, and no counter-instances, provided the observations have the following features:

1. Their providing instances and no counter-instances results from the nature of F's; e.g., it is not merely a result of the way the data were collected, and the hypothesis formed.

2. The observations are relevantly diverse. No amount of raven observation confined to a single forest confirms that all ravens are black.

3. F and G are properties that we would be inclined to group with ravenhood, green and black as "real" properties, as against such "made up" properties as being-a-raven-or-a-goat, weighing either 20.1134 grams of 21.5412 grams or 20.111 grams, or grue.

When we consider the proposal that observing positive instances confirms, we are apt to think of observations that any sensible investigator would make. Those observations have these three characteristics. So it seems that observing positive instances does, in itself, establish the approximate truth of a generalization. But, in fact, the positive instance relation is not, in itself, confirming. The three hedges are important, and, when properly understood, they make confirmation by observing positive instances a special case of confirmation by causal comparison.

That the fit of data to hypothesis must not be a mere artifact of the history of data-gathering and hypothesis-forming is, on the face of it, a causal constraint. But so is the requirement of diversity, when relevant diversity is properly understood. Indeed, when the demand for diversity is properly understood it coincides with the first demand. To confirm that ravens are typically black we need raven data from many different areas. But we needn't have data from many different decades (even if the raven hypothesis is "tenseless") or from observations made by observers wearing many different kinds of shirts. The observations are relevantly diverse just in case it is hard to explain positive observations in the different kinds of circumstances except by appealing to ravenhood's typical tendency to produce blackness.

It might seem, however, that these causal constraints just describe one convenient way to reach the point at which it is reasonable to take the typical truth of a generalization to be more likely than its basic falsehood. Alternatively, in the absence of all causal beliefs, one could confirm by acquiring enough positive instances. The causal constraints describe shortcuts, in which the process of confirmation is shortened by applying background principles that have already been confirmed. Hempel responded to the paradox of the raven in an analogous way.

This defense of the positive-instance rule is only attractive so long as the familiar, "real" properties, not the made-up properties are considered. No amount of observation of instances of hypotheses using the hypotheses in the "grue" camp, as against the "green" camp, would confirm. And, as Sydney Shoemaker has emphasized, our relevant judgments that properties are real are themselves causal judgments.[25] To take something to be a real property is to take it to be a basis for the causal powers of anything that has it. Crulers are not real properties because the change from grue to bleen

---

[25] See "Causality and Properties" in *Identity, Cause and Mind*.

is not a change in causal powers. Being a raven or a goat is not a real, as against a made up property, because being a raven or a goat adds nothing to the causal powers of a raven (or a goat). The real properties of things are the causal factors drawn from our basic repertoire of the factors in things determining how they contribute causally to systems of which they are a part. Thus, there is never confirmation by positive instances except against a background of causal beliefs. Having accepted this, one might as well accept all three conditions for projection. It was never plausible to begin with that enough black raven sightings, no matter how similar, would confirm that ravens are typically black. People imagine that this could happen because they assume that confirmation must be possible in the absence of causal beliefs, when mere empirical regularities are involved. But this is an impossibility.

When the provisos for confirming by instances are rightly understood, such confirmation is a special case of a causal comparison. One produces a situation in which the fact that an unbiased process of observing F's led to the observations of F's that were G's in these circumstances is best explained in causal accounts in which being an F tends to make something G. The positivist canon of method turns out to be one standard rule of thumb for fulfilling a causal principle. That was a moral of the prior discussion of the covering-law model, which turned out to derive its plausibility from implicit constraints, causal when made explicit, on the relevant generalizations and probabilities. The same moral, that the causal theory explains the grain of truth in the positivist rule, will be a refrain in subsequent investigations of positivist accounts of confirmation.

So far, I have been trying to establish a causal dimension in the very simple cases favored by non-causal theories, the confirmation of an empirical generalization in light of an observed instance. When we consider real science in its full complexity, the idea that a confirmed hypothesis is part of a superior causal account is supported in a different way. This idea provides a rationale for standard kinds of criticisms of efforts to confirm. And often no equally satisfying rationale is available, if confirmation is not treated as fair causal comparison.

In general, we only take a finding to give empirical support to a hypothesis if we take the hypothesis to be made true by the process producing the data. All charges made against evidence offered are, in effect, applications of this principle. For example, the charge that evidence is unreliable means that it is the product of a process or processes which would produce it even if the hypothesis were false.

Thus, everyone takes the charge that IQ tests are culturally biased as challenging the use of IQ findings to distinguish between the average intelligence of the groups in question. This is because the test results would then be the product of knowledge, skills, attitudes and character traits unrelated to intelligence. So IQ differences would be the product of factors that would exist anyway, even if average intelligence were the same from group to group. Here, and elsewhere, there is no formalist rule that explicates the criticism in terms that do justice to the actual debate. It is not enough to say that IQ variations are not in general well-correlated with variations in intelligence. If culture is uniform enough, there can be a good correlation, even if the tests are biased against a minority outside the majority culture.[26] In any case, culture-bias criticism is available to those who doubt that intelligence is a magnitude to begin with, susceptible to correlation. Of course, a positivist, like anyone else, can deny that groups with different average IQs do differ in intelligence. But this is supposed to be the outcome of the criticism of IQ tests, and standard good criticisms cannot be explicated by positivist means.

Another extremely important kind of criticism of claims to confirm ascribes the good fit of hypothesis and data to the ad hoc tailoring of a hypothesis that would otherwise be disconfirmed. No one is impressed when a hypothesis is cooked up by taking each of the multiple major defeats of an outmoded hypothesis to be in some category of unexplained special cases. And our worries about ad hoc adjustments are a natural outcome of the requirement of causal superiority. In effect, the hypothesis has been recommended to us on the ground that the best account of the fit between data and hypothesis entails the approximate truth of the hypothesis. But we learn, say, that the investigators had entertained a different hypothesis, then adjusted it to fit when the data were discovered. Now we have an alternative account. The fit is due to the ingenuity of the investigators in tailoring the hypothesis to the findings, after the fact. This ingenuity in the investigators implies nothing about the pres-

[26] One might claim that the only relevant correlations are within test situations, in Cartwright's sense. But these may be non-existent or, in any case, too uncommon to yield statistically significant results. There simply is no set of black and white children in the United States whose lives have not been differentiated, in many ways, as a result of racism. To declare that inferences from IQ to group differences in intelligence are invalid just for that reason is to endorse an implausibly exclusive reliance on rigidly circumscribed statistical inference—albeit in a good cause. Moreover, the identification of test situations turned out itself to depend on prior causal knowledge.

ence of the alleged regularity in the world. They would be just as successfully ingenious if the regularity did not exist except in the cases observed.

If the perils of ad hoc tailoring are understood in this way, the history of how hypothesis and data arose and interacted can be relevant to whether the data confirm. To the contrary, deductivism operates in a timeless perspective, in which facts about the origins of hypothesis and data are invisible. Thus, Hempel claims that Balmer's hypothesis about lines in the hydrogen spectrum would have been as strongly confirmed if it had simply been tailored to previously observed lines, not borne out by subsequent new findings. "[F]rom a logical point of view, the strength of the support that a hypothesis receives from a given body of data should depend only on what the hypothesis asserts and what the data are: the question of whether the hypothesis or the data were presented first, being a purely historical matter, should not count as affecting the confirmation of the hypothesis."[27] But surely Balmer's general equation for hydrogen is more strongly supported by the actual events, in which it led to the discovery of new lines, than it would have been if it never did anything more than summarize numbers of which Balmer was aware. Ingenuity in tailoring theory to given facts does not give one the power to tailor future observations to the new theory. The new spectral lines reduced the force of the objection, "Clever people can often find neat numerical patterns in the current data, quite apart from any general tendency in the mechanisms producing the data."

Finally, that comparison is causal reasoning is implied by two general features of science as a whole. In the first place, a certain grain of truth in seventeenth-century empiricism has survived centuries of criticism: science is ultimately based on sense experience. Even extreme relativists accept this as a roughly accurate characterization of the framework that scientists actually employ. It is not clear, though, in just what way sense experience is basic. Logically speaking, reports of sense experiences are not especially well-suited to serve as premises for arguments with scientific hypotheses as conclusions. In particular, their tenuous relation to theoretical claims (what sights, sounds and colors are specially related to gravitational metrics?) make them *ill*-suited to serve as premises in deductions supporting theoretical conclusions. Nor is our belief in relevant propositions about sense experience especially high. A typical sci-

[27] *Philosophy of Natural Science* (Engelwood Cliffs, N.J., 1964), p. 38.

entist is much more reluctant to give up the belief that the sun is approximately 93 million miles from the earth than he is to suppose that a sense experience has been misdescribed or misremembered or that it is not veridical. Yet nearly all of use believe that sense experience is in some way basic to science. In the present account of confirmation we can explain how it is. It is causally basic. The ultimate justification of scientific hypotheses is their role in the best account of the causes of the overall pattern of our sense experiences. What Newton said was justified by its role in explaining what Tycho Brahe saw.

More specifically, our means of resolving the deepest controversies about the nature of reality is the rating of explanations of sensory appearances and what they reveal against the background of truisms about such appearances and the corresponding realities. Many of the truisms that people share even in the face of radical differences in belief concern features which sight, touch, hearing and smell reveal, e.g., "Some objects are bigger than others," and the causal relations of these features to sensory appearances, e.g., "The apparent shape of a middle-sized object seen close-up in moderate sunlight usually is a product of its similar real shape." If we can rationally resolve the most fundamental scientific disputes that arise, on the order of disputes in seventeenth-century science, we do so by taking advantage of the fact that disputants often agree, in part, in how the world appears to their senses. We accumulate such areas of agreement and interpret them employing shared truisms about the causal relation between sensory appearances and sensible reality. In short, it is a fact about our interactions with each other and our environment that our deepest scientific controversies are fairly resolved through arguments relying on shared principles concerning the causes of sense experience. This is how science is based on sense experience. Suppose, on the other hand, that spontaneous inescapable conviction, on sufficient reflection, that a proposition is true were always a result of its truth; that, as a consequence, what is self-evidence on sufficient reflection to one person would be to all; and that such propositions were an adequate foundation for theoretical science. Suppose, in short, that Descartes were right. Then the crucial levers for fair argument would not attribute causes to sense experience, but to episodes of reflection and irresistible conviction. From this perspective, the controversy between empiricism and rationalism is a dispute over the principles of the causes of human experiences and attitudes, principles which, once settled, provide a framework for scientific reasoning. And that is just what Descartes and Locke thought they were discussing.

Also, the causal account is implied by the fact that science sometimes yields *knowledge* of features of the world. For knowledge of contingent truths does depend on appropriate causal relations between facts and data. As Goldman points out toward the beginning of "A Causal Theory of Knowledge," someone who sees lava on a field does not know a volcano was once nearby if that lava was put there by a fanciful landscape architect. He does not know a volcano was once there even if his inference is geologically wise and a volcano was there. The process producing the data must include the existence of a nearby volcano.[28] Except when we are under the spell of a philosophical theory, we do take science sometimes to produce knowledge, though perhaps only knowledge of approximate truths. The causal account of confirmation permits us to maintain this judgment. The confirmation which scientists achieve, when successful, consists in the possession of data best accounted for as a result of processes including the fact to be explained. Thus, successful hypothesis and confirming data have the causal relation that knowledge requires.

## THE BEST CAUSAL ACCOUNT

How should causal accounts be rated, to see whether a hypothesis is part of the best account of the data? Positivism supplies answers to this question, whether in old-style deductivism or newfangled Bayesianism. I will consider these approaches in detail, in the next three chapters. But already, in light of the discussion of explanation, the positivist ways of rating causal accounts are not very promising. If explanations are not distinctive kinds of deductions or probabilistic derivations, it seems unlikely that choice among them will be governed by general, a priori rules concerning entailment or probabilities.

There is one other current general answer to the question of how to rate rival causal accounts. It is contained, above all, in Kuhn's least relativist writings.[29] In this proposal, explanations are to be rated according to a diverse catalog of virtues: good fit with the data, depth, fruitfulness, congruence with received general theories and (per-

---

[28] "A Causal Theory of Knowing," pp. 72f.

[29] For example, "Objectivity, Value Judgment and Theory Choice" in *The Essential Tension* (Chicago, 1977). See also Bas van Fraassen, *The Scientific Image* (Oxford, 1980), pp. 87–89.

haps) simplicity. All such lists are roughly similar and seem roughly right. They are useful warnings against the one-sidedness of formalist approaches, which tend to devalue depth and fruitfulness at the expense of good fit to the data. At the same time, all of these lists of diverse explanatory virtues are deeply disappointing.

The problem is that every important choice of a scientific hypothesis requires a trade-off between a loss of virtue on some dimensions and a gain on others. No one has proposed a remotely satisfactory general rule for judging such trade-offs. And yet there are cases—all the most interesting ones—in which a choice requiring a trade-off has become the right one to make. Thus, a hypothesis that is relatively fruitful and deep is bound to fit the data less precisely than a rival whose only goal is to summarize current data. The ambitious alternative will have implications for many subject-matters, including some relatively deep factors which are relatively hard to identify. On account of the uneven development of science, the auxiliary principles used to study some of these many fields are bound to be wrong, in part, and to lead to false implications. Ambition produces empirical inaccuracies—even if the ambitious hypothesis is true. The dismissal of an ambitious hypothesis as too speculative because of such anomalies is not always and in principle misguided. Yet it would be misguided in many cases.

As an example of a choice that was right when a trade-off was required, consider the acceptance of Newtonian mechanics, even after Laplace had removed anomalies in Newton's accounts of the moon, the tides and sound, Leverrier and Galle had used Newtonian mechanics to discover Uranus, and Bessel had observed stellar parallax. Surely, at this point, it was reasonable to accept the three laws of motion and the universal law of gravitation. Once acceptance is distinguished from literal belief, even tough antirealists would concede that acceptance had become the reasonable choice. Yet there were still dissenters, certain devout anti-Copernican scientists, for example, who only accepted summaries of the phenomena of motion, such as the latest table of (geocentric) astronomical observations, the latest tidal tables, and artillery engineers' tables for projectiles. And this acceptance of surface phenomena, with a rejection of theoretical causes, *still* at this late date, fit the data more accurately than the more ambitious Newtonian choice. Even after Laplace, Leverrier and Galle, the fit between Newtonian mechanics and celestial phenomena was not perfect. Moreover, though Laplace had removed gross anomalies in Newton's theory of the tides, tides still did not behave as a Newtonian would expect.

Similarly, consider Darwin's case for natural selection. He presents a variety of phenomena, well-explained by the theory of natural selection, that pose difficulties for the hypothesis of species-by-species creation. But he also acknowledges the existence of distinctive difficulties for his own theory, for example, the non-existence of relatively simple or of transitional lifeforms in the fossil record available to him. To suppose that some general rule dictated his choice among hypotheses is to adopt the fiction that there is a general rule for counting and weighing anomalies. And yet, Darwin was surely justified in preferring the hypothesis of natural selection to that of the independent creation of each species.

Finally, consider the fate of the rule that is the most promising tool for coping with anomalies, the rule that conformity to received fundamental principles is a virtue. We often use this rule to dismiss wild theories explaining the anomalies from which every science suffers, for example, some farfetched effort to explain the stomach's mysterious failure to dissolve in its own hydrochloric acid. But if conformity to background principles were an absolute requirement, quantum mechanics could not have triumphed over classical physics. Certainly, general relativity, until recently favored by three isolated sorts of empirical findings,[30] could not have been a rational choice, if theoretical conservatism was in general overriding.

I have emphasized natural-scientific examples of successful trade-off because there is a counsel of despair according to which deeply important disagreements in the social sciences never have a rational resolution. Those of us who are less cynical, however, find an abundance of successful trade-offs in the social sciences, as well. Thus, narrative histories are bound to encounter fewer anomalies than those appealing to underlying social forces. The former only rely on common-sense psychological principles, while the latter rely on those principles together with others which are more novel, harder to apply, and in need of more refinement. Yet it could be reasonable to choose a social forces explanation, say, of the French Revolution, over one confined to narratives of powerful people and appeals to common-sense psychology.

Evidently, in the choice of hypotheses, as in most other kinds of choice, the right alternative to choose need not be singled out by general rules. At the same time, when we look at the criticisms of empirical arguments in various fields, the same basic kinds of

[30] See Kuhn, "The Function of Measurement in Modern Physical Science," in *The Essential Tension*, pp. 188f.

charges seem always to be made. There seems to be this much to the standard positivist claim that there is a logic of justification, but no logic of discovery: there is no general training that enables people to make discoveries in every field, but a grasp of the arguments in some broad and important fields seems to make people good judges of who is arguing well in any field so long as they grasp the relevant vocabularies. A theory of confirmation ought to make explicit the workings of this critical capacity. How can it, if the rating of causal accounts is not the result of applying general a priori rules to the alternative accounts and to the data relevant to their assessment?

My strategy will be to describe the principles for deciding which explanation is best that are appropriate in different contexts of argument. In particular, the context will differ according to how much of the framework is in dispute. At level I, the question of which rival explanation of the data is best is completely isolated. The principles relevant to this question are the same in every current framework. So the task of confirmation theory is simply to describe the role that the given, shared principles play in the choice of a causal account over its rivals. At level II, there is disagreement about what principles to use in doing the work described in level I. And yet, there is some actual agreement among investigators on principles that rational people have disputed at other times (or might have, even if their course of experience were normal). The theory of confirmation at this level describes how a basis for fair comparison can be found in spite of the disagreements. Finally, at level III, all that is relevant to choice and shared is the sort of truism that no rational person actually disbelieves. The role of confirmation theory, here, is to make the role of such truisms explicit, since they usually go without saying, and to establish their special status, as a means of countering various skeptical arguments.

Such a theory is complete, since it covers every context of rational dispute. But it does not lay down a canon of rules that yield answers to questions of the form, "Does this body of data, D, confirm this hypothesis H?", once the contents of D and H are analyzed. For the framework principles connecting data and hypothesis are determined by the actual evolution of hypothesis-making and data-gathering. The theory describes jobs that must be done, but not the content of the principles that do them (except, to a limited extent, at level III). Some of the principles connecting data and a hypothesis are always specific to the subject at hand and (with special and limited exceptions at level III) they are only valid a posteriori.

In these respects, the following theory of hypothesis choice resembles certain holistic forms of positivism, in which the ultimate issue of confirmation is whether the data confirm the conjunction of the hypothesis that is being investigated and the background assumptions governing the investigation; this question is resolved, in these holistic views, by the existence of appropriate relations between the data and the conjunction, relations effectively described by general a priori rules concerned with deductive relations, probability shifts or simplicity. As it is developed in this chapter and defended in the next three chapters, the current theory differs both in the way the goal of confirmation is pursued and in the ultimate basis for its fulfillment. Isolated hypotheses can be confirmed, by arguments that are fair in the given social context. And, what is more important, there will be no general, topic-neutral rules, concerning the favored relations between propositions and propositional attitudes, that describe the confirmation-making fit between hypotheses and fairly chosen auxiliary principles, on the one hand, data on the other. I will often emphasize that the simpler classical positivist stories of how D confirms H make confirmation too lonely, since other characters do not appear when they should. This is not a preliminary to a more holistic positivism, but the beginning of an argument, continued in the next three chapters, that the historical surroundings of H and D cannot be given their proper role without abandoning the positivist project of basing scientific method on a canon of topic-neutral rules, the same for all fields and all times.

Because it is not part of the latter project, this theory of confirmation does not look like mathematical logic or the mathematical theory of probability. Its capacity for interesting formal results is strictly limited, like what is known in the trade as "the baby logic course" as distinct from a philosophy department's "real logic course." For the practice of science, the main pay-off of such a theory is to help advance disputes that look irreconcilable by exposing confusions about the kinds of disagreements that are at work. For philosophy, the main pay-off consists of showing how various forms of relativism and dogmatism can be avoided, in the absence of a positivist canon of rules.

## Level I

In the simplest context for confirmation, the principles relevant to comparing causal accounts of the data are the same in every current framework. Sometimes, the confirmation of an empirical generalization is this straightforward. This might happen when a purely technological achievement, an advance when assessed in everyone's framework, is used to confirm a value for a constant in an empirical law. However, arguments at level 1 are more characteristic of choices among rival hypotheses as to why a particular event took place. Certainly, this is where the theory of level 1 confirmation is most useful in shedding light on areas of real confusion. So it will be convenient to speak of level 1 as the context for choosing event explanations. The adaptations to other choices are reasonably straightforward.

Confirmation at level 1 is a sifting process in which background beliefs are applied to data to see whether it is more likely that the tested hypothesis is an adequate description of an underlying cause than that some rival is, instead. Suppose we are given a body of data and a hypothesis to the effect that an event E happened because of a causal factor H. Our problem is to determine whether the data confirm the hypothesis. The data will consist of observed facts of one or more of these three kinds:

1. Facts to the effect that the situation in which E arose had characteristics C.

2. Characteristics, C′, of other situations, matched with characteristics of respective sequels, E′.

3. A variety of facts, I, which might be interpreted as causally connected with a fact of one of the first two kinds, or a factor described in a competing hypothesis.

Whether these data support the hypothesis depends on the construction of a checklist of likely causes of E, and its adjustment in light of the data. Any shared belief might play a role in this process of adjustment, but certain roles are so standard they deserve to be singled out: the connection of the characteristics C′ and E′ of other situations with the causal analysis of the situation at hand; the interpretation of the facts I, so that they help to discriminate between H and its rivals; the application of standard causal patterns; and the assessment of H for adequate causal depth. If H would be the sole survivor of the sifting, when all of the framework has been applied to the data, then the hypothesis "E occurred because of H" is confirmed by the data.

## Causal Checklists

By "a causal checklist," I mean a list of alternative factors more likely than any rival disjunction of rival factors to have caused the explanandum. The data, as a whole, confirm the hypothesis if, together with background principles, they validate a checklist with one member, H. This is the outcome of a sifting process in which, as more and more data are taken into account, the shortest checklist including H gets shorter and shorter over the long run, until it has H as its only entry.

The sifting of data begins with some causal checklist, validated by background principles and the mere statement of the phenomenon to be explained. The shortness of the initial list is a measure of the initial plausibility of the hypothesis, assuming it is on the list. The goal of confirmation is to shorten the checklist to one item, more likely to be an adequate description of underlying causes than anything else admitted as possible by the framework. The goal is reached by showing that the data as a whole are more likely to have arisen if E had underlying causes adequately described in the favored account than they are if some rival item is valid. The basic maxim used, in employing contingent background principles to reach this goal, is truistic, even valid a priori: if actual phenomena are more likely to have arisen as a result of process P than as a result of an incompatible process P', then their occurrence makes P more likely than P'.

Because causal sifting is intrinsically comparative, it is not enough to show that H is a likely cause of the data. If the data are a likely product of a process involving H, but also are likely on a rival account, we lack the leverage to promote H to confirmed status. Suppose, for example, that we are testing Neumann's explanation of the Nazis' rise to power as due to the need of the industrial and banking establishment for a repressive, expansionist regime with a popular base in the conditions of the Great Depression. That traditional conservative politicians in Weimar Germany acted in the interests of big business would result from the process of big-business dominance of politics which Neumann describes. But it would result, just as surely, from the process described in the rival account in which traditional conservatives are wedded to the status quo, Social Democrats committed to reform it, Communists to destroy it from left-wing motives, and Nazis committed to destroy it from ideological motives that served no underlying social interest. On the other hand, it *is* relevant to confirmation that the Nazi regime supported big business in fact even when the Nazis' populist rhetoric dictated otherwise, and that Hindenburg invited Hitler to become Chancellor after the Nazis' electoral strength declined. For in current frameworks, this is a likely outcome of political and social processes entailing Neumann's account, but not of any entailing the truth of rival hypotheses.

What happens when some of the data are more likely given the truth of H than on some rival H′, but vice versa for other data? The mention of likelihoods in the question may make statistical inference seem the inevitable basis for an answer. But careful accounts of such inference suggest a different answer that I will develop further in Chapter Seven. If the alternatives on the checklist all fit an appropriate statistical model, then there will be a calculation by which successes and failures can be balanced. But usually no such model can be assumed. And even if it can, the choice of this abstract causal structure itself requires a justification that statistical inference does not provide.

Though the problem of a balanced overall judgment of successes and failures has arisen in the context of event explanation at level 1, it is, in a sense, *the* central problem for the theory of confirmation. Positivist accounts of confirmation always seem inadequate due to their one-sided emphasis on a single kind of success: deductions that fit the data. The natural response is to develop a diverse catalogue of virtues. But this seems to be no solution, since reasonably chosen hypotheses often are inferior on some dimensions of virtue, and have a mixed record on a given dimension of virtue. No general rule is remotely promising as a means of balancing these successes and failures.

The idea that confirmation is fair causal comparison suggests that these trade-offs are to be made by pursuing a causal account of the relevant pattern of success and failure in the history of science so far. The crucial question is whether the failures are due to basic falsehood in a hypothesis, as compared with its rivals, or to defects in auxiliary beliefs that have so far been employed. Though the successes and failures may be due to technical and quantitative considerations, this historical way of summing up is apt to be common-sensical and qualitative.

The way to solve problems of trade-off is suggested by Darwin's response to the empirical anomalies arising from his theory, for example, the gaps in the fossil record. (As it happens, his reasoning is at level 1, since it depends entirely on shared views of the reliability of auxiliary fields, based on shared principles of assessment.) "Such is the sum of the several chief objections and difficulties which might justly be urged against my theory. . . . I have felt these difficulties far too heavily during many years to doubt their weight. But it deserves especial notice that the more important objections relate to questions on which we are confessedly ignorant; nor do we know how ignorant we are. We do not know all the possible transitional gradations between the simplest and the most perfect organisms; it cannot be pretended that we know all the varied means of distribution during the long lapse of years, or that we know how imperfect the geological record is."[31]

Here, successes and failures are being balanced not through a calculation, but through a choice among different explanations of the history of data-gathering and theorizing. Darwin is assessing the "first-order" successes and failures of his theory, the results of applying framework principles directly to data, assessing them in light of other, second-order principles, bearing on the status of the former, first-order pattern. For example, he is relying on the *shared* second-order principle ("*we* are *confessedly* ignorant") that the reconstruction of the early history of the earth's surface is especially difficult and uncertain. In light of these second-order principles, he argues that the failures of his theory are more apt to be due to the uneven development of the sciences than to the falsehood of the theory as against its current rivals. That a hypothesis almost always triumphs in comparisons based on shared and secure auxiliary principles, yet sometimes fails where auxiliary insight is dim is most easily explained by blaming the failures on the latter auxiliaries. In short, having assessed the causal fit of rival hypotheses with individual pieces of data, Darwin sums up by arguing that the overall pattern of fit is most likely to result from a certain overall state of scientific knowledge, namely, the basic truth of his theory combined with the special difficulties of framing valid background principles where the theory currently fails. That is the general way in which trade-offs are assessed. It only reduces to calculations in very special cases.

That the balance of explanatory virtues is established by arguing for a certain causal account suggests that the catalog of virtues is itself a list of phenomena that are typical signs of the same causal process, the data's being due to what the favored hypothesis describes. Far from being independent intrinsic advantages, the standard virtues are simply rules of thumb for constructing an argument that a hypothesis is part of the best causal account of the data. This construal is especially far from the usual treatment of the cardinal virtue, accurate fit with the data. And yet, by taking even this virtue as a rule of thumb for making causal arguments, we can do justice to the *un*importance of accurate fit in special cases. Just as one would expect on the causal perspective, whether accurate fit is important depends on the history of how it arose. Fit resulting from

[31] *The Origin of Species*, p. 440.

seventeen successive totally ad hoc modifications in a hypothesis is not an important virtue, because it is as apt to reflect agility in the modifiers as it is to be caused by the process the hypothesis itself describes. After all, agility in ad hoc modification has no tendency to produce future instances of the concocted hypothesis. Nor is disconfirmation through bad fit any more fundamental. It is quite misleading, albeit true, to respond that a hypothesis must be abandoned if it contradicts a proposition known to be correct. Actual conflicts with data always depend on some framework principle in addition to the hypothesis, either a principle used to connect hypothesis with data, or a principle, implicit in the acceptance of data, about what kinds of detection are reliable. Bad fit can be due to falsehood in the hypothesis or to falsehood in the auxiliaries. As Darwin's argument shows, bad fit ceases to be an important vice as soon as the framework makes falsehood in the auxiliaries the more likely explanation.

From a deductivist and, especially, a Bayesian perspective, causal sifting is a crude version of the more precise reasoning that is the primary subject-matter of confirmation theory—rather as proofs that are good enough in practice are always rough compared with the subject-matter of proof theory. Later, I will argue that the deductivist and Bayesian ideals are often inferior means of scientific inference, and that they involve considerable unclarity. But this argument is best postponed, in part because the relevant Bayesian principles deserve careful explication. The other model for confirmation that conflicts with the present one is Scriven's, which departs in the direction of greater simplicity. Especially because it, too, emphasizes a kind of causal sifting, it is important to see that it is, through oversimplification, as farfetched as the overly sophisticated alternatives.

When explanations are not required to conform to the covering-law model, then, in Scriven's view, they begin with a truistic list of possible causes of the event in question. If we are lucky, we will discover only one possible cause in the actual situation in which the event arose, so that we may conclude that it explains the event. If we are not so lucky, we may still be able to eliminate all but one alternative by excluding a possible cause when a necessary intermediate step in its producing the effect is missing. If elimination cannot proceed this far, given the data, we have no rational basis for deciding whether one or another cause explains the event in question.[32]

[32] See "Causes, Connections and Conditions in History" in William Dray, *Philosophical Analysis and History* (New York, 1966), pp. 253f.

This idealization is just as farfetched and crippling as the contrary idealizations of deductivist and Bayesian theories. In practice, we can never eliminate all possible causes but one. In the home territory of Scriven's model, medical diagnosis, we can never eliminate every arcane allergy which might be a cause of a sore throat. Moreover, even supposing that truisms yield a list of the *likely* causes, we often cannot eliminate all but one by looking for necessary intermediate steps. Causes do not typically leave their footprints in this neat way. Scriven's own example is a case of psychological explanation. Did Mark Anthony flee the battle of Actium out of fear or out of a desire to be with his beloved Cleopatra? Our resource is supposed to be the search for necessary intermediate steps or their absence. But even if the historical record were ideal, it would not discriminate in this fashion. For there is no necessary intermediate step either in flight from fear or flight from passion. Acting out of either motive, Mark Antony could behave in the same way. Even if we had access to all his inner twinges and thoughts, we might not be able to read off his motives. Cowards like to be with their beloveds and passionate lovers also experience fear.

What we do here, as in countless everyday cases, is to apply framework principles and inferences from differential likelihood to perfectly accessible evidence. Suppose that Antony's biographer discovers that he stood up to danger on the many other occasions when no private passion was drawing him from the scene. Framework principles about the stability of adult character traits make this a likely outcome of a character which would have led Antony to overcome fear at Actium, an unlikely outcome of a character permitting cowardice at Actium; and the principles make it likely that he did have one or the other of these traits (i.e., personality development produces certain relatively definite and stable attitudes toward regularly encountered fears). That Antony fled from love is now confirmed.

Situations in which more than one possible cause is present but only one may be operating do not just figure in philosophers' examples and in cases which produce no difficulties in practice. A theory of confirmation that cannot deal with Antony at Actium also cannot resolve a single important controversy in the social sciences. In the social sciences, the leading representatives of rival schools of thought are bright enough to appeal to causes that really were present in the situations at issue and that really are possible causes of the sort of event that is to be explained. (This is less common in natural-scientific disputes simply because causes that exist for one side often do not exist at all for the other.) For example, the changes in religious outlook that Weberians emphasize and the changes in the rural and the international economy to which Marxists appeal really were characteristic of the dawn of modern capitalism. Good Weberians and good Marxists know this. Neither side bases its argument on the absence of intermediate causes necessary to the other side—whatever that might mean. Rather, they argue from diverse background principles and facts made relevant by those principles.

For philosophical purposes, the notion of a causal checklist is useful in describing how explanations can be confirmed without confirming covering-laws. The most likely cause when the sifting is done need not be likely to produce the phenomenon in question, according to a general, empirical law. Recall how the doctor, using standard diagnostic questions and tests, quickly sifted out all rivals to the hypothesis that streptococcal infection caused the sore throat without having even a sketch of general conditions in which a streptococcal infection produces soreness in a throat.

For purposes of practical criticism in the science, the notion of a causal checklist is most useful in redirecting disputes in the social sciences which have become interminable and fruitless because the arguments are not directed at the real basis for disagreement. The argument is conducted as if disputants were at level 1, when in fact one side forms causal checklists in accordance with principles the other side rejects. Consider, for example, the so-called revisionist account of the origins of the Civil War. The revisionists claim that the war was due to the effective propagandizing of fanatics, above all, the abolitionists, unwilling to tolerate compromises that established leaders, North and South, would otherwise have accepted. They often appeal to statements by leading Southerners, offering a variety of compromises and protesting that extreme measures were due to extreme Northern demands.[33] In opposition to the revisionists, many historians argue that if these compromises had been accepted, Southern leaders would simply have demanded more. The slave economy, they argue, required continual expansion, as cotton agriculture exhausted the land, and also required the repressive use of political power against whites as well as blacks, as conflicts with homesteaders grew along the frontier. Whatever the Southern magnates may have believed they would have done, they would not in fact have accepted second-rate status in a shabby economic role,

[33] See, for example, James G. Randall, "A Blundering Generation" in his *Lincoln, the Liberal Statesman* (New York, 1947).

without a fight. And the need of the slave economy to expand, if it was to prosper, was bound to conflict with rival interests of manufacturers, artisans, farmers, and others outside of the slave economy.[34]

Revisionists often carry on their side of the dispute through biographical accounts of leading political figures. But the leading issue concerns the bases on which such data is converted into causal checklists. Should our initial checklists be shaped by the principle that plantation owners were guided by the pursuit of the states of affairs they consciously desired, given the resources they had at hand? Then, the biographical data may support the revisionist side. Perhaps leading Southerners sincerely wanted compromise. Or are the plantation owners at least as likely to have been guided by the need for great wealth and power and the social setting that would sustain it, an objective interest that is effective even if it is not their reason for belief or action? Then, the initial checklist includes objective political-economic factors which are not to be excluded on the basis of their absence from sincere self-portrayals of motives. Broad principles of psychology are at issue, which cannot be resolved by marshalling data about what people consciously desired. The argument may well depend on evidence drawn from situations similar to, but different from the ante-bellum United States. Here, a covering-law theorist would be right to insist that underlying psychological principles be made explicit. However, as we have seen, these principles need not have the form or the role of covering-laws.

Certain standard roles in the choice of event explanations are implicit in the arguments of the first two chapters. I will discuss them briefly, here.

### Extrapolators

The process of sifting for causes is not limited to data which characterize the situation in which E occurred. Data from other situations may be relevant. If so, they are made relevant by principles playing the roles of extrapolators and interpreters.

Extrapolators make characterizations of conditions and events in other situations sufficiently analogous to affect causal comparison in the case at hand. Framework principles may extrapolate by dictating that in certain other situations, events resembling E in certain ways are apt to have similar causes. Then, the operation of a cause

---

[34] The most compelling and influential version of this argument is Eugene Genovese, *The Political Economy of Slavery* (New York, 1967), esp. ch. 10.

C′ in that situation makes similar causes of E more likely. Alternatively, extrapolators may tell us that certain situations are analogous in that similar causes are apt to have similar effects. Counter examples are certified as relevant by appeal to this kind of extrapolator. C was supposed to cause E, but in a situation in which similar causes have similar effects, the similar cause C′ was followed by no similar event, E′.

The method of controlled experiment is an ideal case of extrapolation, in cases where the alternative causal factors are known with precision and are susceptible to control, and the extrapolators tell us that the same factors from the checklist have the same effects in the circumstances compared. Suppose we wonder whether the shrinkage of the bacterial colony in the petri dish, which followed the introduction of the antibiotic solution, was caused by it. We construct a second set-up, a petri dish in which a colony of the same bacteria is present and all the factors that might have caused the shrinkage are present except one: the antibiotic. We accept principles establishing that the same total combinations of causally relevant factors will jointly have the same effect where bacterial death is concerned, and the principle that such shrinkage does not occur for no cause. The colony does not shrink in the second dish. So every cause of the prior shrinkage is eliminated except the antibiotic solution, which must have been the cause. Note that without these causal principles, the experiment would have told us nothing. In particular, we cannot employ a general principle, "If a phenomenon occurs when a property is present, but not when it is absent but everything else is the same, then the presence of that property is its cause." In a nondeterministic universe, such as our own, the principle is invalid. Another factor might be the cause in the first instance, but just have happened not to operate in the second instance. In any case, all other properties are never the same in a controlled comparison. The most we can hope for is control over the possible causes of such events. Indeed, the most we can hope for is control over factors likely to function as causes.

*Interpreters*

Observed facts which do not characterize the situation in which E arose or causally analogous situations, may nonetheless be highly relevant, when combined with background principles. In combination, they may yield characterizations of the circumstances of E or of causally analogous situations which function, then, as data bearing on the hypothesis that C caused E. Indeed, such facts, in themselves far removed, may directly imply the superiority of a hypothesis. Thus, in the case of Lee's diary, a principle of diary interpretation led from the observation that Lee wrote, "Richmond has fallen. Sherman's march has cut the Confederacy in two. Therefore, I have decided to surrender," to the conclusion that Lee's despair over those events was the most likely cause of his surrender. Using "interpreters," the task of giving a causal account of the data is developed further through a principle which tells us that some fact outside of the process producing E is apt to have a certain cause, a cause which is part of the process producing E (or part of an analogous process, made relevant by extrapolators). The diary entry is caused, in part, by Lee's giving up out of despair over Grant's and Sherman's victories. A telescope image is caused by the orbitings that result in the eclipse that is to be explained.

Obviously, interpretative principles are ubiquitous in all sciences. Indeed, it is a matter of tactics and context whether a finding is to be classified as a datum or as an inference from data and an interpreter. We want our description of the epistemological situation in which the hypothesis is assessed to be an effective tool for criticizing or defending the hypothesis. If no one in current disputes would challenge a finding of particular fact, we may take it to be a datum. But if it might be challenged on grounds of inaccuracy, we want our description of the situation to be a useful non-question-begging means of judging those challenges. So the controversial finding is not taken to be a datum. Instead, we see whether it can be derived from data and a defensible interpreter in the background. The so-called observational-theoretical distinction is context-dependent and pragmatic, so far as the analysis of confirmation is concerned. Conversely, the widely shared idea that this distinction *is* context-dependent supports the present strategy of analyzing confirmation in terms of different levels of disagreement and the roles they play.

*Patterns and Depth Measures*

As evidence is sifted, two filters should always be applied to causal checklists. Causes worthy of inclusion as possible explanations must be sufficiently deep to explain. And they should fit standard causal patterns. I have nothing to add to the previous account of how beliefs concerning reality, science and benefits of science yield standard causal patterns. The role of depth measurement was also implicit in the causal model of explanation. Background knowledge provides a depth measure if it yields the conclusion that one factor on a checklist is deeper than another which, hence, does not explain. However, certain background principles play a distinctive but subtle role in measurements of depth, which deserves separate mention.

It is roughly true that a cause, X, of Z is undermined by a deeper cause Y if Z was bound to happen anyway given the absence of X and the presence of Y. But, as we saw, this is not precisely right. Y may be undermining even if, in the absence of X, there was a small chance that Z would not have occurred. When historians argue that social forces deeper than this or that mistake of Weimar politicians led to the Nazi seizure of power, they are not concerned to deny that, had Hitler not been made Chancellor, the Nazi leadership just might all have been killed in accidents. And these fatal accidents might have been due to activities which were precluded by the leaders actually settling in Berlin when Hitler was made Chancellor. What is important is that these possible fatal events did not happen and that their occurrence would have been abnormal. Conversely, when social-forces historians say that the Nazis would have triumphed anyway had Hindenburg not underestimated Hitler, they mean that an appropriate chain of actions would have occurred, in the *normal* course of events. Thus, principles describing the normal tendency of the causal factors in question play a role in the assessment of depth.

Sometimes principles of normal tendency are so obvious that they go without saying. Everyone accepts that the simultaneous accidents eliminating the whole Nazi leadership would be extraordinary. But sometimes a disputed principle of normal tendency is a main source of an explanatory disagreement. Often, when this is so, the debate is, nonetheless, conducted on other, less relevant grounds. Here again, the causal model of confirmation serves to clarify areas of relevant dispute.

Again, the debate over the revisionist interpretation of the coming of the Civil War is a useful example. Revisionists frequently repeat moderates' arguments of the 1850s which suggested the prudence of compromises restricting slavery to the Southeast. They emphasize the prudence and realism of these compromises: while plantation owners would have been reduced to a much less substantial economic and political role, they would have avoided widespread death and ruin in their ranks, through civil war. Opponents of the revisionists, especially those emphasizing economic factors, reiterate the ways in which slave-based plantation agriculture needed continual expansion to thrive and to remain a basis for substantial political leadership. Both claims about the effects of compromise may be valid. Both sides would probably accept that in the economic setting a civil war would not have occurred if the leading figures on both sides had continually tried to avoid great bloodshed through moderation. How, then, can the revisionists' opponents claim, nonetheless, that the expansive tendencies of the slave economy and the contrary needs of the non-slave economy explain the coming of the Civil War? The basic disagreement concerns principles of normal tendency. The revisionists regard it as normal for people such as the Southern magnates to give up great wealth and power without a fight, to avoid the risk of widespread destruction. Their opponents regard it as normal for such people to take great risks to preserve their special status. If the latter principle of normality is right, then it might be true that the causal chain leading to the Civil War includes fanatics' goading initially moderate elites *and* false that this process explains why war ultimately replaced compromise. Short of conduct abnormal for the elites, war would have broken out anyway. Depending on which principle of normality is chosen, the availability of compromise will either support the revisionists, or prove as irrelevant as the hypothetical accidents among the Nazis. Yet the actual arguments are, unfortunately, not directed at this choice of general principles. Rather, each side marshalls more and more of its own distinctive kind of evidence. Here as elsewhere, knowledge of the structure of confirmation at level I is useful as showing that level I tactics of confirmation are being employed when investigators, like it or not, are in a level II disagreement.

## Level II

When principles for rating hypotheses in light of data are themselves in dispute, we are in the more troubled context that I have called level II. Even some disputes about choices among explanations of particular events have turned out to be resolved at this level. More typically though, level II is the context for choices among fundamental theories competing for dominance of a major field. When theoretical differences are deep they include disagreements as to how to test theories in light of data. Thus, partisans of Ptolemaic and Copernican astronomy employed different principles for rating celestial hypotheses in light of telescope observations. In political sociology, relatively conservative "pluralist" investigators take victories and losses in votes in official forums to be a measure of the power of interested social groups. But partisans of a theory that a ruling class or power elites dominate take such official processes, i.e., elections and the like, to be ways by which government action is adjusted to suit one of the dominant group's interests, namely, their interest in acquiescence. Alternatives appear on the official agenda when which is implemented is much less important for the dominant minority than the occurrence of a choice acceptable to society at large through a process that promotes general acceptance of the status quo. Given this framework, what doesn't get on the agenda is a better measure of power than who wins in the votes. So Dahl's influential argument that the "Economic Notables" of New Haven are not dominant because they lose votes in official forums is as question-begging as a Galilean argument that the Copernican hypothesis is shown to be correct by telescopic observations of the brightness of Mars.[35]

The theory of confirmation at level II is a theory of how there can be valid arguments that a hypothesis gives the best account of the data even when there are relevant disagreements over principles for rating hypotheses. The task is to engage in causal sifting, as described at level I, without supporting a hypothesis in a way that is unfair. The basic rule which guarantees fairness is simple. In criticizing a rival to the hypothesis one favors, one should, in the final analysis, use principles contained in the current framework most favorable to the rival. This process of fair comparison is most straightforward when one can resolve a framework difference by testing the disputed framework principle in light of further, shared principles. In effect, a disagreement contributing to level II dispute is resolved in light of further data in a level I argument. Many of Galileo's arguments against Aristotelian science are of this kind. Thus, confronting arguments from the Aristotelian principle that unforced sublunar motion soon comes to rest, he tests it against a shared background, by reminding Aristotelians that loose objects in a cabin in a steadily moving ship, even a bird in flight, are not all hit by the stern side of the cabin. (As he points out, if steady pushing by the air were responsible, then, by common principles, the bird would experience difficulty in flying sternwards, within the cabin.)[36]

---

[35] See Robert Dahl, *Who Governs?* (New Haven, 1961), especially pp. 66 and 72. When G. William Domhoff restudied Dahl's original data, which included extensive interviews with leading New Havenites, Domhoff found a very different, radically non-pluralist view of power in New Haven among the interviewees. See Domhoff, *Who Really Rules?* (New Brunswick, N.J., 1978), pp. 19, 111f. I discuss this and related problems of fair comparison in the assessment of political power, in *Analyzing Marx*, chs. 3 and 4.

[36] *Dialogue Concerning the Two Chief World Systems*, tr. S. Drake (Berkeley, 1967), pp. 186f.

Often, fairness is guaranteed by a different tactic, showing that data undermine a rival hypothesis when interpreted using principles most favorable to it, which one does not oneself accept. Thus, Einstein is being utterly fair to classical electrodynamics when he argues that the Michelson-Morley experiment undermines that theory: interpreted using classical electrodynamics, the Michelson-Morley data would show that the absolute rotational velocity of the earth is zero, and from the standpoint of mechanics, including classical mechanics, this must be wrong. The argument is fair even though the data permit no inference from data to absolute velocities in Einstein's own framework. He is "assuming for the sake of argument," in the course of confirming special relativity.

Often, confirmation at level II has aspects of both strategies of fairness. Copernicus takes planetary observations to confirm his hypothesis, even though he must use as many epicycles as the Ptolemaics, in order to explain the data. An important basis for his superior rating of his own hypothesis is his avoidance of equants, mechanisms in which a circular motion is only uniform in relation to a point other than the center. Copernicus says that equants "seem to violate the first principle of uniformity in motion."[37] It is certainly true that the whole astronomic enterprise was an effort to attribute periodic motion to tendencies that were uniform, and that no one should take equants to satisfy this constraint. After all, any motion is uniform with respect to some moving point. Granted, as with most fundamental physical concepts, it is hard to make the underlying notion of uniformity precise while remaining fair to all frameworks. What Copernicus could claim more precisely (in the assuming for-the-sake-of-argument mode) is that equants were not qualified for inclusion in the neo-Aristotelian repertoire of physical causes of motion that *Ptolemaic* astronomers used. If, on the other hand, we ignore the role of causal comparison in the argument over the two cosmologies, Copernicus' emphasis on equants becomes a puzzling appeal to wholly "aesthetic" considerations. And this is, in fact, Kuhn's verdict in *The Copernican Revolution*.[38]

If the arguments of this book are right, and positivist accounts of confirmation are inadequate, then the rules of fairness create an urgent problem, whose solution is the remaining task of level II theory.

[37] Preface to *De Revolutionibus Orbium Caelestium*, in Thomas Kuhn, *The Copernican Revolution* (New York, 1959), p. 139.

[38] "This device [the equant] is of particular importance because of Copernicus' aesthetic objections to it. . . . Copernicus' arguments appeal . . . to his [the typical contemporary astronomer's] aesthetic sense, and to that alone" (ibid., pp. 70, 181).

If there are no general a priori rules determining whether any given body of data confirms or disconfirms any given hypothesis, there will, presumably, be some fields that lack a basis for a sound assessment of whether data confirm a hypothesis. In itself, this is not troubling, except to positivists. It is common sense to suppose that some fields are so new, speculative or deeply divided that a fair claim to have confirmed a hypothesis in light of the data cannot be made. Psychopathology circa 1930 and geology in the eighteenth century look like cases in point. What is troubling is that the best-established natural sciences of the present day have their origins in scientific revolutions where framework differences were extensive and deep. If the revolutionary alternatives were never confirmed by fair comparison, their eventual acceptance as the only sound framework for theorizing and research design was dogmatic. Our reliance on current theories developed in such a framework would depend on ancestral dogmatism, and be dogmatic itself, as a consequence. That is a verdict which should not be accepted unless we have made a thorough search for bases of fair comparison across the broad framework differences typical of scientific revolutions. A major task of level II theory is to aid in that search.

In the social sciences, the need for guidance toward fair tactics of comparison is more practical and urgent. Disputes, here, often continue for generations, with different sides organized into schools of thought applying different framework principles. At least for relatively open-minded observers, it really is a question whether more than confirmation-in-a-framework can be claimed.

To some extent, the location of fair tactics of comparison is simply case-by-case history of science, directed toward finding shared principles which can be used in ranking accounts of shared data. The shared principle of uniform motion to which Copernicus appealed is one example. In addition, there are certain broad kinds of principles which have always provided eventual tactics of fair comparison. I will call these principles, principles of causal simplicity, because they play a similar role to the virtues of formal simplicity in many positivist theories of confirmation. Principles of causal simplicity justify a non-question-begging charge that something which stands in need of explanation has not been explained. Thus, they are means of ranking causal accounts as better or worse according to whether they minimize the number of explanatory loose ends. In this chapter and the next I will argue that this virtue of minimal anomaly is the only virtue of simplicity relevant to comparison.

More formal or aesthetic considerations of simplicity are out of place in a general theory of confirmation.

Principles of causal simplicity are of three kinds. Principles of uniformity tell us that in certain systems, similar causes tend to have similar effects or similar effects tend to have similar causes; if deviations from this tendency occur, they must be due to a specific causal factor creating the deviation. In extreme cases of uniformity all deviation is ruled out, and, in the systems in question, the same cause is said always to have the same effect (or vice versa). Thus, since the triumph of Newtonian mechanics, motion has been taken to have the same fundamental causes everywhere, affecting trajectories in the same ways. Even before, the causes of celestial motions were taken to be the same fundamental mechanisms throughout the heavens, working in the same ways. More commonly, the principle of uniformity is less strict, but a useful lever for comparison, nonetheless. In all schools of thought in the social sciences, the same causes are taken to have the same effects in all modern industrial capitalist societies—prima facie, as lawyers put it. The hedge is important. In every approach, certain anomalies are admitted, if only by relegating them to a category of irreducible national differences. Still, if a phenomenon is traced to a cause in one society which did not have that effect in another society, that *is* an anomaly, counting against the original hypothesis, unless a further cause of the difference can be confirmed. Thus, whether ultimately lethal or not, it is a problem for Neumann's explanation that United States government did not become fascist when there was pressure for international economic expansion in the setting of an industrial depression and working-class discontent. By contrast, there is no framework principle of uniformity requiring that the same causes have the same effects in absolutely every society. It would be interesting to learn why nomadic raiders do not become internally repressive when they expand under conditions of poverty and discontent, but it does not count against Neumann's theory if no cause can be found for this difference from the Weimar Republic.

A second category, principles of stability, imposes the same kind of constraint on changes in a system that the previous principles impose on comparisons between systems. Such a principle tells us that a certain kind of phenomenon does not change unless something makes it change. Again, extreme cases exist where principles of stability preclude all change. An extreme principle of stability in physics tells us that the basic processes governing motion throughout the universe obey laws which do not change from era to era. A less strict principle of stability, fundamental to all human sciences, puts a premium on stability in the ways an individual responds to events, throughout his or her adult life. People do change in personality, temperament or character, but these changes have causes. So a hypothesis is fairly rated the worse if it explains someone's action as a departure from his or her previous ways of responding, without offering an independently supported account of the cause of the change.

Finally, some principles of causal simplicity are principles of composition, stating that certain things, phenomena or processes have certain constitutents. These principles regulate the choice of causal accounts by connecting them with principles governing the behavior of the constituents. If fairly chosen principles imply behavior in the constituents which would tend to make the alleged causal process ineffective, the corresponding causal account has a loose end. There is a need for an independent argument modifying the principles of constituent conduct or locating a countervailing factor in the over-all circumstances. Thus, a macroeconomic account of a recession is the worse if it conflicts with what is known about the psychology of the business people who made the crucial investment decisions. Many teleological theories of evolution are ruled out by what is known of the mechanisms of heredity. Principles of composition provide entry for the claim that constraints on individual causal links favor certain hypotheses about large-scale or deeper causes.

When differences between rival frameworks are so extensive that confirmation seems hopeless, principles of causal simplicity often provide the crucial leverage. For all the differences between Galilean and Aristotelian physics, in both frameworks different basic forces must tend to influence trajectories in different ways. This shared version of "same effect, same cause" makes Newton's argument for the universal law of gravitation especially devastating. For no difference remains, to be produced by an additional basic force, once Newton's one force is identified. Having shown that the force of attraction between the earth and sublunar bodies influences trajectories in the same way as the earth influences the moon's orbit, Newton can fairly argue, "[T]he force by which the moon is retained in its orbit is the very same force which we commonly call gravity; for, were gravity another force different from that, then bodies descending to the earth with the joint impulse of both forces would fall with a double velocity."[39]

[39] *Principia*, bk. 3, proposition 4, p. 408. Newton appeals to the first two Rules of Reasoning, here, and they are, as a whole, distinctly Galilean. However, Aristotelians

In the social sciences, fair arguments directed across chasms separating schools of thought almost always rely on shared principles of causal simplicity. When fair and careful Marxists argue for the principle that class interests are as likely as conscious reasons to shape basic political beliefs they appeal to facts such as these. In the English Civil War, every anti-Royalist faction had emerged from the same religious tradition, was sincerely committed to religious justifications based on the Bible, and interpreted the Bible according to the same interpretative principles. Yet they reached radically different conclusions, which corresponded to different class interests. Before the invention of the cotton gin, plantation owners in the southern United States typically regarded slavery as an evil, whose disappearance should be encouraged as quickly as social stability would permit. When the cotton gin made plantation agriculture in the deep South enormously profitable, the typical view soon changed to the opinion that slavery was a positive good. As far as they go, these considerations are relevant and fair, unlike, say, an argument presupposing that the economically dominant class determines the dominant ideology. They are fair because relevantly non-Marxist frameworks cannot explain the indicated data without violating shared principles of causal simplicity. It is a shared principle that people growing up in the same region and within the same culture should be led, by similar causes in their background, to embrace similar basic political beliefs. That the similar conscious commitments led to such different political outlooks is an anomaly within a non-Marxist framework in which conscious reasons are given priority and no cause of the differences can be found.

Of course, principles of causal simplicity are not the only basis for weighing evidence without begging questions. But they are almost always available, and can almost always be used (eventually) to show that one or another rival cannot account for the data without generating explanatory loose ends. The fear that background principles will either be insufficient or question-begging as bases for confirmation seems to be misguided. By contrast, as we shall see, formal considerations of simplicity provide no adequate rationale for the comparison of rival hypotheses.

Apart from their role in making fair comparisons across deep divides, principles of causal simplicity are important in another way. Like Humean principles of the uniformity of nature in positivist theories, the totality of principles of uniformity and stability sup-

---

also accept the Rule II injunction to attribute the same causes to the same effects, so far as possible, where the efficient causes of motions are concerned.

port claims to have confirmed general laws on the basis of the observation of a limited number of cases. Based on arguments concerned a (practically) infinitesimal part of the known universe, Newton could propose a universal law of gravitation, on the basis of principles of uniformity and stability. An account of the data attributing them to forces operating within the solar system, but not elsewhere, would have an explanatory loose end: what accounts for the difference between the mechanics of solar-system and non-solar-system trajectories? Without the principles of uniformity, made explicit in the "Rules of Reasoning in Natural Philosophy," in the *Principia*, this non-universalizing account might be just a sensible recognition of the diversity of nature.

Despite the functional similarities to Humean principles, principles of causal simplicity are very different in two respects. They are not general, applying to science as a whole. Thus, there is no universal principle of uniformity underlying the limited uniformities of history and the stricter uniformities of physics. Also, they are contingent and subject to defeat by empirical data. The laws of chemical combination, once thought to be always the same, whatever they are, now seem to have been different right after the Big Bang. In the debates at the origins of modern geology, it was sometimes assumed that the main causes of geological change were always and everywhere the same, either always slow and incremental, or always fast and catastrophic. Now it is clear that different kinds of processes operate at different times and in different regions.

## LEVEL III

The differences in the frameworks that investigators employ have turned out to be accompanied by surprisingly powerful similarities, similarities that are often a sufficient basic for fair causal comparison. Suppose, however, that we no longer take for granted shared technical principles that have arisen as science develops. The initial framework for comparing hypotheses in light of data consists only of truisms which no reasonable person doubts. In this situation, arguments from data take place at what I have labelled level III.

Some of the truisms at level III are the principles of reliable perception on which all sciences depend in counting phenomena among the data, for example: middle-sized objects usually have the approximate shapes and colors which eyesight reveals to normal people seeing them in moderate sunlight, close-up. Many others are constraints on causal accounts, employed after the data are determined. The human sciences obviously rely on such truisms as this: when an intelligent person regularly prefers one thing to another, the person is usually motivated by a desire or acts out of habit. A variety of truisms are also concerned with the behavior of inanimate objects. The common-sense core of the principle of inertia tells us that when a non-living thing abruptly takes a different course from its previous one, some force external to it is normally responsible. At the core of the great technical principles of conservation is the truism, which we learn at considerable cost in pain, that a weighty body has an impact when it is stopped.

Speaking of these principles as truisms suggests that they are both universally held and true. Both judgments stand in need of some refinement. The truisms defining level III are universal to the extent that all reasonable humans become committed to them in response to experiences such as almost all humans have. Perhaps some reasonable blind people don't acquire all of these commitments, but they would if they were not blind. No doubt, intelligences travelling near the speed of light would have different commitments. In addition, the truisms are true only in virtue of considerable vagueness and important hedges. There is much vagueness in the notion of persisting in the same course, which helps to explain why Aristotle and (probably) Galileo thought circular motion could be unforced, while Newton took it to require constant causal intervention. In general, there is a need to hedge by taking the truisms as valid, prima facie, for the normal state of affairs. In other words, our commitment is to accept a hypothesis described in the truism unless there is a special reason not to believe it. Even when all principles employed are at level III, the special reason may, in fact, be supplied, by appropriate data and other truisms used to interpret the data. Indeed, pioneers of a science often use truisms to overturn what seems obvious, if not literally truistic. As Sagredo puts it, in praise of Salviati and, implicitly, their common author, Galileo, "Usually he unravels questions that seem not only obscure but repugnant to nature and the truth, by reasons, observations, or experiences that are well-known and familiar to everyone."[40] Thus, it seems obvious that a very light object cannot move a very heavy one, at least when the former is not thrown with great force. But if, as Galileo's Salviati suggests, we hang a huge cannonball from a hook, then hang a small weight beside it, from the same hook, we see that the cannonball has

---

[40] Galileo, *Two New Sciences*, p. 89.

moved from the vertical, and this refutes the obvious, when interpreted using truistic principles.[41]

Confirmation in a level III context is important to some scientific enterprises because their whole framework is truistic. This is the case with biography, narrative history and economics, at least in traditional practice. (As economics shows, a truistic framework can produce elaborate and esoteric structures when it permits the application of mathematics to deal with complex combinations.) In such cases, the theory of level III adds no new methodological insights to the theory of level I.

The situations in which the theory of level III does make a distinctive contribution are philosophical controversies about the scope of reason. In the final chapters of this book, I will appeal to level III truisms to resolve the central question in the current debate over scientific realism: are there important current theories that are the one who says, '*You*'ve had a good snooze,' and spending the rest of reasonable framework that a possible disputant might apply? Questions of *confirmation* are settled, and settled non-dogmatically, when all alternatives implicit in actual frameworks are fairly judged. But further questions about merely possible frameworks remain. The truisms at level III play an essential role in answering them, because commitment to these truisms is an independent mark of being a reasonable person. For someone with the usual human experiences, being reasonable is, in part, having these relatively specific beliefs, with all their vagueness and hedges.

In philosophy, it is more common to take general logical principles and general principles of inference as marks of rationality. But, on the face of it, the truistic responses are marks of rationality as well. A rational human is committed to the law of the excluded middle, to making inferences to the best explanation—and to believing his or her own eyes in appropriate circumstances (described, with the needed vagueness, by the truism about visual perception). Someone with our experiences who believes, without special justification, that the feeling of impact is an independent sequel to his jaw's stopping a moving fist, not an effect of it, is, by that token, unreasonable, as much as someone who does not accept modus ponens. So, for that matter, is someone who believes, without a special justification, that the color of something depends on whether it has been observed.

The truistic beliefs are only marks of rationality for those who

---

[41] Ibid., pp. 290f.

have had the standard experiences. So it might seem that their power is a consequence of the application of more general rules to those experiences. Aside from the doubts, Goodmanesque and otherwise, that the rules have such power, the contrary idea that the truisms are independent marks of rationality is supported by the special certainty of our most banal beliefs. I am certain, as you probably are, that automobiles exist. Skeptics sometimes ask us to consider possibilities such as this, "You might, in a moment, have the experience of waking up under a tree, being approached by someone who says, '*You*'ve had a good snooze,' and spending the rest of your life in what seems to be a car-less world." Unless we can rule out this possibility in appropriate ways, we ought to abandon our certainty. Presumably, there is more to be said against this possibility than that such things have never occurred, or that the experiences could not be veridical, because there are cars. I can say analogous things of hypothetical experiments counting against the latest theories in physics. But a belief in quarks is not an appropriate object of certainty. A modern person's belief in cars is.

The special status of belief in cars is this. Given the prior course of experience, the belief could not be mistaken unless truisms as to what normal people seem to see (close-up, in moderate sunlight) and seem to remember (clearly, distinctly, with good connections to apparently remembered sequels) are wrong. If a situation were to arise like the story the skeptic tells, all general principles of inference might point in the direction of abandoning the belief. For example, if the new phase of experience continues long enough, explanations of one's total data as due to a dream-like state followed by contact with the real, car-less world might be best as rated by any general standard ever proposed. But commitment to the specific truisms is an independent dimension of reasonableness. So reason and evidence would not dictate abandonment of the old belief. Given the bizarre experiences the skeptic evokes, the belief that there never were cars becomes *a* reasonable alternative. But it is also reasonable to cling to the belief, "I used to be in a real world with cars. I have been transported to a carless place. The transport is mysterious, utterly inexplicable." Certain banal beliefs command more than tentative assent because reason and evidence cannot dictate the switch to their negation. The independent status of level III truisms explains this immunity.[42]

[42] For further discussion of topic-specific truisms and reasonableness, in the context of recent efforts to revive skepticism, see my "Absolute Certainty," *Mind* (1978), pp. 46–65, esp. pp. 54–65.

To avoid misunderstanding: truisms are not being portrayed as non-contingent or as incapable of justification, one by one. Each truism could be false, and commitment to it might have been unreasonable if past experience were different. Moreover, each truism is justifiable by causal comparison, using other truisms as framework principles. What is valid a priori is that a reasonable human with standard experiences is committed to the truisms, in all their vagueness and with all their hedges. Or perhaps one should say "committed to the basic validity of the truisms, as a whole."

I will postpone until Chapter Ten the case studies in which the banalities of level III combine with remarkable data to rule out the possibility of rational rejection of some (by no means all) of our important current beliefs about unobservables. The basic strategy will be to reconstruct actual scientific arguments for these beliefs, in a way that reveals their ultimate reliance on level III alone. Meanwhile, this first look at level III may have made it easier to suppose that such humble principles might have such power.

Just as one would expect, it will not turn out to be the case that all confirmed science can be based on level III arguments. Fair causal comparison can make a preference for belief over disbelief reasonable and non-dogmatic, even though the opposite preference would be reasonable in a possible framework that has not actually arisen. This would not be the case if general a priori rules of reasonable inference are the ultimate basis for confirmation. So one distinctive consequence of the present view of confirmation is that there may well be confirmed hypotheses that a reasonable person might have rejected in light of the evidence available. And when one looks at the history of science, this situation seems common. In Newton's actual context, his theory of sound was confirmed. But a framework biased against corpuscular hypotheses, similar to Mach's in the nineteenth century, might have been around, might have handled the data as well and might have rendered a contrary theory reasonable. Indeed, once Huyghens and others had developed the concept of energy further, Einstein's most basic arguments for relativity theory would have made the relativistic alternative to Newton's physics reasonable for possible disputants who were bothered a great deal by Newtonian dependence on special frames of reference, but bothered much less by departures from the Newtonian constancy of mass. (Of course, they would have to be tolerant of computational complexity, and smart enough to develop the Lorentz transformation and tensor analysis before new electrodynamic data had motivated these feats!) Very likely, the latest confirmed theory of processes in the atomic nucleus will turn out in retrospect, ten years from now not to have been the only possible reasonable response to the data. Where confirmation exists, a framework for reasonable dissent is sometimes possible. As we shall see in the discussion of scientific realism, such a framework is not always possible, however. The role of level III truisms in the crucial causal comparisons will make the difference.

The theory of confirmation as causal comparison now needs to be tested by comparison, itself. I will begin with the deductivist approach.

# CHAPTER FIVE

# Deductivism: Plain and with Simplicity

POSITIVISM offers many rivals to the causal theory of the previous chapter. They promise certain distinct advantages. If they can be made to work, then the judgment that a body of data confirm a hypothesis can be based on a simple group of precise and general rules and can always be assessed through conclusive proofs. Since the causal theory does not promise these benefits, it must be justified, in part, through a criticism of the costs that go with them. This chapter and the next two will be devoted to such criticism, directed first at deductivist theories and then at Bayesian ones.

Of course, one can never prove that it is impossible for any version of a major philosophical approach to succeed. But I will be describing certain extremely fundamental and recalcitrant obstacles to both approaches, deductivist and Bayesian. These obstacles have blocked every version of each rival approach up until now. It is initially implausible that any version could overcome them. No progress has been made in overcoming them. Indeed, it is often the case that the pioneers of each program were sensitive to such obstacles and worried about them, while subsequent writers in the same tradition have simply failed to confront them. Also, I hope to show that the positivist approaches to confirmation are a practical disaster if adopted as a working hypothesis or an ideal to be pursued. It is tempting to try to fit arguments to a deductivist or Bayesian model, since a methodology guided by techniques of logic and mathematical probability gives an investigation the aura of physics, the most prestigious science. However, a deductivist or a Bayesian ideal of confirmation will turn out to be so one-sided, that its pursuit would destroy most sciences (including physics!), and really does distort the social sciences, where such positivist ideals are, in fact, pursued. These ideals are systematically biased toward certain kinds of hypotheses, for example, superficial or familiar ones, even where those hypotheses are inferior.

If the causal approach provides the best account of those uncontroversial scientific judgments which are the "data" of the philosophy of science, and if this situation is unlikely to change, then such an approach should be preferred over its rivals. If, moreover, the alternatives are disastrous as ideals to be pursued, then their rejection is not merely justified, it is urgent.

## DEDUCTIVISM DEFINED

Consider the central question of confirmation theory, "When does a given body of data, D, confirm a hypothesis, H?" A theory of confirmation is "deductivist" if it offers a general answer, providing a necessary and sufficient condition for confirmation, specified in terms of logical relations between H, D, and (perhaps) other propositions. By "logical relations," I mean relations affecting logical entailment. Clearly, one aspect of the relevant logical relations between H and D will be this: H must entail D, or a relevant part or feature of D, at least when H is taken in conjunction with appropriate supplements. Deductivism is attractive because the following idea is attractive: a hypothesis is tested by seeing whether inferences it licenses from some phenomena to other phenomena correspond to sequences that are actually observed. Deductivist rules of confirmation describe the kinds of successful deductions that confirm.

Sometimes, "deductivism" or similar labels are used more narrowly, as when "hypothetico-deductive" confirmation is distinguished from confirmation by the observation of instances. These narrower usages are special versions of the broad one in question here. Thus, in an instantial theory, confirmation is basically the deducibility of an observed sequel from the hypothesis supplemented with the observation of an antecedent.

Because a whole approach is to be undermined, not just a version of it, the definition of "deductivism" should be broadly understood. While a deductivist theory offers a general answer to the question of when confirmation takes place, it may do so by presenting a disjunction of alternative routes to confirmation. The list of alternative appropriate logical patterns must, however, be complete. In describing the appropriate patterns, a deductivist theory may specify that certain deductive roles are to be fulfilled by propositions in certain broad epistemological categories, i.e., "theoretical" or "observational." Apart from this extra-logical element, however, a deductivist theory does not discriminate between different kinds of propositions. Above all, it does not lay down one description of the nature of confirmation in one field, another in another field. An important moral of deductivism is supposed to be: given a hypothesis, the investigator's commitments to other propositions, and the data encountered, we can determine whether confirmation exists by a single set of general rules, the same for every science.

In addition, "deductivism" is meant to include Popperian approaches, in which *dis*confirmation is identified with the entailment, in appropriate ways, of consequences incompatible with the data, and the closest a hypothesis comes to confirmation is "corroboration," i.e., not yet being disconfirmed despite efforts to do so. This refusal to make a sharp distinction between corroboration theories and traditional confirmation theories calls for arguments that fundamental problems of the latter affect the former as well. I will make those arguments after a survey of basic problems of the more traditional theories.

Finally, and most importantly, deductivism should be permitted to use the notion of simplicity. From the beginning, the notion has played an important role. In many ways, modern deductivism had its origins in the writings of philosophically minded physicists and chemists in Central Europe toward the end of the nineteenth century, for example, Kirchhoff, Mach and Hertz. Their basic idea was that science is a means of economizing in our dealings with nature, by providing propositions which simplify the deduction of unobserved events from present knowledge.[1] Similarly, in the most recent phase of the debate over confirmation, deductivists have relied on the notion of simplicity in discussing the long-standing problems of how to distinguish between permissible changes in auxiliary principles and unacceptable ad hoc modifications, and of how to distinguish between derivations which confirm theories and derivations of no empirical significance. Thus, Hempel writes, in remarks characteristic of recent deductivism, "[I]f more and more qualifying hypotheses have to be introduced to reconcile a certain basic conception with new evidence . . . , the resulting total system will eventually become so complex that it has to give way when a simple alternative conception is proposed. . . . Testability-in-principle and explanatory import [described in deductivist terms that are unadorned with considerations of simplicity] . . . are . . . only minimally necessary conditions that a scientific theory must satisfy . . . [A] good theory . . . offers a systematically unified account of quite diverse phenomena."[2]

---

[1] See, for example, G. R. Kirchhoff, *Vorlesungen ueber mathematische Physik*, vol. 1, *Mechanik* (Leipzig, 1874); Ernst Mach, "On the Economic Nature of Physical Inquiry" (1882) in his *Popular Scientific Lectures* (New York, 1895); H. Hertz, *The Principles of Mechanics* (1894; New York, 1956), Introduction.

[2] *Philosophy of Natural Science* (Englewood Cliffs, N.J., 1964), pp. 30, 75.

While the appeal to simplicity is a familiar aspect of deductivism, it has never been clear what a deductivist could mean by the notion. By the nature of the program, simplicity must be specifiable by a general description of appropriate logical relations. But there are few proposed descriptions of what those logical relations are and all of them are quite controversial. Worse yet, ordinary judgments of simplicity depend on individual tastes and interests, just the sort of subjective factor that deductivists want to make irrelevant to confirmation.

It would be unfair to assume that deductivists cannot interpret the relevant notion of simplicity as a general structure among logical relations. It would also be unfair to identify deductivist appeals to simplicity with any specific interpretation that has actually been proposed. To cope with this problem of fair criticism, I will proceed by stages. First, I will consider the problems deductivism encounters if it does not appeal to simplicity. Then, I will consider informal appeals to simplicity, relying on assessments of simplicity that are compelling in the absence of a well-developed explication of this term. Finally, I will consider one recent analysis of simplicity, Elliott Sober's, an analysis which is especially plausible, clear and typical, and intended to give new power to the deductivist approach.

## Simple Deductivism

Previous chapters have contained frequent occasional criticisms of simple deductivism, i.e., deductivism which is simple because it does not make use of the elusive and complex idea of simplicity. Some objections have been direct, others implicit in attacks on the covering-law model. To avoid undue repetition, I will just summarize and organize these past criticisms.

One problem with simple deductivism is that it cannot tell us what relations to the data confirm a theory, without including too much or including too little. The underlying difficulty is that the difference between relevant deductive premises and irrelevant excess is a matter of causal relevance, not of logical connectedness. Theories referring to unobservable entities need to be connected to data using auxiliary principles. If any accepted propositions can serve as auxiliaries, then data confirm the most bizarre hypotheses imaginable, if they confirm anything. Just take some confirmed hypothesis as the auxiliary principle. For example, the moon is made of Camembert would be confirmed by the data of Newton's time, since it entails the astronomical implications in the *Principia* when combined with the three laws of motion and the universal law of gravitation, taken as the auxiliaries. (That the Absolute is made of Camembert is, through similar tactics, confirmed now and forever—an especially poignant result since the classical positivists were specially dedicated to excluding cognitively meaningless hypotheses from science.) Of course, the hypothesis about the Camembert moon would do no work in the astronomical derivations. Seeking to exclude absurdities, deductivists have sometimes proposed that what is confirmed is only the core that remains when we subtract all that is logically inessential in a deduction of data.[3] But this requirement is much too exclusive, leaving important parts of major theories quite implausibly unconfirmed. We could not say that the atomic theory of matter is confirmed by the classical derivations of the gas laws, Avogadro's Number and laws of chemical combination. For only a few parts of the theory, having to do with valence and the composition of gases, are directly involved. On this basis, the use of other aspects of the theory, say, to explain phenomena of heat conduction, would be a leap of faith, unsupported by those past successes. Worse yet, though implausibly restrictive when actual inferences are considered, the new deductivist criterion turns out to be as permissive as the first, when the full range of available derivations is considered. For the old type of pseudo-confirming derivation, e.g., from the *Principia* combined with "The moon is made of Camembert," we simply substitute a logically fancier one. Let the indispensable auxiliary be "Either the moon is not made of Camembert or the *Principia* premises are true" while the hypothesis remains "The moon is made of Camembert." Now the "auxiliary" does not do all the work of entailment.

This first problem, of distinguishing relevant from irrelevant deductions, is primarily a problem about theoretical hypotheses. When a hypothesis concerns unobservable entities or processes, a deductivist must be fairly liberal in counting deductive patterns as confirming. By contrast, for generalizations involving observable properties, the relevant confirming relation seems definite and obvious (unless confirmation occurs indirectly, though the confirmation of a theoretical proposition supporting the generalization). Such a generalization seems confirmed by the observation of positive instances. Indeed, this is the prime example of a logical relation

---

[3] See, for example, Hempel and Oppenheim, "Studies in the Logic of Explanation" (1948) in Hempel *Aspects of Scientific Education* (New York, 1965), p. 248; cf. Hempel, "Empiricist Criteria of Cognitive Significance" (1950, 1951) in ibid., pp. 113–17.

which seems to be intrinsically confirming. Without it, deductivism would have very little initial plausibility. It is important, then, that this route to confirmation is blocked by a second fundamental problem. Some generalizations are confirmed by positive instances, but some are not. And the difference between those that are appropriate material for confirmation and those that are not seems, as before, a matter of causal relevance, not a matter of logical form. Propositions of identical logical form may fare very differently. What counts is whether, in the best reconstruction of how the data arose, they are due in part to a causal factor tending to make the generalization true.

The main examples of this problem for deductivism were Goodman's grue hypothesis and generalizations from mere coincidences, such as the three-weights law for ravens. The two kinds of examples are complementary. Goodman's use of specially constructed predicates shows that any purely formal rule of confirmation supports equally well statements that contradict each other wherever they describe the unobserved. So a preference for a hypothesis extending to the unobserved could never be justified. It might seem that deductivists could cope with this problem by using the few abstract epistemological distinctions at their disposal. Sophisticated deductivists only take extrapolation from instances to be the means of confirming laws concerning observable properties. It is not clear that "grue" is observable. But "weighing either 23.112 grams or 41.845 grams or 56.924 grams" is certainly observable. And the claim that the law was confirmed by taking the respective weights of the three ravens is, on reflection, quite implausible, reflecting another aspect of the deductivist neglect of the causal background, the neglect that also allows confirmation of "All emeralds are grue."

A third set of problems concerns the comparative nature of confirmation. If we neglect this dimension of confirmation, then, it has turned out, non-confirmed hypotheses (such as Mischel's delayed-gratification hypothesis) are counted as confirmed, the belief states that are the subject-matter of confirmation theory cannot be adequately defined, the boundaries of approximate truth cannot be measured, and our account of those event explanations that are "pseudo-explanations" for Hempel will be either too permissive or (as with Hempel) too restrictive. Moreover, among event explanations, a specific type of comparison is called for, the type that establishes adequate causal depth. Yet deductivism, even in the present broad understanding, lacks any comparative dimension. Confirmation connects, or fails to connect, a single hypothesis with the data through deductions which involve, at most, already accepted auxiliary principles.

It might seem that the definition of "deductivism" should simply be broadened a bit more to include theories which impose a requirement of comparison and rate rivals according to deductivist principles. This possibility should certainly be considered. However, the fundamental break with traditional deductivist assumptions should also be acknowledged. A major motivation of deductivism has been to show that the context in which a hypothesis is compared with the data affects only the pragmatics of confirmation, not the existence of confirmation itself.

Suppose that a deductivist makes the break with the past and acknowledges that confirmation requires comparison with relevant rivals. The neo-deductivist claims that the comparison is to be guided by rules singling out certain favored logical relations. Even if goodness of fit with the data were the only dimension of comparison, the problems would be formidable. Given the best available auxiliary principles (the only means we often have of connecting hypotheses with data), one hypothesis will typically conflict with some data, its rival with other data. How should the two hypotheses be compared, to determine which fits better? Mere counting of successes and failures seems a silly means of judgment, on the face of it, and in any case is usually quite nondecisive. On each hypothesis, the events which do not fit the theory will be indefinitely numerous. The seriousness of the anomalies is what needs to be weighed. However, there is no plausible rule for such weighing that is solely concerned with logical relations. And the real problems of trade-off are much more severe. Comparison takes place on diverse dimensions. For example, a relatively superficial theory or one tailored to the data after the fact may fit the data very well, but be worse on balance than a deeper and more fruitful theory which fits the data less well. Yet there is no attractive model of a feature of logical structure which balances one confirmatory virtue against another.

The one genuine deductivist hope for coping with the requirement of comparison is to identify the best hypothesis as the best means of simplifying derivations of the data and to try to interpret simplicity as a matter of logical form. I will soon consider this project in detail. For now, it is important to see what a desperate gamble it is. On the face of it, simplicity is not a matter of entailment relations. No one would have supposed it is, if this were not a promising means of saving deductivism, or some positivist program that is similarly imperiled by scientific practice.

A further problem of deductivism is that of distinguishing, on purely logical grounds, between tactics by which reasonable hypotheses are defended in the face of recalcitrant data and tactics by which even the most dubious hypothesis would be preserved. A hypothesis is often modified after the fact, so that recalcitrant data are treated as special and peripheral exceptions. Appeals are often made to the need for facilitating circumstances which are powerful enough to bring about the phenomenon in question, without further general specification of those circumstances. Counter-instances are often put to one side as taken from insufficiently similar situations, without specification of what would count as sufficient similarity. Deductivists have generally treated these tactics as always, by their very nature, unacceptable, if they cannot be avoided when all is made explicit. If confirmation is not comparison, and hypotheses are matched one-by-one with data, there is no alternative. Since confirmation must be an aspect of testing, i.e., of subjecting hypotheses to possible disconfirmation, the always available defenses cannot always be permitted. Since they must be excluded on grounds of logical form, they must be excluded wholesale, if they are excluded in particular cases. In the chapters on explanation, I argued that a variety of quite respectable hypotheses, some of them accepted parts of natural science, would have to be dismissed, as a consequence.

Indeed, when one considers the empirical anomalies that well-established theories can sustain for decades, even centuries, the tolerable burden is awesome. Until the last few decades, the hypothesis that matter is made of molecules, combined with the best-established theories of force, entailed that no floor could hold a person's weight. The modern theory of radiation, combined with the best-established hypotheses concerning celestial matter, entails that the night sky should be full of light. Until recently, the most advanced physiology implied that the stomach would dissolve itself in hydrochloric acid. No doubt, people were reasonable to suppose that the falsehood of the consequences, in each case, reflected falsehood in some relatively peripheral part of the premise, not the molecular hypothesis, Maxwell's equations, or elementary descriptions of the nature of digestion. The auxiliary beliefs combining with the basic theory must be relevantly false, though we do not know how (or did not know when the theories were already confirmed). Still, though this defense is sometimes acceptable on balance, it is not without cost. It had better not be, since any absurd theory can in principle be defended against contrary evidence in defenses with just this logical form. To rule out the absurdities, simple deductivism would have to rule out virtually every interesting theory we possess.

Finally, deductivism makes it difficult, in at least two ways, to fit confirmation into the broader epistemological context. Science contributes to empirical knowledge. Empirical knowledge has an intrinsically causal aspect, involving causal interaction between knowers and the facts they know. Confirmation is the means by which beliefs are formed in science. But, if deductivism is right, there is nothing intrinsically causal about confirmation. So science could not be a source of knowledge. Also, science, at least outside of pure mathematics, is largely based on sensory experience. But sensory experience is only centrally important because it is the raw material for causal reconstructions singling out scientific hypotheses through the use of truisms. Since deductivists take confirmation, the basic means of belief formation in science, to have no intrinsically causal element, they can offer no plausible account of the central role of sensory experience. That data have a favored relation to sense perception is an additional assumption, typically made, but not motivated or explicated by the basic theory of confirmation. This is ironic, since deductivists often take themselves to be the modern heirs of classical empiricism.

In light of these problems of a deductivism which does not appeal to constraints of simplicity, everything depends on the effectiveness of such appeals. Suppose that the goal of empirical laws is the simple summary of phenomena, the goal of theories the simple summary of laws, and the goal of science the simplification of our total calculations in dealing with nature. Going through the list of problems just developed, it is plausible that we might solve all but the last by appeals to these functions. Perhaps we can distinguish deductive patterns which confirm from those that do not by considering whether they establish that these simplifying functions are served by the hypothesis in question. Newton's *Principia* shows that mass-and-motion sequels can be derived from antecedents in a simple and uniform way. The same mass-and-motion facts are entailed if "The moon is made of Camembert" is added to Newton's laws, but that addition is a complication, not a simplification. By the mid-nineteenth century, the atomic theory of matter could, with simple supplements, entail a variety of empirical laws in different realms. Not all of the atomic theory was mobilized in these derivations. But a more complex statement would have resulted if hedges were introduced putting to one side the unused residue. "Grue" seems a more complicated predicate than "green." The disjunctive generalization about weights of ravens complicates ornithology, as compared with the standard assumption that bird weights may occur anywhere in species-specific intervals. As for the comparative dimension of confirmation, it might be thought to obey the rule that the rival which contributes to the simplest consistent system of science-plus-data is to be chosen. Finally, tactics of revision and defense might be admitted or condemned according to whether they complicate or simplify our derivations of observable facts.

These judgments of simplicity and their uses are obviously controversial. For example, one might wonder, even at first glance, whether a science in which empirical laws are derived from the atomic theory and relevant bridge laws really is simpler than a science which uses the empirical laws without further underpinnings. Moreover, even if the ratings of simplicity are defensible and the pursuit of simplicity does constrain confirmation, it might prove impossible to analyze simplicity as a feature of logical form. The relevance of simplicity would then establish the inadequacy of deductivism. Still, the strategy of imposing constraints of simplicity and explicating the constraints in a deductivist way is a plausible response to most of the problems surveyed. No other response can even claim this much. The fate of deductivism as a program likely to succeed stands or falls with the appeal to simplicity.

## The Irrelevance of Corroboration

At least in the United States, the dominant deductivist theories primarily explicate empirical support for a hypothesis, with confirmation by positive instances as the central paradigm. Half a century ago, Popper developed a different approach, in which disconfirmation, "falsification" as Popper usually puts it, is the primary notion. He was moved, in part, by important doubts about the positive-instance rule. The rule seems to elevate a fallacy, generalization from a single case or a limited number of cases, into a fundamental principle of scientific method. Of course, extrapolation to the general is sometimes warranted when a background of appropriate principles licenses it. But then methodology should concern itself with the justification of these substantive assumptions, not avoid this problem through sanctification of the positive instance rule.

Doubts such as these could lead to a causal theory of confirmation. They didn't lead Popper in this direction and couldn't, since he is as firmly committed as Hempel to analyzing causal talk away in favor of talk of regularities and entailments.[4] Instead, Popper developed a theory of testing in which disconfirmation is the central notion. Disconfirmation is treated in a deductivist fashion, as the discovery of data logically incompatible with the hypothesis. A hypothesis which has not been disconfirmed, despite efforts to find such data, is said to be "corroborated." Corroboration has the same implications for scientific practice as confirmation. Rational people use corroborated hypotheses to explain, and make plans on the assumption that a corroborated hypothesis is true. However, rational people do not actually believe in the truth of a hypothesis, not even its likely truth, because it has been corroborated.[5]

According to Popper, the rejection of confirmation for corroboration is a fundamental shift in the philosophy of science. I have labelled it a variation within the deductivist approach. Behind this matter of labels is a substantive question. Does the shift remove any of the fundamental difficulties of traditional deductivism, or in any case, suggest new and promising solutions? In fact, as the following survey shows, each problem with standard deductivism has a direct analog for Popperian deductivism. For both approaches, the appeal to simplicity is the only way out that holds any promise of success.

1. If corroboration were merely the non-existence of data contrary to implications, then extravagant speculations would be corroborated, just because they are so far removed from actual observations. For example, that planets of stars other than the sun have Camembert moons is corroborated. Even to require, as Popper does, that a corroborated hypothesis must actually have been put in jeopardy, is not enough. The conjunction of general relativity and the new Camembert hypothesis might be put in jeopardy and survive, without its being rational to rely on the conjunction, as corroborated. What we would like to say, in this case, is that the data would only be relevant to general relativity. Given the general need to rely on auxiliary hypotheses, one cannot lay it down that data are irrelevant to a proposition whenever another proposition is needed to make appropriate deductive connections. The tempting proposal, here, to exclude excess, is that a hypothesis is only corroborated if all its parts have been subjected, independently, to a possible disconfirmation, and have survived. That is the success that the Camembert-relativity conjunction does not enjoy, if only the relativity part is put in jeopardy. But this requirement is the falsificationist version

---

[4] See Karl Popper, *The Logic of Scientific Discovery* (New York, 1968), pp. 59–62.
[5] See ibid., ch. 10.

of the more traditional requirement that premises be minimal. And it has the same failing. Vast stretches of fundamental theories are rationally employed before these parts have themselves been matched, deductively, against the data. The main option left is to take only the simplest surviving alternative to be corroborated, and Popper has increasingly emphasized this rule. But note that the appeal to simplicity is no less urgent and no more promising here than in more typical deductivist theories. In both cases, it is a last resort in the same project, saying what counts as sufficient closeness to the data, using a general rule of reasoning that is concerned with logical form.

2. Though generalizations are not confirmed, for Popper, by the observation of positive instances, they are falsified if a negative instance is observed. So, through failure to falsify, "All emeralds are green" and "All emeralds are grue" have both been corroborated. In general, by gruifying predicates we can show that contrary explanations in terms of the unobserved and contrary plans for future contingencies are always equally corroborated. Since corroboration is supposed to be a basis for rational choice, this means no corroboration ever occurs.

3. It is as necessary and as hard to incorporate the comparative dimension into falsificationism as into standard deductivist theories. It may be unreasonable to rely on a hypothesis which *has* passed potentially falsifying tests, because those successes were just as likely if a rival hypothesis was true. (Consider the chocolate-bar study.) Moreover, the deduction of false implications using the best auxiliary principles we have does not falsify a theoretical hypothesis, in itself. Every theory is burdened with such anomalies. The solution to such problems is to take falsification to be comparative. Falsification means succumbing to a superior rival. But, except for the usual appeal to simplicity, there is no evident deductivist way to make the needed comparisons, given their real complexity.

4. On a deductivist basis, ad hoc revisions and ad hoc appeals to the absence of sufficiently facilitating circumstances or sufficiently similar ones must all be accepted or all rejected, because of their logical form. If all are accepted, there is no falsification. If all are rejected, perfectly acceptable hypotheses must be rejected as non-corroborated.

5. The fit with epistemology is even worse than in standard deductivism. As before, the account of rational scientific practice offers no basis for the claim that science contributes to empirical knowledge (given its causal nature) or the claim that science is based

on experience (given the peripheral deductive role of experience-reports). Worse yet, a new paradox is introduced into the theory of rationality. Rational people are said typically and standardly to base plans and explanations on propositions which they do not take to be more likely than not to be true.

## THE INADEQUACY OF BOOTSTRAPPING

Clark Glymour's description of how theories are confirmed by "bootstrapping," in his book *Theory and Evidence*, is the most powerful new version of deductivism to be developed in recent years. While it is an effort "to locate general, content-free principles determining the relation of evidence to theory," it is motivated by extensive reflections on the failings of classical efforts of this kind, for example, Hempel's, Carnap's and Reichenbach's. If this new deductivism is defeated by the same problems as the old, that is good evidence that deductivism (at least if it does not emphasize simplicity) is fundamentally misguided.

"The central idea," Glymour explains, "is that hypotheses are confirmed with respect to a theory by a piece of evidence provided that, using the theory, we can deduce from the evidence an instance of the hypothesis, and the deduction is such that it does not guarantee that we would have gotten an instance of the hypothesis regardless of what the evidence might have been."[6] Were it not for the proviso that the successful instantiation is not guaranteed, only confirmation-with-respect-to-a-theory, irrelevant to non-believers in the theory, would seem to have been described. Using the proviso, Glymour argues that genuine confirmation of individual hypotheses is yielded by this "bootstrapping," even though one part of a theory is used to support another. For instances of a hypothesis *are* produced, by applying another part of the theory to the data, when the same procedure might have yielded *counter*-instances. Thus, in Newton's *Principia*, a prime example for Glymour, the second law of motion is applied to the periods and distances of Jupiter's moons to yield an instance of the law that celestial objects attract each other with a force inversely proportional to the square of their distance. The agreement is not an artifact of the theory, since the second law is just as capable of instantiating other laws of force. Moreover, a well-confirmed theory will be one in which parts used to yield instances of other parts are similarly supported, in turn. "[O]ur faith

[6] *Theory and Evidence* (Princeton, 1980), p. 127.

in the instances of any hypothesis in the theory depends on our faith in the linkages used in obtaining those instances, and our faith in the linking hypotheses in turn depends on linkages, and so on."[7] Thus, in Glymour's account of Book III of the *Principia*, the argument that the force attracting the moon is the same as gravity depends on the principle that the force obeys an inverse square law, which is in turn supported by applying the second law to astronomical data. Glymour might have added that the second law itself is instantiated by Galilean experiments, if they are interpreted in light of the first law of motion.

Though Glymour claims that "confirmation proceeds along the general lines I have suggested,"[8] occasional vague hedges make it unclear just how strict or complete his proposals are meant to be. Moreover, many of his discussions can be accepted as penetrating criticisms of particular forms of skepticism about the testability of theories even if they are rejected as general descriptions of how evidence supports theories. The most revealing inquiry, for present purposes, is to see whether, and, if so, why there are fundamental barriers to identifying evidential support for a theory with successful bootstrapping. It will turn out that successful bootstrapping, like the other confirmatory virtues, is a rule of thumb, typically indicating a way of supporting a hypothesis through fair causal comparison. If it typically works it often fails, in the same general ways as classical deductivist accounts failed. And the causal theory best explains both why the bootstrapping strategy is sometimes quite misguided and why it is a handy rule.

The old problem that extends most immediately and directly to this new deductivism is assessing the significance of deductive success obtained through ad hoc tailoring of hypotheses to recalcitrant data. It is easy to produce successful bootstrapping in this way. If part of a theory is defeated by the data, amend the linking hypothesis so that the former succeeds, and, if need be, find a suitable amendment in the further linkages relevant to the latter. Such tailoring sometimes improves science. For example, quantum mechanics emerged from the old quantum theory through such a revision, the amendment of mechanics so that the quantization required by some data was no longer in flagrant conflict with other data. Sometimes, the need for such tailoring is a sign of defeat, not a basis for successful confirmation. Which verdict is justified de-

---

[7] Ibid., p. 151.
[8] Ibid., p. 137.

pends on whether the best explanation of the successful bootstrapping is the existence of the causal processes described in the bootstrapped hypotheses employed, or merely the ingenuity of the scientific tailors. (Thus, quantum mechanics results from suspending certain classical assumptions that had always been somewhat arbitrary as constraints on causes in nature. Mechanics was not merely tailored to fit the data.)

Of course, bootstrapping is often an important accomplishment, as many of Glymour's examples show. From a causal perspective, it is easy to see why. Often, one can point to a success with this formal pattern and argue that this success would be a fluke if the theory in question were not basically correct. If the theory were basically false, each part is unlikely to mobilize data in a way that supports the others. However, ad hoc modification threatens this assessment by supporting an explanation of mutual support that is causally independent of the theory's truth.

To the contrary, in his very brief discussion of ad hoc modification, Glymour proposes that the causal and historical phenomenon of ad hoc modification might be expected "to correspond to one or more logical distinctions."[9] But this guess seems implausible. Balmer's formula for the hydrogen spectrum has just the same logical form, and initially had the same deductive role, as generalizations defended through ad hoc modifications. For example, it has the same form as generalizations about the sequence of masses, densities or climates of the planets, counting outward from the sun, generalizations which have often been revised as new planets are discovered. Balmer's law was soon judged an important advance, while the latest planet "laws" have mostly been non-confirmed curiosities (assuming all actual planets were not known to have been discovered). An important difference is historical, not logical, the fact that Balmer's formula was confirmed after the fact by novel observations.

Another leading problem with the old deductivism is its inability to account for the confirmation of reasonably ambitious theories without opening the floodgates to absurdly excessive hypotheses. While Glymour's deductive strategy is partly developed in response to such difficulties, the old problem simply reappears in a new format, appropriate to the new deductive pattern.

Confirmation, once achieved in parts of a theory, can instantly extend to the whole, including parts with a very different subject-matter. For Glymour, this coverage, when justified, reflects a preference

[9] Ibid., p. 154.

for theories that are better-tested, in ways suggested by the bootstrapping strategy. Suppose there is a unifying theory (say, Daltonian atomic theory) entailing other, more piecemeal propositions (say, the laws of chemical combination, the classical gas laws, and certain laws of heat conduction). Then bootstrapping may connect the unifying theory with diverse evidence, producing actual congruence where the evidence might have yielded conflicting results. For example, atomic theory applied to chemistry entails that a mole of a pure gas always contains the same number of molecules, and this leads to consequences elsewhere, namely, in molecular thermodynamics, which are borne out, but might have been falsified. Taken apart from the unifying theory, each piecemeal hypothesis is less susceptible to such cross-checking.[10] Thus, good inferences to global theories might seem to reflect the fact that confirmation is bootstrapping: cross-checking is more strenuous and confirmation is stronger when bootstrapping is centered on a single ultimate target.

This admission of theories that are subject to cross-checking is certainly not license for the silly "confirmation" of "The moon is made of Camembert," since nothing like an instance of the latter hypothesis is yielded by applying Newtonian principles to data. But the preference for concentrated over diffuse testing has to be substantial, to support the ambitious inferences in question, and if it is, it will support bad inferences of its own kind.

In causal terms, preference for a unifying hypothesis, on the ground that a network of bootstrapping inferences supports it, involves dismissal of the possibility that the correlations in the results are false correlations, produced by processes at variance with the unifying hypothesis. Yet often, when we reject a well-bootstrapped hypothesis because we think the correlations false, the causal account we prefer is more piecemeal and disconnected, less well-tested in Glymour's terms. Glymour offers so-called "causal modelling" as the epitome of the bootstrapping strategy in the social sciences, and it happens to provide many examples of the pitfalls of false correlation.[11] The explanation of income inequalities is one

[10] Ibid., pp. 153, 162.
[11] Herbert Blalock, the pioneer of "causal modelling," acknowledges such pitfalls in frequent shrewd asides. Their total effect is, unintentionally, devastating. Thus, he mentions, almost in passing, "[D]isturbing influences must be explicitly brought into the model. But at some point, one must stop and make the simplifying assumption that variables left out do not produce confounding influences. Otherwise, causal

actual subject of a great deal of causal modelling. Embarrassingly enough, a unifying theory in which height is the main determinant of income, with parents' income, schooling, and location effective so far as they influence height, is bootstrapped about as well as any.[12] Each part of this hypothesis would do a reasonably good job of accounting for correlations in the data, often with help from other hypotheses tested against correlations, in their turn, with further use of linking hypotheses. No one takes this hypothesis seriously, which is to say that everyone prefers even the standard patchwork of piecemeal explanations, according to which part of income equality is based on parents' income and socio-economic status, part based on independent factors in schooling, part on region, part on racial and sexual prejudice. At a more serious level of controversy, a unifying hypothesis in which income inequality is attributed to differences in ability bootstraps reasonably well if ability is measured in thoroughly conservative ways, for example, if years of schooling and foremen's judgments are taken to be good measures of ability. There is a common-sensical criticism that much schooling is so obviously irrelevant to degree of competence on most jobs, that the high correlations of schooling and income suggest that something other than ability is at work. There is a left-wing criticism that points to the fact that the same correlations are explained if what conservatives take to be measures of ability in fact reflect processes primarily establishing and assessing acquiescence in one's social status. Both criticisms seem powerful, even if neither directs the cross-checks of bootstrapping toward a rival unifying hypothesis. Common sense is too piecemeal for this, while left-wing theories are often too qualitative to account for the structures of correlations emphasized by causal modellers.

Evidently, a rule to give substantial preference to unifying hypotheses which can be cross-checked by bootstrapping requires a hedge: "unless the cross-checking succeeds on account of causes at variance with the unifying hypothesis." But then, bootstrapping is not a promising basis for confirmation. For if we know how to distinguish false correlations from those that reveal actual causal connections, we have virtually the whole of the theory of confirmation. To return to the original example, a claim that the diverse evidence

---

inferences cannot be made." *Causal Inferences in Nonexperimental Research* (New York, 1972), p. 176.

[12] More precisely, degree of approach to a tall-and-slender ideal would be the unifying factor. See Samuel Bowles and Herbert Gintis, *Schooling in Capitalist America* (New York, 1976), p. 97.

coordinated by the atomic theory confirms it *unless* the coordination is a coincidence reflecting other kinds of causes, would not bring data to bear on the atomic theory. For opponents of the atomic theory were quite willing to commit themselves to piecemeal causal accounts, in which, for example, chemical affinities explained some phenomena, the "phenomenological" gas laws others. On their view, successful Daltonian bootstrapping was a coincidence, about the causes of which they were agnostic. Being piecemeal is not always a vice, as the social sciences show. No deductive structure seems to establish when it is a vice. The old problem of showing when theory building has moved too far beyond the data has returned in a new guise.

The final problem for bootstrapping that is relevant here (the strategy is not meant to shed light on the other problems of the old deductivism) is the essential role of comparison. That a theory connects with data in a bootstrap network of deductions does not depend on the nature of rival theories and their frameworks.[13] But this dismissal of comparison makes it impossible to respond to two striking problems produced by the identification of confirmation with bootstrapping: no interesting theory has ever literally been bootstrapped; and important theories have been confirmed without bootstrapping.

Glymour's prime examples of successful bootstrapping are Newton's arguments in Book III of the *Principia* and the support given to the atomic theory of matter when Avogadro's Number was assessed using different, potentially conflicting parts of the theory. But in these cases disconfirmation took place, if the strategy of bootstrapping is literally construed. One part of the theory yielded a counterinstance to another. By applying the inverse square law to the distance from earth to moon, Newton gets a value of "15 feet, 1 inch, and 1 line 4/9" for the acceleration of the moon in one second. By applying the second law of motion to pendulums, he obtains a value for gravitational acceleration of "15 . . . feet, 1 inch, 1 line 7/9."[14] The values do not agree. And Newton is notorious for favoring the particular measurements most supportive of his work. Elsewhere in the *Principia*, the differences are much greater.[15] As for the boot-

---

[13] See *Theory and Evidence*, p. 140.

[14] *Principia*, ed. F. Cajori (Berkeley, 1962), p. 408.

[15] For example, prior to totally ad hoc corrections, the velocity of sound derived using Newton's physics of contraction and dilation is 979 feet per second, while Newton accepts a value of 1,142 feet per second, based on standard methods of measurement (*Principia*, pp. 382f). Without similar ad hoc tailoring, even more farfetched

strapping of atomic theory, as late as 1913, studies of radioactivity yielded a value of 60 × 10²² for Avogadro's Number, studies of displacement in Brownian motion a value of 68.8 × 10²², and studies of the passage of light through crystals yielded a value of 75 × 10²².[16] Only physical theories have such a structure that one part applied to data could, in principle, entail an instance of another. Physical theories are the realm where bootstrapping could confirm, and there it never does.

Of course, Newton was right to take the agreement between the two accelerations as close enough. Perrin was not being foolish when he glossed the table of determinations of Avogadro's Numbers from which the above figures are taken with the exuberant comment, "One is seized with admiration before the miracle of such precise agreement coming from phenomena so different."[17] Yet in general, departures from expected values that are just as small can defeat a hypothesis. Newton is also being reasonable when he takes the failure of rival cosmologies to account for tiny perturbations in orbits to count against them. What determines whether a departure from expected values is small enough for confirmation is fair causal comparison. Newton and Perrin are right if the best explanation of the values obtained, fairly treating all current frameworks, is that the values obtained are due to the basic truth of the theory, compared with its rivals, together with the difficulties in precisely measuring the observable phenomena. After all, departures from Newtonian values which are no larger than Newton admits in connection with lunar acceleration made the orbit of Mercury a disconfirming case for Newtonian celestial mechanics, when relativity theory became its rival.[18]

The other large gap in a theory of confirmation based on bootstrapping is the existence of confirmation where bootstrapping is unavailable. Glymour admits, in passing, that there are cases in which the hypothetico-deductive model works (i.e., the only relevant deduction is the deduction of an empirical regularity from a theoretical hypothesis), but the confirmed theory cannot lift itself by

---

and atheoretical, the value for the highest tide derived from his celestial mechanics is three days too late (ibid., pp. 439, 665).

[16] Jean Perrin, *Les Atomes* (Paris, 1914), p. 293.

[17] Ibid.

[18] In fact, I think that the argument from congruence was not especially important in the triumph of the atomic theory. But the issue can be postponed, for the sake of the present argument. Certainly, atomic theory was not disconfirmed circa 1913, as a bootstrapping account of theory-testing implies. See Chapter 10, below.

its bootstraps. Thus, Bohr, in his early papers on the quantum theory, derived Balmer's formula and a few other regularities from a quantum model of the atom. But the theory he confirmed was not sufficiently rich to instantiate a theoretical hypothesis in one part by applying a theoretical hypothesis in another part to the data. Similarly, as Glymour notes, relativity theory lacks connections with the data of the bootstrapping sort. He might have added that modern quantum physics does not fare much better. On account of sheer computational complexity, the theory has only been applied to a very few, extremely simple systems, in the derivations that bootstrapping requires. Thus, although the explanations of standard chemical regularities is an important vindication of quantum physics, questions about anything more complex than a helium atom are settled using atheoretical rules of thumb such as the "free particle approximation."

Glymour proposes that hypothetico-deductive reasoning is enough only where it is supported by shared assumptions that certain kinds of evidence are "natural" means of testing certain kinds of hypotheses.[19] But this response is doubly unsatisfying. Quantum theory and relativity theory are the leading cases of innovations that involved the rejection of previous views as to what is a natural assumption in physical theorizing. Besides, most departures from bootstrapping violate the deductivist premises that the hypothetico-deductive approach shares with the bootstrapping model. So a residual appeal to the hypothetico-deductive approach cannot save the deductivist program. Darwin is admitting an absence of bootstrapping *and* of any other deductivist success when he says, "It is good thus to try our imagination to give any form some advantage over another. Probably in no single instance would we know what to do, so as to succeed. It will convince us of our ignorance on the mutual relations of all organic beings; a conviction as necessary as it seems difficult to acquire."[20] Given the absence of general non-tautological principles of selective advantage, part of his theory does not entail another part, given the data, *and* the theory plus part of the data does not entail other parts of the data. More precisely, any derivation requires such pervasive reliance on ad hoc claims about selective advantage and the like that any absurdity could be confirmed if this much ad-hocness were allowed, in general. The theory is simply nondeductivist. Also, as with most such theories, to say that

[19] *Theory and Evidence*, pp. 169–71.
[20] *The Origin of Species*, ed. J. W. Burrow (Baltimore, 1968), p. 129.

its support depends on a natural assumption about how such a theory should be tested is simply to ignore the nature of the ingenuity required in its support. Darwin's reasoning was not conventional or routine. It was "natural" only in that it was reasonable in ways that a theory of confirmation should explain.

If we take Bohr and Darwin to be engaged in fair causal comparison, their arguments work well. And the same perspective does justice to bootstrapping as a typical basis for triumph in fair comparison. Thus, the best means of filling the gaps in Glymour's theory also implies that the discovery of a bootstrap pattern is a typical means of constructing a fair argument from causal comparison. The same can be said of important hypothetico-deductive triumphs, discoveries that data can be deduced using the hypothesis in question. The discovery of such connections typically, though not always, points to an argument from fair causal comparison. Both the old and the new deductivism take useful rules of thumb in fair causal comparison and make them rigid rules of method.

I hope that deductivism now seems hopeless, unless it pervasively relies on appeals to simplicity. It is time to see whether such reliance offers a prospect of salvation.

## FORMAL SIMPLICITY: AN INFORMAL ACCOUNT

The criteria for hypothesis choice which might save deductivism are criteria of *formal* simplicity, the playing of a deductive role of a simplifying kind. The crucial contrast is with causal simplicity, the reduction of explanatory loose ends identified through empirical, substantive principles. A hypothesis gains in formal simplicity (in this section, I will often call this virtue "simplicity" without qualification) if it simplifies deductive processes in one of two ways. On the one hand, it may figure in simpler deductions of observed phenomena than are otherwise available. In this way, the pseudo-physics consisting of Newton's physics plus "The moon is made of Camembert" is obviously less simple than mere Newtonian physics. Similarly, derivations from a linear equation will often be simpler, as requiring less auxiliary information, than derivations based on higher-order equations. One can tell how much additional y is produced by a unit of x without knowing what part of the x-y curve is in question. On the other hand, the simplification may consist of unification. Formal simplicity increases when a hypothesis unifies a variety of diverse deductions, showing that they can be interpreted as the consequences, in turn, of a uniform general premise, applied to various specific circumstances or processes. Thus, while it did not, for many decades, simplify any particular derivation, the atomic theory of matter did unify the combined account of gas thermodynamics, chemical combinations, and heat conduction.

While the two varieties of formal simplicity are quite different, they are the two important aspects of simplicity in science, if science is a deductive mechanism for making inferences about unobserved but potentially observable phenomena. According to this view, the basic deductivist image of science, scientists are essentially concerned with developing a repertoire of premises with which we can make deductions about as yet unobserved phenomena on the basis of our knowledge of observed phenomena. This enterprise can be simplified in two ways, by simplifying the individual derivations and by simplifying the repertoire of premises.

The explication of formal simplicity, so far, has been quite vague. The question of what makes for simplicity in a derivation or in the statement of a body of knowledge has not been subjected to further analysis. In this section, I will avoid such further explication in fairness to the deductivist project. There is no accepted analysis of formal simplicity. But the appeal to formal simplicity is attractive prior to such analysis. It is only fair to investigate this appeal on the basis of the more natural assessments of simplicity from case to case, before looking at a particular, controversial explication.

Also in the interests of fairness, I will begin this investigation by looking at the area where the appeal to formal simplicity is most apt to advance the case for deductivism, if it ever does. Suppose two hypotheses are both deductively accurate, i.e., both have all true implications among the data when supplemented with accepted auxiliary principles and statements of initial conditions. Suppose that one of them makes a greater contribution to formal simplicity. If, in such cases, the simpler hypothesis is to be preferred, we may have a deductivist means of comparing rival hypotheses and a means of admitting theoretical advances while excluding irrelevancies. On the other hand, if simpler doesn't mean better even in these straightforward comparisons, the appeal to simplicity is very unlikely to overcome the problems of deductivism.

In fact, some well-confirmed and important hypotheses do poorly when rated according to formal, as opposed to causal simplicity. As usual, evolutionary theory is a great embarrassment to deductivism. Biology including evolutionary theory is substantially less simple than biology without it. To entail observational consequences or taxonomic laws of species characteristics, the theory needs to be supplemented by a variety of auxiliary hypotheses concerning organic function, ecological circumstances, differential survival, and, sometimes, embryological and genetic mechanisms. These hypotheses are often complex. They are, basically, ad hoc, amounting to the assumption of selective advantage for a trait on the basis of prior knowledge of selective success. Evolutionary theory does not simplify the derivation of phenomena, unobserved or, for that matter, observed. It does not formally simplify the body of biological knowledge, since the supplements are usually more complex and ad hoc than the regularities they explain. Thus, a mere description of the fossil sequence from *Eohippus* to the modern horse is simpler than the Darwinian paraphernalia used to explain it. By adding a variety of novel propositions, without any corresponding simplification, evolutionary theory reduces the formal simplicity of science. An enormous gain in causal simplicity results. For a variety of regularities which ought, according to all rival frameworks, to have causes only have causes assigned once the evolutionary principles are added. But this kind of simplicity is causal attribution governed by substantive framework principles, not deduction governed by a priori and formal rules.

The supposed paradigm of confirmation by simplification, the triumph of heliocentric astronomy, is in fact an example of the failure of the confirmed alternative to be simpler, just like the triumph of Darwinian evolution. Copernicus' complete system requires just as many circles as contemporary Ptolemaic systems, and is no more accurate.[21] On balance, Copernicus' system probably displays less formal simplicity, since, for example, he needs to ascribe three independent circular motions to the earth. Any advantages of his system are advantages of causal simplicity, determined by substantive, shared framework principles such as "the first principle of uniformity in motion" that makes equants a defect in Ptolemaic astronomy. Kepler's system does not fare much better. A system of Ptolemaic circles can fit the same phenomena as an elliptical system, to as close an approximation as one pleases. More circles are required, but, on the other hand, Kepler's elliptical motions are much more complex. Compared with Ptolemaic calculations, the calculation of successive positions becomes extremely difficult. In fact, Newton deals with this problem by reducing it to a problem involving circular motion.[22] The advantage of Kepler's system is that it respects the prin-

---

[21] See Kuhn, *The Copernican Revolution* (New York, 1959), pp. 169–71.

[22] *Principia*, pp. 112f. Goldstein notes, in a standard contemporary textbook in me-

ciple of uniformity in motion, and is a promising start toward filling the great gap in previous astronomy, the lack of a plausible explanation of the mechanics of planetary motion. Indeed, Kepler developed his second law on the basis of speculations about such mechanisms.[23] Even Newton's system is no obvious triumph of simplicity, since precise derivations of orbits in a more-than-two-body Newtonian system seemed difficult even to Newton, and turned out to be impossible in principle. The clear triumph was rather the explanation of what produces planetary motion.[24] In sum, simplicity looms very small in the part of science that provides its most standard illustration.

In claiming that the theory of evolution complicates science, I emphasized the complexity of the supplements through which the theory is deductively connected with empirical facts. This might seem unfair, since the unification of science is a distinctive aspect of simplicity. The theory of evolution, as opposed to the supplements which connect the theory with phenomena, is simple. Why not count it as unification if a simple theory entails a variety of empirical regularities, when joined with supplements however complex? The problem is that the original difficulties about the scope of confirmation return in full force, once we remove limits on the complexity of auxiliary principles. Absurd theories are now licensed, through the power of their supplements. For example, chemistry based on Aristotle's four elements can now triumph over the relative complexity of the periodic table. We simply derive empirical facts using elaborate supplements concerning the properties of the four elements and of their combinations in various circumstances. The only hope of excluding these absurdities without excluding worthwhile theories is an insistence that a hypothesis simplify the totality of science, including the structure of supplement and deduction which links up statements about different phenomena.

It might seem that deductivism should be allowed its own version of the preference for hypotheses with fewer explanatory loose ends:

---

chanics, "Indeed, it can be claimed that the practical need to solve Kepler's equation to accuracies of a second of an arc over the whole range of eccentricity fashioned many of the developments in numerical mathematics in the eighteenth and nineteenth centuries." *Classical Mechanics* (Reading, Mass., 1981), p. 102.

[23] See Kuhn, *The Copernican Revolution*, pp. 214–16, where Kuhn shows that even the development of the first law significantly depended on Kepler's view of celestial mechanics.

[24] I argue for this primacy of mechanics in the fair comparison of cosmologies in Chapter 9.

a hypothesis is superior if it is a premise in derivations of answers to more questions. However, this revision also fails. For one thing, deductivists must take explanation, here, to be deduction according to the covering-law model. Otherwise, the injunction to reduce explanatory loose ends abandons the deductivist approach. But in its explanations of regularities, the theory of evolution does not conform to that model. Other, quite legitimate hypotheses, e.g., functionalist hypotheses in social anthropology, have turned out to share these features. In the second place, the requirement that as many answers as possible be derivable has an intrinsic tendency to compete with the more standard aspects of formal simplicity. Rivals offering more answers tend to have additional, more speculative elements, connected to the data through additional supplements. Sometimes, as in the case of evolutionary theory, confirmation results. But often, it does not. A theory answering questions about violations of locality in quantum mechanics by appealing to evil demons at the sub-quantum level is not confirmed. The revised deductivism asks us to choose hypotheses according to intrinsically competing considerations, which cannot be ranked in a rigid lexical order. Yet it provides us with no way of balancing these considerations. And, within the deductivist approach, there is no hint as to how this gap might be filled.

Deductivists sometimes admit that evolutionary theory is a recalcitrant case, but treat it as a special one. In fact, the sacrifice of formal simplicity for causal simplicity is common in all theoretical sciences. We must judge a proposed theory in light of our present knowledge of relatively superficial empirical regularities that the theory is supposed to explain. Often, a theory is confirmed when the latter regularities are sparse, even though they are important levers for fair comparison. In such cases, science with the theory is apt to have less formal simplicity than a "phenomenological" alternative that states the few empirical regularities and denies the existence of any deeper causes. Thus, Newtonian science is more complex and no more accurate than a phenomenological alternative stating Keplerian regularities, Galilean principles of terrestrial motion, the tidal tables and the speed of sound. (Admittedly, there are a few astronomical phenomena, in the *Principia*, that have no simple non-Newtonian statements. But on the other hand, Newton's derived values for the speed of sound and tidal regularities are grossly inaccurate. Someone just concerned with formal simplicity and deductive accuracy would find the phenomenological alternative at least as good, probably better.) Certainly, nineteenth-century regularities stated phenomenologically make for simpler total science than atomic theory and its derivations of those regularities. Perhaps atomic theory, opposed by scientists as insightful as Kelvin, Helmholtz and Poincaré, was *not* confirmed in the nineteenth century.[25] Still, atomic theory circa 1880 surely was not *disconfirmed*. It would be if formal simplicity were an important confirmatory virtue.

Indeed, far from supporting the appeal to formal simplicity, the fruitfulness of fundamental physical theories ultimately undermines it. Suppose that rational physical science did evolve through the choice of the formally simpler alternative. Then the ultimate fruitfulness of physical theories, their capacity to entail old laws and supply new ones in a variety of fields outside the initially confirming ones would be quite miraculous. It is as if the simplest scheme for classifying my birthday cards would be a fruitful clue to the contents of the map room in the New York Public Library. On the other hand, there is no miracle if the causal theory of confirmation describes the best scientific practice. The basic theories are descriptions of what matter is made of and of how its constituents and aspects interact. They are chosen as describing causal processes governing certain phenomena. If matter has a certain structure and that structure governs certain phenomena, it is very likely to have an effect on other phenomena, as well. So the basic description will be fruitful elsewhere.

The attack on formal simplicity so far has concentrated on simple situations of hypothesis choice in which two competing hypotheses have equal deductive accuracy so that superiority must be decided on other grounds. The standard deductivist case studies used to motivate appeals to formal simplicity, for example, deductivist accounts of the vindication of heliocentric theory or of the triumph of the atomic theory over more superficial "phenomenological" physics, all have this structure. But in the real world of science, candidates for acceptance may differ in deductive accuracy. And the more accurate need not win. When this complication is admitted, the deductivist appeal to simplicity looks even less promising than before.

Any interesting theory entails some false observational consequence when combined with supplements which are as well-warranted as we can require for purposes of confirmation. There is always some point at which instruments interpreted within the

[25] On the opposition to atomic theory, see Bellone, *A World on Paper* (Cambridge, Mass., 1980), and Chapter 10, below.

supposed limits of their accuracy assign boundary conditions to theories which yield observational entailments conflicting with magnitudes which are also observed. Far from overthrowing all theories, these anomalies are often regarded as mere curiosities. That contemporary physics combined with the best assessments of the energy of stars yields the prediction that the night sky will be bright is a puzzle that challenges physicists. But it is not a challenge to basic physical theory.

In the causal account of confirmation, the deductive inaccuracy of important, well-confirmed theories is no surprise. Indeed, it is to be expected. The different fields of science develop unevenly. So if a hypothesis about a broadly important aspect of reality is true, we would expect it to have false implications when joined with some auxiliary hypotheses from less "ripe" fields, used to make deductive connections with the data. In any case, what we are pursuing in science is the approximate truth of a hypothesis, as against the basic falsehood of its rivals. The departures from precise truth are bound to lead to significant, observable falsehood in some particular cases. This is not to say that inaccuracy does not matter in the causal account. Rather, reflection on deductive inaccuracies is part of the process of fair comparison of causal accounts of the relevant history of data-gathering and of science in general. Within relevant frameworks we ask whether the best explanation of the deductive inaccuracies attributes them to the uneven development of science, the limitations of approximate truth, or the falsehood of the hypothesis, as compared with relevant rivals.

By contrast, the deductivist approach is deeply troubled as soon as deductive accuracy is seen to be one dimension of choice among several, and a matter of degree. There are now two kinds of deductive virtues, accuracy and simplicity. Hypotheses must be compared for deductive accuracy, and comparison cannot consist of discarding a hypothesis as soon as an inaccuracy is found. But merely counting inaccuracies is an arbitrary and unsatisfactory means of comparison. In the causal theory, we compare in a process of fair historical reconstruction, asking whether the inaccuracies concern standard problems, well-developed fields of science, and so forth. If, in a deductivist approach, we look for purely formal characteristics distinguishing crucial inaccuracies from peripheral ones, none seems to be available. Worse yet, even if the judgment of relative fit with the data is straightforward, other considerations are competing and potentially overriding. Often, a deeper theory fits the data more loosely than more superficial ones, as in the case of Newton's physics and nineteenth-century atomic theory, compared with their phenomenological rivals. To yield an assessment of these cases, deductivism would have to include formal rules for balancing deductive accuracy, the advantage of "phenomenological physics," with formal simplicity, which, for the sake of argument, we might take to be the advantage of the more theoretical alternatives. No such rule is laid down in the deductivist literature.

## AN ANALYSIS OF SIMPLICITY

Deductivism needs to go beyond our intuitive piecemeal judgments of simplicity, to construct an adequate theory of confirmation. By doing so, it might still save itself. Perhaps our informal ideas about simplicity, like our pre-theoretic ideas about entailment and proof, are only vague and unreliable sketches of the concepts which are needed for scientific purposes. In all fairness, then, we should look at analyses of simplicity which are general, clear, framed in a vocabulary appropriate to deductivist rules, and intended to contribute to a deductivist theory of confirmation. For reasons of space, I will only discuss what I take to be the best account of this kind, Elliott Sober's, in his book, *Simplicity*. Fortunately, his discussion, the only booklength one in the literature, is not at all idiosyncratic. For example, it resembles Popper's and Kemeny's proposal that simplicity is high falsifiability. Thus, it is a good paradigm, apart from its intrinsic merit.

Sober begins by stating the goal of science which dominates the deductivist image of science, as previously described. "By enabling us to anticipate the course of our sensations, hypotheses make the results of observation less surprising and less informative. . . . [R]equiring that theories inform us is equivalent to requiring that the world be made that much less able to tell us something new."[26] Simplicity, as he analyzes it, is informativeness of this kind. Relative to a given question, one hypothesis is simpler than another if it requires less minimum extra information (Sober uses the abbreviation MEI) to answer the question. Answering a question is entailing an answer, in conjunction with the extra information. The amount of content in the MEI set for the hypothesis and in the set of propositions defining the alternative answers to a question are determined by general rules referring solely to the internal syntax of the hypothesis and the question. The details are not important, for pres-

---

[26] Elliott Sober, *Simplicity* (Oxford, 1975), p. 1.

ent purposes. What is important is that the analysis scrupulously observes deductivist constraints.

So far, only simplicity relative to a given question has been described. But we are interested in simplicity, not simplicity-relative-to-a-question, and these two kinds of judgments may conflict. Relative to Goodman's question, "Is this grue?", "All emeralds are grue" is simpler than "All emeralds are green." But we take it to be the more complex proposition. And relative to "Is this green?", it *is* more complex, since we need to know both whether this is an emerald and whether it was observed before the grue-defining time. Sober's analysis of simplicity (*simpliciter*, not relative to a question) is suggested by this example. Simplicity is necessarily relative, not to a particular question but to a set of predicates which we take to be the natural means of describing the world. In effect, the questions as to whether these predicates do or do not apply to arbitrarily chosen individuals are taken to be the question set with respect to which simplicity is defined.[27] If one hypothesis is simpler than another relative to each natural question which they both can answer, then it is simpler. If comparisons relative to different questions yield contrary results, then the questions must be weighted for importance in resolving questions of simplicity. As for the determination of what predicates are natural and how important they are—as Sober describes the procedure, it introduces an element of circularity into the analysis, without, it seems, rendering it uninformative. A predicate is natural and has a certain weight if it is part of the weighted predicate family the use of which would preserve most of our intuitive judgments of simplicity, when the further analysis proceeds in Sober's way.[28] Sober acknowledges that other bases for choice of the predicate family, and perhaps other approaches to naturalness and relative weight are worth investigating.

In some respects, this analysis conforms to ordinary ratings of simplicity. A law limited to a special case is less simple by this standard than a law without the limitation, since the MEI for the former law includes the additional information that the condition is met. A law describing a natural process uniform over time is simpler than a law describing a changing process, since in the former case information as to time of occurrence is not part of the MEI. A hypothesis of an elliptical orbit is more complex than a hypothesis of a circular one since one needs more information to determine the curvature

[27] Ibid., p. 25.
[28] Ibid., pp. 27f.

of the curve at various arbitrarily chosen points. In other respects, the analysis departs from ordinary judgments. For example, a hypothesis does not become less simple as it is conjoined with additional propositions. Since simplicity is relative to the total family of natural predicates (i.e., to all the questions they determine) the MEI for answering the relevant questions will often decrease, so that the elaborate conjunction is simpler. So long as new conjuncts are not less simple themselves, elaboration never reduces simplicity. Since these departures from ordinary usage are dramatic, Sober is not prepared to recommend his analysis as an explication of the ordinary notion. Rather, it is supposed to integrate most aspects of the ordinary notion into a concept which plays a central role in the theory of hypothesis choice. It "provides both an explication and a justification of the use of simplicity in hypothesis choice," telling us what we ought to mean if we say that hypotheses ought to be chosen for their simplicity, when they fit the data equally well.[29] In particular, Sober proposes that this dictum be understood in the following way. Let k be the minimum degree of fit between data and hypothesis which a reasonable person requires if he or she is to choose the hypothesis. This is "the caution threshold which we bring to bear in a particular situation of hypothesis choice."[30] If two hypotheses are both above the threshold, the simpler should be chosen. If neither is, neither should be chosen. If one is and one isn't, the one above the threshold should be chosen. If both are equally simple, the one fitting the data better should be chosen.

For present purposes, the question is not whether Sober's analysis of simplicity succeeds as a whole, but the narrower one of whether it provides a means for deductivism to succeed in overcoming the obstacles it has encountered. These questions are closely related, however. Since it is not an accurate summary of ordinary usage, Sober's analysis ought only to be accepted as defining a methodologically useful concept related to the ordinary notion. In particular, it ought to function in the best theory of hypothesis choice, Sober's favored terrain. If deductivism turns out to be inferior to the causal approach, in which formal simplicity gives way to causal simplicity, then there is no point in adopting Sober's analysis. At best, it should be adopted as the most charitable reconstruction of what deductivists have appealed to, when they have falsely claimed that formal

[29] Ibid., p. 19.
[30] Ibid., p. 34.

simplicity, together with deductive accuracy, is the basis of confirmation.

The problems of deductivism remain when we take simplicity as Sober defines it to be a confirmatory virtue. The analysis does help, not by contributing to the theory of confirmation, but by revealing limitations of formal simplicity and confusions which have made appeals to that notion attractive.

The problem of confirming theories without confirming absurdities and irrelevancies remains, as resistant as ever, though it takes on some distinctive details. Simplicity seemed to help, here, because the genuine theories are vindicated by their simplifying role as premises for entailing data. If simplicity means making experience redundant, it is not clear, initially, how theories help. To take a typical example, at any given time, the capacity of the best phenomenological physics to answer the "natural" questions to which it is addressed seems as great as the capacity of the molecular-kinetic theory to answer those questions. Indeed, given the inevitable inaccuracies in theoretically determined values, the theory will answer the question less accurately than the best phenomenological alternative. Sober points out, however, that extra content may add to informativeness in the following way. The logically stronger hypothesis may offer an alternative way of resolving a question along with the ones the sparser hypothesis supports. Adapted to the present example (his own are taken from optics), the kinetic theory permits us, in principle, to derive a fact about the temperature of a gas from attributions of mass and velocity to molecules. Or, we can proceed as the gas laws allow, basing the calculation on pressure and volume inputs. The availability of an alternative means of calculation renders a hypothesis more informative, both intuitively and according to Sober's detailed technical analysis.

The production of alternative ways of answering questions about observables is the only kind of simplification which seems available, here, to warrant theories describing relatively deep causal mechanisms. Certainly, it is the only warrant mentioned in Sober's book. So what theories are chosen or rejected will be very sensitive to what is counted as a way of answering a question about observables. If we were to insist that the answers relied on phenomena that are actually observable by current means as providing their auxiliary information, there would be no appropriate independent means of measuring molecular magnitudes in the vindication of molecular-kinetic theory. In general, on account of their extra burden of empirical uncertainty or inaccuracy, theories describing unobservable entities would typically be excluded in favor of laws correlating observables, if actual means of observation are required. To avoid this over-restrictiveness, we must require no more than that relevant inputs be determinable in principle. And the irrelevant, merely "practical" barriers to determination may be much more than technological. As in the case of "selective advantage" in evolutionary theory or assumptions about atoms and molecules in the nineteenth century, we may have no idea what an independent measurement based on data would be like.

When we stretch simplicity-as-informativeness as far as we have to to admit legitimate hypotheses, absurdities creep in. If the kinetic theory is admitted, so is the hypothesis that temperature-pressure-volume relations among gases reflect agitation by tiny, claustrophic gas demons. Granted, the demon theorists cannot give us independent demonic measurements to apply, in actual calculations. But this is no more than the drawback of evolutionary theory or nineteenth-century atomic theory. As always, there is no deductivist measure of how far a theory can stray from the data without getting lost.

The second major problem with deductivism concerned the difference between generalizations which are confirmed by positive instances and those that are not. In Sober's account, the discrimination between the two kinds of hypotheses is written into the contents of the family of natural predicates. "All emeralds are green" is preferred as simpler than "All emeralds are grue," "All ravens range from approximately three to six grams" as simpler than "All ravens are 3.114 grams or 4.512 grams or 6.012 grams," because the natural questions about mineral types concern colors, not "crulers," the natural questions for bird species concern ranges of weights. The "because" is misleading, though. Sober proposes that we construct the family of natural predicates to fit the judgments of simplicity. Our preference for efficiency in answering certain questions is assumed to be right.

The result of this assumption is a substantial gap in confirmation theory. Although we do not describe bird species through disjunctions of highly precise weights, we do describe chemical elements through disjunctions of highly precise atomic weights. This is not a mere preference, but a rational response to data. That the chemical world may "naturally" be described in this way is an outcome of the theory of the periodic table. But the choice of such deep theories is the area where the appeal to simplicity is most urgently needed. The circularity is quite general. Simplicity is relative to a favored vocabulary. The choice of a favored vocabulary depends on the choice of a theory. The choice of a theory depends on simplicity (if there is anything to the deductivist appeal to simplicity). Perhaps deductivism can break out of the circle. But, at a minimum, the dependence of simplicity judgments on empirical theories means that deductivism's special problems with theory confirmation will infect the appeal to simplicity in the account of how laws, even observational ones, are confirmed by positive instances.

Finally, consider Sober's general account of how to compare hypotheses. Its most striking feature is its insensitivity to differences in empirical support among unequally simple hypotheses above "the caution threshold." This is a remarkable feature. If there was such a thing as a caution threshold for theories of species formation, Lamarck's and Darwin's were both above it. Lamarckian evolution is simpler since, for example, information about the geographic isolation of a species is not needed. On Sober's account, then, Darwin was wrong to recommend his more complex theory on the grounds of superior empirical support. Similarly, Kepler was wrong to recommend his more complex theory over a rudimentary seven circle Copernican theory, which fits the data fairly well.

There is one conception of science in which restriction to thresholds makes sense, and these counter-examples have no weight. Suppose we take any deductive inaccuracy to be lethal. A threshold of caution represents the amount of trying-to-derive-false-implications, without success, that must precede theory choice. Copernicus' theory and Lamarck's are simply falsified, and, so, need not be compared with rivals for relative support. In general, once the threshold is reached, all depends on simplicity, since any further non-falsification just tells us once again that the hypothesis has passed a test it might have failed. This is, of course, a natural extension of Popper's approach to confirmation. By the same token, it does not fit the facts of science. Deductive inaccuracy is not lethal. Lamarck's theory, seven-circle Copernican theory, and, for that matter, Newton's theory were in the running, and were only defeated by competitors whose theories fit the evidence better.

Apart from the problems of traditional deductivism, the criterion of simplicity-as-informativeness creates a new one. We certainly prefer informativeness in hypotheses. But greater informativeness is not a basis for preferring a hypothesis as more likely to be true. And likelihood in light of the data is the subject-matter of the theory of confirmation.

"All ravens are black and say 'caw-caw' " is more informative than

"All ravens are black."[31] But this judgment in no way implies that "All ravens are black" is less likely to be true. This irrelevance of simplicity to questions of truth makes it hopeless to use the notion to resolve such central problems as confirming theories without confirming irrelevancies. That the demon theory of heat lacks simplicity turns out to tell us no more than the obvious: the theory is vague. But in comparison with rivals, this is no more of a defect than the disadvantage of "All ravens are black" as against "All ravens are black and say 'caw-caw.' " So no light is shed on the irrationality of accepting the demon theory as excess, not at all confirmed.

In principle, it might have been bad strategy for philosophers to single out the question, "Is this more likely than not to be true?" as a distinct subject-matter, independent of such other interests in propositions as the interest in informativeness. Perhaps they should have constructed a general theory of hypothesis choice, with empirical support and simplicity as two aspects, as *Car and Track* develops rules for car choice, with fuel economy and maneuverability as two aspects. This is probably Sober's own position.[32] But previous examples show that philosophers of science have, in fact, been wise to isolate a distinct kind of choice as their object of study. If we mix empirical support and simplicity in the way prescribed by Sober's own general theory, we are led to the choice of Lamarck over Darwin, rudimentary Copernicus over Kepler, and other choices which reject the better-confirmed alternative. Yet no other rule for ranking empirical support and simplicity in a general theory of hypothesis choice seems any better. The general theory of hypothesis choice is as much a chimera as the general theory of how to chose a time of day. We need to ask, "Choose for what?" If we are choosing for confirmation, we are never choosing for formal simplicity.

Sober's is one of a cluster of analyses in which simplicity is ease of testability.[33] Yet there are other approaches outside this cluster, such as Goodman's, emphasizing the sparseness of the vocabulary of a theoretical system. Despite this diversity, the same examples and similar arguments work to the same effect whenever a concept of simplicity is used to save deductivism. For example, the rational preference for more complex theories, Darwin's over Lamarck's,

[31] See ibid., p. 28.
[32] See ibid., pp. 164–66.
[33] See also Popper, *The Logic of Scientific Discovery*, pp. 140–42; John Kemeny, "The Use of Simplicity in Induction," *Philosophical Review* (1953), pp. 391–408; and, in the recent literature, Michael Friedman, "Explanation and Scientific Understanding," *Journal of Philosophy* (1974), pp. 5–19.

say, or Kepler's over the rudimentary version of Copernicus', must be dealt with. The only available tactic is to emphasize the greater success of the less simple hypothesis along dimensions of hypothesis choice other than simplicity. In each case, the emphasis on these other dimensions must become so great that the other dimensions become the whole story of confirmation.

If the appeal to simplicity is such a failure, why is it so great a temptation? Perhaps the biggest benefit of Sober's analysis is its helpfulness in locating the real, though misleading, attractions of the view that formal simplicity and empirical fit are the two major grounds for confirmation.

The fact that one hypothesis is more informative than a rival (in Sober's sense) is often important raw material for an argument that the best account of the data entails the approximate truth of the former, even though neither rival is in deductive conflict with the data. Less information is, in general, required to derive implications of the former hypothesis, and this suggests (in itself, all else being equal) that false implications were more apt to have been uncovered if the former hypothesis were really false.

It might seem, then, that formal simplicity is itself a virtue, for purposes of confirmation. But this has turned out to be wrong. On the broad construals of formal simplicity that admit the demon theory of gas dynamics along with the molecular theory, formal simplicity had better not be a virtue, since otherwise the demon theory would be superior to the body of superficial gas laws. On narrower construals, excluding such absurdities, molecular theory, Darwinian theory and other rationally superior theories would also be defeated by mere superficial rivals. All that can be said is that formal simplicity figures in an important rule of thumb: "See if the hypothesis requires less MEI than its rival, to answer relevant questions. That may be part of a fair argument for its superiority in causal comparison." This no more shows that formal simplicity describes a confirmatory virtue than the rule, "See if someone resists cajoling; this may be part of an argument that he or she has moral integrity" shows that stubbornness is in itself a form of moral integrity. Moreover, the rule of thumb could not describe an independent virtue, since the whole theory of confirmation is implicit in the selection of certain questions as the relevant, "natural" ones. As usual, deductivism takes one standard clue in the construction of causal comparisons and makes it seem an essential part of confirmation.

Because "Pursue informativeness" is just one rule of thumb among others, when we know the specific kind of MEI employed and the nature of relevant rivalries the appeal to simplicity sometimes has no weight. IQ-based arguments for the intellectual inferiority, on average, of blacks often include the claim that the equation of IQ with relative intelligence makes intelligence theory more informative, while preserving deductive accuracy. Questions about intelligence are answered on the relatively concise basis of test scores. But when the actual history of IQ testing is joined with the leading egalitarians' accounts of racism and of racial bias in education and psychology, the inequality in average IQ scores is what would be expected if blacks and whites were equal in intelligence. Hypotheses about intelligence including the equation with IQ will still be more informative. But given the actual context of the dispute over alleged racial differences, this will not add to the likely truth of the IQ-based hypotheses. Indeed, in the best rival frameworks, the informativeness of hypotheses including the IQ-intelligence equation *distorts* the nature of intelligence, because the latter is an objectively vague phenomenon.[34]

Quite apart from its function in the rule of thumb, formal simplicity, as Sober defines it, is a virtue for many purposes of hypothesis choice. Indeed, most processes of belief change in science can be described as the pursuit of more informative hypotheses. For one thing, in the normal moments of science, when received beliefs are applied, not tested, the dominant goal is to refine and develop the beliefs, i.e., to make them more informative. There is an apparent paradox, here, since scientists are not typically interested in mere lists of observations, least of all during the confident "normal" phases of science. Sober's analysis is useful in removing this paradox, distinguishing informativeness in hypotheses from the proliferation of data. But, despite its importance, the shift to more informative hypotheses is just a shift to something more informative. It is not, as such, a shift to hypotheses which are more likely to be true, in light of the data. Given the same source of information, ornithologists prefer a report describing the typical colors of a new species to one that does not. This is not because they take reports including colors as more likely to be true than color-neutral ones.

---

[34] I do not mean to suggest that the IQ intelligence equation and its racial uses fit observed magnitudes well whenever joined with generally accepted auxiliary hypotheses, but only that the deductive fit that actually exists is much less important than usually supposed. For descriptions of significant failed "test implications," see Bowles and Gintis, *Schooling in Capitalist America*, ch. 4; and Ned Block and Gerald Dworkin, "I.Q. Heritability and Inequality" (1974) in their *The I.Q. Controversy* (New York, 1976).

There is another goal that makes informativeness important. Once we understand basic causal connections, our further concern often is to use this knowledge for efficient prediction and control. This supports a preference for the informative, but a preference which need have nothing to do with testing and confirmation. Suppose that we know that the tensile strength of an alloy varies with temperature. Given a scattergram, we will choose the best-fitting straight line over the best-fitting quadratic curve, unless the fit of the former is enormously inadequate. The linear equation is more informative, since it tells us, without further information, the rate of change of tensile strength at an arbitrary point on the curve. The quadratic equation only yields this information if the actual temperature is known. It is reasonable, then, to prefer the linear equation as a better means of coping with reality. But it is not reasonable to prefer it as a better means of describing the nature of reality. One sign of this difference is our relative insensitivity to looseness of fit when we choose the best-fitting linear equation over the best-fitting higher-order one. Even if the latter fits substantially better, as assessed, say, by the least-squares method, we usually prefer the former, unless the line is extremely ill-fitting. This attitude toward data is cavalier, if we are wondering whether the real relation between temperature and tensile strength is linear, but quite reasonable if we seek the hypothesis which is an economical means of coping with reality.

Similarly, given their inability to measure the size and mutual repulsion of molecules, Maxwell and Boltzmann sometimes employed hypotheses because the latter were simple and informative in just Sober's sense. And they always clearly distinguished their uses of such hypotheses from other derivations which really did confirm. Indeed, Boltzmann, in this spirit, often worked with the ridiculous assumption that molecules are infinitesimal.[35]

When we add these pragmatic reasons for hypothesis choice to

[35] See Ludwig Boltzmann, *Lectures on Gas Theory* (Berkeley, 1964), p. 318; and, on the simplifying assumption for the force of repulsion between gas molecules, ibid., p. 168. Of course, fitting a curve to a scatter-gram can be relevant to confirmation. The existence of a best-fitting curve of a certain kind may be likely if one phenomenon affects the other in a certain way, unlikely on rival hypotheses. This fit will be confirming on any reasonable account, causal, deductivist or Bayesian. It has no special bearing on formal simplicity. What does seem important is our preference for simplicity among equally well-fitting curves, even when we lack specific substantive prior beliefs that the causal relations are described in some lower-degree equation, with allowance for small and random interference. This preference is relevant to formal simplicity, but irrelevant to confirmation.

others which support different kinds of formal simplicity (simplicity of notation, ease in systematic exposition, ease in computation), it appears that the pursuit of formal simplicity dominates the choice of hypotheses. No wonder that "Simplicity" is such a tempting answer, when people realize that testing is comparison, and ask what, besides deductive accuracy, determines the relevant comparisons. The temptation should be resisted, however. Formal simplicity dominates hypothesis choice because confirmation, comparing-which-is-testing, is such a small part of hypothesis choice.

I have been denigrating simplicity in realist language, taking confirmation to be the pursuit of truth. But the same points can be stated in a more neutral way. Contemporary anti-realists accept that what is normally called theory-testing is a reasonable practice. They also think (or obviously should) that the goal of this practice is not simply the choice of a hypothesis as most useful, on balance. Otherwise, geocentric astronomy was the one to chose in the nineteenth century, when it was still the best alternative for contemporary practical purposes, for example, the construction of navigational tables. As I argued at the beginning of Chapter Four, "acceptability," in van Fraassen's sense, needs to be distinguished both from warranted belief and from general usefulness. For an anti-realist, then, testing involves finding empirical support for a specific kind of choice. This is a kind to which formal simplicity is not directly relevant, despite its importance for other kinds.

## THE PERILS OF DEDUCTIVISM

I have been arguing that deductivism is philosophically misguided. If so, it is a practical disaster as well. If we compare theories with an eye on deductivist virtues alone, the result is bias in favor of relatively superficial and socially respectable theories. Especially in the social sciences, these biases in method have encouraged real distortions in theorizing and research.

By a bias toward the superficial, I mean an unjustified preference for theories denying the operation of causal factors which are relatively hard to observe. This bias arises, independently, from at least three aspects of deductivism: the rejection of the hedges and defenses on which deeper theories usually depend; the neglect of causal depth in assessing explanations; and the neglect of the actual context of scientific development in the choice among hypotheses. The neglect of context is important because, by their nature, deeper hypotheses are more apt to produce deductive inaccuracies. These failures can only be assessed if one takes into account the tautology that it is harder to develop and apply auxiliary principles connecting relatively hidden factors with the data, even when those factors exist and exist in the form described by the relatively deep theory.

This bias towards the superficial has considerable influence in the social sciences, today. For example, it contributes to the dominance over economic theory of relatively shallow hypotheses taking economic distributions, technologies and (among Keynesians) distinctive investors' psychologies as given, and explaining other phenomena as the outcome of market processes. The prestige of these approaches is not due to actual predictive success, which is virtually nil.[36] Since proponents regard predictive success as the main criterion of acceptability, why don't they try another approach? The main justification, most vigorously expressed in Milton Friedman's *Essays in Positive Economics*, is that there is no other approach which could in principle achieve the scientific acceptability which the dominant approach pursues. The other approaches, institutionalist, historical or Marxist, appeal to factors involving social conflict, political influence or international political competition whose general effects cannot be described accurately without rendering the theories tautological, in the same way that Darwin's theory is. Also the latter approaches contain ready-made means of explaining away recalcitrant data on the grounds that circumstances were not of the right kind, where "the right kind" is not independently determined. In short, although the dominant kinds of economic theories may not, in fact, satisfy deductivist tests, the alternatives cannot even be tested, according to deductivist rules of method. This really is a difference between the theories in the mainstream and the theories outside it. However, a methodological preference based on this fact is an unjustified bias toward the superficial.

To take one other example, consider the dominance of social psychology by literature of the following form, of which the candy-bar experiment was just an especially vivid example. Various psychological factors are "operationalized" by associating them with magnitudes which any wise amateur would recognize as crude, partial,

---

[36] For a bleak assessment from an era of general optimism about the power of economic theory, see S. Schoeffler, *The Failures of Economics* (Harvard, 1955). The burden of predictive failure is even heavier now, after the combination of high unemployment and high inflation in the 1970s, high interest rates and economic expansion in the 1980s. For a relatively recent mordant assessment of the state of the art, see Joan Robinson, "What Are the Questions?" and "The Abdication of Neo-Classical Economic Theory" in her *Collected Papers*, vol. 5 (Oxford, 1979).

and potentially misleading measures. A hypothesis is tested by the statistical analysis of correlations among these magnitudes. It is recommended on grounds of good statistical fit. Almost invariably, the correlations might reveal something other than the causal connections described in the hypothesis. A rival cause, excluded by the operationalization, might be at work. Or a third factor may be producing a "spurious," only apparently causal connection (in the way in which racism can create a spurious connection between distrust of authority, on the one hand, being poor, on the other). The salient rival hypotheses are not investigated, usually not mentioned at all.

At one time, such emphasis on operationalizing and then applying techniques of statistical analysis may have seemed to be a means of achieving the basic unanimity among psychologists which physicists are supposed to enjoy. That turned out to be an empty dream. At most such research has produced new material for explanation, which sometimes creates a new possibility of confirmation by revealing correlations best explained by one alternative. Festinger's work on cognitive dissonance is a good example of such highly productive quantitative research, producing leverage for hypothesis comparison which would otherwise be unavailable.[37] But though these successes fully justify this kind of research, they do not justify its paradigmatic status. Fieldwork, historical data, and the testimony of sensitive participants in psychological processes can also yield important raw material for explanation. However, the drive to "operationalize" *is* justified within the deductivist conception of confirmation. The alternatives supported by other techniques are too vague, too permissive of ad hoc defense and too prone to tautological hedges to be distinguished from obviously absurd alternatives, by a deductivist.

The other general bias of deductivism is a bias toward old and respectable hypotheses. If a theory is new, or has not been applied by many sympathetic investigators with adequate resources, deductive inaccuracies are apt to be great and informativeness limited, through want of extensive, refined research and well-developed auxiliary principles. Often, these disadvantages are a mark of real inferiority. The neglect of the hypotheses has reflected the good

[37] See Leon Festinger, *A Theory of Cognitive Dissonance* (New York, 1962); Roger Brown, *Social Psychology* (New York, 1965), pp. 584–608. The basic mechanism, the tendency of beliefs to adjust so as to justify conduct already engaged in, is all too familiar, prior to controlled experiment and statistical analysis. But the ease with which such adjustment occurs and its power to overcome contrary tendencies are surprising and important findings.

judgment of a scientific community with finite resources. But it is also possible for this neglect, and the resulting deductivist disadvantages, to reflect social processes having nothing to do with the truth. The appeal to these social and historical factors influencing research will then play an important role in the case for a new or disreputable theory. Because it neglects the historical background (both internal and external to science) deductivism has an unwarranted conservative bias.

The crucial examples are in the social sciences, and the uncontroversial ones are, of course, judged retrospectively. At the turn of the nineteenth century, cranial measurements and observations of technological inferiority were widely used to justify anthropological theories based on the alleged intellectual inferiority of non-white non-literate peoples. Pioneering egalitarian anthropologists, such as Boas, could not initially claim the same wealth of successful deductions. In retrospect, we can see that the hypothesis of inferiority was not confirmed, despite its deductive superiority. The development of a more egalitarian anthropology required excruciating long-term fieldwork, new kinds of linguistic talents, and new forms of broadened sensitivity—all of which was just beginning at the turn of the century. Though the new anthropology required great resources and encouragement, almost all resources and encouragement had gone to rival programs, for reasons having much to do with turn-of-the-century imperialism, but little to do with the truth.[38]

The prestige of the mainstream style of economics, as previously described, may be a modern case in which deductivism has had a distorting effect, producing undeserved credit, wherever the truth may ultimately lie. Mainstream economic theory derives much of its prestige from its capacity to generate models establishing deductive connections among a wealth of economic data, within an appropriately chosen economic period. This is the stuff of respectable economic journals (which also reveal dramatic modifications of the models as new economic crises produce new data). Rival approaches to the mainstream have produced no such abundance of deductive connections. But this advantage of mainstream economics is partly an artifact of the kinds of data available. In a modern economy, firms and governments want and support the gathering of enormous quantities of data concerning supply and demand, the output of one sector and the input of others, present investment and in-

[38] See George Stocking, *Race, Culture and Evolution* (New York, 1968).

dices of future growth. In contrast, as budding Marxist economists discover to their dismay, it is extremely difficult to find usable statistics concerning the intensity of work, the real rate of return on investment to all the firms, managers, lenders and property owners involved, or the degree of mechanization. Indeed, it is hard to find usable unemployment or poverty statistics. The official definition of the poverty line does not depend, in anyone's view, on principled social theorizing. The official unemployment statistics do not reflect difficulties in getting a first job, despair of finding a new job or discouraged and reluctant choices of housework or part-time work. While there are conceptual problems in defining the needed magnitudes, they are no deeper than those involved in the definition of real Gross National Product, the Consumer Price Index, and the money supply. And this is the paucity of data afflicting the non-respectable approach that is most straightforwardly quantifiable, Marxist economics. In short, the dominant economic theories get the data they need for appropriate deductions because this is the kind of data needed by the dominant economic entities. But what is important for the dominant economic entities need not be most revealing of economic processes.

Many philosophers of science who have grave doubts about deductivism, still adopt it as a working hypothesis. If well-confirmed theories do not actually conform to deductivism, still, they believe, deductivism describes the ideal that science should pursue. Or in any case, until an equally precise alternative comes along, it can do no harm to investigate the nature of confirmation by refining and elaborating deductivism. The compromise is wrong, on both counts. Deductivism is a bad ideal, since the hypotheses which approach it more closely are often worse. Deductivism is a harmful assumption in practice, since it encourages unfair comparisons. It should no longer be used.

# CHAPTER SIX

# The New Positivism

Positivism seeks the general a priori principles that make a given body of data evidence for or against a hypothesis. There seem to be just two sorts of relations among propositions that are so absolutely general and so susceptible to a priori reasoning that they could be the material for such rules. First, there are the relations of logical form that positivists have traditionally investigated, trying to construct a deductivist account of confirmation. Second, there are relations among the probabilities attaching to propositions, those relations whose a priori structure is usually described by interpreting the mathematical theory of probability. As the obstacles to deductivism grow, it becomes a more and more attractive option for positivism to make confirmation theory a branch of probability theory, interpreting the latter so that it lays down rules for rational belief. And in fact, this option, to which I have given the usual label, "Bayesian," is the most creative branch of positivist philosophy of science today. Salmon, Jeffrey, Rosenkrantz and Horwich are just a few, important representatives of the trend.[1]

A number of these writers are also powerful critics of traditional positivism. In light of the last two chapters, this is not surprising. The comparative dimension of confirmation, which positivism initially neglected, makes the turn to probability theory extremely attractive.

In the real world of hypothesis choice, there is no natural yardstick of comparison framed in terms of deductive relations. Admittedly, if empirical anomalies were not attached to valid hypotheses, there would be one natural deductivist yardstick, namely, the counsel of perfection: eliminate all hypotheses that entail a consequence

---

[1] See, for example, Wesley Salmon, *The Foundations of Scientific Inference* (Pittsburgh, 1967), ch. 7, and "Carl G. Hempel on the Rationality of Science," *Journal of Philosophy* (1983), pp. 555–562; Richard Jeffrey, *The Logic of Decision* (New York, 1983), chs. 11 and 12, and "Bayesianism with a Human Face" in J. Earman, ed., *Testing Scientific Theories* (Minneapolis, 1983); Roger Rosenkrantz, *Inference, Method and Decision* (Dordrecht, 1977), and "Does the Philosophy of Induction Rest on a Mistake?" *Journal of Philosophy* (1982); Paul Horwich, *Probability and Evidence* (Cambridge, 1982).

conflicting with observations, when joined to independently accepted auxiliary principles. Of course, a flood of difficulties would still enter into the question, "On what basis are the auxiliaries to be accepted?" And an infinite number of contrary hypotheses would do equally well by this standard, including absurdities, gruified and otherwise. In any case, once the existence of acceptable anomalies is admitted, not even the counsel of perfection survives, question-begging and incomplete as this standard would be. The remaining deductivist precedures for comparison, even ones as ingenious as Sober's, all have the look of artificial devices invened to save an approach that is in trouble.

In contrast, probability theory seems manifestly destined to regulate the comparison of rival hypotheses. Its very axioms speak of the respective probabilities that one or another mutually exclusive possibility is actually the case. Everyone who reasons about conditional probabilities often sounds like a scientist engaged in crucial episodes of comparison, comparing the probability of the evidence on one hypothesis against its probability on rivals, to see how probable the former hypothesis is given what was observed.

In sum, the arguments of this book make Bayesian confirmation theory the best version of positivist confirmation theory. To use phrases that are important to the Bayesian account itself: it is the version most likely to be true if positivism is, in fact, valid.

My argument will be that this best version of positivism is defeated, in the final analysis, by the problems that defeated oldstyle positivism. Though the Bayesian respect for comparison is a real difference, the two approaches turn out to be the same in another, basic way, a shared exphasis on successful prediction.

In the most common and intuitively appealing account of Bayesian inference, explanatory success enters into the confirmation of a hypothesis only so far as it amounts to predictive success, i.e., the effectiveness of the hypothesis in supporting the expectation of events that really do occur. Confirmation occurs on the basis of general and a priori principles prescribing the impact of successful prediction on the hypotheses employed. In this respect, the most common form of Bayesianism (deriving from the work of Ramsey and De-Finetti) is identical with deductivism—with the shared proviso that "prediction" includes retrodiction, the expectation that a certain event has occurred in the past. In this chapter, I will describe the considerable appeal of this approach to confirmation, and argue that it is the only remotely promising way of developing a new positivist account of confirmation by mobilizing the probability calculus. The new emphasis on probability cannot depart from the old emphasis on prediction without intolerable costs.

In contrast to this continuing emphasis on prediction and general a priori rules, I have been developing an account of science in which explanation consists of causal description, which need not be effective in predictions. Confirmation is a byproduct of the explanation of data, and the choice of an explanation as best depends on a background from which specific (and, often, a posteriori) principles cannot be eliminated. The major problems with deductivism resulted from the gap between its predictive, a priori and general outlook, and this causal, contingent and specific one. When Bayesianism is comparing with the facts of scientific rationality, old, deductivist problems will re-emerge, just as important and just as recalcitrant. Once again, the need to say when ad hoc revision is allowed, in response to negative test results, will be urgent and unfulfillable. The problem of admitting theories that go beyond empirical regularities, without admitting nonsense, will return, essentially unchanged. Because the work of science is not sufficiently tied to causal reconstruction, legitimate hypotheses will be excluded and non-starters allowed to compete. The assessment of tests will be distorted through insufficient emphasis on the history of controversy leading up to the tests.

So that this indictment does not sound one-sided, proper credit should be paid to Bayesian reasoning, as well. For one thing, Bayesian reasoning works, undeniably, where we know (or are ready to assume) that the process studied fits certain special though abstract causal structures, often called "statistical models." To illustrate one very common model, a "Bernoulli process," Bayesian reasoning does guide us in choosing among hypotheses about the mix of red and blue marbles in an urn, on the basis of samples drawn from the urn—if we know that the marbles are uniform and thoroughly mixed, the drawings are blind and the marbles returned and thoroughly mixed after each drawing. However, when we choose among hypotheses in important scientific controversies, we usually lack such prior knowledge of causal structures, or it is irrelevant to the choice. As a consequence, such Bayesian inference to the preferred alternative has not resolved, even temporarily, a single fundamental scientific dispute.[2]

[2] Claims to the contrary are sometimes made for fundamental questions in population genetics. See R. C. Lewontin, *The Genetic Basis of Evolutionary Change* (New York, 1974), ch 5, for some reasons to be skeptical of these claims. Of course, Fisher and his successors made powerful use of statistical reasoning, first to show that nat-

The other concession involves, not special situations, but an epistemological principle of the widest range. This might be called the "likelihood principle": the strength with which a body of data supports a hypothesis as against rivals is the greater as the data are more likely should the hypothesis be true and less likely should the rivals be true. In this sense, the ideal limit of confirmation is the case in which the data are certain should the hypothesis be true, but impossible should it be false; and confirmation grows as this ideal is approached.

In any sound theory of confirmation, nothing is more fundamental than the likelihood principle. And, as we shall see, much of the appeal of the Bayesian approach comes from the appearance that it gives this principle its proper importance. But Bayesian confirmation theory does not just consist of endorsing this basic truism. Rather, it claims that this truism is entailed by a compelling general interpretation of probability theory, and that it and other results of the interpreted theory are the rules that govern hypothesis testing. (Without such claims, Bayesianism could not vindicate the positivist emphasis on the effectiveness of general a priori rules.) But neither proposal is at all obvious. For example, one idea expressed in the likelihood principle, as usually understood, is that data confirm in the degree to which the favored hypothesis explains them more easily than the rivals. It is by no means obvious that an interpretation appropriate to the theory of probability captures relevant aspects of explanatory power. In any case, even if the likelihood principle was an outcome of probability theory, it is by no means obvious that it and other such outcomes would be the whole story of confirmation.

Indeed, my criticisms of the Bayesian approach in the next chapter will largely amount to a distinction between the likelihood principle as a valid basis for scientific reasoning, and anything probability theory can provide. The likelihood principle is only a valid principle of extremely broad scope if "likely should the hypothesis be true" is taken to mean "better explained assuming the approximate truth of the hypothesis." But the Bayesian strategy is to explicate excellence in explaining evidence, and other basic terms of appraisal, using interpretations of the mathematical theory of probability. On any such reading (which would be a misreading),

---

ural selection is compatible with the mechanisms of inheritance, then to develop alternative possible ways in which species might change. But they were not applying probabilistic techniques for revising or assessing beliefs in light of data, any more than Maxwell, Clausius and Boltzmann did so, when they used statistical reasoning about molecules to defend the molecular-kinetic theory.

the likelihood principle distorts scientific reasoning, if it is extensively applied.

I will discuss Bayesianism in stages. In this chapter, I will describe in detail what the Bayesian approach says, and why what it says is so plausible. In the next chapter, I will argue that the approach encounters the same problems as deductivism and some new problems of unclarity, as well. There, I will often be contrasting Bayesian prescriptions with the practice of such paradigmatic investigators as Darwin and Newton. Finally, at the end of the next chapter, I will describe some ways in which the Bayesian approach is not just wrong in the abstract, but harmful in practice.

I will begin by discussing the two most elementary questions about the Bayesian approach, how Bayes' Theorem follows from the axioms of the mathematical theory of probability and how this theory might be so interpreted that it has something to say about confirmation. In part, this investigation of basics is needed because of a brute educational fact. People with a solid standard background in philosophy, even in the philosophy of science, often know little about probabilistic reasoning, even if they know a lot about logical deduction. As a result, the philosophy of science these days sometimes seems split into two subcultures, one that elaborates Bayesian models and one that simply ignores them. People in the second group often attack positivism without considering the most recent and the best version of it, while people in the first group often ignore doubts that would bother those for whom formal techniques have no intrinsic appeal. The Bayesian approach is too important to be segregated in this way.

Even for experts, a survey of basics may have its uses. Because the jargon of probability theory sounds so much like the vernacular of all scientific reasoning, there is a tendency to blur the distinction between the uncontroversial derivations that Bayesians employ and the controversial philosophical uses to which they put those findings. Looking at the basic questions of how Bayes' Theorem is derived and how formal results in probability theory can, in general, be interpreted should make it clearer just what the Bayesian approach could say that is both plausible and directly relevant to confirmation.

## DERIVING BAYES' THEOREM

There are different, even contrary general analyses of what probability is. But partisans of these different analyses usually take the general truths about probability to be the consequences of a single, amazingly sparse set of axioms and definitions, which they interpret in their favored ways. When studied without commitment to one or another controversial interpretation, this axiomatic structure is often called "the mathematical theory of probability" or "the probability calculus," as distinct, say, from "the frequency theory of probability," i.e., *the* theory of probability, according to the frequency interpretation.

In one standard presentation, the axioms of mathematical probability are these, omitting niceties that will only be of interest to those who already know them.

Axiom I. For anything, A, with a probability, its probability, $P(A)$, is a real number not less than 0 or greater than 1.

Axiom II. If $A_1, \ldots A_i, \ldots A_n$ are mutually exclusive and exhaust all possibilities, the sum of their probabilities is 1.

Axiom III. If $A_1$ and $A_2$ are mutually exclusive, then the probability that at least one is the case is the sum of their individual probabilities.

These axioms need to be supplemented with "definitions," equating mathematical functions of individual probabilities with further probabilistic notions. Otherwise, even such a simple principle as that the fair odds favoring A over B are $P(A)/P(B)$ cannot be derived, since "odds" does not occur in the axioms. Although they have the logical form of definitions, many of the equivalences introduced are just as important and substantive as the above three axioms, i.e., just as important and just as far advanced beyond the requirement of basic linguistic competence. (Someone can violate the axioms while still knowing the meaning in English of "probability," and the same can be said of many such "definitions.") The most important "definition" by far, sometimes presented as a fourth axiom, is that of "conditional probability." By this "definition": the probability of B given A equals the probability of A and B divided by the probability of A, i.e.,

$$P(B|A) = \frac{P(A,B)}{P(A)} .$$

Of course, if this "definition" were simply a device for deriving further formulas, whose non-mathematical parts were not meant to have any connection with meanings in actual discourse, the equation could simply be stipulated. But the same can be said of the axioms. In fact, both axioms and "definition" are meant to fit sound vernacular reasoning about probabilities, in which talk of the probability of something given something else is pervasive. (The mathematical theory is really uninterpreted only in the weak sense that it is unprejudiced among the rival analyses of probability.) Since "the definition of conditional probability" is neither a stipulation nor a mere summary of ordinary usage, it is confusing to speak of it as definition. The confusion is dangerous because the controversial move in interpreting the mathematical theory is often precisely the claim to have described how good reasoners should intend their statements as to the probability of something given something else.[3]

The three trivial-looking axioms and the "definition" of conditional probability entail "Bayes' Theorem," a result so powerful that it gives the whole probabilistic approach to confirmation its name. According to Bayes' Theorem,

$$P(B|A) = \frac{P(A|B) \cdot P(B)}{P(A|B)\,P(B) + P(A|B_1)\,P(B_1) \ldots + P(A|B_n)\,P(B_n)}$$

where $B, \ldots B_n$ are mutually exclusive and exhaust all possibilities. A rigorous derivation of the theorem from the axioms and definitions is not difficult. But it makes newcomers either feel that the result must be trivial or wonder what it is in the premises that could justify such an important result. An argument that dispenses with axiomatic formalities makes it clearer why the theorem really is important and attractive and indicates some main steps in the formal derivation as well.

First, consider the rationale for equating conditional probabilities with other probabilities in the way described by the "definition." The probability that A and B are both the case is the probability that A is the case and that, given this, B is the case. In other words, the probability of there being both states of affairs (events, truths or whatever) is the probability of there being one and of there being the other, given that there is this one. So the joint probability is the probability that A is the case times the probability that B is the case given A. First, we look at the probability of getting A. Then we dis-

---

[3] I will not be arguing that the mathematical theory is false unless empty of content. I will be arguing, in this chapter and the next, for two claims which jointly reduce the importance of the mathematical theory: the theory, at best, describes rules appropriate to certain special kinds of sound reasoning about probability; and these kinds are not the centrally important kinds in the testing of hypotheses. In other words, the mathematical theory at most lays down good rules for reasoning about probability (likelihood, etc.) in very special epistemic contexts; and sound reasoning about probability goes on, most commonly and importantly, outside these contexts. Questions of precision and vagueness will *not* be the issues, here.

count for the further probability of getting B, once we have A. Hence,

$$P(A,B) = P(A) \cdot P(B|A).$$

This is just another expression for the equation in the "definition":

$$P(B|A) = \frac{P(A,B)}{P(A)}.$$

Alternatively, we can build up $P(A,B)$ in reverse stages, starting with B, rather than A. So, applying this reasoning to the numerator in the above ratio, $P(A,B)$:

$$P(B|A) = \frac{P(A|B) \cdot P(B)}{P(A)}.$$

And now, we are very close to Bayes' Theorem. If the various $B_i$ are mutually exclusive and exhaustive of all possibilities, then A must come about in one of these $B_i$ circumstances (where $i = 0,1 \ldots$ or n and $B = B_o$). The probability of A is just the probability that A comes about in circumstance B or that A comes about in circumstance $B_1$, etc. By previous reasoning about joint probabilities, each disjunct is $P(A|B_i)P(B_i)$. Directly applying the third axiom, the probability that one of these $(A,B_i)$ situations is the case is the sum of the probabilities of each situation. So:

$$P(B|A) = \frac{P(A|B)\,P(B)}{P(A|B)\,P(B) + \ldots + P(A|B_n)\,P(B_n)}, \text{Q.E.D.}$$

Note that the "definition" was the rabbit in the hat. Understand the rationale for it, and Bayes' Theorem is ripe for justification.[4]

Bayes' Theorem is an exciting result, because it seems to express the likelihood principle. (Whether it really does, at least as that principle is meant in the best scientific practice, is another matter. For now, I am trying to make the best case for the Bayesian approach.) Suppose that B is some hypothesis, H, being tested. It and the other $B_i$'s are a set of rivals, covering all possibilities. A is a bit of evidence,

---

[4] I have sketched a justification of Bayes' Theorem that is compelling, but neutral among the competing interpretations of probability. Often, the latter supply distinctive justifications of their own. Horwich, *Probability and Evidence*, pp. 30f., could serve as the basis for an argument from a subjectivist standpoint. For an argument based on a modern revision of the "classical" interpretation, see Rosenkrantz, *Inference, Method and Decision*, pp. 48–52. Of course, each of these special arguments introduces the question (to which we will soon turn) of whether the underlying interpretation makes probability theory the basis for scientific inference.

e, that further testing might reveal. The question, "What is the probability of H given e?" sounds like the question of to what level the probability of H should be revised, if e is observed. Bayes' Theorem seems to give a rule connecting that revised probability, should e be observed, with present ones, prior to the observation of e. The rule is that the prior probability should be adjusted in proportion to the probability that e occurs given H, but inversely to the probability that e happens somehow or other, regardless of whether H is the case. And the probability of e's occurring via H increases in its ratio to the probability of e's occurring anyhow (via H or not) if and only if the probability of e's occurring via H increases in its ratio to the probability of e's occurring when H is not the case. This seems to be precisely how evidence favors the truth of a hypothesis as against its falsehood, according to the likelihood principle. Moreover, if we want to know what the revised odds for H as against some particular rival, H′ should be, the theorem seems to tell us to multiply the prior odds, i.e., the ratio of prior probabilities, $P(H)/P(H′)$ by the ratio of the conditional probabilities of e given the respective hypotheses, i.e., by $P(e|H)/P(e|H′)$. The revised odds are, by definition, the ratio of the "posterior probabilities," the ones conditional on e. And the denominators in the Bayesian expressions for these posterior probabilities, being identical, divide out in the ratio. It is standard technical usage to call the probability of evidence given a hypothesis a likelihood. So the revised odds are the prior odds times the ratio of likelihoods. This seems to be the likelihood principle applied to the case in which we assess evidence for a hypothesis as against a given rival, not necessarily the synoptic one, "H is false." It is reassuring that Bayes' Theorem does not require us to know the likelihood on every possible rival, much less the probability of each of the latter, in comparing any two rivals. After all, such comprehensive knowledge is usually unavailable.

I have adopted cagey locutions about what Bayes' Theorem "seems to express" for two reasons. The axioms, the definitions and the informal rationale for the theorem say nothing about the revision of beliefs, indeed, nothing about time at all. Whether talk about revision of belief can be inserted into probability theory in ways that make it useful and true is exceptionally controversial. Also, however convenient the technical usage of "likelihood" may be, we must not assume that the likelihood principle, a colloquial principle in actual disputes, is or should be bound by it. "More likely on the hypothesis" often means "easier to explain on the hypothesis" when rival hypotheses are compared. It is quite controversial whether the latter phrase means "having a higher probability given the hypothesis."

One objection to the interpretation of Bayes' Theorem as a rule for revising beliefs is quite misplaced, however, namely, that the rule, if true, is useless, since it tells us, in a complicated way, to do what we would do anyway. People often do not revise beliefs as Bayes' Theorem seems to dictate. In many of these cases they, *quite uncontroversially*, should. Suppose a coin is either fair and normal or has two heads. You initially think the probability is two-thirds that the coin is fair. All you know about it is that it was drawn from a thoroughly mixed jar of coins, two thirds of them fair and normal, the rest two-headed. Now you learn that in two tosses, the coin came up heads both times. What probability do you now assign to the coin's being fair? Most people respond with an assessment much higher than the Bayesian one. Yet given the background knowledge, the Bayesian value can be made utterly compelling, as the rational one to assign. One can fit the intuitive justification of the theorem, as given above, to the particular facts governing the coin-drawing and coin-tossing. The resulting posterior probability is a mere one in three chance of fairness. Far from threatening the reading of Bayes' Theorem as a rule for the revision of beliefs, the departures from actual revisions complete its allure. Bayes' Theorem seems to stand to actual practice in revising beliefs as arithmetic stands to guessing "How many?" by looking.

## What Is Probability?

People often agree that the mathematical theory appropriately interpreted yields all general truths about probability but disagree over the interpretation. The different interpretations are explicit, general analyses of probability and allied notions, meant to do two things. Each is supposed to make the mathematical theory, so interpreted, a source of all and only the general a priori truths about the subject-matter the interpretation describes. And each is supposed to provide rules for assigning probabilities to an indefinitely large class of important items. Some of the interpretations standardly defended are, straightforwardly, rivals, since they assign different probabilities in the same cases. All the standard options are controversial, since they are regarded by some as incoherent, or as making assignments that are either arbitrary or too limited to capture a substantial part of what probability is.

To know what a Bayesian is offering in his or her probabilistic theory of confirmation, we need to know which interpretation we are to adopt. It might seem, to the contrary, that the ensuing controversies could be avoided through the instruction to understand the relevant probabilistic expressions just as they are ordinarily understood; the further controversies over the general, explicit interpretations would, then, concern the further, different issue of how to analyze that meaning. Unfortunately, this attractively naive proposal is quite inadequate. To make probability theory an account of rational hypothesis choice, we must assign probabilities where our naive understanding provides none. What was the probability that the universal law of gravitation was true, at the moment when it occurred to Newton? What is the probability that the planets revolve in elliptical orbits with foci very near the center of the sun, given the truth of Newtonian theory's main contemporary rival, Cartesian vortex theory? To make probability theory applicable in these and virtually all other interesting cases of scientific debate, we need a rationale for assigning probabilities that only an explicit and general analysis can provide.

Just as misplaced hopes for common-sense usage can block the demand for a general analysis, so, too, ironically, can a flight into abstraction and formal techniques. The mathematical theory of probability yields important insights, in fields as diverse as physics, genetics and epidemiology, when it is applied in reasoning about specific situations. These successes, together with the availability of common-sense judgments of probability, might seem to give the theory the status often accorded pure mathematics and, sometimes, pure geometry. It might be a theory of certain abstract magnitudes (call them "Probabilities"), not fully defined by any standard general interpretation; these magnitudes characterize all possibilities, and our difficulty assessing them in a particular case is just a limitation of our present knowledge and understanding. Though it is not part of any Bayesian's official program, this conception often seems a working hypothesis when, for example, a Bayesian dismisses vast areas of undefined probability as doubtless subject to natural extensions of his favored way of assigning probabilities, or offers a Bayesian result in confirmation theory as plausible quite apart from whether his favored interpretation is accepted.[5] But the flight into

---

[5] See, for example, R. Rosenkrantz, "Why Glymour *Is* a Bayesian" in Earman, ed., *Testing Scientific Theories*, pp. 88–91, and "Does the Philosophy of Induction Rest on a Mistake?" p. 80; and W. Salmon, "Carl G. Hempel on the Rationality of Science," pp. 559–61 (cf. Hempel's warnings about the problem of understanding the pertinent probabilities, in ibid., p. 570).

abstraction has an enormous cost, in the present context. The abstract magnitudes are supposed to correspond to magnitudes ascribed to hypotheses in good empirical reasoning. Since empirical reasoning is not explicitly an application of the probability calculus, the true laws of Probabilities might, in principle, say nothing in general about confirmation. And there is no argument from an abstract theory of Probabilities to a general theory of confirmation that does not employ one of the standard interpretations.

There are other current projects that gain support from misplaced formalization of commonsense talk of magnitudes, together with a flight into abstraction where concrete phenomena must, in fact, be accounted for. They are efforts to solve enduring, substantive problems through formal techniques in the social sciences, for example, in neoclassical economic theory and "causal model building." Since many people already regard these projects as examples of misplaced formalism, I offer them, not as an argument against the Bayesian approach, but as a means to evoke an attitude towards Bayesianism that the arguments of the next chapter will support. The formalist projects in the social sciences are all based on important truisms, for example, "People who have trouble clearing inventories will take the lowering of their prices to be one useful means to clear them," "One way to assess the existence of an alleged causal connection is to see whether appropriate correlations obtain." That the truisms are neither as univocal nor as universal as the like-sounding principles of the formal theory is often not recognized, at all. If it is, the determinate, general principles of the formal theory are defended in artificial and distorting ways. Thus, price determination for capital goods and labor power is made to fit the same model as consumer goods by implausible ad hoc postulates, of declining returns to scale and so on. The possibility that a correlation may reflect a "third cause" missing from a causal hypothesis is dismissed unless it adds to the formal simplicity of the over-all model. Alternatively, the abstract features of the formal theory are investigated in great detail without any effort to show the theory governs actual processes (cf. the scrutiny of "Probabilities"). Yet the theory is supposed to say something about concrete phenomena—inflation and unemployment, say, or the causal relation between race and wages. As the division of labor in systematic discussions is skewed toward the abstract, the use of the theory to account for realities becomes ever more arbitrary and inaccurate.

Whether because of the triumphs and prestige of the physical sciences, or ingrained ways of thinking in a highly monetary society, or both, excesses of formalism surely do occur. Later, I will be trying to show that the Bayesian approach is an excess of formalism, in which truisms about likelihood (plausibility, simplicity, and so forth) are given one-sided readings, and abstract results are developed at too far a remove from the problems to be solved. For now, it is enough to see that these temptations are a danger. This makes it all the more important to specify the interpretation under which the theory of probability is supposed to fill the gaps in the old positivism.

The diversity of interpretations might be an enormous complication in assessing the Bayesian approach. There are, however, good reasons to believe that just one of the extant analyses, sometimes called the "subjectivist" interpretation, is a plausible means of making probability theory into a theory of confirmation. Very roughly, the subjectivist interpretation takes probability to be degree of belief by a coherent believer. Since the advantages of the subjectivist interpretation are, in large part, the disadvantages of the alternatives, I will first describe the problems of those rivals. They are, using common labels, the classical, the logical and the frequency interpretations.

## THE CLASSICAL INTERPRETATION

The classical interpretation, the outlook of most of the pioneers of probability theory, assigns the basic probabilities according to a principle of indifference: divide all possibilities into a set of alternatives such that there is no reason to favor one over the other; then each is equally probable and has a probability of 1 divided by the total number of alternatives in the set. For example, if all that is known about a car is that it took between one and two minutes to make a trip, then nothing favors its arrival in the interval between one and one and one-half minutes over its arrival in the interval between one and one-half and two. Its making the trip in the former interval has the probability 1/2. This principle has succumbed to fundamental difficulties, as terminally as any principle in philosophy. The problem is that the indifference principle licenses contradictory probability assignments, corresponding to different ways of dividing all possibilities into a set of equally reasonable alternatives. The same kind of reasoning as supports the first probability assignment in the car example leads to the conclusion that an average speed between thirty and forty-five miles an hour has the same probability, 1/2, as an average speed between forty-five and sixty. But this contradicts the first assignment, which tells us that the probability is 1/2 that the car moved at an average rate between a mile a minute and a mile a minute and a half, i.e., between 30 and *40* miles per hour. This is Bertrand's Paradox in Wesley Salmon's illustration.[6]

Recently, Rosenkrantz has developed a new version of the classical interpretation, and recommended it as the basis for an "objectivist" Bayesian philosophy of science. In part, his interpretation involves a more general version, derived from information theory, of the classical principle of indifference, a version that he calls the "law of maximum entropy." Much more important for present purposes is his adoption of a strategy for coping with Bertrand-type arguments which was developed by the physicist E. T. Jaynes. A question of what probabilities are to be assigned often imposes certain constraints of invariance. Certain kinds of differences in the properties of the situation are not supposed to affect the outcome and, hence, the probability assignment. When these constraints of invariance, combined with reasoning from indifference, produce just one probability assignment, Bertrand paradoxes are avoided and the question of what probabilities to assign has turned out to be well-formulated. Otherwise, it may be that contrary assignments are supported—but this is simply a sign that the question was ill-formulated. Thus, the question, out of all context, of how probable it is that a chord of a given circle will be greater than a side of an inscribed equilateral triangle is ill-formulated. By classical reasoning (including neo-classical reasoning from "maximum entropy"), equal probabilities might equally partition possible angles of the chord with the perimeter or possible distances of the mid-point of the chord from the center. Different answers to the question result. But in most contexts, invariances are imposed. Perhaps the question concerns chords made by a straw tossed on a little circle on the floor. The straw is tossed "at random," i.e., the circle is much too small for aiming, even unconscious aiming, to affect the outcome. Then small changes in the size of the circle will not affect the outcome. Neither will small displacements of the circle. And, of course, rotating the circle about its center will not. These invariances permit just one answer to the question, when combined with classical reasoning from uncertainty. (The answer is 1/2, as it happens.) So the question was well-posed.[7]

---

[6] See *The Foundations of Scientific Inference*, pp. 66–68. Bertrand's original example concerned two partitions of possibilities yielding two answers to the question, "What is the probability that a chord of a circle may be greater than the side of the inscribed equilateral triangle?" See H. Poincaré, *Science and Hypothesis* (New York, 1952), pp. 183–86, for a concise and intriguing discussion.

[7] Rosenkrantz, *Inference, Method and Decision*, pp. 73–77.

Still, it could be the case that the question of what probability to assign a scientific hypothesis is almost always badly formulated by Jaynes' criteria, even when good reasoners would freely apply colloquial talk of probabilities, as in the likelihood principle. It is disappointing, then, that Rosenkrantz' detailed applications of his neo-classical interpretation to hypothesis choice all concern fields of science that are explicitly engaged in mathematical reasoning concerning probabilities, for example, statistical mechanics and modern genetics. These are the kinds of case where one would expect the neo-classical interpretation to be satisfactory even if it were not a valid account of how to assign probabilities to hypotheses in general. By Bayesian reasoning, then, they have no weight in justifying a Bayesian theory of confirmation.

At times, Rosenkrantz emphasizes similar turns of phrase in objectivist Bayesian principles and informal principles for assessing hypotheses.[8] But to take the former as revealing the rationale for the latter is to suppose that the two sorts of principles are talking about the same kind of thing, the former more precisely. That formal and informal assessment are not so related is suggested by one of Rosenkrantz' own main examples of scientific reasoning engaged in when the context is too indefinite for Jaynes' criterion and the law of maximum entropy to be applied. He praises, as "a beautiful example" of informal assessment of evidence Thor Heyerdahl's argument for the hypothesis

> that the cultural flowering that occurred in ancient Meso-America had sources (Sumerian, Egyptian, Hittite, or Phoenician) in the Near East. Heyerdahl protests the tendency of "isolationists" to dismiss the parallels between these cultures singly, rather than confronting them collectively, for there is a compounding of improbabilities. That one or two such parallels should arise by mere coincidence does not strain credulity, but the probability of finding well over a hundred by chance seems infinitesimal.[9]

Rosenkrantz explains how this argument might be strengthened by programming a computer to count similarities among cultures in an ethnographic survey conforming to a uniform, accepted typology. The computer might count the parallels, say, between Sumerian and Peruvian cultures and compare them with the average count of similarities among cultures chosen at random. If the former degree

[8] See "Why Glymour *Is* a Bayesian," pp. 88–91.
[9] Ibid., p. 89.

of parallelism were much higher than the latter, then Heyerdahl is vindicated by adopting the informal pattern of reasoning most closely resembling objectivist Bayesian reasoning about precise and well-formulated probability questions.

Of course, stodgy academic archeologists would protest that parallels Heyerdahl ascribes to cultural influence can also be due to "convergent evolution." Convergent evolution is the development of independent but similar responses on account of similarities in environments and in the activities, social, instrumental, and aesthetic, the similar environments encourage. But the academics must admit that there are no solid grounds for any general assessment of which factor, cultural influence or convergent evolution, is more important in producing similarities. So, by classical reasoning from uncertainty, the Bayesian computer could produce an impressive increment to the probability of Heyerdahl's hypothesis. The problem is that the stodgy academics are right in their disdain for Heyerdahl's views. There are some specific phenomena that do lend themselves to good arguments for cultural influence, even though, in general, emphases on influence as against convergent evolution are no better than idiosyncratic. Parallels in written language are one such indicator, since written languages are rare and their elements arbitrary. Because of similar arbitrariness in the initial choice and conservatism in subsequent usage, multiple parallels in proper names in myths and folklore are also relatively hard to explain except on a basis of interaction. And sometimes (Polynesia is the classic example) a pattern of geographic distribution in practices, language and physiological characteristics may be hard to explain, except on a premise that entails a migration. The academics can point to over a century of efforts to justify Heyerdahl's kind of hypothesis, at least since the discovery of the Mayan ruins. They can note that the relatively definitive arguments about cultural influence have not been developed successfully, despite much trying, while the speculative sort of argument abounds. The best explanation of this pattern, best on the basis of shared principles for explaining scientific activity, is that there was little if any transoceanic influence. It is the same with flying saucers. If saucer lore were true, it would be hard to explain why no clear photograph of a close encounter, untainted by fraud, has been produced. Eventually, a definitive record of an uncommon but repeated transient event is made, however unlikely this is in a given case. Photographs exist of cars crashing by accident and of murders *in flagrante*. The reader will also recognize in this pattern of negative reasoning the converse of Darwin's argument that natural selection is the best hypothesis on balance: in the areas where all accept that science is least speculative, the wild theories do worse.

Common-sense explanation of the pattern of success and failure overwhelms reasoning that ought to be extremely powerful, on an objectivist Bayesian model. It does so even though the common-sense reasoning applies the likelihood principle, rating a hypothesis the worse because its pattern of success and failure is less likely given its truth than given the truth of its major current rival.

## THE LOGICAL INTERPRETATION

Evidently, the classical interpretation can only exclude contradictory probability assessments in special cases, not typical of the real world of scientific reasoning. Another, non-classical way that paradox can be avoided is by stipulating that the partitioning into alternative possibilities must be described only in certain standard ways, too limited to generate contradictory assignments. That is one advantage of Carnap's "logical interpretation." In this interpretation, probability statements, when explicit and complete, should be stated in an appropriately regimented pattern, and have two parts. On the one hand, a proposition is described which states the evidence relative to which the probability is assigned. In the logical interpretation, a probability relative to nothing is as much a contradiction in terms as leftness relative to nothing. For the rest, a probability statement says that the hypothesis is assigned a certain magnitude by a certain rule connecting hypothesis statements and observation statements according to their logical relations. The rule may be any one of a continuum of methods fitting a general pattern that Carnap describes in detail. All the methods are concerned with relations of logical form, and all embody the intuition that the probability of a conjunction is raised when a conjunct is observed. Admissible methods differ, above all, in the rate at which probabilities of conjunctions are raised as conjuncts are observed. Until the actual method of inference is understood, the probability statement is incomplete.[10]

One problem with the logical interpretation is that it avoids contradiction at the price of arbitrariness. Someone's probability assignments are relative to choices of a style of describing evidence

---

[10] See Rudolf Carnap, *Logical Foundations of Probability* (Chicago, 1962). See also the illuminating discussion in Salmon, *The Foundations of Scientific Inference*, pp. 68–79.

and to choices of a method, choices which are not themselves subject to justification. Though the logical interpretation has fallen into disuse, Carnap's response is much the same as a standard defense of the flourishing subjectivist interpretation: the arbitrariness corresponds to a real indeterminacy in probabilities. The truth of a probability-assignment, given the evidence, really is only relative to unjustified choices as to how possibilities are to be divided up, how much impact evidence is to have on belief, and so forth. To insist otherwise is like supposing that the rightness of a spice is independent of prior, sometimes unjustified choices of the other ingredients in a stew.

Two further problems account for the differential survival of subjectivism, despite this similarity. For one thing, it is very hard to say which Carnapian choice one actually makes when one infers, as Carnap presents the options. By which method is one learning from experience? The elaborations of Carnap's scheme that seem to provide answers tend to collapse it into the subjectivist interpretation. In the second place, the logical interpretation is, explicitly and unlike the subjectivist one, an extension of deductivism. In effect, Carnap was looking for a way of extending the deductivist account of the confirmation of a hypothesis by an instance to the question of the degree to which propositions are confirmed. On the face of it, every problem with deductivism will return when degree of evidential support is equated with "probability of the hypothesis given the evidence" on Carnap's reading. For all the "methods" have it in common that relations of logical form determine the probabilities, according to absolutely general rules.

Before turning to the last two items on the list of interpretations, an unlisted one, the objective propensity interpretation, deserves brief praise and dismissal. On this interpretation, the probability of an outcome for a given process in a given situation is the objective tendency of that process to have that outcome in that situation. The probability of A is a gauge of the power of A-production, with absolutely inevitable A-production set at "1" and total incapacity for A-production set at "0." Given the theory of explanation defended in the first half of this book, the objective propensity interpretation is the best reading of uses of probability *within* explanations of phenomena. But it is not and is not intended to be a means of converting the mathematical theory of probability into a theory of choice *among* explanatory hypotheses, to find the one whose probability of truth is highest. More precisely, it is only a candidate for this role in certain particular versions which convert it into a form of the frequency interpretation, to which I will now turn.

## THE FREQUENCY INTERPRETATION

In their high level of abstraction, the classical and the logical approaches are at a far remove from most concrete activities in which we freely talk of probabilities. The remaining interpretations naturally emerge from reflecting on certain procedures in which probability talk is endemic: sampling (the frequency interpretation) and betting (the subjectivist interpretation).

According to the frequency interpretation, a probability is the relative frequency with which a certain process (experiment, phenomenon, etc.) would have a certain characteristic over an indefinitely large number of occurrences. More precisely, the probability is the limit to which the cumulative relative frequency would converge, as the number of trials increases without limit. Of course, if we claim to know this magnitude with certainty, we will be defeated by Keynes' quip that in the long run we are all dead. But warranted belief seems enough for science. And frequentists have a rule to justify an assignment of a probability: assign the probability corresponding to the relative frequency with which the process has been observed to have the outcome in trials of the appropriate kind.

For the rule to be applied it is essential that the reference class, the kind of previous trial over which frequencies are taken, be appropriate. Suppose I wonder whether Silky Sam will win at Aqueduct tomorrow. Assume that frequentists are right to suppose that what I want to know is the frequency with which Silky Sam would win if he were to race in just tomorrow's circumstances in an indefinitely large number of races. (We will come back to the obvious worry that Sam would soon be dead.) What class of processes should be taken as providing the relevant frequency of wins? If I only look at races just like tomorrow's, the project of estimating probabilities is hopeless. Even two simple characteristics, the precise attendance combined with the precise size of the parimutuel betting, will probably single out just tomorrow's race. So the reference class would be empty, and a probability estimate impossible. Looking at enormously broad classes, e.g., assigning the frequency with which horses have won in all races in North America, involves an inane dismissal of relevant facts about Silky Sam. Even looking at the frequency of Silky Sam's wins may obviously be too broad, if, say, he is a specially good mudder and I know it will rain tomorrow.

I have followed a typical pattern in the literature, by illustrating the problem of the appropriate reference class with an example of the assessment of the probability of a particular event. However, precisely the same problem arises when we do justice to the realities of assessing the probability that a kind of phenomenon has a kind of characteristic. What is the probability that chickens of the Rhode Island Red kind will end up on someone's dinner table? An extrapolation of the frequency with which this fate has befallen Rhode Island Reds might ignore relevant facts drawn from the fate of other breeds, say, Golden Bantams. But an extremely broad class, say, all chickens, will also yield irrelevant frequencies, neglecting the fact that different breeds are sometimes developed for different uses.

Efforts to analyze the appropriateness of reference classes either work within the conceptual repertoire of the frequency interpretation or go beyond it, appealing to causal notions. The first, frequency-bound approach produces a false analysis. The second renders the frequentist theory of probability inappropriate as a basis for a theory of confirmation.

Salmon, improving on Reichenbach, has developed the standard version of the more frequency-bound approach.[11] The appropriate reference class, he proposes, is the broadest "homogeneous" class including the item in question. In arriving at the probability assessment for A, we refer to its frequency in the largest class, B, not partitioned by a further property, C, whose presence or absence affects the probability that A occurred. In other words, we have non-homogeneity just so long as

$$P(A|B) \neq P(A|B \text{ and } C).$$

But how will the probabilities in this rule be assessed? If the frequency interpretation is not to defeat itself, they must be assessed according to observed relative frequencies. The result, however, will typically be a tiny reference class, obviously too small to be appropriate. Like other sensible people, Salmon and Reichenbach want the reference class for the assessment of the probability that Jones will die of lung cancer to be, roughly, the class of people of Jones' age, of his general physical condition, smoking his number of cigarettes, with his environment of pollutants, of his sex, of his ethnic background and with his family history of cancer. However, with all actuarial information available, we can almost certainly partition further. The frequency of death from lung cancer in the sensible

[11] See *The Foundations of Scientific Inference*, pp. 90–92.

reference class will surely be further differentiated on partitioning for many such trivial factors as living beside pear trees or in green houses. In terms of frequencies, the broadest homogeneous reference class including Jones will be much too small. It might, for all a good epidemiologist knows, consist of someone living in a green house under a pear tree, smoking three packs a day, who did not die of cancer. An estimate of certain freedom from lung cancer death results for a similarly situated Jones. It is small consolation.

The natural response is to interpret homogeneity causally, not probabilistically. A class is homogeneous if it is described by all properties of the subject in question affecting the characteristic in question. But what determines whether a property, C, is such a factor, tending to affect the characteristic in question, E? Frequentists have been attracted to a frequency analysis of causal hypotheses: C tends to cause E just in case E's occurrence is positively correlated with the presence of C. But Cartwright's work, discussed in Chapter One, shows that this analysis fails, for fundamental reasons. As shrewd statisticians have long been aware, causation and correlation are routinely dissociated by the actions of third causes in the background. The general association between causal influence and correlation is, at most, this: C tends to cause E just in case the occurrence of E is correlated with the presence of C in every population where everything is influenced by the same *causal* factors, save for the variation in C.

Reference classes are appropriate in virtue of causal homogeneity. But finding what is a causal influence, i.e., an ingredient in causal homogeneity, requires justified background beliefs about what other factors are causal influences. And the justification of such a belief cannot simply consist of an extrapolation from observed correlations. So the understanding of "appropriate reference class" that assigns acceptable probabilities makes it impossible to assign them until after we have means of justifying causal beliefs. Understood in this way, the frequency interpretation cannot be a foundation for confirmation theory. At most, it will show how confirmation theory, once established, extends to statistical hypotheses.

That causal beliefs should influence inferences from frequencies to probabilities is obvious enough in practice. If I know that Jones has been depressed and think that depression sometimes helps to cause cancer, I will assess the actuarial facts one way, only treating a class of depressed people as homogeneous for him. If I do not believe that depression has any independent causal impact on cancer, I will proceed in another way. If I am unsure of the causal impact on cancer, my statistical inferences will take some other, intermediate form. If the effect of causal beliefs on assessments of probability works to the disadvantage of the frequentist approach, it makes the subjectivist approach all the more promising. For subjectivists continually engage in plausible and explicit reasoning concerning the probability that a characteristic has a certain probability, *given* that it is governed by a certain causal structure, which has yielded certain data so far.

Similar defects, and similar advantages for subjectivism, arise when we face the fact that Silky Sam will die. The frequency with which Sam *will* win, as the number of trials is increased indefinitely, converges on 0, since Silky Sam dies in a finite amount of time. Or, if we imagine an indefinitely large number of trials in a finite life, say, one race in the first half of Sam's life, one in the third quarter, one in the seventh eighth, etc., we will be faced with an indefinite number of irrelevant losses from exhaustion. This motivates the non-indicative formulation: the probability is the limit to which the frequency of winning *would* converge if the number of trials were indefinitely large. But what do we know of what Sam would do if he were able to run an indefinitely large number of races? Really, we know nothing about what such a superhorse would do, or what Sam would do if he were such a superhorse. Or perhaps we know that such a superhorse would then win infallibly, which is not the guide to handicapping which probability should provide. This suggests that statements about probabilities are statements about objective propensities (which the actual Silky Sam will actually carry into the race). These statements guide predictions about frequencies-in-trials when the sequence of trials does not require substantial modification of the causal factors that would actually govern a given trial. That Sam might run ten races in similar conditions and with a similar internal state is not unrealistic, and an assessment of the probability of his winning at .10 supports the belief that he will then win once.

Whether such a mixed interpretation is an objective propensity interpretation, a frequency interpretation or both is not important, here. What is important is the presence of complex causal claims as part of the very meaning of the probability assignment. If the standard frequentist rules for assigning probabilities were the right basis for these claims, their importance might be all to the benefit of frequentist theories of confirmation. But Cartwright's argument shows that this response is doomed. And really, no one has tried to defend the implausible claim that frequentist rules for extrapolation are the basis for the judgment of what would actually happen in the causally realistic sequence of causally similar trials. As the basis for probability assignment, we are now left with the usual motley of arguments, e.g., about Silky Sam's stamina and the length of tomorrow's race, his ability to run on muddy tracks like tomorrow's, and so forth. Once again, the acceptable frequency interpretation shows at most how confirmation theory could be extended to specifically probabilistic hypotheses, once the basic theory of confirmation has already been established. As before, the defect makes the subjectivist approach all the more attractive. The relevant probability assignments have no special basis in samplings and no intrinsic connection with frequencies in infinite series. It seems most plausible to take them as reflections of degrees of belief in an outcome, and to consider how they are supported by degrees of belief in hypotheses bearing on that outcome.

When we look at the most interesting choices between rival scientific hypotheses, not to the bettors' or actuaries' predictions that are the normal stuff of probability calculations, a final problem emerges. There is no appropriate reference class. Consider theories offering rival complete accounts of the causal factors influencing a common subject-matter, for example, Aristotelian and Galilean physics, Cartesian and Newtonian astronomy, Newtonian physics and general relativity, or classical and quantum mechanics. In each case, the old theory had a series of triumphs, was defended in response to anomalies, not all of which were successfully explained away, and was replaced by a new theory, explaining many of the residual anomalies but introducing some anomalies of its own. The empirical arguments justifying the change involved a small number of experiments, observations or derivations that were crucial indicators of reality according to shared premises of both rivals. If the story of these hypothesis choices is probabilistic, the crucial inferences begin with the assignment of certain probabilities to the rival theories and continue with the application of generally accepted likelihoods to data, using Bayes' Theorem. If the frequency interpretation is relevant, the prior probabilities and the likelihoods are derived from frequencies in an appropriate reference class. But what is the class? Suppose the dispute between Newtonian celestial mechanics and Cartesian vortex theory is being reconstructed. If the reference class for the theories themselves is all astronomical theories, the nil observed success rate in the past makes the probability of success for either nil. And zero probabilities are not changed by Bayes' Theorem. More plausibly, one might take the appropriate reference class to be theories sharing the many characteristics that both Newton and Descartes took to be essential to valid astronomical theorizing. But then, the reference class consists of just Cartesian and Newtonian celestial mechanics, both in dispute. So no probability can be assigned from observed frequencies.

Often, the problems for a frequentist account of theory choice are supposed to center on the prior probabilities, suggesting that subjectivity in the priors reflects the subjectivist nature of plausibility, while the frequency interpretation captures the really objective likelihoods, the objective means of scientific comparison. But the problems of frequentism are at least as serious for the likelihoods. In the present illustration, the likelihoods would surely include the high probability that the planets will have periods in proportion to the 3/2 power of their solar distances (Kepler's third law), if they are governed by Newton's gravitational force, and the low probability that they so behave if they are moved by vortices in Cartesian material filling all of space. How would a frequentist justify these probability assignments? The natural justifications produce an assignment of certainty, a probability of 1, to the higher likelihood, 0 to the lower likelihood. These extreme assignments are entailed by beliefs that Newton and the Cartesians accept at the outset of the dispute, as Newton shows in Proposition 52 of the *Principia*. It follows from those shared beliefs that there are no vortex-filled heavens obeying Kepler's third law. Here, as elsewhere, by dismissing the possibility of ad hoc revisions of auxiliary beliefs, this basis for frequency-assignment turns an important test into an absolutely decisive one. But the dismissal is as unjustified here as it was for simple deductivism. Ad hoc modification is no lethal defect, as its frequent presence in the *Principia* shows.

Suppose, then, that less extreme likelihoods are assigned to the classic tests, reflecting the non-existence of absolutely decisive observations. In the present case, relevant intermediate frequencies must be assigned to reflect the legitimacy, in principle, of Cartesian appeals, after the fact, to unsuspected variations in the density or slipperiness of the celestial medium. The problem, here as elsewhere, is that the moderate likelihoods do not correspond to any justifiable frequency ratio. Indefinitely many ad hoc Cartesian defenses and, for that matter, indefinitely many imaginable inaccuracies in Newtonian background principles would produce logically possible worlds at variance with the standard expectations. Of course, none of these worlds is the actual one—but that is what we learn in light of the vindication of the Newtonian account, not in the course of vindicating it. Kepler's third law is much easier to explain on a Newtonian than on a Cartesian basis. To express this relative ease as a difference in relative frequency is just as artificial and indefensible as expressing plausibility comparisons in this style.

The frequency interpretation is natural when we know a great deal about many causal factors influencing a characteristic, are ignorant of crucial facts about the other influences, and want to assess the impact of the known facts. That is the typical division of knowledge and ignorance for gamblers and actuaries. But it is not the situation in choices among rival theories. There, the rivals offer complete accounts of the relevant causal factors, and we are asking which complete account is true. No wonder, then, that the frequency interpretation immediately looks artificial and strained, when applied to theory choice.

## THE BEST BAYESIANISM

Almost all these arguments lead to a subjectivist interpretation of probability as degree of belief. In part, this is by a process of elimination. Degree of belief is the only remaining natural association of our ordinary talk of probability which suggests a general interpretation of the probability calculus. But the support is really much more specific. The previous interpretations yield cogent probabilistic inferences when certain facts about the process studied can be presupposed. If the crucial partitionings are causally relevant, we have the right reference class for frequency extrapolation or for plausible Carnapian inferences from state descriptions. If we are dealing with certain standard processes of drawings from an urn, a certain principle of indifference is sound and turns out to be remarkably productive: take all sequences of m drawings containing n red marbles as equally probable, no matter what the order in which the colors are drawn. Applications of previous rules for probability assignment are sound relative to the probability that reality fits one or another model. So our confidence in these various rules, from case to case, is relative to assignments of probabilities to diverse hypotheses about how the world is. It is hard to see what the latter, fundamental probability assignment could be if it is not (very roughly) the degree of belief that reality fits the appropriate model.[12]

[12] The one problem of rivals that is not a gain for subjectivism is this last one, of assigning likelihoods in a way that admits the legitimacy of ad hoc modifications. Or

Still, for this degrees-of-a-belief approach to make probability theory into a theory of inference, we need an explicit, general analysis of how appropriate probabilities are to be assigned, and further arguments connecting these assignments to processes of probability revision. For one thing, people's spontaneous answers to the question, "Where, from zero to one does your belief lie?" often lead to violations of the mathematical theory. For example, they often assign zero to blank uncertainty, so that all possibilities of weather tomorrow might have a total probability of zero. Beliefs in evidence, hypotheses and likelihoods often are related in an un-Bayesian way, and an argument that Bayes' Theorem should have been observed is often unavailable without a general analysis of the relevant probabilistic notions. Moreover, in most cases that are important to the theory of confirmation, we urgently need a general analysis to answer questions about degree-of-belief that have no intuitively compelling answer. How could one determine a seventeenth-century astronomer's degree of belief that stellar parallax would soon be observed given the truth of the heliocentric hypothesis? (Though parallax was not observed until 1837, Galileo was not dismayed by contemporary failures to detect it.) How should a modern astronomer assess her own degree of belief in the Big Bang hypothesis, or her degree of belief that red-shift data will continue to be observed even if the Big Bang hypothesis is false? (Big Bang and Steady State are not, after all, the only alternatives.) In addition to the general need for an appropriate measure of credence, it is not clear how an interpretation of the probability calculus could be a useful guide in the revision of beliefs, as against simply registering their changes over time. Ramsey provided the basic answer to the problem of measurement, DeFinetti to the problem of guiding belief revision.

Ramsey's basic idea consists of "defining the degree of belief in p by the [least favorable] odds at which the subject would bet on p" and interpreting the probability calculus as the rules someone must observe if he is prepared to take all bets suiting his degrees of belief and if he wants to avoid the elementary irrationality of making "dutch book."[13] "Dutch book" (by antique English chauvinist analogy with "dutch uncle" and "dutch treat") is a bet that the bettor is bound to lose, whatever the outcome.

---

so I shall argue. Rather, this failing of frequentism is important as showing that corresponding subjectivist difficulties have no cure in a frequentist or partly frequentist Bayesian program.

[13] F. P. Ramsey, "Truth and Probability" (1926) in H. Kyburg and H. Smokler, eds., *Studies in Subjective Probability* (Huntington, N.Y., 1980), p. 40.

This is the basic idea, but it will not do in this simple statement, as Ramsey was well aware. You may be willing to bet at even odds that a coin will come up heads at the next toss when I am not, not because of our different degrees of belief in the fairness of the coins but because of our different evaluations of monetary losses in bets. Losing money is a more serious loss to me, penny for penny. I am not more pessimistic about the coin, but my despair at losing is relatively high, compared with my glee at winning. So Ramsey needed to construct a way of measuring someone's desirabilities and to extract assessments of probabilities from it, using the odds-making idea.

Putting aside this complication (and other, less serious ones) for a while, degree of belief in p is the greatest fraction of a dollar that the believer would put up in a bet that yields $1 if p is true, nothing if p is false. This interpretation makes a certain reading of "the degree of belief in p given q" both natural in itself and an important ingredient in the argument that probability theory is the totally compulsive bettor's guide to avoiding "dutch book." Ramsey's words in defining this conditional attitude deserve to be quoted at length, since his careful warnings have often been forgotten.

> We are also able to define a very useful new idea—'the degree of belief in p given q.' This does not mean the degree of belief in 'If p then q,' or that in 'p entails q,' or that which the subject would have in p if he knew q, or that which he ought to have. It roughly expresses the odds at which he would now bet on p, the bet only to be valid if q is true. Such conditional bets were often made in the eighteenth century. . . .
>
> This is not the same as the degree to which he would believe p, if he believed q for certain; for knowledge of q might for psychological reasons profoundly alter his whole system of beliefs.[14]

Probability theory, on Ramsey's degree-of-belief interpretation, might be useful to a compulsive gambler worried about "dutch book" and certainly advances the abstract philosophical project of defining "degree of belief." But it seemed of little use for other tasks of inference. The basic advance, here, was DeFinetti's. He showed how people who were certain that a process had various abstract features but were unsure and in disagreement about its probable outcome might nonetheless be compelled to assign identical likelihoods, and be guided by Bayes' Theorem toward eventual consensus in their probability assignments. Suppose we are all certain that we are studying drawings from an urn of the philosophically familiar sort: thoroughly mixed, with a finite number of uniform marbles, with replacement and thorough mixing after each draw. We are all interested in the proportion of red marbles in the urn, our only new evidence will be drawings from it, and each of us will only change his or her estimate of proportions to the extent required by the new evidence. Otherwise, we are neither certain nor agreed concerning the proportion of red marbles. Each of us has a distinctive "probability distribution," i.e., a set of degrees of belief (à la Ramsey) in the alternative possibilities of one or another proportion. DeFinetti showed that our shared certainty about the structure of the drawing process entailed a shared assignment of values to the likelihoods, "x is the probability that of m marbles drawn n will be red, given that the total proportion of red marbles is actually p/q." More generally, he showed how a likelihood assignment is derived whenever there is agreement on certain structural properties embodied in this example, which make the process fit an important, though by no means universal model, "Bernoulli processes." So long as we all remain committed to the model, we ought, rationally, to remain committed, draw after draw, to the likelihoods DeFinetti derives. His argument also made it clear that each of us, in this situation, would be irrational not to change his or her probability distributions to new values calculated by modifying the old ones in light of the evidence and the fixed likelihoods, in accord with Bayes' Theorem. So long as the background assumptions are made and the results of the drawings are accepted, such Bayesian revision has a further consequence. No matter how different our initial distributions, our revised distributions become more and more alike as evidence accumulates, becoming as close as you please in a finite number of draws.[15]

A unique assignment of likelihoods can also be derived from the assumption of conformity to other models. More important, for present purposes, revision according to Bayes' Theorem turns out to be uniquely rational and to produce convergence whenever in-

[15] DeFinetti's classic exposition of these techniques of inference is "Foresight: Its Logical Laws, Its Subjective Sources" (1937) in Kyburg and Smokler, eds., *Studies in Subjective Probability*. The same anthology includes a highly informal and very charming expression of DeFinetti's views, "Probability: Beware of Falsifications!" (1977). Robert Winkler, *Introduction to Bayesian Inference and Decision* (New York, 1972), is an extremely lucid guide to Bayesian inference, as applied to Bernoulli processes and several other statistical models. See also Jeffrey's discussion of DeFinetti in *The Logic of Decision*, pp. 186–90.

vestigators continually agree on likelihoods, share the same characterizations of the new facts constituting new data, and are committed to modifying degrees of belief only to the extent that new data dictate. In effect, DeFinetti and his successors showed that this situation (fixed and common likelihoods, shared evidence and the commitment to "stick to the evidence") obtains in a variety of interesting cases where the initial probability distributions can be quite different, and leads to convergence through Bayesian revision. When likelihoods are fixed, Bayesian revision is always one way of doing the necessary work of revising degrees of belief to avoid "dutch book." And it is the strategy that involves the least alteration of the old distribution, consistent with the likelihoods and evidence.

In light of previous sections it seemed that if probability theory is to become the theory of confirmation, probabilities must be "subjective," i.e., degrees of belief as defined by Ramsey or as in some alternative general analysis. This conclusion about the probabilities in a Bayesian theory with a chance of success has considerable impact on the rest of the theory's content. Given non-subjectivist interpretations of probability, a probabilistic theory of confirmation might include general rules dictating a certain assignment of probabilities for everyone accepting the same total body of evidence (say, accepting the same frequencies in homogeneous classes). But subjective probabilities can vary from person to person, even given the same evidence, subject only to the minimal constraint that dutch book could not be made.

If its probabilities are subjective, the whole weight of a probabilistic theory of confirmation will be on the ways in which people revise their initial probabilities. The basic premise of the theory will be as follows. Evidence, e, supports a hypothesis, H, just in virtue of the fact that the subjective probabilities of the investigator about to encounter e entail that $P(H|e)$ be higher than $P(H)$ (and, similarly, e supports H as against H' just in case the subjective probabilities of the investigator in question at the verge of the encounter entail that $P(H|e)/P(H'|e)$ be higher than $P(H)/P(H')$); if disagreement among scientists is ended by rational arguments from data, it is because such Bayesian revision produces convergence.

This theory might fail for one of three reasons. Either investigators can make good arguments from data when they are not in the Bayesian situation of shared likelihoods, fixed prior to the evidence, shared evidence and commitment to stick to the data—so that Bayesian considerations do not explain why their reasoning is good. Or (an even more troubling failure) preferences resulting from Bayesian revision might actually be less reasonable than contrary preferences. Or the subjectivist interpretation might be fundamentally unclear when applied to the measurement of degrees of belief in scientific hypotheses. In the next chapter, I will argue that this best version of the Bayesian theory fails on all three counts.

In principle, there might be theories of intermediate strength, saying much less than this full-blooded Bayesianism but much more than that Bayesian revision is appropriate in certain quite special situations and that the likelihood principle is valid. But this option would have to be justified by arguments that a specific Bayesian strategy is characteristic of a vast but less than universal type of scientific inference. At present, there are no non-universal Bayesian strategies substantially broader in scope than inferences with the standard statistical models. And those models do not fit most choices among scientific theories. For either the causal structure of the processes described by the theories departs from standard models, or the question of which model the subject-matter fits is itself in dispute. At any rate, subsequent arguments will usually have a bearing on the intermediate proposals that might naturally come to mind.

If residual positivism is one part of the attraction of Bayesian confirmation theory, another part, undeniably, is the need to respond to certain advances in the philosophy of science. Claims that data confirm hypotheses turn out to depend on further, substantive background principles. It has seemed, then, to many, that confirmation only exists as a matter of objective fact (not an artifact of a non-justified background) when confirmation consists of Bayesian revision. The probability distributions are arbitrarily different, then, and yet convergence is rational. Often, I will be illustrating two ways in which confirmation can be objective, but non-Bayesian, in spite of background dependence. Inference from the best explanation can still be rationally compelling when it violates Bayesian constraints. And convergence, not dictated by Bayes' Theorem, can depend on substantive, specific principles of rock-bottom common sense, which it is irrational for anyone to deny.

# CHAPTER SEVEN

# Anti-Bayes

THE traditional objection to Bayesian (i.e., subjectivist Bayesian) reasoning is that the prior probabilities can be arbitrary.[1] Bayesians have a great deal to say about how initial degrees of belief should be revised in light of evidence. But any initial system of belief states is allowed, if it meets a minimal requirement of coherence: were the believer to take all bets supported by his or her degrees of belief, "dutch book" would never be accepted.

In fact, given the essential role of framework principles in confirmation, this alleged disadvantage is, if anything, a virtue in a broadly positivist account of confirmation. In general, all that one can require of the initial ranking of hypotheses and the initial expectations of evidence given each hypothesis is that they fit the investigator's background beliefs. Working in a broadly positivist style, seeking rules to specify this fit that are general, valid a priori and determinate in light of the investigator's propositional attitudes, it is hard to see what could regulate this fit other than the subjectivist requirement of coherence. Coherence includes traditional requirements of logical consistency, since "dutch book" can always be based on inconsistencies. It is also a precise and general description of how some probabilistic belief states, e.g., those concerning what data-like events have probably happened, cohere or fail to cohere with others, e.g., those concerning probable regularities or underlying theoretical mechanisms. Closer regimentation either seems too limited to special cases, as with frequentist or classical proposals, or it seems to ignore the realities of good scientific inquiry. Thus, a further requirement that there be a favored kind of event description, corresponding to "hard data," believed in with certainty, ignores both the essential role of uncertain observations and the standard possibility that a general belief may be maintained by casting doubt on conflicting observation reports. As a general description of the prior belief state of a rational inquirer, the Bayesian approach seems not arbitrary, but appropriately flexible.

---

[1] See, for example, Salmon, "Carl G. Hempel on the Rationality of Science," *Journal of Philosophy* (1983), p. 559; Putnam, *Reason, Truth and History* (Cambridge, 1981), p. 190; van Fraassen, *The Scientific Image* (Oxford, 1980), pp. 22, 35f.

I will be arguing that the Bayesian approach to confirmation is really worst where it is usually assumed to be best, in its description of how initial beliefs should be revised in light of evidence. The difficulties will all have the same general form as the most basic problems of deductivism. On the most natural reading, the Bayesian rules are too restrictive, excluding important, valid parts of science; the rules cannot be made liberal enough without making them too liberal, so that absurdities and bad reasoning are let in, or there is a total failure to provide usable tools of criticism. What is even more striking is the ultimate identity in the reasons for these shared failings in the new positivism and the old one. Bayesian reasoning cannot account for the confirmation of hypotheses that are part of the best explanation of the history of science so far, but are inferior as bases for prediction. And this is the old deductivist problem of excluding hypotheses that are superior sources of explanation but not superior means of deducing some data on the basis of others. Bayesian rules that exclude the ad hoc modification of likelihoods after threatening evidence is encountered are too restrictive; yet no general rule is available that admits acceptable theories without permitting everything to be believed no matter what the data. This is the old problem with empirical anomalies. Because of the uneven development of science, good theories that are at a relatively far remove from the data will be inferior to more superficial rivals, on a Bayesian account. And this is, in essence, the old deductivist problem of showing why theories are not excessive whenever they go beyond the data. Much ingenuity is now devoted to elaborating the Bayesian approach, not because it strikes anyone as obviously without flaw, but because it seems a promising research program, whose problems are apt to be the novel difficulties of any new approach. In fact, it is the latest version of a long-standing positivist program. It makes no fundamental headway in coping with the problems that affect the old, deductivist version.

Often, I will be contrasting Bayesian reasoning with bits of informal causal reasoning in the explanation of episodes in scientific inquiry. The likelihood principle will turn out to come to no more, in general, than the idea of confirmation by causal comparison: a hypothesis is confirmed if the history of theorizing and data-gathering is better explained on the basis of its approximate truth than on that of any of its relevant rivals; hence, it is confirmed most strongly if phenomena of science are extremely hard to explain unless it is approximately true. What regulates applications of the likelihood principle is, in general, nothing more than the maxims of fairness and the causal theory of explanation. The relevant framework principles are supplied either by the actual development of science or by the commonsense core of all frameworks. When the hypotheses are radically different, the levers of comparison will be vague, as are the maxims of fairness and the likelihood principle itself. So, the Bayesian approach may seem attractive because it is precise and clear. At the end of this chapter, I will argue that this appearance is an illusion. Despite over half a century of enormous ingenuity and brilliant partial applications, the basic concepts of subjective probability are still murky. To "explicate" the likelihood principle by Bayes' Theorem is to replace a vague valid principle with another that is either extremely unclear or based on false assumptions. Since the theory of logical deduction is not afflicted with corresponding conceptual problems, the new positivism has a burden which deductivism did not carry.

In assessing the Bayesian approach, a good place to begin is with some powerful and important argument from empirical facts, which might naturally be summed up in ways that sound Bayesian. If the approach does not work here, that is good evidence of its basic falsehood. Darwin's *The Origin of Species* is full of such arguments. The following argument about geographic distribution is perhaps the neatest of all.

> The most striking and important fact for us in regard to the inhabitants of islands, is their affinity to those of the nearest mainland, without being actually the same species. Numerous instances could be given of this fact. I will give only one, that of the Galapagos Archipelago, situated under the equator, between 500 and 600 miles from the shores of South America. Here almost every product of the land and water bears the unmistakeable stamp of the American continent. There are twenty-six land birds, and twenty-five of those are ranked by Mr. Gould as distinct species, supposed to have been created here; yet the close affinity of most of these birds to American species in every character, in their habits, gestures, and tones of voice, was manifest. So it is with the other animals, and with nearly all the plants, as shown by Dr. Hooker in his admirable memoir on the Flora of this archipelago. The naturalist, looking at the inhabitants of these volcanic islands in the Pacific, distant several hundred miles from the continent, yet feels that he is standing on American land. Why should this be so? why should the species which are supposed to have been created in the Galapagos Archipelago, and nowhere else,

bear so plain a stamp of affinity to those created in America? There is nothing in the conditions of life, in the geological nature of the islands, in their height or climate, or in the proportions in which the several classes are associated together, which resembles closely the conditions of the South American coast: in fact there is a considerable dissimilarity in all these respects. On the other hand, there is a considerable degree of resemblance in the volcanic nature of the soil, in climate, height, and size of the islands, between the Galapagos and Cape de Verde Archipelagos: but what an entire and absolute difference in their inhabitants! The inhabitants of the Cape de Verde Islands are related to those of Africa, like those of the Galapagos to America. I believe this grand fact can receive no sort of explanation on the ordinary view of independent creation; whereas on the view here maintained, it is obvious that the Galapagos Islands would be likely to receive colonists, whether by occasional means of transport or by formerly continuous land, from America; and the Cape de Verde Islands from Africa; and that such colonists would be liable to modifications; —the principle of inheritance still betraying their original birthplace.

Many analogous facts could be given: indeed it is an almost universal rule that the endemic productions of islands are related to those of the nearest continent, or of other near islands.[2]

The previously cited argument about bats is an enchanting subsidiary to this inference. "Why, it may be asked, has the supposed creative force produced bats and no other mammals on remote islands? On my view this question can easily be answered."[3]

It is natural to summarize Darwin's overall argument in probability talk, and Darwin himself often sums up in this style. Certain facts about distribution are much more probable given that species arise through natural selection than they are given that species arise through individual creation, i.e., through the agency of a force creating each species without prior ancestors and adapting it directly to its environment. So the facts greatly increase the probability that the former hypothesis, not the latter is true. The question is whether this obviously reasonable and Bayesian-sounding argument really corresponds to a reasonable use of Bayes' Theorem applied to subjective probabilities.

[2] *The Origin of Species*, ed. J. W. Burrow (Baltimore, 1968), pp. 386f.
[3] Ibid., p. 383.

NON-PREDICTION

The first consideration suggesting otherwise is that, among Darwin's subjective probabilities, the likelihoods relevant to the rival theories were equal and were 1. Darwin was certain of the geographical distributions. If he were a betting man, he would put up as much as a pound for the bet: if evolution takes place according to natural selection, win a pound if species endemic to islands almost always closely resemble those on the nearest continent or other nearby islands; otherwise the bet is off. He would pay *precisely the same amount* for the bet: if species arise from individual creation, win a pound if the same island fact obtains; otherwise the bet is off. (Of course, this presupposes that Darwin took biological theory as relatively speculative, and would not change his views of elementary zoological data just on the basis of considerations of grand theory. Obviously, he *was* that sensible.) Since the likelihoods are the same, the observation cannot shift the odds for one hypothesis or another via Bayes' Theorem. So Darwin would be wrong to take the geographic facts as confirming, if confirmation were Bayesian revision.[4]

It might seem that this limitation merely corresponds to the trivial fact that Darwin was aware of the relevant evidence by the time he wrote *The Origin*. It might seem that the relevant confirmation occurred at some point in the past when he was weighing one theory against the other and first encountered the geographical data. But, on reflection, this is a biographical speculation on which the assessment of Darwin's argument should not depend. Darwin knew a great many geographical and biological facts, perhaps including the above, long before he wrote *The Origin*, even during the many years in which he took transmutation of species to be impossible. Perhaps at the very early time at which he first learned the relevant facts of geographic distribution, his other biological views were so different, fragmentary or even muddled as to be quite irrelevant to likelihoods that might be located in his actual and excellent argument.[5]

If Darwin and others sharing his grasp of geographic facts could not take his superb argument as confirming if the Bayesian analysis is right, that is, in itself, good evidence that the analysis is wrong.

---

[4] That Bayesians cannot account for the assessment of hypotheses in light of old evidence was first proposed by Glymour. See *Theory and Evidence* (Princeton, 1980), pp. 85–93.

[5] I only mean to show, here, that the status of Darwin's argument is not sensitive to these various biographical possibilities. In fact, we know a great deal about the actual timing of Darwin's intellectual gains. I will make use of this knowledge in the next section.

Still, there were, no doubt, readers of *The Origin* who did not know those geographical facts before they read them, and whom Darwin meant to convince. To see that even this limited success is not always available on a Bayesian reading, one has only to turn to that paradigm of scientific argument, Newton's *Principia*. Almost all the empirical arguments of the *Principia* are of two kinds: extremely compelling arguments based on facts (mostly astronomical) *known to all competent* readers, many of them known from pre-Copernican times; and extremely unconvincing arguments concerning facts discovered by Newton and his collaborators, unconvincing because Newton must rely on highly speculative auxiliary hypotheses in his arguments, for example, unsupported speculations about the "spring and tone of the air" and "reciprocal motions" in tidal waters. Certainly, the *Principia* would be a much less convincing book were it not for arguments of the former kind. Those arguments can always be summarized in a Bayesian-sounding way: "This fact is much more likely given the three laws of motion and the universal law of gravitation than on any other available hypothesis." But if we take this talk too seriously, and suppose that a calculation of subjective probabilities is called for, the arguments are powerless to confirm for any of the readers whom Newton meant to convince.

The issue is not the relativity of Bayesian confirmation to the beliefs of the individual investigator. In many ways, this is the strong point of the Bayesian approach. Rather, the problem is the exceptionally tight connection between prediction and confirmation in this approach. Even in deductivism, all that is required is that an observation be deducible, with the hypothesis as a premise, in a derivation of the right logical form. The form was supposed to be such that the existence of the datum could, potentially, have been predicted via knowledge of the premises. But no one required that the datum actually be news. On the other hand, if probabilities, especially likelihoods, are interpreted in the subjectivist way, then Bayesian revision must be solely concerned with shifts from actual ignorance to actual knowledge of data. A naive reader of the best Bayesian accounts of confirmation might think that it makes the situation of scientific investigators like the situation of bettors, when, generally, it is not. It appears that the naive reader is right.

## BAYESIAN REPLIES

The general anti-Bayesian objection that theories are often confirmed on the basis of facts already known was first made by Glymour in *Theory and Evidence* (1980). Bayesian philosophers of science have since replied in detail. Theirs is the first major counteroffensive in the controversy over Bayesian philosophy of science. A look at the responses (which fairness requires in any case) will make it clearer how close Bayesian confirmation theory is to the old positivism and how far it is from the theory of confirmation as causal comparison.

The rebuttals have been of two kinds. Some identify a new kind of discovery, involving the old evidence but going beyond it, as the subject of distinctive expectations based on the hypotheses in question. Others interpret Bayesian confirmation as concerned with timeless relations. The first kind of response, which Glymour briefly discussed in his book, is the more popular. Daniel Garber has developed it in the most detail, with subsequent refinements by Jeffrey and others.[6]

When a hypothesis, h, is confirmed by old evidence, e, the distinctive likelihood that makes confirmation possible is, for Garber, the likelihood of "the *discovery* of some generally logical or mathematical relation between h and e." Garber adds, "I shall often assume for simplicity that the relation in question is some kind of logical entailment."[7] Thus, to use one of Garber's examples, Newton could not take Kepler's Second Law to have a greater probability conditional on the truth of his own three laws of motion than conditional on their falsehood. For Newton was certain of Kepler's Second Law already. But when he was engaged in testing his theory, Newton was initially uncertain of whether the Second Law could be derived from the three laws of motion (or so Garber, Glymour, Jeffrey and others assume). In his belief system, the likelihood that a derivation exists was greater given the truth of his mechanics than given its falsehood. So the discovery of the derivation was confirming.

On this account, the investigator who uses old evidence to confirm cannot be logically omniscient, i.e., cannot already be aware of the logical (and mathematical) relations between all of his or her beliefs. And this creates a problem for traditional subjectivism, which Garber discusses in detail. Traditionally, the subject-matter of subjective probability theory is supposed to be a person aware of all log-

---

[6] See Daniel Garber, "Old Evidence and Logical Omniscience in Bayesian Confirmation Theory," and Richard Jeffrey, "Bayesianism with a Human Face," both in J. Earman, ed., *Testing Scientific Theories* (Minneapolis, 1983). See *Theory and Evidence*, pp. 90–92, for Glymour's relatively sympathetic response to an earlier version of Garber's proposal.

[7] "Old Evidence and Logical Omniscience," p. 104.

ical relations, since otherwise "dutch book" can be based on the subject's ignorance. Garber's solution is to relativize logical awareness to the given context of hypothesis choice. Bayesian confirmation theory, as he sees it, is a tool addressed to the needs of investigators coping with particular problems of hypothesis choice with whatever resources they actually possess. While the hypotheses that an investigator confronts will have definite, more or less elaborate internal logical structures and logical relations to possible data, Bayesian guidance for the investigator need not impose requirements of coherence which he or she could only fulfill if entirely aware of that structure and those relations. Instead, Garber proposes, we should relativize requirements of coherence to the situation at hand. We should treat the hypotheses and evidence statements in question as "unanalyzed wholes from the point of view of the problem at hand" and only impose restrictions on logical compounds from these relatively atomic sentences.[8] Garber shows that scientifically interesting questions of derivability will typically be left open when an investigator fulfills the resulting weakened and problem-relative requirement of coherence.

On reflection, this revised Bayesian account seems more similar to the old one than it first appears, and also highly dependent on traditional deductivism. To begin with, though the new model is more flexible than the old in admitting certain phenomena as discoveries, its attitude toward time is just as rigid. Confirmation only comes when an initial expectation—now including expectations about logical relatedness—turns out, in the future, to have been prophetic. By way of contrast, Garber asks us to "suppose that S constructed h *specifically* to account for e, and knew, from the start, that it would. It should not *add* anything to the credibility of h that it accounts for the evidence that S knew all along it would account for. In this situation, there is not confirmation."[9]

---

[8] Ibid., p. 222.

[9] Ibid., p. 104. Garber says, *in toto*: "In this situation there is not confirmation, at least not in the relevant sense of the term." But the hedge about a relevant sense is puzzling, here. Presumably, Garber is speaking of some distinct and important sense that people attach to "confirmation" even if they are not committed subjectivist Bayesians, at least not for the moment. Indeed, the example is introduced to show that sometimes even Glymour would regard an encounter of hypothesis with data as nonconfirming because, in a certain way, the encounter is too old. But when Garber, in a footnote, explains what the "relevant sense" of "confirmation" is, it is a sense in which e confirms h just in case the subject's learning of it would heighten his or her degree of belief in h. So the relevant sense of confirmation is stipulated to be one in which confirmation requires revision of belief in light of something new. Of course, every-

In fact, it is quite possible for a hypothesis that began as the outcome of an effort to account for certain evidence to be confirmed by that outcome. Indeed, that might even be the case with Newton's laws of motion and Kepler's Second Law. The derivation of a general form of Kepler's law is Proposition 1, Theorem 1, in the *Principia*, presented with great intuitive force and central to all that follows. It was probably one of Newton's motivating projects to develop a more precise version of the qualitative mechanical explanations of Kepler's system that others had offered.[10] So it would not be amazing if the derivation of the Second Law had been the means by which Newton arrived at this first two laws of motion. Suppose that a notebook of Newton's is discovered in an attic tomorrow, and shows that this is so. Since the derivation was not preceded by ignorance of whether it existed combined with an expectation that it probably would if the laws of motion were valid, we must now conclude that Newton's mechanics was not confirmed by its capacity to explain Kepler's Second Law. Surely, this is wrong.

In the case of Darwin, the origins of his hypotheses are quite well-known, and the arbitrariness of Bayesian attitudes toward time is even more vivid. When Darwin began to doubt that species had independent origins, he developed his natural selection hypothesis largely in an effort to explain certain facts he had encountered as naturalist on the H.M.S. *Beagle*, including the fact, in the passage presented above, that endemic Galapagos species are quite similar to those on the adjacent mainland. Darwin never *expected* the Galapagos facts to be a consequence of the theory of natural selection. Theory and empirical argument did not follow this sequence.[11] On the other hand, the facts about bats on remote islands seem to have been gathered to shore up Darwin's case, after he had developed his theory. So, on the new Bayesian account, we must say that the ca-

---

one accepts that confirmation in this sense requires revision of belief in light of something new—including people who deny that confirmation requires revision in light of something new, apart from special senses of the term. Since the Bayesian replies are not meant to establish a trivial or question-begging position, I will omit the appeal to special senses. It will turn out that the Bayesian perspective on time is too rigid for any Bayesian theory of confirmation that is not trivial or question-begging.

[10] See Kuhn, *The Copernican Revolution* (New York, 1959), pp. 247–52.

[11] Darwin wrote in his diary, "In July [1837] opened first notebook on Transmutation of Species. Had been greatly struck from about the previous March on character of South American fossils, and species on Galapagos archipelago. These facts (especially the latter), origin of all my views." *The Autobiography of Charles Darwin*, ed. Francis Darwin (New York, 1958), p. 150; see also pp. 41f.

pacity to explain Galapagos facts did not confirm Darwin's hypothesis, but the capacity to explain bat facts did.

It is not even true that theories developed out of certain efforts to explain will be justified by at least some subsequent derivations, in Garber's way, whenever they are supported by the evidence as a whole. For example, the Bohr-Rutherford theory of the atom only had important explanatory connections with the phenomena from which it was developed.

In light of the example I took from *The Origin of Species*, a further problem of the revised model stands out. Though the Bayesian approach is initially attractive as a promising cure for the defects of deductivism, the new version presupposes that deductivism is basically sound. What an investigator pursues in trying to confirm h is supposed to be a certain kind of "logical or mathematical relation" with evidence, which can, for purposes of simplification, be treated as a relation of entailment. Similarly, Glymour, in his original sketch of a possible Bayesian reply, speaks of "the discovery of a certain logical or structural connection between a piece of evidence and a piece of theory."[12] In fact, every effort to specify the desired relation in terms of logical form has failed, for fundamental reasons. If we attribute to Darwin any goal that a deductivist account of confirmation has described, his supposed hope that the theory of natural selection will bear the corresponding logical or mathematical relation to the data would turn out to be a false hope. So, according to the new Bayesianism, his theory was disconfirmed.

Is this deductivism essential to the Garber-Jeffrey proposal, or just a dispensable personal inclination of theirs? It might seem that every expectation concerning the future vicissitudes of a hypothesis given its truth could be admitted as relevant to confirmation, without requiring that the relevant vicissitudes be of some favored kind, e.g., the entailment of phenomena. On the face of it, though, this is a disappointing proposal. A theory of confirmation ought to help explain why Newton's actual argument was more powerful than that of a schoolboy whose belief in the laws of motion is heightened because he expects his schoolteacher to endorse the laws, should they be true, and endorsement is given. Worse yet, "wild" likelihoods, not fitting background beliefs, will confirm, if nothing is said to restrict the kinds of expectations that are potentially confirming.

Consider the outlook of a dizzy would-be supporter of Galileo who thinks that Galileo's cosmological beliefs are more likely to be

---

[12] *Theory and Evidence*, p. 92. Garber identifies himself as the author of this Bayesian response, in "Old Evidence and Logical Omniscience," p. 124.

true than Ptolemaic ones (degree of credence: .60), but thinks that Venus is, to the same degree, more likely to have phases given the Ptolemaic system than given the Copernican. In traditional Bayesianism, this belief system is excluded on grounds of incoherence. The All-Shrewd Bookmaker could get the Galilean simpleton to make a bet at 3:2 odds that the beliefs distinguishing Copernican from Ptolemaic astronomy are false, combined with a 7:4 conditional bet that Venus has phases, the condition being the falsehood of those Copernican beliefs and the truth of their Ptolemaic rivals. He is no astronomer, but being a good logical analyst, the All-Shrewd Bookmaker sees that he will make money if the Copernican beliefs are true (so that the conditional bet is off), and also make money if they are false (so that Venus will not have phases). But in the new Bayesian format for describing relevant belief systems, there is no way to exclude many wild likelihoods, such as the simpleton's, which fail to cohere with background beliefs. In recording likelihoods that will be relevant to someone's choice among certain hypotheses on the basis of certain phenomena, we suspend requirements of logical omniscience, context by context, taking differential expectations of the relevant phenomena as given even when they are in conflict with the actual logical structure of the investigator's beliefs. We admit a Newton who is unaware that certain of his beliefs entail others of his beliefs, so that the discovery of the relation can raise a probability. On a similar note of psychological realism, we must admit belief systems like the Galilean simpleton's.

The simpleton expects Venusian phases to be observed if the Ptolemaic system is true, and, to his dismay, phases are observed, confirming the Ptolemaic system. A theory of confirmation does not have much point if it has no tools for setting him straight. In particular, the Bayesian account of scientific rationality requires such tools of criticism. Likelihoods play no special role in producing convergence if the same evidence can, in general, be likely on one hypothesis for one investigator, on its opposite for another. Yet the general rules that would exclude wild likelihoods on a priori grounds are the old positivist prescriptions of relations of logical form connecting hypothesis and data.

There are, of course, alternatives to the deductivist account of the desired connections between hypotheses and evidence, namely, causal theories such as the one I have proposed. It might seem that Garber and Jeffrey could take the desired relation to be one of explanation (as they do often put it), while accepting that the causal element in explanation cannot be analyzed away. The problem is that once explanation is given an autonomous role in confirmation,

Bayesian accounts are undermined. Like deductivist proposals, they turn out to be rules of thumb for constructing appropriate arguments from the best explanation, useful in special circumstances but distortions if imposed as general rules.

If what good investigators want is a hypothesis that explains the evidence, a capacity not to be analyzed and specified in other terms, then it is obviously arbitrary to deny that a hypothesis can be confirmed when it is designed in a successful effort to explain certain evidence. That it does explain is crucial, not that it fails to fit the particular temporal pattern in which the investigator first framed it, then formed a special expectation that it would explain, then discovered the explanation. No doubt, it is typically a point in favor of a hypothesis, all else being equal, that its triumph fit the latter pattern. When a hypothesis is developed to explain certain data, this can be ground for a charge that its explanatory fit is due to the ingenuity of the developer in tailoring hypotheses to data, as against the basic truth of the hypothesis. If an otherwise adequate rival exists, this charge might direct us to a case for its superiority. But such a rival does not always exist, and the advantages of having first been developed, then tested against the data are not always compelling. As usual, positivism takes a limited rule of thumb for making a fair argument of causal comparison, and treats it as a universal, determinate rule, functioning on its own.

In the other general kind of Bayesian reply to the problem of old evidence, the usual subjectivist view of confirmation is replaced by another, in which confirmation does not depend on discovery and revision. In the end, this very different kind of reply is as rigid in the relation between time and confirmation it imposes and as regressive in its deductivist assumptions as the appeal to logical discovery.

Horwich's version stays the closest to traditional subjectivism. Confirmation, he proposes, exists "if and only if reason requires that with background assumptions, B, anyone's conditional degree of belief in H given E, should be greater than his unconditional degree of belief in H. . . . [W]e can now account for confirmation by known facts. . . . For it is natural to identify the evidential force of such information with what ought to have been the epistemic effects of its acquisition. In other words, we might say that E, which is known to be true, is evidence for H, by virtue of the fact that, given our beliefs before E was discovered, $P(H|E)$ should have been greater than $P(H)$."[13]

[13] Horwich, *Probability and Evidence* (Cambridge, 1982), p. 52. More precisely, the

Since the crucial relation is the timeless one linking B, P(H|E) and P(H), this is a relatively atemporal view of confirmation. It is, in its way, just as rigid about the significance (or insignificance) of timing as views that require discovery. In particular, it has the reverse problem, underemphasis on timing. Garber was, surely, not all wrong in saying that a hypothesis is not confirmed when designed to explain the evidence in question. While confirmation often does exist in such cases, it is usually weaker than it would be on a basis of discovery. General relativity was enormously strengthened when its novel predictions about the interaction of mass and light were subsequently borne out. The use of Newton's celestial mechanics in the discovery of Uranus was an enormous vindication, at a time when the truth of the universal law of gravitation was by no means uncontroversial. In contrast, Bohr's early quantum model was, everyone agreed, more weakly confirmed than it would otherwise have been because the phenomena it explained were simply those it was devised to explain. A theory of confirmation that makes these questions of timing invisible neglects phenomena that are clearly relevant to the comparison of hypotheses—and that ought to be if confirmation is fair causal comparison.

The other liability of Bayesian rebuttals, the tendency to presuppose the basic truth of deductivism, emerges when one considers problems in determining what background beliefs are relevant to the judgment that reason dictates the probability assignments on Horwich's analysis. Granted, Horwich's treatment of confirmation contains a hedge that makes his subject-matter somewhat different from deductivists'. He proposes to analyze the relativized locution "E confirms H relative to B." But he is certainly concerned to find rules locating the particular background beliefs relevant to our usual statements of confirmation, which are not explicitly relativized. And his rule is not simply to take all actual beliefs as relevant if they determine the crucial probability assignments, given the requirement of coherence. This could not be his rule, since it would generate Glymour's problem about old evidence.

Horwich says that the background consists of the subject's beliefs "before E was discovered." But this rule introduces irrelevancies, which could produce the wrong assessment of a hypothesis. In point of biographical fact, many pioneers of quantum theory had, as their old evidence, E, anomalies of classical physics that they had known

---

first explication, mentioning H, E and B, is a definition of "E confirms H relative to B." I will discuss the hedge soon.

since they had begun to acquire sophisticated physical insight. Perhaps Bohr's unsophisticated schoolboy beliefs before he learned of the classical anomalies had so excessively emphasized certain kinds of underlying continuity that the facts of observed discontinuity he later encountered would not have been made more likely by discontinuities at the atomic level. His favorite high school physics teacher taught him that energy must change continuously, even if particles change location discontinuously. Who cares what was likely for Bohr in high school? Who cares if Kepler's Second Law would have been less likely given the three laws of motion, for Newton at a tender age, dominated perhaps by mystical theological musings and still ignorant of basic Keplerian astronomy?

Should we consider, instead, what beliefs the subject would have, if he or she were not aware of the evidence in question? Taken literally, this proposal is just as mired in psychological irrelevancies, as Ramsey made clear when he introduced the subjectivist interpretation of conditional probability.[14] Newton's physics is confirmed by the totality of old evidence on which he relies. If he had not known these facts, perhaps he would have arranged his system of the world on the basis of Scriptural interpretation. Whether the derivation of Kepler's Second Law would be probability-raising against that background is hardly relevant to the argument of the *Principia*.

Suppose, then, that we put biographical speculation to one side, and simply subtract the already known evidence from the given background to get the assumptions on which reason is to work. That would be too liberal. Unsupported inferences would now be self-supporting, via background beliefs they introduce. There is a familiar vice in reasoning, often a product of wishful thinking, in which one forms background beliefs because they make certain known facts evidence for a conclusion. Hoping that I have reached Maine, I see five people in a row wearing red plaid shirts, I form the belief that people in Maine have a distinctive preference for red plaid shirts, and I conclude that I have arrived. If the relevant background is simply my current belief state minus the evidence in question, then, at the end of this process the hypothesis that I am in Maine would be confirmed by the past evidence of plaid-shirt-sightings, according to Horwich's proposal. But surely my claim to have

[14] In the previously quoted passage from Ramsey "Truth and Probability" (1926) in H. Kyburg and H. Smokler, eds., *Studies in Subjective Probability* (Huntington, N.Y., 1980), p. 40.

confirmed arrival is defective, as any reasonably skeptical fellow traveler would point out.

In locating the relevant system of background beliefs, we should not be too true to the past, for irrelevant biographical quirks are introduced. But we should not be too true to the present, or hasty inferences are admitted. Presumably, Horwich would admit only a logically purified version of present belief. We subtract out, not just the evidence immediately in question, but background beliefs that are not adequately motivated by the rest of the subject's evidence. The account of adequate empirical motivation cannot itself be confined to episodes of confirmation by successful prediction, since old evidence can adequately support a background belief. What we need to carry out this program is an atemporal account of the relations between propositions and evidence that make those propositions appropriate premises for subsequent scientific argument. The only program for finding such relations that does not undermine the Bayesian approach is the old positivism, deductivism. And indeed, Horwich says of "the orthodox . . . theory of scientific methodology . . . Hempel's hypothetico-deductive model," "I think that this is approximately right, as far as it goes. But it is silent on a wide range of important matters. It fails to account for the testing and adoption of statistical hypotheses . . . It provides no measure of the *degree* of confirmation . . . And it gives no account of when a hypothesis has been sufficiently confirmed to justify any confidence in it."[15] A harsher verdict on the old positivism deprives Horwich of the means for identifying the background against which likelihoods of old evidence are assessed.

Finally, for Rosenkrantz there is no problem about old evidence, since likelihoods are, in his view, "timeless relations."[16] He is well aware that the corresponding theory of confirmation gives no special weight to vindications of a hypothesis in which it predicts or explains phenomena different from those which it was first developed to explain. For example, the phenomenon of light-bending by the sun would no longer be, as most think it is, stronger confirmation of relativity theory because of its timing. He dismisses this "old chestnut" that timing is sometimes a source of strength as an unreflective prejudice. But his sole basis for doing so is a description of a few important theories which were accepted on account of their capacity to explain old evidence that they were designed to explain. This is

[15] *Probability and Evidence*, pp. 11f.
[16] "Why Glymour *Is* a Bayesian" in Earman, ed., *Testing Scientific Theories*, p. 85.

only a good argument that timing is never relevant if there is a single perspective on the relevance of timing which fits all rational theory choices—an assumption which is as pervasive in the new positivism as it is implausible. Indeed, the Bayesian literature is notable for containing adamant and general claims about the relevance of timing, of utterly contrary sorts. Thus, while emphasis on novel derivations is a mere common prejudice for Rosenkrantz and, for Horwich, is only appropriate for those who lack first-hand knowledge of a theory's content, both Garber and Jeffrey take the discovery of a new derivation to be the only possible way in which a hypothesis can be confirmed by its capacity to explain.[17]

As for the identification of the timeless relations, Rosenkrantz accepts that it often proceeds by informal techniques, well-removed from the precise constraints of his ingenious neo-classical interpretation of probability. For example, there is, he supposes, an objective likelihood that the perihelion of Mercury would advance in the way it does given the truth of relativity theory. It is hard to see on what objective but non-causal basis such a likelihood could rest, except the deductive relations between general relativity and the facts about Mercury. It is hard to see how the confirming kind of derivation could be further specified, except by making the appeals to formal simplicity, minimal content and the avoidance of the ad hoc characteristic of deductivism. After all, some deduction of the advance of the perihelion is available on basically Ptolemaic premises. And, in fact, Rosenkrantz' practice in justifying the crucial likelihood assignments is deductivist in all these ways. In his rationales for assigning likelihoods, the high likelihood of the evidence given the theory corresponds to the existence of a deduction of the former from the latter in a way that embodies familiar positivist formal virtues. Again, the new positivism presupposes the basic adequacy of the old.

In constructing a general interpretation of the probability calculus that makes it into a theory of confirmation, a Bayesian is faced with two choices. Though the probability calculus says nothing about time, the theory of confirmation is about learning from evidence, which takes place in time. So the general interpretation will say whether timing is relevant and, if so, how. Also, the probability calculus provides no means of assigning probabilities. A Bayesian needs a rule that, at the very least, assigns likelihoods. The first

---

[17] See Horwich, *Probability and Evidence*, p. 117; Garber, "Old Evidence and Logical Omniscience," pp. 103f.; Jeffrey, "Bayesianism with a Human Face," p. 148.

round of debate over Bayesian confirmation theory suggests that no right choice is available in response to either of these needs. Any rule about timing that makes probability theory an effective guide to confirmation will be intolerably one-sided, leading to false assessments of important propositions. As for the problem of likelihood-assignment, if actual expectations are freely admitted as producing relevant likelihoods, nonsensical arguments are counted as confirming. But as Bayesianism is made stricter to exclude such non-sense, it becomes an extension of traditional deductivism.

Indeed, the ultimate reliance on deductivism helps to explain the frequent and puzzling expressions of agreement between Glymour and the Bayesians, in the course of their debate. Bayesian accounts of confirmation by old evidence in Garber's and Jeffrey's style are "correct," Glymour has remarked (almost in passing), although they do not discuss the questions of logical form that are "really important and really interesting."[18] Reportedly, Glymour readily concedes that old evidence poses no problem for objectivist Bayesians such as Rosenkrantz.[19] This is as it should be. Bootstrapping is an extremely elegant and subtle deductivist strategy. Bayesianism is incorrect because deductivism is incorrect, in the substance of its rules for confirmatory derivations and in its neglect of the diversity of relations between historical patterns of discovery and strength of confirmation.

## THE RETURN OF AD-HOCNESS

The gap between inference from the best explanation, which Darwin and Newton certainly accomplished, and inference from successful prediction has turned out to create a special difficulty for Bayesianism. But the general phenomenon, that the realities of confirmation are distorted when explanation and prediction are conflated, is a familiar problem of positivism, in its traditional, deductivist form. It becomes even clearer that nothing has really changed when we look at some of the ways in which Darwin's or Newton's arguments might have been resisted.

Suppose we examine the force of Darwin's geographical argument for the audience that fits the Bayesian approach the best. Someone approaches *The Origin* ignorant of the facts about distribution, and with a higher degree of belief in individual creation

[18] *Theory and Evidence*, p. 93.
[19] Rosenkrantz, "Why Glymour *Is* a Bayesian," p. 85.

than in natural selection; in his belief system, before encountering the data, it is highly probable, given the truth of individual creation, that distinctive species on islands and distinctive species on the adjacent mainland will be related as distinctive species are in the world at large; but the probability is high that island species and mainland species have the special relation Darwin describes given the truth of species creation through natural selection. For a Bayesian, the rational force of Darwin's argument is the rational force of the proposal to revise belief according to the Bayesian relation between likelihoods, individual probabilities and the resultant probabilities-conditional-on-evidence.

In fact, though Darwin's argument is good, reason does not, by any means, force the creationist to revise degrees of belief on Bayesian grounds. He could, as many scientists did, resist the revision of the probabilities of hypotheses by changing his *likelihoods* in response to the evidence. If one were to try to restore the power of Bayes' Theorem to produce convergence, by adding a general rule prohibiting such responses, one unfortunate result would be a disproof of Darwin. With the prohibition of ad hoc revisions of likelihoods, open-minded investigators in Darwin's time could not have given any significant credence to Darwin's theory. For Darwin, too, had to avail himself of ad hoc defenses, whose pattern is identical when described in terms of subjective-probability theory.

Because actual creationists these days make such terrible arguments, it is important to reconstruct the logic of the reasonable response that could be made to the argument about islands. In the only version of creationism that Darwin and his fellow scientists took very seriously, species arise when they are created, without ancestors, by a force that intelligently adapts them to their respective environments. How this creative force works is a mystery, but a mystery with parallels in Darwin's theory. Darwin realized that life first arose on the earth at a certain point in time, and he had no idea of the nature of the process producing this result. For that matter, he had no idea why offspring generally resemble parents or why resemblance occasionally breaks down in the ways that permit natural selection to operate. Similarly, both Darwin *and* the creationists freely admitted that they could not predict when traits are adaptive, on the basis of mere descriptions of the traits and the relevant environments. Concluding the thought-experiments in Chapter 3, "The Struggle for Existence," Darwin cheerfully proposes, "It is good thus to try in our imagination to give any form some advantage over another. Probably in no single instance should we know what to do so as to succeed."[20] In essence, modern biologists can do no better. The mutations contributing to actual species formation are each of them so small in selective advantage that the advantage cannot be assessed by any known technique.

In this situation of shared ignorance, a creationist can, reasonably, revise his likelihoods in response to Darwin's evidence. He might conclude, contrary to his initial assumption, that the environments on islands and adjacent mainlands must be similar yet different in ways that make distinctive but similar species the most adaptive choice for a creative intelligence. As for the initially surprising facts about bats and specially remote islands, specially remote islands must be well-suited for bats, albeit in peculiar ways, but not for other mammals. Prior to Darwin's data, the creationist would not have expected this. And what the relevant environmental features are, he cannot say. But claims about adaptiveness are often after the fact inferences from the observed traits and distributions of species—notoriously and in *both* theoretical frameworks.

The creationist has revised his likelihoods to preserve his probability distribution. Unless it is supplemented by a general rule excluding such maneuvers, the Bayesian approach provides absolutely no rationale for resolving disputes. No general rule comes to mind except a general requirement that likelihoods be kept fixed, no matter where they lead. But that theory of testing would be much too restrictive. For example, Darwin's own theory would fail.

As Darwin freely admits, some "grand facts" are sharply at variance with strong expectations given his theory, expectations that the best scientists of his time would have formed. "[A] crowd of difficulties will have occurred to the reader. Some of them are so grave that to this day I can never reflect on them without being staggered."[21] If some facts of geographic distribution support his theory, some are quite unexpected, for example, the presence of similar "alpine" species on isolated mountain tops located literally at opposite ends of the earth.[22] On the theory of natural selection, the best geologists would have expected to find in the fossil record forms intermediate between the ones actually found. Certainly, they would have expected that the lowest fossil-bearing strata that had been excavated would include only simple species, not the quite advanced ones actually present.[23] Darwin responds to these difficul-

[20] *The Origin of Species*, p. 129.
[21] Ibid., p. 205.
[22] Ibid., p. 359.
[23] Ibid., pp. 309, 312f., 340–42, 439f.

ties (and they are all among those *he* states) with admittedly speculative hypotheses, which he did not and would not have adopted before the anomalies were discovered. In some cases, he admits to having no auxiliary hypothesis of any plausibility with which the contrary appearance can be explained away. Of the problem of the lowest strata, Darwin writes, "The case at present must remain inexplicable; and may be truly urged as a valid argument against the views here entertained. To show that it may hereafter receive some explanation, I will give the following hypothesis."[24] An admittedly quite unsupported theory of the metamorphosis of strata follows, which has turned out to be false.

Of course, *The Origin* is, in fact, a magisterial empirical case for the theory of natural selection. How can this be so, when both sides employed the tactic of ad hoc revision? With his usual acumen about the logic of scientific disputes, Darwin provides the key, which I used before in developing the causal theory of confirmation: "Such is the sum of the chief objections and difficulties that may justly be urged against my theory. . . . I have felt these difficulties far too heavily during many years to doubt their weight. But it deserves especial notice that the more important objections relate to questions on which we are confessedly ignorant; nor do we know how ignorant we are."[25] The phenomena that natural selection cannot explain but that individual creation can are clustered in certain areas: areas where the effects of natural selection would obviously depend on additional causal factors which were obviously very imperfectly understood, as yet. This dependence on auxiliary fields and the fragmentary and uncertain status of these fields (historical geography, for example, or the metamorphosis of sedimentary rocks) are admitted by all sides to the dispute. Elsewhere, where data are more secure and auxiliary hypotheses better established, natural selection explains a vast array of facts that are not explainable using the theory of individual creation.

Darwin is reminding us that the total shape of success and failure has this pattern, and that no analogous claim can be made for the theory of individual creation. (It is because of this reliance on the total pattern that *The Origin* had to be a long book.) The best explanation of this pattern of success and failure is that the problems of the natural selection theory are due, not to its basic falsehood, but to mistakes and ignorance in auxiliary fields; in contrast, the failures

[24] Ibid., p. 314.
[25] Ibid., p. 340.

of individual creation theory are best explained as due to the non-existence of its basic mechanism. Darwin's overall argument is a common-sensical explanation of the history of an explanatory project, not an application of Bayes' Theorem. As noted in the last chapter, negative analogues to Darwin's reasoning can defeat Bayesian defenses of hypotheses, for example, arguments from surprising evidence to the truth of flying-saucer lore or of speculations concerning ancient cross-cultural contact.

An interpretation of the probability calculus tells us nothing about hypothesis choice, unless we are required to keep likelihoods rigid. For revisions in the assignment of hypothesis can always be avoided by revising likelihoods instead. The ad hoc response of the creationist shows how easy such evasion is. Darwin's own, legitimate practice shows how distorting a general rule against revising likelihoods would be.

It might seem that Darwin's solution to his problem of ad hocness is a key to the right Bayesian response to this problem in general. Instead of simply treating the present scientific consensus as the basis for likelihoods, we might acknowledge that the scientific community has doubts about the actual validity of its present consensus, and work with an array of likelihood distributions, each conditional on relevant background principles, believed to some degree. Aside from the enormous computational complexities, the ramified theory would fail in two fundamental ways. First of all, the likelihoods that distinguish this from the unadorned Bayesian theory are likelihoods conditional on the falsehood of the consensus, e.g., the probability, given the falsehood of the present geological consensus, that it is probable, given the truth of the theory of natural selection, that intermediate forms will frequently be present in the fossil record. Who has any firm degree of belief about such conditionals? These probabilities conditional on the falsehood of the actual consensus amount to transient sentiments, too fluid from time to time and from scientist to scientist to support convergence within the amount of time that good arguments have properly compelled agreement. In the second place, even in this very ramified form, the Bayesian approach is concerned with predictive success and failure. But the actual pattern of success and failure to be explained is a non-predictive pattern of explanatory success and failure, not the predictive success and failure governed by the subjectivist version of Bayes' Theorem. At least this is often true, as in the case of Darwin's theory.

When hypotheses are revised ad hoc, vagueness or complicating hedges are frequently introduced. The Bayesian literature does contain discussions of why these frequent characteristics of hypotheses revised ad hoc are relatively undesirable. Vague or hedged hypotheses are relatively hard to falsify, and so, as Rosenkrantz puts it, they have relatively low "cognitive growth potential."[26] On the average, the likelihood of evidence on such a hypothesis is closer than otherwise to its likelihood on the most probable rivals. But, to begin with, Bayesian disadvantages in growth *potential* will not produce *actual* rational convergence, if likelihoods are frequently revised after the fact. And investigators are often in a situation in which such revision is legitimate. In the second place, it is not a good rule to choose the hypothesis with the highest cognitive growth potential. Usually, that hypothesis conflicts too sharply with the evidence thus far. Attempts to find a rule for choice in the face of trade-offs between growth potential and empirical fit ultimately rely on the sort of deductivist oversimplification discussed in Chapter Five. Finally, it is not always true that the ad hoc revision that deserves to lose has low cognitive growth potential as its basic defect. Natural selection is not obviously less vague than creationism, when all ad hoc revisions are made by both sides. The crucial judgment is Darwin's common-sensical weighing of how serious the difficulties are. If Cartesian vortex theory had been revised to require that the celestial medium swirls so as to produce precisely Newtonian trajectories, that would be a paradigm of undesirable ad hoc revision, as Newton himself proclaims.[27] But the inferior, ad hoc hypothesis would not be less falsifiable than Newton's theory. In general, the effort to connect Bayesian measures of growth potential and content with the perils of ad hocness involves the same implausible hope as Hempel and Glymour express in defense of deductivism: that the results of objectionable tactics of revision will be singled out by their logical form.

The problem of ad hoc revision in Bayesian confirmation theory is essentially the same as a central problem of deductivism: every theory entails some false observations when joined with the best-established data and auxiliary hypotheses of the time; if we permit some of these anomalies to be blamed, ad hoc, on errors in the observations or auxiliaries, not independently ascertained, there is no general rule that tells us when such an ad hoc defense is inappropriate; but if it is appropriate everywhere, testing is impossible. At first, the Bayesian approach might seem a more promising means of

[26] See "Why Glymour *Is* a Bayesian," p. 74.
[27] *Principia*, ed. F. Cajori (Berkeley, 1962), p. 394.

coping with anomaly and ad hoc revision, since conflicts with the data are not taken as lethal, but as matters of degree, in the comparison between a hypothesis and its rivals. But the deductivist problem of assessing revisions of premises simply returns as the problem of assessing revisions in likelihoods. If likelihoods were kept rigid, rational belief in many good theories would have to be lowered to an implausible degree. If likelihoods can be bent to suit the facts, Bayes' Theorem cannot account for the real force of compelling arguments. The basic distortion, common to both the new and the old positivism, is the conception of theories as means of forming expectations, not repertoires of mechanisms from which accounts of phenomena can be extracted.

## THE INACCESSIBILITY OF THEORIES

In deductivism, the problem of assessing ad hoc revisions was one side of the larger question of describing how far acceptable hypotheses can stray from the data. The other side was the problem of admitting theories with a content that exceeds the mere statement of currently observed regularities. If such excessive premises for deducing observations are never confirmed, the greatest scientific achievements are excluded. But once such excess is allowed, there seemed to be no way to exclude obvious absurdities. The Bayesian approach has a similar problem in accounting for the status of the best scientific theories. Just as these theories are inflated means of deducing available data, they are inflated and inferior bases for forming expectations.

A theory, as I am using the term here, is a description of causal factors that are relatively hard to observe or measure, factors which are held to shape phenomena that are relatively easy to observe or measure. For every theory, at any given time, there is an alternative that might be called the "phenomenological" rival, a term that late nineteenth-century opponents of the molecular theory of matter used to describe their more superficial approach. The phenomenological rival makes two kinds of statements. It states all the well-established observations of the time bearing on the phenomena that the deeper theory proposes to explain. In addition, it expresses agnosticism about the underlying causal factors, if any, producing these phenomena—typically, these empirical regularities. The phenomenological rival (as I intend the phrase at present) does not assert the non-existence of the factors alleged in the theory. It expresses total ignorance as to whether those factors exist. The subjective probabilities assigned to the possible states of any underlying reality are, in the jargon of probability theory, "diffuse." Clearly, this belief state is a rival to the committed theorist's. A rational scientist must often decide between such options.[28]

In the new, Bayesian positivism, the theoretician's dilemma takes the following form. A phenomenological rival would almost always be preferred to any theory (even to the tentative belief that a theory is approximately true) if scientists were to revise beliefs according to Bayesian inferences. This is true even in the many cases in which a preference for a theory (i.e., for its approximate truth) would be rational, in point of fact.

By definition, a theory makes claims about factors that are relatively hard to observe or measure. Given the latter difficulties, many current beliefs as to what these factors are like, if they exist, are apt to be wrong. At the same time, a theory asserts that the hidden factors have a definite causal impact on what is observed. Theories, after all, are advanced on account of their capacity to explain phenomena. The mistakes about the theoretical factors and the connections between those factors and what is readily observed will combine to produce false expectations about the data. More precisely, the associated likelihoods, the bets that a scientist would make about the data given that the theory is true will often turn out to favor statements conflicting with observations. The phenomenological rival is not burdened by similar difficulties in describing deep factors. Since it only asserts well-established empirical regularities, it will be a basis for likelihoods that fit observations better than the theory.

Newton, for example, made serious mistakes about tidal friction and about the relation between motion, heat, and conductivity in the invisible constituents of air, and remained in ignorance of important facts about gravitational influences originating beyond the orbit of Saturn. As a result, the expected values for tides, the speed of sound and Saturn's orbit were wide of the mark. A partisan of a phenomenological approach to motion would have no commitment to "deduce the phenomena" from beliefs about those underlying factors, so no false observational expectations arise. Similarly, Daltonian chemists encountered central and abiding difficulties in determining the number of atoms in molecules of free gases. Many mistakes and false observational expectations resulted. Their more phenomenological colleagues did not claim to have better means to assess the ultimate composition of gases. Rather, their expectations

[28] There are substantial problems in representing agnosticism through a distribution of subjective probabilities. But these are real problems for the Bayesian approach, not means of defending it from criticism. For the agnostic attitude does exist and is crucial to rational science.

about the data did not depend on beliefs about ultimate composition. As a result, there was always an observationally superior phenomenological rival.

Deductivists sometimes tried to turn the anomalies of the best theories to the advantage of the deductivist account. They pointed out that derived values conflicting with the best observations at a given point in time often turned out to fit subsequent improved observations, a powerful vindication of the theory. Deviations in Saturn's orbit turned out to be due to a mass beyond the orbit of Saturn, which Newton speculatively surmised, Leverrier precisely described on theoretical grounds and Galle observed. The molecular theory of gases makes it plausible that the Boyle-Charles law is not quite right, and more refined observations established that the theoretical law most plausible on molecular-kinetic grounds, Van der Waals' law, does fit the data. But these developments provide no basis for showing that a theory is preferable to the best phenomenological description, on either a Bayesian or a deductivist view. When observation is improved, belief simply shifts from one phenomenological description to another, the new best one.

In every case in which a preference for the theoretical description seems desirable, the idea of confirmation as causal comparison provides a satisfying rationale. The failures of the theory being tested are best explained as due to the difficulties of investigating factors that the theory itself describes with basic truth. Or rather, this is the best explanation of the total pattern of failures and successes. By contrast, the evidential fit of the phenomenological rival is best explained as a consequence of its avoiding the special risks of ambitious causal description. Such risk avoidance is a sign of gambler's prudence but no special sign of rational access to truth. In addition, the best shallow description often succeeds because it has stolen the observational fruits of theorizing (e.g., the Leverrier-Galle result, Van der Waals' law), while leaving unexplained the fruitfulness of the theory.

In Glymour's celebrated explanation of why he is not a Bayesian, his criticism of the Bayesian approach to confirmation begins with the problem of justifying theories. "The first difficulty is a familiar one. . . . [T]he collection of 'observational' consequences of the theory will always be at least as probable as the theory itself; generally the theory will be less probable than its observational consequences."[29] In the subsequent debate, this particular criticism has not had much impact. Given the deductivist context of Glymour's

---

[29] *Theory and Evidence*, p. 83.

criticisms, this should not be surprising. Glymour's deductivism encounters problems of justifying inferences to theories, problems whose proposed solutions are not very different from Bayesian strategies and in no way more promising. If "bootstrapping" supports theoretical claims we want to preserve, it also occurs when bootstrapping auxiliaries are the result of desperate and absurd ad hoc defenses. A unifying theory will be favored over piecemeal lists of regularities if one favors concentrated over diffuse testing; but the possibility that the cross-checks are false correlations needs to be ruled out, and the grounds for doing so are not clear. Some theories are justified in the hypothetico-deductive way, even though no bootstrapping is available. (Here, I am simply summarizing objections developed at length in Chapter Five, above.) Glymour's responses introduce further criteria for preference, to single out the preferred theories. He expresses the hope that ad hoc revisions will produce hypotheses with distinctive and objectionable logical structures, assumes that appropriate formal structures of cross-checking justify the belief that correlations are causally revealing, and takes the occasional triumphs of purely hypothetico-deductive reasoning to be supported by "natural" connections between kinds of evidence and kinds of theories. All of these standards of preference have Bayesian analogues, which are as likely to support belief in theories as against mere empirical summaries as the deductivist standards are likely to separate well-grounded theories from flimsy speculations. The hedges and vagueness of many ad hoc revisions are also a typical price of the accuracy in mere empirical summaries, as against underlying theories. A preference for concentrated over diffuse testing is also a preference for hypotheses more easily shown to be false if they are false. In both cases, a Bayesian preference for high cognitive growth potential is as plausible a ground for hypothesis choice as Glymour's, and as likely to support the choice of standard theories. Similarly, the appeal to "natural" evidence is no more plausible than a reliance on certain conditional probabilities, as founded on deep-seated background beliefs. Because Glymour's treatment of theory and evidence stands or falls with analogous Bayesian proposals, Rosenkrantz's long rebuttal to "Why I Am not a Bayesian" could bear the apt title "Why Glymour *Is* a Bayesian."

Some contemporary Bayesians and informal Bayesians of the past have welcomed the inaccessibility of theories. Belief in forces, as against mere trajectories, hydrogen molecules, as against mere hydrogen, is helpful, they acknowledge, but philosophically controversial. The controversies might be resolved by taking the corresponding theories to be economical summaries of empirical regularities and fruitful guides to forming hunches about new regularities. As such, the theories would not be used to describe reality, any more than most memory aids, vivid images or instructive metaphors. Rather than puzzling about the ontologically suspect entities, one is always free to seek merely the best phenomenological description, in forming beliefs about what is true.

In the last section of this book, I will examine the main philosophical arguments for such an anti-realist perspective. For now, the crucial issue is whether the new, Bayesian positivism can be defended by showing that the inaccessible theories concern alleged entities that are suspect, special philosophical arguments to one side. In fact, the neglected hypotheses may concern entities which are hard to observe, but neither strange nor controversial otherwise.

Consider Robert Koch's powerful argument that tuberculosis is caused by a certain kind of bacillus. He cultured the bacillus from tubercular human lung tissue, administered it to rabbits who then developed tuberculosis, cultured the same bacillus from their diseased tissue, injected it into other rabbits and thereby produced tuberculosis again. The demonstration was convincing to all. Yet, given the weaknesses of immunology in his day, Koch's hypothesis led to false expectations that the best phenomenological description would not have produced. For example, Koch expected that tuberculosis symptoms would be common among infected humans, whereas in fact, infection is usually contained at a non-symptomatic level. Koch thought that if the bacillus caused tuberculosis, a vaccine containing weakened bacilli would prevent it, as Pasteur's vaccines prevented anthrax, rabies and several other diseases. Tragically, Koch's preparation gave people tuberculosis. If belief should be governed by Bayesian revision using subjective probabilities, the bacterial theory of tuberculosis should have been disbelieved. Yet Koch's argument from the best explanation quickly commanded assent, and deserved to, in spite of its many observational anomalies. Bayesian confirmation theory is not just biased against ontologically suspect proposals. It excludes hypotheses that are routine for everyone except an anti-realist philosopher of science.

## NEGLECTING HISTORY

A final, basic defect in deductivism was its neglect of the history leading up to a test. A description of a deductive pattern would only be sensitive to what the evidence turned out to be, not to when it was gathered. It might seem that (standard subjectivist) Bayesian confirmation theory avoids this problem, since this new positivism is intrinsically dynamic, i.e., is concerned with revision over time. As we have seen, the basic problem is the same. Though temporal, the Bayesian pattern is too rigid to register with accuracy the implications of the history leading up to a test.

Consider the prime example of the deductivist neglect of history, Hempel's indifference to the relative timing of Balmer's development of his formula and the observations of the various spectral lines of hydrogen. The Bayesian approach is not at all indifferent to such matters of timing. But the difference they make for Bayesians is implausibly great. The fit between the Balmer formula and lines observed by the time Balmer developed his formula is given no confirming power at all. For the likelihood of already known lines occurring is 1, regardless of whether the formula is correct. Only the subsequent lines confirm, which is, in its way, as farfetched as deductivist indifference to timing. For an even more farfetched conclusion, consider the assessment of the Bohr-Rutherford model of the atom. Bohr and Rutherford supported the model by deriving a few important and previously puzzling regularities, including the Balmer series, from their hypothesis. A Bayesian would have to say that if the derived phenomena had already been observed (the actual situation), there was no confirmation. On the other hand, if the same phenomena were observed after derivation, the rational degree of belief in the model would be raised enormously, indeed, would be close to one, since the odds, apart from the theory, that spectral lines and black-body radiation should follow the relevant laws would be virtually infinitesimal. This is surely a wild exaggeration of the difference that timing makes. And earlier in this chapter, variations of this standard Bayesian approach turned out to be just as exaggerated, in other directions.

The inaccessibility of theories is really just a special case of Bayesian insensitivity to the historical context; it is a case in which the uneven development of auxiliary fields is neglected. In general, Bayesian assessment is distorting if the availability of data and auxiliary principles that raise degrees of belief by Bayes' Theorem is actually due to factors independent of the validity of the hypothesis in question. As we have seen, a systematic bias toward the superficial results. There can also be more specific distortions, when the social context of science has encouraged certain directions in research for reasons unconnected with the rational pursuit of truth. (Once the emphases in research were adopted, everything else may have been rational, scientific and impartial.)

## WHERE'S THE HARM?

The bias toward the superficial and the response to extraneous influences on research are both examples of real harm done in contemporary social science by a roughly Bayesian paradigm of statistical inference as the epitome of empirical argument. For instance, the dominant attitude toward the sources of the black-white differential in United States unemployment rates (routinely the rates are in a two to one ratio) is "phenomenological," in the present sense. The employment differences are traced to correlates in education, locale, occupational structure, and family background. The attitude toward further, underlying causes of those correlations is agnostic, in the sense previously described. Yet on reflection, common sense dictates that racist attitudes and institutional racism *must* play an important causal role. People do have beliefs that blacks are inferior in intelligence and morality, and they are surely influenced by these beliefs in hiring decisions. Much hiring is strongly influenced by recommendations by family, friends or acquaintances, and this must produce disadvantages for blacks in a society where there is de facto social and residential segregation and whites do most of the hiring. This is true even if those white people are quite non-racist. On the face of it, this common-sense reasoning is not just the a priori hunch of one group of investigators. It reflects routine encounters with facts about decision-making together with commonsense psychological principles based on everyday facts. But these facts and principles are, as it were, already in the archives, not material bearing on future discoveries for reasoning from differential likelihoods. In addition, when we attempt to specify the nature and causes of racism, answering such natural questions as why anti-black racism has persisted in the United States for so long, the causal theories must rely on highly controversial auxiliary principles that often give rise to expectations conflicting with the data. Thus, an overemphasis on Bayesian success in statistical inference discourages the elaboration of a type of account of racial disadvantages that almost certainly provides a large part of their explanation.

As a further example of a bias stemming from neglect of the context of research, consider how the actual state of economic data-gathering affects two rival accounts of the 1983 economic recovery in the United States. According to one, the recovery was basically due to the stimulus of deficit spending together with whatever shifts in household and capital budgeting have normally produced upturns in the business cycle. According to a rival hypothesis, there is an additional basic factor, increased labor discipline based on long-term high unemployment that reflects explicit priorities of the Carter and the Reagan administrations: as the threat "if you don't like it here, try to find a job somewhere else," became more and more bloodcurdling, firms were able to count on more intense work, on an increasing lag between profit gains and wage gains (if any), and, in general, on lower labor costs. Their inclination to invest increased, as a result. The second hypothesis is quite popular among those concerned with the concrete facts of capitalist production, quantified or not, for example, workers, business people, Marxists and writers for the business pages of the *New York Times*.[30] Among academic economic theorists (as opposed to policy-oriented advisors) the second hypothesis is much less popular, and in terms of testing against well-established data, one can see why. Enormous and ingenious work is constantly done producing comprehensive and up-to-date statistics on the Gross National Product, consumer spending, the money supply, capital outlays and consumer confidence. There is no corresponding abundance of data on the intensity of work, workers' attitudes toward their jobs, employers' expectations about their workers, or even labor costs. Sporadic, fragmentary or rough assessments are what is available. This difference has a great deal to do with the usefulness of some statistics but not others for decision-making by governments and firms. The difference is quite unconnected with the truth or falsehood of the hypothesis emphasizing the sociology of production. Yet the trend in data-gathering severely limits the possibility of raising the probability of that hypothesis in a Bayesian way. In general, the shape of the actually available data limits the Bayesian capacities of an economics based on the structure of production, in ways for which common

[30] See, for example, the front-page article of the October 7, 1979 "Business and Finance" section, "The Economy: A Quick Fix Won't Work," praising the Carter administration for its realization that "If there's to be a savior, it will not be innovative gimmicks but a good old-fashioned recession, intended to bring aid to the problems of inflation . . . [in essence, by bringing wages down]." The June 4, 1985, "News Analysis" concerning the United Airlines strike (p. A13) notes, "Seeking to moderate wages and benefits and to alter often costly work rules, many companies are taking actions that would have been unthinkable a few years ago, illustrated by their willingness to continue operations during work shutdowns, by recruiting new workers and by welcoming old workers who cross picket lines. . . . 'Employers discovered a few years ago how relatively easy it is to get another work force, and that continues to be true,' said Audrey Freedman, labor economist at the Conference Board." In addition to the employers' recent discovery, President Reagan's firing of striking air traffic controllers is singled out as "impetus for new militancy among employers."

sense would discount in a final assessment, but Bayes' Theorem does not.

I am not remotely proposing that Bayesian philosophy of science, sophisticated or in some crude version, is the main causal factor distorting social research. Rather, these examples of implicit bias are meant as arguments against the policy of adopting the Bayesian model as a working hypothesis, despite its problems as described in previous sections. People have often adopted the covering-law model in just this spirit, when they are not prepared to defend it as actually valid. One needs some orientation in reflecting on methodological issues, and a defective model can be useful here, if it is not apt to distort judgment in practice. But the Bayesian model does distort judgment.

1. It supports excessive attachment to superficial or easily tested hypotheses (a relatively uncontroversial case being "phenomenological" physics as against the atomic theory).

2. It discourages the ad hoc revisions that are especially important in the defense of a novel or wide-ranging hypothesis (for example, Newton's or Darwin's).

3. It encourages the neglect of reflections on facts already known, based on common-sense principles (as in the assessment of the pattern of success and failure for Darwinism and creationism).

At most, talk of subjective probabilities should be treated as a kind of slang for applying the likelihood principle and other rules governing inference from the best explanation. More precisely, Bayesian reasoning is methodological slang except in the special and limited cases where reason and evidence compel us to keep likelihoods rigid, revising beliefs to the minimal extent required by uncontroversial facts we are encountering.

## WHERE'S THE CLARITY?

Taking Bayesian talk as slang, compared with pre-Bayesian discussions of what explanation is best may seem bizarre to the point of perversity. The new positivism, like the old, gets much of its appeal from the appearance that it has rendered vague notions clearer. Obviously, the history of rational science is a story of changing degrees of belief in alternative hypotheses. Whatever else it does, the Bayesian account of this process seems to increase clarity by analyzing degrees of belief as subjective probabilities, explicated in the style of Ramsey and his successors.

In fact, this appearance of heightened clarity is largely an illusion.

I will conclude this examination of the new positivism with a sketch of the deepest and most recalcitrant obstacles to the subjectivist explications of degrees of belief: the interaction of probability and desirability; irrelevant features of the betting model; and the elusiveness of measures for ignorance.

## PROBABILITY AND DESIRABILITY

The foundations of subjective probability would be relatively simple if people put equal but opposite value on equal gains and losses of money (or something else that comes in identical units), and if people's desire for a given gain or aversion to a given loss was not affected by their individual circumstances. It would, then, be plausible to take the rough-and-ready gambling measure of probability as strictly accurate. The probability of A would be the greatest amount \$.X that the subject would put up in a bet yielding \$1 just in case A occurs. But the obvious falsehood of those assumptions of linearity makes the simple gambling measure frequently and obviously false. In the example mentioned in the previous chapter, you and I might very well have the same degree of belief in a coin's coming up heads the next time, but still put up different stakes for the dollar bet, because I find losses more undesirable, relative to gains. In some circumstances, every sane person violates the simple gambling measure. What sane starving person, with just enough money for a square meal, would stake it on the next toss of a coin at even odds, just because he or she believes the coin to be fair?

To avoid these difficulties, we need to assign degrees of desirability to stakes and outcomes in the crucial bets, in a scale with the formal properties of the Fahrenheit scale of temperatures. Then, having assigned degrees of desirability according to the particular subject's preferences, we can speak of bets in which the gains and losses are (say) equally desirable for the subject, without relying on dubious assumptions about what people in general prefer. One of Ramsey's major achievements was to describe a plausible technique for constructing and applying such a desirability thermometer, for any rational person whose degrees of belief are to be assessed.[31]

First, Ramsey describes a way of finding a proposition, N, which has a subjective probability of 1/2 for the subject. N is such a proposition if it has two properties:

[31] See "Truth and Probability," pp. 36–39 for Ramsey's original, very concise proposal, and Jeffrey, *The Logic of Decision* (New York, 1983), chs. 1–3, for a detailed and thorough exposition.

(a) it is "ethically neutral" in the sense that the subject is always indifferent between any given situation in which N is the case and an otherwise identical situation in which N is not the case;

(b) given two other propositions, A and B, one of which (i.e., the truth of one of which) is preferred to the other, the subject has no preference between the gambles (1) A if N is true, B if N is false and (2) B is N is true, A if N is false.

Thus, assuming one cares about money, but doesn't care about a coin's coming up heads as such (i.e., this is ethically neutral), one regards the coin as fair if one is indifferent between the gambles "$100 if heads, nothing otherwise," "Nothing if heads, $100 otherwise."[32]

Using N, Ramsey, in effect, proposes the following technique for constructing someone's desirability thermometer. Take any convenient proposition (event, state-of-affairs) as the zero point. For some purposes $0, i.e., no monetary gains or losses, might be convenient, for others, a tautology, e.g., "either getting or not getting that plate of pasta." Then, stipulate that the unit in the scale is the difference between the desirability of the zero-point and the desirable of something else. It *might* be convenient to make the desirability of a $1 gain the something else, but anything will do. We can now use N to locate propositions with all degrees of desirability in the scale, if we assume, as Ramsey always does, that our subject is rational and, *as such*, must combine preference and belief in the following way. If he or she is choosing between having X for certain and getting either Y or Z, but not both, then he or she is indifferent as between the choices if and only if:

$$X = Y \cdot P + Z (1 - P),$$

where X, Y, and Z refer to the desirabilities of the respective outcomes, and P is the probability of Y, for the subject. More generally, Ramsey assumes that rational people always evaluate situations with different possible outcomes according to the sum of the desirabilities of the outcomes weighted by the respective probabilities. Using this principle and the known probability of N, we can divide up the scale between "zero degree" and "one degree" into halves, fourths, etc., as finely as needed. This process begins by assigning one-half degree to something, H, such that the subject is indifferent between

---

[32] For simplicity's sake, I will be playing fast and loose with the differences between propositions, their truth, corresponding gains and losses, and desirabilities—wherever the context makes it clear what is intended. Strictly speaking, the gain is "the truth of A," so the illustration, strictly, should be a gamble "making it true that you get $100 if heads, and otherwise making it true that you get nothing."

(1) H's certainty and (2) getting the one-degree outcome if N, the zero-degree outcome, otherwise. In other words, H is the most the subject would bet to get the one-degree item if N. Thus, if the desirability of money is linear for him, and N is a certain coin's coming up heads, 50 cents will be assigned a desirability of 1/2, if 0 = $0, 1 = $1. One can find events with desirabilities 2, 4, 6, etc., by a process that begins with the location of something T, such that the subject is indifferent between (1) the one-degree item and (2) a situation in which he gets T if N, the zero-degree item if not-N. One can then divide up the intervals between these points, using N and further intermediate items. In this way, any degree of desirability is associated with some item. The resulting desirability thermometer is then applied to any further item, D, by finding the item S, on the scale such that the subject is indifferent between D and S.

Ramsey uses the desirability thermometer to measure probabilities by a sophisticated version of the gambling strategy. If we are assigning a probability to A, which happens to be ethically neutral, then, the procedure is the same as the crude gambling strategy, but with units of desirability instead of money. Assuming, as Ramsey always does, that the desirability of a gamble is the desirability of the outcomes weighted by their probabilities and summed, then

$$M = 1 \cdot P(A) + 0 \cdot (1 - P(A))$$

when the subject is indifferent between getting M (i.e., anything "worth" M) for certain and getting the one-degree item if A, otherwise the zero-degree item. So P(A) equals M, what the subject would bet to get 1 unit of A. But many things are not ethically neutral. In the general case, the outcome of the bet on A will be getting the unit and getting A, if A occurs, getting zero and the absence of A, otherwise. Ramsey assumes that the probability of A will always adjust the value of the possible outcome, getting 1 degree of desirability plus A. If the subject is neutral between the gamble on A and the certainty of something with desirability M, then, by Ramsey's principle of rational choice:

$$M = (1 + A) \cdot P(A) + (0 + \text{not-A}) (1 - P(A)).$$

This reduces to

$$P(A) = \frac{M - \text{not-A}}{1 + A - \text{not-A}}.$$

Of course, this account of Ramsey's procedure leaves out many details. Moreover, there are now other ways of defining subjective probability, similar to Ramsey's but significantly different. The most important alternative, due to Jeffrey, develops the idea that a subject's rating of propositions as better or worse "news" reflects, in systematic ways, both his preferences among individual outcomes and his assessment of their probabilities. *All analyses of subjective probability, however, depend upon Ramsey's assumption that the desirability of a situation with exhaustive, exclusive alternative outcomes is the sum of the desirabilities of the outcomes weighted by their probabilities.* This is the basic tool for constructing the desirability scale and extracting probabilities from it. But the assumption is extremely doubtful. And even if the assumption is right, our actual departures from Ramseyan rationality make it impossible to apply Ramsey's (or Jeffrey's) thermometer to real people's preferences.

*Risk Aversion*

Risk aversion is one obstacle to measuring degrees of belief in the subjectivist way. If aversion to risks were solely a matter of finding certain losses more undesirable than gains of the same magnitude are desirable, Ramsey's strategy would overcome this obstacle. But risk aversion has an additional component, for many people who seem to be rational. For example, many people say they would support no action that increases the risk of nuclear war. Presumably, then, they would not pay someone five dollars to do something that will yield them $20, with probability P, and yield nuclear war, otherwise—no matter how high P is. Someone's refusal to regard such a bet as desirable need not reflect the belief that the undesirability of a nuclear war is infinite. He or she might regard some nuclear wars as less undesirable than others, while wars by certain imaginable but, fortunately, undiscovered means are even worse than nuclear war. The nuclear cost is finite, but not a justifiable risk, certainly not for $20. There seems to be no general problem in assigning a degree of probability to the nuclear outcome. One might simply tell a story about a mad Air Force general with Bingo equipment. Yet given the Ramseyan concept of rationality, the refusal to bet of the people I have described would have to be irrational. Given any desirability of the worse outcome, there has to be some probability that discounts it enough and raises the chance of the twenty dollar outcome enough for the bet to be worth $5. To say that Ramsey's rule may be rejected is simply to say that a rational person may have an aversion to risk that is not fully explained by the size of the bad outcome that would be risked. That seems quite possible, and yet it violates the rule by which Ramsey extracts probability from preference. Bizarre dutch books can be constructed on the basis of the violation. The subjects can avoid them—as we all would often do—by simply refusing to take bets on certain outcomes.

For a less grisly example of the same element in risk aversion, consider the attitude expressed in the following statement: "I would pay the same amount for a gamble that would give me $1 million if a fair coin came up heads (otherwise nothing) as I would for a gamble which would give me $8 million (otherwise nothing) if a fair coin came up heads twice in a row. But I would prefer simply being given $1 million to a bet in which I receive $9 million if a fair coin comes up heads, otherwise nothing." This statement does not seem a confession of irrationality. The first sentence presumably reflects a certain tendency to value the change from non-rich to rich more than the change from rich to super-rich. The second part expresses an additional disposition to prefer sure things. But the statement as a whole is quite incompatible with the subjectivists' way of combining probabilities and preferences. Extracting desirabilities from the first part of the statement in Ramsey's way, $8 million is twice as desirable as $1 for the subject. But then, she ought to prefer a fifty-fifty chance of $9 million to a sure $1 million. Again, there is a residual aversion to risk-taking that is not just a non-linear rating of desirabilities.

If these examples simply showed that subjective probabilities cannot be assigned when people are in certain strange situations, they would be relatively unimportant. In fact, they confirm, through extreme and clear illustrations, what is plausible in general: aversion to taking risks exists, over and above a tendency for gains to be less valued than losses are disvalued. If rational people can have this independent risk aversion, they can have it in varying degrees. As a result, no present analysis will assign them subjective probabilities reflecting degrees of belief. You and I may place the same bets on the coin's coming up heads, assign the same desirabilities to stakes and outcomes, but have different degrees of belief. The reason is that we have different aversions to gambling, cancelling out the different degrees of belief.

Actually, the situation is worse than this. Even if rationality required adherence to Ramsey's principle of choice, real people often do depart from his rule. Independent risk aversion is often an ingredient of choice. So, even if this factor would play no role in assessing the probability distribution of an ideally rational person, it would be important in assessing the distribution for most, perhaps all humans. One must determine to what extent the subject is risk-averse and discount for this, in assigning desirabilities and subjective probabilities in Ramsey's or Jeffrey's way. But there is no means to do this.

Of course, one can simply propose that the disvalue of anxiety be counted as part of Ramseyan calculations, making everyone rational again. But until an anxietometer is developed, there will be no clear sense to talk of "the disvalue of this amount of anxiety." In any case, the proposal seems wrong. A calm person might not like risk, even if she experiences little anxiety.

In sum, it is doubtful that the degrees of belief of rational people fit the subjectivist analysis, and, hence, the probability calculus. Moreover, any assignment of degrees of belief to actual people must rest on judgments that are unjustified and unclear.

*Bad Bets and Good News*

Much of the attractiveness of subjectivist probability theory is due to the power of Ramsey's questions about wagers to clarify people's degrees of beliefs. When one puts the problems of the previous section to one side, a good way to make someone's degrees of belief more precise is to ask, "How much would you bet in a wager that in which you get a dollar if things turned out that way?" In practice, actual techniques of Bayesian decision-making often begin with the interrogation of experts to evoke probability distributions, using just such questions about wagers.[33] No one could doubt the usefulness of such questions. The clarifying power of Ramsey's kind of question is an important argument for the validity of the probability calculus, taken as rules governing a rational person's degrees of belief: informal statements of degrees of belief are clarified by associating them with corresponding preferences among bets; if the elementary irrationality of accepting dutch book is to be avoided, those preferences must obey the probability calculus.

Unfortunately, the useful, Ramseyan device of investigating betting propensities is too concrete for purposes of conceptual clarification. The only alternative available avoids the misplaced concreteness of Ramsey's method, but at the cost of losing its clarifying power and the resulting argument for subjectivist probability theory.

If someone proposes a wager in which he pays you ten thousand

[33] Indeed, Robert Winkler's superb textbook, *Introduction to Bayesian Inference and Decision* (New York, 1972), is, in a sense, a businessperson's manual for interrogating experts using Ramseyan questions, and making use of their answers through Bayesian reasoning in DeFinetti's style. See, for example, pp. 19-30, 95-104.

dollars if you are not shot in the head at noon tomorrow, this will lead you to revise your degrees of belief in matters bearing on your health. Yet your response to bets was supposed to determine the degrees of belief you would have had if you weren't engaged in betting. Again, the extreme example illustrates a pervasive phenomena. The fact that we are responding to a wager is a datum influencing our view of the world, yet wagers are Ramsey's instrument for investigating the structure of that view, apart from the bet. It might seem that we should simply accept that the bookmaker is honest—i.e., does not tamper with outcomes, has no inside information and can pay off—in the reasoning that fixes probabilities. But it isn't clear that the factual judgments that this assumption suspends are always irrelevant. If someone offers to pay me $5 at noon tomorrow if I am dead by tomorrow morning, I will surely be affected by knowledge of the difficulty of payment, in ways that should not affect probability assignment. If I assume for the sake of probability-calculation that there will be no payment problem, then this hypothesis implies further, vast modifications of my beliefs. In any case, accepting that any bet could be made good is bad policy, for probability theory in general. For certain standard paradoxes are best avoided by questioning the actual capacity of a bettor to make good on the best. Above all, the notorious "St. Petersburg paradox" involves a fantastic offer which, by standard probability calculations, merits an infinitely large wager; yet surely reasonableness never entails an impossible action, making an infinite bet. The best explanation of reasonableness in face of the St. Petersburg offer is that no one can be in a position to make the fantastic offer. The wager is a bit elaborate, but the crucial limitation is mundane; not enough non-inflated money could be around to back up a guarantee to make good whatever the outcome.[34]

If subjective probability isn't about betting, what is it about? On the basis of the above considerations and others, Richard Jeffrey proposed the main alternative to Ramsey's analysis. In this interpretation, subjective probabilities are most directly concerned with the subject's preferences for discovering that one or another proposition is the case. The crucial question is not, "What would you bet?" but "How good would this news be?"[35]

[34] In the St. Petersburg paradox, a game is proposed in which a coin is tossed until it comes up heads; on the nth toss, on which it first comes up heads, you will be paid $2^n$ dollars, no matter how high n should be. See Jeffrey, *The Logic of Decision* (New York, 1983), pp. 139–43.

[35] See ibid., chs. 4–10.

Though the details are quite complex, Jeffrey's basic idea is simple, yet ingenious. Someone's degree of belief that A is the ratio of what his disappointment would be on learning that A is not the case (i.e., his disappointment on passing from ignorance to this knowledge) over the extent to which he cares whether A or not-A.[36] I would be delighted to receive a million dollars in tomorrow's mail. I care a great deal about the gap between what my financial state would be if this happens and what it would be if this doesn't. But I will not be very disappointed if my mail is empty of a million. The tiny proportion of my caring taken up by my disappointment reflects the utter improbability the event has for me. More precisely (the rough formulation in terms of disappointment is mine, not Jeffrey's), Jeffrey relies on the same principles of rationality that Ramsey freely uses, and applies them to the desirability of news items. Non-news, the null point against which real news is measured, is any tautology, say, A or not-A. Jeffrey's probabilistic equation for the desirability of non-news is:

$$A \text{ or not-A} = A \cdot P(A) + \text{not-A} (1 - P(A)).$$

This can be rewritten as a formalization of the disappointment measure:

$$P(A) = \frac{(A \text{ or not-A}) - \text{not-A}}{A - \text{not-A}}.$$

Of course, Jeffrey, like Ramsey, needs to construct an appropriately determinate scale of desirabilities, on the basis of which probabilities can be assessed. The construction is too complex to summarize, here. What is important is the difference between Jeffrey's and Ramsey's data for assessing desirabilities and probabilities. Ramsey's data are the subject's preferences among wagers. Jeffrey's data are the subject's preferences among different bits of news. For example, just as Ramsey divided up his scale using a 1/2 probable proposition derived from bets between which the subject was indifferent, Jeffrey finds a way of extracting equiprobability from preferences among news items, for partitioning purposes. At a crucial point, he needs to assume that for every proposition A, there are two propositions, B and C, such that A is the disjunction of B and C, B and C are mutually exclusive, and B and C are equally probable. Of course, the last clause must be analyzed away, in the general

---

[36] If A is something bad, for example, a beating, substitute "joy" for "disappointment" on learning that A is not the case.

project of analyzing probability. It is replaced by the conditions: news items B and C are ranked together, in the subject's preferences, and so are not-B and not-C.

How does a subject determine his or her preferences among bits of news, e.g., among disappointments or rejoicings? That news would be a disappointment or an occasion for rejoicing is usually a datum, that does not have to be *determined* by the subject, except by imagining and responding to what is imagined. (Even if reflection is needed, it usually requires no explicit thought about probabilities, so the preference is a datum for present purposes.) But Jeffrey's technique requires preferences among disappointments and preferences among rejoicings. Also, whether one would exchange the truth of a certain bit of news for the truth of another often seems an appropriate psychological datum. I can tell you right away that if it were snowing, I would be indifferent to the Great Weathermaker's offer to substitute sleet (and vice versa). But Jeffrey's technique depends on the further aspect of preference that could lead me to be more disappointed by news of snow than news of sleet even if I would be indifferent to exchanges of one for another. Except in extreme cases, *these preferences require reflection on one's degrees of belief.*

If the weatherman says that it may snow or it may sleet, a good way to clarify her degrees of belief is by asking, "Which would you rather bet on?" A bad way is by asking, "Supposing you would exchange snow for sleet and vice versa and that news of snow would make you just as unhappy as news of sleet, would news of non-snow be more or less or just as much an occasion for rejoicing as news of non-sleet?" She could not possibly give an accurate response except by reflecting, " 'No snow' would be less desirable if I thought snow was the less probable outcome in any case. Now, do I?" One might as well ask directly which she thinks more probable, just the sort of question that was to be clarified. And the preferences that figure in Jeffrey's constructions are, in crucial cases, vastly more elaborate than these. Of course, the difference in clarifying power of the two techniques is just a matter of degree. Sometimes, one has no stable preferences among Ramseyan bets until one has explicitly reflected on probabilities. But the difference in degree is vast.

In the extensive range of cases in which Ramsey's questions do clarify degrees of beliefs, he can claim his probability theory is a demand of rationality, i.e., a product of the need to avoid dutch book.[37] Jeffrey *could* claim that his theory describes the degrees of

---

[37] Because of the problem of risk aversion, other, contrary demands of rationality may also be relevant. But Ramsey certainly describes one dimension of rationality.

belief of those whose preferences among propositions are regulated by the principle that net desirability is desirability of outcomes weighted by degree of belief in the outcome. But he could not claim to make it clearer what a degree of belief is, or to show that the belief structures governed by the principle of weighting desirabilities by degrees of belief are of special interest. In fact, Jeffrey's primary intention was to provide a coherent subjectivist model for the probability calculus, not to explicate "degree of belief" or to argue against people who regard subjectivist theory as vacuous.

Ramsey's and Jeffrey's techniques represent two horns of a dilemma for anyone who takes probability to be the clear version of our usual rough principles for reasoning about the uncertain. Ramsey can promise clarification of the informal notion, but at the cost of introducing irrelevancies. Jeffrey can avoid irrelevancies, but at the cost of losing the clarifying power that made subjectivist theory attractive in the first place.

### The Burdens of Ignorance

Ignorance is a large part of science, in some ways, the largest part. Admittedly, in a well-established science there is often a consensus, at a given point in time, about the basic lore of the science, a consensus that often includes a global theory of the basic mechanisms governing the phenomena studied, together with auxiliary hypotheses that are routine and uncontroversial means of interpreting data. Moreover, in most well-established sciences, respectable disputes at the level of important theory usually involve just two or three substantially different alternatives. Yet, despite this appearance of certainty, thoughtful investigators with even a smattering of the history of their field are epistemologically modest. They accept that the global theory dominating current lore (or, all the current respectable rival hypotheses) may turn out to be inferior to an indefinitely large number of fundamentally different theories and corresponding auxiliary hypotheses, of whose nature they are quite unaware.

If science is to be represented by degrees of belief, measured in a probabilistic way and subjected to Bayesian revision, the depths of uncertainty concerning hypotheses not yet under consideration must affect the degrees of belief in current hypotheses in a variety of ways.

(1) Given an investigator's degree of belief, B, in the global theory dominating the lore, his or her degree of belief that one of the possible rivals to it is the actually true one is immediately assigned by the first axiom of the probability calculus. The probability assigned to the rest of the possibilities must be $1 - B$. Conversely, degree of be-

lief in the possible rivals entails degree of belief in the standard theory. And the same calculation works, just as immediately, when the question is whether some hypothesis outside the present array of respectable alternatives is true, or whether the dominant global theory (or the disjunction of respectable rival hypotheses) is *approximately* true. (For simplicity's sake, I will usually frame discussions in this section in terms of the truth of a single theory. But the extensions to the more complex questions about disjunctions or approximate truth will be immediate, within a Bayesian framework.)

(2) When belief in a theory is revised in a Bayesian way, it is not enough to put into the denominator the respectable, specific current rivals, i.e., the likelihood of the evidence on those rivals adjusted for the probability of the rivals. That would be as unreasonable as revising belief in one's neighbor's temperament on the basis of his scowl this morning, without taking it into account that he may be scowling for some reason of which one is quite unaware. In adjusting degrees of belief, the investigator must assign a certain degree of belief to the possible truth of quite unforeseen theories *and* a certain likelihood to the evidence given those theories.

(3) When scientists say they want their theories to fit the data, what they mean is somewhat ambiguous. They may have it in mind that the theory should fit the empirical laws relating certain properties of phenomena which the theory seeks to explain. In this way, the molecular-kinetic theory of gases fits the laws relating temperature, pressure and volume in gases. On the other hand, they may have it in mind that the theory should fit the raw data, the evidence by which they assign the properties to phenomena that the theory seeks to explain. The data, here, include the thermometer readings and pressure gauge readings that establish relations between temperature and pressure. But scientists never possess laws from which the magnitudes of raw data can be derived, and they never will. The readings from dials, meters and digital displays are always influenced by uncontrollable and unpredictable factors. That is why the precise replication of an experiment is a sign, not of success, but of cheating. The fit between theory and raw data is indirect: the raw data are interpreted to yield the laws that the theory is supposed to explain. But this interpretation will depend on beliefs about possible factors whose specific nature or effect is unknown. Something is wrong with current beliefs concerning the specific causes of data—otherwise any deviation from theoretical expectations would indicate the falsehood of a theory. The investigator has to decide to what extent unknown distorting factors have shifted the raw data

away from the true values of the magnitudes under investigation. For a Bayesian, this decision must be a bet on whether the auxiliary hypotheses currently relied on are wrong when they interpret data in ways that conflict with laws that are currently given credence. Often, one has no idea which current auxiliary is false, must less what the truth is apt to be.

Subjectivist probability theory was developed, above all, as a tool for decision-making under uncertainty. So it might seem ideally suited to describe people's belief states in regions of maximum uncertainty. In fact, subjective probabilities that are supposed to reflect such belief states are arbitrary, epistemologically irrelevant or incomplete.

The neat relation alleged between belief in a canonical theory (the global theory dominating current research) and belief in all possible rivals is suspicious, on the face of it. It is not that this degree of belief cannot be fixed by subjectivist means. No doubt, a physicist with a sense of humor could give a sincere answer to the question of how much he would bet on the truth of general relativity, as against the truth of some possible rival, perhaps quite unknown at present. But these quantities vary from physicist to physicist and from week to week in ways that usually reflect nothing more than change in mood. Though subjective probabilities are supposed to be the most precise measure of a physicist's view of the world, they seem largely to obscure it. In asking for the degree of a scientist's belief in a theory, we are interested in such matters as willingness or reluctance to use it in explanations, willingness or reluctance to use values derived from it in further derivations. These epistemologically important inclinations are affected, for example, by the presence of a specific rival which explains phenomena that have resisted explanation by the canonical theory. But they are usually unaffected by the shifts between high and low spirits that produce different subjective probabilities.

For many Bayesians, this result would be both expected and welcome. In their view, the probabilities that a scientist assigns to rival hypotheses are not, in themselves, rational. Rather, the rationality of a scientist is to be praised or condemned on the basis of his disposition to revise beliefs in the face of evidence in appropriate ways.

However, rational raising of confidence in a theory must depend on two kinds of likelihoods, the likelihood of evidence given the truth of the theory and its likelihood on the condition that some rival, perhaps an unknown rival supported through an unknown auxiliary science, is true. And bets on how likely evidence is given the falsehood of all current theories of the evidence in question measure the most ephemeral attitudes imaginable. No one who isn't already committed to a Bayesian philosophy of science would care whether a present-day scientist thinks it likely that Pluto would have its perturbations given that nothing remotely like general relativity is correct. Worse yet, since these bets would reflect transient moods, varying from scientist to scientist and week to week, there would be no tendency for Bayesian revision to produce an ultimate consensus as to whether a known, specific theory is probably right.

By contrast, if confirmation is causal comparison, a hypothesis is confirmed if it triumphs in a causal argument that is fair to all current frameworks. If the resulting belief cannot be shown to triumph in an argument that would be fair to possible, but as yet non-existent frameworks that failure does not make the belief dogmatic. The line between dogmatism and non-dogmatism has a social aspect.

For certain hypotheses, something more can be said, or so I shall argue in the next three chapters. Given current evidence, the denial of certain hypotheses would be irrational in any possible framework, because a deviant framework would have to reject some truism, the acceptance of which is a mark of rationality. These truisms, however, will be topic-specific, tied to particular subjects such as perception, motion, feeling or behavior. They are not the absolutely general, topic-neutral rules that are the ultimate bases of rationality in positivism, both new and old. In the Bayesian approach, the historical aspect of confirmation is represented by the degrees of belief that individuals actually have, interpreted in Ramsey's or Jeffrey's way, and the non-dogmatic element in belief is represented by the rules of the probability calculus. Because it is both individualist and topic-neutral, the Bayesian approach cannot draw the line between the dogmatic and the non-dogmatic in a plausible way.

It might seem that these doubts involve too literal a reading of the Bayesian model. Often, Bayesians seem really concerned to see whether an actual ranking of hypotheses would be the inevitable outcome of a hypothetical history, in some ways like the reconstructions I have emphasized in my alternative theory of explanation. We imagine the scientific community in a situation in which they only have pretheoretical ideas about reality. Otherwise, their probability distributions express total uncertainty. The crucial question then becomes, "How would rankings of hypotheses develop if the nature and sequence of evidence and theorizing is as it actually was, and beliefs are revised in the Bayesian way?" We would not expect the resulting credence *intervals* between hypotheses to be the same for all, since different people are willing to abandon beliefs in light of evidence at different rates. But the credence rankings might end up the same for all. Then and only then, the preferences have been confirmed. The question of whether a present theory is confirmed will be the question of whether its truth would be ranked ahead of its falsehood in this hypothetical process. What is non-dogmatic is what can be vindicated by Bayesian reasoning from actual evidence, starting in a hypothetical state of blank uncertainty (apart from the evidence).

Something like this model is implicit in many presentations of Bayesian philosophy of science. But apart from the question of whether it fits the facts of rational comparison (previous case studies suggested it doesn't), the model is quite unclear. In the subjective interpretation of probability there is no convincing way of representing the state of total uncertainty with which the hypothetical history begins.

The initially tempting proposal is to represent blank uncertainty using a principle of indifference. Taking the best sort of case for probabilistic reasoning, the assessment of the initially unknown size of a magnitude, the probability distribution is to be such that equal intervals are equally probable. One problem, here, is the production of contradictory assignments of probabilities when different, equally appropriate expressions for the unknown factor are chosen. This is the problem that defeated the classical interpretation. Even if the embarrassing abundance of alternative probabilities is ignored, a further problem remains. The shape of the distribution just does not represent the state of blank uncertainty in a rational person. Suppose you know that an urn contains red and blue balls, but know nothing more. Given equiprobability for all combinations, it is fifty-fifty that the proportion of red balls will be at least one-half. Three drawings are conducted (with subsequent replacement and mixing), and only one red ball is drawn. If you really had been in total ignorance, you should surely regard a 1/3 proportion as most likely, now. But you cannot, if the initial probability distribution is revised by Bayesian reasoning. For the attitude that there is a .5 probability of at least a 1/2 proportion will still exercise some weight. On the most natural representations of equiprobability for a Bernoulli process, you ought to be most inclined to a ratio of 4/10 after the three draws.[38] The problem here cannot be the use of Bayes'

[38] See Winkler, *Bayesian Inference*, p. 201.

Theorem in revising probabilities. For this is one of the special sit-uations in which Bayesian revision can be made rationally compel-ling for everyone. Rather, something must be wrong with the rep-resentation of the initial blank uncertainty.

The working Bayesian statistician responds by associating blank uncertainty with a U-shaped curve. Proportions of red balls around 1/2 have the lowest probabilities, while other proportions, higher or lower, are assigned probabilities increasing without bound as they approach 0 and 1, respectively. The curves do have the desired property of yielding completely to subsequent evidence. But they do not remotely describe the initial attitudes of the subject toward the respective possible proportions. Worse yet, the probabilities as-signed by the curves add up to more than one.[39] No one has yet de-scribed the probability distribution that does three things: expresses the current attitudes of the totally uncertain subject, expresses the impact of subsequent evidence on such a subject, and assigns values compatible with the probability calculus.

At this point, one further retreat into subjectivity is available. In science, blank uncertainty is not an actual attitude, but a hypotheti-cal construct. So far, that construct has only been important in de-veloping an analysis of rational preference among theories. So if preferences among theories are non-rational, the problems of ex-pressing blank uncertainty are immaterial.

Though some might accept that preferences among theories are matters of taste, fewer would say the same about preferences among superficial laws describing empirical regularities. Taking this fur-ther step implies, not some distinctive theory of testing, but the view that testing does not occur in science. However, the distinction be-tween the phenomena described in empirical laws and the raw data by which those phenomena are observed would force this further step, if preferences among theories are declared non-rational. For the assessment of a proposed empirical regularity requires theoret-ical beliefs about mechanisms underlying the regularities. Our tol-erance of deviations from expectations about raw data reflects our awareness that auxiliary beliefs are somehow defective. This aware-ness is not the product of independent stable inclinations toward ri-val auxiliary beliefs. Often, the empirical anomalies would result from any specific alternative that we would take seriously. Rather, what sustains our vague skepticism about the auxiliaries is a com-mitment to beliefs about underlying mechanisms that would make

---

[39] See ibid., p. 202.

the laws true. With these theoretical beliefs we have a reason to resist tampering with the laws (as Ohm had a reason to resist tampering with Ohm's Law because it fit beliefs as to the nature of electricity). Without any theoretical beliefs, no confidence in any current law is rational, since all conflict with some raw data.

It might seem, to the contrary, that we can extract regularities from raw data using "curve fitting," without assumptions about underlying factors. To take the best case for this view, suppose the mathematical relation between two continuous magnitudes is under investigation. The raw data can be presented in a scattergram, and a best-fitting linear equation found, i.e., a line among the dots such that the average squared value of apparent deviations in the dependent variable is at a minimum. Isn't this the only reasonable choice of a function relating the quantities under investigation?

The choice is only reasonable if further underlying assumptions are. If the direction of causality is reversed, deviations ought to be assessed along the other axis, and a different best fitting curve may result. Moreover, the best-fitting linear equation will not fit as well as the best-fitting quadratic, and so on for higher and higher degrees. Admittedly, equations of higher degree are harder to apply, since more information is required to employ them in answering standard questions, in particular, questions about rates of changes. But a ban on non-linear relations is inappropriate, since some relations surely are quadratic, e.g., the relation between time spent and space covered in free fall. There is no general principle regulating the trade-off between the simplicity of lower degree equations and the accuracy of higher degree ones. Rather, the choice of a type of equation as describing the real phenomena presupposes a corresponding commitment concerning the causal structure underlying the production of raw data. One has no basis for choosing the best-fitting linear equation if one has no basis for supposing that (1) a given change in one magnitude always produces a proportionate change in the other, and (2) further factors, not influencing the two magnitudes in question, do influence the raw data that are the best means of measuring these magnitudes. Often, choices among alternative curves are heavily influenced by ambitious theoretical programs, for example, Galileo's physics as it influenced his view of laws of free fall, Kepler's Platonism, and Newton's physics, which sustained the absolutely crucial but utterly non-linear principle that periods of rotation around a celestial body are as the $3/2$ power of distances from its center.

The impact of preferences among theories on preferences among regularities is even clearer when we take into account the possibility of distorting factors that remove raw data from true values in a sys-tematic, not a random, way. Even if there were a general a priori rule dictating, say, a linear curve for certain scatter-gram distribu-tions, the best-fitting curve is a misleading guide to the real relation, when such a systematically distorting factor is at work. And the question of whether such a factor is at work is an issue concerning theories of what produces surface phenomena. For example, dur-ing much of the nineteenth century it was reasonable to take appar-ent departures from the Boyle-Charles gas law in extreme condi-tions as systematic distortions in the raw data, so that pressure-volume temperature phenomena really are as the Boyle-Charles law describes them. Thermodynamic isolation is hard to achieve, even approximately, and attempts to achieve it might well have been tainted by excessive hopes that standard controls would work in ex-treme conditions. The relevant experimental set-ups were similar enough to make systematic distortion likely. What changed this as-sessment was the triumph of the molecular-kinetic theory, which supported an alternative empirical law, not the development of bet-ter experimental controls.[40] Similarly, theoretical considerations led Newton, quite reasonably, to adopt descriptions of the "apparent diameters" of Jupiter and Saturn to which no actual visual experi-ence corresponded. Like everyone else, Newton meant something quite particular and quite susceptible to modification on the basis of theories when he spoke of "apparent diameters" of planets, namely, the angles of the cones of light passing from the planets to the sur-face of the earth, as those cones would be if undistorted by interven-ing media. No regularities here are detectable without telescopic ob-servation, and no telescopes of the time were undistorting. Newton arrived at appearances that fit his theory only through complex and speculative theoretical arguments about distortions in telescopes. His interest is not in the apparent apparent diameter, but in the true apparent diameter! This is a good epitome of the sort of empirical phenomenon scientists seek to describe.[41]

No matter how atheoretical their inclination, scientists are inter-ested in relations between properties of phenomena, not in lists of readings from dials of instruments that detect those properties. How one passes from the latter to the former depends on one's de-grees of belief in theories governing those properties. Partly be-

[40] See Aaron Ihde, *The Development of Modern Chemistry* (New York, 1964), p. 403.
[41] See *Principia*, pp. 402f., 523 and "The System of the World," pp. 563–66.

cause of problems in assigning degrees of belief to unknown and unspecified alternatives, the subjectivist interpretation produces no clear and convincing measure of scientists' degrees of belief in their theories. As a result, it can provide no clear and convincing measure of degrees of belief in empirical regularities.

Here as elsewhere, Bayesian philosophy of science obscures a difference between scientists' problems of hypothesis choice and the problems of prediction that are the standard illustrations and applications of probability theory. In the latter situations, such as the standard guessing games about coins and urns, investigators know an enormous amount about the reality they are examining, including the effects of different values of the unknown factor. Scientists can rarely take that much knowledge for granted. It should not be surprising if an apparatus developed to measure degrees of belief in situations of isolated and precisely regimented uncertainty turns out to be inaccurate, irrelevant or incoherent in the face of the latter, much more radical uncertainty.

## Conclusion

We ought to extend to theories of science the same tolerance we extend to scientific theories: anomalies are acceptable, as a rule, so long as there is progress in explaining anomalies away; such progress is a sign that the remaining anomalies reflect difficulties in investigating reality, not the basic falsehood of the theory itself. In this chapter, together with Chapter Five, I have tried to show that there has been no such progress in the positivist theory of confirmation. The classical version, describing rules solely dependent on logical form, gives a fundamentally inaccurate account of hypothesis choice. In the new version, adding relations derived from probability theory, the old problems all reappear. In addition, the new version has its own distinctive problems of clarity. It is relatively clear how to assign deductive relations to propositions, relatively unclear how to assign probabilities to them.

The shared assumption that produces the recurrent distortions is that confirmation is established by applying general, a priori rules, solely concerned with the internal features of propositions and propositional attitudes, rules that are the same in every field. To the contrary, in the theory of confirmation as causal comparison testing is governed by specific and, often, contingent principles, different ones salient in different fields, applied in light of the specific histories of each field. This theory accounts for the aspects of rationality that elude the others. By the normal scientific argument from superiority in accounting for relevant phenomena, it should be preferred.

So far, I have used the theory of confirmation as causal comparison to assess particular scientific disputes. In the next and last section of this book, I will extend this theory in an effort to solve the general problem that dominates philosophy of science at present, the problem of scientific realism: are we ever justified in condemning disbelievers in a kind of unobservable entity as wrong?

First, I will argue that a certain question about historical relativity that naturally emerges from the account of confirmation I have defended is the only version of the issue of scientific realism that remains an open question in the present day. Previously, I argued that confirmation only requires fairness to frameworks that are actually employed. But this leaves open a further question, which certainly should not be dismissed, even if it is not associated with the term "confirmation." Are there empirical arguments the conclusion of which could not be reasonably avoided by any possible rational disputant accepting current data, because such dismissal would require a framework that could not be reasonable, in light of current data? This is the natural extension of the idea of fair causal comparison to the question of whether reason and evidence alone can compel acceptance of a hypothesis. This question applied to arguments for the existence of unobservable entities will turn out to be the only live issue in the current debate over scientific realism. Both leading realists *and* leading anti-realists are careful, these days, not to appeal to a positivist account of scientific justification. As a result, I will argue, the question about possible reasonable frameworks is the only one that can divide them.

After using the anti-positivist account of confirmation to define the issue of scientific realism, I will argue that it sets the stage for solving the problem, as well. At present, many of us find the debate over scientific realism unsatisfying, on both sides. What anti-realists claim is unbelievable. But realist arguments are inadequate. I will argue that this dilemma results from the influence on both sides of the positivist worship of generality. At crucial points, anti-realists suppose that rational theory-choice is governed by pursuit of the formal virtues that dominated positivist theories of confirmation. For their part, leading realists assume that belief in unobservables is vindicated by discovering some general pattern of success in the use of scientific theories and applying a corresponding general principle warranting belief in approximate truth wherever this general pattern is found. I have argued that the positivist virtues do not regulate hypothesis choice. I will argue that the general principles of inference that realists now employ either are false themselves or require patterns of success that would be false history of science.

The issue of scientific realism can be resolved, and realism about some important kinds of unobservables sustained, by rejecting outright the attempt to base methodological judgments on general rules. If reason and evidence compel belief in certain statements about unobservables, this is because relevant arguments can be based on topic-specific truisms, which people with relevant experiences can only reject on pain of irrationality. I will apply this image of reason in the defense of a number of kinds of unobservables—including molecules, which are traditionally at the center of the debate. My strategy will be to avoid grand philosophical arguments from general patterns of success in favor of reconstructions of the scientific arguments that actually convinced investigators that agnosticism about a kind of unobservable was not a reasonable option.

One goal of these final chapters is to defend realism. (I have already confessed to finding anti-realism unbelievable—although I will frequently be emphasizing the many grains of truth in current anti-realist writings.) Another goal is to develop an approach to the issue of realism that sheds light on more practical or more specific problems. I will conclude by showing how the choice of a realist or an anti-realist position concerning a field has important consequences for subsequent research, by describing how this choice should be made, and by arguing that in at least one field, quantum physics, the present approach to realism makes possible an understanding of what the leading theory is actually about.

# PART THREE

# Realism

# CHAPTER EIGHT

# The Issue of Realism

WRITING toward the end of the eighteenth century, Kant said it was a scandal that philosophers had not proven the existence of the external world in the face of over a hundred years of skeptical and indealist criticisms. On the similar question of the reality of the distinctive entities postulated by scientific theories, present-day philosophy of science is at least as scandalous. Most characteristic methods and outlooks of modern philosophy of science can be traced to the last quarter of the nineteenth century, when philosophically minded physicists and chemists, especially in Austria and Germany, tried to show how the fruits of classical mechanics, Maxwellian electrodynamics and atomistic chemistry could be retained without commitment to the distinctive entities of each theory. As we would now say, they questioned "scientific realism." Far from being resolved over the course of time, their basic questions about the reality of theoretical entities are the hottest topics in the philosophy of science today. What is even more embarrassing, the history of the dominant opinion about scientific realism has the rhythm of changing fashions in the width of neckties, not of a continuing approach to some permanent consensus. Writing in 1902, Poincaré can dismiss belief in invisible processes underlying physical theories as a confusion about the obvious goals of science, either largely due to ignorance or the result of a peculiarly English style of theorizing.[1] Yet for Schlick, in 1932, realism is a deep and pervasive tendency among philosophers and, especially, among scientists in their philosophical moments.[2] Putnam, in his essays of the 1960s, could take an anti-realist, instrumentalist account of science as dominant, his own realist views as heretical. Yet at the beginning of *The Scientific Image*, van Fraassen could suggest that realism was the emerging trend from which his anti-realist "constructive empiricism" deviates.[3] If present-day opinion has any novelty, it is that realists and

[1] *See Science and Hypothesis* (New York, 1952), pp. 172, 177, 211–13. See also Pierre Duhem, *The Aim and Structure of Physical Theory* (1905; New York, 1981), pp. 76–80.

[2] See "Positivism and Realism" in M. Schlick, *Philosophical Papers*, vol. 2 (Dordrecht, 1979), especially pp. 267, 270f., 274f., 278f.

[3] *The Scientific Image* (Oxford, 1980), pp. 4f.

anti-realists seem about equally numerous at the same time, in contrast to the usual oscillation in which each camp dominates for about twenty years.

## TWO IMAGES OF REASON

When controversy is so cyclical and evenly divided, one cause may be a tacit, distorting assumption, shared by both sides and insuring that arguments from both sides will be defective. Many of my specific criticisms and proposals will support such a diagnosis of the debate over scientific realism. What is shared is an image of scientific rationality according to which fundamental questions about science are to be resolved by applying to the relevant facts general and abstract principles of scientific reasoning, the same for every field—"topic-neutral" principles as philosophers would once have called them. "The principle of induction," "inference from the best explanation," "preference for simplicity," and "methodological conservatism" will suggest some leading candidates. For positivists, the data, i.e., observational findings, are the only facts to which the relevant principles are applied. For anti-positivists, including such leading realists as Boyd, the relevant facts may include the existence of certain theoretical frameworks, actually governing the assessment of hypotheses in light of data. In either case, the question of whether unobserved theoretical entities exist depends on the content of utterly general and abstract principles of inference, and their implications when applied to the facts.

This worship of generality is, I think, a legacy of positivism that haunts us in the debate over scientific realism. I will argue in the next two chapters that the debate is stalled. Realists have not offered any sufficiently compelling inference from data to theoretical belief. On the other hand, it is unbelievable that agnosticism concerning certain unobservables, microbes and molecules, for example, is still a reasonable option. Leeuwenhoek's work on microbes, Einstein's and Perrin's work on molecules make agnosticism unreasonable, though standard defenses of realism cannot account for the compelling force of their arguments. They cannot, I shall finally argue, because topic-specific truisms play an essential role when a case for unobservable entities is rationally compelling.

Putting science to one side, for a moment, most of our rational beliefs, including rational beliefs about what there is, seem to depend on relatively specific principles. Unlike most people in the history of the species, I believe that there are buildings more than ten stories tall. I believe this because I have seen them. Not only have I seen them, I have been in them, sometimes looking out the elevator as it stops at floor after floor, even, on some unlucky occasions, walking upstairs to above the tenth floor. My belief seems to rest on such specific principles as this one, about sight: the gross external features of material things typically are as sight reveals them to be, if they are not far away and are seen distinctly in moderately bright, non-colored light. More precisely, this, like other relevant principles, is to be followed unless some reason to the contrary arises. Similarly, I think there are traveller's checks in my drawer because I distinctly remember putting them there, distinct memories are typically valid, no one has been at the draw, and visible objects don't normally disappear.

Of course, these various topic-specific principles, specifically concerned with vision, memory, non-disappearance and so forth, could be justified by appeal to the course of experience, assessed in light of a principle of inference to the best explanation. The best explanation of the familiar correlations of sight, sound and touch is the familiar world-picture of people interacting with things which entails, in turn, the typical reliability of sight. But it is far from obvious that the familiar world picture can be rated the best explanation on the basis of wholly general considerations. After all, the familiar world-picture leaves open a variety of important explanatory questions that do not arise in ontologically simpler rivals. Questions of why non-mental processes, hitting, for example, sometimes have mental sequels, say, pain, are prime examples of such open questions, which scientific extensions of common sense have barely begun to close. In contrast, the outlook of subjective idealism, positing nothing non-mental, raises no such question. That the truisms are part of a superior explanation cannot just reflect their providing more explanations than subjective idealism, neutral monism, eliminative materialism or some other philosopher's simplification. Reckless speculations often promise the same abundance of hypotheses. Presumably, the philosopher's simplification is worse because unlike the truistic world-picture it does not explain what stands in urgent *need* of explanation. Regular sequences among sensations stand in need of explanation, as standard causal connections (say, between being hit hard and feeling pain) do not. It would be mysterious that pain regularly follows visual experiences of fist trajectories' seeming to end at the surface of one's body, if the painfulness of hitting did not explain the regularity. In contrast, it is only a disappointment, not a mystery, if the means by which hitting produces pain are not known. Distinctions between what stands in need of explanation and what doesn't seem to be presupposed in our rating of the standard world-picture as best among rivals. Yet these distinctions are not obviously grounded on a further, absolutely general principle, unconcerned with any specific relation between feelings and material happenings.

In any case, even if the topic-specific truisms on which we rely could be derived from utterly general principles and particular data, the truisms would have an independent role in determining the limits of rationality. Skeptics have sometimes described bizarre circumstances which would force us to choose between the topic-specific truisms and topic-neutral principles of inference. "Imagine that two minutes from now you seem to have the experience of waking up beside the Great Wall of China. And then someone seems to tell you, in a familiar way, '*You've* had a good snooze.' And then. . . ." Ultimately, I argued in Chapter Four, it could become reasonable to adhere to substantive principles about the continued validity of what sight and memory seem to reveal, even at the cost of explanatory inferiority as assessed by any topic-neutral standard. Relying on topic-specific principles, one might reasonably accept the existence of an inexplicable split in one's life. Given the actual course of experience—as against the bizarre imagined patterns—one can take the most basic specific principles about sight, memory and non-disappearance to be justified by the facts and one's favorite topic-neutral inferential principles. Even so, the former are just as much "in the archives," just as much ultimate standards against which proposals are tested, as the latter. To put the matter baldly: I might rationally prefer an inferior explanation of my experience, if the alternative would be to doubt that my name is "Richard Miller" and I have a mother.

My proposal will be that scientific rationality, including the assessment of the real existence of postulated entities, often depends on specific and substantive principles in just the same way as ordinary rationality seems to. Indeed, the most basic principles are the same. In particular, when scientific inferences to the existence of unobservables make agnosticism about these entities unreasonable, the inferences rely on common-sense principles or developments from them, as the principles are refined and extended on the basis of common sense together with (often extraordinary) data.

I will develop this image of scientific rationality as I assess the current debate over scientific realism. Meanwhile, a glance at certain episodes in the history of science should make it plausible that topic-specific truisms play a special role in the judgment of whether the distinctive, unobservable entities of an empirically successful theory exist.

Throughout most of the nineteenth century, physical scientists debated whether molecules existed, even if they granted that the molecular theory of matter fits the data and provides the best explanations of many phenomena. For example, by the middle of the century, the law of multiple proportions, which Dalton elegantly explained using a molecular theory, was well-established. The molecular-kinetic theory of heat was, throughout most of the century, the only plausible explanation of the gas laws and of the interconvertibility of mechanical energy and heat. The molecular hypothesis provided the best explanation of differences and analogies routinely encountered in organic chemistry. In 1858, Cannizzaro could use molecule theory to explain certain striking similarities in estimates of atomic weight derived using independent branches of the theory itself. By 1860, the existence of molecules was an inference from the best explanation. Yet many creative, reflective scientists, Poincaré and Mach, among many others, did not believe in the actual existence of molecules, even at the beginning of the twentieth century. What changed the verdict from mere "empirical adequacy" to "existence" was, above all, the investigation of Brownian motion, in which Einstein was the leading theorist, Perrin the leading experimenter. As Einstein's first paper makes clear, Brownian movement can furnish a "weighty argument" for the existence of molecules because it brings to bear specific principles concerning the causes of motion, for example: when little particles deviate from their paths, that is evidence that something causes the deviations; if the random motion continues in the same manner for an indefinitely long period of time, that is evidence that the deviations are not due to internal capacities of the particles; if the random motion continues unabated while the observable state of the medium is uniform, the impact of unobservable discontinuities is apt to be at work.[4] The point is not just that Brownian motion studies were relevant to the molecular theory (which no one denies), but that quite special background principles concerning motion and its causes made the studies relevant to the more special question, "Granted that many and various phenomena behave as if matter were made of molecules, is matter really made of molecules?"

[4] Einstein, "On the Movement of Small Particles . . ." (1905) in Einstein, *Investigation on the Theory of the Brownian Movement*, ed. R. Fuerth (New York, 1950), pp. 1f.

To take one other example (both will be analyzed in detail later on): when the existence of microbes gained quick and permanent credence, general principles of inference from the general shape of success do not seem to have been at work. Anton van Leeuwenhoek, a soft-goods merchant of little education, quickly and permanently convinced the best and most skeptical scientists that his microscopes revealed little living things much smaller than the eye can see. Yet his reports were astounding, a number turned out to be wrong, and microscope optics was rudimentary. All that Leeuwenhoek could rely on—or needed to—were common-sense principles about what sight reveals and about the relation between motion and life. For example, what seems to have compelled belief was not some general pattern of success so much as the humble truism that an instrument which makes blurry, barely visible phenomena become clear and distinct is, all else being equal, to be given tentative credence when it also produces smaller appearances corresponding to nothing visible at all. (Soon, I will give grounds for taking Leeuwenhoek's animalcules to be unobservable in the only sense of the term that makes scientific realism an interesting question.)

## Redefining the Issue

Despite—or rather because of the long life of the debate over realism, the issue at stake is often in flux. Scientific realism is always some version of the following vague idea: scientific research often puts people in a position to claim that kinds of things exist that are unobservable. However, from time to time, the particular aspects of this vague idea that are in dispute are determined, to a high degree, by changing conceptions of scientific justification.

Although the current round of the debate over realism has already generated a vast literature, the current issue is elusive, with charges of misrepresentation from both sides. The main problem is that the previous round was dominated by conceptions of scientific justification that both sides now reject. Thirty years ago and more, when anti-realism was epitomized in Carnap's, Nagel's, Russell's and Reichenbach's work, the attack on unobservables developed certain antirealist tendencies in classical positivism. As deductivists, the classical positivists were under strong pressure to say that a scientific hypothesis is solely confirmed by its own test implications, i.e., by observable relations among observables that the hypothesis itself entails. More liberal doctrines, allowing auxiliary hypotheses an essential role in the entailments, always ended up certifying as confirmed absurdities that the positivists wanted to exclude. So there was good reason, given the deductivist image of science, to claim that belief in a hypothesis was always unjustifiable where the latter did not speak of observables. What seemed to be justification of something more was just a matter of pragmatic tactics (Reichenbach), or of deep-rooted but quasi-aesthetic inclinations (Carnap), or was not really concerned with unobservables at all (Russell, Nagel, and Carnap elsewhere). This denial of justifiability is what the issue of anti-realism and, hence, of realism, used to be about.[5]

Similarly, at least in the golden age of classical positivism, the realm of the observable was understood in special ways. In Russell's pioneering writings of the 1910s, the observables were taken to be sense data, in the final analysis. In subsequent, more charitable views, Carnap's for example, the protocol for evidence, as against theoretical conclusions, was still supposed to impose some special vocabulary, to which the scientist gives unique epistemological status. So the old issue of realism also depended on whether theory language and observation language could be distinguished in some non-arbitrary way.[6]

If the new issues were the old ones, it would now be easy to resolve the debate. The previous attacks on deductivism and its Bayesian successors were, a fortiori, attacks on the deductivist way of being anti-realist and its Bayesian analogues. It used to be thought that hypotheses were only testable by observing test implications they entail. That claims about unobservables were untestable was a consequence of this assumption. But this assumption has turned out to be false. A Bayesian revival of the old argument, in which a purely observational belief system always triumphs on account of the more accurate observational expectations it supports, would meet the same fate. In addition, there is a well-established literature, by Putnam, Grover Maxwell, Austin and others, widely held to have demolished efforts to construct a distinctive observation language.[7]

[5] See Hans Reichenbach, *The Philosophy of Space and Time* (1927; New York, 1957), esp. pp. 10–37, and his *Experience and Prediction* (1938; Chicago, 1970), esp. pp. 145–56; for Carnap at his most tolerant, "Empiricism, Semantics and Ontology" (1950) in his *Meaning and Necessity* (Chicago, 1956), and for a more reductionist view, "Testability and Meaning" (1936) in H. Feigl and M. Brodbeck, eds., *Readings in the Philosophy of Science* (New York, 1953); Russell, *Our Knowledge of the External World* (1914; London, 1926), esp. chs. 3 and 4, and "The Relation of Sense-Data to Physics" (1914) in his *Mysticism and Logic* (London, 1918); Ernest Nagel, *The Structure of Science* (New York, 1961), esp. ch. 6.

[6] See Russell, "The Relation of Sense-Data to Physics," and Carnap, "Testability and Meaning."

[7] See Putnam, "What Theories Are Not" (1962) in his *Mathematics, Matter and Method* (Cambridge, 1980); Grover Maxwell, "The Ontological Status of Theoretical

In fact, to end the whole debate on the basis of attacks on the old foundations for anti-realism would mean refusing to take current anti-realists at their word. The leading anti-realists, as well as the leading realists, are often prominent opponents of both aspects of classical positivism, and, in any case, strenuously avoid basing their arguments on the old premises. Realists, of course, frequently suspect that positivism is required to sustain the other side. But their hunch will turn out to be strictly wrong, although suggestive of much that is right.

How is the current issue to be defined? In the earlier round, anti-realists denied that statements going beyond the observable had any justification. When one looks at the scientific literature, there seem to be many such justifications. Maxwell's "On the Dynamical Theory of Gases" and Einstein's "The Elementary Theory of the Brownian Motion" certainly look like justifications of statements about unobservables, in particular, about molecules. With their special view of confirmation, positivists could argue either that these weren't really, in the final analysis, justifications of the truth of molecule statements—or that the molecule statements were really, in the final analysis, statements about observables. But current anti-realists claim to be relying on no such special view of confirmation. So what can self-described anti-realists now be saying that merits their self-description? Similarly, scientists frequently argue from a theory-laden description of a phenomenon to a theoretical conclusion, say, from measurements of the charge and spin of an elementary particle to conclusions about its "charm." If these are full-fledged and complete justifications, it is hard to see what the problem could be about believing in unobservables. The theory-laden descriptions of phenomena easily justify belief in unobservables; indeed these phenomena include the existence of unobservables. Old-style anti-realists could describe the kind of justification that was missing, appealing to the old distinction between vocabularies. The phenomena described could not be ultimate data, because the descriptions included non-observational terms. Foresaking this distinction, what can an anti-realist say? Even more basically, how can any rejection of belief in unobservables, however nuanced, be clear, if the old distinction between vocabularies is abandoned? Finally, the anti-positivism of current realists poses problems about the scope of *their* position. Before the transformation of our picture of science which

Entities" in H. Feigl and G. Maxwell, eds., *Minnesota Studies in the Philosophy of Science*, vol. 3 (Minneapolis, 1962); J. L. Austin, *Sense and Sensibilia* (Oxford, 1962).

Kuhn, Feyerabend and others produced, it seemed that realists were offering a basic inventory of what there is, or, in any case, claiming that triumphs of theories among rational scientists were always steps toward that goal. Except for occasional anti-realist asides, the *Encyclopedia of Unified Science* is dominated by such claims.[8] Nowadays, realists accept that there can be competing, equally good descriptions of the world, that good science is not always cumulative and convergent, and that what confirms in one framework may not in another, equally good. What approval of belief in unobservables do they, then, intend which anyone would want to refuse? Though all these questions are related, I will, to some extent, separate them, first discussing observability, then the scope of realism, and finally the anti-realist limit on justification. My goal is to find the version of anti-realism that has the best chance of being valid and genuinely anti-realist, assuming the failure of positivism.

## OBSERVABILITY

In the vague statement of realism, namely, that research often puts people in a position to claim that something unobservable exists, "unobservable" is probably the term that cries out loudest for explication. Obviously, "unobserved" would not do, since no one is so anti-realist as to deny that scientists could be in a position to claim that unobserved Canada goslings are being born deep in the Yukon. But in a broad sense, the kinds of alleged entities, for example, molecules and electrons, to which any anti-realist wants to be uncommitted *are* observable. Physicists observe electrons passing through cloud chambers. Some crystals are single giant molecules, observable by the naked eye. Even electrons can be seen with the naked eye, when speeds near that of light give them substantial mass and energy. Many kinds of molecules can be seen using an electron microscope. And we see sets of molecules all the time, e.g., you see the set of molecules constituting this page. Indeed, one important attack on anti-realism has been that the position is vacuous, since everything is observable, unless the scope of "unobservable" is narrowed through an arbitrary or question-begging stipulation.

What the set of molecules constituting this page and the giant molecule-crystal show is that the observable had better not be identified as something of a kind that is sometimes seen, heard, touched, or otherwise observed. More precisely, an anti-realist should not

[8] R. Carnap, C. Morris and O. Neurath, eds. (Chicago, 1938–55).

take this route if he or she offers no reason to suppose that molecules, electrons, and so forth do *not* exist. In fact, modern anti-realists *are* this modest; they are more like agnostics than atheists. So they have no reason to reject page-wide sets of molecules and crystal-sized molecules as candidates for observability.

What anti-realists can do is to regard observables as things the presence of which can be detected by certain means, to admit that appropriately detectable molecules (and so forth) may be observables, but to deny that status to non-detectables of those kinds. In effect, they will take talk of page-wide sets of molecules, molecular crystals and enormously energetic electrons to be just a fancy way in which certain people refer to pages, crystals and flashes. (Similarly, a non-Catholic takes the Pope to be referring to someone in the latter's use of "the saint who translated the Bible"—even though the non-Catholic may have no belief in the existence of saints.)

Now, however, cloud chambers and electron microscopes intrude, suggesting that the wide scope of detectability renders anti-realism vacuous. Any entity in a theory is, in principle, detectable. One response has been to reject the troubling detection processes as too tainted by inference to count as observation. The scientist observes the vapor trail (the image on the fluorescent screen) and only infers the presence of an electron (a molecule). But surely, the routine practices of very well-trained cloud-chamber and electron-microscope users are no more tainted by inference than paradigmatic observations of ordinary, medium-sized material objects. Anti-realists are expected to distinguish belief in electrons from belief in chairs, but many beliefs in electrons within cloud chambers depend on inference no more than the usual belief in the presence of a chair "on the basis of observing, by sight, the presence of chair-surfaces." And some observers' reports of the presence of chairs rely very heavily on inference.

Just two ways seem open to the anti-realist. One is to accept the attempted *reductio*, put chairs on a par with electrons, and count nothing as truly observable but sense data, sensations, qualia, raw feels, or the like. Apart from its intrinsic difficulties, this conception would not capture the distinctive issues at stake in the current debate over *scientific* realism. For whatever reason, sane people do not doubt that chairs exist, yet a number of them refuse to commit themselves to the distinctive entities of many successful scientific theories. If the debate over scientific realism has a point, it is to clarify this specific kind of doubt, then justify or end it.

The only path that seems to remain is Bas van Fraassen's. Van

Fraassen takes observability to be the possibility of detection by the unaided perceptual apparatus of normal human beings. What is normal and what is possible, here, are determined "within science." In other words, anti-realists and realists, in their debates, determine what is observable by consulting the best natural science of their time. Anti-realists, as much as realists, use the best science of the time, as a device for distinguishing the part of human coping that could be a matter of sensory perception from the part that could not. The anti-realists part company in their assessment of what humans can achieve when they go beyond the limits of sensory perception.[9]

In this conception of the observable, "normal human being" is to be given a fairly strict reading, while "possible" is to be given a charitable one, within the limits of the laws of nature. A human subspecies with electron-microscope eyes is to be counted as abnormal. So observability-via-those-eyes is not observability.[10] But van Fraassen is not agnostic about dinosaurs, or about the dimness of light on Pluto. No human has detected these things with unaided senses, but such detection is possible, i.e., not incompatible with laws of nature. Note that, although dinosaurs are observable, on this view, many animals are, unobservable, viz., microbes, living things too small for the unaided eye to see.

Van Fraassen's conception of observability is, at once, faithful to the current views of justification that are the framework for the realism dispute today and a plausible means of excluding from the observable what anti-realists have always wanted to exclude. In addition, this conception may seem refreshingly close to what the anti-speculative scientist has in mind when he or she resolves to "stick to the data." But in fact, when anti-realism is understood in van Fraassen's way, vacuity is avoided at some cost in arbitrariness in the distinctions it emphasizes.

For one thing, the non-vacuous version of anti-realism will often rest enormous methodological distinctions on differences that seem too small or irrelevant, from the standpoint of many people who are otherwise unprejudiced in the realism dispute. For the physical possibilities governing human observation don't always plausibly cor-

---

[9] See *The Scientific Image*, pp. 56–59. Presumably, anti-realists will also doubt that epistemology produces established truths, when it relies on theories of unobservable mechanisms to determine the limits of what humans can observe. But few philosophers are so proud as to regard it as a reductio if a position makes philosophy edifying, useful, organizing—but not a body of well-established truths.

[10] Ibid., p. 17.

relate with different attitudes concerning what exists. The dimness of light on Pluto is observable, since human astronauts could detect it with unaided eyesight. But the coldness of Pluto is not observable, since humans cannot detect it without instruments. They would die instantly if they tried. So the anti-realist, persuaded of the adequacy of modern astrophysics where observables are concerned, must say, "The dimness of light on Pluto exists, though no one has ever seen it, but I have no belief that the coldness of Pluto exists, since theory tells us it would instantly kill humans." Or suppose that well-confirmed astronomic theory tells us of the existence of certain configurations on the surface of the sun that are a mile across, and also tells us of other, structurally different ones, that are .9 mile across. If human astronauts would have to melt just as they got close enough to the sun to see surface configurations less than a mile across, the anti-realist must say, "I believe in the existence of the Z-configurations, 1 mile across, though no one has seen them, but not in the existence of the Q-configurations, predicted by the same body of theory, since theory tells us they would be over 500 feet too small to be seen without one's melting."

The other problem concerns the all-pervasive differences between observable magnitudes (on the present understanding of the phrase) and the magnitudes that physical scientists actually have in mind when they speak of the "observable phenomena" that theories should fit. Part of this problem is the infinite coarseness of any observable differences compared with the differences regulated by differential equations. But apart from such issues of coarseness and fineness, it is troubling that the simplest quantitative "observable regularities" in physics, say, the Boyle-Charles gas law, are different from all quantitative relations that are observable in the present sense. Since no one proposes to reconstruct physics on the basis of weighing by hand, judging distance purely by sight and taking temperature by feel, the literally observable magnitudes will be, in effect, numbers indicated by dials and gauges on instruments. These are the most important magnitudes human scientists detect without using instruments, in turn. But the relations among these magnitudes never correspond to the "empirical regularities" with which physicists are concerned. Even if we take the smoothest curves in a cumulative scattergram of volume and pressure, there will be some departure from the gas laws. Physical scientists almost always dismiss such differences as the results of "experimental error" causing the readings to depart from the actual phenomena. This shows that the phenomena, for them, are the results of interpreting instrument readings using theories of the instruments and their objects; that is, "the observable" in the jargon of quantitative physical science is not observable in the jargon of non-vacuous anti-realism.

Since present-day anti-realists do not want to reject current theories as *dis*confirmed, they are faced with a dilemma. In some sense, the best-established theories are to be admitted as non-disconfirmed because they are close enough to the literally observed magnitudes. But, on the one hand, if "close enough" is not a relative judgment, based on the comparison of a hypothesis with its rivals, then it is hard to see why Ptolemaic astronomy or Lamarckian evolution is not confirmed. In the abstract, neither is very far from observed magnitudes. On the other hand, if "close enough" means "closer than rivals," then every current theory is disconfirmed. For a list of relations established by precise but superficial curve-fitting will always fit the data better. While a realist might dismiss the latter relationship as insufficiently supported by background theories to vindicate a rival, the anti-realist can hardly adopt this tactic. For he or she is, precisely, an agnostic between concerning the truth of theories as against truth limited to mere generalities linking observables.

The problem of magnitudes, like the prior problem of methodological discontinuities, shows that anti-realism is further than one might think from the attitude of the working scientist who seeks to avoid speculative commitments. Do these problems undermine the whole anti-realist project? It is premature to revive the old strategy of ruling out anti-realism through reflections on "observability." Presumably, the anti-realist will conclude that a theory is a useful, simplifying fiction, not to be taken too literally even in its observational parts. Similarly, initially implausible judgments about Plutonian coldness and solar swirls might show that scientific talk is more a matter of useful fiction than one had thought. One might have thought that science is revealing what is true, not just organizing data in a satisfying way, whenever it speaks of qualities of a kind that humans often detect with unaided senses. Plutonian coldness and small solar swirls show that observability—and, hence, access to truth, for the anti-realist—does not project in this way, from some instances of a kind to others.

## THE SCOPE OF REALISM

I have summarized scientific realism as the view that scientific research often puts someone in a position to assert the existence of kinds of things that are posited in successful theories, but unobservable. This is very different from the following view, which might be called the One True Inventory theory: on the basis of all relevant evidence and theorizing, a rational person could accept just one inventory of the locations, kinds and relations of material things. Recently, Putnam and Rorty, among others, have attacked the One True Inventory theory, and at least implied that it is part of the realist interpretation of science.[11] In fact, while the One True Inventory theory is certainly false, this does not undermine scientific realism as such.

One reason why scientific realism can be true if the One True Inventory thesis is not is that the latter imposes a demand on every subject matter (that only one complete description fits it), while realism is more modest. Realism is the view that we are often in a position to make certain existence claims, not that we always are. So it does not exclude isolated indeterminacies. For example, the One True Inventory theory is defeated by such humble creatures as the tiny flagellates, living in the arctic snow, that contain chlorophyll yet lack cellulose cell walls. In one taxonomy, they are plants, in another, equally rational, they are animals. Yet that there is no fact of the matter as to whether there is a plant in the relevant pieces of snow hardly makes it dogmatic to insist that plants exist. After all, they unequivocally exist in many flowerpots. Certainly the existence of equally good inventories of arctic life forms does not show that the denial that molecules exist is as defensible as its affirmation.

Of course, if scientific justification were the application of a canon of determinate general rules concerned with logical form, if the goal of realism were to justify statements in theory language on the basis of statements in observation language, and if every scientific statement were governed by a fixed and determinate set of observational criteria *then* realism would require belief in the One True Inventory. The application of all the rules to all the evidence would license one set of hypotheses in observation language. And the application of the observational criteria would then license one set of statements in theory language. But this connection between realism and the One True Inventory depends on a framework to which neither side is committed any longer. Again, the current issue is confused by importing the framework of the old debate.

Even within those fields of theorizing in which a realist claims to be in a position to assert that a kind of entity exists, a certain plural-

[11] See, for example, Putnam, *Reason, Truth and History* (Cambridge, 1981), pp. 49f., 54f.

ism in inventories is permissible. The realist can accept that a complete inventory, not explicitly mentioning the kind of thing in question, could be just as reasonable and just as accurate as one that does explicitly assert the existence of that kind. For claims that each inventory is complete are not exclusive, so long as the assertions in each are entailed by the assertions of the other. This pluralism is characteristic of the most interesting and important cases in which more than one option for complete description exists, the alternative descriptive repertoires for fields of physical science.

For example, as Putnam aptly notes, there is more than one complete way of describing the processes in the domain of quantum physics.[12] In the so-called Schroedinger picture, dynamical change consists of change in states corresponding to change in wave functions; dynamical magnitudes are timeless relations between wave functions. In the Heisenberg picture, dynamical magnitudes change, while the states that they relate are timeless.

Certainly, there is no one true inventory of the components of quantum processes. But physicists do not think that they are any the less able to assert that what is depicted in the Schroedinger picture exists. (They may have anti-realist doubts on other grounds, but not on this.) A precise but non-technical analogue to the Schroedinger-Heisenberg duality shows why. I can describe all processes involving the physical colors that physical objects have by taking surfaces to have some color properties at some times, others at other times. This is analogous to the Schroedinger attitude toward dynamical magnitudes. Or I can take surface colors to change over time, as Heisenberg takes dynamical magnitudes to be variable. The color property green does not become the property red when an apple ripens. But the surface ceases to have the former and acquires the latter. In the Heisenbergian format, the surface color changes. I can regard each inventory of color facts as complete, even though one does not mention surface colors and the other does not mention color properties. (I won't be this permissive if I think that some exclusive metaphysics, such as nominalism, must be correct. But surely this is not the only rational assumption.) Reason and evidence compels belief that color properties exist (in my permissive view) even though the surface-color inventory is a complete one. For statements in this inventory entail that color properties exist. That an ap-

---

[12] See *Realism and Reason* (New York, 1983), pp. 39f. I do not mean to suggest that the transition from such examples to an anti-realist perspective is easy or obvious for Putnam. Some of my discussion will resemble the options Putnam himself offers realists on pp. 40 and 42, including my subsequent simile of map projections.

ple has the surface color red entails that its surface has the color property red, and, of course, vice versa. The two modes of description are related as a map in the Mercator projection is to a map assigning the same locations in the polar projection; they are not related as maps are when one locates a mountain at a latitude and longitude where all is flat in the others. This entailment of statements in one mode of description by statements in the other is very much a part of the analogy with physics. Indeed, most physicists were only satisfied that either of the quantum inventories was true when Schroedinger convinced them that each entailed the other.[13]

What a realist must deny is that in all fields of theorizing there are equally good, complete inventories that are incompatible in the sense that assertions made by one do not entail assertions made by the other. This denial of pluralism is not obviously right, but it does not fly in the face of such uncontroversial options as the Schroedinger-Heisenberg duality. Because the rejection of pluralism is not total, here, and non-exclusive difference is always permitted, the realist claim should be sharply distinguished from the One True Inventory theory.

How often must scientists be in a position to claim that unobservables exist, for scientific realism to be true? The worship of generality that I criticized before can make the only option seem to be: whenever a theory postulating unobservables is rationally preferred as empirically adequate, i.e., as an adequate basis for predicting and explaining observable phenomena. Empirical adequacy must always be a sign of truth if it ever is. When we look at the history of science, a new kind of option emerges. The very rational Poincaré circa 1902 denies that molecules exist, while accepting the empirical adequacy of molecule theory; the very rational Einstein and Perrin, circa 1907, argue that the existence of molecules has become the only rational conclusion in light of new data and theorizing; and they seem to have convinced the aged Poincaré.[14] Scientific realists should be given the following option, even if the philosophers among them have rarely taken it: when scientists are justified in taking a theory which postulates unobservables to be empirically adequate, they are often (*not* always) in a position to insist that the postulated entities exist. The cases in which they are in this position, at

[13] For a classic description of the Schroedinger-Heisenberg contrast, see Dirac, *Principles of Quantum Mechanics* (Oxford, 1981), pp. 111–16.

[14] For Poincaré's earlier position, see *Science and Hypothesis*, pp. 152, 164, 178f., 186f.; for his later position, see "Les Rapports de la Matière et de l'Ether," *Dernières Pensées* (Paris, 1963), pp. 68–70. I will discuss this episode in detail in Chapter Ten.

least in the best-established sciences, are relatively frequent, involve many unobservables, are important, and do not depend on tricky logical constructions from observables. Even if there is no general strategy for sound inference to unobservables, exemplary arguments for important kinds of unobservables can be given. If someone says all this, he or she is a scientific realist worthy of the name. I will be arguing that the scope of valid realism is no broader than this.

## REALISM AND REASON

Before, I described modern anti-realists as more like agnostics than atheists. Making such similes more precise, i.e., describing the precise criticism intended of certain beliefs in molecules and the like, is absolutely essential for an understanding of the realism debate. Yet, on both sides, the criticism (or defense) involved is surprisingly hard to grasp.

Certainly, modern anti-realists (in disanalogy to Berkeley and other traditional idealists) do not make arguments that molecules do not exist. They have abandoned deductivism and the notions about meaning that deductivism supported, according to which testable theoretical claims were really, in the final analysis, about observables. Having accepted that molecule talk really does refer to unobservables in the final analysis, they would be claiming to know a great deal about the unobservable if they denied that molecules exist. Yet, even though they do not argue for the non-existence of molecules, present-day anti-realists sometimes seem to make a claim that would have much the same impact on belief in molecules: people who believe in unobservables take on a burden of proof which they can never, in fact, support. Thus, van Fraassen says, "[A] realist will have to make a leap of faith," and elsewhere, "[A]cceptance of a theory involves as belief only that it is empirically adequate," the virtue he sharply distinguishes from the true description of actual theoretical entities.[15] If not the analogue of atheism, this sounds like the very aggressive agnosticism that condemns all belief in God as unreasonable, while stopping short of the claim that God does not exist.

In fact, modern anti-realists have not been proposing that belief in molecules is unreasonable. And, more important, their actual position, though genuinely anti-realist, is more defensible than this.

[15] *The Scientific Image*, pp. 36, 12.

The plausible and genuinely anti-realist position in post-positivist philosophy of science is the following. Evidence and argument never make belief in the existence of something unobservable the only reasonable option (even as a tentative belief in the approximate truth of an existence claim), thus making all basically different rivals unreasonable. The surprise that anti-realists seek to create is not that belief in molecules is unreasonable, but that disbelief in molecules is still a reasonable option.

One kind of rival to standard theories is so omnipresent in current anti-realism that one can use it in an alternative formulation of the position itself. Adapting the usage of previous chapters, there is a "phenomenological rival" to any theory committed to unobservable entities. Someone who adopts this phenomenological alternative thinks, "Best-informed, ideally reasonable believers in the theory reach true conclusions when they use the theory to make statements about observables. But I have no idea whether they are right when they make statements about unobservables." The phenomenological rival to the theoretically committed science of the time consists of belief in its observable part, agnosticism about the rest. Since anti-realists are at pains to show that the phenomenological alternative is reasonable, they may seem to claim that theoretical commitment is unreasonable. But all they need, to be anti-realists worthy of the name, is the claim that reason and evidence never compel abandonment of the best phenomenological rival in favor of its fully committed counterpart.

Any position more anti-realist than this would be extremely hard to defend in the current state of the discussion of confirmation. How could it be thought that people who believe in molecules cannot justify their belief? The experts among them would point to certain classical investigations, say, Perrin's observations of Brownian movement, and describe how these findings point to the existence of molecules, when interpreted in accordance with certain physical principles, say, in Einstein's way. Of course, someone might object to this justification by casting doubt on the physical principles used, say, by doubting the applicability to Perrin's tiny latex spheres of Stokes' law concerning movement through a medium of uniform viscosity. But these concrete and answerable objections are never the worry of philosophers who are concerned that belief in molecules is excessive. Rather, a philosopher who regards such belief as unreasonable will think that if the Einstein-Perrin argument justifies belief in the molecular hypothesis, it must have a further analysis in which it connects the molecular hypothesis to data via general, a priori principles. And the disbelieving philosopher will doubt that the right principles could connect data with hypotheses asserting the existence of unobservables. In other words, aggressive agnosticism would require commitment to a positivist approach to confirmation. And this is very far from the intention of modern anti-realists. Van Fraassen, Putnam and Rorty are prominent critics of positivist confirmation theory, who, in fact, regard realism and positivism as related symptoms of the worship of the methods of modern science.

On a close reading, modern anti-realists typically turn out to be saying that disbelief in theoretical entities is always one reasonable option, but to be saying no more than this. Thus, van Fraassen glosses his characterization of realism as a leap of faith with the remark, "The decision to leap is subject to rational scrutiny, but not *dictated* by reason or evidence."[16] What is not dictated need not be forbidden, or even unsupported. Elsewhere, he makes it clear that belief in molecules is not a mistake, for him, but rather the belief that those who disbelieve in molecules are unreasonable.[17] Similarly, that theory acceptance only "involves," as belief, belief in empirical adequacy means, in practice, that it entails nothing more. Some scientists will believe in the postulated entities, as well. After all, some scientists read Boyd's writings and Putnam's of the 1970s and are convinced. They *and* their more phenomenological colleagues are reasonable, for an anti-realist. Probably, this tolerance of diversity is part of Putnam's rejection of "metaphysical realism." Clearly, it is Rorty's intention in trying to replace confrontation with "conversation" among diverse epistemic communities, including, as just one among others, the Western post-Renaissance scientific community with which he allies himself.[18] Modern anti-realism is a principle of tolerance.

This understanding of the issue between realists and anti-realists seems fair to the texts, and it is certainly the fairest basis for the arguments I will be making. Those arguments will be directed against the tolerant form of anti-realism, and so would work, a fortiori, against the harsher versions. Finally, this reading creates a parallel between the question of scientific realism, and debates that have always seemed similar, and have often flourished at the same time, viz., debates over the objectivity of value judgments, especially

[16] Ibid., p. 37.

[17] Ibid., p. 217.

[18] See Richard Rorty, *Philosophy and the Mirror of Nature* (Princeton, 1980), pp. 318, 390f.

moral judgments. After all, moral relativists need not deny what others assert in their moral judgments. They have been at pains *not* to deny that the killing of innocents is bad. What they do deny is that standard affirmations are the only rational judgments in light of relevant data. This is the way to understand anti-realists on the existence of molecules, as well.

Because modern anti-realism is best seen as a tolerant outlook, the burden of proof on realists is heavy. If they only had to show that belief in unobservables is reasonable, it would be enough to point out familiar empirical arguments employing physical principles, arguments actually found in the best scientific writings. Then, the burden would be on anti-realists to show that these arguments are not really good enough. In fact, realists also have to show that there is something unreasonable or uninformed about any practice of scientific inference confined to an alternative framework in which the existence of the crucial unobservables is not implied by the data. Because this burden is so heavy, even the most powerful realist writings have been implausible at just this point.

Consider, for example, what is, in many ways, the pioneering realist contribution to the current debate, Boyd's "Realism, Underdetermination, and a Causal Theory of Evidence." Here, and in subsequent writings, Boyd shows that standard theoretical commitments are justified by the usual evidence, once substantive background principles are taken to be indispensable in making observations into evidence for hypotheses. However, as Boyd is aware, a modern realist has a further need to show that basically different commitments are typically *un*reasonable in light of the same evidence. To fill this gap, Boyd relies on a methodological conservatism similar to Goodman's and, in its own way, just as implausible.

Midway in his article, Boyd comes to grips with a non-standard catalogue of physical forces that Reichenbach constructed, which seems to be a rival to the standard catalogue in physics. Reichenbach's construct will be discussed in detail in Chapter Nine. The basic tactic is the positing of a force that distorts so uniformly that its distinct physical contribution produces no distinctive observations. The non-standard catalogue has the same consequences for observations as the standard one. If physicists had used it, they would have made the same guesses, in seeking new relations among observables. But, of course, they have used the standard catalogue, instead.

Boyd assumes, at least for the sake of argument, that realists need to defend standard theories from rivals of Reichenbach's sort. His defense relies on a conservative principle, that a received theory which has contributed to successful prediction and control is to be believed in preference to an alternative that merely might have been used so successfully.[19] He is also concerned to show that commitment to received and successful theories is preferable to other alternatives, guesswork, for example. But the dismissal of non-standard theories that could, demonstrably, have worked is essential to the argument against Reichenbach's alternative, and fully in the spirit of the modern realism debate. It is not enough to show that the standard inference is reasonable. The radically different alternative must be shown to be unreasonable.

Unlike Goodman, Boyd does not take his methodological conservatism to be valid a priori. He proposes that it could be supported as part of an empirical assessment of scientific methodologies themselves. Methodologies are justified by their actual contributions to scientific practice, and the preference for received theories has in fact contributed in appropriate ways, for example, through its role in experimental design.[20]

The problem with Boyd's way of supporting the distinctive burden of the modern realist is that his conservatism is implausible in light of the actual history of science, and would have posed a barrier to actual scientific progress. The proposal that the non-standard catalog of forces, which could have done as well, is just as well-justified, embodies a skeptical attitude toward standard physics which has often been reasonable and has often contributed to progress. For example, the instrumental reliability of classical mechanics was, basically, the work of people who construed it as a theory of motion in absolute space. But after reliability had been established, and before significant predictive anomalies had arisen, Mach showed that mechanics could have been developed into just as reliable a science without the assumption of absolute space. He demonstrated that predictions turn out just as well if physicists abandon the Newtonian distinction between a universe with a still center of gravity and one with a center of gravity moving at uniform velocity. And he urged that this alternative physics was at least as reasonable as Newton's. The response, "But the man actually responsible for the derivations actually believed in absolute space," seems Newton-worship, not

[19] See "Realism, Underdetermination, and a Causal Theory of Evidence," *Nous* (1973), pp. 7f.
[20] See ibid., pp. 3, 9f.

real refutation.[21] Similarly, Einstein noted, on the way to general relativity, that classical mechanics did not owe any reliability to the classical distinction (roughly) between a constantly accelerated system within which there is no gravitational attraction and a non-accelerated system within which gravity acts. (Think of the "pseudo-gravitation" when an elevator starts to ascend.) In addition, that gravitational attractiveness and resistance to acceleration should be two utterly different ways of determining mass that always turn out the same should not, he thought, be accepted as a mere empirical equation, in the classical way. Because it avoids distinctions and assumptions that he took to be arbitrary or mystifying, general relativity was, in his view, at least as reasonable as classical mechanics, indeed, superior, quite apart from further experimental tests.[22] It seems a bad reply to remind him, "These weren't the plausibility judgments of the people who actually established the reliability of mechanics."

In the previous discussion of Goodman, I tried to show that questions of what theory was actually established first lack substantial prima facie weight. But even someone who is unconvinced ought to have doubts once the epistemology of science is made an empirical inquiry, in Boyd's way. For refusing to take alternatives seriously just because they have not been shown to be better than standard theories would, in fact, have impeded scientific progress. It would have impeded the development of general relativity, special relativity (to which Mach's arguments made an important contribution) and electrodynamics (with its growing neglect of Faraday's and Maxwell's original mechanical models).

## THE LIMITS OF TOLERANCE

While they are more tolerant than realists, anti-realists do not regard all alternatives to current theories as equally reasonable. Of

---

[21] See Ernst Mach, *The Science of Mechanics* (1883; Chicago, 1942) and, for related doubts bearing on the Newtonian idea of force, H. Hertz, *The Principles of Mechanics* (1894; New York, 1956), Introduction. Einstein's first full-scale presentation of general relativity, which in no way appeals to distinctive empirical expectations, begins with an argument of Mach's. See "The Foundation of the General Theory of Relativity" (1916) in Einstein, Lorentz, Weyl, Minkowski, *The Principle of Relativity*, ed. A. Sommerfeld (New York, 1952).

[22] See "On the Influence of Gravitation on the Propagation of Light" (1911) in *The Principle of Relativity*, pp. 99–101 and "The Foundation of the General Principle of Relativity," pp. 111–115. There is a superb non-technical account in Einstein and Infeld, *The Evolution of Physics* (New York, 1942), pp. 220–60.

course, if a hypothesis is incompatible with actual observations, past or present, they will reject it as unreasonable in light of data. But almost all would go much further, in two ways. For one thing, almost all anti-realists think we often have reason to believe that a hypothesis will or will not fit future observations, and they take reasons for or against the fit with observations, past, present *and* future, to be reasons for accepting or rejecting the hypothesis. In addition, they regard different theories as more or less acceptable in light of observations even when those theories (like most fundamental ones in science) by themselves entail nothing about observations. A consistent anti-realist will have problems upholding both kinds of discrimination as reasonable. However, some realists to the contrary, these problems, though serious, are solvable.

Taking up the latter problem first, how should an anti-realist assess the empirical adequacy of a pure theory which itself says nothing about observables? For a theory that must be connected with data via auxiliary hypotheses, a *realist's* ideal of empirical adequacy can be compatibility with all data, on the basis of all *true* auxiliary hypotheses. But this cannot be an anti-realist's ideal, since the auxiliaries refer to unobservables. Indeed, the set of all auxiliaries includes all theories, in the final analysis. To say that the auxiliary hypotheses must themselves fit all the data is not much help, since they will, in part, make statements about unobservables, and the problem is to discover how those parts can "fit the data." (Note that there will always be rival auxiliaries with the same observational entailments, which would not license the inference to the pure theory in question.) Given these problems of defining the ideal goal of empirical adequacy, an anti-realist might be tempted to look at the actually available auxiliaries, not dreaming of ideal ones, and identify observational fit with compatibility via hypotheses actually believed at present. But if current beliefs determine empirical fit, a cheap realist victory is in the offing. In point of sociological fact, there is often sufficient consensus concerning the auxiliaries to make a great many beliefs about unobservables empirically adequate, as against all basically different rivals. And for anti-realists, empirical adequacy, as against other, allegedly pragmatic virtues, is relevant to truth.[23]

[23] See, for example, van Fraassen, *The Scientific Image*, pp. 4, 12, 87f. An anti-realist who took empirical adequacy to be irrelevant to truth could not be rationally committed to the truth of empirical regularities concerning observables, and, also, could not take theories to be falsified when their empirical inadequacy is discovered. Boyd emphasizes the problems anti-realists face in defining empirical adequacy in "Real-

Two courses are now open to an anti-realist who wants to rank hypotheses about unobservables in something like the normal way. One is part of van Fraassen's strategy of dispensing with belief in favor of mere acceptance. He stipulates (or proposes, the desired connection with normal usage is unclear) that a hypothesis is "empirically adequate" just in case it is compatible with the actual course of observable phenomena, past, present and future.[24] Thus, hypotheses confined to realms of unobservables are bound to be empirically adequate. "Gases consist of unobservable molecules" and "Gases consist of unobservable little people" are both empirically adequate, though in a quite uninteresting way, since any observable world-history is compatible with both. As van Fraassen would emphasize, they have the same models among the observable phenomena.

Of course, this is only true if the hypotheses are taken in isolation, not supplemented with standard auxiliary principles. But at this point, it seems self-defeating for anti-realists to give auxiliary principles an intrinsic role in the definition of empirical adequacy. By the same token, van Fraassen's model-theoretic approach is especially promising because it can treat theoretical hypotheses in isolation.

Of course, van Fraassen thinks rational people should only accept the hypothesis concerning molecules, not the leprechaun hypothesis. But acceptance, he proposes, is utterly different from belief where hypotheses about unobservables are concerned.[25] To *accept* the molecule statement is to use it as a preferred basis for developing predictions about the course of observables. This is rational, because it would, for example, be very much more complicated, and unnecessarily so, to use the leprechaun statement to predict the behavior of gases given initial observable conditions. More precisely, the needed auxiliaries would either be complications (new and special laws of how the little people fly) or useless as guides to future observable laws ("the little people make observable gas laws true"). These vices and virtues are just pragmatic, though, according to van Fraassen. They are appropriate grounds for using a hypothesis, but not for believing it. Scientists who construct astronomical tables for navigators use a geocentric two-sphere universe to do so, because working with a heliocentric theory makes for pointless complica-

---

ism, Underdetermination, and a Causal Theory of Evidence," pp. 2–7, and in subsequent writings.

[24] See *The Scientific Image*, pp. 12, 47.

[25] See ibid., 12f., 86f., 156f.

tions. Everyone sees that they do not believe the view of the universe they use. For van Fraassen, preferring molecular-kinetic theory as a basis for prediction and research design in thermodynamics in itself implies no more about actual belief. So the superiority of a molecule statement can be defended, even though on this account there is no basis for defending belief in it.

However, the denial that literal belief in a purely theoretical statement is justifiable seems a heavy and unnecessary burden for an anti-realist. Van Fraassen accepts that we have justified beliefs concerning empirical regularities linking observable phenomena past, present and future. Compatibility with past and present observations may be one standard we employ here. But it cannot be the only one, since an infinite number of alternative extrapolations must be rejected, from grue-type bizarreries to alternative well-fitting curves of different algebraic forms. The further criteria used in these justifications of empirical beliefs about the future seem just the same as those employed in distinguishing among wholly theoretical statements. So why suppose that they provide no justification for beliefs about the latter?

The same conclusion, that theoretical statements can be empirically justified beliefs, emerges when we ask what the other virtues apart from empirical adequacy really are. "Simplicity" will not really do, though it is usually the first on the list. Boltzmann's statistical thermodynamics forces much more complex derivations than classical thermodynamics. But even Boltzmann's critics did not suppose it should, just by that token, be given the status of the leprechaun theory of gases. Rather than supposing we have clear and clearly pragmatic notions, when we lack them, it would be truer to our current understanding of scientific reasoning simply to say that the empirical justification of theoretical statements has aspects going beyond compatibility with observables. But then there is no reason to suppose that the justifications are too pragmatic to justify beliefs.[26]

Once it is clear that van Fraassen's position, and anti-realists' in

---

[26] As a matter of philosophical (and practical) psychology, distinctions between acceptance and belief can also become farfetched. A constructive empiricist working in statistical mechanics makes guesses about observables, designs experiments, chooses her research projects and guesses how the molecular model may have to be revised—by asking what would be the case if the molecular theory were basically true. The claim that she does not believe in the basic truth of the theory sounds like certain examples of farfetched casuistry about intentions, for instance, "The Joint Chiefs of Staff will never really intend the death of civilians in case of nuclear war, because they are only interested in Moscow and other Russian cities as military targets."

general, is essentially one of tolerance, it is also clear that anti-realism need not deny that theories can be empirically justified beliefs, even when the theories say nothing about data when taken in isolation. The alternative, more modest approach to observational fit is implicit in Putnam's attacks on metaphysical realism. An anti-realist can let empirical justification, i.e., justification in light of data, be whatever it is. Though epistemological issues may become very relevant in the defense of anti-realism, there is no need to take on special epistemological doctrines in defining the position. The anti-realist is saying that when all data are in and all relevant ideas have been developed, for every theory referring to unobservables which is empirically justified, rival theories, including a phenomenological rival, will be at least as well justified. (That is, tentative belief in the approximate truth of a basically different rival will be at least as well justified.) Perhaps, "Gases are made of little people" will not be among the survivors. But other rivals, including the best phenomenological rival will.

Van Fraassen's notion of empirical adequacy is too useful to do without entirely. It helps to describe certain positions and epistemological temperaments that are extremely important in the realism dispute, for example, those expressed in a preference for phenomenological alternatives. However, anti-realists need not be burdened with the principle that an empirically justified belief is always a belief in empirical adequacy. To have it both ways, I will associate "empirical adequacy" with van Fraasen's notion of empirical fit and related narrow notions, but make no assumption that "empirical justification" is similarly narrow, for anti-realists.

The remaining difficulty in discrimination affects the vast majority of anti-realists who take many beliefs about relations between observables, past, present, *and* future, to be rationally compelling in light of the data. These anti-realists do not believe they have crystal balls, revealing the future in magical ways. The beliefs about the as-yet-unobserved are dictated by rational scientific inference from the already-observed. Positivists used to say that such reasoning was based on utterly general, a priori principles for extrapolation. But Goodman showed that the classical principle of induction could not yield coherent beliefs about the future, and no alternative a priori principle, including Goodman's own proposal, seems an adequate basis for scientific reasoning. It might seem, as a consequence, that anti-realism is incompatible with the normal anti-realist commitment to the truth of many empirical regularities. If rational belief in such regularities is not based on a general, a priori principle of extrapolation, then, it might seem, it must be based on specific beliefs concerning the underlying causes of our observations. If disbelief in the former is unreasonable, so, it might seem, is disbelief in the latter. And belief in relevant underlying causes seems likely to include belief in the real existence of posited entities at stake in the realism dispute.[27]

Is it true, though, that the commitments supporting our extrapolations must be of the kind that anti-realists reject? More precisely, if the tools we ultimate use in making assertions about the as-yet-unobserved are not limited to general a priori principles, must they include principles about the operation of unobservable causal mechanisms? To avoid pointless linguistic legislation about what must count as an unobservable mechanism, it is helpful to look at actual cases in which scientists have taken themselves to adopt an anti-realist perspective. At least in the physical sciences, such episodes are frequent and have sometimes contributed to scientific progress. Mach, in many ways the founder of modern anti-realism, rejected the molecular theory of matter in favor of "phenomenological" laws of thermodynamics, conductivity and chemical combination; and he took laws of the conservation and equivalences of energy as fundamental, not something to be explained. Hertz advanced electrodynamics by divorcing it from mechanical models under the slogan, "Maxwell's theory is Maxwell's equations." Bohr, Heisenberg, and other pioneers of modern quantum mechanics helped to free physics from the contradictions of early quantum theories by taking probabilities of momentum and location measurements to be the ultimate subject-matter, not the locations and momenta themselves. These all seem to be moves in the direction of anti-realism. And they all have something in common. If we put to one side questions of the fineness and accuracy of observation, they are proposals to limit a part of physics to the description of propensities for some observables to be associated with others. It is in this sense that the mere commitment to "$PV = kT$" is less realist than commitment to Boltzmann's "Gases are composed of unobservably tiny, elastic molecules, in constant motion."

When consistent anti-realists extrapolate, they depend on certain beliefs as to the propensities of certain observables to be associated with certain others, e.g., the ("anti-grue") propensity of a limited

[27] Cf. Boyd, "On the Current Status of the Issue of Scientific Realism," *Erkenntnis* (1983), p. 76. Though this quick argument that the normal anti-realist position is incoherent turns out to be too quick, I will soon be sketching a longer argument for a similar conclusion.

range of colors (not "crulers") to occur in gems of given kinds, the distributions being roughly uniform over time. Of course, realists rely on the same kinds of propensities in their extrapolations. The difference is that anti-realists never think that a further explanation of these propensities, in terms of unobservable mechanisms, is dictated by reason and evidence.

Since he counts the crucial propensities as observable phenomena, the anti-realist presumably takes the observation of an instance of such a propensity to be the observation of the propensity. The usage is a bit artificial, but surely not intolerably so. What would be intolerable is an understanding of the issue that makes it beside the point whether it would be unreasonable to accept the phenomenological gas laws, the combination principles summed up in the periodic table and the visible phenomena of Brownian movement, while denying that molecules exist.

## DEFENDING REALISM

In defining the issue of realism, I have, in effect, been constructing the best version of anti-realism, the one most likely to be valid if any form of general skepticism about unobservables is correct. Along the way, I have argued that many versions of anti-realism are incoherent, arbitrary, or unnecessarily committed to doubtful principles. But, although I have already expressed realist inclinations, I hope it is clear that the best version surviving is coherent, rests on distinctions worth taking seriously, and does not obviously undermine essential practices of science. If wrong, it is an important error, from which realists can and should learn.

In the rest of this book, I will argue that realism is right. I will offer a radical revision of now-standard realist inferences to the best explanation, developing the new kinds of inference in response to anti-realist criticisms of the standard ones. Here, the alternative image of rationality, in which topic-specific truisms are as fundamental as rules of inference, will be crucial. But first, a book-length defense of realism is possible.

## A BOOK-LENGTH ARGUMENT

The book-length argument relies on the premise that at least one of these two propositions is true.

1. In the best-established sciences, strong, universally shared beliefs of scientists concerning approximate, observable relations

among observables, some of them as yet unobserved, are often rationally compelling, i.e., unless new evidence comes along, belief in the basic falsehood of these mere regularities is unreasonable.

2. In the best-established sciences, when a theory is universally chosen by the experts as the one to apply, in assessing other hypotheses, in designing experiments and in looking for new empirical regularities, that preference is often rationally compelling. A rival choice is unreasonable unless new evidence supports it or an important and persistent defect in the current theory is resolved in a new one, in light of shared background principles. Of course, the standard choice is not *assumed* to be a matter of belief in the theory's truth, or else premise 2 would assume the truth of realism. What is rationally compelling is the use of a theory as a basis for research, which might, here, be acceptance-without-belief, as with van Fraassen.

Most anti-realists respect science enough to accept either 1 or 2. In fact, most accept both. So an argument based on these premises would be effective, directed against them. And its effectiveness is not just ad hominem. Each premise is quite plausible. When properly informed, we (a "we" at least as broad as in most plausibility arguments!) regard it as quite unreasonable for someone to propose that the Boyle-Charles gas law is wildly wrong for gases at normal conditions, or to propose that it would be just as effective to base chemical research on a totally non-molecular model—unless the dissenter offers surprising new evidence or a novel, satisfying solution to definite, outstanding theoretical problems.

The hedges in each alternative premise are important, especially the one about "best-established sciences." If there are empirical regularities or theoretical models on which all expert economists or psychopathologists agree, the mere assertion that those choices are dictated by reason and evidence would not be the basis for a very compelling argument. Many of us have far less trust in these experts. To avoid either begging the question or injecting unnecessary controversies, it is probably best just to understand the relevant sciences as the standard fields that investigate material phenomena without claiming to offer insight into mental phenomena. These are the natural-scientific fields listed in a respectable university's catalogue, with their firm establishment dated in standard ways.

Also, there is the usual complication about "mere" empirical regularities. The familiar empirical regularities of science, Boyle's Law and Snell's Law, for example, are not literally relations among observables. Presumably, an anti-realist will take them as approximate indications of relations among the really observable phenomena, for example, numbers read off of certain dials. Still, all kinds of decisions are routinely based on these approximate indications, such as the decision whether to extrapolate from given data or the decision whether to take the best linear relation as the right basis for extrapolation. Premise 1 says that these decisions are often rationally compelling. As a rule, I will speak of the usual empirical regularities, the ones among temperatures rather than thermometer readings. This usage will not be misleading, *unless* there is something wrong with anti-realist reconstructions of science.

The realist argument that can be based on premise 1 or premise 2 depends on the theory of confirmation as causal comparison. According to this theory, the actual hypothesis choices mentioned in these premises are rational if they are the outcome of scientists' efforts to show that the causes of relevant histories of data-gathering and theorizing include mechanisms making the hypotheses in question true. In the actual cases in question, many of the causes posited in this reasoning are unobservable (sometimes because a hypothesis about unobservables is ultimately supported, sometimes because an empirical regularity is justified on the basis of reasoning about unobservables). Not only is this one account of the reasoning leading to the hypothesis choices, it is the only account of the goals of scientists that makes their actual choices as rational as 1 or 2 requires. *And, according to 1 or 2, those choices are not just reasonable, they are the only reasonable options in light of the evidence.* So crucial steps in the supporting justifications must be the only reasonable options in light of the evidence. Some of those steps posit unobservables. So realism is true.

As a first illustration of the role of theories in justifying commitments to empirical regularities, consider the traditional prime example of a mere empirical regularity, Boyle's Law that the pressure of a gas varies inversely with its volume at constant temperature. As a basis for simple extrapolation, Boyle possessed the observations of Richard Towneley, an obscure gentleman-dilettante. Boyle fully accepts that mere extrapolation should not compel belief, here. His argument for Boyle's Law is, almost entirely, a process of fair causal comparison, drawing on far-flung data and background principles, meant to vindicate a theory of unobservables, namely, that the air consists of unobservable "springy particles."[28] This is the crucial

---

[28] Excerpts from *New Experiments Physico-Mechanical, touching the spring of the air and*

premise which, in turn, is used to support the extrapolation of the law from its instances. To take another example, crucial to twentieth-century physics: throughout the nineteenth century, scientists were unsure of the empirical relation between the specific heats of different substances. The simple proposal of Dulong and Petit seemed to be wrong in several cases, especially for relatively complex substances or low temperatures. But the problem might have resided not in Dulong and Petit's proposal but in certain difficulties in experimental design or certain systematic errors in assessing crucial constants. Early in the twentieth century, scientists achieved a consensus concerning the right law (much more complex than Dulong and Petit's). The acceptance of the law depended, not on progress in observations, but on the vindication of quantum theory, as best explaining the relevant data.[29]

In modern physical science, there is not a single empirical principle which is firmly believed by all without crucial reliance on a theoretical underpinning. This need for an underpinning in theory is frequently asserted by scientists with no ax to grind in the realism dispute. Thus, in a typical comment on an effort to ascertain an empirical regularity by purely observational means, Feynman criticizes the engineers' friction law as not to be taken literally because "this friction law is one of those semiempirical laws that are not thoroughly understood."[30] He explains that a believable general law relating the observable phenomena of friction would have to be supported by reasoning from intermolecular forces. What is even more striking, practicing scientists who are adamant anti-realists acknowledge the essential role of theories in any compelling justification of an empirical law. Thus, Poincaré's *Science and Hypothesis* is a magisterial work of modern anti-realism, to which the most impressive anti-realist arguments can still be traced. Yet, to cite one passage out of many, Poincaré fully acknowledges that curve-fitting depends on "convictions" about unobservables, for example, about continuity and discontinuity. "But for this conviction, the problem would have

---

*its effects* in Stephen Brush, ed., *Kinetic Theory*, vol. 1 (Oxford, 1965), p. 44. For further background, see Brush's Introduction, pp. 3–6.

[29] Before, I argued that the mere fact, derived from Goodman's "new riddle of induction," that extrapolations require substantive commitments is not enough to vindicate realism. Here, I am arguing from the nature of specific preferences in the actual course of science, together with the assumption that these preferences were the only reasonable ones.

[30] Richard Feynman et al., *The Feynman Lectures on Physics*, vol. 1 (Reading, Mass., 1963), ch. 12, p. 5.

no meaning; interpolation would be impossible; no law could be deduced from a finite number of observations; science would cease to exist."[31]

That justifications of theory choices (the subject of premise 2) also involve commitment to the truth of theories of unobservables was a recurrent theme of my previous discussion of confirmation. Newton's, Darwin's and all other fundamental arguments for theories are efforts to show that the mechanisms in the repertoire of the theory are involved in the best causal account of the history of data-gathering and theorizing. And what does not exist cannot cause. Moreover, a good argument that a relevant causal account is best mobilizes shared framework principles that partly refer to unobservable causes, e.g., whatever it is that keeps planets in regular orbits or that causes organisms to "breed true."

An argument for realism of this kind proceeds in just the style of scientific argument as anti-realists see it. This kind of argument is an effort to "save the phenomena," in this case, the rationally compelling nature of various choices that scientists have made. The argument does not presuppose that everything stands in need of explanation, or that a hypothesis that explains more is always, by that token, better than one that explains less. Rather, it depends on a specific characteristic of rational choice: if a choice is rational, and its rationality is by no means self-evident, it should be possible to show that it is the best means of reaching a certain goal. The description of underlying causes turns out to be that goal in the case of the choices in question. Finally, there is no assumption that theory acceptance is theory belief, only that acceptance is sometimes the best strategy given the evidence.

An argument for realism of the kind just outlined must be book-length. This book, up through now, is such an argument. For one thing, it is essential both to show that the crucial choices can be based on confirmation as causal comparison and to show that no rival account of their rationality works. Here, problems that tend to be neglected as mere matters of detail in standard disputes about realism assume crucial importance, for example: the inadequacy of simplicity as a criterion for choice among hypotheses; the existence of standard and central theories that are not predictively reliable, since they entail no observations even when supplemented by current auxiliary hypotheses; the irrelevance, in general, of probabilistic inferences, unless they are construed as claims of explanatory ade-

---

[31] *Science and Hypothesis*, p. 286; see also pp. xxv, 22f., 31f., 142f.

quacy. In the second place, if confirmation as causal comparison is to have a realist use, then positivist analyses of causal explanation need to be ruled out. If the covering-law model were valid, then theories, as used in the crucial inferences, could be treated as fictions. That the history of data-gathering is best explained on the basis of molecule theory could simply mean that the relevant sequences can be subsumed under the law that observables behave as if there were molecules. It is crucial that the explanations must actually describe molecules as making things happen. So the first part of this book, the theory of causal explanation, is as relevant as the rest to this defense of realism.

"But doesn't fictionalism permit an anti-realist to give unique status to causal comparison, in quite a different way? Granted, scientists who are making the crucial choices of empirical laws and theoretical hypotheses act as if they were sifting causes of data through the fair use of framework principles, principles often referring to unobservables. But this could be the only reasonable procedure, even if they do not believe in the truth of the principles and the existence of the causes when unobservable. After all, people who calculate navigational tables are being reasonable when they act as if they believed what they really think false, namely, that the earth is at the center of two celestial spheres on which the other celestial objects ride." Of course, it sometimes is reasonable to use a proposition one does not believe. But the specific question at hand is whether the choices that are being taken as uniquely reasonable, in premises 1 and 2, would have this status if the causal comparisons that sustain them were uses of fictions. A consequence of the detailed case studies in Chapters Four, Five and Seven is that causal comparison, construed in the fictionalist way, would lack this rational force. The application of principles that are, on the whole, not believed, to see whether observables behave as if governed by certain causes, not claimed to exist, would be reasonable, if at all, as a means of arriving at formally simple summaries of observations, or some other familiar positivist goal. But if that is the goal pursued, then the choices endorsed in premises 1 and 2 should not be made. Rival options, more superficial, formally simpler, less burdened with anomaly, and so forth, are more reasonable. The tolerance of anomaly, the preference for causal depth, the reliance on causal rather than formal simplicity, the weighing of failures against successes and many other aspects of arguments as paradigmatic as Newton's, Darwin's and any shrewd curve-fitter's are not reasonable ways of pursuing the goals that a fictionalist might reasonably pursue. On the other hand, fair causal comparison deserves unique status, and can convey it to certain hypotheses it supports, if the goal is to find a nondogmatic way of learning truths about the world, on the basis of arguments about the actual causes of observations.

The link between realism and that respect for science which is expressed in the disjunction of 1 and 2 is only as firm as the preceding chapters are well-argued. I have nothing to add to strengthen the latter. However, even if there are no relevant defects in those discussions of confirmation and explanation, the force of the present argument is limited in three ways. First, it assumes a certain respect for science that some important anti-realists lack. Some have proposed that a radically different empirical law or a radically different research program is always reasonable, in light of the data, even if no one actually would dream of adopting it. Feyerabend certainly says this, Rorty probably, Putnam possibly. Earlier, this was Poincaré's way of remaining anti-realist, despite his acknowledgment that theories of underlying mechanisms support standard extrapolations. Thus, the assumption that certain choices are uniquely reasonable is a significant gap in the argument. It would be filled by a case for realism that did not presuppose so much trust in science.

Certainly, it would be useful to have an argument for realism that did not just presuppose our normal invidious comparison between what experts in physics know and what experts in sociology know. If this presupposition cannot be lifted, then realism is just part of the dogma of a shared faith. And that is very close to the anti-realist position.

The same need for a further argument arises, when we consider a burden of proof that most realists assume. All scientific realists think that there are more things in the world than merely phenomenological alternatives posit, and that it is often unreasonable to deny this. In addition, most realists take this claim about science to be supported by scientific arguments. They think that early twentieth-century scientists discovered that molecules exist and that Mach and Poincaré had been incorrect in taking the molecular hypothesis as merely a convenient model. The first stage in the argument for this conception of science's capacity for discovery might basically be bibliographical. One might describe the classic papers arguing for the unobservables, say, Einstein's and Perrin's writings on Brownian motion. But the next stage in the argument is much more troubled. Anti-realists have a variety of responses to the effect that the scientific arguments show nothing more than that certain empirical regularities exist (e.g., the laws of diffusion for Brownian particles), that certain theories (e.g., the "classical," non-molecular version of thermodynamics) clash with the data and that certain research programs will be fruitful. If scientific realism is to be based on scientific arguments, it must be possible to develop the classic scientific arguments further so that they are defended against these anti-realist objections.

Finally, we are bound to learn something, whatever the answer, if we pursue the question: are there arguments from the data that make beliefs in unobservables rationally compelling, arguments which do not simply presuppose that many hypothesis choices in science are rationally compelling? In defending "no" as the answer, anti-realists have tried to show that such an argument always ignores relevant alternatives or assumes that merely optional beliefs are dictates of reason. Even if the realist arguments can ultimately be made good, it would be amazing if anti-realists did not reveal that many common assumptions about science are too rigid or too dogmatic.

In the next two chapters, I will try to show that many scientific arguments for unobservables can be defended as making disbelief in unobservables unreasonable—once philosophical misunderstandings about reason, reference and the nature of physics are removed. But before this second kind of argument is developed, the first should be put to a further philosophical use, clarifying the issue of realism itself.

## REALISM, TRUTH AND JUSTIFICATION

A certain conception of the basic issue between realists and anti-realists has become extremely influential, through powerful writings of Putnam and Dummett. The basic issue, as they understand it, concerns the relation between truth and justification. Roughly, anti-realism is to be understood as the claim that truth is justification carried to the ideal limit. No doubt, disagreements on this claim about truth have been the crux of many past debates about realism in science and in mathematics. But given the conception of scientific justification developed in the previous chapters, this can no longer be a useful characterization of the issue of scientific realism. Any defensible characterization of idealized scientific justification will be one that realists need not divorce from truth.

For example, in recent writings, Putnam has contrasted the "metaphysical realist," "externalist" perspective with his own "internalist" perspective. Sometimes, the perspective he attacks is presented as the One True Inventory theory.[32] Yet clearly the latter, which can be defeated by a few, apparently isolated examples, is not the basic target. (Whether those examples really have quite general implications is a further question, but more a matter of the shape of Putnam's argument than the nature of his conclusion.) In the most perspicuous characterizations of his internalist perspective, he presents this outlook as a way of looking at truth. "[T]ruth is an *idealization* of rational acceptability. We speak as if there were such things as epistemically ideal conditions, and we call a statement 'true' if it would be justified under such conditions." "The most important consequence of metaphysical realism is that *truth* is supposed to be *radically non-epistemic.*" "[I]f metaphysical realism were right and one could view the aim of science simply as trying to get our notional world to 'match' the world in itself, then one could contend that we are interested in coherence, comprehensiveness, functional simplicity and instrumental efficacy only because these are instruments to the end of bringing about this 'match.' But the notion of a transcendental match between our representation and the world in itself is nonsense." "The supposition that even an 'ideal' theory (from a pragmatic point of view) might *really* be false appears to collapse into *unintelligibility.*"[33]

The various virtues that Putnam mentions are, of course, the virtues that figure in positivist theories of confirmation. If previous arguments are right, these virtues do not describe empirical justification, and they fail to do so for reasons with no direct bearing on the possibility of falsehood should ideal justification be attained. Rather, the positivist version of justification cannot account for phenomena of rationality that Putnam, too, wants to save, e.g., the rationality of shifting to Newton's theory or to Darwin's in light of Newton's or Darwin's arguments. Putnam, indeed, was a pioneer in undermining the positivist account of justification. I am suggesting that the characterization of realism that he has borrowed from Dummett does not fit his own rejection of positivism.

A realist would certainly want to say that a theory could be ideal from the standpoint of the positivist virtues, without being true.

[32] See, for example, *Reason, Truth and History*, p. 49.

[33] Ibid., p. 55; "Realism and Reason" (1976) in his *Meaning and the Moral Sciences* (London, 1982), p. 125; *Reason, Truth and History*, p. 134; "Realism and Reason," p. 126. See also Michael Dummett, "Realism" (1963) in his *Truth and Other Enigmas* (Cambridge, Mass., 1978), p. 146: "Realism I characterize as the belief that statements of the disputed class possess an objective truth-value, independently of our means of knowing it."

Any construal of "realism" has to express realists' inclination to deny that human thoughts, tastes and interests basically determine the right answers to most questions about reality. And the total catalog of positivist virtues is too strongly dependent on human thoughts, tastes and interests to fit this inclination. At the same time, it certainly is conceivable—for realists and non-realists alike—that a theory should be ideal from the standpoint of the positivist virtues and yet be false. Indeed, a theory can even have these virtues to the fullest extent possible and not be *justified*. For example, the stricter understandings of simplicity, coherence and the like would have made phenomenological rivals to Newton's and Darwin's theories ideal. Yet Newton's and Darwin's theories were epistemically better. Indeed, because of the dependence of choice of empirical laws on choice of theories, the positivist virtues (narrowly understood) do not even single out ideals for someone seeking empirical regularities. Newton's theory (like the molecular theory of gases, later on) implied distinctive empirical regularities that a rational scientist would have accepted, on theoretical grounds, even though different regularities are contained in a phenomenological rival richer in positivist virtues. On the other hand, given the more liberal understandings of these virtues, hypotheses can be as ideal as any but as little justified as "The Absolute is made of Camembert." Of course, there are difficulties imagining the ideal limit of positivist virtue. But these are just the difficulties of imagining any ideal limit.

Suppose, now, that we accept the post-positivist account and take empirical justification to be causal comparison as previously described. It becomes quite unclear how to frame the issue of realism as a question about justification and truth. Justification will be ideal when a theory is entailed by the best causal account of all the evidence, when all rivals are considered. What counts as ideal is further specified by describing what circumstances make the causal account *definitively* the best. A first proposal might be that the epistemic situation is ideal if the ratings are relative to a final set of background principles truly describing the mechanisms that guide data-gathering and theorizing. Then, it will certainly be inconceivable that the ideally justified theory is false. Every theory plays a role in assessing some evidential claims, so every theory entailed by an ideal causal account was already part of the assumed true background. No realist makes truth so radically non-epistemic that this ideal world of science could, nonetheless, contain falsehood.

In the above depiction of ideal justification, justifications of relevant statements depend not just on data, but on background propositions, and a justification relying on a false proposition is, by that token, an inferior justification. When we look at the phenomena of justification without prejudice, this view of the matter seems right. Suppose I rely on my memory to answer "Yes" when asked whether Lincoln's successor as President had a last name beginning with "J." I answer "Yes" because my memory is that Jackson succeeded Lincoln. Though my answer is justified to some extent, the justification is not very good. It is not simply that I do not *know* that some Mr. J. succeeded Lincoln (as Russell proposed in connection with a similar example). I am not very well-justified.[34]

Still, there is another way of looking at the goal that scientists are pursuing when they justify hypotheses. One might try to describe it as some desired end state in the process of fair comparison of rival causal accounts, describing the end state without reference to truth. Here, questions of the relation between ideal achievement and conceivable falsehood do turn out to be interesting and open. But they are not a means of defining realism.

To construct an ideal goal for the game of fair comparison is difficult, if pursuit of this goal is supposed to dominate science. (If it does not dominate science, it is not, presumably, the standard of empirical justification.) Scientists are not, literally, interested above all in finding hypotheses that withstand all further criticism, in the game of causal comparison. Otherwise, they would like vague hypotheses or extremely well-hedged ones, like "There is life on some planets infinitely far from the earth." Nor is their primary goal the development of a hypothesis that will be justifiable come what may. Though positivists may have exaggerated the phenomenon, scientists often do regard it as bad practice to make a hypothesis so fundamental in the framework for assessing evidence that every potential refutation is explained away, ad hoc. Yet this is a very good way to achieve justifiability, come what may.

How, then, can one devise a post-positivist epistemic ideal, that does not presuppose so much truth in the theoretical framework that the connection between truth and justification is downright uninteresting? At the end of Chapter Four, I described one way, and no other seems available. In pursuing a question, scientists do seem to seek situations in which the only acceptable explanations of the history of data-gathering and theorizing entail a certain hypothesis; ideally, the justification for any rival explanation would have to violate basic principles of common sense in ways that entail unreasonableness. When victory in causal comparison is this perfect, there is

---

[34] See Russell, *The Problems of Philosophy* (1912; Oxford, 1959), pp. 131f.

a reconstruction of the history of science, entailing the favored hypothesis, relying only on the background principles that are the common property of all sane people. If this situation has been reached, and no new data or theoretical alternatives would disturb it, justification would be ideal.

This ideal justification does seem a dominant goal of science (even though a weaker triumph, involving fair treatment of current technical frameworks is good enough for confirmation). But present-day realists are surely not to be separated from anti-realists by an alleged tendency of theirs to divorce this ideal justification from truth. After all, I can:

(a) be a realist about the existence of trees, taking this to be a fact independent of human thoughts, tastes, and interests;

(b) take belief in trees to be justifiable on the basis of truisms that are independent constituents of being reasonable; and

(c) be unable to conceive of trees' never having existed without conceiving of some bizarre course of experience which would deprive tree beliefs of support by those (well-hedged) truisms, or set them at variance with other independent and fundamental truisms.

What people whom we usually think of as anti-realists would often deny, and what a realist might insist on is that the truisms, what I previously labelled level III, are the ultimate framework principles for much of science and that their acceptance is a fundamental, independent part of being reasonable. Anti-realists with positivist leanings take formalist, pragmatic or Bayesian constraints to be, instead, the ultimate framework for science, while anti-realists who reject positivist accounts of justification usually think that our ultimate frameworks are no more reasonable than radically different ones. Indeed, if the arguments of the next two chapters are right, insistence on the role of truisms in science and reason is the only sound basis for being a scientific realist. The first half of the claim upon which a realist might insist, the fundamental relation between topic-specific truisms and technical science, has been neglected because of the worship of generality on both sides of the realism dispute. But the second half raises issues that are familiar from Feyerabend's writings and from the wars over Wittgenstein's and Moore's writings. As veterans of those wars are well aware, the beliefs that only a philosophical skeptic would question are sometimes taken to be fundamental only as a matter of social and psychological fact. If, for example, people in another culture were to put the belief that life is literally a dream "in the archives," making it a standard for assessing evidence and arguments, they are not unreasonable, in this view; they are not unreasonable even if their experience is no different from our own. People who call themselves "realists" have typically rejected this view. People who call themselves "anti-realists" have often been receptive to it. So these positions about justification are a good diagnostic of which side someone is on. But the issue is about the kind of justification available, not about the relation between ideal justification and truth. Moreover, nothing is gained, here, by reflection on justification at some ideal limit when all evidence is in. The realist position is that current hypotheses can be justified from level III, using current data. Reference to ideal situations just forces us to contemplate situations that are eternally unfamiliar to us.

As usual, Putnam's analysis conveys an important lesson to realists. If they want to stay realists, they had better not be positivists. Otherwise, they will be forced to separate truth from maximum epistemic virtue, and be wrong, perhaps unintelligible, as a consequence. Such anti-realist lessons for realism will abound in the next chapter, a survey of the state of the realism controversy today.

# CHAPTER NINE

# Learning from Anti-Realism

LIKE many, if not most arguments in twentieth-century philosophy in the English language, current arguments for the existence of unobservables are, in effect, refinements of a passage in Russell's little book, *The Problems of Philosophy*. Russell asks, at one point, what reason one has to believe in a world of matter causing one's sensations. His answer is that this hypothesis is part of a uniquely powerful explanation of regularities in the course of one's sensations. One finds, for example, that after several hours the visual sensations one is inclined to associate with seeing one's cat end, as a rule, in visual sensations of a cat beside a bowl, accompanied by auditory sensations of whiney meows. What better explanation, Russell asks, than that the sensations are of a real cat who has become hungry in the meantime? And if cats exist, so does matter.[1]

Attempts to show that belief in the unobservables of science is the only reasonable response to the evidence have been variations on Russell's basic strategy. In this sense, Smart's application of Russell's argument to the problem is the beginning of modern scientific realism, while Boyd's major transformation of Smart's argument has become the paradigmatic case for scientific realism. To see whether realism has been justified, so far, means seeing how good these arguments are. My ultimate conclusion will be that they need to be transformed once more, in the context of a different image of rationality.

By the early 1960s, many philosophers had lost interest in Russell's problem of answering general skepticism about the material world—as usual, without coming to any enduring consensus about the right answer. The energy that had been bound up in this problem had started to be displaced onto the debate over skepticism concerning unobservable entities in science. In this context, Smart set the terms for the defense of scientific realism with his strikingly clear and vivid application of Russell's strategy. The best current scientific theories, Smart points out, are the best explanations of a vast number of regularities among observables, the ones that the most

---

[1] See Russell, *The Problems of Philosophy* (Oxford, 1959), p. 23.

expert scientists derive from those theories. He condemns disbelief in the entities required by the theories as amounting to the acceptance of "cosmic coincidences." Thus, speaking of a theory T′ which is a phenomenological rival extracted from a current, full-fledged theory T which does refer to unobservables, he says, "the success of T′ is explained by the fact that the original theory T is true of the things that it is ostensibly about; in other words by the fact that there really are electrons or whatever is postulated by theory T. If there were no such things, and if T were not true in the realist way, would not the success of T′ be quite inexplicable?"[2]

Smart's challenge is extremely intimidating if a good anti-realist answer would have to consist of an explanation of relevant regularities that is as good as the best current scientific theory, while postulating no unobservables. But that would be an inappropriate demand. Smart is arguing against people who think that the empirical regularities in T′ do not stand in need of further explanation, not against people who think they have a super-explanation different from any scientific theory. The non-believers in the literal truth of T already accept that "the success of T′" is, in a sense, a cosmic coincidence, but of a quite non-miraculous kind. The world is *bound* to be orderly with respect to some properties, disorderly with respect to others. The empirical regularities in T′ and other successful general statements about observables involve the properties among which there happens to be order. Though Smart is concerned to separate science from religious faith, he sounds, on this reading, like the man who used to circularize the Harvard Philosophy Department with proofs of a God who leaves clues to His orderliness around the universe. The proofs were along the following lines: "Venus is the SECOND planet from the Sun, the Earth the THIRD planet, and the ratio of the mass of Venus to the mass of the Earth is TWO THIRDS. What better explanation is there than that God has left this as a clue?"

On a more plausible reading, Smart is asking for an explanation, not of regularities among observables, but of the success of scientists, relying on current theories, in describing observables. The demand is not to explain why pressure times volume is proportional to temperature, rather than to something else, but to explain why scientists are so successful when they use theories to arrive at state-

---

[2] J.J.C. Smart, *Between Science and Philosophy* (New York, 1968), pp. 150f. For an earlier version of the argument, see *Philosophy and Scientific Realism* (London, 1963), p. 39, where Smart speaks of the "phenomenalist about theoretical entities" as compelled to "believe in a *cosmic coincidence*."

ments of empirical regularities. If someone who has already seen the day's races at Hialeah describes characteristics of the winners, we do not suppose he has special insight into the causes of horses' winning. But if someone predicts the winners day after day, we are usually quite impressed, think an explanation required, and assume that the explanation will involve the bettor's inside information about the processes resulting in victory. Similarly, Smart is arguing, the successes of scientists in coping with data demand an explanation. We know that guesswork does badly in these matters. And, he is proposing, there is no satisfying explanation that does not entail that scientists have inside information about the processes producing the regularities.

Smart's loose talk of "cosmic coincidences" and his own use of humble analogies is, in itself, a virtue. We lack any general theory of the point at which it is unreasonable to take a regular phenomenon as a given tendency, leaving it unexplained even though an explanation is available. Some reasonable people, of an explanation-loving temperament, are strongly inclined to believe in the best explanation of any regularity. Others, of an anti-speculative temperament, are averse to taking on extra commitments for explanatory gains. Nonetheless, there are some cases in which everyone of any epistemological temperament should find the burden of coincidence excessive and choose the explanation. Smart simply proceeds by vivid description of particular burdens of coincidence, sometimes mobilizing analogies in which the rational need for explanation is clear. In this, I will follow him.

The problem with the second version of Smart's challenge to anti-realists is that it has a non-realist answer, on any accurate view of the success of science. Scientific theories have a very different history from the eternally successful banalities that Russell was trying to justify, such as that cats eventually get hungry. Scientists are constantly trying to describe regularities and construct theories that imply true empirical laws. They frequently *fail*, on both counts, and create new descriptions and theories in response. That the latest theories in this process fit the data up until now is explained by their being the latest theories, i.e., the current survivors. If a tout keeps revising his cumulative list of assertions about victories in light of the latest track results, the non-defeat of the horses on the latest list need reflect no inside information. The success of current scientific theories need be no more validating.

Of course, a few sciences display a relatively long-term pattern of success in which, for the last century or two, what is once established in the way of theory continues to fit the data approximately, if the phenomena are not too small or too far removed. But other sciences, once the province of highly insightful investigators, have turned out to fit the data very badly. Astrology, caloric thermodynamics and humoral pathology are three examples. And yet other sciences, such as economics and psychopathology, keep switching from one temporarily successful framework to another, without any long-term, cumulative pattern. A claim that science in general displays the pattern of long-term success would depend on a criterion for science that is too question-begging for a defense of realism on the basis of success: the "real sciences" are the ones which at present have a good long-term record. One might as well argue that a string of successful bets is not just a random lucky streak by contending that the other, losing bets were not real bets, at all.

In addition, the successful sciences often explain away apparent failures through ad hoc revisions of theory or reinterpretations of data. For example, now, as always, the most successful sciences are afflicted with multiple anomalies, simply assumed to result from unknown defects in auxiliary principles affecting the interpretation of data. Also, the most successful sciences are themselves repeatedly redefined, by dismissing questions as peripheral to the science when it cannot answer them. Thus, phlogistic chemistry was centrally concerned with questions about the observable qualities of compounds and their elements which Lavoisier and Dalton did not try to answer.[3] Newton counted it as important that an astronomical theory reveal how planetary phenomena (including climates) manifest God's benevolence and sense of beauty.[4] Finally, standing behind the appearance that a theory has constantly been in use throughout a long period of diverse and consistent predictive success there is often a very different reality: qualitative changes at the level of theory to reduce the repeated burden of empirical anomaly. Thus, "modern, Copernican astronomy" has shifted from a system of natural, circular motions (Copernicus) to elliptical motions with a special sun-centered source (Kepler) to universal gravitation based on a subtle fluid (Newton, in the final analysis) to universal gravitation based on action-at-a-distance (Newtonism, by the time of Laplace) to variations in the space-time metric (Einstein). Similarly, the atom of atomic theory today is quite unlike the atom of Dalton's atomic theory, or Boltzmann's or Bohr and Rutherford's, or even Fermi's.

[3] See Kuhn, *The Structure of Scientific Revolutions* (Chicago, 1970), pp. 99f., 107.

[4] *Principia*, ed. F. Cajori (Berkeley, 1962), pp. 417, 544–46.

In sum, scientific inquiry as a whole is apt to produce some patterns of cumulative empirical success in any case, even if full-fledged scientific theories are never literally true. For scientists define their sciences, reinterpret their data, budget their research time, and connect new theories with old ones in ways that would produce such patterns in the absence of truth. What would demand an explanation is a world-history in which science as a whole usually has the cumulative pattern, despite a rigid adherence to received theories. But this is not the real history of science.

To be more plausible than Smart's argument, a defense of realism must seem to display two features, at once. It must look like an appeal to scientific practice in the real world of frequent scientific failure and revision, in contrast to the more or less constant triumph that Smart's argument implies. And it must describe a kind of success that would be unlikely if scientific theories were not true. Because it seems to answer both needs, Boyd's argument has become the central one in the debate over scientific realism.

Like Smart, Boyd emphasizes the predictive and instrumental reliability of the leading present-day sciences. Unlike Smart, Boyd emphasizes that these sciences are the result of particular methods, which give scientific theories themselves a distinctive guiding role.

In his crucial argument, Boyd begins by pointing out that the actual methods of the sciences, or in any case, the well-established natural sciences, are biased toward reliance on theories of unobservables, in ways that both realists and anti-realists would accept as a feature of scientific practice. Boyd singles out, as a prime example of such reliance, the use of theories in experimental design. When scientists are deciding whether to accept a hypothesis, which may itself be about observables or have definite implications concerning observables, they put it to the test by seeking the situations that are most likely to show the hypothesis is wrong, if it is, in fact, wrong. (Where they wish, anti-realists can gloss "wrong" as "not fitting all observable phenomena.") In deciding which test situations are crucial in this sense, and in carrying out their tests, scientists rely heavily on background theories about the unobservable causes of observable events. Boyd's main example is the design of an experiment to test a hypothesis about the way in which an antibiotic destroys a species of bacteria. We test the hypothesis, viz., that the drug destroys cell walls, by comparing it with the rivals that are most likely to be true, according to our theories, using theories also to evaluate the tests. Thus, genetics, cytology and chemistry might tell us that interference with cell division is a likely alternative, needing to be excluded. In determining which hypothesis to prefer, the auxiliary theories will again come into play, singling out certain observable phenomena, say, certain rates of shrinkage of clumps in Petri dishes, as more likely on one hypothesis than on another. A hypothesis that survives such sifting is accepted, used in further investigations, and, Boyd would surely add, is even maintained in the face of certain subsequent anomalies.

Boyd does not claim that hypotheses established by this method have always proved empirically adequate. What he does propose is that this method, and other theory-dependent ones, "contribute" to the kinds of scientific success that interest anti-realists, i.e., predictive and instrumental reliability.[5] In his original paper, Boyd presented this as a claim that "need hardly be argued."[6] As subsequent writings make clear, he takes the claim to be based on a more or less obvious fact, "the astonishing predictive reliability of well-confirmed scientific theories,"[7] i.e., those that are initially vindicated through the extensive use of the theory-dependent methods. His case for realism is, in large part, an inference from the contribution of this and other theory-dependent methods to predictive and instrumental success. "But, I suggest, the only explanation for the reliability of this principle [the one basing experimental design on judgments of vulnerability based on current theories] lies in a realistic understanding of the relevant collateral theories. . . . [S]uppose that these guesses [about where hypotheses are most likely to go wrong, if they are wrong] are so good that they are central to the success of experimental method. What explanation besides scientific realism is possible?"[8]

Though this may sound like Smart's argument, it seems to avoid

[5] "Realism, Underdetermination, and a Causal Theory of Evidence," *Nous* (1973), p. 3.

[6] Ibid., p. 11.

[7] "On the Current Status of the Issue of Scientific Realism," *Erkenntnis* (1983), p. 54.

[8] "Realism, Underdetermination, and a Causal Theory of Evidence," p. 8. As Boyd develops and defends his argument from the explanation of success, he describes other considerations, which can play an independent role in defending realism, and have in some of his subsequent writings. For example, that only realists can, consistently, acknowledge the epistemic legitimacy of scientific practices whose rationality is accepted by all is an especially prominent theme in his "*Lex Orandi est Lex Credendi*" in P. Churchland and C. Hooker, eds., *Images of Science* (Chicago, 1985). Concentrating on the central argument of Boyd's 1973 article will be a useful organizing device, since his other arguments play a role as means of defending the central inference. These other arguments will be discussed in his chapter and the next.

both pitfalls of the latter. Scientists' tendency to rely on experimental designs that rely, in turn, on collateral theories is, in itself, independent of their tendency to abandon hypotheses that fit data badly in favor of hypotheses that fit the data well. In principle, the former tendency could interfere with the discovery of empirically adequate statements. If, as Boyd claims, theory-dependent methods contribute enormously to empirical adequacy, so that, for example, pharmacological reasoning relying on theories is more reliable than more superficial methods, then the explanation cannot simply be that the successful hypotheses produced are merely the current survivors. Why shouldn't investigators pursuing more superficial methods, and not relying on collateral theories, do an even better job empirically? The good fit of current theory to current data was no more surprising than the good fit of clothes in my current wardrobe to my current body; but the success Boyd describes, in which the search for truth about observables seems constrained by commitments about the unobservable, seems analogous to the good fit of clothes a tailor has made, based on measurements of my foot. The tailor must know something about anatomy, involving parts of me he has not observed. At the same time, the success Boyd emphasizes is credible. His argument does not require an obvious fantasy in which the basic theories of science have all thrived for millenia.

Boyd offers his principles of experimental design as one example of the way in which methods relying on current theories contribute to predictive and instrumental reliability. Another might be the tendency I described in a previous chapter, to revise a regularity based on "curve-fitting" when theoretical considerations support another kind of curve as the one to fit to the data. Stated generally, Boyd's argument has four steps.

1. Methods relying on theories of unobservable causes guide scientists in the testing and consequent acceptance of hypotheses.

2. These methods contribute to the predictive and instrumental reliability of the systems of hypotheses established through their extensive use.

3. This contribution stands in need of an explanation.

4. The only satisfactory explanation is that the theories used in the productive methods are approximately accurate descriptions of underlying causes. It would be a miracle, otherwise, if the methods were so productive.

The fair way to assess this current paradigm of realist argument is by judging the current anti-realist responses. They are of four kinds, as well.

a. When we look where Boyd wants us to, at physical sciences with "astonishing predictive reliability," we also discover a history of repeated basic failures to describe unobservable causes in an empirically satisfactory way. Step 2, even if literally correct, is utterly one-sided. It leaves out the fact that the methods usually produce basic mistakes about unobservables, with no cumulative pattern of success concerning unobservables. When the failures are taken into account, the history of science justifies skepticism about any positive assessment of science going beyond the approximate reliability of some fields in the realm of prediction and control.

b. For every theory well-established by scientific methods, there is another theory, just as well-justified by scientific methods, which basically differs from it, concerning unobservables. For every theory justified by its contribution to predictive reliability, there is another theory, fundamentally differing about unobservables, that would have contributed as well, and is, hence, as well-justified. Step 4 is wrong. The alternative explanation of success is that the theories employed are one selection among many different sets of just-as-good theories that would contribute just as well to predictive reliability. In a way, the realist argument is too good. It shows why there is always equal reason to support incompatible theories concerning unobservables, so that realism must be false.

c. The contribution to predictive success made by the use of collateral theories does not stand in need of explanation. It amounts to a regularity that a reasonable person might simply take as a given. Step 3 is false.

d. In addition to general methods of inference, scientists rely on certain background assumptions about the world in framing hypotheses *and* in interpreting data as successful predictions which vindicate the hypotheses. It is not unreasonable to adopt contrary assumptions. And relative to the contrary frameworks, contrary theories are vindicated, by applying to actual data possible reasonable methods. Step 1 leaves out certain non-rational constraints on scientific practice narrowing the array of hypotheses that are actually accepted. Scientific realism turns out to be dogmatic when those non-rational factors are taken into account.[9]

While each kind of argument can be seen as an objection to

[9] Argument d, the relativist objection, could be a form of b, the argument from equivalence. But explicit arguments from equivalence were pioneered by classical positivists whose epistemological inclinations were often quite anti-relativist. It is best to separate the two lines of attack, to match the natural ways of sorting out the literature.

Boyd's, each is, of course, an argument for an anti-realist position, in its own right. In fact, every major current argument for anti-realism is of one of these kinds. This double meaning of the list of objections is a tribute to the power of Boyd's work. In examining these anti-realist claims, in turn, I will investigate them in both connections. In the rest of this chapter, I will discuss the first two objections, based on theory change and on empirical equivalence. I will try to show that these objections are extremely productive failures. They do not refute realism or the standard arguments for it. But the defense of realism from these attacks produces fundamental clarifications of what realism means and of what theories of meaning, truth and reduction a realist can accept. I will begin the next and last chapter by arguing that the third objection, based on the absence of an appropriate need for explanation, is correct, as a response to Boyd's and Smart's defense of realism. The contribution that genuinely theory-dependent methods have made to reliable prediction and control does not stand in need of a further explanation. In describing a new way of defending realism, I will show how it depends on real explanatory needs, and how it copes with the anti-realist appeal d, to alternative evidential frameworks.

## FAILURE AFTER FAILURE?

Both Boyd's and Smart's arguments are inferences concerning belief in unobservables drawn from the actual history of success in the best-established sciences. So it is fair for anti-realists to point to failures in just those sciences as counter-balancing the arguments from success. And they have done so, to considerable effect.

Above all, realists must contend with the appearance that the best-established sciences are highly prone to failure precisely at the level of unobservables. Where the prediction and control of observables are in question, the leading physical sciences are, after a certain point in early modern history, triumphant processions. Once phenomena of a certain kind are subjected to prediction or control, up to a certain level of accuracy and a certain degree of remoteness from everyday observations, they almost always remain predictable or controllable on the basis of similar empirical laws, in successive transformations of the science. Meanwhile, the accuracy and extensiveness of the successful prediction or control typically increase, and new kinds of observable phenomena are subdued. However, the succession of theories of the unobservable used in prediction and control is, not a triumphal procession, but a row of tombstones.

Just within the last three hundred years, the epitaphs speak of the demise of caloric, phlogiston and the ether. Even when it is not clear that a fundamental entity turned out not to exist, the reigning conception of its essential properties has always turned out to be vacuous, in the past. Thus, the casualties include gravity as Newtonian described it, Newtonian mass, space and time, atoms as Dalton conceived them, molecules in Maxwell's and Boltzmann's treatment, and electrons as Lorentz and Rutherford conceived them. The partial "successes" here—for example, the fact that belief in atoms is still reasonable though not belief in atomic properties essential for Dalton—seem the product of a self-serving tendency to retain the same term in successor theories, even when ancestor theories turned out to be fundamentally wrong. So, an anti-realist can plausibly claim, the failures are a better indication of our real grasp of what there is in the realm of unobservables.

The best account of the overall record seems to be: in the best-established sciences, the dominant theories of unobservables are, at any given time, usually good models for purposes of prediction or control; when they encounter widespread anomalies, scientists have been able to replace the models in crisis with different models, and these models have turned out to be effective for most of the old subject-matter and new material besides; similarly, if people immersed in an earlier model find its respective explanations satisfying, people immersed in the new ones will, too, for most of the old subject-matter and new material besides. This is, of course, an anti-realist account of the history of science. This conception of science as most unstable just where realists look for the basis of its triumphs was vividly stated and strikingly illustrated by Kuhn's first book, *The Copernican Revolution*, almost thirty years ago. He concludes:

> Only the list of explicable phenomena grows; there is no similar cumulative process for the explanations themselves. As science progresses, its concepts are repeatedly destroyed and replaced and today Newtonian concepts seem no exception. . . . Because they provide an economical summary of a vast quantity of data, Newtonian concepts are still in use. But increasingly, they are employed for their economy alone, just as the ancient two-sphere universe is employed by the modern navigator and surveyor. They are still a useful aid to memory, but they are ceasing to provide a trustworthy guide to the unknown.[10]

[10] *The Copernican Revolution* (New York, 1959), p. 265.

One of the main reasons why the debate over realism has stalled is that philosophers of science, realist and anti-realist, have no credible means of assessing the best realist response to this argument from failure. The best realist response is that, with a few exceptions, the consensus in the mature sciences has proved to be *approximately* correct in statements about what exists in the realm of unobservables. After all, we do not put gravitational attraction, Daltonian atoms, Newtonian mass, space and time, pre-quantum-theory molecules, or energy as described in classical physics into the same wastebasket as caloric and phlogiston. We are inclined to accept formulations of the difference along these lines: Caloric and phlogiston simply do not exist, but it is approximately, though not strictly and literally true that gravitational attraction (Daltonian atoms, etc.) exist.

The problem is that we lack a useful account of what it is to claim mere approximate truth for a theoretical statement. The demand for a more detailed account of approximate truth, here, is not just pedantry, or merely of interest for the theory of meaning, reference and truth. To determine whether belief in unobservables is rational, we need to determine whether abiding approximate truth is the kind of real success that would counterbalance the admitted failures. According to some anti-realists, the tendency to regard defeated theories as, nonetheless, approximately right simply reflects a preference for a certain style of history writing that makes progress salient, "Whiggish" history, as Rorty calls it.[11] To vary his analogy, the physicist who regards Galileo, Newton, Dalton and Maxwell as approximately right is thought to emphasize in retrospect the aspects of the old criteria that have not yet been disconfirmed, like the math teacher who establishes the basic competence of his students by retrospective revisions of grading, choosing a curve that guarantees that most were "A" or "B" students, year after year. In contrast, realists need to describe a way of assessing past theories as approximately right that makes the approximate rightness of old theories evidence that theorizing gives access to distinctive kinds of facts, concerning unobservables.

For present purposes the state of the art in semantics is disappointing. The working scientist's notion of approximate truth is useless, the notion suggested by positivism is both useless and unbelievable, and post-positivist theories of meaning are underdevel-

[11] See, for example, *Philosophy and the Mirror of Nature* (Princeton, 1980), pp. 287, 344.

oped just where help is needed. In scientific practice, the judgment that a theory is approximately true tends to mean that it usually yields observational findings with reasonable accuracy, but not always and precisely so. In this spirit, a physicist is apt to respond to philosophical inquiry—perhaps in an exasperated tone of voice—by saying that Newtonian mechanics is approximately right, though of course it does not work well near the speed of light or at atomic dimensions. But this approximate observational fit, admitted by all sides to the realism dispute, is clearly of no use to the realist seeking to assess qualitative and structural changes in the content of successive theories.

Among philosophical accounts of meaning, the ones characteristic of positivism suggest a rigid and universalized version of the working scientist's notion. Distinctively positivist proposals about the meaning of theoretical statements (for example, Carnap's in "Testability and Meaning") identified them with what would normally be taken to be the assertions of the test results that would confirm the statements. Approximate truth, here, would be approximate observational fit. But the semantics is too biased toward anti-realism to be used in the realist reply. All of science, now, turns out to be about observables. And the theory of meaning is wrong. It yields a hyperkinetic view of scientific meanings, in which theories change meaning whenever a basically new way of measuring a magnitude is accepted. Even more unbelievably, the major advances in science, far from showing that a former view of matter was wrong, will simply replace one subject matter with another. Bohr and Rutherford seemed to be disagreeing with Dalton when they claimed, "Atoms are structures with discrete parts." But their means of identifying atoms were so different that they would not be disagreeing, but changing the subject, on the positivist view of meaning.

The alternative, post-positivist accounts of scientific meaning emphasize the causal interactions between language users and their environments. They were developed by Kripke, Putnam and others largely in an effort to counter the view that meanings are in constant flux, from time to time, person to person, and culture to culture. Quite appropriately, those who developed the causal approach concentrated on terms of which it is not just approximately true that they refer to what exists, "water," "dreaming," and "Moses," for example. In slowing down the hyperkinetic view, they needed to rely on relatively uncontroversial examples. And it was hard enough to analyze clearcut truth and falsehood, without investigating the grey area of approximate truth. Thus, though a post-positivist theory of approximate truth must grow out of Putnam's and Kripke's writings, this work does not itself contain criteria for the assessments on which realists may rely.[12]

Given this state of the art in semantics, it is best to begin slowly, going by cases. There are a variety of distinctions that we are actually inclined to make among different kinds of literally false theories—putting philosophical preconceptions to one side. A useful account of approximate truth can be developed by finding the most attractive rationales for these distinctions. One moral that will emerge is that realists need to adopt a characteristic insight of anti-realists. For theoretical statements, including the positing of unobservable entities, claims of approximate truth are relative to quite specific goals and contexts. The goals are purposes that theories were actually meant to serve, quite specific purposes that are not accurately summarized as the goal of true description, even true description of causes. The historical contexts are two-fold: the bearing of the theories on the subsequent development of science and their impact on extra-scientific interests. Anti-realists have always insisted that theoretical success, by its very nature, is relative to culture, interests and history, both scientific and extrascientific. So far they are right. But the goals and contexts involved in what is claimed, in claims of approximate truth, do not guarantee actual success in achieving it, as the math teacher's goal and context guaranteed his "achievement." An approximate grasp of the nature of unobservables can still be a real achievement of many scientists.

My procedure will be to infer an account of when a strictly false theoretical statement is approximately true from relatively uncontroversial judgments of strict and literal truth, fundamental (not merely strict and literal) falsehood and approximate truth. Then I will apply the account that emerges to the controversial judgments of approximate truth that figure in the realist's ledger of theoretical success and failure.

The relatively uncontroversial judgments are:

1. What Aristotle referred to in using *hudor* (the word everyone translates as "water") does, strictly and literally, exist. His belief that there is hudor in the world was strictly and literally true.

[12] See, for example, Saul Kripke, "Naming and Necessity" in G. Harman and D. Davidson, eds., *The Semantics of Natural Language* (Dordrecht, 1972), and Putnam, "The Meaning of 'Meaning' " (1975) in *Mind, Language and Reality* (New York, 1979). The frustration with semantic hyperkinesis that influenced much of this work is especially prominent in such predecessors as Putnam's 1962 "Dreaming and 'Depth Grammar' " in ibid.

2. Caloric, phlogiston and demons simply do not exist. The respective existence claims are fundamentally false.

3. The theory of evolution in Darwin's *The Origin of the Species* is approximately true.

Though these ratings are standard, it turns out to be hard to construct justifications for them in light of certain facts pointing toward quite different ratings. Aristotle had certain deep-rooted, fundamental beliefs about the essential properties of hudor that are false and, indeed, attribute properties that nothing actually has. These beliefs are at least as far removed from reality as corresponding believers' commitments concerning the nature of caloric, phlogiston or demons. Darwin's theory is taken to be approximately true by biologists who take many fundamental aspects of the theory, extremely important to Darwin, to be utterly false. Nonetheless, a satisfying rationale for the usual ratings can be constructed. It includes a rationale for ratings of approximate truth. I will argue that by this standard, realists are right in their judgment that Newton's physics, including his claim that gravitational attraction exists, is approximately true. This will be my one explicit application of the account of approximate truth to a controversial rating, but its central and typical status is accepted by all sides, and extensions of the basic strategy elsewhere will be obvious.

As a relatively clear example of a theory referring to something real but attributing essential properties to it that it lacks, consider an important part of Aristotle's chemistry. Aristotle has definite, deeply held views about the essential properties of what he calls "hudor." It is one of the four sublunary elements, in particular, the cold-moist one. And its distinctive function in physical changes is to cool. If told that hudor was a combination of two substances that are gases, when uncombined (hence forms of air, the hot-moist element), he would not simply disagree, but take the statement to violate essential properties of hudor. Using his basic principles of chemical reasoning, Aristotle shows that steam cannot be a form of hudor.[13] Nonetheless, Aristotle was using "hudor" to refer to something that does exist, namely, water, which is HOH.

The demise of what eighteenth-century physicists meant by "caloric" is a clear contrast to the survival of what Aristotle meant by "hudor." On the face of it, the overthrow of the caloric theory is like the overthrow of Aristotelian chemistry. Caloric was supposed to be a massless fluid, with a constant total magnitude, whose changes of

[13] See *De Generatione et Corruptione*, II, 2–4 and *De Caelo*, 305 b 9–15.

distribution constituted heat phenomena. Beginning with Rumford's work, a series of arguments and findings showed that caloric does not exist. Rumford argued that nothing has the alleged essential properties of caloric, since more heat can be generated to an indefinite extent by mere friction. In light of the work of Rumford and his successors, we do not say, "Caloric exists, only it is molecular kinetic energy." We say, "Caloric does not exist." With a similar lack of charity, we do not say, "Phlogiston exists, only it turned out to be oxygen," or "Demons exist, only they are psychotic personality disorders." Why not, when we are so charitable to Aristotle and hudor?

The most powerful post-positivist accounts of meaning were developed by Kripke, Putnam and others, largely to show how terms could preserve their reference in the face of massive shifts in beliefs about the essential properties of what they refer to. It is important, in these theories of meaning, that Aristotle was actually guided by the presence of batches of HOH in his usage of "hudor." In that usage, he was an HOH detector, though an imperfect one, and the evolution of language, down to present applications of "water" has tended to pass along that capacity. Not surprisingly, this relatively objective feature of reference, which was developed to account for survivals of reference, does not help us to understand the present cases of demise. Users of "caloric," "phlogiston" and (in many cultures) "demons" are detectors of heat, oxygen and psychosis. They are imperfect, making certain systematic mistakes. But so was Aristotle, when he spoke of water.

In Putnam's semantics, part of the meaning of a term is its "stereotype," the circumstances for applying the term that someone must recognize in order to grasp its meaning.[14] It might be granted as one distinction between "hudor" and "caloric," that the stereotype of "hudor" is the same as that for "water," and that the same cannot be said for the stereotype of "caloric" as compared with any term in twentieth-century physics. But surely an account of scientific meanings should provide a rationale for descriptions of the stereotype of "caloric," not just introduce such descriptions as premises. In his crucial memoir, Rumford said,

> And in reasoning on this subject, we must not forget to consider that the most remarkable circumstance, that the source of the Heat generated by friction, in these Experiments, appeared evidently to be *inexhaustible*.

[14] See "The Meaning of 'Meaning,' " pp. 247–52.

It is hardly necessary to add, that anything which any *insulated* body, or system of bodies, can continue to furnish *without limitation*, cannot possibly be a *material substance*[15]

Here, Rumford takes conservation to be part of the stereotype of "caloric" (and of "material substance"). Rumford is offering an estimate of a distance beyond which "caloric" cannot be stretched. "Caloric is a material substance that can be inexhaustibly generated" is absurd. It is doubtful that Rumford took this as an obviously valid summary of every contemporary's actual usage. Caloric theorists, including physicists as distinguished as Laplace and Poisson, were notoriously daring and unpredictable in their ad hoc proposals about the workings of the substance. In any case, Rumford obviously thinks his argument to be especially important because the abandonment of conservation restrictions would be unreasonable, even if actually proposed by a caloric theorist. We need to understand why.

"Caloric" was introduced for an explanatory purpose, to account for heat phenomena in terms of the normal dynamics of fluids. Rumford showed that this purpose could not be served. In light of his work, and the work of his successors, the concept of caloric lost its point. That is why it is absurd to say, "Caloric exists, but mere friction creates more and more of it," or "Caloric exists, and is mean kinetic energy." Similarly, phlogiston was postulated to maintain a relatively neat correlation between the material composition of objects and their current observable properties. And the explanatory point of talk of demons is to explain bizarre behavior as due to malevolent forces from outside of the person who acts so strangely. That is why it is absurd to say, "Phlogiston exists, and is oxygen" or "Demons exist, and are personality disorders." On the other hand, "hudor" was not introduced to serve an explanatory purpose, or, at any rate, no technical one that was undermined by Lavoisier and Dalton.

In general, scientific concepts forever bear the imprint of the basic explanatory purposes for which they were introduced. When they lose their point, they lose their extension.

If it were clear that "gravitational attraction" and other fundamental terms of relatively good but strictly false scientific theories had not lost their point, i.e., that the basic explanatory goal for

[15] Benjamin Thompson, Count Rumford, "An Experimental Inquiry Concerning the Source of the Heat which is Excited by Friction" in *Count Rumford on the Nature of Heat*, ed. S. C. Brown (Oxford, 1967), p. 70.

which they were introduced could be fulfilled, the way would now be open for a reconciliation between realism and the ledger of scientific success. It would be true that gravitational attraction exists, just as much as hudor does. We could say that Newton spoke the truth in saying that universal gravitational attraction exists, though he was wrong to identify it as proportional to a product of intrinsic masses, independent of velocity, over the square of absolute distance. But the real situation of entities in once-confirmed but false theories is more complex, here and in most other cases. One basic explanatory purpose of Newton's physics is to explain motion as due solely to the activity of matter, without giving space or time a fundamental causal role, like the causal power of the center of the universe in Aristotelian physics. The distance between bits of matter affects the strength of the action of the one on the other. But this is the only role of mere space. In short, the vindication of the "corpuscular philosophy" is one of Newton's basic goals, a main motivation for introducing such entities as the force of gravitational attraction. This goal turned out to be unfulfillable. By the end of the nineteenth century, the goal was already suspect, since Maxwell's equations, if fundamental, require a fundamental force depending not just on distance, but on velocity and past trajectory. And the arguments for special relativity showed that Maxwell's equations do describe a fundamental process, with no further mechanical analysis. In special relativity, the main causal agency in matter, for Newton, is to some extent, a passive reflection of mere change in location: mass increases with velocity, according to relativistic mechanics. What is even more striking, in general relativity there is no force exerted by mass; instead, the local metric of a spatio-temporal region governs motion, there. It turns out to be false that matter, as against space, is the source of activity. Since a main explanatory purpose of introducing universal gravitational attraction cannot be served, Newton's belief in this force was a false one. This negative judgment is suggested by the prior account of our judgments of hudor and caloric, and standard presentations of relativity theory concur.

Still, Newton's belief in gravitational attraction might be approximately right, and gravitational theory might be approximately true. In his use of "gravity," Newton was an (imperfect) detector of space-time metrics, as Einstein was at pains to show,[16] and his failure

[16] See Einstein, "The Foundations of the General Theory of Relativity" (1916) in

is less straightforward, his goals more complex than caloric theorists'. To see whether approximate truth is indeed the right judgment, it will be helpful to look first at a clearer rating of a theory with complex goals and mitigated failures, the judgment that Darwin's theory is approximately true.

We are taught that the theory of how species evolve in Darwin's *The Origin of Species* as approximately right. This is the typical verdict of modern biologists (when they assess the actual content of the book, as against certain twentieth-century programs often labelled "neo-Darwinist"). We know of this verdict before we read *The Origin*. So we are struck, or should be, by the fact that Darwin insists on the following major points, which are false or controversial according to biologists who take the book to be approximately right.

1. Lamarckian inheritance of acquired characteristics frequently occurs, even though it is not the main factor in the rise of new species. Thus, Darwin thinks it "probable" that the drooping ears of many domestic animals are "due to the disuse of the muscles of the ear, from the animals not being much alarmed by danger."[17]

2. In the changes that create new species, the new traits are always advantageous to the individual.

3. In the successive great epochs of the flora and fauna of the earth, the basic trend is one of progress, the triumph of new forms because they are superior in competition with old ones.

4. Domestic breeding with artificial selection, the model for the theory of natural selection and the source of its very name, employs the same processes of variation as the formation of new species in nature.

An accurate summary of *The Origin* could largely consist of these four statements. Indeed, 2–4 pervade Darwin's own "Recapitulation and Conclusion." Yet many modern biologists believe all of the following contrary statements.

1'. Lamarckian inheritance never occurs.

2'. The changes that create new species are often due to the triumph of non-advantageous mutations in isolated populations as a result of random "genetic drift."

3'. The fauna and flora of one great geological epoch are not typically superior to those of the preceding one. The old forms often were destroyed in an unusual, relatively brief episode. The basic

Einstein, Lorentz, Weyl, Minkowski, *The Principle of Relativity*, ed. A. Sommerfeld (New York, 1952), pp. 157–60.

[17] *The Origin of Species*, ed. J. W. Burrow (Baltimore, 1968), p. 74.

characteristics distinguishing the successor forms are largely due to chance.

4'. Domestic breeding is, to a significant extent, a process of segregating out and grouping factors already present in the gene pool of the species. By contrast, actual mutations dominate the formation of new species in nature.

These four ideas are a good measure of how far Darwin is from presenting a latter-day consensus. For want of a better term, I will call them the "anti-adaptationist" perspective, stretching a common label for an important school of thought in contemporary biology. (Of course, 1' is more or less universal among biologists.) For want of a handier label, I will call Darwin's allegiance to principles 1–4 the adaptationist perspective. In this part of his explanatory project, Darwin tries to show how organic evolution is a process of improved adaptation, extending through the history of organic life.

Why do reflective, historically informed anti-adaptationists take *The Origin* to be approximately correct? Here, there is no temptation to answer, "Because the theory generally yields true predictions." The theory yields no predictions. Rather, in their assessment, biologists give much weight to the evolutionist strategy of Darwin's book, which can be summed up in the following principles.

A. Except at the very lowest level of complexity, the members of a species are always descendents of members of another species.

B. The variations that triumph and accumulate in the rise of a new species are of the same kind as departures from average type that occur at present within a given species.

C. No individual causal link in a process of species formation involves a purpose of creating an organism adapted to the environment, or anything like such a purpose. No purposes are links in the causal chain except such familiar goals as surviving, mating, and propagating and preserving offspring.

D. The basic source of new traits is variation and change in reproductive material, through processes with no inherent tendency to create a well-adapted organism.

The contrast is to some extent with Lamarckian evolution, which denies D, and is in tension with B and C. But, above all, the contrast is with the consistent object of confirmation-by-comparison in Darwin's book, the theory that substantially novel species arise, without ancestors, as a result of a creative force inherently tending to produce organisms adapted to their original environment. This had been the dominant view of most of the best and most qualified investigators before the 1850s, including the young Darwin himself.[18] The many anti-creationists before Darwin had mostly been naifs, unaware of the scientific difficulties of their position. While one of Darwin's goals was to vindicate adaptationism, another was to vindicate evolutionism, in the form of principles A–D. The evolutionist goal is to show how new species result from individuals' purposeless deviation from type. And the achievement of this goal is not now questioned by informed and reasonable investigators.

Evidently, the consensus that *The Origin* is approximately right requires a ranking of Darwin's achievement in principles A–D as more important than his arguable failure, in principles 1–4. Why rank success and failure in this way? Apart from the actual role of Darwin and like-minded contemporaries in the history of science and the actual bearing of scientific disputes on extra-scientific interests, *there would be no rationale* for this verdict. It depends on the fact that the contest between evolutionism and creationism is more important for us humans than that between adaptationism and anti-adaptationism, even supposing that present-day anti-adaptationists will win. Darwin's advocacy of principles A–D was in fact preceded by a creationist consensus, and post-Darwinian progress, even if it will ultimately vindicate anti-adaptationism, has depended on the triumph of those principles. Moreover, the victory of Darwin's evolutionism fundamentally changed people's deepest beliefs and attitudes about God and nature. Nothing of that magnitude hinges on the contest between adaptationist and anti-adaptationist biology.

Suppose, by way of contrast, that there is a planet of alpha-Centauri on which the intelligent inhabitants were always atheist, materialist Lamarckian evolutionists, until someone wrote a book advancing all the Darwinian principles described above. Later, biology moved in parallel with ours. For these scientists, it might be reasonable to question whether the Centuroid Darwin was approximately right. Anti-adaptationists might believe, and reasonably so, that Darwin was brilliant but fundamentally wrong, through a failure to make a clean break with the even more extreme adaptationism of the Centuroid Lamarck. The only relevant difference is that our planet's history of science, culture and sentiment is not in fact the same.

[18] See *The Autobiography of Charles Darwin*, ed. Francis Darwin (New York, 1958), pp. 175, 178, and esp. p. 45: "It has sometimes been said that the success of the *Origin* proved 'that the subject was in the air.' . . . I do not think that this is strictly true, for I occasionally sounded not a few naturalists, and never happened to come across a single one who seemed to doubt about the permanence of species."

Outside of the philosophy of science, it seems truistic that approximate truth is a matter of quite specific contrasts, ranked in importance according to definite purposes. This is so even when numbers are in question. It is obviously absurd to say, "Yes, it is approximately five o'clock, though I don't know whether you asked in order to catch a train, to record an astronomical observation, or to tell whether this is a time of day at which you're usually hungry."

The judgment that a false scientific theory is approximately true is the judgment that certain aspects of the theory are true, and that its superiority in these respects to definite alternatives is more important than the failures of other aspects, defeated by other alternatives. The rating of the success as more important than the failure is valid if it reflects the actual role of the theory's original triumph in the development of scientific theories and its impact on extra-scientific interests.

This conception of the approximate truth of theories also applies to the approximate truth of those central statements that assert the existence of entities posited in a theory. The case of gravitational attraction illustrates how such verdicts affect the ledger of success, in the dispute over realism.

As noted before, Newton posited a new kind of entity, the universal force of mutual attraction of matter to matter, as part of an explanatory strategy of attributing motions solely to causal powers of bits of matter. The relevant complexity in deciding whether the gravitational hypothesis is approximately true is that the corpuscular philosophy was ambiguous in a way of which its proponents were not fully aware.

Broadly and roughly speaking, Newton's explanatory goal is to explain trajectories by attributing them to the powers of matter interacting with matter. But this is too broad and too rough for the assessment of his success. For one thing, it is not clear what can be counted as matter. In the *Principia*, Newton takes matter to be "hard," to take up space, to resist changes in its state of motion in the ways described by the first two laws of motion, and to be subject to gravitational attraction. But all of these are said to be properties we learn "by our senses" to be features of matter.[19] Newton is receptive to modifications and extensions of these criteria. And he had better be, since he is well aware that non-gravitational forces exist, magnetism for example, and that he has no well-supported notion of

[19] See *Principia*, pp. 399f.

how they operate.[20] In any case, a definition of the Newtonian out-look restricting material agency to *Principia*-type matter, "impenetrable" or "ponderable," would have the absurd consequence that the vindicators of Newtonian physics, in everyone's estimation, were actually overthrowing it. Above all, Laplace, the great consolidator of the Newtonian revolution, would be accorded this counter-revolutionary status. For Laplace believed in caloric, which was not hard and, in important versions of the theory, was not ponderable. The most useful construal of "matter," faithful to Newton's own open-mindedness and to the vicissitudes of recognizably Newtonian physics, would employ the notion of a core concept, introduced in Chapter Two, in connection with causation. Matter is whatever is subject to a material process. At the core of the notion of a material process are such elementary varieties as pushing, pulling, hitting, and squeezing. The core is expanded as required to explain regularities which, all agree, stand in need of explanation.

Using this broad conception of matter, we can define two aspects of Newton's explanatory project, to both of which creative scientists subscribed for over two centuries. On the one hand, Newton has a deep commitment to explain trajectories by tracing them to forces of attraction or repulsion of matter (in the broad sense), forces dependent only on the internal properties of the interacting bits of matter and the distances between them. In short, the Newtonian project is, in part, mechanistic.[21]

Yet there is another way of describing Newton's break with the Aristotelian outlook. There must be such a less restrictive alternative, when one reflects on the history of science. For even in Newton's time, Huyghens and others thought that mechanistic explanations were the wrong approach to light trajectories. In the nineteenth century, being a mechanist about optics, magnetism and electricity was seen as a controversial and risky enterprise even by the great physicists who pursued it. Even philosophers who think that Newton turned out to be utterly wrong (except as an approximate predicter) in the twentieth century, do not think that this judgment was a live option for good physicists circa 1830.

The other aspect of Newton's project that is worth singling out is its materialist aspect. Trajectories are to be explained by appealing to the powers of matter and the laws governing material influences. This can be done by someone who does not think that all such pow-

[20] See ibid., pp. 414, 547.

[21] In the last paragraph of the *Principia*, Newton makes it clear that he has such a very general strategy in mind, and also that he takes it to be especially speculative, in the absence of "a sufficiency of experiments" (p. 547).

ers and processes work through mechanistic attraction and repulsion. What the materialist project does exclude, above all, is an outlook in which a location has causal power, with no further explanation of that power in terms of the influence of matter on matter. If we are interested in Newton as the consolidator of the Galilean revolution, this is the aspect to emphasize. What Newton and Galileo and Descartes (and Huyghens and Laplace) all find uniquely repellant is any outlook in which the center of the universe or the center of an epicycle is said to draw things to it solely because of the place it is. As Newton puts it, "That forces should be directed to no body on which they physically depend, but to innumerable imaginary points . . . , is an hypothesis too incongruous."[22]

The mechanistic bias of Newtonian physics is, to some extent, undermined by relativity theory. But, quite as much as in the *Principia*, trajectories, including celestial ones, are caused solely by material agencies, obeying universal laws. Einstein makes this point emphatically in his Foreword to the *Dialogue Concerning the Two Chief World Systems*, where he treats Galileo as precursor to Newton:

> Let me interpolate here that a close analogy exists between Galileo's rejection of the hypothesis of a center of the universe for the explanation of the fall of heavy bodies, and the rejection of the hypothesis of an inertial system for the explanation of the inertial behavior of matter. (The latter is the basis of the theory of general relativity.) Common to both hypotheses is the introduction of a conceptual object with the following properties:
>
> (1). It is not assumed to be real, like ponderable matter (or a "field").
>
> (2). It determines the behavior of real objects, but it is in no way affected by them.
>
> The introduction of such conceptual elements, though not exactly inadmissible from a purely logical point of view, is repugnant to the scientific instinct.[23]

---

[22] "The System of the World" in ibid., p. 553. That space is "isotropic" is often said to be the revolutionary idea that Galileo and Newton exploited. But the central ambiguity re-emerges when one asks what this isotropy amounts to. If only the internal properties of masses are supposed to have an ultimate causal role, then only Euler, Hertz and a few others advanced an isotropic physics. If only distances count in addition, as regulating the strength of influence of the internal properties of particles, then isotropy was continually in controversy until it was defeated in the early twentieth century. As a characteristic of science after Newton and Galileo, isotropy would have to be materialism, in the sense just defined.

[23] *Dialogue Concerning the Two Chief World Systems*, tr. S. Drake (Berkeley, 1967), p. xii.

The preservation of the materialist part of Newton's explanatory project, the fact that Newtonian judgments of gravitational attraction are (fairly) reliable indicators of the local space-time metric and the approximate agreement in observational consequences of the new theory and the old are the basic support for a verdict of approximate truth.

Indeed, to say that relativity theory preserves the materialist part of Newton's project is to say much too little. This goal is fulfilled more strictly and completely in relativity theory than in the *Principia*, and this was a major motivation for the modern theory, itself.

The trick, as usual, is not to interpret findings of relativity theory in terms of pre-relativistic notions. In special relativity, the mass of a given object depends on its instantaneous velocity, and this may make it seem that the basic causal powers of matter are affected by something immaterial. But in relativity theory, all the relevant properties of space and time reflect the workings of a material process, field propagation. In all his writings, including the fundamental essays, Einstein presents special relativity as the result of two principles, the Galilean principle that "the laws by which the states of physical systems alter are independent of the alternative, to which of two systems of coordinates, in uniform motion . . . relatively to each other, these alterations of state are referred"[24] and the electrodynamic principle that electromagnetic change "is always propagated in empty space with a definite velocity . . . which is independent of the state of motion of the emitting body."[25] Thus, Minkowski can speak of relativity theory as "an electromagnetic image of the world."[26] Space-time is what transmits waves according to Maxwell's equations. While mass is no longer independent of velocity, space and time are now material, i.e., essentially features of the process of electromagnetic propagation. Indeed, a spatio-temporal entity, energy, rather than mass, is the fundamental material magnitude. This and other changes permit Einstein to go even farther from Aristotle than Newton could, in fulfillment of Newton's materialist goal. For Newton, the strength of gravity, and, presumably, other forces as well, depends on distance, which is a property of immaterial space. For Einstein, the relativistic magnitudes corresponding to distance are as material as any properties, and, in any case, action at

[24] "Does the Inertia of a Body Depend upon Its Energy-Content?" (1905) in *The Principle of Relativity*, p. 69.

[25] "On the Electrodynamics of Moving Bodies" (1905) in *The Principle of Relativity*, p. 38.

[26] "Space and Time" (1908) in *The Principle of Relativity*, p. 91.

a distance no longer exists. The basic laws are "structure laws. They connect events that happen now and here with events which will happen a little later in the immediate vicinity."[27]

Similarly, when one hears that spatio-temporal metrics replace gravity, in general relativity, this sounds like a wholesale defeat of the corpuscular outlook. Indeed, that this is a kind of return to Aristotle has been a truism of anti-realist history of science.[28] But in fact, general relativity was an important vindication of the materialist side of Newton, and an even more radical rejection of what Newton broke with in Aristotelian physics. In the *Principia*, the three laws of motion do not hold in all coordinate systems, as Newton is well aware. Set up a coordinate system fixed to a working carousel and, with respect to it, ball bearings left to themselves will neither remain at rest nor move in straight lines. Usually, Newton copes with this problem by proposing to take the "fixed stars" as adequate reference points for all actual scientific purposes. But eventually, they became inadequate for the purposes of many Newtonian astronomers. And in any case, this practical advice does not provide the literal meaning of the laws of motion. Literally, they are true relative to absolute space (or, in alternative formulations of Newton's basic ideas, relative to quite special, "inertial" coordinate systems). So the most basic principles of Newtonian mechanics have an Aristotelian taint. Space, conceived of as something unaffected by material processes, plays a crucial role in governing material motions. In a dramatic illustration of the causal powers of Newtonian space, Mach asked physicists to imagine a two-body system consisting of equal masses, each describing the same orbit, relative to the other. In Newtonian physics, one body would be a sphere, one an ellipsoid if the former is at rest in absolute space. Absolute space flattens spheres. In his first full-fledged account of general relativity, Einstein takes this thought-experiment to illustrate the fundamental defect that his theory removes.[29]

General relativity pushes physics even further in the materialist, anti-Aristotelian direction than special relativity. Its motivating principle, as Einstein emphasizes, is that, *"The laws of physics must be of such a nature that they apply to systems of reference in any kind of motion"*—even claiming equal validity in systems accelerating with re-

---

[27] Einstein and Infeld, *The Evolution of Physics* (New York, 1942), p. 251 (where the immediate allusion is to Maxwellian field theory, but the characterization is extended to general relativity a few sentences later).

[28] See, for example, Kuhn in *The Copernican Revolution*, p. 99.

[29] "The Foundation of the General Theory of Relativity," pp. 112f.

spect to one another. The alternative is to give causal power to "the privileged space [i.e., the absolutely non-accelerating coordinate systems] of Galileo." And this is objectionable because such a space "is a merely *factitious* cause," not a material one.[30] In the development of the new theory, variations in the local space-time metric do play a role analogous to the force of gravity. But these variations are governed by the distribution and motion of matter.

Was Newton's usage of "gravitational attraction," like Aristotle's usage of "hudor," reference to something that exists, within a false theory? Now we are in a position to resolve this question on the basis of general principles of reference, truth, and approximate truth. In his employment of "gravitational attraction," Newton is, in many respects, similar to Aristotle. Newton is an (imperfect) space-time metric detector, as Aristotle is an (imperfect) HOH detector. Moreover, the reliability has important connections with the detector's beliefs, as we should certainly require for continuity of reference. Some properties by which Newton recognizes gravitational attraction are, roughly speaking, properties of the space-time metrics to which he is responding. And similarly for Aristotle's usage of "hudor" and HOH. The major difference is that subsequent findings have partly undermined the explanatory goal with which "gravitational attraction" was introduced, so that the concept has lost its point, in part (the mechanistic part). To this extent, "gravitational attraction" is like "caloric," rather than "hudor." So we shouldn't say—as we do not—that gravitational attraction exists and is the local space-time metric.

Nonetheless, it is approximately true that gravitational attraction exists, when this theoretical statement is judged by the standards that were latent in the verdict on Darwin's theory. The verdict on Newton requires weighing the mechanistic aspect of his project against the materialist one. There is, if anything, even less doubt of the just verdict, here. In the development of science, it was the denial that any individual location or nonmaterial agency ultimately governs the motions of matter that provided the basis for all subsequent progress. By contrast, the bias toward Newtonian forces of attraction and repulsion as the ultimate causal agents was always qualified and controversial. Outside of science, it was the materialist aspect of the rejection of Aristotle that produced the enormous reversals of perspective and sentiment associated with such phrases as "the Copernican Revolution."

[30] See ibid., p. 113; Einstein's emphases.

It is a real achievement of past science that the existence of gravitational attraction is an approximate truth. This is not just an artifact of a "Whiggish" way of writing the history of science. The Whig historians wrote the political history of England in a way that guaranteed that major episodes would be triumphs of forces striving for a parliamentary constitutional monarchy. They were committed in advance to dismissing setbacks as minor when these defeats went against the alleged trend and to interpreting successes as progressive in intent; in these commitments, they were oblivious to actual historical effects and intentions. In an especially silly example, the action of backward-looking barons, in extracting the Magna Carta from King John to protect traditional feudal privileges, was interpreted as a triumph of early enlightened partisans of the Whigs' favored Lockean principles. In contrast, the routine ratings of the approximate truth of scientific achievements seem to be decidedly non-Whiggish, respectful of the purposes, effects and extra-scientific contexts of the actual historical activities. Success is not guaranteed by this way of rating it. After all, the positing of caloric, phlogiston, or demons is rated a failure in this scheme, a fundamental falsehood rather than an approximate truth.

Admittedly, the above assessment of gravitational attraction depends on stretching the concept of matter to cover cases that Newton would not have had in mind. But the extensions were well-motivated, indeed perfectly natural, for the working scientists who were part of these developments. These extensions are not just devices of "Whiggish" philosophers interpreting the history of science. For Huyghens and Fresnel, it was natural to take waves that lacked corpuscular parts to be material, nonetheless. For Einstein and his successors, it is natural to deny that inertial coordinate systems and absolute space function as material causes.

At any rate, among important false theoretical statements whose approximate truth realists defend, the positing of universal gravitational attraction is the hardest to defend. By the standards that have emerged, it is much more obvious that Dalton's atomic theory, the molecular-kinetic theory of Maxwell, Clausius and Boltzmann, and Leeuwenhoek's reports on microbes are approximately true. Thus, Maxwell's main goal is to show "that a very considerable part of the energy of a hot body is in the form of motion. . . . The motion we call heat [is] . . . a motion of parts too small to be observed separately."[31] Quite explicitly, this goal is the main point of positing mol-

---

[31] Maxwell, *Theory of Heat* (London, 1904), p. 311. Maxwell's cagey "a very consid-

ecules. A few lines later, he introduces the term as follows: "A molecule may therefore be defined as a small mass of matter the parts of which do not part company during the excursions which the molecule makes when the body to which it belongs is hot."[32] Clearly, his main goal in positing molecules has not been undermined in subsequent science. Admittedly, he has the further goal, which has been undermined, of showing that all forms of energy are kinetic energy, governed by classical mechanics. But he treats this as a separate goal, and, quite prophetically, singles out its vulnerable point. "The internal motion of a single molecule is of a very different kind."[33] Boltzmann is even more emphatic. "[W]e can hardly doubt that in gases certain entities, the number and size of which can roughly be determined, fly about pell-mell. Can it be seriously expected that they will behave exactly as aggregates of Newtonian centres of force, or as the rigid bodies of our mechanics?"[34] Though Maxwell is writing in 1871, Boltzmann in 1895, it is hard to imagine a modern theorist describing the most vulnerable points in the classical theory of molecules more accurately, in light of the quantum-mechanical revolution.

Suppose that the ledger of success and failures is recorded by the techniques I have described, and that it includes the following entries. Dalton, in saying that atoms exist, Maxwell and Boltzmann, in saying that molecules exist, and Newton, in saying that gravitational attraction and mass exist, were at least approximately right, in the statements they made. Or rather (to avoid begging the question of realism), they were approximately right, if their claims are assessed from the perspective of present-day physical theory. Would the total ledger be the basis for a justification of scientific realism? Very likely, not. After all, every verdict of "approximate validity from the modern perspective" is associated with verdicts of important partial failure. And the ledger also includes the demise of caloric, phlogiston, the ether, chemical affinity and other alleged entities of the past. Surely, we lack a standard of tolerable coincidence so well-calibrated that it tells us that this amount of success would be an intolerable coincidence, unless it is explained as due to the existence of

---

erable part" reflects his awareness that he has only plausible speculations to offer about radiant heat and the internal motions of molecules. See pp. 336–38.

[32] Ibid., p. 312.

[33] Ibid., p. 336.

[34] From a letter which Boltzmann wrote, in English, to *Nature*, in 1905; see the Translator's Introduction to Boltzmann, *Lectures on Gas Theory* (Berkeley, 1964), p. 16.

many kinds of unobservables like those described in theoretical science. The ledger is not a basis for a realist inference to the best explanation, and it does not play that role for Boyd. He is arguing from an alleged contribution of theory-based methods to predictive and instrumental success, not from a tendency of earlier theories to be included in later ones. The above account of approximate truth is only a way of neutralizing a single, important anti-realist argument. If the ledger were the record of consistent failure that Kuhn describes, the reasonable inference would be that theorizing is not a reliable means of discerning features of the unobservable. The actual ledger seems to be between the extremes of continual triumph and wholesale failure. Realists and anti-realists will have to look elsewhere to make their cases.

Using the notion of approximate truth, the option of realism is preserved. But, as usual, an important lesson for realists remains. Belief that scientific theorizing has led to approximate knowledge of unobservable underlying mechanisms is only reasonable if a copy theory of scientific knowledge and truth is abandoned. For what saves fundamental theoretical entities from the fate of caloric and phlogiston is a method of assessing approximate truth in which explanatory goals, historical consequences and extra-scientific interests play a basic and independent role. The rationales for the crucial verdicts must rate goals by their historical importance. Neither the goals nor the standards by which the goals are rated can be summarized as "the true description of the causes of such-and-such phenomena," in an effective rationale for claims of approximate truth. The right model for an approximately true description of unobservable causes is not a fairly congruent copy. A better model would be good-enough advice, that is, advice good enough for the needs and future development of the advisee. There is no valid copy theory of approximate truth, if scientific realism is correct.

## EMPIRICAL EQUIVALENCE

Throughout the long history of the realism debate, anti-realists have frequently appealed to considerations of empirical equivalence. In such arguments, they claim that for every theory T, whatever the evidence for it might be, there is some rival theory T′, radically different in what it says about unobservables, which is just as well-confirmed in light of the evidence. So a belief in the approximate truth of T, where it speaks of unobservables, is never dictated by reason and evidence.[35]

Arguments from equivalence depend on two claims. One is the claim of general empirical equivalence, that for any T at any time there is a T', just as well confirmed by the current data. The other is an anti-dogmatic premise, that in a situation in which the data confirm T' as strongly as T, one should not take belief in T to be the only reasonable alternative for a fully informed person. In the current realist literature, Boyd's response to this argument is the most powerful and influential. In essence, his objection is that the anti-dogmatic premise only holds in a limited sense, in which the premise of equivalence is invalid. Questions of how well-confirmed a hypothesis is are properly resolved by applying background theories in assessments of plausibility. There is nothing dogmatic, here, in applying a background theory that has actually been used in experimental design (say, the standard catalogue of forces, in Reichenbach's example), in preference to an alternative that only might have been used, even one that makes just the same observations just as likely (the non-standard catalogue, including the uniform distorting force). But once such conservatism is allowed to be non-dogmatic, then the process of confirmation governed by it will not sustain the premise of equivalence. Even after a Reichenbach presents T' and its associated framework, T may be the only reasonable alternative for a fully informed person because the fact that T was actually, successfully used is relevant information. Certain basic theoretical claims, serving as standard background assumptions, are better-confirmed than alleged "equivalents" just because of their actual entrenchment as part of successful scientific practice, and their connections with data via other, actually entrenched background principles. Given this standard repertoire of background principles, one can discriminate between further theories and their rivals, contrary to the premise of equivalence.[36]

---

[35] Of course, in the sense described in the last chapter, anti-realism as such is the claim that evidence never justifies a statement about unobservables in a way that makes disbelief unreasonable. Here, I mean to single out certain arguments that, more specifically, proceed by showing that evidence could not single out a theory as best because of the very nature of confirmation or the very content of the theory itself. By contrast, anti-realist arguments from past failure depend on the actual history of science, while denials of the need to explain crucial tendencies are specially directed at the nature of explanation and its role in realism. Still, there is no need to insist that all these paths to anti-realism are independent. All that matters is that the anti-realist literature be carved up in a convenient way, without major omission.

[36] See Boyd, "Realism, Underdetermination, and a Causal Theory of Evidence," pp. 3f., 7–12.

I have already argued that Boyd's conservatism really would be dogmatic. If those arguments are right, then realists need to attack the claim of general equivalence more directly. Certainly, this claim is in need of support. Why should we suppose that our actual current evidence (to take one set of data that is highly important to us) always supports a rival to a standard theory that is so different from it that the latter cannot be approximately true if the former is true? This sounds like an unlikely fate for theorizing, when this practice has been advanced for so long by so many intelligent men and women. Equivalence arguments are distinguished, above all, by the ways in which they answer this challenge. And there has been a dramatic shift in the kind of answer typically given—dramatic in itself, that is, but usually unannounced.

When many philosophers of science were committed to deductivism, this general theory of confirmation supported the general equivalence claim. On any attractive account of the kind of entailment of data that confirms, there was a means of constructing a rival, T′, that was confirmed just as well. Usually, the best phenomenological rival could play that role, since its laws seemed to have all the theory's observed "test implications" among their confirming instances. Of course, there were deductivists who did not want to become anti-realist, because of the quality of their respect for science and for normal scientific discourse. But it was always a struggle to resist anti-realist conclusions. Many of Hempel's essays of the 1950s, for example, "The Theoretician's Dilemma," are records of this struggle.[37]

If previous arguments are right, deductivism is a defective basis for assessing equivalence claims or any claims about science. And these days, leading anti-realists do not commit themselves to deductivism. The old outlook does survive in certain accounts of theory acceptance, as distinct from belief. Van Fraassen and Putnam sometimes assume that the general and formal virtues on which the deductivists eventually relied, including, for example, simplicity, govern theory choice. They then point out that crucial virtues here, such as simplicity, are not, even on the face of it, reliable indicators of truth. But if previous chapters were basically right, deductivism never yielded an adequate rationale for belief *or* acceptance.

More and more, a different kind of argument for equivalence, always important for anti-realists, has become dominant. Specific fundamental theories are supposed themselves to have the conse-

[37] See "The Theoretician's Dilemma" (1958) in his *Aspects of Scientific Explanation* (New York, 1965).

quence that they cannot be distinguished from a certain rival or rivals on any empirical grounds. An argument based on Reichenbach's construct is sometimes employed and is usually in the background. The pair of alleged equivalents consists of the current catalogue of forces joined to the best current physical geometry, on the one hand, and the catalogue expanded to include a universal deforming force with a suitable physical geometry joined to it, on the other. The equivalence arises from specific features of current force theory and physical geometry. Our understanding of how to determine whether lines are straight rests such determinations on hypotheses about forces. Our understanding of how to determine what forces there are rests such determinations on assumptions that certain lines are straight. Once the details of this circularity are understood, current physical theory seems to require that the combination of non-standard force theory and the geometry to which it leads be as well-confirmed as the combination of standard force theory and its geometry.[38]

Similarly, van Fraassen has emphasized an infinite equivalence suggested by Newton's *Principia*. Though it makes no difference for observations what the constant velocity of the center of gravity of the universe, or any closed system of masses, is, Newton takes such an assignment of velocity to be meaningful, and asserts the actual absolute velocity of the center of gravity of the universe to be 0. His theory is, by his own account, empirically equivalent to each of the infinite rivals in which another constant velocity is assigned.[39] Responding to the temptation to suppose that subsequent discoveries might resolve the ambiguities, van Fraassen borrows an elegant argument of Poincaré's, which suggests that the conjunction of one "resolving" hypothesis with the mechanics it "vindicates" will be em-

[38] This is a common reading of Reichenbach, *The Philosophy of Space and Time* (1927; New York, 1957), pp. 10–37. Whether it is a correct reading of Reichenbach is doubtful, for reasons that I will discuss. But on its own account, the argument is important. It certainly has been advanced in influential writings of Adolf Gruenbaum. For an early, important statement of the argument, see Poincaré, *Science and Hypothesis* (New York, 1952), pp. 72–84.

[39] See *Principia*. pp. 6–12, 419, and, most graphically, "The System of the World," p. 574: "Because the fixed stars are quiescent one in respect of another, we may consider the sun, earth, and planets, as one system of bodies carried hither and thither by various motions among themselves; and the common centre of gravity of all (by Cor. IV of the Laws of Motion) will either be quiescent, or move uniformly forwards in a right line: in which case the whole system will likewise move uniformly forwards in right lines. But this is an hypothesis hardly to be admitted; and, therefore, setting it aside, that common centre will be quiescent."

pirically equivalent to the conjunction of a rival mechanics and a suitably altered "resolving" hypothesis. Classical electrodynamics is the only modern theory in which velocity, as against acceleration, seems to play an appropriate role. If classical electrodynamics had been correct, only one velocity assignment would have been permitted by the electrodynamic data, given the electrodynamic hypothesis that two electrified bodies moving with absolute velocity v attract each other with force F(v). But a different velocity assignment is permitted given the non-standard hypothesis that F(v) is only created by v + w, i.e., by velocities v higher than a threshold absolute velocity w, in effect, the velocity of the ether. The initial problem of distinguishing absolute velocities on non-electrodynamic grounds guarantees that the "resolving" hypotheses will be indistinguishable.[40] Appealing to a different but related episode in physics, Putnam has emphasized the empirical equivalence of two versions of classical electrodynamics, field theory and the "retarded potential" account in which electrodynamic changes at one point exert action at a distance at later times without the intervention of physical fields.[41] Finally, different interpretations of quantum physics are sometimes taken to yield empirically equivalent theories.

By turning specific sciences against themselves, these arguments avoid reliance on dubious philosophical accounts of confirmation in general. But the virtue of specificity can become a vice, in an argument for a general conclusion. Why should we generalize from one or two or even ten pairs of empirically equivalent rivals to the conclusion that every fundamental theory has such a rival? In particular, there is a question that naive sophomores ought to ask (though

---

[40] Bas van Fraassen *The Scientific Image* (Oxford, 1980), pp. 48–50. See also Poincaré, *Science and Hypothesis*, pp. 242–44.

[41] See "Equivalence" in his *Realism and Reason* (Cambridge, 1983), pp. 44f. Most of the other examples of equivalence in this essay are, I think, problems for the One True Inventory theory, rather than realism itself. For example, I think that the geometric examples are best used in an anti-reductionist argument to show that the full array of geometric objects should be accepted if any are, rather than defining away some in favor of others, say, points in favor of spheres or vice versa. (Quine's arguments about set-theoretic definitions of "number" can, and have, provoked a similar response.) Putnam also discusses equivalence arguments based on Reichenbach's writings. However, Putnam accepts that alternative descriptions which are genuine rivals according to these arguments may be two ways of saying the same thing, in interpretations of relativity theory that are now standard. See ibid., p. 42. Since Putnam's general remarks on the connection between equivalence and anti-realism are both tentative and open-minded, the electrodynamic example is especially important. It is the one example in which scientists with no strong philosophical prejudice have thought that alternatives cited by Putnam really were exclusive.

such is the worship of physics that I have never encountered one who asked it). All the examples in the now dominant arguments for equivalence are from physics. Is this just an accident? Why suppose that all theoretical science is prone to empirical equivalence if physics is?

As an example of the typical absence of empirical equivalence, at least outside of physics, consider the elementary theory of an important kind of biological unobservable, namely, bacteria. The theory includes the following principles. There are extremely tiny one-celled living things, quite invisible to the naked eye. They have cellulose cell walls and a much simpler internal structure than *Daphnia* and other barely visible creatures. They reproduce by splitting and are all descendents of other, similar living things. They breed true, i.e., the basic form and habits of offspring are distinctive and closely similar to parents', throughout the life cycle, if environmental circumstances are similar.

Though these principles seem truistic, now, I have emphasized aspects of basic bacteriology that were once extremely controversial. For example, some of the greatest chemists of the nineteenth century, such as Berzelius and Liebig, were partisans of spontaneous generation. They took the simpler microbes often to be the products of reactions among non-living substances. In opposing spontaneous generation, Schwann, Pasteur and Tyndall faced an enormous obstacle. Necessary processes of sterilization and isolation could, quite plausibly, be taken to interfere with reactions involved in spontaneous generation. Schwann made the first great strides in the argument that apparent cases of spontaneous generation were due to contamination by microbes and their spore. After boiling a nutrient broth for an appropriate period in sealed flasks, he exposed some flasks to ordinary air, others only to air that had been super-heated and then allowed to cool. Typically, only the former flasks supported microbial life. Pasteur and Tyndall went a step further, finding mechanical ways to eliminate dust from the air in contact with sterilized media, procedures that involved neither heating nor passage through special chemicals. As an important benefit, Pasteur was able to examine the eliminated material, in his filters, and he did discover microbes and spores that developed into microbes. As for the principle that bacteria breed true, it only emerged from controversy in the late 1870s, largely as a result of Koch's ingenious procedures for raising pure cultures and his painstaking monitoring of those cultures, hour after sleepless hour.[42]

---

[42] See W. Bulloch, *The History of Bacteriology* (New York, 1979), chs. 3, 4, 8 and 9.

Bacteria are unobservable, in the only sense that is relevant to a coherent anti-realism. They are unobservable by unaided human organs of perception. What is the theory, contradicting elementary bacteriology, that is just as well confirmed by current data? Of course, a partisan of spontaneous generation can still say, "There is a process of spontaneous generation, I know not what, the unfolding of which is blocked, I know not how, by every current procedure of sterilization." But if confirmation is the comparison of causal accounts of the data, we should rate this hypothesis very low. In explaining why microbes sometimes appear, sometimes do not, in nutrient media, opponents of spontaneous generation can rely on a definite hypothesis about the role of microbes and their spore, supported by a variety of independent empirical considerations. In the competition among causal explanations, the appeal to a definite factor, indicated by a variety of independent reasons, is to be favored over the appeal to an unknown factor, supported by no non-question-begging considerations.

Similarly, there is no just-as-good rival T' to the basic theory of molecules, genes or continental drift, although the relevant data cannot be sketched as quickly. In each case, all rivals in light of current data must appeal to an unknown distorting factor, the existence of which is supported by no independent reasons of anything like the weight of those supporting the standard factors. Granted, this consideration only defeats empirical equivalence if confirmation is a process of the fair comparison of causal accounts and if that process cannot be analyzed in a positivist way. For example, if the preference for formal simplicity were crucial to the explanatory comparisons, then these comparisons could be said to be irrelevant to truth, as van Fraassen does claim.[43] If the covering-law model were right, then certain highly non-standard theories, for example, that bacteria occasionally arise spontaneously but only when unobserved, might be "logically, though not pragmatically adequate," the sort of possibility that troubles Hempel in his reflections on scientific theories. Here, as elsewhere, the case for realism is utterly dependent on the discussions of confirmation and explanation in the preceding chapters.

But isn't there some definite rival, say, to elementary bacteriology, receiving its fair evidential support in a framework of background hypotheses that are just too foreign to us for us to construct and entertain them? The failure to find this theory T' might be, as Rorty suggests it is in general, simply a failure or limit in us, reflecting only

[43] See *The Scientific Image*, pp. 87f.

"the sense in which a procedure is reliable because we cannot imagine an alternative."[44] Yet surely, we do have a good reason to suppose that a definite, independently supported alternative to elementary bacteriology does not exist. Smart people looked hard for such an alternative throughout the nineteenth century and did not find it. If this is a normal question about what doesn't exist, the argument that the equally good rival does not exist is as compelling as the argument that unicorns do not.

In fact, Rorty and like-minded anti-realists take the question of whether some non-standard rival could be supported in a fair comparison on the basis of the data to be a very special question, governed by some specific reason favoring tolerance. In Rorty's eloquent and influential book, *Philosophy and the Mirror of Nature*, this special rationale is, in effect, an extrapolation from Quine's arguments in the 1950s against attempts to base empirical justifications on alleged analytic truths establishing rigid and detailed connections between hypotheses and the evidence that could confirm them. The connection between a subject-matter and standards of evidence that might govern the judgment of hypotheses about that subject-matter is very loose (Rorty notes). A variety of different standards might be used without abandoning the old subject-matter for a new one. The connection between questions and evidential standards used to resolve them is so loose (he claims) that the most entrenched hypothesis always has some rival that survives fair comparison when relevant but bizarre standards are made to accompany the latter.[45]

In fact, the connection between a subject-matter and relevant standards of evidence is not so loose, in general. When a child cries, we take it to be in pain, uncomfortable, or in some way upset. Perhaps, someone can sometimes give a special reason to suppose that the crying child is not in the least distressed. But in the absence of a special argument, someone who does not take crying to be evidence of discomfort in a child is unreasonable. In fact, this and a few other similar departures from basic standards of evidence would constitute a failure to grasp the concept of pain.

Since such reflections are sometimes developed into cheap arguments against skepticism, it is important to keep in mind just what the imagined dissenter is doing. We are not dealing with someone professing to know additional facts about the child, or someone who

---

[44] *Philosophy and the Mirror of Nature*, p. 284.
[45] See, for example, ibid., pp. 268–73.

already has a specific, plausible skeptical argument. We are not dealing with someone who has had utterly different experiences from normal human ones. For the relativism that was to be defended was the universal possibility of radically non-standard belief in the face of standard evidence; that a non-standard scientific hypothesis might be justified if non-standard evidence were encountered is trivial, and has never been controversial. In effect, we are asked to suppose that someone with normal human experiences has a completely adequate grasp of the concept of pain, when he or she does not see that a child's crying puts a burden of proof on someone who thinks that the child is in no distress. In a similar way, someone with the usual human experiences does not grasp the concept of red if he does not take the question of whether something looks red to most people to have any bearing on the question of whether it is red; he doesn't grasp the concept of life if he takes movement, growth and reproduction to have no bearing on the question of whether something lives; he does not wholly grasp the concept of accurate perception if he does not accept that making the blurry clear has a bearing on visual accuracy. Intrinsic evidential connections are very loose, but not that loose.

Without using the word, I have been introducing Wittgenstein's notion of a criterion (at least on one construal of it), as a means of defending scientific realism. "Crying is a criterion of distress, not just a symptom" would summarize much of the previous paragraph. The use of Wittgenstein's work to defend scientific realism may seem perverse. Certainly, Wittgenstein regarded a certain worship of scientific progress as a major spiritual disease of our times.[46] To some readers, the *Investigations* seems based on a theory of meaning with dramatically anti-realist implications. Moreover, discussions of behavior and sensations in the *Investigations* and of mathematical controversies in the *Remarks on the Foundations of Mathematics* strike some readers as more sophisticated (or murkier) versions of reductionist claims familiar from logical positivists with anti-realist inclinations concerning science. However, when Wittgenstein's work is seen in its historical context, it becomes natural, indeed, almost inevitable, to use it in a certain kind of defense of realism, in present circumstances. The later Wittgenstein's explicit project is to show how distorted views of language and thought drive philosophers to conclusions that are unbelievable, often absurd. The several distorted starting points he examines have two features in common.

---

[46] See, for example, the Foreword to the *Philosophical Remarks* (New York, 1975).

First, thinking, talking, inquiring and coping are treated as excessively independent of one another; more specifically, the activities toward the thought end of the spectrum are treated as states to be analyzed independent of activities closer to the coping end. Second, each great sphere of activity is supposed to be governed throughout by utterly general rules of reason, an assumption that expresses "our craving for generality."[47] Thus, the beginning of the *Investigations* is dominated by warnings expressing both concerns: "Here the term, '*language-game*' is meant to bring into prominence the fact that the *speaking* of language is part of an activity, or of a form of life. Review the multiplicity of language-games in the following examples, and in others."[48]

In the *Investigations*, Wittgenstein is often describing how one-sided, overly generalizing views of thought and language distorted the philosophy of mind in the *Tractatus* and in Russell's early twentieth-century writings, a philosophy of mind tending toward solipsism as its characteristic absurdity. In the *Remarks on the Foundations of Mathematics*, he is often concerned with the contemporary stalemate between the classical and the intuitionist approaches to the non-finitary parts of mathematics. If one forgets these special goals and expects a general theory of meaning, then a murky version of logical positivism, behaviorist and nominalist in tone, is apt to emerge. But this is to succumb to the craving for generality, not to attack it. On the other hand, if one accepts Wittgenstein's program at its face value, then the discussions of behavioral criteria in the *Investigations* (e.g., of the relation between pain and crying), are of a piece with the emphasis on the supreme role of topic-specific truisms in knowledge and justification, a main theme of his last major writing, *On Certainty*. The overall project of the later Wittgenstein is to show how absurdity and stalemate arise when thought is rigidly separated from coping and reason is entirely based on general rules. And now, thirty years after Wittgenstein's death, appreciation of the interaction of meaning, inquiring and coping (e.g., in the analysis of approximate truth) and resistance to the craving for generality (e.g., in the investigation of the limits of reasonableness) might play a role in resolving a great current stalemate, the scientific realism dispute. Of course, this suggestion is just program and slogan. The proof of the program will lie in its detailed applications. But if the applications become plausible, this quick historical digres-

[47] "Blue Book" in *The Blue and Brown Books* (Oxford, 1958), p. 17.
[48] *Philosophical Investigations* (Oxford, 1967), remark 23.

sion may be worthwhile. For there will be a point to cultivating a combination of traits that is now somewhat unusual: respect for the rationality of technical science and the access to truth it offers combined with respect for Wittgenstein and the rationality and diversity of inquiry outside of science.[49]

In general, the connection between a subject-matter and the standards of evidence governing it can be tight enough to force a dissenter into a dilemma, when the data are in: either acknowledge that a burden of proof has not been supported or acknowledge that the subject has been changed, so that there is no dissent. This is quite compatible with the Quinean discussions, emphasized by Rorty, of how loose the connection between meaning and evidence is, in other ways, and how useless it is for many standard philosophical purposes. In such essays as "Two Dogmas of Empiricism," Quine was attacking a certain use of the distinction between the analytic and the synthetic (linguistic truths and empirical truths, definitions and empirical equivalences) that was characteristic of classical positivists. Taking a proposition to be analytic had been assumed to be the start of a good argument that it was immune from revision on empirical grounds. Quine showed that such arguments were, at best, intolerably question-begging. In contrast to Quine's positivist targets, realists are claiming that tentative belief in approximate truth is sometimes the only rational option in light of the actual state of the evidence. Once a positivist account of justification is abandoned, such claims ought to be based, in part, on well-hedged principles concerning prima facie considerations, commitment to which is a mark of rationality for anyone whose actual evidence includes experiences typical of human beings. Because the goal is to give unique status to tentative beliefs in certain approximate truths given our actual evidence, there is no need to assert any immunity from revision that Quine was attacking in his seminal essays.[50]

[49] I have developed this view of Wittgenstein further in "Solipsism in the *Tractatus*," *Journal of the History of Philosophy* (1980), pp. 57–74 and "Wittgenstein in Transition," *Philosophical Review* (1977), pp. 520–44. My article "Absolute Certainty," *Mind* (1978), is an effort, in this spirit, to extract at least one of the morals of *On Certainty*. See also Rogers Albritton, "On Wittgenstein's Use of the Term 'Criterion' " in G. Pitcher, ed., *Wittgenstein* (Garden City, N.Y., 1966), and Norman Malcolm, "Knowledge and Belief" (1952) in his *Knowledge and Certainty* (Ithaca, N.Y., 1963).

[50] Perhaps the vague, hedged, topic-specific, prima facie claims as to what would be reasonable for anyone with our experience are linguistic or, in any case, conceptual truths as against empirical truths. I do not know whether this is so, largely because I do not know whether the distinction is at all defensible. What is important for present

The attractions of the specific examples of empirical equivalence derived from theoretical physics are now powerful, by contrast. Reichenbach, van Fraassen, Putnam and others describe definite alternatives, which seem equally good on any fair comparison. Given fundamental parts of standard frameworks for assessing relevant evidence, the same observations seem just as likely on the basis of each rival hypothesis. Certainly, it seems wrong to claim, here, that an alternative criterion for assessing hypotheses has strayed so far from the norm that the subject has been changed. This makes it understandable that the examples from physics are so important for anti-realists. But given the absence of such equivalence elsewhere in science, the inference to pervasive equivalence looks all the more doubtful.

Suppose, for the sake of argument, that it is rational not to believe in any description of unobservables yielded by a well-confirmed theory in theoretical physics, because some radically different, incompatible theory is always equally well-confirmed. This would not in the least affect the rationality of disbelief in bacteria, molecules (as posited in chemistry), genes or continental drift. At most, the anti-realist conclusion about physics shows the equal rationality of believing that bacterial, molecular, genetic or geological phenomena are made up of one sort of micro-constituent or made up of the other. Let us assume that in the framework of classical physics, it is equally rational to believe that bacterial (or molecular, or genetic, or . . .) processes are governed by fields or by delayed effects, that bacteria (etc.) have one absolute velocity or that they have another. This does not make it rational, within that framework, to disbelieve in bacteria, molecules, genes or continental drift. That would be like supposing it was rational to believe that sexual intercourse did not exist during the millennia in which it was equally reasonable to believe or to disbelieve that sperm contain homunculi.

One should only make the inference from indeterminacy in theoretical physics to interdeterminacy in all other fields if one is a reductionist, i.e., if one thinks that the terminology of every scientific theory should be definable in the terminology of physics. Unless one is a reductionist about genetics, chemistry, bacteriology, and geology, for example, one should not make the inference from A to B:

A. Any version of physics at the quantum level that asserts the existence of unobservable entities is a theory that it is reasonable to disbelieve, in light of current—and, indeed, all future—evidence.

purposes is that the present uses of topic-specific truisms do not depend on such a classification of them.

B. It is unreasonable to deny that genes, sugar molecules, bacteria or continental drift exist.

Yet B is concerned wholly with unobservables. (Continental drift is unobservable, since human perceptual rhythms are too fast and human memories too perishable to detect it without further aid.)

What Putnam and van Fraassen do show is that scientific realism is most defensible if it is non-reductionist. Only that is not an argument against scientific realism, since reductionism is an independent and discredited position. Indeed, reductionism is another ghost of positivism haunting the current debate. The classical positivists assumed that the statement "Things of kind A consist of things of kind B" must, like all methodologically basic claims, assert a distinctive entailment relation, in this case, between A-theory and B-theory. Since physics does describe the ultimate constituents of all other subjects of empirical science, the positivists took definitions (or bridge laws, equivalences, or reduction sentences) converting statements outside of physics into statements in physics to be an inherent goal of science. But that this is so has always been one of the less plausible assumptions of the positivist project. Certainly, when scientists defend interesting claims about constituency, say, that humans are made out of proteins or that life processes are electrochemical processes in proteins, they do not advance arguments with any tendency to support reductive definitions. "Human" remains the right term for the structure of protein that humans are.

The tendency to generalize from the familiar examples of empirical equivalence is physics-worship. But it is physics-worship strongly encouraged by positivist philosophy, which led to the insistence that the epistemic status of physics be part of the epistemic status of any natural science. Thus, arguments from empirical equivalence have turned out not to undermine realism, but to lend further support to a lesson for realists: don't be a positivist. Unless this warning is heeded, realism is threatened, either quite directly, through the implications of deductivism, or indirectly, through the physics-worship produced by the positivist conception of reduction.

## EQUIVALENCE IN PHYSICS

Even if the epistemology of physics need not affect the epistemology of every science, the former subject is important, to put it mildly. Moreover, as part of a reply to major contemporary arguments for realism such as Boyd's, arguments about physics could have real force, even if the force is ad hominem. For presumably

Boyd is, above all, appealing to the history of physics when he claims that reliance on theories has made an enormous contribution to prediction and control. But how are the arguments from specific empirical equivalences actually supposed to support anti-realism in physics?

The question is not stupid because an equivalence must be of a quite particular kind to support anti-realist claims about the field in question. The alternatives must be, not just different, but incompatible. In particular (since this is the particular issue of realism), the existence of a kind of unobservable posited in a standard theory must be denied in some equally well-confirmed alternative. Finally, the existence of equal confirmation must not depend on false empirical premises, the falsehood of which might be revealed by subsequent inquiry. None of Reichenbach's, van Fraassen's or Putnam's examples has all of these features.

I have already argued that alternative formats for quantum physics, such as the Schroedinger picture and the Heisenberg picture, do not involve incompatible claims. There are also alternative interpretations of the formalisms, some of which are genuine rivals. But these interpretations, in their controversial features, are philosophical reflections on physics, not a direct outcome of shared background principles. In any case, I will argue in Chapter Eleven that only one of the basically different interpretations is correct, a realist but highly nonclassical interpretation, made possible by the view of explanation and confirmation that I have defended.

The two catalogs of forces that Reichenbach discusses would be a bad example of empirical equivalence in other ways. First of all, the kinds of forces mentioned in the standard catalog are also present in the nonstandard one. Similarly, the kinds of physical entities in the space-time theory associated with the standard catalog exist in the other space-time theory; or rather, the statement that the former exist is approximately true in the latter theory, according to the notion of approximation that I developed earlier. Granted, an unobservable entity in a given situation may have a different magnitude, depending on which alternative is adopted. But in the dispute over realism the issue is supposed to be whether standard theories are approximately correct when they assert the existence of kinds of unobservables. That belief in a theoretical entity can be unequivocally justified even when some rival assessments of its magnitude or causal role are empirically equivalent is only surprising to someone who takes the whole task of theories to be economical prediction. On this assumption, the claim that a theoretical entity exists might seem to have no confirmable content if distinguished from the assertions of magnitudes and causal roles that lead to predictions. But this view of the whole task of theories is an anti-realist assumption.

In the second place, commitment to the nonstandard catalog would involve false belief, the acceptance of which would lack needed justification. Because of its relation to spatio-temporal determinations, the nonstandard catalog is never in itself incompatible with observations that fit the standard alternative. But its rejection is justified by Einstein's basic principle of invariance, and by the (hedged, prima facie) principle that action-at-a-distance does not take place, when these are combined with data about electromagnetic phenomena. The result is relativity theory, in light of which the uniform distorting force hypothesis can be disproved. The ultimate background principles, here, are not preferred as a mere matter of convention or of antiquity. Rather, they are supported by data combined with truisms. Thus, Einstein writes of Faraday that he "must have grasped with unerring instinct the artificial nature of all attempts to refer electromagnetic phenomena to actions-at-a-distance between electric particles reacting on each other. How was each single iron filing among a lot scattered on a piece of paper to know of the single electric particles running around in a nearby conductor?"[51] In the nineteenth century, such considerations led to distinctive problems, the problems of mechanical theories of the ether. So incomplete information and inadequate theorizing would have made it wrong to say that the non-standard catalog was less justified than the standard one, convenience to one side. But it would come as no surprise to a realist that false theoretical frameworks due to incomplete information or inadequate theorizing often make it impossible to single out one rival as empirically justified. For a realist, empirical equivalence is typically a sign of incomplete understanding.

Indeed, Reichenbach's own use of his example, as against the uses often ascribed to him, was in support of the conclusion that genuine rival hypotheses about space-time do not survive confrontation with the data. The real Reichenbach's moral is that the meaning of geometric ascriptions and the meaning of force ascriptions cannot be fixed independently of each other. Once the real interdependence is understood, the alternative geometry-force theory pairs are seen

[51] "The Fundaments of Theoretical Physics" in *Essays in Physics* (New York, 1950), p. 56.

to have the same meaning, in his own view.[52] Admittedly, Reichenbach's reasoning in support of this conclusion often implies an account of meaning that would lead to the version of anti-realism that classical positivism often produced: the whole content of a theory is exhausted by its test implications among observables. "Reichenbach the anti-realist" need not be a figure of myth if "Reichenbach the conventionalist" is. What is important for present purposes is that Reichenbach could not have been true to the spirit of contemporary physics if he had used his examples in an argument that genuine rival hypotheses are empirically equivalent.

The allegedly equivalent electrodynamic-mechanical pairs of van Fraassen and Poincaré are bad examples for the same reasons as the force-geometry pairs extracted from Reichenbach. The standard kinds of entities exist in all cases. And the equivalences depend on a false theory, pre-relativistic physics.

Finally, consider the two approaches to classical electrodynamics that Putnam contrasts. To begin with, both are pre-relativistic falsehoods. Also, their history reveals a capacity of theorists' to avoid advancing theories that are both empirically equivalent hypotheses and genuine rivals. When Faraday and Maxwell were actively seeking a mechanical explanation of propagation in the ether, ether phenomena were taken, by informed theorists of all persuasions, to be denied in retarded-potential theories. But during this period, the two approaches were not empirically equivalent. The movement of uncharged bodies was expected to cause vibrations in the ether, if it existed. Maxwell thought those vibrations were the source of radiant heating.[53] Indeed, as Einstein later remarked, empirical findings of the most ancient vintage made it likely that masses would move ether, even when uncharged.[54] For the most elementary phenomena of refraction show that matter and light interact. So robust ether theories were disconfirmed by experiments that showed the non-existence of "ether drag," for example, the failure of a rapidly rotating wheel to affect light propagation in its neighborhood. By the end of the nineteenth century, belief in the ether probably amounted to nothing more robust than a belief that electromagnetic fields tend to be propagated in absolute space according to Max-

[52] See Reichenbach, *The Philosophy of Space and Time*, pp. 14–19, 287ff. Putnam's "The Refutation of Conventionalism," in his *Mind, Language and Reality* is a wonderfully clarifying discussion of both the argument that Reichenbach made and the argument that is often attributed to him.

[53] See *Theory of Heat*, pp. 336–38.

[54] See Einstein and Infeld, *The Evolution of Physics*, p. 124.

well's equations. But then it is not clear that the appropriately weakened positing of ether involved an existence claim that retarded-potential theories reject.

For these reasons, the crucial case studies seem useless for present-day anti-realists. And yet, anyone reading these case studies feels that they describe evidence that anti-realists can use. How?

The plausible argument in which these examples do play a crucial role is an inference from the explanation of the history of physics. It is striking that fundamental theories in physics have almost always had empirically equivalent rivals. This can be explained from an anti-realist perspective. In physics (the explanation goes), reason and evidence only dictate commitment to the adequacy of a theory as a model that actual trajectories fit. Here, theories are used as general descriptions of possible world-histories of where bodies are when, and the theories are adequate if actual world-history is among those allowed. In positing novel kinds of unobservable entities, physicists have said more than that certain trajectories (i.e., relative trajectories) have, do or will occur. So it is genuinely anti-realist to suppose that all that is rationally compelling is belief in the fit with trajectories. Beyond this, a scientist may prefer one way of describing possible trajectories to others, on the basis of simplicity, convenience, or some other intellectual taste. But these inclinations will vary from scientist to scientist, except under the temporary pressure of a dominant culture, personality or clique. So diversity concerning unobservables combined with identical expectations concerning observables ought to be the norm.

The fact to be explained is that a fundamental physics has often, in the past, guaranteed that a rival physics would be as well-confirmed by the data as it is, whatever the data might be. Clearly, realism by itself will not explain this. If the goal of physics is the true description of the causes of motion, it is, if anything, surprising that the enterprise has been so afflicted with equivalence. A realist about physics needs to appeal to special facts about the history of the field that are compatible with the characterization of its goal as the true description of causes, facts that explain the pervasiveness of empirical equivalences in the past and that indicate a dramatic reduction of empirical equivalence at present. Those facts consist of the uneven development of physics for most of its history, with a wide-ranging capacity for describing trajectories, but a relatively sparse and speculative capacity to describe the causes of trajectories. The clue to this diagnosis is another common feature of the anti-realist examples: they are about force. The dramatic reduction of equivalence in the recent past is the triumph of relativity theory.

Physics is the general science of motion. It is a remarkable fact about physics that its capacity to describe its distinctive phenomena, where bodies are and when, has been extremely advanced since Babylonian times, if not before. Since ancient times, scientists have had a conception of space and time permitting meaningful spatio-temporal description of any body. Moreover, they have possessed the means to justify spatio-temporal characterizations of indefinitely many bodies. These wide-ranging means are vision and geometrical optics. With respect to the spatio-temporal framework for description, these means of description only determine the facts subject to the transformations of projective geometry. But such determinations are definite enough to be highly useful. What is at least as astounding is the survival of the basic means of description, and their basic adequacy, for millennia. The geometric optics of the ancient world is still the first approximation to modern optical theory. Though the telescope was a useful aid, it was not a crucial one until the nineteenth century. The decisive heliocentric arguments were Kepler's and Newton's, and they relied, in essence, on naked-eye data. Until the twentieth century, the only basic conceptual innovation in the description of trajectories was Galileo's treatment of velocity as a real physical magnitude (not a mathematical artifact, like the average Florentine male), and Newton's development of a mathematical analysis of this and other rates of change. But both could develop their apparatus from Hellenic geometry.

When we turn to the causal part of physics, the picture is utterly different. In most of the history of the field, scientists' general grasp of the causes of trajectories has been utterly impoverished, compared with their ability to describe trajectories. This uneven development of causal theory and description is by no means universal in science as a whole, or a necessary feature of a science of motion. In chemistry, accurate description of the subject-matter has typically depended on an improved grasp of underlying, unobservable mechanisms. Thus, the fundamental distinction between mixtures and true compounds is laden, not just with theorizing, but with controversial and fundamental theorizing. The accurate description of the history of life on the earth had to wait, almost entirely, for eighteenth- and nineteenth-century developments in geological and biological theorizing. In physics itself, one can imagine a situation in which mechanics is well-developed before optics. In an imaginable early civilization, scientists are especially impressed by the banalities to which Galileo can appeal in his rudimentary theory of inertia, for example, the familiar calamities that ensue when a wagon is abruptly stopped. Mathematicians develop the calculus early, aided, perhaps, by the importance of certain hydraulic technology governed by rates of flow. Meanwhile, the skies are too overcast too often for the early development of astronomy. But this was not the actual fate of physics. In the realist explanation, the actual gap between actual description and causal theory is the reason why empirical equivalence was the distinctive burden of physics, for so long.

Geometrical optics fixes relative positions, subject to projective transformations. In general, it can do no more. In principle, mechanics can do much more, ruling out descriptions as incompatible with the ways in which motions are caused. But the same Hellenistic astronomers who developed astronomical descriptions as accurate and simple as those of Copernicus had no satisfactory mechanics of celestial motions, and, indeed, soon stopped caring about the subject.[55] Not surprisingly, very different models used by the best ancient astronomers were, and were known to be, empirically equivalent, given the framework of background principles to which ancient astronomy was confined. An infinite variety of distances between orbits, indeed, a variety of orderings of planetary orbits were equivalent. Using telescopic observations, Galileo made some arguments for one fundamental determination (from which some others would have followed), the superiority of the heliocentric hypothesis over the geocentric. But his arguments were specious. Until stellar parallax was observed, in the nineteenth century, optical findings alone could not be decisive in resolving this dispute. In particular, Brahe's system, in which the sun revolves around the earth while the moon and planets revolve around the sun, allowed for the phases of Venus. Galileo's awareness that a mechanical argument was needed is reflected in the fourth and final book of his *Dialogues Concerning the Two Chief World Systems*, a theory of the tides. Tides, he says, are the "trace or indication of the earth's behavior in regard to motion or rest."[56] Without the fourth book, the *Dialogue* would be an (unintended) argument for the empirical equivalence of the two world systems, should parallax prove to be unobservable. But Galileo's theory of the tides is false, and his mechanics is too flawed, in general, to decide the cosmological issue.

Very broadly speaking, Newton filled this gap. More accurately,

[55] See Kuhn, *The Copernican Revolution*, pp. 80f., 104f.
[56] *Dialogue Concerning the Two Chief World Systems*, p. 417.

he reformulated the issue, and established a position that was closer to what Copernicans had in mind than to what Aristotelians had in mind. The earth and the sun both revolve around the center of gravity of the sun-and-planets system, and that center is very close to the center of the sun. That this center of gravity itself is at rest was quite explicitly, a stipulation on Newton's part, for which no argument was available.[57] In general, Newton's method was to use the three laws of motion to derive force assignments from data, which are then used to impose limits on further trajectories.[58] Since the whole job of a force is to change velocity, absolute constant velocities cannot be established. Yet, in Newton's apparatus for description, different absolute velocities can be stated. So, though Newton's additions to the theory of causes of motion ended the empirical equivalence of the Copernican and Ptolemaic systems, an infinite variety of further equivalences remained.

There were three possible responses to this gap between descriptive capacity and causal insight, and, for almost three centuries after Newton, all were live options. As Leibniz thought, ascriptions of absolute velocity, distance, and location might all have been vacuous, like the claim, "This is to the left—absolutely, not relative to some particular reference point." Or, as Poincaré proposed, alternative Newtonian ascriptions of velocity and location might have described genuinely different but empirically equivalent possibilities, any further preference being dictated by pragmatic or conventional considerations. Finally, as Maxwell thought and Newton hoped, some supplement to Newtonian physics might have enabled scientists to single out a frame of reference in which the absolute magnitudes could be ascertained. This third option is clearest once one appreciates Maxwell's basic reason for belief in the ether. His motive is not primarily to show that electrodynamics can be reduced to a Newtonian theory of stress and its propagation. Rather, he argues, quite plausibly, that energy does not just disappear and reappear, and that it is always in something. "In fact, whenever energy is transmitted from one body to another in time there must be a medium or substance in which the energy exists after it leaves one body and before it reaches the other, for energy, as Torricelli remarked, 'is a quintessence of so subtle a nature that it cannot be contained in any vessel except the inmost substance of material things.'" [59] Given such

[57] See *Principia*, p. 419, Hypothesis 1.
[58] See ibid., pp. xviif.
[59] *A Treatise on Electricity and Magnetism* (New York, 1954), pt. 2, II, p. 493.

findings as the non-existence of ether drag, it would have been more reasonable to identify this medium with space itself than with anything taking up space. Space is what propagates electromagnetic disturbance according to Maxwell's equations. So, *pace* Poincaré and van Fraassen, evidence and reason could have dictated that the ether does not move. If there had been a special spatio-temporal framework in which Maxwell's equations are valid, it would have determined the correct ascriptions of absolute magnitudes.

Of course, it turned out that there is no such favored frame of reference, as Michelson and Morley's experiment showed and as Einstein had supposed very early in his thinking. Everyone now agrees that Maxwell's way of resolving Newtonian indeterminacies is not available. The only question is, which of the other two alternatives is represented by relativity theory. Often, classical positivists took Einstein to be claiming that alternative world-descriptions were empirically equivalent, with preference accorded on pragmatic or conventional grounds. But this is neither Einstein's argument nor his method, in practice. In his presentations of the basic theory, relativity theory does not emerge from operational definitions of distance and duration, the experimental findings of Michelson and Morley and others, and the imposition of pragmatic or conventional constraints to single out a favored form a description. Rather, Einstein always begins with a statement of fact: that moving bodies emit light with a definite, constant velocity, in all directions, with respect to every inertial frame of reference. This reliance on factual claims, rather than empirical equivalences and their pragmatic resolution, is essential to all of the distinctive inferences that lead to our calling it Einstein's Theory of Relativity, not Lorentz' or Poincaré's. If he had been concerned to establish empirical equivalence, Einstein could not, for example, have made his most dramatically anti-Newtonian argument, that mass increases with velocity, so that nothing can be pushed to move faster than the speed of light. Unless the route to equivalence was blocked by using the standard Maxwellian equations and the basic principle of invariance to interpret the data, a Newtonian mechanics joined to a non-standard electrodynamics would be as well-confirmed as Einstein's non-Newtonian mechanics joined to standard electrodynamics. Given this equivalence, it would have been simpler, more convenient, more economical and more familiar to use Newtonian mechanics in coping with mechanical problems, so that there would have been no grounds for preferring relativistic mechanics. This was, indeed, Poincaré's position in his last years.[60] To cite one other example of Einstein's intense opposition in practice to the strategy of "operationalize, establish equivalence, resolve it on conventional or pragmatic grounds," the more realist approach is essential to the crucial conclusion in general relativity that a perfectly constructed and synchronized accelerating clock slows down.[61]

Rather than exploring consequences of empirical equivalence, Einstein and those who followed him were pursuing Leibniz' option, and pushing it further than Leibniz would have dreamed, not just to location, distance and velocity, but to time of occurrence and simultaneity. The effect of such relativizing is to destroy empirical equivalence and to do so without a general anti-realist semantics in which meaning simply consists of observational test implications. What seemed genuinely different spatio-temporal descriptions, among which the evidence cannot decide, are different ways of describing the same reality, like "Cincinnati is to the left of New York, when you face north" and "Cincinnati is to the right of New York when you face south." Einstein, Minkowski, Weyl and others ended an ancient gap between spatio-temporal description and causal theory, in part by changing the ancient framework for spatio-temporal description. (In the latter, they are prefigured by Newton's reformulation of the central issue in cosmology.)

I have been sketching an explanation of why genuine alternatives have often been empirically equivalent in past physical theories, an explanation which is meant to show that such equivalence is not intrinsic to all of physics. Because the reduction of indeterminacy in the latest chapters of this story is not derived from the nature of justification or meaning in general, the reduction of indeterminacy as physics has progressed need not have occurred and may not be general, even today. Alternative Newtonian descriptions could have turned out to be genuinely different, but empirically equivalent. For one thing, the theories through which Einstein ends the equivalence might ultimately have proven false. It is not an a priori truth, after all, that elementary particles in synchrotrons acquire enormous mass as they speed up. Moreover, there may be fundamental gaps between description and causal theorizing elsewhere in physics, in particular, in nuclear physics. A realist ought to expect some such gaps, and consequent empirical equivalence. If science is the

[60] See "Les Rapports de la Matière et de l'Ether" (1912), pp. 82f., and "L'Espace et le Temps" (1912), pp. 108f., both in *Dernières Pensées* Paris (1963).

[61] See "The Foundation of the General Theory of Relativity," p. 116.

pursuit of causes, and the notion of a cause is governed by the special constraints described in Chapter Two, then it would be a fluke if science could ever provide means that, in principle, answer all the questions that science poses. But realism is the view that evidence and reason often compel an answer, not that they always do.

Could this sketch of the history of empirical equivalence in physics be accepted by an anti-realist? With suitable reinterpretation, it certainly could. The story is simply retold as the development of increasingly comprehensive and unified models for trajectories. If certain characters, such as Einstein, trusted to realist inclinations, that just shows that realist tactics sometimes help to advance the development of unified, comprehensive and empirically adequate theories.

But I have not been using this history to show that an anti-realist view of physics is wrong. Rather, it is directed at what remains of the argument from empirical equivalence, once positivism is abandoned. This argument reduces to a claim that the actual history of empirical equivalence in physics only has a plausible explanation on an anti-realist view of physics. Realists, I have tried to show, can also explain the actual shape of the history of physics, as due to the initial gap between descriptive capacity and insight into causes and the closing of that gap in the course of two millennia.

What is surprising and revealing about this history is that a conceptual revolution, the relativistic view of space, time and force, saves the day for realism. On account of the writings of Kuhn and Feyerabend, it has often seemed that realism is best suited to dull histories of science, in which the most basic ways of describing a subject-matter never change, once a field is mature. But basic ways of describing reality have sometimes condemned a fundamental science to pervasive empirical equivalences about rival hypotheses. The lesson for realists is that they must be as accepting as the other side of the occurrence of genuine conceptual revolutions in mature sciences.

## ALBERT EINSTEIN: ANTI-POSITIVIST

I have made a double claim about Einstein's arguments for relativity, that he means to exclude possibilities in classical physics that genuinely different theories of space and time might be empirically equivalent, and that the basis for this exclusion is the actual invariance of certain causal processes (above all, electromagnetic propagation), not a general, anti-realist view of meaning that identifies the meaning of a theory with its observational implications. No careful reader of Einstein's work has doubted the first half of this interpretation. Clearly, Einstein is not Poincaré. But many careful readers have doubted the second half. In effect, they have supposed that Einstein is Reichenbach—or Schlick or Mach. In a way, the dispute is less important than it seems. When one comes to Einstein's later writings, and those of his most influential and creative followers, from Minkowski to Wheeler, the verdict is again unanimous. Obviously, the premises in these writings are claims about actual invariance in causal processes that are for the most part unobservable, not anti-realist theories of meaning. Still, the realist form of Einstein's later presentations might be taken to reflect the pressures of the later debate over quantum mechanics. And the realism of many of his successors might simply reflect a tendency for analysis and argument not to be pursued as far as it used to be, when a once-novel theory has triumphed and become near dogma in its turn.

I have already noted, on several occasions, the evidence for the realist reading of Einstein's classic papers on relativity, including special relativity. The premises offered are actual principles of invariance concerning "[t]he laws by which the states of physical systems alter,"[62] or concerning a real cause as against "a merely *factitious* cause."[63] (At the very start of the reflections leading to these papers, Einstein was concerned with problems of describing one and the same process in the framework of classical mechanics and the framework of Maxwellian electrodynamics.[64] Such worries about consistency will turn out, similarly, to depend on a realist construal of both alternatives.) When he drew conclusions from his reasoning, they often depended on his use of these physical principles of invariance in preference to an observational reduction of theoretical meanings. Thus, he is not open to Poincaré's observationally available alternative, the possibility that classical mechanics might be acceptable, if combined with a non-Maxwellian electrodynamics. When invariance arguments leading to general relativity require the abandonment of "definitions" of time in terms of clocks, he abandons the "definitions" with no sign of reluctance.

Obviously, Einstein did regard it as a defect in a theory if it asserts the genuine difference of alternative descriptions that, on the same theory, must be empirically equivalent. But this is a defect according

[62] "Does the Inertia of a Body Depend upon Its Energy-Content?" p. 69.
[63] "The Foundation of the General Theory of Relativity," p. 113.
[64] See "Autobiographical Notes," tr. P. Schilpp, in Schilpp, ed., *Albert Einstein: Philosopher-Scientist* (Evanston, Ill., 1949), p. 53.

to any philosophy of science (though not a lethal defect according to every one). A theory is the worse for posing questions that cannot possibly be answered unless the theory is false.

Still, there is more to the common reading than lingering positivist prejudice. Often, Einstein presents thought-experiments concerning idealized observers, their ways of measuring and their ways of communicating, and proposes that the significance of a basic magnitude is established by associating it with such a procedure. Thus, early in his first paper on relativity, he notes, in connection with the description of the motion of a particle, "Now we must bear carefully in mind that a mathematical description of this kind has no physical meaning unless we are quite clear as to what we understand by 'time.' " He then describes how distant clocks might be synchronized using light pulses, and takes this description to yield "a definition of 'simultaneous' or 'synchronous,' and of 'time.' "[65] This is an important step in his argument for his first truly revolutionary conclusion, the relativity of simultaneity to a temporal frame of reference. Given the free usage of such terms as "meaning" and "definition" among physicists, nothing here is strictly incompatible with the realist reading. Since the clocks are assumed, at critical junctures, to be accurate (for example, accurate in measuring local processes), the description of measurement is appropriately theory-laden. The emphasis on associating magnitudes with idealized measurement procedures could express the goal of constructing a physics that does not pose unanswerable questions. What is harder to explain is Einstein's predilection for such apparent operational definitions, throughout his classic papers. Why is it so important for him to imagine how magnitudes might ideally be fixed, if he is not a positivist who thinks that the meaning of a term does, strictly and literally, consist of its observational test implications?

Einstein's frequent use of apparent operational definitions is the joint result of two tendencies, his project of removing unanswerable questions from physics and a task he shares with all revolutionary scientists of showing that what seems to be inconceivable is conceivable. By its nature, a revolutionary science appeals to possibilities that seemed inconceivable in the old science, i.e., either inconceivable in themselves or in combination with obvious facts. So it has been crucial to show, to the contrary, that phenomena that could only reveal familiar states of affairs if the old science is to be believed are just the ones that would reveal novel states of affairs, if the new

[65] "On the Electrodynamics of Moving Bodies," pp. 39f.

framework is adopted. Galileo's Simplicio thinks that a rock could not conceivably fall from the top of an earthly tower in the way it obviously does, if the earth were moving. His Salviati gets Simplicio to admit that this trajectory is just what one would expect on the hypothesis of earthly rotation, if one abandons the Aristotelian idea that continued motion requires pushing in favor of what we would now call a principle of inertia.[66] On a quick and anachronistic reading of this passage, Salviati might seem to be defining "unforced motion" in terms of observational implications, on the way to showing that the rock's falling along the rotating tower is unforced motion. But really, he is separating out the observations associated with the uncontroversial rock-tower relations, on the way to showing that they only require that the rock's motion be forced should the tower be turning if one unfairly imports further theoretical presuppositions from the framework of the Aristotelian system. On reflection, it is clear that Salviati cannot be reducing physical descriptions to their observational implications, since his discussion is part of a Copernican argument that the rock really has a natural tendency to continue moving in a circumterrestrial circle. An observationally equivalent Aristotelian description would be false.

Similarly, Einstein needs to offer frequent apparent operational definitions in order to combat the tendency to reject his revolutionary pronouncements as inconceivable. In part, these frequent passages are a reminder that what one imagines when one imagines a classical situation, for example, absolutely simultaneous events, is the same as what one imagines in imagining a relativistic situation, say, events that are simultaneous in one's local frame of reference. The appearance of a genuine reductive definition is stronger here than in Galileo's case because the same passages also serve a second goal, of showing how physics can avoid a certain important (though not always lethal) defect: presenting as genuinely exclusive possibilities among which there could be no justified choice.

This account of Einstein's apparent positivism as a matter of limited tactics, not general belief, has the advantage of resembling his later self-portraits. This suggests that his later views were his earlier ones, as well. Though Einstein's interest in epistemological issues is always apparent, his explicit statements date from the last twenty years of his life. The conception of science he advances then is explicitly opposed to classical positivism, implicitly opposed to positivism in the broad sense that I have described. Apart from certain

---

[66] *Dialogue Concerning the Two Chief World Systems*, pp. 138f., 148, 165f.

matters concerning which Einstein's statements are vague in his own appraisal, his conception parallels the present anti-positivist view of scientific reasoning.[67]

Einstein distinguishes two kinds of virtues that we seek in a scientific theory, "external confirmation" and "inner perfection" as he calls them in one passage, with both phrases in scare quotes.[68] One virtue is closeness of fit with the data. The other is the capacity to render the data intelligible. In pursuing the first goal, one seeks hypotheses that would be singled out as correct by the totality of sense experience. Thus, one tries to avoid a certain *embarras de richesses*, the acceptance of concepts that make it possible to pose questions that cannot be resolved on the basis of the totality of sense experience alone.[69] Pursuing the goal of "intelligibility," on the other hand, one applies principles that one needs to make sense of the course of experience, developing new concepts as tools for this purpose. The task begins with the application of truisms and continues with their modification as obstacles to intelligibility are encountered.[70]

Einstein's discussions of each kind of virtue are both delicate and sensible. For example, he emphasizes that ad hoc tailoring is sometimes an acceptable way of preserving empirical fit. And he notes that the pursuit of intelligibility, i.e. of "the 'naturalness' or 'logical simplicity' of the premises [is] . . . a kind of reciprocal weighing of incommensurable qualities."[71] The epistemological systems of philosophers single out one kind of virtue as overriding, often construing it in a narrow way. Thus, positivists such as Mach take the avoidance of the embarrassment of riches to be all important, and insist that concepts be defined in terms of observations, so that the totality of observations would determine the right answer to every question. To philosophers, as Einstein expects them to be, a scientist will seem "an unscrupulous opportunist."[72] For he will sometimes emphasize one virtue, sometimes another. None is overriding in general. In particular, the content of physical theories cannot be restricted to observations, because (among other reasons) intelligibility requires

[67] Einstein's extensive discussions with a bearing on present issues begin with "Physics and Reality" (1936; see *Essays in Physics*) and achieve their most detailed and most clearly anti-positivist development in "Autobiographical Notes" and "Reply to Criticisms" (1949) in *Albert Einstein: Philosopher-Scientist*. My sketch will largely rely on the 1949 essays.

[68] "Autobiographical Notes," p. 23.

[69] "Reply to Criticisms," p. 680.

[70] See, in particular, ibid., pp. 673f.

[71] "Autobiographical Notes," p. 23.

[72] "Reply to Criticisms," p. 684.

guidance by background principles, initially truistic, that are not dictated by the course of sense experience. In this sense, they are "freely chosen."[73]

Still, "science without epistemology is—insofar as it is thinkable at all—primitive and muddled."[74] The respective virtues in which philosophers specialize are real. Mach is important to the development of relativity theory because it was so important to recognize that such assumptions as "the axiom of the absolute character of time" were arbitrary, i.e., were conceivably wrong and yet could not be assessed by any means available to classical physics. Determined to avoid such arbitrariness at all costs, Mach detected it in classical assumptions that would otherwise have remained "anchored in the unconscious." "The type of critical reasoning which was required for the discovery of this central point was decisively furthered, in my case, especially by the reading of David Hume's and Ernst Mach's philosophical writings."[75]

If the present replacement for positivism is basically correct, Einstein stands at the origins of post-positivist philosophy of science. In his confession of unscrupulous opportunism, he is an epistemic Huck Finn, apologizing for his epistemological insight. Acceptance of the diversity of virtues, acknowledgment that none is overriding, and the development of basic concepts out of the use of substantive background principles are, in his view, a desertion of philosophy. Or in any case, this is the explicit self-mockery of a famous wit. Intended or not, the real joke is on us philosophers.

## The Best Lesson

So far, the objections to arguments for realism have not defeated them, but have clarified and refined realism itself. But there is a further type of objection, concerned, not with the history of failed the-

[73] See "Autobiographical Notes," p. 49, where Mach is criticized for "a philosophical prejudice" against such freedom. For other statements that either explicitly criticize classical positivism, or are obviously incompatible with it, see "Autobiographical Notes," pp. 21, 23; "Reply to Criticisms," pp. 588, 674, 678, 679.

[74] "Reply to Criticisms," p. 684.

[75] "Autobiographical Notes," p. 53. See "Physics and Reality," p. 26, for a similar connection between relativity and positivist views of meaning. Of course, it is also hard to imagine orienting oneself to the new space-time facts without the help afforded by operational definitions. They are heuristics, which can be discarded later, connecting new realities with earlier ways of thinking without importing old assumptions that must be abandoned. See "Reply to Criticisms," p. 678 and the charming conversation in W. Heisenberg, *Physics and Beyond* (New York, 1971), p. 63.

ories or with empirical equivalences, but with the option not to explain at all in cases where realists require explanations. Realists have often been criticized for supposing that a reasonable person must accept the best explanation of certain regularities when, in fact, it is also reasonable to be agnostic. When Mach and Ostwald took "phenomenological" physics to be at least as good as molecular theories, they were claiming that a non-explanatory option was rational. In the same spirit, van Fraassen takes Sellars and other leading realists to rely on the false premise "that every universal regularity in nature needs an explanation."[76]

Are present-day realist arguments from the successful use of theories, above all, Boyd's argument, guilty of insisting on a need for explanation where none exists? I will argue for just this verdict. Certainly, Boyd's argument does not depend on the simple excessive commandment to believe the best explanation of every regularity. Still, it is excessive, I will argue, if more plausible and more complex. There is, in fact, no contribution to science as a whole that theory-dependent methods have made which stands in need of an explanation. The moral of these criticisms will be that no inference from a general pattern of scientific success is a sound basis for scientific realism. But this defeat for standard realist arguments is best studied as part of a defense of realism. For it suggests what the materials for a new defense should be, topic-specific principles about how the world works and how we perceive it, much closer to the banalities of common sense than to the laws of logic.

[76] See *The Scientific Image*, p. 21.

# CHAPTER TEN

# A Defense of Realism

## Two Temperaments

In his exemplary argument for scientific realism, Boyd is making an inference from the best explanation of a certain tendency. In the best established natural sciences, there is a strong tendency, he claims, for theory-dependent methods of designing and interpreting tests to contribute to the predictive and instrumental reliability of hypotheses developed by means of such methods. The best, indeed the only explanation of this tendency is, he proposes, the approximate truth of those theories. So it is unreasonable not to believe in the existence of something like the entities postulated by the theories.

What is troubling about this argument is that it is not in general unreasonable to accept that a hypothesis is the best, indeed the only explanation of a tendency, while not believing it is even approximately true. Granted, when a hypothesis is the best explanation, that makes belief one reasonable option. And there is a speculative but reasonable epistemological temperament (very common among philosophers!) that is expressed in a general inclination to take up this option. But there is another epistemological temperament, also reasonable, expressed in a disinclination to believe what is the best, indeed the only explanation, merely because it has this explanatory status.

That the more skeptical temperament is reasonable is clearest in those cases where it has actually contributed to scientific progress. Throughout most of the nineteenth century, the best, indeed the only explanation of the regularities embodied in Maxwell's equations was that they were due to stresses produced by torsion in a physical substance. Certainly, there was no other explanation of why an electromagnetic change at one point produces an electromagnetic change at a distant point after a regular delay. Yet the scientists who accepted the tendencies in the equations without accepting the hypothesis explaining them (Hertz's "Maxwell's theory is Maxwell's equations") were reasonable.[1] They were reasonable

---

[1] See Hertz, *Electric Waves* (London, 1900), p. 21.

before empirical anomalies burdened ether explanations. And they proved to be right.

It is clear enough in everyday life that general belief in the best explanation is just an expression of one temperament. People of a very speculative cast can find, and embrace, a best explanation of virtually anything, every half-overheard conversation, every regularity noticed in the neighborhood. As their friends sometimes suggest with a smile, their beliefs are not dictated by reason.

It might seem that Boyd's inference must be rationally compelling because it just depends on the truism that explanation is desirable, not the less compelling claim that the best explanation should always be believed. The explanation of a regularity is a distinct gain, and, in his inference, the gain seemed to be acquired at no cost.

The case of electrodynamics suggests that this assessment of scientific gains and losses cannot be right, since agnosticism was reasonable even before the ether theory encountered specific difficulties. For both scientific realism and ether theory, the problem seems to lie in the means by which the explanatory gains are achieved. Scientific realists and ether theorists explain regularities among observables by positing new kinds of entities. Among those entities, new kinds of regularities are supposed to exist. So the number of unexplained regularities is reduced in one place, to be increased elsewhere. Moreover, since the explanatory hypothesis says more than a mere statement of the regularities it explains, those who adopt it take on an added risk of being wrong. Such speculative risks can make non-explanation reasonable, as the ether hypothesis shows. Every gain in explanations is accompanied by costs of kinds that can, in general, make non-belief a reasonable option.

Of course, a great variety of compelling empirical arguments, indeed, I claimed in Chapter Four, all compelling empirical arguments, can be stated as inferences from the best explanation. Here is a banal example. Night after night one sees cheese disappear from the cupboard; the bits of cheese left have little sharp tooth-shaped marks in them; flour dust on the cupboard shelves reveals tiny mouse-foot-shaped imprints. In the absence of contrary data, this is wonderfully compelling evidence that a mouse is getting into the cupboard. But surely this is an inference from the best explanation.

Seeing why this and other routine inferences are compelling is both a step toward showing why the standard argument for realism do not work and what a new argument would have to be like. In the inference to the mouse, we can rely on specific principles according to which certain phenomena stand in need of an explanation. Cheese doesn't just disappear, without any cause. Tooth-shaped imprints and apparent footprints are caused by similarly shaped objects pressing down. Or, more precisely, it is unreasonable to deny that these phenomena have those causes unless one has a strong and specific case for doing so. The cheese-disappearance phenomena need causes, and among the possible causes, mouse invasion is most likely by far.

The governing consideration here is not the optional one, namely, belief in the best explanation, but one that a reasonable person must respect, namely, "Avoid dramatic anomalies, sharp conflicts with rationally compelling principles about how the world works." But the issue of scientific realism is precisely whether reason and evidence ever dictate belief in a principle about the work of unobservable causes.

There is something ambiguous about the notion of the best explanation. If what is best is what is licensed by topic-neutral principles describing a general pattern that is actually in the data, then the corresponding realist inference must meet a challenge which, I shall argue, always defeats it: the possibility that people of a relatively anti-speculative temperament would reasonably reject conclusions supported by such principles. The principles just express one epistemological temperament. On the other hand, if what is best is determined by topic-specific principles of how the world works, then the question of realism is begged if it is simply assumed that such principles can support belief in unobservables and, at the same time, be rationally compelling for all. What anti-realists deny is precisely that a substantive hypothesis about unobservables is ever that compelling. Yet the status and power of topic-specific principles are never established in contemporary arguments for realism.

## An Anatomy of Agnosticism

The notion that there is one kind of anti-speculative temperament is a simplification, and not just because a practice of inference can express this temperament to a greater or lesser degree. There are two different bases for a refusal to believe the best explanation. Only one is usually at issue in the realism dispute. But the other could play a role. And, in any case, the distinction between the two bases for agnosticism will make it clearer what the dispute is most commonly about.

A good example of the kind of agnosticism that is not central to the philosophical dispute, though it is the more important by far in science, is the response to the viral theory of cancer. There was a brief period in the 1950s in which viral accounts of cancer were the best explanations of the total data. Yet few researchers were so speculative as to believe, even tentatively, in a general viral hypothesis. It is not that they thought that the occurrence of cancer stood in no need of explanation. Rather, they thought the best explanation was not good enough to be believed.

More precisely, the first form of agnosticism is non-belief based on inadequate confidence that the best explanation of current data would not be disconfirmed by subsequent data. As the case of the viral theory shows, such agnosticism may be reasonable even when the issue is tentative belief, belief on the part of someone who is willing to abandon belief in light of imaginable subsequent evidence. Tentative belief requires adequate confidence that the imaginable disconfirming circumstances will not occur.

Though it is extremely important in science, the thrust of anti-realist arguments has not been to show that this first form of agnosticism is always reasonable, when hypotheses refer to unobservables. Anti-realists typically claim that agnosticism about unobservables would be reasonable even if all relevant observable phenomena were known to have been observed. For example, van Fraassen would certainly claim that even absolute conviction about the empirical adequacy of a theory might accompany non-belief in its truth. Given their usual attitude toward empirical laws, i.e. generalizations about observables, anti-realists could not rely on the more routine form of agnosticism. They are trying to give belief in hypotheses about unobservables a systematically different status from belief in empirical regularities. Yet both beliefs are challenged, to the same degree, by lack of confidence about non-defeat by further data.

There is another form of agnosticism that is central to anti-realist arguments, and that is common and productive in both science and everyday life. It is exemplified in the attitude toward the ether hypothesis of Poincaré, Mach and the other nineteenth-century scientists who are the most striking precursors of modern anti-realism. Their non-belief in the hypothesis was not based primarily on the concern that it might be defeated by further data. Even if they had been confident that the ether hypothesis would not have been defeated by further data they would not have believed it. Quite apart from the possibility of empirical defeat, the best explanation of electromagnetic phenomena need not, in their view, be accorded even tentative belief; they were willing to take Maxwell's ether version of his total theory as the best means of summarizing all the data that would ever be relevant, without even tentatively believing the ether hypothesis. So they did not believe in any further cause of electromagnetic regularities, quite apart from empirical doubts about Maxwell's cause. In previous sections, I emphasized this aspect of scientific agnosticism by speaking of the denial that regularities stand in need of an explanation. In science and in everyday life, it corresponds to a willingness to accept unexplained coincidences ("The crows had to perch somewhere and that is where they happened to perch") as against an agnostic lack of confidence in the support for an explanation ("Do we really know enough about the crows to say that they stopped there because they were tired?").

In general, someone directs the more relevant, second type of agnosticism at a hypothesis if:

1. he judges the hypothesis to be the best explanation of the data;

2. he does not, even tentatively, believe it is approximately true;

3. he does not justify this non-belief on the grounds that the hypothesis might be defeated by further data.

Anti-realists do suppose that this agnostic attitude is always one reasonable option where hypotheses about unobservables are concerned. This is merely one special case of their general claim that a framework not requiring belief in a hypothesis about unobservables is always a reasonable option. But the defense of the agnostic framework for assessing hypotheses is important, since it is often the only alternative framework that can be made definite and plausible. In contrast, anti-realists do not commonly suppose that there is always a possible reasonable belief threshold that is higher than the evidence concerning unobservables; i.e., they do not think that hypotheses about unobservables may always reasonably not be believed simply on the basis of insufficient confidence that further data would not defeat them. Later, I will argue that they show good judgment in leaving this common form of skepticism unexploited. Until then, I will simply impose the standard assumption that the possible disputants to be considered do not have abnormally high belief thresholds.

By making it clearer what the relevant need for explanation amounts to, this anatomy of agnosticism also makes clearer the force of the topic-specific truisms at level III. According to these truisms, a fact of one kind is, prima facie, a sign of another. That someone is crying is, prima facie, a sign that he or she is in discomfort. That something makes the blurry clear and distinct is, prima facie, a sign that it makes invisible details visible. The force of the lawyer's term, "prima facie," is this. Suppose that someone takes the relevant phenomena to have the indicated explanation, and takes the total current data to include no indication that the explanation is false. Suppose, in addition, that he or she has adequate confidence that the hypothesis would not be defeated by further data. Then it is unreasonable not to believe, tentatively, that the hypothesis is true. If someone cries and otherwise acts as if in a state of discomfort, then it is unreasonable not to take him to be in pain unless one moves slowly in these matters for fear that one might be proved wrong. In the case of magnification, a shrewd investigator might well be worried, say, that what seem to be revelations of invisible details might prove to be distortions in the glass, artifacts of lighting, or the like. What is unreasonable is the position that the glass has made the blurry look clear and distinct, that the hypothesis that it magnifies fits all the facts, that there are no grounds for fear that reliability will be disconfirmed, and that, nonetheless, the hypothesis that the glass truly magnifies should not be accorded tentative belief.

## RELYING ON THEORIES

If realists only claimed that practices relying on commitment to the truth of theories make some contribution to predictive reliability and if they argued for the truth of every theory that provides the best explanation for such a contribution, then their inference would be obviously biased toward the more explanatory temperament. The principle that would force a realist conclusion from this pattern of success would be the general, unadorned demand that has already proved to be excessive, "Always believe the best explanation." To accept without further explanation that theory-dependent methods sometimes contribute to predictive success is no more unreasonable, on the face of it, than accepting Maxwell's equations, and no explanation of them, even though a mechanical theory of the ether provides the best explanation.

Of course, Boyd has a more compelling argument to offer. The observation that it is often reasonable not to believe the best explanation is—so far—troubling for his approach to realism, but nothing more. He makes strong claims about the contribution of theory-dependent methods, claims that might seem to produce his relatively modest realist conclusion in virtue of a principle that is compelling, as "Always believe the best explanation" is not. The contribution of theory-dependent methods to reliable prediction and control is said to be "astonishing."[2] Out of this enormous contribution, Boyd is only trying to extract the relatively modest conclusion that "scientific methodology produces (typically and over time) approximately true beliefs about theoretical entities."[3] Boyd can appeal to rough but quantitative notions as to how much is tolerable in the way of unexplained success, when an explanation, involving only a flexible and vague commitment, is in fact available. Since no precise limit to tolerance, here, would be rationally compelling, loose talk of the enormous and the astonishing is quite appropriate. And if the contribution of theory-dependent methods is as enormous as Boyd claims, then the acceptance of this success without even the vague explanation he proposes should probably exceed the limits of anyone's tolerance. "Accept the typical approximate truth of the theoretical assumptions on which these successful methods depended, when the alternative is to take such astonishing predictive gains as lacking an explanation" would be the appropriately vague basis for a compelling inference.

Have theory-dependent methods made such an enormous contribution, though? They certainly have if even the routine pharmacological reasoning in Boyd's example of the antibiotic depends on belief in the approximate truth of theories. But it does not.

In the example, the hypothesis that the drug acts by dissolving cell walls is ultimately promoted to the status that everyone, realist and anti-realist alike, regards as desirable and attainable, that of a preferred basis for asserting tendencies among observables. Even someone with an anti-realist view of pharmacology would be interested to know how fast relevant clumps in petri dishes shrink when exposed to the drug, how fast symptoms disappear, and whether other chemicals, breaking down clumps of organic matter in similar ways, have a significant chance of alleviating the same symptoms. If the wall-destruction hypothesis is empirically adequate, i.e., if, in the context of current science, it provides true descriptions of relations among observables, it points the way to answers to such questions. If she accepts current theories, the pharmacologist (in Boyd's example) will suppose that interference with cell division is the most likely alternative to cell-wall destruction. In addition, auxiliary hy-

---

[2] Boyd, "On the Current Status of the Issue of Scientific Realism," *Erkenntnis* (1983), p. 54.

[3] Ibid., p. 69.

potheses will dictate, say, that the effect of the drug is, in the former case, relatively slow. (The bacteria are only vulnerable when they divide.) So fast shrinkage of the observable colonies in the petri dishes will give relatively strong support to the initial hypothesis, leading to its use in predicting and controlling observable phenomena. *But all that is relied on, here, is belief in the empirical adequacy of current theories.* In what they say about empirical tendencies among observables, current theories imply that the drug will tend to be associated either with relatively fast shrinkage or with relatively slow shrinkage, and that, in the former case, there will be further tendencies involving cure, solvent properties, and so forth. Very likely, it will be psychologically impossible to keep all these tendencies in mind, without thinking of real living things with real cell walls, multiplying through real splitting. But that is no justification for strict and literal belief. No one works with the molecular kinetic theory without imagining elastic spheres bouncing off one another—and no modern scientist believes that gases are actually composed of elastic spheres.

This is not to deny that there are important cases in which scientific arguments depend on belief in unobservables; it is only to deny that these cases are as common and as productive as the example in Boyd's 1973 paper suggests. In particular, there is irreducible dependence on a theory when a scientist argues for a novel empirical tendency or for a controversial rating of a theoretical hypothesis on the basis of features of the former theory that are independent of previous derivations of empirical laws.[4] In such situations, some characterizations of the theoretical entities have already been linked to empirical laws via auxiliary hypotheses. The scientist argues that if the established features of the entities really exist and work to a certain effect, other features are likely to exist and to work to a certain effect. And yet this does not follow from commitment to the empirical adequacy of past uses of the theory. The scientist is using intra-theoretic considerations to justify commitment to novel auxiliary hypotheses. In sum, theory-dependent plausibility plays a role in scientific reasoning, and cannot always be replaced by reliance on empirical laws that have already been derived. What is plausible to a believer in a theory (at a given time) need not be plausible to a believer in the empirical adequacy of the theory (at that time).

---

[4] Boyd singles out this kind of reasoning as the theory-dependent methodology that is central to his argument, in "Realism, Underdetermination, and a Causal Theory of Evidence," *Nous* (1973), pp. 8f., and *"Lex Orandi est Lex Credendi"* in P. Churchland and C. Hooker, eds., *Images of Science* (Chicago, 1985), pp. 9, 18.

Here are some typical examples of genuinely theory-dependent arguments.

1. Clausius' and Maxwell's work in the 1850s showed that the laws of Boyle and Gay-Lussac concerning the thermodynamics of gases, and other familiar phenomena, as well, could be explained on the hypothesis that gases consisted of tiny bits of matter, in constant motion, with a relatively long path between collisions as compared to their size. More precisely, the usual gas laws followed if attractions between these molecules were neglected, and if they were treated as point masses. But what was known about matter made it extremely implausible that tiny bits of matter would exert no force on one another when extremely close. And, of course, the bits of matter would be expected to have size—indeed, substantial collective size, since solids were supposed to consist of molecules that virtually touched one another. Van der Waals showed that certain kinds of deviation from the standard gas laws followed when plausible assumptions about intermolecular force and molecular size were adopted. Anyone taking an argument from molecule theory to Van der Waals' law as justifying the latter is making a genuinely theory-dependent inference. For there was nothing in the received body of empirical regularities that made the novel empirical expectations likely—indeed, the contrary was the case.

2. Dalton mobilized the atomic theory to explain the laws of definite and of multiple proportions. Suppose that A and B are both substances that cannot be broken down into observably different substances. Then, the ratios by mass in which they combine do not vary continuously, but are a few ratios of relatively small integers. Moreover, if m is one combining ratio of A and B, while n is another, m/n will also be a simple ratio. More accurately, these are approximately the observed results of chemical analysis, and they are approximated more closely as techniques become more reliable. Dalton's explanation is that elementary substances are composed of identical, indivisible bits of matter, while compounds are composed of identical combinations of these atoms (i.e., molecules, as we would now call them); each atom only makes a small number of attachments, characteristic of its kind. It follows that combinations are in simple and non-continuous ratios. If the claims about unobservable constituents are true, not just summaries of observable tendencies in chemical combination, then the spatial configuration of atoms in molecules should have an important influence on chemical activity, whenever the configuration of atoms in a given molecule is stable, and is repeated throughout the substance. More specifically,

if one takes the spatial talk in Dalton's theory as true, not just diagrammatic, then complex and rigid configurations will affect capacities to attach and, hence, to react chemically. But the same numbers of atoms of the same respective kinds can be locked in quite different configurations if the molecules are sufficiently complex. So, on the atomic hypothesis, there ought to be cases in which two substances can be broken down into the same chemical constituents, in just the same ratios, even though the substances have different chemical properties. In the usage invented by Berzelius, there ought to be isomers. Berzelius was guided by this reasoning in the researches that established that racemic acid and tartaric acid are isomers.

3. The genetic material incorporated in both parents is blended, in turn, in each of their offspring. At any rate, this was the received and plausible view in Darwin's lifetime. It is plausible, then, that a single tiny departure from the types of genetic material found among all other members of a breeding population should be highly diluted in its influence on the traits of all offspring, even more diluted among all grandchildren, and so forth. Darwinian speciation through individually small deviations from type is, then, impossible. The tiny mutations postulated by Darwin will be too diluted too quickly to become fixed in a population. More precisely, although actual breeding records (the available data) concern relatively gross traits, belief in the blending theory as true, not just a convenient summary of the records, makes the quantitative inference that blocks Darwinism extremely plausible, as Darwin's most thoughtful critics took it to be.[5]

4. Until the mid-twentieth-century, the best explanation of the gross geological features of the earth's surface was that they were due to sedimentation, erosion, volcanic activity and the crinkling of a gradually cooling crust. If one treated this model of the earth's activity as true and applied the leading physical theories to it, it was highly implausible that the continents drifted with respect to each other. The fluidity required by the drift would preclude the crinkling. Starting with Antonio Snider in 1858, some geologists had appealed to similar fossilized life forms in now distant places as evidence for continental drift. But believers in theories had grounds for dismissing their hypothesis. (Even now, when plate tectonics is

---

[5] The most impressive argument of this kind was Fleeming Jenkin's essay on *The Origin* in 1867. Darwin himself was impressed, indeed was "fairly disgusted to find how much I have to modify." For Jenkin's essay and Darwin's responses, see David Hull, *Darwin and His Critics* (Chicago, 1973), pp. 303–44.

the core of geology, there is no well-established theory of how the plates move.)[6]

5. Electromagnetic changes at one point are followed by changes at a different point with a delay governed by definite laws. If one seeks to explain this phenomenon, it is implausible to attribute it to action-at-a-distance. In effect, charged bodies would have to be equipped with telepathy, memories and stopwatches to obey the laws. Given nineteenth-century data, someone committed to explaining what is observable will have grounds for supposing that electromagnetic fields are propagated through stresses or other structural changes in an all-pervasive medium. Moreover, by 1860 the best explanation of heat phenomena was the kinetic-molecular theory. But hot bodies can radiate heat through a space devoid of molecules. So, if one believes in the ether as a universal medium for energy propagation and in kinetic-molecular theory as well, one is justified in supposing that radiant heat is a perturbation in the ether caused by the motion of molecules.[7] Since such motions are subject to continuous variations in nineteenth-century mechanics, the emitted energy of radiant heat must be subject to continuous variations. This provides the basis for the theory of radiant heat that Rayleigh developed and Planck and others overthrew.

When one looks at the writings of good scientists, one discovers that some, as great as Maxwell and Berzelius, are inclined to believe what intra-theoretical plausibility suggests while others, as great as Darwin and Hertz are inclined to be agnostic. Standard realist arguments imply that a scientist should not have the more agnostic attitude toward theoretical science as a whole, because reliance on intra-theoretic plausibility has been such a success. But the above sample is typical. The record of such reasoning is mixed at best. Van der Waals and Berzelius were led to brilliant discoveries by the kind of reasoning that misled Darwin's most thoughtful opponents, kept continental drift at the margins of geology for over a century, produced frustrating dead ends in Maxwell's work and wildly false laws of radiant heat in his immediate successors'. So far as general principles of inference show, a reasonable person could deny that the successful uses of intra-theoretical plausibility that shine among the failed ones are so frequent that they stand in need of an explana-

---

[6] See the superb popular account by J. Tuzo Wilson, a pioneer of plate tectonics, "Continental Drift," *Scientific American* (April 1963), pp. 86–88; see also Patrick Hurley, "The Confirmation of Continental Drift," *Scientific American* (April 1968), pp. 52f.

[7] See Maxwell, *Theory of Heat* (London, 1904), pp. 336–38.

Relying on Theories — 459

tion, an explanation appealing to the approximate truth of the theories that scientists use. And this freedom not to believe is all that anti-realism requires.

There are other kinds of reasoning that logically, not just psychologically, depend on commitment to the truth of theories. But in these cases, too, the record of success and failure is decidedly mixed. As Putnam has noted, a certain kind of intolerance of contradiction presupposes a realist treatment of the theories involved. If T and T′ make statements about the same kind of unobservable, if the empirical laws entailed by each are consistent with those entailed by the other, and if T is inconsistent with T′, this is not a problem standing in need of a solution provided that T or T′ or both are simply treated as convenient summaries of the respective laws.[8] Thus, there is no problem in accepting that light, in any non-accelerating frame of reference, behaves *as if* it were propagated in a stationary medium, while believing that a substance that is stationary in one frame of reference is moving in every other one that has a velocity relative to the first. This is as easy as believing that a friend behaves as if he were Dmitri Karamazov, while believing that Dostoyevsky's novels are pure fiction. One isn't shocked that his father is not named "Fyodor." As the same example from physics shows, the realist attitude that makes the conflict of T with T′ a genuine and urgent problem can lead to fundamental discoveries. In contrast, for example, to Poincaré's calm acceptance of the contradiction between classical mechanics and classical electrodynamics, Einstein took the conflict to be an urgent problem, justifying the bold hypotheses, dramatic conceptual shifts and complex calculations of relativity theory. This result of the realist attitude is impressive. Indeed, along with modern molecular theory it is the most impressive yet. But on the other hand, when Maxwell was intolerant of contradictions between electrodynamics and mechanics, he pursued dead ends. Darwin's vacillations in the face of the contradiction between evolutionary theory and contemporary genetics are widely regarded as his weakest moment.

A certain understanding of genuine theory dependence has emerged, which undermines even the subtlest current arguments for realism when combined with the history of science I have sketched. A method is genuinely theory-dependent just in case it depends on expectations that are only reasonable for someone who

[8] "Explanation and Reference" (1973) in *Mind, Language and Reality* (New York, 1979), pp. 210f.

believes that relevant theories are approximately true. Weaker forms of dependence abound in which theories are actually used in successful reasoning by investigators who would have found it difficult, perhaps impossible to reach the same conclusions without the theories. The pharmacologist's reasoning is an example of this pervasive psychological dependence. But the contribution of merely psychological dependence can be explained as due to the heuristic importance of theories in summarizing vast congeries of tendencies among observables. Even those who demand an explanation of success need not appeal to truth, here. It might seem that there is a third sort of dependence, in which the expectations are only reasonable for someone who always prefers the hypothesis that would be most likely to be true if the most defensible current background theories *were* true. This is a different and relevant option if such an attitude is reasonable on the part of someone who only takes theories to be useful fictions. But, I argued in Chapter Eight, such a fictionalist position is, in fact, unreasonable. Background theories do not deserve such a privileged position, if they are fictions.

A realist inference from success must be an inference from the successful contribution of genuinely theory-dependent methods. Sometimes, those methods have contributed to reliable prediction and control (Van der Waals, Berzelius). Sometimes, they have detracted from predictive reliability and control (Maxwell, Rayleigh). There is an explanation of this pattern, namely, that the positive cases are due to the approximate truth of the theories used, the negative cases to their falsehood, at least in those aspects that contributed to the failures. But surely, reason does not require belief in this explanation. A reasonable person might take it as a given that theory-dependent methods sometimes contribute to reliable prediction and control, as they do to other virtues, and sometimes detract from each of these virtues. Each epistemological temperament is sometimes a basis for successful and internally consistent science. And that is the end of the matter. In contrast, it would be unreasonable just to take it as a given that genuinely theory-dependent methods have contributed with enormously greater frequency than they have detracted. If this were the case, it would be unreasonable not to accept Boyd's explanation. But the pattern of success that would demand an explanation has not occurred.

That theory-dependent methods make an enormous contribution on balance is sometimes qualified with the hedge that they do so in mature or well-established sciences. But nineteenth-century physics has always seemed mature and well-established. And the-

ory-dependent reasoning, there, failed about as often as it succeeded. At present, fundamental physics has two well-established
branches, one of which (relativity theory) is an outgrowth of theory-
dependent reasoning, the other of which (quantum mechanics) is
the outcome of agnosticism about deep-seated causal principles.
Most of the creators of quantum mechanics were proudly willing to
assert what was implausible in light of all current views of unobservable processes, *without* vindicating a suitable alternative view. The
standard realist argument requires a standard of maturity that science has not grown up to, so far. This does not mean that realism is
wrong, but it does mean that the standard defense of realism is
wrong. A case for realism cannot be based on an accurate, non-question-begging description of the extent to which the use of theories
has typically been successful.

## THE MANY CASES FOR REALISM

If this criticism of the standard arguments for realism is right, a
valid argument will not be all-embracing. It will not describe a general pattern of success characteristic of many sciences, and show
that reason dictates acceptance of a corresponding realm of unobservables, wherever this pattern is found.

"The" argument for realism is an indefinitely, but by no means
infinitely large number of arguments making disbelief in particular
kinds of unobservables unreasonable, in light of the data. The arguments are further developments of cases for unobservables in the
literature of science, as against the literature of the philosophy of
science. Some of the unobservables whose existence turns out to be
rationally compelling are: tiny living things, too small for the naked
eye to see, of whose existence Leeuwenhoek gave the first account;
molecules, the compelling case for which is largely based on Einstein's theoretical arguments and the investigations of Perrin and
his colleagues; genes, based in part on Mendel's and Morgan's
work; electrons, on the basis of Millikan's findings, among others;
and continental drift, for which Tuzo Wilson contributed some of
the most impressive arguments. In each case, the only task of the
philosopher of science is to show that the standard accounts ultimately depend on beliefs that scientists of all epistemological temperaments share, beliefs that only a philosophical skeptic would
profess to doubt. There is a remaining, general philosophical task,
which I will take up later, of showing that the needed commitment
to these truisms is not itself dogmatic. But this task is not as specific

to the philosophy of science and not as urgent, in any case, since present-day anti-realists are, in effect, committed to the basic truisms on which these cases for realism rest. *Indeed, since present-day anti-realists cannot escape such commitments, the arguments for unobservables that employ those truisms show how anti-realism defeats itself.*

These days, anti-realists do not think that the observational part of science, in which they do believe, consists of propositions that, on account of their very content, are indubitable for any observer who sincerely reports them. They do not think that the realm of observables can be defined in terms of any favored vocabulary. They do not think these things for the good reason that fifty years of epistemological criticism has established that there is no such privileged kind of proposition, and that philosophers' best candidates for this privileged status could not even support commitment to the routine characterizations of middle-sized objects on which scientific observation always depends.[9] Moreover, anti-realists do not base their trust in our typical capacity to perceive shape, color, texture, and the like on some general principle of inference to the best explanation. For such principles would dictate realism, when applied to the empirical regularities that theories explain. Yet anti-realists still distinguish between observation and theory, claiming that the former is more trustworthy than the latter. What is the basis for their trust? None is left except commitment to truisms such as this, as precepts that every rational person ought to accept, at least if he or she has a course of experience similar to actual human beings': if the eyesight and touch of several observers seem to reveal that something is a middle-sized object with a certain shape, that is a reason to believe that it does have that shape. But there are other precepts, just as truistic and fundamental, that can, in principle, support belief in objects that are not ordinary or middle-sized, for example: if a non-living thing is in constant erratic motion, that is reason to believe it is constantly being pushed to and fro; if something makes the barely discernible clear and distinct, that is reason to suppose it can make the invisible visible. These are examples of the principles that figure in the many cases for unobservables. So the present approach, re-

9 See, for example, Otto Neurath, "Protocol Sentences" (1932) in A. J. Ayer, ed., *Logical Positivism* (New York, 1959); W. V. Quine, "Two Dogmas of Empiricism" (1951) in his *From a Logical Point of View* (New York, 1953); H. Putnam, "What Theories Are Not" (1962) in his *Mathematics, Matter and Method* (Cambridge, 1980); G. Maxwell, "The Ontological Status of Theoretical Entities" in H. Feigl and G. Maxwell, eds., *Minnesota Studies in the Philosophy of Science*, vol. 3 (Minneapolis, 1962); J. L. Austin, *Sense and Sensibilia* (Oxford, 1962).

lying on topic-specific principles, has the advantage of relying on no more than present-day anti-realists implicitly grant.

Of course, in the old days, when anti-realists claimed that empirical knowledge was only about logical constructions out of sense data, they had a basis for rejecting the crucial truisms, which are not compelling if construed in this old style. But the epistemological framework for the realism controversy has been changed—as usual, not self-consciously enough to change the outcome.

For reasons of space, I will confine myself to sketching the first two items in the above list of arguments for realism: microbes and molecules.

It will be obvious how similar arguments might be extracted elsewhere. It will also be obvious that similar arguments need *not* be latent whenever one theory of underlying causes is the best of the actual rivals in a science that has gained increased reliability through theory-dependent methods. For example, it has sometimes turned out, in retrospect, that the best theory conflicted with truisms as basic as those it respected and that a possible, but non-actual rival could have been as well-supported, as a result. Thus, Newtonian mechanics, with its characteristic entities (absolute space and time, universal gravitational attraction and conserved mass), could not have been defended against all possible rivals, even when rock-bottom truisms are combined with eighteenth-century data. Mach's anti-Newtonian argument, with which Einstein begins his paper on general relativity, would have been perfectly accessible to any post-Galilean scientist. It is an anomaly that mere spatial orientation should flatten a sphere. Moreover, wave theories of light were always at least as well confirmed as Newton's corpuscular theory, indeed, most of the time have been better-confirmed. And if light is a wave phenomenon it is implausible that the speed of light in vacuo, emitted from a moving body, should be faster in some frames of reference than others or faster in some directions than others. The regularities in refraction indicate that the speed of a wavefront is determined by a basic property of the light itself, together with properties of the media, if any. That basic properties of matter do not depend on the frame of reference chosen is a fundamental Galilean principle. And since light seemed to have no mass, it was unlikely that it moved more quickly in the direction of a moving light source; the emitter creates the light, but cannot push it. In sum, one can imagine a seventeenth-century Einstein—more ingenious, it is true, than Newton and Einstein combined—criticizing Newtonian physics and constructing a relativistic alternative at least as well-confirmed. This is not to say that Newtonian physics was not well-con-firmed. Confirmation is superiority over actual rivals. But present-day anti-realists are asking whether theories are more reasonable than all possible rivals, in light of actual data. Perhaps someday the artificiality of the distinctive methods of modern quantum electro-dynamics will turn out to be a clue to some just-as-good rival to quantum mechanics, which is available in principle today.[10]

By basing realism on a series of little arguments, we allow for such possibilities of local anti-realism, which are plausible on the face of it. Reason and actual evidence often dictate tentative belief in the approximate truth of a theory and of existence claims about vast kinds of unobservables. But "often" does not mean always, not even for theories that are the best actually available, as the Newtonian ex-ample shows. A case for unobservables must be clear about how much is being established, and must display good judgment about the connection of what is established with the full array of relevant truisms. If such connections must be the basis for the argument dic-tating belief, it is quite unlikely that reason and evidence always dic-tate belief in the best current theory.

[10] The suspect procedure is "renormalization," which requires, not the usual neg-lect of arbitrarily small terms, but the neglect of certain infinitely large ones. Renor-malization is basic to determining the fundamental magnitudes in electron charge and electron mass. Without it, the basic equations of electron motion would, for ex-ample, be undetermined. Yet, in a recent work, Feynman, a co-inventor of renor-malization, says it is "what I would call a dippy process! . . . I suspect that renormali-zation is not mathematically legitimate"; *QED* (Princeton, 1985), p. 128. In an earlier, technical presentation of quantum electrodynamics, he labelled his creation "just a dirty-looking prescription"; *The Theory of Fundamental Processes* (New York, 1962), p. 144. Though the need for renormalization suggests that quantum electrodynamics may not be the only possible reasonable response to the data, Feynman obviously thinks quantum electrodynamics is a confirmed theory, the only reasonable response given current frameworks. He can make this claim in spite of the mathematical in-consistencies. For those problems might reflect details of mathematical presentation that are relatively peripheral to the basic physical claims of the theory. Thus, the standard means of describing continuous magnitudes in quantum mechanics, the Dirac delta function, lacked a mathematically consistent description for decades, and was always in use, with serene confidence that the mathematical details would be worked out. In addition to illustrating the difference between confirming a theory and showing that reason and evidence alone dictate its acceptance, quantum electro-dynamics illustrates the continuing role of approximate truth in assessing even the best-established and most exact sciences. For Feynman, quantum electrodynamics is "the jewel of physics—our proudest possession," in contrast to the guesswork of much nuclear physics (*QED*, p. 8). Yet his ultimate argument is for its approximate truth, in contrast to the falsehood of all relevant current rivals. See *QED*, p. 129; *The Theory of Fundamental Processes*, pp. 18, 145.

## MICROBE HUNTING

Microbes provide a good introduction to the localized arguments, based on topic-specific principles, that establish the existence of unobservables. The premises of the arguments are elementary, and the data are familiar, indeed are now part of the personal knowledge of many curious teen-agers. I will rely on the data and the largely implicit arguments in Leeuwenhoek's original correspondence with the Royal Society. But I urge anyone who thinks disbelief in unobservables is always a rational option to get a microscope and acquire similar data.

Anton Leeuwenhoek was a prosperous soft-goods merchant and hard-working amateur scientist, most of whose important scientific work was done in the 1670s. Though he showed great practical ingenuity in coping with problems of lens grinding and, especially, illumination, he had no substantial knowledge of theoretical optics or, indeed, of any other branch of theoretical science. His basic scientific reports, letters to the Royal Society in London, are written in plain Dutch, the only language he knew, and begin with the apologies, "first . . . I have no style or pen with which to express my thoughts properly; secondly . . . I have not been brought up to languages or arts, but only to business; in the third place, . . . I do not gladly suffer contradiction or censure from others . . . my observations and thoughts are the outcome of my own unaided impulse and curiosity alone."[11] Though Leeuwenhoek was eager to let visitors examine specimens under his microscopes, he would not permit them to disassemble and closely study the microscopes, being jealous of his craft secrets. Yet, on the basis of his letters, the approximate reproduction of many of Leeuwenhoek's results, and visits to look through Leeuwenhoek's microscopes, the best scientists of this great age of science, including such skeptical and rigorous investigators as Robert Hooke, accepted Leeuwenhoek's remarkable claims in their most basic aspects.

Here is part of the series of observations that led to the ultimate conclusion that there are utterly invisible living things. The examples are all taken from Leeuwenhoek's letters or contemporary accounts of his work.

Initially, Leeuwenhoek used some of his equipment to look at small but visible objects. Like curious teen-agers instructed by modern microscope kits, he looked at bee stingers and grains of sand, for

[11] Clifford Dobell, *Antony van Leeuwenhoek and his "Little Animals"* (New York, 1960), p. 42.

example. Details that one can barely make out in a blurry way, looking very carefully at such objects with a naked eye, stand out much more clearly and distinctly under apparatus such as he first used. Seen close-up with the naked eye, bee stingers look very vaguely barbed or feathery. Seen close up, many grains of sand look rough, and at least approximately faceted. Putting these objects under the microscopes, Leeuwenhoek saw distinct rows of barbs in the one case, what "looked like the finest crystal with facettes"[12] in the other. Even more propitiously, he looked through the equipment at tiny but barely visible animals, cheese mites and the recently discovered "water fleas," which would now be called *Daphnia*. One can barely see these creatures, if one knows where to look, and, in a blurry way, one can see the general arrangement of their grosser parts. Under the microscope, they seem to have corresponding distinct parts, appearing with certain details that are otherwise unobservable, e.g., the facets of the mites' eyes. Leeuwenhoek, of course, concluded that the details that clearly appeared under the apparatus really existed. When later equipment made those details loom larger, and other phenomena appeared, entirely unseen before, he trusted in the new equipment as revealing yet smaller aspects of reality.

Leeuwenhoek's first description of utterly invisible living things, in 1674, is a report on some cloudy water he had collected from a nearby pond. Its tone is conveyed by the following passage, in which the first detailed observations of green alga are followed by the first reports of entirely microscopic Protozoa:

> [E]xamining this water next day I found floating therein divers earthy particles, and some green streaks, spirally wound serpent-wise, and orderly arranged, after the manner of the copper or tin worms, which distillers used to cool their liquors as they distill over. The whole circumference of each of these streaks was about the thickness of a hair of one's head. . . . Among these there were, besides, very many little animalcules, whereof some were round-ish, while others, a bit bigger, consisted of an oval. On these last I saw two little legs near the head, and two little fins at the hindmost end of the body. . . . And the notion of most of these animalcules in the water was so swift, and so various, upwards, downwards, and round about, that 'twas wonderful to see: and I judge that some of these little creatures were above a thousand times smaller

---

[12] Ibid., p. 66, from a contemporary's report of a visit to Leeuwenhoek.

[i.e., in volume] than the smallest ones I have ever yet seen, upon the rind of cheese, in wheaten flour, mould, and the like.[13]

His next report begins:

> I discovered living creatures in rain, which had stood but a few days in a new tub, that was painted blue within. This observation provoked me to investigate this water more narrowly; and especially because these little animals were, to my eye, more than ten thousand times smaller [again in volume] than the animalcule which Swammerdam has portrayed, and called by the name of Water-flea, or Water-louse, which you can see alive and moving in water with the bare eye.[14]

In reading Leeuwenhoek's various reports, sophisticated scientists had no general reluctance to doubt him, sometimes finding his anatomical speculations almost as quaint as we do. But, to bring the story to its happy close, the Royal Society soon accepted the remarkable finding that there was a variety of living things, smaller than the eye can see. In a letter to Leeuwenhoek of 1677, Hooke emphasized the profusion of animals in solutions of black pepper, Leeuwenhoek's most fertile medium:

> [T]he Members . . . have ordered me to returne you both their thanks . . . and also an account of what hath been done in order to verify your observation concerning the small animalls you have first discovered in Pepper-water. . . . I could discover divers very small creatures swimming up and down in every one of those steepings and even in Raine it self and that they had various shapes & differing motions, yet I found none soe exceedingly filled and stuffed as it were with them as was the water in which some cornes of pepper had been steeped. Of this the President & all the members present were satisfied & it seems very wonderfull that there should be such an infinite number of animalls in soe imperceptible a quantity of matter. That these animalls should be soe perfectly shaped & indeed with such curious organs of motion as to be able to move nimbly, to turne, stay, accelerate & retard their progresse at pleasure. And it was not less surprising to find that these were gygantick monsters in comparison of a lesser sort which almost filled the water.[15]

[13] Ibid., pp. 110, 111.
[14] Ibid., p. 117f.
[15] Ibid., p. 183.

The principles of scientific optics play no significant role in early discussions of "animalcules," though Hooke was fully capable of such theorizing, and could have called on his fellow member Newton for a consultation. Rather, two elementary principles are constantly relied on. Though they are so basic that they go without saying, they are repeatedly evident, just below the surface of these writings about the unobservably small.

The first principle is that a procedure is typically reliable if it seems to reveal clearly and distinctly what is, on close observation, unaided by that procedure, visible in a blurry way. Using this principle, Leeuwenhoek and Hooke can establish, step by step, both the validity and the scale of investigations of the tiny. Leeuwenhoek's first letter to the Society concerns investigations of such items as "the sting and sundry little limbs of the bee."[16] Validated as making the barely visible clearer, these early microscopes provide a standard against which one can evaluate later apparatus, such as the stronger microscopes revealing the invisible structure of human hair and the eye of a louse. What is vaguely present in the earlier microscope is clearly and distinctly present in the later, along with new phenomena not previously seen at all. So the new microscopes can be relied on when they seem to reveal little creatures smaller than the width of a hair, a tenth the diameter of a louse's eye, a tenth the length of a cheese mite, and so on through the almost obsessive comparisons in Leeuwenhoek's writings. Suppose, by contrast, that the first microscope had been, by some fluke, an extremely high-powered device in which invisible Protozoa loomed large. Far from inspiring rational belief, the first microscope would have been a curiosity, a new and frightening kind of kaleidoscope.

The other principle concerns motion and life: if something has distinct and fairly stable boundaries, if it frequently and unpredictably changes its state of motion with respect to its environment, if the changes are not caused by any external factor, and if they are associated with the movements of its parts, then it should be taken to be alive, unless there is evidence to the contrary. Movement, in short, is a sign of life. Leeuwenhoek and Hooke constantly emphasize the variety of movements of the animalcules. By contrast, the status of yeast was highly controversial until well into the nineteenth century.

Of course, the underlying principles concerning detection, motion and life do not yield certainty, when properly understood.

[16] Ibid., p. 42.

Leeuwenhoek might have been engaging in chicanery, projecting distorted images of guppies into his apparatus. The whole toy industry is largely based on the fact that an articulated object, propelled by a moving part, need not be a living thing. The most the principles yield is a prima facie case. If the conditions are met, one ought to accept the conclusion unless there is some definite reason not to do so. Even this may be too strong. In science, if not on Anglo-American criminal juries, when the conclusion is an unexpected belief, it is routinely checked by considering the most likely contrary causal accounts of the data, and eliminating them. Thus, the Royal Society could eliminate the possibility that chicanery or, more likely, wishful thinking distorted Leeuwenhoek's account by duplicating his more surprising findings with similar apparatus. Still, once all currently likely specific rival hypotheses are eliminated, it is unreasonable not to accord tentative belief to the conclusions of the elementary principles.

Despite all the hedges, these principles can move all reasonable people, of the most diverse epistemological temperaments, to the same conclusion, if they mobilize appropriate data. No one who has played with a decently constructed microscope for a while has seriously doubted that the more articulate and mobile things that seem to be revealed in pond water are, in fact, living things. Though they cannot be seen without instruments and the theory of those instruments is fairly esoteric, the status of the apparent animalcules as living is no more in doubt than the status of the first kangaroo one sees, with one's naked eyes.

In the case of microorganisms, the role of elementary principles is relatively clear and immediate. It might seem that this marks off the argument for this kind of unobservable as a very special case. In particular, in physics and chemistry, arguments for the existence of an unobservable kind of thing explicitly rely on technical principles, which a reasonable person could doubt. In fact, the role of topic-specific common-sense principles is basically the same in the physical sciences, when propositions are given the status that realism requires. Granted, crucial parts of the arguments that compel tentative belief are esoteric. But when an argument really does make disbelief in a kind of unobservable unreasonable, this special force depends on support from specific principles of the same kind as the ones on which Leeuwenhoek relied. The argument that, historically, vindicated realism concerning molecules is representative of the role of such truisms in realism about entities in physical theories.

## FROM MOLECULAR HYPOTHESIS TO
## MOLECULAR TRUTH

In the realism dispute, appeals to microbes are always a bit shame-faced. The most defensible versions of anti-realism rate microbes as unobservable. So the appeals to microbes are fair. But everyone knows that anti-realists would rate microbes as observable, if they could.

By contrast, molecules are the paradigm of a posit that anti-realists regard as simply a convenient device for summary and prediction concerning observables. Yet, though this is the best-explored terrain in the realism dispute, the actual history of the scientific controversy over molecules does not fit either anti-realism or standard arguments for realism. This history has two main phases. One, taking up the first half of the nineteenth century, is the familiar story of how studies of combining ratios, analogies in chemical behavior, vapor densities and specific heats led to the physical chemistry summed up in modern chemical formulas and the periodic table. In the other, much more rapid phase, played out from 1905 until 1912 at the latest, phenomena of motion, above all, Brownian motion, were used to justify and refine the theory of molecules. If present-day anti-realists *or* realists were right, each phase should have had the same outcome (i.e., the second should have been an anti-climax). On the anti-realist view, the nineteenth-century studies should have established no more than the empirical adequacy of molecule theory, a conclusion on which the early twentieth-century work could not improve. Given the realist style of inference from general patterns of success, the first phase should have made disbelief in molecules unreasonable, so that, again, the twentieth-century phase was simply more of the same, so far as the very existence of molecules is concerned.

These assessments fly in the face of the actual responses of good scientists. After the first phase, agnosticism about molecules was the preferred option for many good scientists, through the end of the century. It was only the work on Brownian motion that closed off this option, converting scientists, such as Poincaré and Ostwald, who had believed in no more than the empirical adequacy of molecule theory. Both philosophical outlooks make early twentieth-century scientists' claims that the Brownian motion studies finally verify the existence of molecules look naive and historically ignorant—a rather implausible conclusion when the naifs must include Poincaré and Einstein. The problem is the common image of scientific rationality that realists and anti-realists share, the one in which reason is governed by general, topic-neutral principles. Any such principle that is at all attractive fits both phases equally well. Perhaps it is time to reassess the realism dispute through the respectful study of scientific practice that has transformed the philosophical analysis of confirmation. When scientists have claimed to have found ways to establish whether a thoroughly useful theory is, also, true, they have something to teach philosophers. What turns out to explain the actual shift in the scientific view of molecules is the other image of rationality, in which topic-specific truisms play a basic and independent role.[17]

For purposes of convenience, the developments in the earlier phase can largely be divided into more purely chemical work, relying on combining ratios and analogies in chemical activity, and work depending on gas laws and thermodynamics, appealing to vapor densities, specific heats and the like. Dalton (1808) used the atomic hypothesis to explain the laws of definite and of multiple proportions. The argument was impressive. But, even assuming atomic theory, it did not give strong support to particular atomic formulas or atomic weights, since there was as yet no basis for deciding the number of atoms in a free molecule of the most common elements.[18] In the 1820s, Mitscherlich, Berzelius and others supplied this lack, for many substances, by the study of chemical isomorphism. The molecular theory suggested that atom-for-atom substitution within a molecule should produce a substance with analogous chemical properties. Mitscherlich and Berzelius found that reactions which molecular theory interpreted in that way did tend to have this re-

[17] Here are two pedantic digressions. Should one call it "the molecular theory" or "the atomic theory"? In light of quantum mechanics, the former label seems best, since the theories in question work well at the molecular level, and generally fail when they speak of the internal structure of atoms. But nineteenth-century usage happens to be "the atomic theory" and "the atomic hypothesis," where accounts of chemical composition are concerned. I will generally favor "molecular," but sometimes use "atomic" to avoid anachronism. Similarly, I will sometimes speak of the *molecular-kinetic* theory in thermodynamics, to acknowledge that some saw matter as molecular, but heat as non-kinetic. The second elaboration concerns the close focus on Brownian motion. Other work, such as studies of ionization and of the radiometer effect, played a supporting role. See, for example, Boltzmann, *Lectures on Gas Theory* (Berkeley, 1964), p. 25. But most neutral observers took the Brownian motion studies to be the turning point. And the other work marshalled truisms about movement in ways analogous to the Brownian motion studies.

[18] An atomic weight is the ratio of the mass of an atom of the element in question to that of a standard substance, assigned a standard number as its weight. The ultimate standard was 16 for oxygen, giving hydrogen a "weight" very close to 1.

sult. And they used such structural reasoning to assign a variety of weights and formulas.

Three years after Dalton's *A New System of Chemical Philosophy*, Avogadro (1811) stimulated a parallel and interacting series of studies, involving the explanation of thermodynamic phenomena and of the role of volume in reactions among gases. He explained Gay-Lussac's law that gases combine in integral ratios by volume, on the basis of the molecular theory, combined with the hypothesis that equal volumes of different gases, at the same temperature and pressure, contain the same number of molecules. Pressure-volume-temperature relations in gases can be explained on the same basis. In the 1820s, Dumas and Gaudin employed Avogadro's hypothesis to assign a variety of atomic weights, implying a vast number of formulas, through the determination of the density of vaporized substances. Meanwhile, Dulong and Petit (1819) had developed a principle like Avogadro's, that could be applied both to volatile and non-volatile substances: the amount of heat required to raise by one degree Centigrade a gram-atom of any elementary solid (i.e., its atomic weight expressed in grams) is the same. In other words, they showed that this principle approximately fit facts already established concerning atomic weights, and that the further weights assigned were compatible with known phenomena of combination.

The determination of atomic weights was crucial to most uses of molecular theory. The fit of the weights assigned by these different routes, one to another and with other relevant findings, was only approximate. However, in his paper of 1858, Cannizzaro could show that the fit was striking, despite the different methods used, that it tended to improve as techniques became more sensitive, and that the most serious discrepancies were removed by theoretical modifications that were extremely plausible if molecular theory as a whole was true. His presentation at the Karlsruhe Conference two years later is widely accepted as a turning point, after which the molecular theory became the working hypothesis of all the leading chemists. As a participant remembered, years later, "The scales seemed to fall from my eyes. . . . [M]ore and more the old atomic weights of Berzelius came into their own. As soon as the apparent discrepancies between Avogadro's rule and that of Dulong and Petit had been removed by Cannizzaro, both were found capable of practically universal application."[19]

[19] See Aaron Ihde, *The Development of Modern Chemistry* (New York, 1964), p. 229. Chapters 4–8 of Ihde's book are a detailed narrative of the development of atomic

Here is a prime example of how decades of experiment and theorizing can convince the scientific community that a theory is, by far, the best explanation of diverse and important data. Were all, or nearly all, good, reasonable and thoughtful scientists who were convinced of the superiority of the theory also convinced of its truth? No, not in 1860 or at any other time in the nineteenth century. Mach and Poincaré are just the most eminent, creative, and emphatic of the many agnostics.[20] They regarded the molecular theory as, at best, an economic means of summarizing empirical laws. Thus, Ostwald, an important chemist and perhaps the most widely read textbook writer in the field, would introduce atomic theory in his texts with anti-realist glosses such as this (1904): "In general a hypothesis is an aid to *representation*. . . . [T]he atomic hypothesis has proved to be an exceedingly useful aid to instruction and investigation, since it greatly facilitates the interpretation and the use of the general laws. One must not, however, be led astray by this agreement between picture and reality and combine the two."[21] Writing forty years after Cannizzaro's paper, Boltzmann, who was engaged in deriving the thermodynamic consequences of literal belief in the molecular constitution of gases, expresses isolation and despair: "In my opinion it would be a great tragedy for science if the theory of gases were temporarily thrown into oblivion because of a momentary hostile attitude toward it. . . . I am conscious of being only an individual struggling weakly against the stream of time."[22]

So far, the history of molecular theory is a powerful case against realism. Reasonable scientists of a relatively agnostic temperament seem to have accepted that the existence of molecules was part of the best explanation of extremely diverse phenomena, without believing in molecules. The case is all the more impressive since Glymour, among other present-day realists, has singled out the nineteenth-century phase as a paradigm of how to establish the truth of a theory.[23] And yet, just ten years after Boltzmann's declaration of isolation, the state of informed opinion had utterly and perma-

---

theory from Dalton to Cannizzaro. Most of Jean Perrin, *Atoms* (New York, 1923), ch. 1, is a concise, lucid and careful statement of the nineteenth-century case for atomic theory, sketched by a leader in the twentieth-century phase.

[20] Mach, "On the Economic Nature of Physical Inquiry" (1882) in his *Popular Scientific Lectures* (New York, 1895), is a characteristic and highly influential statement. For Poincaré on the molecular hypothesis, circa 1903, see *Science and Hypothesis* (New York, 1952), pp. 152, 164, 212.

[21] *The Principles of Inorganic Chemistry* (London, 1904), pp. 149, 151.

[22] Foreword to part 2, *Lectures on Gas Theory*, p. 216.

[23] See *Theory and Evidence* (Princeton, 1980), pp. 226–63.

nently shifted. In the 1908 Preface to a new edition of his *Outline of Physical Chemistry*, Ostwald announced:

> *I have become convinced that we recently came into possession of experimental proofs of the discrete or particulate nature of matter, proofs which the atomic hypothesis vainly sought for centuries, indeed, for millennia.* The separation and measurement of ionized gases, on the one hand, which the long and splendid researches of J.J. Thomson have crowned with complete success, and, on the other hand, the agreement of Brownian motion with the demands of the kinetic hypothesis, which was established by a series of investigators, finally and most completely by J. Perrin, justify even a cautious investigator in speaking of an experimental proof of the atomic nature of extended matter.[24]

Two years later, this excitement of conversion has given way to the assertive blandness of his new textbook treatment of the atomic theory: "[T]he weight relations of chemical compounds can be perfectly and clearly expressed by the supposition of the existence of atoms. This makes it seem very probable that substances are actually so constituted, and this view has been confirmed by discoveries in utterly different fields."[25] In 1912, Poincaré, perhaps the most committed anti-realist of all great scientists, declared, "[A]toms are no longer a useful fiction. . . . The atom of the chemist is now a reality."[26]

The most important factor in this change, acknowledged by all, was the work on Brownian motion in which Einstein was the leading theorist, Perrin the leading experimenter. Einstein's papers, beginning in 1905, develop the argument with his usual elegant simplicity.

Brownian motion is a phenomenon discovered by Robert Brown, a botanist, in 1828. Small particles in dilute solution in a liquid are in constant irregular motion. Brown first observed the phenome-

---

[24] Preface (November 1908) to *Grundriss der allegemeinen Chemie* (Leipzig, 1909); Ostwald's emphasis. Ostwald is alluding to studies by Thomson and his co-workers in which uniform masses of ionized gas were isolated and their diffusion rates explained in ways precisely analogous to the work on Brownian motion. See Perrin, *Atoms*, pp. 176f.

[25] *Introduction to Chemistry* (Stuttgart, 1910; rpt. New York, 1911), p. 32.

[26] "Les Rapports de la Matière et de l'Ether" in *Dernières Pensées* (Paris, 1963), pp. 68f., 70. Stephen Brush has useful comments and voluminous references concerning the early twentieth-century triumph of molecular theory in *Kinetic Theory*, vol. 2 (Oxford, 1966), p. 6, and in the editorial apparatus of his edition of Boltzmann, *Lectures on Gas Theory*, pp. 13–17, 23–25, 215. See also Mary Jo Nye, *Molecular Reality: A Perspective on the Scientific Work of Jean Perrin* (London, 1972).

non in solutions of pollen, and thought a force specific to living matter was responsible. He abandoned this view when it turned out that quite inanimate particles, chalk scrappings, for example, behave in the same way. Another obstacle to vitalistic explanations was the fact that the movement is constant, and continues with the same liveliness so long as the temperature is maintained. The particles in slides from Perrin's laboratory are still dancing to this day. By 1905, two further facts had been established. The liveliness of Brownian motion varies directly with the temperature and inversely with the viscosity of the solvent. And, apart from temperature, no other known physical factor produces the movement. In particular, electromagnetic forces, convection currents and capillary actions were all shown to be irrelevant, by standard means.

Einstein begins his 1905 paper with what is, in effect, a powerful qualitative argument that the molecular hypothesis is true if osmotic pressure due to Brownian motion exists. (Amazingly, he had developed all the ideas of the paper, as descriptions of a hypothetical test, before he knew that Brownian motion existed. He admits to only a vague awareness of the literature on it, in the paper itself.) Suppose that a pure liquid, of a kind that does not have discrete parts unless the molecular hypothesis is true, fills a horizontal tube, closed at both ends. We insulate the tube from outside heat, electromagnetic fields and other external forces, and wait until the energy states that are supposed to characterize a continuous substance are in equilibrium. There is a piston in the middle of the tube, with a semi-permeable membrane. Particles of small but microscopically visible size are introduced into the tube, on one side of the piston. The membrane, permeable to the solvent medium, is impermeable to the particles. If the fluid is not made up of molecules, there is nothing capable of moving the particles, except for the force of gravity against which there can be no insulation. They will simply fall to the bottom of the tube. By the same token, if the particles are in constant irregular horizontal motion, with a net diffusion toward the other end and consequent pressure on the piston, something in the liquid is moving the particles. And motions of discrete parts of the liquid are the only such sources not already ruled out. In short, the osmotic pressure, i.e., the pressure on the membrane due to its semi-permeability, is evidence for the molecular theory. "According to the classical theory of thermodynamics . . . we would not expect to find any force acting on the partition. . . . But a different conception is reached from the standpoint of the molecular-kinetic theory of matter."[27]

[27] "On the Movement of Small Particles . . . " (1905) in Einstein, *Investigations on the*

This qualitative argument, which takes up three short paragraphs at the beginning of Einstein's paper, has a certain power that the more elaborate and quantitative arguments of mid-nineteenth-century atomists lacked. Faced, for example, with Dalton's appeals to ratios of combination, agnostics could propose that the ratios were regular tendencies standing in need of no explanation. There is no need for actual atoms and valences to make them true. And, indeed, leading textbooks, such as Ostwald's, took Dalton's accomplishment to be simply the discovery of such "chemical equivalences." On the other hand, it is a shared principle of reasonable people of all tendencies and schools of thought that when a non-living object constantly and erratically changes course, something external typically makes it change course. More precisely, this is to be concluded if a potential source of change can be identified and if there is no strong reason for supposing that change is spontaneous. It is not reasonable to suppose that dead leaves may be dancing spontaneously, quite apart from the influence of the wind, even if it is reasonable to suppose that Dalton's proportions reflect an uncaused tendency of certain substances to combine chemically with others in certain ratios. That there is osmotic pressure due to Brownian motion is a powerful argument for the molecular hypothesis, since it mobilizes the commonsense basis for all technical principles of inertia.

Still, Einstein's initial, qualitative argument is weak in certain respects. It depends on the assumption that external forces have been excluded and that internal equilibrium has been achieved. That standard means have been used and that no relevant disturbing factors have been found, despite much trying, was a substantial argument in favor of corresponding descriptions of experimental setups used to study Brownian motion in the early twentieth century. Still, such arguments have often proven misleading, depending on methods of isolation and detection that turned out to be defective. In the second place, though the qualitative argument gives reason to suppose that the liquid contains discrete moving sub-microscopic structures, they might still be different from what molecule theorists had in mind, perhaps so very different that they ought not to be called "molecules." Einstein's achievement, which takes up most of the 1905 paper and its successors, is to exclude these possibilities

---

*Theory of the Brownian Movement*, ed. R. Fuerth (New York, 1956), p. 3. By "the classical theory," Einstein means the attempt to base thermodynamics on differential equations concerning observable properties. In the classical theory, substances that are observably uniform and stable are treated as continuous and without internal motion.

in the standard way, through quantitative derivations. He shows that if the motive force on the particles is due to the action of sub-microscopic objects with the most basic and essential properties of molecules—random, independent motion of bits of matter much smaller than the Brownian particles and constituting the chemical substance in question, then an experimentalist should observe certain magnitudes, magnitudes which are highly unlikely to arise unless the motive force is of this kind.

Einstein's basic derivation concerns the rate of diffusion of Brownian particles through the solvent medium. Suppose that spherical particles of known diameter are introduced into a solvent. Then, Einstein shows, certain purely empirical laws provide one measure of the diffusion coefficient, i.e., of the ratio of the rate of diffusion at any point to the change in density of the particles at that point. On the other hand, the molecular-kinetic theory dictates another expression for the coefficient, in an entirely different way, depending on the most elementary and distinctive claims of the theory. Equate the two expressions, and a distinctive relation between the average displacement of a particle and the time elapsed results.

Both believers in molecules and agnostics accepted as a matter of empirical law that there is a diffusing force on the suspended particles that will produce an osmotic pressure on a semi-permeable membrane, in a process governed by precisely the same pressure-volume-temperature relations as expressed in the classical gas laws. In his first paper, Einstein shows that this is to be expected on the molecular-kinetic theory. But he notes that "an understanding of the conclusions reached in the present paper is not dependent on a knowledge . . . of this paragraph,"[28] and he omits the derivation from most subsequent accounts. The ambivalence is appropriate to his reasoning. The expression for the diffusing force can be established, through observation, without commitment to molecular theory, but it had better be an outcome of the latter if the theory is ultimately to be vindicated.

Everyone also accepts that a particle moved through a medium by a force is slowed down by the resistance of the medium. "This frictional resistance cannot in general be deduced theoretically. But when the dissolved molecule [a term Einstein is using, indifferently, for Brownian particles and chemical molecules] can be looked upon approximately as a sphere, which is large compared with a molecule of the solvent, we may ascertain the frictional resistance according

[28] Ibid., p. 4.

to the methods of ordinary hydrodynamics, which do not take account of the molecular constitution of the liquid."[29] The reasoning from osmotic pressure and the relevant hydrodynamic principle, Stokes' law, leads to an expression for the diffusion coefficient involving the temperature, the empirical constant in the classical gas law, the radius of the spherical particles, the viscosity of the solvent, and Avogadro's Number, the number of molecules that there would be in a gram molecule of a gas if Avogadro's Hypothesis is true. By 1905, various branches of physical chemistry provided values for the latter, based, for example, on phenomena of viscosity and electrolysis.

"The molecular theory of heat affords a second point of view, from which the process of diffusion can be considered. The process of irregular motion which we have to conceive of as the heat-content of a substance will operate in such a manner that the single molecules of a liquid will alter their positions in the most irregular manner thinkable."[30] Einstein's main achievement is to derive an expression for the diffusion coefficient solely from this distinctive and essential part of the molecular theory. The alternative expression equates the coefficient with one-half the ratio of the mean square of the displacement of a particle to the time that has elapsed in the course of the displacement. Thus, combined with empirical laws that all accept, the molecular theory has the distinctive consequence that the two expressions are the same. Equating and rearranging terms, this amounts to the claim that mean displacement of Brownian particles, in the course of diffusion, equals the square root of the time elapsed times a term involving the temperature, the constant in the gas law, the radius of the spheres, the viscosity of the solvent and Avogadro's Number.

The task for the experimenter is to manufacture tiny, uniform spheres of known dimensions, to exclude external forces so far as possible, and to cope with the problems of measuring mean displacements for rapid and irregular movements. Starting in 1908, Perrin and his colleagues successfully took up this heavy burden.

[29] "The Elementary Theory of the Brownian Motion" (1908) *Investigations on the Theory of the Brownian Movement*, p. 73. This essay is Einstein's clearest single account.

[30] Ibid., p. 76. Randomness is essential to the molecular theory. Clausius, Maxwell and Boltzmann constantly rely on it in explaining observed thermodynamic regularities. At an even more elementary level, if the molecular motions in a fluid of uniform temperature were not random, a substance in thermal equilibrium would often have an observable structure, displaying just the discontinuities that are not, in fact, observed.

Their labors involved months of sorting tiny latex particles by means of centrifuges. Eventually, cameras, stopwatches and microscopes were combined in a direct test of the displacement hypothesis. Initially, Perrin exploited the tendency for the molecular collisions and the force of gravity to create a distinctive vertical distribution at equilibrium. It was these studies, above all, that converted molecular agnostics from Poincaré's earlier view that the atom is a useful fiction, to his later one, that the atom of a chemist is a reality.

Why was this argument so compelling? The few realists who have studied this episode in detail have emphasized the use of the diffusion equations to estimate Avogadro's Number.[31] The estimates are in fairly close accord with one another, and with other estimates arrived at by quite different means. But what Einstein emphasizes is the availability of a molecular account of a phenomenon of motion, in which Avogadro's Number figures as an empirically determined constant. More importantly, an appeal to the coincidence of differently developed numerical estimates cannot, remotely, account for the distinctive outcome of the twentieth-century argument, as compared with the nineteenth-century ones. For Cannizzaro could also point to a variety of coincidences in important magnitudes, when they are estimated using independent parts of molecular theory. A variety of different routes warranted similar atomic weights. Indeed, atomic weights are, if anything, more important to molecular theory than Avogadro's Number. Given early twentieth-century ignorance about intermolecular forces, molecule theorists might, in principle, have accepted substantial departures from Avogadro's hypothesis. But it is hard to imagine how the molecular theory could be maintained in the face of gross violations of the Daltonian approach to chemical combination.

It is important to distinguish two kinds of doubt about the truth of the molecular, or any other theory. If someone accepts that Brownian phenomena stand in need of a causal explanation, but worries that the apparent success of the molecular explanation is due to inadequate experimental controls or false auxiliary hypotheses, then the coincidence of different values for Avogadro's Number is highly relevant to these doubts. And this is the kind of doubt that motivated Einstein's intricate argument, as against his initial reflections on osmotic pressure. However, if someone is inclined to deny that the Brownian phenomena stand in need of an

---

[31] See, for example, Nye, *Molecular Reality*, ch. 4.

explanation, the coincident values are not an appropriate response, any more than the coincident atomic weights had been half a century before. Like Mach, Ostwald and Poincaré, someone who is moved by the agnostic temperament will take the coincidence as showing that atomic theory is both an accurate and an economical way of summarizing empirical regularities, not that it is true.

Modern anti-realism is the position that the second kind of doubt is always reasonable. What destroys this position in the second phase of molecular theory, as against the first, is not general pattern, but specific content. Without a definite and powerful argument, it is unreasonable to suppose that non-living things that constantly deviate from their courses in an irregular manner do so without being caused to deviate by something external to them. This truism establishes the need for a causal explanation of Brownian phenomena. Once the need is established, Einstein's and Perrin's technical arguments answer relevant doubts as to whether the molecular explanation is the one to believe. Here, the coincidence in estimates of Avogadro's Number is relevant.

Of course, in 1860, there had been a number of areas in which molecular theory did not seem to fit observational findings. Different estimates of the atomic weight of an element did not perfectly coincide. Much worse, important auxiliary principles, such as Dulong and Petit's principle concerning specific heats, were sometimes in substantial conflict with the data. It would be unfortunate for my argument if molecular theory were less burdened with anomaly around 1908. This better fit could be taken to lift molecular explanations above a threshold, to a level at which the best explanation should, in general, be believed. Topic-specific truisms would play no role in describing the crucial difference.

In fact, the burden of anomaly was greater in the triumphant phase of molecular theory. The coincidence of different estimates of Avogadro's Number was, of course, not perfect. And, much more important, in the early years of the twentieth century, the best molecular theorists knew that their theories were all importantly false, in ways that they could not yet correct. For example, the falsehood of Dulong and Petit's principle had become well-established, especially for low temperatures. And Maxwell and Boltzmann had shown that on any current conception of molecules, the molecular theory of heat dictated this false principle. Similarly, molecular thermodynamics seemed to require a view of radiation on which a gas, when heated in a nearly closed cavity, would radiate at all frequencies, with an intensity approaching infinity as the frequency increased. In effect, Rayleigh had shown that when we look at an opening in a furnace, our eyes should be burned out by X-rays. In 1908 it was known, of course, that this is false. Molecular theory, circa Einstein and Perrin, was more anomalous than molecular theory circa Cannizzaro and Berzelius. The new areas in which the empirical fit was good were decisive. But what made them decisive was not some generally important formal property, but their bearing on compelling truisms concerning motion, its causes, and the difference between what is living and what is not.

This emphasis on truisms may seem philistine. Notoriously, modern science goes far beyond common sense and sometimes even puts it in doubt. It may seem wildly conservative to give any scientific priority to principles that thoughtful people accept in hunter-gatherer societies.

This appearance of conservatism would only reflect a misunderstanding of the special content and the special role of the truisms. The underlying principles only dictate belief prima facie and in the absence of special reasons to the contrary. Sometimes these reasons exist. Thus, given the evidence available around 1913, Bohr had special reasons to suppose that certain non-living things minutely change position erratically but spontaneously, namely in the quantum jumps of elementary particles. I am only proposing that Bohr would have been unreasonable to posit jumps without those special considerations, and that those special considerations were only rationally compelling if they rested on other parts of the common-sense background, for example, the elementary principles of light and shadow.

In addition, the role of the elementary principles is quite limited. The usual question of evaluation in science is which rival explanation of the data is to be preferred, on the basis of scientists' shared background principles, which are almost all technical. The question of realism, whether the rational preference is a uniquely justifiable belief in approximate truth, is a very special one, with a distinctly philosophical tone. The usual tasks of science are to apply technical principles to new data, to establish or refine hypotheses, to find improved values for theoretically important constants, to predict, control and explain specific phenomena. The special task of the common-sense background is to establish certain theories as ones to which every possible reasonable person possessing present data should extend approximate tentative belief. This is only an urgent task in special contexts. But whose contexts have been accorded much importance in philosophy. And the neglect of the work of specific and substantive principles, there, has added considerably to the excessive prestige of general and formal methods.

## HESITATION AND BELIEF

The burden of scientific realism is to show that certain explanations are not just best but needed: no reasonable person possessing relevant data could refuse to believe, tentatively, in their approximate truth. In the cases for molecules and for microbes, the topic-specific truisms make it unreasonable for anyone to fail to count the data—say, Leeuwenhock's or Perrin's—as supporting the explanation in terms of unobservables. But is it unreasonable to stop short of belief in the explanation on the grounds that the evidence does not provide strong enough support? I have been assuming that belief thresholds are not that high. At least for a while, this assumption should be lifted, to see whether higher thresholds would be reasonable.

If truisms are to help settle the issue of realism, it must be unreasonable for anyone with normal human experiences to deny them. When this much is said for a principle, the principle itself had better not say too much. In fact, the relevant truisms claim very little. Certain phenomena are merely said typically to be prima facie signs of a certain state of affairs. For example, that something makes the blurry clear and distinct is a prima facie sign that it reveals real features when it makes the invisible visible. In absence of a definite argument to the contrary, it is unreasonable not to count the apparent image as relevant, in a positive way, to the hypothesis that the apparent features actually exist. Clearly, reasonable people will differ in the amount of positive relevance they give to the appearance. Where some reasonable people will tentatively believe hypotheses about the shape of invisible stuff beneath the bottom lens of the microscope, others will want additional microscope observations, or more evidence of other kinds. Reasonable people differ in their belief thresholds. So a hypothesis that is a mark of reasonableness may single out phenomena as evidence without singling out sufficient evidence to compel belief.

How, then, can topic-specific principles help to settle the issue of scientific realism, when this is the issue of whether non-belief is ever irrational, for all possible investigators responding to certain data? Where the specific issue of scientific realism is concerned, a secure, relatively neat answer is possible, limited in scope, like most such solutions. The issue is whether people accepting the normal range of observations as their data are always reasonable to reject further conclusions about the unobservable. Accepting van Fraassen's reading of "observable," are people with the normal trust in unaided sense perception as revealing truths always in a position not to believe claims about entities that are not detectable by their unaided senses? Here, a normal belief threshold is presupposed, very low compared to a philosophical skeptic's. Concealed in the proviso that scientific realist arguments must be rationally compelling for any possible person possessing current data, is the understanding that those people have the normal willingness to believe hypotheses, for example, concerning real congruence, shape and color, when they are supported by phenomena that the basic truisms rate as evidence, for example, perceptions of congruence, change and color. Without this willingness, unaided sense perception would not provide data for empirical justifications.

In short, if belief thresholds could be arbitrarily high, then belief in molecules would fail to be compelling, not because of a problem about unobservables, but because relevant disputants never accepted that a pointer points near "2" on a dial. The normal threshold, which defines the debate about unobservables, is low enough to make the case for microbes and the case for molecules compelling for anyone with that threshold.

The limitations of this response are disappointing. Unless more is said about willingness to believe, there is some temptation to take shared belief thresholds to be nothing more than pervasive conventions, so that a higher threshold would be an unseemly type of self-assertion, but nothing more. And if the cut-off for doubt is purely conventional, there is room for some vague hope, on the anti-realist's part, that a reasonable person might limit commitment to a few, narrow inferences based on sense perception, enough to supply the normal range of data but too few to sustain a case for unobservables.

A broader, though more speculative view of the scope of belief might start with the distinction between real and empty doubt. One doesn't really doubt a proposition if one would not hesitate to act on it in any situation of realistic stress. By a situation of realistic stress I mean a circumstance in which the costs of not acting on the proposition are substantial if it is true (so that hesitation is stressful) but the costs of acting on it should it be false are not set unrealistically high. That Hume would not have hesitated to act on the belief that coaches exist, in such normal situations as the one he confronted most times he crossed the street, is good reason to suppose that he did not really doubt that coaches exist. On such grounds, a biographer might note that Hume did not really doubt that coaches exist, while describing Hume's feelings of uncertainty about the existence of coaches when he contemplated skeptical arguments in his study. Admittedly, Hume might have hesitated to act on his real belief in coaches when the cost of inaction should the belief be true was insubstantial. This could merely reflect the relaxed state of mind that is available when one is unconcerned about consequences. If Hume would have hesitated to bet a farthing on the existence of coaches, that does not, in itself, amount to real doubt, since Hume was a rich man. On the other hand, purely hypothetical hesitation in the face of unrealistic costs of being wrong does not establish real doubt, either. Perhaps I would hesitate to act on my belief that there are cars, if I were convinced that someone would commit me to eternal hellfire if I were wrong.[32] But this shows nothing more than the paralysis of the will that extreme fear creates. (Like most bizarre situations for evoking attitudes, it also introduces bizarre new reasons for belief that could, irrelevantly, change my belief state.) Real belief, the contrast to real doubt, is like hardness or rigidity, in being relative to normal stresses. A surface is hard if normal stresses do not break or dent it. A hard wall can be shattered by an atomic bomb.[33]

If this speculation is basically right, then real doubt and real belief are only features of beings with practical concerns and with threats in their environments. More precisely, there otherwise would be no way to draw the line between real doubt and belief, on the one hand, and, on the other, merely having feelings of uncertainty or conviction and making corresponding assertions—as Hume did in his study. So far, this is a lesson such as anti-realists teach. They emphasize the role of extra-scientific concerns in the assessment of scientific justification. But once the role of hesitations and threats is clearer, it becomes much less plausible that the actual limits of doubt are merely deep-seated conventions. Someone with our basic concerns, in a world that threatens as our world does, cannot have reasonable doubts in certain quite attainable situations. Someone who really has a much higher than normal belief threshold will, for example, hesitate to drink water coming from the familiar faucet of the kitchen sink, even if he is thirsty, because of the possibility that a poison is gushing out. If he has only the usual evidence bearing on

---

[32] Compare H. Frankfurt, "Philosophical Certainty," *Philosophical Review* (1962), pp. 321f.

[33] I defend this conception of doubt and conviction in more detail in "Absolute Certainty," *Mind* (1978), pp. 47–54.

relevant threats, and if he has our basic concerns (for example, there is some substantial cost to never readily drinking from a faucet), then he seems not just different but unreasonable in his hesitation. Given the apparent connection between hesitation, concerns, threats, and real doubt, this would mean that his real doubt is unreasonable doubt.

My proposal is that reason and normal human experience require not just commitments concerning what counts as evidence but also commitments concerning the connection between evidence and belief. Just as it is unreasonable not to take certain facts as evidence for certain propositions, it is also unreasonable to maintain real doubt in light of certain evidence. The belief threshold that forces belief in molecules is our normal threshold, at which real doubt must, rationally, cease. So belief in molecules is the only reasonable response to the data. It might not be the response of a literally carefree being. But this shows, not that belief in molecules is belief about a mind-dependent entity, but that belief itself depends on certain mental facts about believers which are of a not-so-obvious kind.

Present-day anti-realists emphasize alternative frameworks in which observations are assessed as evidence, rather than alternative connections between admitted evidence and actual belief. This is quite appropriate, since they have rejected the broader forms of philosophical skepticism, in accepting a realm of data much broader and more normal than the sense data of the early positivists. I will share this emphasis from now on, as I did before this section. From now on the normal belief threshold should be understood, at least when a framework includes the usual truisms, against a background of normal human experiences. Given the diversity of evidential frameworks currently asserted, this leaves room enough for bizarre alternatives.

## TOLERANCE AND NONSENSE

If the present style of realism can seem disrespectful of technical science in its emphasis on pre-scientific banalities, it can seem much too respectful in another way. The processes of inquiry by which the best-equipped and best-informed people now reach conclusions about unobservables have developed out of a quite particular cultural environment, which first triumphed in Europe in the course of the seventeenth century, with the defeat of Ptolemaic astronomy as its pivotal scientific campaign. It might seem that modern justifications of beliefs in unobservables are only rationally compelling given the standards of justification embedded in modern culture. Other people, with a different culture, could, in each case, encounter the same data, understand the same arguments, but rationally persist in contrary beliefs. Of course, this is an objection, not just to the kind of realist argument I have developed, but to realism as such, as defined in Chapter Eight. It is the major anti-realist argument that remains to be considered in detail.

Rorty's *Philosophy and the Mirror of Nature* is the most influential book of the last few years to argue that realism would be a philosophy of intolerance. "We are the heirs," Rorty writes, "of three hundred years of rhetoric about the importance of distinguishing sharply between science and religion, science and politics, science and philosophy, and so on. It made us what we are today. . . . But to claim our loyalty to these distinctions is not to say that there are 'rational' and 'objective' standards for adopting them. . . . [S]cientific inquiry . . . is made possible by the adoption of practices of justification . . . and such practices have possible alternatives. But these 'subjective conditions' . . . are just the facts about what a given society, or profession, or other group takes to be good ground for assertions of a certain kind."[34] Feyerabend has defended the same position in even more vivid and provocative ways.[35]

One outlook that Rorty and Feyerabend are attacking is positivism in the broadest sense of the term, the target of this book, as well. For they are saying, in part, that there is no general description of the scientific way of arriving at the truth which is both valid a priori and capable of justifying beliefs as uniquely rational in light of the data. Indeed, I have gone further, as Feyerabend does and Rorty might. There is no general description of the scientific way of arriving at the truth which is effective, by itself, in assessing justifications, and there are no valid principles that describe what belief should be in light of the data, whatever the data are. Putting these points of agreement to one side, Rorty and Feyerabend disagree, in the fol-

---

[34] *Philosophy and the Mirror of Nature* (Princeton, 1980), pp. 330f., 385.

[35] See *Against Method* (London, 1975), where Feyerabend recommends an "epistemological anarchism" in which one "takes great interest in procedures, phenomena and experiences such as those reported by Carlos Castaneda, which indicate that perceptions can be arranged in highly unusual ways and that the choice of a particular arrangement as 'corresponding to reality,' while not arbitrary (it almost always depends on traditions), is certainly not more 'rational' or more 'objective' than the choice of another arrangement: Rabbi Akiba, who in ecstatic trance rises from one celestial sphere to the next and still higher and who finally comes face to face with God in all his Splendour, makes genuine observations once we decide to accept his way of life as a measure of reality" (p. 190).

lowing claim, with the anti-positivist realism I have been defending: whenever the specific data available to us modern people, heirs of the Scientific Revolution, lead everyone of us who possesses all those data to believe a scientific hypothesis, someone, with a relevantly different background, could grasp those data, understand our arguments, and rationally persist in a different conclusion, without possessing extra data that would surprise us and lead us to question our views. Of course, there are a variety of ways of explicating "data," and some, no doubt, would render it unclear again where the line between anti-positivism and anti-realism should be drawn. But Rorty and Feyerabend do not, on the whole, rely on any such special analysis. At least in their main arguments, they accept, from case to case, any specification of the data that is not historically inaccurate and that does not make the arguments from data intolerably question-begging. This straightforward willingness to let distinctions between data and hypothesis be settled by the context of argument is one reason why their relativism is a powerful challenge to non-positivist readers with realist inclinations.

Why, though, should we accept that rational dissent is always possible? Granted, there are sometimes cases in which people rationally respond to the same data with different views. "Phenomenological" and molecular accounts of the behavior of gases, circa 1870, are a scientific case in point. My reasonable belief that someone is shy and a friend's reasonable belief that he is arrogant are a pattern for innumerable everyday examples. But realists don't (or shouldn't) say that such disagreement is never fully rational; so the common stuff of relativist history of science, particular episodes in which revered scientists have claimed without warrant that disagreement was irrational, are not to the point.

In the course of this chapter, the cases that have turned out to be crucial for non-positivist realism are certain ones in which a dissenter concerning the subject-matter in question must either acknowledge a burden of proof or fail to address himself or herself to the subject-matter. If, in addition, meeting the burden of proof must involve presenting extra data of a surprising kind, then scientific realists have all they require. For they demand nothing more than tentative belief, which might be withdrawn if new and surprising data were encountered. The animalcules hypothesis, circa 1680, the molecular hypothesis, circa 1908, and the hypothesis that a baby is at least uncomfortable, when crying, all seem to have the required unique reasonableness. Anti-realists need to show that situations with this structure do not really exist, at least in theoretical science.

There is just one kind of consideration presented by Rorty, Fey-erabend and like-minded anti-realists which has a tendency to un-dermine the appeal to inherent burdens of proof. It is an argument from different ultimate standards of evidence, embodied in Rorty's discussion of an unlikely hero of his philosophy of tolerance, Robert Bellarmine, the Vatican official who condemned the aged Galileo to house arrest for life. Though the anti-realist objection is, I shall ar-gue, wrong, it is also enormously revealing: of the relation between rationality and evidence, semantics and epistemology, and philo-sophical and everyday categories.

The crucial evidence for Bellarmine's alleged philosophical acu-men is a letter he wrote to Paolo Foscarini, a Provincial of the Car-melite order who was a follower of Galileo.[36] Bellarmine begins by accepting that Copernican astronomy may be used "hypothetically," which Rorty interprets as meaning that a Copernican model may be a useful predictive and heuristic device. In Rorty's view, Bellarmine then shows that his own rejection of Copernican astronomy as false is not unreasonable. "When he said that it [Copernican theory] should not be thought of as having wider scope than this, he de-fended his view by saying that we had excellent independent (Scrip-tural) evidence for believing that the heavens were roughly Ptole-maic. What determines that Scripture is *not* an excellent source of evidence for the way the heavens are set up? Lots of things, notably the Enlightenment's decision that Christianity was mostly just priest-craft. . . . [T]he 'grid' which emerged in the later seventeenth and eighteenth centuries was not there to be appealed to in the early seventeenth century, at the time that Galileo was on trial."[37]

Rorty's Bellarmine is a threatening figure for the present style of realism, much more so than just another illustration of the unsur-prising fact that creative scientists have sometimes claimed undue certainty. Rorty's Bellarmine acknowledges that the successes of Copernican astronomy impose a burden of proof on a dissenter. He supports this burden of proof by appealing to passages in the Bible. Moreover, his disagreement with Galileo is not based on alleged ac-cess to surprising data. Galileo could have recited by heart the Bib-lical passages Bellarmine cites (for example, "The Earth abideth forever; the Sun also riseth and also goeth down, and hasteth to the place whence he arose"). Rather, Rorty's Bellarmine is applying a

---

[36] The letter is most accessible in Giorgio de Santillana, *The Crime of Galileo* (Chi-cago, 1955), pp. 98–100.

[37] *Philosophy and the Mirror of Nature*, p. 329.

standard of evidence that Galileo doesn't apply, the appeal to what the Bible says as a source of truth concerning the general properties of the material world. If this was a basis for rational dissent, for Bellarmine, it might seem some such basis can always be invented. Just imagine a Scripture that is committed to classical thermodynamics, as against the molecular-kinetic theory of heat, and so on.

It will be useful to begin with quibbles. The philosophically astute Bellarmine of recent histories of science and of philosophy is not the Bellarmine of history.[38] And the reasons why the actual Bellarmine was an uninsightful dissenter suggest the reasons why the Bellarmine of anti-realist writings (call him " 'Bellarmine' ") does not really undermine the case for realism.

In his discussions of Copernican astronomy, Bellarmine does an indefensible job of marshalling relevant data, according to the standards of evidence of his own subculture. (In fact, throughout the Galileo case he seems no better than a suave Counter-Reformation hatchetman. Presumably, it was his virtues elsewhere that led to his canonization.) Writing to Foscarini, he appeals, not to the Bible as such, but to "the interpretation of the sacred texts as given by the holy Fathers." The appeal to traditions in interpretation is essential. There are too many inconsistencies within the Bible for it to be accepted without interpretation. Indeed, the basic heliocentric passages are from the Old Testament, which a Christian cannot accept without liberal interpretations of important passages. But there had, in fact, been no consensus among the Church Fathers that the astronomy of the Bible was to be accepted as literal truth. Until the Counter-Reformation, the Church had been open to astronomical speculation. For example, that the earth moves was a clearly proclaimed belief of the famous and respected medieval theologian, Nicholas, Bishop of Cusa.[39] Bellarmine was misreading his evidence, in the institutional interests of the Counter-Reformation Church. To create "Bellarmine," the dissenter from science an anti-realist might find useful, we need to alter the actual Bellarmine's culturally endorsed system of ultimate reasons, his "grid," as Rorty calls it, imagining a "Bellarmine" who possesses a basically consistent Bible and functions in a Church that uses it literally, as a source of truth.

Bellarmine was also a bad scientist, or, rather, a dilettante, in a

[38] For other recent accounts of Bellarmine in which respect verges on admiration, see Feyerabend, *Against Method*, pp. 192f., and Harry Frankfurt, *Demons, Dreamers and Madmen* (Indianapolis, 1970), pp. 181–85.

[39] See Kuhn, *The Copernican Revolution* (New York, 1959), pp. 196f., 233–35.

way that weakened his argument and makes it strictly irrelevant to the issue of realism. In the letter to Foscarini, he accepts "that on the supposition of the Earth's movement and the Sun's quiescence all the celestial appearances are explained better than by the theory of eccentrics and epicycles."[40] This was not true. Because stellar parallax could not be observed, Tycho's geocentric system explained celestial appearances just as well. The question could only be settled, indeed, could only be properly defined, with future improvements in physics. But of course, Rorty is not just claiming that reason and evidence admitted geocentric astronomy in Galileo's time, but excluded it in Newton's. So, in changing Bellarmine into the philosophically relevant "Bellarmine," we need to broaden the scope of the evidence, imagining that "Bellarmine" knows the data available to Newton and follows Newton's arguments.

If the historical record is modified this much, but no more, "Bellarmine" is as unreasonable as Bellarmine. To appreciate his dilemma, one must be sensitive to both kinds of problems that afflicted the real Cardinal, the nature of his standards and the nature of his data. Given all the data that really have a bearing on the cosmological question, "Bellarmine" 's answer is unreasonable in his framework. As the framework is modified more and more, under pressure of the data, it becomes the framework of someone who isn't disagreeing with Galileo about the reasonableness of alternative astronomies.

By the 1630s, if not long before, voyages of discovery and the expansion of international trade had produced data that made it unreasonable to rely on the Bible as a source of general truths about the material world. There had turned out to be whole societies throughout the world, made up of people as moral and as thoughtful as Christians, who often had scriptures contradicting the Christian Bible, who had no special disposition to accept Christian beliefs once they were announced and who, indeed, were the less prone to conversion the more developed their culture was. The reliability of what Christians took to be the word of God stood in need of justification in these circumstances, and had none. It was unreasonable under these circumstances to insist that the Koran and the basic texts of Buddhism reflected the doings of humans long ago who were mistaken about superhuman attributes and much else besides,

[40] De Santillana, *The Crime of Galileo*, p. 99. Since Copernicus' full-fledged system is highly epicyclic, Bellarmine must have entirely depended on popular accounts, presumably, Galileo's above all.

while insisting that the Bible had a different status. Well-protected by social station and geography, Montaigne could make discreet suggestions of this kind. But Galileo would have been crazy to. Still, to regard Galileo's religious acquiescence as justified belief is to make it a standard of evidence who can put whom under arrest.

In both "Bellarmine" 's and Bellarmine's frameworks, the argument from the diversity of intelligent informed opinion takes a specific and especially powerful form. God is supposed to be rational, powerful, benevolent and just. Evidently, he has permitted people who seem just as deserving of the truth as Christians to have fundamental scriptural beliefs fundamentally different from Christians'. Evidently, God has reasons, which we cannot fathom, for creating and overseeing a world in which many people have scriptural beliefs that are monstrously false. So "our" scripture may be monstrously false.

It might seem, though, that "Bellarmine" 's framework has been misconstrued. Perhaps he takes the literal truth of the Christian Bible as never standing in need of any justification, come what may. He: (1) believes that God has given true scripture to Christians and false scripture to Muslims; (2) accepts that he has no reason to offer in justification of this belief; and (3) regards further beliefs of his, depending on this distinction among scriptures, as reasonable beliefs about the material world. In other words, "Bellarmine" is saying, "I think there is a person who has done utterly remarkable things, a person whom no living human observes. I realize that millions of others have similar beliefs about unobserved all-powerful people and are quite mistaken. I have no reason to offer suggesting that they are wrong and I am right. Nonetheless, my belief is reasonable." Someone who sincerely says this doesn't understand what persons are, what beliefs about people are, or what reasonableness is. If you believe that someone whom you have never observed has done certain remarkable things including the creation of a true all-encompassing scripture and if you admit that millions of others have a similar belief, but are wrong, that creates a burden of proof. The burden of proof is as inherent as the one that weighs on a person who claims that a crying infant isn't really even uncomfortable. Of course, in the theological case there have been arguments, independent of appeals to the Christian Bible, for the distinctive validity of the Christian Bible. I will assume, as even most Christians do these days, that those arguments are simply defective. Certainly, anti-realists, who think it impossible to prove any unobservable entity exists, will not find them compelling.

If this argument were to suggest that religious people were typically unintelligent, it would be the sort of arrogance that sometimes gives atheism a bad name. But in fact, it fits the phenomena of religious belief very well. Believers are not like "Bellarmine." Some take their beliefs to be supported by the specific arguments to which I just alluded. Others, at least when pressed, take their belief in God to be a matter of attitude, not a belief about the world such as might resolve a question in astronomy. Others take their religious beliefs, at least the more specific ones that could in principle decide astronomical matters, to be matters of faith as against reason, absurdities that are embraced but are not rationally defensible. Finally, some stretch the notion of "God" so very far that a basic physical force or moral principle would count as God, just as much as a person. In short, people have independent reasons, allegedly fair to an atheist's framework, for their scriptural standard, or accept that they are not concerned with reasonable belief about the world, or make it quite unclear just what their belief is about. None of these options successfully preserves a Biblical argument that the sun also riseth while the earth abideth, in the face of data available by Newton's time.

This reply to "Bellarmine" suggests similar critiques of others whose dissent is supposed to be not unreasonable. Thus, Putnam asks us to imagine a devotee of a guru of Sydney (Australia) who says things that are absurd to us. If the faith in the guru is sufficiently deep-seated, our ultimate ground for rejecting it, in Putnam's view, will be that it is "sick."[41] Yet the reply to "Bellarmine" suggests an argument that we would surely make, if we had some hope for the devotee: there are gurus in Perth, Brisbane, and on most blocks in Greenwich Village, with as many guru qualities as the guru of Sydney, but saying radically different things.

Of course, such attempts to end disagreement by means of reason depend on the existence of certain data. And this is not just true in the limited sense that the particular beliefs defended are only supposed to be specially rational in light of the data possessed—a contingency that positivists certainly accepted. In addition, if the data were different, it might be impossible for any side in the controversy to claim to have the only rational position (in light of the data). *What*

---

[41] See *Reason, Truth and History* (Cambridge, 1981), pp. 131–35. This is a very truncated version of Putnam's claim. He points to a variety of "virtues" missing from the devotee's outlook. However, their absence is taken to be a sign that human cognitive flourishing has been stunted, a conclusion more aptly expressed in judgments of sickness than in independent judgments of false belief.

*kinds of justification are available to us is a contingent matter*. In a world in which well-attested miracles only occurred in one faith, the structure of reason might be very different.

## THE WORLD AND WORDS

It might seem that the above arguments are too specific in the different frameworks they compare. Perhaps humans can only take seriously a few ultimate standards with a bearing on the subject-matter of science, say, the standards that modern secular people find common-sensical together with reliance on gods, gurus, divination, oracles and the like. And perhaps the actual data count against the standards that modern secular people find bizarre. Still, this might seem to be just a fact about what humans take seriously. Whatever the effectiveness of actual anti-scientific arguments, it might seem that there must be some standard that some possible rational being could bring to bear to negate scientific inferences from any body of data. So any conclusiveness a scientific belief possesses will reflect a limitation of human beings, not a limitation on the non-human world. This is a conclusion that anti-realists willingly accept. Indeed, it seems to be the essence of Rorty's outlook.[42]

In fact, the defeat of religion when it contests with science is symptomatic of a much more general problem for ways of learning about the world that are opposed to the common-sense foundations of science. If the former ways of learning are significantly related to the common-sense ways, then the former can be defeated in light of the actual data; if those ways of learning are not significantly related to the common-sense core, they are not ways of learning about the world. The crucial limitation is not what humans can be like, either actually, by their nature, or conceptually, but what could count as the world.

There is, to begin with, something misleading about the proposal that people have had standards of evidence contrary to any that modern secular folk respect. Non-scientific frameworks presuppose a core of common-sense ways of learning about the world which is the same as the core of the scientific framework. In any case, this is true of any outlook that could produce a reasonable dissent from science. Bellarmine and "Bellarmine" presuppose that they can tell by looking what words are in a book, or else they are hardly in a position to reject a cosmology as conflicting with passages in Scripture.

[42] See, for example, *Philosophy and the Mirror of Nature*, p. 284.

Augurers had better think that they can reliably detect natural phenomena by looking in addition to augury, or else they will not be able to make out the spots on their birds' livers. This presupposition of ordinary ways of learning by extraordinary ones is the systematic reason why the extraordinary ones can be put in a few groups: hearing or reading what an extraordinarily knowledgeable person knows, when that knowledge cannot be acquired by scientific means, or interpreting some phenomenon, observed in a standard way, according to principles that cannot be justified from the standpoint of science or common sense. At the same time, each kind of extraordinary and non-scientific way of learning has been shown, in many instances, to be unreliable, given the ordinary ways of learning it presupposes. Scriptures, gurus and means of divination contradict one another and contradict the observed facts. This puts a burden of proof on non-science that it has not sustained.

To be defensible, an extraordinary framework for evaluating data must make a cleaner break with our ordinary ways of learning. But there is a problem, here. If beings do not employ anything like our ordinary ways of learning, then they are not talking about the same kinds of things as we. So they cannot disagree. Suppose that Bellarmine had not thought that seeing a point of brightness in the same part of the sky night after night was even strong prima facie grounds for supposing something existed in that direction; and so on through the common-sense presuppositions of Galilean science. It is not that he has special scientific arguments to the contrary; he does not accept the standard burdens of proof. Then Bellarmine would not be talking about stars, and couldn't disagree with Galileo.

The appropriate and common anti-realist response is to accept the conclusion that the subject-matter changes with the framework, but to put the conclusion to anti-realist uses. A framework that is so different from ours that the same beliefs are never justified by the same evidence will be the framework of beings who never talk about the same kinds of things as we. Still, we have no reason to suppose there is something missing from the ontology of beings with this framework. Nothing in our inventory of the world would be in theirs. But, the anti-realist proposes, their failure to believe in our kinds of things is not unreasonable, just different from our practice. We and they live in different worlds and have different ways of world-making.

The most important current criticism of this claim about possible differences is Donald Davidson's, in "On the Very Idea of a Conceptual Scheme." Davidson notes that we are often asked to imagine people who have beliefs about the world, but differ from us in all their beliefs. Yet, he argues, to have beliefs is to have a language, and we cannot "make sense of there being a language we could not translate at all."[43] The alleged complete difference in beliefs would, he shows, produce a complete failure of translatability. He infers that the notion of the totally different framework is, in fact, unintelligible.

Because Davidson's immediate goal is to describe a limit on thought and language, as we can imagine them to be, his essay can be and has been put to anti-realist use—although this does not seem his ultimate intention. Once positivist accounts of justification are rejected, it is easy to see why these uses are attractive. If positivist conceptions of justification are wrong, then justification depends on a framework of beliefs. Dissent is only unreasonable if it is ruled out by arguments that are impartial among relevant competing frameworks. But dissent from all our beliefs has turned out to be not something we can refute, just something we cannot imagine. We lack the shared framework that a judgment of unreasonableness presupposes, though because of the same lack a judgment of unintelligibility is appropriate. So the special status of our most basic beliefs seems to reflect a limit on what we understand, features of how we construct any image of the world, as opposed to basic truths about the world common to all our images.[44]

My proposal is that Davidson's basic line of criticism is right, but that it needs to be directed away from the issue of what we can imagine in the way of thinking or language, and toward the issue of what could be a world. That we cannot conceive of a language we could not translate at all is not very plausible, in any case. Communication by language is one of a few alternative explanations we have of certain patterns of behavior. Surely, such an explanation could be supported by elimination of the rest, even when efforts to translate are defeated. Suppose that many Saturnians do increasingly complicated things as they mature, but only if other Saturnians make sounds in their direction, with just the acoustic structuredness of Earth languages. Like chimpanzees as opposed to cats and ants, they are not at all creatures of instinct. Yet when we try to assign meanings to the sounds we are always defeated, in standard ways, for example, by landing in the trap of assigning blatantly contradic-

---

[43] "On the Very Idea of a Conceptual Scheme" (1974) in his *Inquiries into Truth and Interpretation* (Oxford, 1984), p. 192.

[44] This sometimes seems a moral that Rorty is deriving from Davidson's writings in *Philosophy and the Mirror of Nature*, pp. 298–311.

tory beliefs to these generally thriving creatures. To say that they have a language we cannot understand in the least seems no stranger than my saying that I know, from observing the responses of Indian friends at concerts, that Indian music must have a large-scale structure, though I have no idea what that structure is.

However, the idea of a radically different framework goes much further than the assertion that beings may think when we can't understand their language. It is not just that we can't determine what they are saying about the world with a given piece of their language. They are supposed to be describing a world without talking about any of the relatively specific kinds of things one mentions in everyday life, science, or philosophy. They do not talk about people, plants, animals, rocks, clouds, mesons, genes, distances, sequence in time . . . and yet they have a world and talk about objects. If they did apply the more specific, less metaphysical categories, then they would accept certain burdens of proof, in making their assertions, that would drive them to our conclusions, if they had our data.

To accept that these beings are, nonetheless, talking of a world or objects, is to accept the tyranny of philosophical words. It is as if our human guide to Saturn assured us that the Saturnians are speaking about objects and describing their world, but added that they never (much less now) talk about these rocks, this dust, the sky or those lights in the sky, each other, space, time, feelings, thoughts or numbers. The best analogy is Wittgenstein's, "Isn't it as if I were to say of someone, 'He *has* something. But I don't know whether it is money, or debts, or an empty till.' "[45]

The tyranny of philosophical words was an important theme at the beginning of this book. I suggested that the positivist account of explanation assumes that it is merely a fact about how people happen to acquire the notion of a cause that they first acquire more specific notions of pushing, hurting and the like. To the contrary, I argued, the concept of a cause consists of just such diverse and specific concepts, together with extensions of them that inquiry forces on us. That there should be causes but no more specific, intrinsically causal processes is as impossible as that there should be numbers but no counting or measuring numbers.

The alleged utterly different frameworks are not really threatening for a similar reason. Something is missing from them. Because they do not describe any of the specific kinds of objects that might provide a core for a concept of a world, they are not means of

---

[45] *Philosophical Investigations* (Oxford, 1967), remark 294.

describing a world. The world is missing, and only excessive respect for the word "world" conceals this absence. This no more reflects a limitation on what we can imagine than does the non-existence of number systems in which counting or measuring numbers play no role. It is not just that we cannot conceive of a total practice of numerical calculation that does not involve counting or measuring. An activity that different from our practice of numerical calculations would not employ numbers. Similarly, apart from the question of whether we can conceive of such activity (and in this case, I think we can), language and mental activity that is not regulated at all by our basic truisms does not describe things or a world.

As usual, realists have a lot to learn from the major anti-realist arguments. One important source of realism is the desire to find something constant in the flux of exposed illusions, refuted arguments and periodically defeated scientific theories. This desire can lead to a feeling that there is a world out there to be described, whatever the fate of particular ways of describing it. The feeling should be resisted. If there is a proof of an external world, or a realm of unobservable objects, it is based on more specific arguments for the existence of trees, or of molecules, rather than the more specific arguments' presupposing a general one. In a familiar, pejorative sense, people who claim to have a concept of the world and of objects, quite independent of anything more specific, are getting metaphysical. The ultimate moral of the argument about framework differences is that realism should not be metaphysical in this sense.

## SCIENCE: WITH AND WITHOUT FOUNDATIONS

In one way, the recent flourishing of controversy over realism has been unfortunate. As it has come to dominate the literature, the philosophy of science has come to seem less and less relevant to practitioners' problems. In contrast, the covering-law model and positivist accounts of confirmation were obviously bits of advice to practitioners, and critics of them were obviously condemning the positivists for giving bad advice.

Indeed, most current approaches to the realism controversy guarantee its practical irrelevance. According to van Fraassen and Rorty, realist rules of inference may be the right rules for our choices, even though they should not determine strict and literal belief. For their part, leading realists try to base their argument on general principles that all sensible investigators are already following in all fields in which relevant uses of theories are well-established.

On my alternative conception of how to argue for realism, the current status of the realism debate is a practical disaster. Whether to deal with theories in a realist way is a live question, whose answer varies from field to field, and does not depend on a general criterion applied to the patterns of success in each field. So each current approach to realism is bound to be wrong in many cases. Only the image of rationality in which topic-specific principles are fundamental can provide an adequate framework for answering the field-specific questions of whether to be a realist. And the practical stakes are high when such questions are asked, as I will now try to show. In particular, the realist controversy comes down to earth at two related points: the connection between research strategies and a realist understanding of the foundations of a field, and the need to avoid the excessive conservatism that excessive agnosticism creates.

Suppose that in some field, the rational acceptance of a hypothesis requires not just belief in its empirical adequacy but belief that it expresses at least approximate truths about entities. Rational assessment includes truth assessment, even for hypotheses about unobservable posits. In this sense, the field has a real foundation, the single realm of entities which hypotheses are expected to describe, at least in part. Taking a field to have such a foundation is a decision in favor of (field-specific) realism. And it has important consequences for the agenda of research.

As arguments from empirical equivalence imply, contradictions between theories are urgent problems for fields with foundations, but not for fields in which acceptable theories need only be acceptable means of summary and prediction. For their part, realists emphasize a related intra-theoretic side of the need for consistency: in a field with foundations, the fact that entities of a kind posited in a justified explanation would be expected to have certain features is a reason to believe that they do, even if those features have not yet been employed in deriving empirical laws. Though these considerations turned out to be inadequate to resolve the issue of realism, they are genuine insights, nonetheless, with an important bearing on the agenda of research. If a field is taken to have a foundation, a contradiction among theories poses an urgent task for research, and directly testing what is intra-theoretically plausible is a fruitful and important project. To these maxims, one can add a third. In a field with foundations, attempting to fill in important gaps in the characterization of posited entities is a worthwhile project.

Geology, for example, is a field with foundations, even though the checkered career of theorizing in the field would make it hard to justify this position in standard realist ways. As a result, when frameworks for explanation posit incompatible causes of observable phenomena, this is taken as a crisis demanding resolution, not a healthy diversity of models. The field entered one such crisis in the mid twentieth century, from which it has not fully emerged. According to the traditional view, major geological features were due to the large-scale cooling and local erosion and sedimentation of a basically stable earth. According to the plate tectonic view, the drift of large, independently mobile portions of the earth's crust was largely responsible. These different models for explanation were associated, as usual, with different strategies of hypothesis choice, since the traditionalists favored hypotheses in which uniform and well-studied mechanical processes were at work, while the drift theorists accepted speculations and gaps at this level. Rather than welcoming this diversity, geologists treated it as a crisis and directed their most creative energies towards its solution. If they had been anti-realists in practice, they could have taken plate tectonics as the useful model for the distribution of life forms and certain special questions about mountains and earthquakes, while retaining the traditional view as the model for the earth's thermodynamics and for most geological phenomena. But geology has a foundation. Earthquakes, the rise of mountains and other geological events do not happen spontaneously, and theories of why they happen ought to describe the activity and effects of real stuff.

Microbiology is another field with foundations. That is why Leeuwenhoek and Hooke, having posited extremely simple and tiny life forms—what we would now call bacteria—could suppose that these life forms took in food, even though these processes of nutrition had not yet been connected with empirical regularities. Whatever the particular degree to which such intra-theoretic plausibility justifies belief, it has an undeniable relevance to research plans. "How do bacteria take in and process nutrition?" was obviously a question that ought to be pursued, as soon as pursuit was feasible. And making pursuit feasible was clearly a useful project. On an anti-realist construal, the question might be no more answerable than whether Hamlet had a sister, and its resolution no more important to the investigation of reality.

As relatively clear examples of fields without foundations, consider literary interpretation and musical analysis. To deny that these are fields of inquiry or to suppose that they are different in kind

from all scientific ones means imposing a positivist theory of explanation or stipulating that a field is only scientific if it has a foundation. A critic defending an interpretation of *Lear* or analyzing the
developments in Mozart's C-minor piano concerto is constantly explaining phenomena—for example, why this character says these
words or why this modulation occurs at this time. The explanations
are almost always governed by theories of something more general,
say of that genre in that historical period or at that point in the cre-
ator's output. Neither the explanations nor the theories include covering-laws such as the positivists demanded. But neither does geology, biology, or, in many cases, physics.

The theory that Elizabethan drama reflects the tensions and discontinuities of nascent capitalism suggests that *Lear* expresses the
clash between the traditional world outlook based on socially prescribed interpersonal loyalties and the new world outlook based on
the fulfillment of individually chosen goals and personal ties. The
theory that Shakespearean drama seeks to dramatize, without a
false ultimate solution, the inherent problems of human existence
interprets *Lear* as a play about growing old and dying. By the same
token, different general theories of literature imply rival accounts
of particular texts. On some views of literary meaning, the right
interpretation of *Lear*, whatever it is, must capture Shakespeare's intentions. On other views, the responses of a sensitive reader to the
text must be organized in relevant ways, with the consequence that
Shakespearean meanings need not be Shakespeare's. Similarly,
what Tovey takes to be a moment in which Mozart solves a problem
he has created about the acoustic contest between soloist and or-
chestra or about the ultimate harmonic coherence of a modulation,
may be what Turner takes as an expression of a comedic and pessimistic view of life.

As one encounters more and more explanations in these fields,
one realizes that many apparently contradictory approaches, interpretations and explanations are, in some sense, all true. But in what
sense? It is tempting to explain away the apparent contradictions, by
supposing that ultimately true, overarching positions make each of
the good rival positions true to some partial degree, quite compatible with the truth of the others, similarly hedged. But this is not an
accurate description of the intentions or the power of the rival approaches. On each of the different interpretations of *Lear*, the
drama is pervaded by different themes. Simultaneously hearing
Lear's first speech both as an attempt to be part of two historical
world outlooks and an attempt to accept and evade old age is like

trying to see the famous figure as a duck and a rabbit, at once. Even more closely, it resembles an attempt to combine two great and different actors' interpretations of the role; in other words, it creates a disheartening mess. Rather, literary interpretation and musical analysis are fields without foundations. Most certainly, they are not fields in which anything goes. But a situation in which different explanatory frameworks are in the field, attributing contrary explanations to the phenomena, is no crisis. For accepting a theory, approach, or explanation only requires belief in its adequacy to cope with the phenomena.[46]

Perhaps there are other, non-aesthetic fields which can be shown to lack foundations. Biography may be a case in point. However, the most important reason why these reflections are not just important for aesthetics is that it is an open and practically important question, for many non-aesthetic sorts of inquiry, whether they have foundations. Practitioners feel this uncertainty and sense its bearing on their agendas for research. Yet the obsession with general principles in the philosophy of science distorts any effort to resolve the issue.

This question about foundations is characteristic of the self-questioning fields of inquiry, in which quite self-respecting practitioners often wonder about the status of the whole enterprise, for example, psychoanalysis, social history, social anthropology, and cognitive psychology. Thus, whether foundations exist is an especially common question in psychoanalysis, taking the subject quite broadly, as the effort to explain enduring emotional problems as due to psychological causes of which the sufferer is usually unconscious. I will take it to be the outcome of any reasonably broad experience of human life that this subject-matter, so described is not vacuous: the non-conscious causes of enduring emotional problems sometimes have a non-physiological description, even when mere self-attentiveness would not be enough to bring them into consciousness. At any rate, this is an interesting possibility, since for a vast number of patterns of suffering and self-defeat, opaque to self-attentive sufferers, no current physiological account is any good. According to some psychoanalytic theorists, of whom Sullivan has probably been

[46] For an interesting brief discussion of the legitimacy of incompatible interpretations, see Joseph Margolis, "The Logic of Interpretation" in Margolis, ed., *Philosophy Looks at the Arts* (New York, 1962). The diverse styles of reading that Barthes advocates, sometimes for the same texts, are an important illustration and refinement of such tolerance. See, for example, the essays in *Image Music Text* (New York, 1977). Derrida's program of putting literature "into the abyss" would be the farthest reach of this pluralism, but it is one for which I can find no justification.

the most creative and influential, psychoanalysis lacks foundations. Sullivan viewed psychoanalytic explanations as attributing phenomena, both in and out of the context of treatment, to "dynamisms," mechanisms affecting how people will feel, respond and behave. But he did not think that reason and evidence would ever single out one description of the unconscious—in general or even in a given individual—as the one approximately true description. In accepting a dynamism, one should only commit oneself to certain expectations about experience and conduct.[47] Other psychoanalysts, of course, have taken the goal of theory to be the description of the nature of the unconscious. This is, most famously, Freud's view, though adamant and clinically productive anti-Freudians, Fairbairn, for example, have shared it. The distinction is not one of open-mindedness versus stubbornness. Freud was refreshingly open to radical changes in his map of the mind, while Sullivan almost never acknowledges that an alleged dynamism has proven inadequate. Rather, this is a disagreement as to whether a field has a foundation, a disagreement motivating different agendas for research. From Freud's or Fairbairn's perspective, it is a sign of crisis that there is now no generally accepted psychoanalytic model of how the mind works. From Sullivan's, this provides no greater motivation for unifying research than the coexistence of different interpretations of Lear or different ways of analyzing the C-minor concerto.

Consider, for example, how the following present-day psychoanalytic controversy has a different bearing on the agenda of research, depending on how the field is viewed. In Kernberg's theory of narcissistic personality disorders, they are due to a lack of fusion of love and hate in the unconscious internalized objects that structure one's emotional life. In Kohut's theory, these disorders are a flight from an unconscious sense of inferiority. On Freud's view of the field, which happens to be Kernberg's and Kohut's as well, the good clinical evidence for each view makes it urgent to determine which is right.[48] If psychoanalysis lacks foundations, this is likely to be a pointless enterprise. Similarly, Freud's inference from the usefulness of the Oedipus complex in explaining neurotic symptoms to its usefulness in explaining gender identity is a reasonable employment of intra-theoretical plausibility if the field has foundations, unreasonable literalism if it does not. And such intra-theoretical questions as whether the super-ego is an object of unconscious love,

[47] See, for example, *Clinical Studies in Psychiatry* (New York, 1956), chs. 1 and 2.

[48] See Otto Kernberg, *Borderline Conditions and Pathological Narcissism* (New York, 1975); Heinz Kohut, *The Analysis of the Self* (New York, 1971).

as well as unconscious fear, have no special appeal on the foundationless construal.

While analysts are rightly troubled by this issue of foundations, their response is typically unproductive. Contrary to popular lore, most analysts, including most whose clinical techniques are Freudian, are inclined toward a dogmatic denial that their field has foundations. Yet, though this could be true, it need not be. Giving up on the project of constructing a map of the mind could bar the way to important work, as did Poincaré's premature denial that physics had foundations in the present sense. On the other hand, when theorists argue for the realist construal, the results are even grimmer. Because of the standard image of scientific rationality, they try to make psychoanalytic reasoning look like reasoning in some other field with foundations, biology, say, or physics. The resulting generalities are lifeless, implausible, or both.

So far I have framed the issue about foundations as the question of whether investigators should require the true description of underlying causes. This formulation is closest to the actual talk of troubled practitioners, "Is there a map of the mind, a structure of the unconscious?" ("Is there really a universal way of structuring reality which is embodied in all mythologies?" "Are there really contradictions in social formations, or is this just a convenient summary of individuals' conflicts?") Once this step is taken, van Fraassen's distinctions between acceptance and belief, truth and empirical adequacy seem the convenient means of distinguishing the main options. However, as the previous analysis of realism suggests, this way of putting the issue can confuse communications between foundationalists and non-foundationalists. After all, people who think there really is a structure of the unconscious often make their arguments within a framework that does, quite uncontroversially, justify corresponding attributions of unconscious structures. They can back up truth claims with reasons. And their anti-foundational opponents admit this. For example, it is a commonplace of modern psychoanalysis that Freudian theorists can absorb non-Freudian work into their explanatory practice, finding Freudian analogues for explanations that non-Freudians have developed. But no one thinks that the status of the field is settled by reasoning about the structure of the mind confined to a special Freudian framework. The question is whether reason and evidence, apart from some special framework, would compel all rational investigators to take one repertoire of mutually consistent mechanisms to govern the phenomena of psychopathology.

That an appropriately compelling argument could just rely on methods that have succeeded in physics or biology is only plausible given the worship of generality common to both realists and anti-realists, at present. On the conception of how to argue for realism that I have recommended, the foundations will be established, if they can be established at all, by arguments in favor of a single repertoire that ultimately rely on topic-specific truisms about what is in need of explanation and what its causes are apt to be. When psychoanalytic arguments for unconscious causes inspire conviction, not just admiration for the explainer's agility, they are almost always close to such truisms. For example, rejecting some of Freud's arguments for the existence of repression, as without any evidential force, while accepting his relatively observational claims, would mean rejecting some principle as truistic as that dramatically inconsistent attitudes, on the part of someone who is not stupid or ill-informed, are apt to have some non-conscious cause. "The patient X," he relates in one example, "was a girl, who had lost her beloved father after she had taken a share in nursing him. . . . Soon afterwards her elder sister married, and her new brother-in-law aroused in her a peculiar feeling of sympathy which was easily masked under a disguise of family affection. Not long afterwards her sister fell ill and died, in the absence of the patient and her mother. They were summoned in all haste without being given any definite information of the tragic event. When the girl reached the bedside of her dead sister, there came to her for a brief moment an idea that might be expressed in these words: 'Now he is free and can marry me.' We may assume with certainty that this idea, which betrayed to her consciousness the intense love for her brother-in-law of which she had not herself been conscious, was surrendered to repression a moment later, owing to the revolt of her feelings. The girl fell ill with severe hysterical symptoms; and while she was under my treatment it turned out that she had completely forgotten the scene by her sister's bedside and the odious egoistic impulse that had emerged in her. She remembered it during the treatment and reproduced the pathogenic moment with signs of the most violent emotion, and, as a result of the treatment, she became healthy once more."[49] Similarly, it takes no special theory to suppose that Breuer's Anna O. has a tendency to keep out of mind feelings and knowledge that would normally be accessible to consciousness. Usually gentle and affectionate, she has violent and angry states which she later ascribes to

[49] *Five Lectures on Psycho-Analysis*, vol. 11 of *The Standard Edition of the Complete Psychological Works*, ed. J. Strachey, pp. 24f.

her "bad self." For several weeks, she can hardly speak at all, then can only speak extremely fluent English; during the time "when she had forgotten her mother tongue . . . if she was handed a German book, she was able straight away to read out a correct and fluent translation of it."[50] Of course, Freud takes his conclusions, as a whole, to be surprising, not truistic. The repression and dissociation allegedly revealed by his data are surprisingly pervasive and effective, he argues, and many details of their workings are unexpected. But common sense, unsuspected data and resourceful argument are the typical means of constructing a surprising view of the world, at least since the time of Galileo.

If foundationalist arguments ought to derive their ultimate compelling force from topic-specific truisms, then psychoanalysis has not yet been shown to have foundations—but not because of the absence of general laws with appropriate deductive consequences, the failure of theories to have a sustained history of predictive and instrumental success, or the absence of extensive "bootstrapping" of the sort Glymour describes.[51] The problem is that arguments using shared, truistic premises often license contrary attributions of underlying mechanisms. So psychoanalysis does not yet have foundations, even though the rival hypotheses may be similar enough for useful clinical guidance. By the same token, it would be an unjustified constraint if everyone were expected to adopt the research strategies proper to fields with foundations. Still, it might turn out that psychoanalysis is such a field. It is good for some to try to establish this option. The present conception of realism and rationality suggests how they should proceed. They should take the existence of plausible rivals, such as Kernberg's and Kohut's theories, to be a challenge, to be overcome by further investigations or by the discovery of a new explanatory framework more compelling than the old ones. Apart from new data, the rational force of the new foundations will depend on mobilizing deep-seated truistic principles about action, thought and feeling. It is a relief that the pursuit of foundations involves a recognizable style of interesting, substantive research, which is actually being pursued, not the reconstruction of current theorizing to fit a prior philosophical or natural-scientific pattern.[52]

[50] Ibid., p. 22; see also Breuer's original case study, Freud and Breuer, *Studies in Hysteria*, vol. 2 of *Standard Edition*, pp. 21–47.

[51] See his discussions of Freud, on the "Rat Man" case in particular, in *Theory and Evidence*, pp. 263–77.

[52] Two examples of such empirical work on the structuring of emotions, related-

In other self-questioning fields, the question of foundations should be pursued in similarly specific ways. To cite one further example out of many, the notion that myths and symbols are a culture's way of organizing thought has certainly led to striking successes in making meaningful what had been opaque. But depending on whether one follows Lévi-Strauss and others in regarding the structure of a culture's thinking as a real phenomenon, one will be excited or dismayed that effort is spent on questions as to whether such-and-such a binary opposition is the organizing principle of thought in such-and-such a culture. Even if structuralist principles were adequate summaries of all relevant data, the foundationalist views and corresponding strategies would not be established. For rival explanations of the same data often exist. And when only structuralists can explain a pattern, the pattern stands in no need of explanation, in other frameworks. At this point in time, what the foundationalist project seems to require is more psychological fieldwork, as compared to the further analysis of myths. The gap is the absence of a compelling psychological argument that the lack of a rigid scheme for classification causes disorientation. Douglas' work on taboos could figure as an especially promising start in pursuing this argument, since she addresses herself to phenomena of disgust and awe that cry out for explanation, and that are explicitly based on locations in classification schemes.[53]

Philosophers of science often try to resolve the issues characteristic of the self-questioning fields. In fact, they would be more helpful if they were more humble. It takes more work within the field to establish whether there is a map of the mind, a structure of thought expressed in myth, and so forth. At most, the philosopher can help the scientist to decide what kind of exploration is most apt to uncover the foundations, if they exist.

## The Dogmatism of Skepticism

Detailed argument to one side, perhaps the main attraction of the anti-realist outlook is the appearance that it liberates science, opening up new options for theorizing what would otherwise be blocked. There is a grain of truth in this idea. An anti-realist outlook does

---

ness and the self, which are obviously useful and which could turn out to have a foundationalist use are Margaret Mahler et al., *The Psychological Birth of the Human Infant* (New York, 1978), and Daniel Stern, *The Interpersonal World of the Infant* (New York, 1985).

[53] Mary Douglas, *Purity and Danger* (London, 1970).

encourage a tactic that has been fruitful, indeed, essential in scientific revolutions. More or less by definition, a revolutionary science appeals to possibilities that seemed inconceivable in the old science. So it is essential for scientific revolutionaries to show that phenomena that could only reveal familiar states of affairs if the old science is to be believed are just the ones that would reveal novel states of affairs, if the new framework is adopted. Faced with people who say they cannot imagine a triangle with more than 180 degrees, Reichenbach shows that their visual imagery precisely captures the look of a Riemannian triangle, if relativity theory is right about the nature of light, rods and causality.[54] Before, I argued that realists are staunch as Galileo and Einstein (on my reading of him) can engage in such liberating reinterpretations. But the anti-realist attitude certainly encourages people to think up such arguments, because of its emphasis on the empirical equivalence of radically different theories. After all, the goal of the revolutionary tactic is to show that the traditional interpretation of phenomenon presupposes principles that a reasonable person might reject. Anti-realists are often especially good at developing such arguments because they think that any theoretical interpretation of any phenomenon is subject to such criticism.

Perhaps it is helpful to imagine oneself an anti-realist when one tries to expand the limits of the conceivable. *In every other respect, however, the impact of anti-realism on theory change is conservative.* And standard realist outlooks encourage their own kind of dogmatism. In contrast, the alternative version of realism that I have been developing, with the image of rationality on which it depends, has this practical advantage: it encourages scientists to break with the past when, otherwise, they might give tradition excessive respect or assess alternative research strategies using dogmatically realist standards.

Anti-realism would have no conservative tendency if reasonable scientific practice was one of extreme theoretical fluidity, a willingness to base research and testing now on one basic theory, now on another radically different but empirically equivalent one, or a tendency to desert a theory as soon as the first empirical anomalies appear. Anti-realism would certainly fit this practice, and realism would not. But anti-realists see, quite as clearly as realists, that greater stubbornness in theory acceptance (putting aside strict and literal belief) has been reasonable and productive. These days, the

[54] See *Philosophy of Space and Time*, pp. 37–58.

best practitioners in most fields of inquiry stick to their basic theories until the burden of anomaly is enormous and long-standing, explaining away lesser anomalies or simply ignoring them.

How can it be reasonable systematically to neglect alternatives whose deductive connections with the data are as secure as one's favorites'? An inference from the allegedly good track record of such stubbornness in the past is as flimsy as all simple inductions, and it requires a distorted reading of the actual record (or so I have argued). The remaining option, which anti-realists have taken, is to base the preference on considerations that are relevant to choice, if not to literal belief, namely, pragmatic, aesthetic and psychological considerations. The typical conservatism of physics, since the seventeenth century, chemistry, since the nineteenth century, and biology, in the twentieth century, must have its rationale in the desire for the simple, the convenient and the familiar. Of course, accurate fit with the data must also be a criterion. However, given scientists' broad tolerance for empirical anomaly, the other criteria must have great independent weight.

Philosophers sometimes propose relatively precise standards of simplicity; I criticized such proposals in Chapter Five. However, those standards are philosophers' constructions, often far removed from practitioners' assessments. In practice, among considerations of simplicity, convenience and familiarity, the first two have rested on the third. What breaks with familiar fundamental principles always produces complications, as complication is standardly assessed. In practice, then, the counsel of anti-realism has been to avoid complications by sticking to the familiar, while avoiding dogmatism by specifying that one's preference is not belief that the familiar is more likely to be true. This is the best counsel that anti-realism can give, in light of the inadequacy of alternative, philosophical accounts of simplicity and similar virtues.

Poincaré's *Science and Hypothesis* (1903) is the ironic paradigm of this conservatism. No one, not even Einstein, has ever shown more vividly that classical physics need not be true, even in its most elementary claims about space and time. No one at this time was better aware of the failure of nineteenth-century hopes of establishing the validity of classical mechanics, or proving the existence of the ether. Indeed, Poincaré is renowned for having proposed a version of special relativity in 1900, summed up in the mot that nature's successful conspiracy to prevent our establishing velocities relative to the ether is itself a law of nature. Yet his brilliance in debunking pretensions to show that classical physics is true always culminates in the defense of basic received ideas as the ones to use, as convenient, simple or psychologically compelling organizing principles. Here are some characteristic examples:

> If . . . we were to discover negative parallaxes . . . we should have a choice between two conclusions: we could give up Euclidean geometry, or modify the laws of optics, and suppose that light is not rigorously propagated in a straight line. It is needless to add that every one would look upon this solution as the more advantageous. Euclidean geometry, therefore, has nothing to fear from fresh experiments.[55]

Similarly, the conservation of mass, while not dictated by experiment, is the hypothesis to use because otherwise mechanics "*would not be so simple. . . . Thus it is explained how experiments may serve as a basis for the principles of mechanics, and yet will never invalidate them.*"[56] The existence of the ether cannot be disproved.[57] Because it conflicts with received thermodynamic theory, and makes derivations "a little more difficult," molecular-kinetic theory, though no less well-confirmed than classical thermodynamics, is a bad choice, which "has cost great effort, and has not, on the whole, been fruitful. . . . [I]f the belief in continuity were to disappear, experimental science would become impossible."[58]

If *Science and Hypothesis* were Poincaré's last work, some of his ultimate conservatism might be taken to express the unwillingness of a pioneering critic of classical physics to abandon the old outlook before a constructive alternative was available. But in fact, the use of anti-realism to reduce the pressure for change is just as much the hallmark of Poincaré's vigorous essays in the last year of his life, 1912. In particular, it characterizes his clear, insightful and eloquent summaries of the very latest work in physics, including Einstein's work in relativity theory. The conclusion of Poincaré's discussion of relativity theory, in the essay "Space and Time," is an exceptionally clear expression of the conservatism of skepticism, and an exceptionally poignant one, considering who is writing and when:

---

[55] Science and Hypothesis, p. 73.

[56] Ibid., pp. 104f. (Poincaré's emphasis).

[57] Ibid., pp. 167f, 174–77.

[58] Ibid., pp. 152, 179, 206. Poincaré's acceptance of the molecular hypothesis at the end of his life is, in the final analysis, a triumph of his good judgment as a scientist over the dictates of his philosophy.

What is to be our position in the face of these new conceptions? Will we be forced to modify our conclusions? Surely not. We had adopted one convention because it seemed convenient, and we said that nothing could force us to abandon it. Today, certain physicists want to adopt a new convention. It isn't that they are forced to do so. They take this new convention to be more convenient. That's all there is to it. And those of a different persuasion can legitimately preserve the old convention so as not to disturb their old habits. For myself, I think that they will do so for a long time to come.[59]

As impressed as anyone could be by Michelson and Morley's experiment, the early evidence for discontinuities in radiation, and all the other burdens that classical physics had acquired at the turn of the century, Poincaré is profoundly skeptical concerning all theoretical belief, yet profoundly conservative in theoretical choices. His writings show why. The skepticism motivates the appeals to the aesthetic, pragmatic and psychological constraints that justify the conservatism. Though the connection in Poincaré's case is especially ironic and clear, it is typical of the role of anti-realism in science. In Mach's opposition to molecular-kinetic theory and in most sophisticated attacks on evolutionary theory in Darwin's lifetime, skepticism in belief also meant conservatism in theory choice.

When realism is based on a general pattern of success supposed to be found, the outcome is dogmatic in practice, though in a different way. The research strategies that are motivated by realism are presented as the only reasonable options for everyone, when they are not—as when a psychoanalytic theorist or a structural anthropologist infers from successful uses of theory-dependent reasoning that there is one true map of the mind. Still, this bias in topic-neutral realism is probably less dangerous, because it is so overt. Unlike anti-realism, this outlook does not seem to be liberating. And realism almost always suggests one worthwhile agenda for research. There should be a realist program in psychoanalytic theory and anthropology.

As usual when a philosophy of science could make a difference in practice, the practical influence of anti-realism is greatest in the social sciences. In discussions of economics and of controversial social theories, one often hears it said that theories are just devices for summary and prediction. The tone is staunchly anti-doctrinaire. This seems like encouragement to take seriously a profusion of rival

[59] *Dernières Pensées*, p. 109.

theories. Yet such anti-realist preliminaries typically lead to the neglect of approaches that stray from the most familiar principles of the field in question.

For example, in Friedman's "The Methodology of Positive Economics," the single most widely read essay on economic method, the idea that economics seeks no more than devices to summarize and predict observations turns out to support exclusive commitment to formally simple principles about rational buying and selling as the right basis for economic explanation. Initially, Friedman's anti-realism seems liberating, to the verge of anarchism. "[T]he only relevant test of the *validity* of a hypothesis is comparison of its predictions with experience. . . . The validity of a hypothesis in this sense is not by itself a sufficient criterion for choosing among alternative hypotheses. Observed facts are necessarily finite in number; possible hypotheses infinite. . . . The choice among alternative hypotheses equally consistent with the available evidence must to some extent be arbitrary, though there is general agreement that relevant considerations are suggested by the criteria 'simplicity' and 'fruitfulness,' themselves notions that defy completely objective specification. . . . [T]o suppose that hypotheses have not only 'implications' but also 'assumptions' and that the conformity of these 'assumptions' to 'reality' is a test of the validity of the hypothesis . . . is fundamentally wrong and productive of much mischief."[60]

One might think that the mischief is the reduction of theoretical diversity. But Friedman immediately specifies that the misguided obsession with "reality" impedes "the attainment of consensus on tentative hypotheses in . . . economics." And that consensus turns out to rely on the most traditional principles of neo-classical economics on an extremely narrow construal. This transformation of a near anarchic view of theoretical belief to a near reactionary view of theory choice is as revealing as the similar transition in Poincaré, and has had enormously greater impact on actual research strategies.

In economics, as in most social sciences, actual predictive success is too slender to resolve a great many outstanding controversies. Even on Friedman's relatively sanguine assessment in this essay, the successes of the dynamic part of economics, the theory of how the economy as a whole adapts to changing conditions, are almost non-

[60] Milton Friedman, "The Methodology of Positive Economics" in *Essays in Positive Economics* (Chicago, 1953), pp. 8f., 10, 14.

existent.[61] So hypothesis choice will largely depend on the pragmatic and formal virtues. Putting the mischief-making question of the "real" causes of economic conduct to one side, economists should rely on the apparatus for making predictions which is relatively simple, convenient, and, also, highly familiar, namely, the neo-classical assumption that economic agents behave as if they were fully informed, fully rational exchangers making virtually instantaneous bargains unconstrained by forces outside the relevant market. Certain problems of inaccurate prediction show that the model should, more accurately, be accepted as approximate only. But it should be preferred to its clumsier, more complex rivals, despite (or, in a way, because of) the fact that none of the alternatives can be validated in the present state of predictive capacity.[62]

As a shrewd and inventive practitioner, Friedman is well aware that simplicity and convenience are determined by familiarity as much as by any ahistorical "objective specification." And familiarity, he notes, is field-specific, a fact that he mobilizes in the following example. "Consider . . . the hypothesis that the extent of racial or religious discrimination in employment in a particular area or industry is closely related to the degree of monopoly in the area or industry in question," that is, the hypothesis that corporate leaders, managers and personnel officers in highly competitive industries make no distinctive contribution to discrimination, since they are under pressure to hire the most skilled, of whatever race or religion. "This hypothesis is far more likely to appeal to an economist than to a sociologist. It can be said to 'assume' single-minded pursuit of pecuniary self-interest by employers in competitive industries; and this 'assumption' works well in a wide variety of hypotheses in economics bearing on many of the mass phenomena with which economics deals. It is therefore likely to seem reasonable to the economist that it may work in this case as well. . . . [T]he background of the scientists is not irrelevant to the judgments they reach. . . . [T]he weight of evidence . . . can never be assessed completely 'objectively.' "[63]

There are indeed, sociological, and common-sensical, considerations contrary to the hypothesis. And one might have thought that the economist would take them into account. Racial antagonism in a

[61] Ibid., p. 42. For a grimmer assessment, from the same period as Friedman's essay, see S. Schoeffler, *The Failures of Economics* (Harvard, 1955).

[62] See Friedman, "The Methodology of Positive Economics," pp. 263, 36, 40 and 42f.

[63] Ibid., p. 29.

workforce might be thought to be in the interest of employers, because it weakens the unity and, hence, the bargaining power of workers. The *Wall Street Journal* has described splits among workers largely due to racial exclusion by crafts unions and praised the resulting wage cuts, in the highly competitive construction industry.[64] Such an interest in racial division might well influence employers both in their more directly political activities and in their contributions to the milieu of the workplace. Also, if there is racism in the media and racial segregation in interpersonal ties, a personnel officer in a highly competitive industry might, one would think, show racial bias in routine, quick but crucial judgments of industriousness and reliability. If the economists' assumption really does discount these possibilities, it must include the familiar assumptions in neoclassical economics that the labor market is a commodity market like any other, that choices on each occasion maximize outcomes (given the distribution of money, technology and commodity preferences), and that rational economic agents do not consider how acts of the kind they choose influence the social framework in which economic choices are made. When the notion of single-minded pursuit of pecuniary self-interest is spelled out in this way, it is both familiar and highly relevant to assessing the contribution, if any, of corporate leaders, managers and personnel officers to racial inequality.

In a way, the agnostic about the real causes of economic conduct takes the non-neoclassical considerations into account. They are a reason for withholding belief from the neo-classical hypothesis about inequality. But in another way, anti-realism makes the diversity of frameworks irrelevant. One must chose some hypothesis as a basis for budgeting research time and resources and for organizing cooperation with other investigators. What the domain of prediction leaves open, the familiar practices of the field can resolve. In the absence of decisive predictive tests, to make arguments about the plausibility of theories of economic conduct, construed as factual claims about motives, is to make mischief, impeding consensus and wasting time.

In principle, the implicit advice of anti-realism, to favor the familiar, could be good advice to us, in seeking to explain social phenomena. More precisely, it could direct us products of advanced industrial capitalist society toward the most reasonable bases for

[64] See *Wall Street Journal*, July 7, 1972, p. 1, "Hard-Hat Split: Non-Union Contractors Winning Sizable Share of Construction Work"; and also the editorial praising the impact on wages of non-union construction workers, March 3, 1972, p. 8; and the report on declining wages in building trades, August 29, 1972, p. 1.

expectations and social choices. Whether the bias toward the familiar is in fact scientifically good depends on whether the institutions in which we live are biased toward the reasonable, when they make certain beliefs respectable and routine. At times, the conservatism of skepticism is not just a matter of methods.

# CHAPTER ELEVEN

# Quantum Reality

MODERN quantum physics has a unique status in debates over scientific realism. It is the one well-established field of natural science that is widely thought to require an anti-realist interpretation for reasons internal to the field itself. Of course, if arguments for a general anti-realist view of science are right, then quantum physics, along with every other field, ought to be seen in an anti-realist way. What is striking—and frightening for people with strong realist inclinations—is that the internal content of quantum physics itself seems to have dramatically anti-realist implications. Regularities dictated by parts of the theory that everyone accepts, regularities which are magnificently confirmed by experimental findings, seem to require an interpretation of the theory according to which it merely describes the final measurements that follow various preparatory observations.

This anti-realist view of the field pervades the writings of almost all of its creators. Indeed, modern quantum physics begins with a paper by Heisenberg at the head of which stands this synopsis: "The present paper seeks to establish a basis for theoretical quantum mechanics founded exclusively upon relationships between quantities which in principle are observable."[1] Late in life, Heisenberg was to

---

[1] W. Heisenberg, "Quantum-Theoretical Reinterpretation of Kinematic and Mechanical Relations" (1925) in B. van der Waerden, ed., *Sources of Quantum Mechanics* (New York, 1968), p. 261. All current forms of fundamental microphysics stem from Heisenberg's replacement of the basic means of description characteristic of classical mechanics, and from the equivalent "wave-mechanical" replacement that Schroedinger presented a few months later. The leading theory of atomic processes before this revolution was the quantum theory that Bohr, Rutherford and others had developed, whose Saturn-like atom and quantum jumps are still associated with current physics in most people's imaginations. The old quantum theory was internally inconsistent and clashed with well-established experimental findings. In acknowledgment of Heisenberg's fundamental advance, "quantum mechanics," i.e., mechanics revolutionized to remove the inconsistencies of the old theory, is sometimes used to refer to all that is distinctive in modern microphysics. As a rule, I will speak of "modern quantum physics" instead, or "quantum physics," where the old quantum theory obviously is not in question. For every field of fundamental physics has since been transformed, in ways suggested by the quantum-mechanical revolution, but often quite surprising even in light of the work of the mid-1920s.

claim, "The laws of nature which we formulate mathematically in quantum theory deal no longer with the particles themselves but with our knowledge of the elementary particles. . . . The conception of objective reality . . . evaporated into the . . . mathematics which represents no longer the behavior of elementary particles but rather our knowledge of this behavior."[2] This interpretation is implicit in the vast majority of good textbook presentations. Above all, the textbooks instruct us that what quantum physics says about physical objects, states and processes is that certain measurement outcomes occur with certain probabilities. For example, the theory tells us, not the probability that a particle is in a given volume element, but "the probability that upon a measurement of its position the particle will be found in the given volume element."[3]

That this anti-realism pervades so much work in quantum physics is especially remarkable when one considers how extremely anti-realist it is. This is not the projection into physics of the open-minded anti-realism of the present day, in which theories are about unobservables, and belief in observables is permitted by reason and evidence, though not required by them. Rather, the traditional view of quantum physics takes the evidence to exclude any microphysics that makes statements about anything beyond tendencies for certain observations to follow certain others. Quantum physics, so conceived, is the projection into physics of the aggressive anti-realism toward which classical positivism tended, the restriction of the whole content of a theory to statements of results of observations.

The traditional view of quantum physics is often called "the Copenhagen interpretation," because of Bohr's leading role in its development. In its final form, influenced, above all, by the need to respond to Einstein's criticisms, Bohr's own version of this view is a strict instrumentalism according to which quantum-physical principles assert nothing more than that certain measurement procedures have certain statistical tendencies to have outcomes of certain classically describable kinds. "[T]here can be no question of unambiguous interpretation of the symbols of quantum mechanics other than the well-known rules which allow to predict the results to be obtained by a given experimental arrangement described in a totally

[2] "The Representation of Nature in Contemporary Physics," *Daedalus* (1958), p. 99.
[3] Eugen Merzbacher, *Quantum Mechanics* (New York, 1970), p. 36. In this and other ways, most of the best textbooks echo Pauli's classic monograph of 1933, most accessible in its revised version, *General Principles of Quantum Mechanics* (New York, 1980); see especially pp. 2–10.

classical way. . . ."[4] Taking quantum physics to be complete, Bohr meant to deny that any description of a further underlying mechanism producing the correlations among measurements could be true. Often, Bohr's allies tried to mitigate his instrumentalism. But their milder doctrines seem to avoid metaphysical shock at the cost of inconsistency. Either the laws of classical physics are said to be true in the course of the interpretation, in respects in which they are declared to be false in the further development of the theory.[5] Or (as I shall argue later on) causal processes are introduced that would violate relativistic prohibitions against action at a distance. Although Bohr's extreme instrumentalism is not the only interpretation that physicists regard as orthodox, it turns out to be more defensible than the more moderate doctrines.

Because it is so bold, Bohr's paradigmatic version of the traditional view has consequences for all of science. For one thing, it is incompatible with the theory of confirmation that I have defended. If confirmation is fair causal comparison, then the approximate truth of quantum physics (which has certainly been confirmed) must be entailed by the best causal account of the statistical distributions in observations. The principles of quantum physics must describe the causal processes bringing about those distributions. However, if Bohr is right, no such processes exist.

What is much more shocking, the instrumentalist view of quantum physics seems to entail a similarly instrumentalist understanding of any science concerned with material processes. Consider a statement in such a science which does not seem to be about observations, for example, the statement that the moon is an enduring, approximately spherical object. A material object has tiny parts, of atomic dimensions. Understood non-instrumentally, the statement about the object asserts that the behavior of the tiny parts is limited so that the large-scale properties, explicitly mentioned, obtain. For example, there must be something preventing the tiny parts of the moon from drifting apart, if the moon is an enduring spherical object. Yet if objects have parts of atomic dimensions, then quantum physics is the science of the behavior of those parts. And, according to Copenhagen instrumentalism, there can be no underlying mechanism governing the quantum events, producing the observed pat-

---

[4] Bohr, "Can Quantum-Mechanical Description of Physical Reality Be Considered Complete?" (1935) in Wheeler and Zurek, eds., *Quantum Theory and Measurement* (Princeton, 1983), p. 150.

[5] See, for example, L. Landau and E. Lifshitz, *Quantum Mechanics (Non-relativistic Theory)* (Oxford, 1977), p. 3.

terns in atomic phenomena and preventing others. So really, one ought to regard all of science as simply concerned with correlations among observations. Part-whole talk, then, would refer to nothing more than the relative fineness of the instruments defining properties in the domain of different sciences.

In the course of a reminiscence of Einstein, an eminent quantum physicist reports, "Einstein suddenly stopped, turned to me and asked whether I really believed that the moon exists only when I looked at it."[6] Einstein may have been exaggerating for effect, but not very much. If the instrumentalist view is correct, the existence of the moon really would consist of nothing different in kind from the fact that a lunar-sighting experience results when someone's peering is prepared in certain ways.

Though Bohr's instrumentalism threatens even piecemeal realism concerning science, it is supported by arguments about particular physical regularities, regularities which are abundantly confirmed by experiment and required by universally accepted parts of quantum physics. These arguments begin with the description of phenomena excluded by classical physics but dictated by well-established parts of quantum theory. They continue with attempts to show that only an instrumentalist version of the theory can provide an adequate account of the phenomena. I will try to stand the case for instrumentalism on its head, drawing the opposite moral from the same non-classical situations. First, I will try to show that the instrumentalist interpretation gives a bad account of those situations—bad by the standards of routine physicists' judgments and of quantum theory itself. Then, I will defend an alternative, realist interpretation of quantum physics, as providing the best account of quantum phenomena. On this interpretation, quantum physics is (as it always seems to be in practice) a theory of unobservables, electrons, for example. It makes statements about unobservables whose meaningfulness and truth do not, in general, depend on the presence of a measurement process. If it resembles classical physics in these ways, quantum physics had better radically differ in others. Of course, quantum physics will be indeterministic, on the proposed interpretation: in general, a complete characterization of a situation will admit, as physically possible, more than one spatio-temporal event in any spectrum of alternative events in that situation. However, indeterminism—which was a feature of the old, inconsistent

[6] See A. Pais, "Einstein and the Quantum Theory," *Reviews of Modern Physics* (1979), p. 907.

quantum theory, as well—has turned out to be just one part of the enormous distance between classical physics and any defensible interpretation of modern quantum physics. On the interpretation that I will propose, the further differences, characterizing modern quantum physics, will fall under two main headings.

First, the distinctive laws of quantum physics and the causal factors that they describe are holistic. The causal factors are dynamical properties of whole systems. The properties dictate propensities for individual dynamical events to occur as the system evolves, for example, the propensity, at a given time, for an electron to be (not just: upon measurement to be found in) a given volume element. The existence of these system properties does not consist of the occurrence of separable properties of parts of the system, i.e., properties that can be completely described without reference to other parts. In contrast to the system properties, dynamical events in the system make no independent causal contribution to the evolution of the system.

Second, the repertoire of basic dynamical magnitudes used in quantum-physical descriptions is not classical. It is not the same as the repertoire of basic magnitudes used in classical physics, or the same as probabilities for the classical magnitudes to occur, or the same as probabilities for the classical magnitudes to be the outcomes of measurements. The departure from classical means of description begins in the most elementary part of quantum physics, non-relativistic mechanics without spin. For there, no reference is made to classical linear momentum. Except for spatio-temporal location, quantum physics uses classical terms as labels for non-classical magnitudes, honoring the older theory on the grounds of partial causal analogies.

Any decent textbook contains many statements along these lines. The equations of quantum physics are often said to determine probabilities for events to occur. When "spin" is discussed, if not before, the student is warned not to treat the dynamical property in quantum physics as a classical property, merely inserted into non-classical laws. Nearly every textbook begins with a description of a so-called superposition, in which properties are combined in a distinctively quantum-physical way, which cannot be described by any conjunction of assertions of separable properties. Still, the only interpretation that is discussed explicitly is, almost invariably, the Copenhagen interpretation. And on this construal, the routine ways of talking are loose ways of talking. The apparent probabilities for events to occur are really probabilities for measurements to have certain results. The fact that quantum state descriptions do not employ separable characterizations of parts of the state is taken to reflect the need to define properties in terms of the total measurement set-up. By restricting the subject-matter of the theory to measurement, one can avoid a radically non-classical scheme for description. For the individual measurement outcomes can be expressed in classical terms. Indeed, this conservatism in description was Bohr's ultimate justification for his instrumentalism.[7]

Why is the realist picture that I sketched so rarely accepted in the final analysis, when it is so freely available? It isn't as if detailed mathematical development, so important if physicists are to use an interpretation, is missing. Feynman's work on probability amplitudes, essentially completed in the 1940s, is the natural framework for this realist account.[8] Admittedly, this work contains certain residual assumptions of a dangerously classical or Copenhagen kind. Such assumptions have been elegantly exposed in Arthur Fine's precise and vigorous work on probability and measurement, starting in 1968.[9] One would think that the realist theory I have sketched would be a common option, if not the dominant one.

In the course of defending a realist interpretation, I will try to show that positivism makes this natural realist option seem unnatural, indeed, quite unacceptable; by the same token, the views of justification and meaning that I have been defending are required to sustain the realist interpretation. In general, assumptions about causation and meaning that are part of the positivist conception of science would set the realist interpretation in conflict with important physical principles. In particular, the realist interpretation would conflict with the prohibition against action-at-a-distance and with the indeterminacy required by the uncertainty principle.

[7] See, for example, Bohr, "Can Quantum-Mechanical Description of Physical Reality Be Considered Complete?" p. 150; see also Landau and Lifshitz, *Quantum Mechanics*, pp. 2f., and W. Heisenberg, "The Development of the Interpretation of the Quantum Theory" in W. Pauli, ed., *Niels Bohr and the Development of Physics* (New York, 1955), p. 28.

[8] Volume 3 of *The Feynman Lectures* (Reading, Mass., 1965) is the most charming and eloquent introduction to this approach. R. Feynman and A. Hibbs, *Quantum Mechanics and Path Integrals* (New York, 1965), is the clearest.

[9] See, for example, "On the General Theory of Quantum Measurement," *Proceedings of the Cambridge Philosophical Society* (1969), pp. 111–22; "Some Conceptual Problems of Quantum Theory" in R. G. Colodny, ed., *Paradoxes and Paradigms* (Englewood Cliffs, N.J., 1972), pp. 3–31; "The Two Problems of Quantum Measurement" in P. Suppes et al., eds., *Logic, Methodology and Philosophy of Science IV* (Amsterdam, 1973), pp. 567–81; "On the Completeness of Quantum Theory" in P. Suppes et al., eds., *Logic and Probability in Quantum Mechanics* (Dordrecht, 1976), pp. 249–81.

Causation by quantum system properties would violate any meaningful prohibition of action-at-a-distance, if the covering-law model is an adequate basis for analyzing causal claims. On the other hand, causation by quantum system properties can be reconciled with the standard prohibition, if the causal status of quantum descriptions is established by a topic-specific scientific argument, of the sort required by the core conception of causality, presented in Chapter Two.

Positivist views of meaning create similar conflicts between realism and good physics. If "momentum" as the term is used in elementary quantum mechanics refers to classical momentum, the theory cannot speak of the possession of magnitudes, but only of the outcomes of measurements. For in a theory that is realist and conceptually classical, the uncertainty principle has no rationale, and, contrary to the evidence, quantum physics is deterministic at the level of events. The realist interpretation requires a break with the classical means of description. But in a positivist framework, no such break is possible. Realist state descriptions would not have meanings that fit quantum physicists' uses of them, if the meanings must consist of entailments in the common vocabulary of classical and quantum physics. And deductivist accounts of confirmation strongly support the assumption that meaning requires such a connection with the common vocabulary. In the alternative anti-positivist view, the needed meanings are acquired by a fair argument from the old theory, sustaining a radically new descriptive scheme.

For the most part, I will be concerned with the interpretation of quantum physics, for example, with the claim that it is only concerned with measurement outcomes. But I will end by considering the bearing of quantum physics on the milder anti-realism that is, these days, much more common in the appraisal of science as a whole. Even if quantum physics does refer to unobservables, it might seem that it need not be believed, only used, when it makes assertions about them. The actual history of quantum physics is very unpromising terrain for the current realist strategy of arguing from alleged contributions of theory-dependent methods. But the topic-specific framework developed in the previous chapter does sustain arguments that some (by no means all) of the posits successfully used in quantum physics actually exist. Though limited in scope, these arguments have the power required by the modern debate. They make disbelief unreasonable in light of the evidence.

Quantum physics seems to pose the main threat, from within science, to the view of science that I presented in previous chapters. I hope to show that just this general view of science has the virtue of making possible an interpretation of quantum physics meeting demands that are routine within physics. In the final analysis, that is what I mean by standing the traditional anti-realist argument on its head. Of course, I will not be able to discuss all of the major alternatives to my specific interpretation. My main intention is to show that a non-positivist view of justification, meaning and causation leaves room for a realist interpretation of a holistic, non-classical kind, and to argue that such an interpretation will be superior to instrumentalist ones, superior by the usual standards for assessing physical theories.

## QUANTUM EFFECTS AND ALLEGED CONSEQUENCES

Here is a phenomenon that illustrates what is, in many ways, the most important distinctive feature of quantum physics, the so-called superposition of quantum states, and the entanglements and interferences among probabilities to which superposition gives rise. The same phenomenon is a compelling and much-used argument for an instrumentalist interpretation. For such an interpretation seems the only way to account for this well-established pattern in nature without lapsing into inconsistency.

A filament emitting electrical energy, a barrier with two holes, and an array of detectors are set up, all in a row. (See Figure 1.) The detectors are tightly packed microchips connected to a loudspeaker. On receiving a charge, each produces a proportionately loud sound. The detectors register incoming charge. If we turn down the transmitter low enough (and if the detectors are sensitive enough), the sounds from the loudspeaker will become a series of isolated clicks, all of the same volume. Charges are arriving in identical units at particular areas. (For convenience, only arrival at one vertical line of detectors will be discussed. Also, this is a fictitious experiment. But similar experiments, on electron diffraction, have often been performed. Quantum physics is the only basis for explaining the real experiments, and it dictates that an experiment prepared in this way would have the outcomes to be described, if controls and detectors could be made sufficiently fine.)

If hole 1 is left open and hole 2 is closed, the cumulative pattern of clicks is curve $P_1$ in Figure 1 (A). If hole 2 is open and hole 1 is closed, a similar pattern is produced, represented by $P_2$. In Feynman's grisly analogy, it is as if electrons, the bearers of the identical charges, were being shot at random from the transmitter, firing like

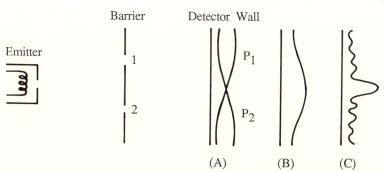

FIGURE 1. Electrical energy is emitted at the left. At the right is a wall of charge detectors, and, in between, a barrier with two holes. If hole 1 is left open while hole 2 is plugged, the cumulative frequency of detection events for various heights along the wall is P₁, plotted in A. Similarly, if hole 1 is plugged and hole 2 is left open, the cumulative frequencies are P₂, also in A. If these frequencies are added at each height, the result is the pattern in B. However, if the experiment is run with both holes open, the result is pattern C.

a machine gun run wild.[10] Physicists can represent the observed cumulative pattern of arrivals at the wall, together with the other cumulative patterns that occur if the wall is moved backward or forward, by means of abstract probability-of-arrival-at-volume-dv-and-time-interval-dt waves, which radiate outward from the single open hole. That electron transmitters are really like machine guns, producing localized particles with continuous trajectories is a speculation, which turns out to be false. That these are the cumulative frequencies of arrival events is hard fact.

Next, both holes are opened. When we wait for a cumulative pattern to emerge, we discover, not B, the result of adding $P_1$ and $P_2$, but C. This pattern is utterly familiar to physicists from other situations. It results from interference between two wave-like phenomena, continuously propagating from two different sources. The waves reinforce each other where peaks meet peaks and troughs meet troughs, cancel each other out where peaks meet troughs. However, anyone who supposed, on the basis of the one-hole experiments, that the process of transmission was a random spewing of indivisible corpuscles will find the pattern surprising. The "bullets," coming out one by one, would not interfere with each other. Indeed, the two-hole experiment by itself ought to shock anyone

[10] R. Feynman, *The Character of Physical Law* (Cambridge, Mass., 1967), pp. 130f.

who thinks that what the filament transmits must either be corpuscles or waves. The clicks are isolated and equal, as if corpuscles were arriving. Presumably, then, corpuscles were transmitted. But in that case, interference would not occur.

On reflection, this set of experiments might seem to present a paradox, and not just for someone who wants everything elementary to be a corpuscle or a wave phenomenon. There are tempting arguments for all the following three statements about the experiment with both holes open. But all three cannot be true, since otherwise B, not C would be observed.

I. *During the time interval between clicks, an electron, in its entirety, passes through one hole, the other remaining empty.*

That this is so is strongly suggested by the fact that electrons are only observed arriving in their entirety, i.e., with the identical elementary charge (and mass, if one cares to measure it), together with the fact that the electrons can only arrive if they pass through one hole or the other. One might resist this inference on the grounds that what sometimes acts like a corpuscle need not always be one. However, the inference receives powerful support from a further empirical finding. If we set up apparatus to ascertain what emerges from the barrier, we always discover a whole electron appearing near one or the other hole in between clicks. If, for example, we were to set up a gamma-ray microscope, such as Heisenberg once imagined, and point it at the right side of the barrier, we would always observe an entire electron emerging from one hole or another.[11]

II. *The probability that an electron arrives at a given detector if it passes in its entirety through hole 1 is the same for an experiment with two holes open as for an experiment with only hole 1 open; and similarly for arrival via hole 2.*

After all, an electron at hole 1 does not know whether hole 2 is empty but unblocked, or blocked. And whether empty or blocked, there is nothing going on in hole 2 to affect the subsequent history of the electron, in between the clicks. More precisely, any proposal that a separate but causally relevant process is going on at the other, electronless hole would be a speculation in need of further support. And such speculations have done very badly, in the face of further experiment and theorizing. For example, there is good reason to be-

[11] Heisenberg, "The Physical Content of Quantum Kinematics and Mechanics" (1927), the first presentation of the "uncertainty principle," in Wheeler and Zurek, eds., *Quantum Theory and Measurement*, p. 83; *The Physical Principles of the Quantum Theory* (1930; New York, 1949), pp. 21–25.

lieve that electrons are not pushed by separate, physical "pilot waves," which might vibrate through unblocked holes that are empty of electrons.

III. *If an electron passes through one hole or the other in its entirety, and if the probability of its arrival at a detector should it go through a given hole is the same as for the corresponding one-hole experiment, then the total probability of arrival at a detector is the probability of passing through hole 1 times the hole-1-only conditional probability plus the probability of passing through hole 2 times the hole-2-only conditional probability.*

This seems to be required by elementary reasoning about probabilities.

Join the three premises to the experimental findings described, i.e., to the pattern C distribution, and a contradiction results. The premises entail pattern B, instead. The parts of quantum physics dictating that pattern C results in the given experimental set-up are accepted and constantly used by physicists of all philosophical persuasions. Which premise is wrong?

So far as considerations of physical theory are concerned, the attractiveness of the instrumentalist view is due to its ability to answer this question and similar ones in an apparently straightforward and highly plausible way. Indeed, the most important textbooks in the history of modern quantum physics began by extracting instrumentalist morals from concise sketches of situations like the one just described.[12]

In the instrumentalist answer to the riddle of the electrons and the barrier, the first premise is wrong. The electron does not pass, unobserved, either through one hole or through the other. The instrumentalist description of the real state of affairs is, roughly, this. (I will be arguing that the roughness is important. The answer is subject to two readings. On one of them, the first premise is meaningless. On the other, it is false. The readings create different, complementary problems. The attractiveness of the instrumentalist solution depends on the possibility of shifting from one reading to another, as each version is put under pressure.) Instrumentalists allege that it is only right to say that the entire electron passes through one hole or passes through the other if the electron is in a situation in which it can be observed through which hole the electron passes. Of course, this failure of an entire unobservable electron to be in

---

[12] See Pauli, *General Principles of Quantum Mechanics*, ch. 1; Dirac, *The Principles of Quantum Mechanics* (Oxford, 1981), pp. 4–13; Landau and Lifshitz, *Quantum Mechanics*, pp. 1–3.

either hole does not reflect a tendency of electrons to split into pieces when unobservable. Rather, premise 1 is excluded by a general prohibition against saying that one of a number of possible alternatives is the case in situations in which there is no means of observing which is the case. We can, in principle, change the given experimental situation and set up apparatus that determines whether an electron passes through 1 or 2; for example, we might illuminate the holes with gamma rays and point Heisenberg's microscopes in their direction. However, if the apparatus is operating, pattern B in fact emerges, so that the three premises, now all true, do not contradict what is observed. Whenever pattern C emerges, we are saved from paradox by instrumentalism, since, in all such cases, no relevant means of discriminating between holes is in operation.

Even if it helps avoid a paradox, Copenhagen instrumentalism might seem an intrusion of philosophy into physics. In the final analysis, it is an avoidable philosophical intrusion, if my subsequent arguments are correct. Nonetheless, physicists who are generally allergic to philosophy are attracted to Copenhagen instrumentalism. For it provides an interpretation of the full-fledged, mathematical theory in terms of the classical physics that everyone learns first. The new physics is interpreted as laying down laws governing the measurement of the magnitudes in the old physics. A brief and utterly sketchy description of some of the mathematical theory will clarify this main attraction of instrumentalism among the scientifically learned but philosophically uncommitted. It will also make clearer a challenge that any interpretation must meet. The mathematical formalism is trustworthy as it is actually employed. An interpretation must justify the successful uses without producing further implications that conflict with empirical findings or create internal inconsistencies.

The most common and, for many purposes, most convenient format for the full-fledged mathematical theory is the so-called wave mechanics first developed by Schroedinger. In this format, as in all standard ones, the states to which the distinctive laws of quantum physics directly refer are states of closed dynamical systems. (A closed system is one not subject to influence from anything that is not a part of the system. Complete characterizations of states of a closed dynamical system describe all factors present at a given time that influence the evolution of spatio-temporal events in the system.) In Schroedinger's format, in contrast to standard alternatives, descriptions of states are built up out of functions that vary in a wave-like way. The wave functions that will serve to represent states can be functions of space and time coordinates. These are the easiest to grasp, but others, for example, functions of time and the quantum-physical analogue of momentum, produce fully equivalent descriptions. By itself, every Schroedinger wave function represents a physically possible state. And there is a principle of superposition that says that if functions represent physically possible states, then the so-called superposition resulting from multiplying each function by a complex number, perhaps different in each case, and adding up the products represents a state, as well. Thus, if $\psi_1$ and $\psi_2$ are wave functions representing states, so is the compound wave function $c_1\psi_1 + c_2\psi_2$.

In Schroedinger's picture, the magnitudes that are labelled with the familiar classical terms, position, momentum, energy and the like, are represented by operators, converting functions to other functions. Very unfortunately for our purposes, the jargon term for these operators is "observables." Their official definition is technical, mathematical and philosophically neutral. To make the philosophical neutrality clearer, I will speak of the operators as representing "dynamical magnitudes." In some cases, applying one of these operators to a wave function produces a function that is the original multiplied by a real number. Then, the wave function that is operated on is said to be an "eigenfunction" of the operator. The eigenfunction is said to represent an "eigenstate," and the real number is called the "eigenvalue" of the dynamical magnitude for a system in that eigenstate. If a system is in an eigenstate of a dynamical magnitude—i.e., if its whole wave function for that magnitude is the single corresponding eigenfunction—then it is certain to have the corresponding eigenvalue of that magnitude. Any state can be represented by a superposition of the eigenfunctions of any dynamical magnitude. The $c$'s in such a superposition are called "probability amplitudes" for reasons that will soon be clearer.

The details of this descriptive apparatus are arcane to anyone uncomfortable in the mathematical territory known as Hilbert space. But the output of this mathematical work is, so far, purely a means of description, analogous to Newton's statements about absolute space and time, as against his laws of motion. In quantum physics, the general law for describing how systems evolve concerns an operator known as the Hamiltonian for the system in question. The law says, very roughly, that the time rate of change for a description in terms of wave functions is given by the application of the Hamiltonian operator to that description. The Hamiltonian is taken to have states of definite energy as its eigenvalues, an interpretation that is a natural extension of the most general and abstract treatment of energy in classical physics (due, not surprisingly, to Hamilton). As one feature of the law of evolution, the "general time-dependent Schroedinger equation," the rate of change of each probability amplitude at a given time depends on all of the amplitudes at that time. What the Hamiltonian for a system is, is determined from case to case on the basis of experimental and theoretical findings concerning the forces, changes, entities, and interactions in the system. As Dirac puts it, in a famous textbook, this is "a special problem which presents itself with each particular dynamical system one is called upon to study."[13] So it is somewhat misleading to call the most general principles of quantum physics a physical theory. In effect, they amount to an instruction, "If you want to find the laws governing the evolution of a system, find the Hamiltonian." In this, they resemble Newton's three laws, which amount to the instruction, "If you want to find the laws governing the evolution of a system, find the forces."[14]

Some warnings are needed before this sketch is used. First, it is, of course, a simplified sketch. For example, the $c$'s are only probability amplitudes, strictly speaking, when the description is put in a certain standard mathematical form. Second, the Schroedinger format is only fully adequate for elementary non-relativistic quantum physics, neglecting the important property "spin," whose closest classical analog is the intrinsic angular momentum of, say, a spinning top. Some further theoretical developments, beyond this most elementary level, are important in interpreting quantum physics at all levels, including the most elementary one. Fortunately, one can describe them, in a vague and qualitative way, using the apparatus of probability amplitudes, an apparatus whose significance can be brought out by investigating the Schroedinger picture. Finally the Schroedinger format is just one of a number of equivalent formats. Indeed, I will rely on another format, Feynman's path-integral treatment, to clarify the relation of elementary quantum mechanics to classical mechanics. All ways of putting quantum physics include a version of the principle of superposition, the apparatus of probability amplitudes, and the use of a Hamiltonian to describe the evolution of a system.

According to the instrumentalist interpretation, the description

[13] *The Principles of Quantum Mechanics*, p. 84.
[14] Cf. *The Feynman Lectures on Physics*, vol. 1 (Reading, Mass., 1963), pp. 10–12.

of a quantum state in terms of amplitudes and eigenfunctions says nothing more about physical reality than that measurements result with certain probabilities if an apparatus is operating that measures the dynamical magnitude in question (i.e., the one whose eigenfunctions are being used to represent a state). Those probabilities are determined by taking the absolute square of each respective amplitude to be the probability that measurement will yield the associated eigenvalues. An absolute square of a complex number is the number times its complex conjugate, i.e., the original number with plus and minus signs reversed before the i's.

Although the most common wave-function representation, in the Schroedinger format, involves eigenfunctions of position, such a wave function for a given time will yield information about much more than position—on this instrumentalist interpretation and every other interpretation. When we take the absolute squares of amplitudes associated with position eigenfunctions, we neglect so-called phase factors, numbers of the form $e^{id}$ (where e is the base of the natural logarithm system). These numbers all have 1 as their absolute square. However, the relation between these phase factors determines the amplitudes for eigenvalues of the other dynamical magnitudes that have different eigenfunctions. So a single Schroedinger description contains information about all magnitudes. Moreover, the Hamiltonian operator, applied to the state description, will determine the subsequent Schroedinger states. The quantum state description, together with the Hamiltonian, contains all information about dynamical tendencies of the system—which means all information about potential measurement results, on the instrumentalist interpretation. The state description determines how measurement tendencies evolve given the various Hamiltonians the system may have.

This instrumentalist interpretation of the mathematical theory seems a neat way of avoiding paradoxes concerning physical processes described using superpositions. The quantum-physical description of the two-hole experiment will assign an amplitude for an electron to pass through hole 1, in between clicks, and an amplitude for an electron to pass through hole 2. What are the probabilities of these alternatives? If there is an apparatus at work for detecting through which hole an electron passes, say, Heisenberg's microscope, then the question has a direct answer. The probability of each alternative is the result of taking the absolute square of the corresponding amplitude in the positional representation. Moreover, the total detection set-up ascertains whether an electron, having passed through a given hole, arrives at a given area on the wall. So corresponding amplitudes for transitions can be squared to yield ordinary conditional probabilities. The ordinary simple and conditional probabilities combine to yield pattern B for arrival at the wall.

Suppose, however, that no measurement apparatus is operating to determine electron locations at the barrier. Then no probability whatever is assigned to passage through either hole. What the state description asserts is that certain magnitudes will be observed with certain probabilities if a measurement apparatus is operating. By hypothesis, the "if" clause, here, has not been satisfied. (It is because the probabilities presuppose measurement that they are best described as probabilities to be found upon measurement, not probabilities to be, independent of measurement.) Still, detection of arrivals goes on at the back wall, so one can speak of probabilities of arrival events. In all versions of quantum physics the amplitude for arrival at a detector on the wall, in this situation, is the amplitude for arrival given passage through hole 1 plus the amplitude for arrival given passage through hole 2. According to the instrumentalist interpretation, this talk of arrival via a hole is just part of an intermediate stage in the calculation of a detection event. It does not correspond to anything real, any more than the analysis of a force into x-, y- and z-components corresponds to the presence of three different processes. The phase factors in each component amplitude in the arrival sum affect the magnitude of the absolute square of the sum. When the calculation is done for different positions along the wall, relations between phase factors produce the interference pattern, pattern C. ($e^{ix}$ is a function of x with real and imaginary parts, each varying in a wave-like way; it equals $\cos(x) + i\sin(x)$.) In contrast, if detection at the barrier has justified the calculation in which amplitudes for passage and amplitudes for transition are individually squared, the probability of arrival at a detector is the square of the amplitude for arrival via hole 1 plus the square of the amplitude for arrival via hole 2. That the two ways of extracting probabilities yield different results should not be surprising to anyone who expects the square of 2 plus the square of 3 to be different from the square of 2 plus 3.

## STRICT INSTRUMENTALISM

Bohr was the great partisan of the strict instrumentalism that denies meaning to the statement that either the electron in its entirety is at hole 1 or it is at hole 2 (i.e., that this is so when no detection apparatus is functioning at the barrier). Of course, this denial is only a way out of paradox if it has a justification. As Bohr was well aware, its justification would have to come, not from an uncontroversial finding of physics, but from a constraint on meaning, applying throughout quantum physics, if not beyond: an alleged description of a possible state of affairs is meaningless in the absence of a means for testing its truth. On these grounds, each disjunct, and, hence, the disjunction could be judged meaningless. Note that the constraint on meaning must be quite strict, if paradox is to be avoided. In particular, it isn't enough to claim that an alleged proposition is meaningless if there is no way in which it could, in principle, be tested by applying an appropriate apparatus. All physicists, including Einstein, the great opponent of Copenhagen instrumentalism, have tried to avoid a theory that admits questions that are unanswerable to this extent. One *can* always test whether an electron, in its entirety, passes through hole 1, by using Heisenberg's gamma-ray microscope. Apparently, Bohr needs the stronger claim (which he certainly did make), that an alleged description of a possible state of affairs is meaningless if no means of testing it is actually in operation.[15]

This strict instrumentalist constraint would require the rejection of unquestioned explanatory achievements of quantum physics itself. For example, it is a great achievement of quantum physics to have explained the radiation properties of the sun and other stars as due to quantum states in the stellar interiors. Needless to say, detection apparatuses for these processes are not functioning inside stars. Indeed, whenever there is a quantum-physical explanation of a kind of phenomena, the instances in which it refers to observed antecedents are an infinitesimal fraction of the whole. For example,

[15] See "Can Quantum-Mechanical Description of Physical Reality Be Considered Complete?" p. 150, and "Discussion with Einstein on Epistemological Problems in Atomic Physics" in P. Schilpp, ed., *Albert Einstein: Philosopher-Scientist* (Evanston, Ill., 1949), pp. 221f., 238. In all of his mature formulations of the strict instrumentalist constraint, Bohr applies it only to quantum physics. The constraint would not be valid, his remarks suggest, if classical physics had been empirically adequate. Yet presumably some general view of meaning is also required to sustain the strict constraint, in addition to empirical findings and considerations of physical theory. I will argue that connections between meaning and observation implied by the deductivist theory of confirmation are that underlying view. Roughly speaking, familiar requirements of testability-in-principle combine with the uncertainty principle, indeterminism and the structure of quantum-physical explanation to make the operation of a classical apparatus a requirement for meaningful description, if quantum physics is complete.

the initial elementary achievements of quantum physics largely consisted of explaining the spectrum of hydrogen. Perhaps spectral events are sometimes traced to an observed process in a hydrogen atom. But of course, the vast majority of hydrogen atoms have never been in a measurement apparatus. Yet the quantum processes underlying their radiation properties are known and meaningfully described.

One response is to subordinate explanation to prediction. Copenhagen instrumentalists often say that the success of quantum theory amounts to nothing more or less than enormous success in prediction. The equations for solar radiation and for radiation from hydrogen atoms might be taken to be, not general descriptions of underlying processes, but tools for prediction, accepted as trustworthy on the basis of past success. Formulas about unobserved quantum states are, then, literally meaningless tools that will always serve to predict what we find if we look.[16]

The problem is that quantum theory as such yields very little in the way of prediction. In dealing with atoms more complex than helium, physicists do not use descriptions of quantum states that they actually regard as valid. The mathematics of the interactions between the electrons is, at present, unmanageable. Still, the explanation of the properties of elements and their compounds is a great triumph of quantum physics. One can use the theory itself to explain certain features of substances. More precisely, the observed features are easiest to explain, in broad outline, by supposing that the atoms involved have the properties quantum theory would lead one to expect. These explanations are better than those supported by any rival theory consistent with basic background principles. Presumably, the enormous further difficulties in using the theory to derive extensive true predictions are due to limitations of a basically true theory, for example, mathematical complexity or problems in framing accurate auxiliary hypotheses concerning tiny, subtle phenomena. The justification of quantum theory on the basis of such explanatory superiority is very different from a justification appealing to predictive success, in a number of ways. First of all, predictive accuracy is no better than many obviously false theories can claim.

[16] Thus, Heisenberg takes a quantum state description of a system that is not subjected to measurement to be "completely abstract and incomprehensible; . . . it . . . , so to speak, contains no physics at all." The state description "becomes a part of the description of Nature" by telling us what the outcomes of experimental interventions would be. See "The Development of the Interpretation of The Quantum Theory," p. 26.

Second, without further assumptions concerning symmetry, continuity, linearity or causal independence, the theory would usually say nothing about observed phenomena. And the assumptions that were initially most plausible often led to conflict with observed phenomena. They were revised to fit. Finally, derivations of precise predictions from premises that are regarded as strictly true are usually unavailable, for the previously noted reasons of mathematical complexity, among others. The predictive success of the theory, as against mere rules of thumb, is slim, even though its explanatory power is enormous.

On the basis of the limited, relative success of the theory, certain methods of approximation can be justified, and used as means of avoiding the unmanageable mathematics. The methods are constantly adjusted, in turn, in an ad hoc fashion. This is hardly the kind of success that would justify the universal acceptance of quantum physics—unless that theory is justified by its superiority in explanatory power, independent of its efficacy as a predictive tool. In other words, if explanation is subordinated to prediction it is hard to see why scientists would trust anything more interesting than the rag-tag of semi-classical approximations, where atoms more complex than helium are concerned.

The strict instrumentalist view, which is supposed to save physics from paradox, would make it impossible to explain vast numbers of phenomena that could otherwise be explained. This is a standard physicist's reason for rejecting a proposal. Of course, the physicists' standard is not the only relevant one. The explanatory costs might be justified by good philosophical arguments. Bohr himself bases his analyses on a theory of meaning according to which talk is only intelligible when it can be fully paraphrased in a fixed vocabulary, the vocabulary of ordinary sense perception, which he identifies with the vocabulary of classical measurement results.[17] This is the positivist theory of meaning discussed in Chapter Nine. It turned out to give a bad account of stability and change in science. It depends for much of its appeal on the deductivist account of confirmation, which fails in its own ways. The stricter instrumentalist answer would mean giving up much science with no good justification.

[17] See "Can Quantum-Mechanical Description of Physical Reality Be Considered Complete?" p. 150; "Discussion with Einstein on Epistemological Problems," p. 109; "The Quantum Postulate and the Recent Development of Atomic Theory" in Wheeler and Zurek, eds., *Quantum Theory and Measurement*, pp. 88f., 126.

## A MILDER DOCTRINE

Is there a less strict instrumentalism, in which it is false, but not meaningless, to say that the entire electron is in one hole or other between clicks? In such a theory, the electronic process taking place in between observations does not involve localized corpuscles with the whole electron mass and electron charge. The localization is the product of observations, brought about by the detectors in the wall or (in the variant experiment) the gamma-ray microscope.

Just this view of quantum physics is often associated with the two-process model von Neumann employs in his *Mathematical Foundations of Quantum Mechanics*. (Actually, it is unclear whether he takes the description of a process prior to measurement as anything more than a description of a tool for predicting measurement results. Still, it is well worth examining the notion that the two processes might both exist.) One process is that described by the time-dependent Schroedinger energy equation. It is continuous, i.e., values are reached via a continuous gradation of intermediate values. And it is deterministic, in that an initial quantum state, generally described through a superposition of wave functions, dictates all subsequent quantum states. The second process consists of measurement interventions. In these episodes, a quantum state, generally a superposition, is made into one of its eigenstates, acquiring the corresponding eigenvalue. The episode is discontinuous, since the other components of the quantum state simply disappear. It is nondeterministic, since it is possible for any of the eigenvalues to be realized. All that is dictated by the situation just prior to measurement is the probability, based on the absolute squares of amplitudes, with which eigenvalues will be created. In this sense, measurement changes a superposition, a "pure quantum state," to an ordinary statistical mixture, in which states with definite classical attributes occur with certain probabilities—and without the subsequent "interference of probabilities" that would be guaranteed by a description in terms of probability amplitudes. Particular entities in a system—for example, electrons in the emitter–barrier-wall system—possess definite physical properties (for example, definite locations) only if the system is in a corresponding eigenstate. In general, this requires the creation of an eigenstate by a measurement.

Suppose that the quantum state descriptions used in depicting the Schroedinger evolution are taken to describe states of an actual deterministic, continuous process. What the description says—on this two-process reading—is that measurement intervention, acting on the state, would, indeterministically, produce one or another of the corresponding spectrum of dynamical magnitudes, with probabilities assigned by the usual calculations with probability amplitudes. More precisely, it says that measurement would produce such values at the time in the state description, and it also dictates measurement probabilities for other times, according to the usual calculations employing amplitudes and Hamiltonians. This interpretation is close to Bohr's. Characterizations of the continuous deterministic processes only conflict if they assign conflicting probabilities to measurements. What is even more striking, a measurement process, even an idealized, perfect process, does not, typically, assign characteristics that would exist in the absence of measurement interventions. Typically, a quantum state is a superposition, which must be physically transformed to produce the definite value assigned in a measurement outcome.

Still, there is an important difference from Bohr's strict instrumentalism. Characterizations of physical states, for example, via a Schroedinger description, are sometimes true, even though no measurement process is taking place. So there is no implication that descriptions in the absence of measurement are meaningless. The assumption, concerning the two-hole experiment *sans* microscope, that there is either an electron in hole 1 or an electron in hole 2 is not meaningless, here. It is false, because the superposition has not yet been "reduced" by measurement.

Because the connection between measurement and meaning is much looser, this milder instrumentalism might seem to avoid the enormous loss of explanatory power produced by Bohr's interpretation. Of course, there will be no explanation of why measurement of identically prepared states has sometimes produced one magnitude, sometimes another. But the latter inability is not specially troubling, since any version of quantum physics that is faithful to well-established claims of the theory will have to allow an analogous indeterminism.

In fact, the milder instrumentalism produces a distinctive explanatory incapacity, that is even more troubling than the stricter doctrines. The notorious problem with the two-process interpretation is the arbitrariness of borders drawn between the continuous quantum evolution and the measurement process. In the two-hole experiment where does the continuous evolution end and the measurement intervene: at the detectors, along wires to the loudspeaker, in the scientist's car, in his brain? This is now a question as to when a real physical process ends. There is no way of answering it, in the two-process approach. So this approach produces the type of unverifiability that everyone, instrumentalist and realist alike, regards as a defect in a science. Quantum physics now poses questions about how to describe reality while making them unanswerable.

Also, the reduction to the eigenstate requires exceptions to basic physical laws, exceptions only justifiable in the name of saving the interpretation itself. It is a well-established theoretical result that superpositions do not evolve into mixtures, according to the time-dependent Schroedinger equation. But the physical system consisting of object to be observed and measuring apparatus is itself a dynamical system, in a "pure" quantum state. Measurement does not simply add a new feature to physical reality, which would not otherwise exist. Measurement requires a violation of laws that would otherwise obtain.

Von Neumann hinted at one way of reducing the arbitrariness of the boundary and of the exemption from normal laws. The idea, which Wigner has developed in detail, is to locate measurement in the observer's consciousness and declare that conscious processes are not subject to the laws governing the rest of reality. Aside from overturning materialism with suspicious ease, this converts quantum physics into a science for solipsists, once the two-process view is applied to the task of interpreting quantum physics. The interpretation of descriptions of pure states will now be that they describe propensities, continuously and deterministically evolving, for measurement interventions to have certain results. The interventions and results are now entirely episodes in a non-material mind. And not just any mind, but one's own. If it is natural to locate measurement in the mind rather than in the detector, then hearing a result from a friend only involves a process of measurement in the mind of the hearer.[18]

The required metaphysics has become bizarre. And it is being sold on the basis of an implausible analysis of measurement. Really, locating the act of measurement entirely in the measurer's consciousness is not natural. It is an arbitrary analysis introduced to prevent the situation in which the two-process interpretation poses questions about physical change and makes them unanswerable.

So far, the two-process interpretation makes quantum physics either defective because it poses unanswerable questions or defective because it gives bizarre and arbitrary answers. Actually, a fa-

[18] Wigner acknowledges the implication of solipsism. See "Remarks on the Mind-Body Problem" in Wheeler and Zurek, eds., *Quantum Theory and Measurement*, p. 173.

mous thought-experiment of Einstein, Podolsky and Rosen shows that matters are even worse.

Einstein and his colleagues argue that quantum physics cannot be complete, by exploiting a fundamental result of quantum physics, the uncertainty principle, together with a fundamental proposition of relativity theory, the principle that instantaneous action at a distance is physically impossible. The uncertainty principle is part of everyone's quantum physics, i.e., there is always the same equation about intervals and probabilities, though it is interpreted in significantly different ways. For example, the principle figures in the standard explanation of why the protons do not suck the electrons into the nucleus of an atom. Einstein and his colleagues present their argument as a challenge to an instrumentalist quantum physics employing a two-process model. For example, they speak of the determination of actual states, according to quantum mechanics, as requiring "the help of further measurements, by a process known as the *reduction of the wave packet*," the instantaneous reduction to eigenstates that von Neumann would soon describe in a precise and systematic way.[19] So it is most useful for the present to introduce the uncertainty principle in the interpretation that a two-process instrumentalism would give it. This is most in accord with Einstein's argument and best fitted to the present task of assessing that instrumentalism. On such a reading, the uncertainty principle says (roughly) that no state is simultaneously certain to give rise to a definite measurement result concerning momentum in a given direction and certain to give rise to a definite measurement result concerning location in the corresponding dimension; the product of the interval within which a momentum result has some probability and the interval within which a position result has some probability is always at least as great as a certain physical quantity, Planck's constant, divided by $4\pi$. Compared with visible quantities, Planck's constant is tiny. It is on the order of an atom's diameter.

Einstein and his co-authors describe a kind of system that must be possible and measurable, according to fundamental principles of quantum physics. In their most concrete illustration, the system contains two particles which are initially separate, interact, separate again, and finally are subjected to measurements at remote regions. The quantum-physical description of the whole system dictates that a momentum measurement for particle 1 will assign, with certainty,

[19] "Can Quantum-Mechanical Description of Physical Reality Be Considered Complete?" p. 140; italics in original.

a definite momentum to particle 2. The principles involved are, in effect, the quantum physical version of the conservation of momentum. So measuring momentum for 1 is a way of measuring momentum for 2. Similarly, measuring position for 1 is a way of measuring position for 2.

Einstein and his co-authors argue that particle 2, at the time when magnitudes of 1 might be measured, must have both a definite momentum and a definite position, regardless of whether any measurement does take place. For, they note, a measurement on 1 of either magnitude could have dictated the value of the magnitude for 2 with certainty, and as a result of an act of measurement that does not change anything in the region of 2. The measurement at 1 cannot change anything at 2, because that would require instantaneous action at a distance. What could be established with certainty and without changing the object measured must be a property of the object, independent of whether or not it is measured. But quantum physics cannot, according to its own principles, make it certain that an object has a definite momentum and certain that an object has a definite position. So, if true, quantum physics must be incomplete.

A one-particle system, without spatial separation, would not have supplied such a strong argument. The act of measurement might then be taken to change the object, giving it a definite momentum, say, and depriving it of definite position, so that there is never a pair of definite objective properties. After all, two-process instrumentalism is based on the idea that measurement indeterministically and spontaneously produces definite magnitudes. So it is natural to take measurement to be capable of destroying definiteness, as well.

In his response, Bohr used a strict instrumentalism account of meaning to reject Einstein, Podolsky and Rosen's criteria for the possession of a property independent of measurement. The measurement of momentum at 1 makes the possession of a definite position at 2 impossible—not because definiteness is destroyed through action-at-a-distance, but because the ascription of a definite physical value as the one actually possessed is only meaningful when a corresponding measurement procedure is in operation.[20] Bohr had already argued, in connection with Heisenberg's original development of the uncertainty principle, that the operation of momentum-measurement procedures of arbitrarily fine sensitivity ex-

[20] See ibid., esp. p. 150; "Quantum Physics and Reality" (1935) in Wheeler and Zurek, eds., *Quantum Theory and Measurement*, p. 144.

cluded the simultaneous operation of correspondingly fine position detection.[21] So the conditions for simultaneously meaningful ascription of a definite momentum and a definite position are physically impossible.

Einstein's response to this strict instrumentalist answer was always to accept its coherence while rejecting the underlying view of meaning.[22] But what of the milder instrumentalism, in which quantum physics describes two processes, in one of which instruments create magnitudes? In the paper with Podolsky and Rosen and in other work, for example, his letters to Born, Einstein unequivocally condemns any interpretation in which reduction via measurement is a real change from one process to another and quantum physics is complete. He condemns such a theory not on philosophical, but on physical grounds, as requiring "spooky actions at a distance."[23] In this he was right. The milder instrumentalism is ruled out by the prohibition of action-at-a-distance.

On the milder, two-process view, two real physical processes exist and interact. The Schroedinger evolution of superpositions affects the measurement process, influencing the probabilities of measurement outcomes. The measurement process causes a superposition of eigenstates to become one eigenstate entirely, which would not happen if the superposition continued to be governed by the Schroedinger process. Suppose that particle 2 is measured for position, in a measurement interaction at particle 2 at time t. Any instrumentalist reading of quantum physics will tell us that, all else being equal, the particle will be certain to have virtually the same position, within a range smaller than that described in the uncertainty principle, when the measurement is repeated a sufficiently short time later. Suppose that at the time, very soon, t', all else is not equal. The momentum of particle 1 is measured at t'. Then the intervention at region 1 must cause a change in the quantum state at region 2, for only in this way could the probabilities for measurement be changed so that the old position measurement is no longer certain and the uncertainty principle is not violated. This must be the instantaneous result of the remote measurement intervention. So

[21] See "The Quantum Postulate and the Recent Development of Atomic Theory," pp. 97–103.

[22] See "Reply to Criticisms" in Schlipp, ed., *Albert Einstein: Philosopher-Scientist*, pp. 667–71, and "Quantum Physics and Reality" (1948), in *The Born-Einstein Letters* (New York, 1971), pp. 172f.

[23] *The Born-Einstein Letters*, p. 158.

spooky action at a distance is required, to sustain this form of quantum physics.[24]

Both versions of the Copenhagen interpretation would create a defective physics, in light of theoretical considerations and standards of assessment characteristic of physics proper. As Schroedinger showed, through an argument so simple it sounds like a joke, the situation is even worse if elementary knowledge, not specific to physics, of macroscopic objects is taken into account. Schroedinger took advantage of elementary knowledge of cats and poisons. "A cat is penned up in a steel chamber, along with the following diabolical device . . . in a Geiger counter there is a tiny bit of radioactive substance, *so* small that *perhaps* in the course of one hour one of the atoms decays, but also, with equal probability, perhaps none; if it happens, the counter tube discharges and through a relay releases a hammer which shatters a small flask of hydrocyanic acid." Elementary knowledge of cats tells us that during this hour either the cat is alive or the cat is dead. But during this hour, the cat is penned up, not subject to observation. On either instrumentalist interpretation, this fact, combined with the state description and elementary knowledge of poisons, dictates that during the hour the cat is neither alive nor dead. It is in a superposition of life and death. "The $\psi$-function of the entire system would express this by having in it the living and the dead cat (pardon the expression) mixed or smeared out in equal parts."[25] Open the steel chamber to observe the cat, and then . . . in Richard Healey's joke about the joke, you might give new meaning to the proverb that curiosity killed the cat.[26]

Does this mean that quantum physics does not provide laws constraining the behavior of macroscopic objects? This response is hardly available to instrumentalists. For they interpret the whole theory as governing observations that we large-scale humans can report without purporting to describe underlying micro-processes. And this response would devastate quantum physics on any interpretation. If the quantum laws do not constrain the macroscopic,

[24] The remote, instantaneous change produces a state corresponding to a statistical pattern in measurement outcomes, not to a single measurement outcome. This might seem to permit a reconciliation with the prohibition against action-at-a-distance, when the latter principle is suitably qualified. I will discuss this option later.

[25] Schroedinger, "The Present Situation in Quantum Mechanics" (1935) in Wheeler and Zurek, eds., *Quantum Theory and Measurement*, p. 157.

[26] R. Healey, "An Interactive Approach to Quantum Mechanics" (typescript, 1985).

they have no bearing on any experiment that a human has ever conducted.

## Toward Quantum Reality

The rejection of premise 1 of the riddle about the two holes seems to require an instrumentalist interpretation of quantum physics. If the usual inferences from observations to hypotheses about the unobserved are not blocked, there is abundant reason to suppose that an entire electron passes through one hole or the other. At first it seemed that considerations of physical theory required that the inferences be blocked and instrumentalism be adopted, to permit the observed interference pattern. However, the instrumentalist answer to the riddle turned out, at best, to deprive quantum physics of most of its apparent explanatory power in the name of a suspect view of meaning. Surely, an interpretation of a theory is better if it does not require the denial of otherwise uncontroversial explanatory achievements on shaky semantic grounds. I will try to develop an interpretation that is better, in this way, by questioning the second premise, while accepting the first. Although the riddle about the two holes is usually supposed to motivate instrumentalism, the better interpretation is realist. It takes descriptions of quantum states to be ascriptions of properties, with real causal power, that exist in the absence of measurement and that are not merely propensities for measurement outcomes to result. Accepting this better interpretation will depend on accepting the alternative to positivism that I have been defending in this book.

If the entire electron either passes through hole 1 or passes through hole 2, how can any pattern other than B result? After all, B, the pattern without interference, seems to be dictated by the other two premises, for which there are excellent arguments:

II. The probability that an electron arrives at a given detector if it passes in its entirety through hole 1 is the same for an experiment with two holes open as for an experiment with only hole 1 open; and similarly for arrival via hole 2.

III. If an electron passes through one hole or the other in its entirety, and if the probability of its arrival at a detector should it go through a given hole is the same as for the corresponding one-hole experiment, then the total probability of arrival at a detector is the probability of passing through hole 1 times the hole-1-only conditional probability plus the probability of passing through hole 2 times the hole-2-only conditional probability.

My argument will be that premise II is false, so that premise III is irrelevant. In quantum physics, there is an identity that might suggest the identity of probabilities claimed in premise II: the probability amplitude for arriving at detector d at $t_2$ having passed through hole 1 at $t_1$ is the same regardless of whether hole 2 is blocked. If hole 2 is blocked, the absolute square is the conditional probability. However, if both holes are open, no such conditional probability is assigned by quantum theory, in any uncontroversial employment.[27] The theory is used to assign probabilities to arrival at a detector, in both cases. When both holes are open, the amplitude for arrival via hole 1 is added to the amplitude for arrival via hole 2, and the sum is squared, producing the interference pattern. The respective amplitudes are not isolated and squared, to yield respective probabilities. When one hole is open the assigned probability is the absolute square of the amplitude for arrival via that hole.

Indentity of probability amplitudes is not indentity of probabilities. By the same token, the quantum state and Hamiltonian answer all questions of the form, "What is the probability amplitude for there being an electron in region $q'$ at time $t'$ given that there was a single electron in q at t?", but they do not answer all questions of the form, "What is the probability of there being an electron in $q'$ at $t'$ given that there was a single electron in q at t?" Quantum physics tells us how states of whole systems govern probabilities for events to happen, and this governance is not the product of causal powers or tendencies of entities or events in the systems. This is a difference, the central difference, between quantum physics and a classical physics moderated through the use of probabilities. Quantum physical laws are not the result of weakening exceptionless generalities into general statements of conditional probability.

The difference between probability amplitudes and probabilities makes it possible to deny premise II without rejecting any uncontroversial use of the mathematical theory. Still, this does not show that there is any plausible interpretation of the theory as a whole in

---

[27] As Arthur Fine has emphasized. See "Some Conceptual Problems of Quantum Theory" and "On the Completeness of Quantum Theory." Similar considerations are fundamental to Feynman's presentations of quantum physics. See, for example, *The Theory of Fundamental Processes* (New York, 1962), chs. 1 and 2; *Quantum Mechanics and Path Integrals*, ch. 1.

which premise II is rejected, but premise I is not. Rejecting II while accepting I is all too characteristic of the rear guard, first led by de Broglie, who tried to assimilate the new ideas of quantum physics to the concepts of classical field theory. In their view, the unblocked but electronless hole contains something that subsequently propagates toward the detector wall and pushes electrons in ways that yield the interference pattern. Such proposals of so-called local hidden variables have always seemed fragile speculations at best. They now are widely judged to be reactionary failures, especially in light of recent experimental findings concerning situations like the one Einstein, Podolsky and Rosen described. What is needed is a general interpretation that rules out the offending ascriptions of conditional probabilities, but that is otherwise banal, i.e., that avoids the rear guard's speculations about novel causal episodes.

The complete description of a quantum state of a system—say, through a superposition of wave functions—entails the physical probabilities, or propensities, for dynamical magnitudes of the system to have values at the time in question. Together with the Hamiltonian for the system, the state description entails all subsequent propensities, so long as the system is closed.

Every expositor of quantum physics sometimes writes this way, even if he or she stipulates elsewhere that "having a value" means "being found to have a value upon measurement." My proposal is that these routine claims about states of systems in quantum physics be taken literally. A state description attributes a real property to a system, the property of having the Hamiltonian-dependent propensities. Like all real internal properties, in science and in nontechnical inquiry, the one attributed in the state description determines the potential causal contributions of the state to subsequent events. In quantum physics, the causal contributions are propensities which, in probabilistic ways, influence dynamical events, i.e., the occurrence of particular values of dynamical magnitudes.

I have begun to use such phrases as "value of a dynamical magnitude" as part of an interpretation of quantum physics, not just as labels for items in the wave-function and operator formalism. By a "value of a dynamical magnitude," I mean location in space and time, charge, mass, spin, and the other basic micro-properties. A complete specification would soon be made obsolete by the latest high-energy physics. The strategy for determining what dynamical values there are is, first, to see what properties of spatio-temporal regions have to be mentioned in adequate explanations of where masses and charges are and when—and then to take the explanation of new spatio-temporal facts involving the newly posited properties as a means of discovering new micro-properties, in turn. A dynamical event is the occurrence of a dynamical value at a time and place. A statement describes a dynamical system at a given time if it describes all factors with a causal bearing on the possible dynamical events to which it refers.

The state description plus the Hamiltonian is a complete characterization of the internal properties of a closed dynamical system. It describes all of the causal powers of the system so long as it is closed, i.e., its whole capacity to influence the dynamical events in its history. The dynamical events themselves have no causal power. So there is no room in this version of quantum physics for the dynamical events to which the rear guard appeal in explaining the observed interference patterns. In contrast to the rear guard's explanations, these patterns result from applying the Hamiltonian to the amplitudes in the description of the state of the whole system and converting to probabilities according to the standard rules, rules which refer to the state of the system as a whole.

The argument for premise II depended on two claims: if an electron arrives at a detector, an entire electron passes through one hole or through the other; the subsequent behavior of an electron that has just passed through one hole is not influenced by the occurrence of a plug in another hole. Anyone who accepts premise I will certainly accept the first claim. However, on the present interpretation of quantum physics, the latter claim is not unequivocally right. It is true that the separable, individual event, the occurrence of the plug material in a region of space, does not influence subsequent dynamical events involving the electron. In the case at hand that would require ghostly action at a distance. However, the system properties characterized in a quantum state description of the system at hand do dictate the subsequent dynamical events involving electrons. And these system properties are different if the plug is present or is absent. If the plug is absent, a complete description of the state at passage time assigns amplitudes to either possibility of passage— say, amplitudes squaring to one-half, in a symmetrical situation. The amplitudes are assigned regardless of where the electron is. If the plug is present, then the correct state-description assigns all the amplitude to passage through the unblocked hole. If one hole is blocked but we do not know which, our ignorance should be expressed by assigning a probability, representing our state of ignorance, to each state description that our knowledge admits. If our knowledge gives equal probability to two alternative state descriptions, then each has a probability of one-half. But these probabilities are not physical propensities and they do not occur within state descriptions. (Also, the difference between an amplitude of $\sqrt{\frac{1}{2}}$ and an amplitude of $-i\sqrt{\frac{1}{2}}$ may be physically significant, even though the absolute squares are the same.) In sum, whether one hole is blocked or is merely empty makes a great deal of difference to subsequent events. So the argument for premise II has a relevantly false premise. But the difference consists of the existence of some properties of the whole system rather than others. It does not consist of the influence of a separable, causally effective property of the electronless hole. So valid prohibitions against action-at-a-distance are respected.

What of the other variant on the two-hole experiment, the operation of a gamma-ray microscope to determine through which hole an electron has passed? Here everyone needs to take seriously the point that Bohr always emphasized in his instrumentalist explanations of quantum physical laws: measurement requires physical interaction. The operation of a gamma-ray microscope is an interactive process involving photons, electrons, the microscope "lens" and some end result involving the microscope indicating passage through one hole or another. The quantum physics of this total set-up dictates pattern B at the back wall (i.e., the one with the array of detector microchips). More precisely, the observed pattern approaches B more and more closely, as the gamma-ray measurement approaches the ideal of perfect accuracy, viz., the state of the total system in which there is no amplitude for the microscope's indicating passage through a hole when there is in fact no passage through that hole. For the barrier with two holes open, and for superpositions in general, it is impossible in principle to achieve this ideal. But uncontroversial quantum physics shows that one can, in principle, get arbitrarily close. (The impossibility of perfect accuracy for superpositions is a problem for any attempt to define superpositions in terms of measurement outcomes. On the present interpretation, it only reflects an impossibility of perfection that thoughtful physicists have always acknowledged.)[28]

---

[28] For the relevant physical analyses of measurement, see David Bohm, *Quantum Theory* (Englewood Cliffs, N.J., 1951), ch. 22; and K. Gottfried, *Quantum Mechanics*, vol. 1 (Reading, Mass., 1966), ch. 4. Of course, one can stipulate that the detection in question be perfect. This entails that there be no superposition of barrier states. Instead, there is a "statistical mixture," in which alternative single-eigenstate situations

A useful image for this interpretation is that of a probability-amplitude wave. Such a wave is not an entity within a system that interacts with other entities the system contains, like de Broglie's pilot waves which pushed electrons around. Rather, the probability-amplitude waves entailed by quantum state descriptions together with Hamiltonians dictate propensities for dynamical events to occur within a system should it have the respective Hamiltonian. Such waves do not push electrons any more than fairness in a coin toss steers the coin. So probability-amplitude waves do not violate the conservation of energy, or observed phenomena of quantization or observed variations under rotation, as pilot waves and their descendents do. Probability-amplitude waves are not probability waves, either, i.e., the probabilities of events are not determined by the probabilities of immediately prior events in the immediate neighborhood. That is why the "interference of probabilities" is possible. Actually, everyone with a smattering of quantum physics has worked with this image. Everyone understands Schroedinger descriptions in this way, except when he or she has been convinced to take the descriptions as just tools for predicting measurement events, the only events that really happen in quantum physics.

Although amplitudes do not characterize fields, as de Broglie and his successors thought, the transition involved in the acceptance of explanations appealing to fields precisely parallels the change involved in accepting quantum physics on this realist interpretation. For almost two generations after Faraday, it seemed to most physicists that field theory must be understood in either an old-fashioned or an anti-realist way. Either field equations were made true by causal factors in the old repertoire, for example, mechanical stresses. Or they merely described a tendency for some dynamical events to be succeeded by other related ones, typically remote in space and time, with no need for causal attribution to a real, intermediate field. As it became increasingly clear, on theoretical and empirical grounds, that neither sort of explanation was adequate, physicists extended the repertoire of basic causes to include fields. This required a changed view of what could be the possessor of a causally effective property. As Einstein emphasizes in praising Lorentz, the full acceptance of field theory required the acceptance of space, not bits of matter, as the ultimate bearer of a field.[29] Similarly,

---

are assigned ordinary probabilities. This would be the rationale for the analysis that Feynman distinguishes from Bohm's in *The Theory of Fundamental Processes*, pp. 2f.

[29] "Autobiographical Notes" in Schilpp, ed., *Albert Einstein: Philosopher-Scientist*, p. 35.

the explanatory failures of rear-guard and instrumentalist interpretations of quantum physics are what motivate the realist construal of the quantum state descriptions that everyone has used all along. Like field descriptions, state descriptions govern dynamical events, and are characterized in terms of the ways they govern them. As in the earlier shift, the most striking change is the acceptance of a new ultimate subject for a basic causal property, in this case, a whole system.

This interpretation, then, has a wonderful virtue of banality. At least in broad outline, it is often entertained. Almost invariably, it is entertained in order to be rejected, in favor of an interpretation in which probabilities to be found upon measurement, not probabilities to be, are the subject matter of quantum physics. The rejection is defended on the grounds of conflicts between realism and established physical findings, for example, the prohibition against action-at-a-distance, superposition and the interference of probabilities, the failure of the "hidden-variables" accounts offered by de Broglie and his successors, and the uncertainty principle.

In the vast literature on the interpretation of quantum physics, Popper has come closest to defending the realist option I have described—but with consequences for the rest of physics that would be anything but banal. He takes the subject matter of quantum physics to be propensities for dynamical events to occur, independent of measurement. He emphasizes that the crucial propensities are propensities of whole systems. From this starting point, so similar to the interpretation I have proposed, he reaches just the conclusions I am trying to avoid. In his view, a realist interpretation, based on propensities, requires that there be action-at-a-distance if quantum physics is true and complete. He is now receptive to the verdict of virtually all physicists that recent experiments have indicated the truth and completeness of quantum physics. His conclusion is that action-at-a-distance may well exist, along with the ether and Newton's absolute space and time.[30] The interference of probabilities is a paradox, in his view, and it is best avoided by adopting an indeterministic hidden-variables theory.[31] Faced with the recent experimental findings that appear to rule out hidden-variables theories, Popper, who is not noted for concessions to the other side of a dispute, has occasionally taken an entirely different tack, admitting the

[30] See K. Popper, *Quantum Theory and the Schism in Physics* (Totowa, N.J., 1982), pp. 20–30.

[31] See "Replies to my Critics" in P. Schilpp, ed., *The Philosophy of Karl Popper* (La-Salle, Ill., 1974), pp. 1137–39.

possibility of experimental defeat. "Although the results of testing so far are not quite conclusive, most of them seem to go . . . in favor of quantum theory and perhaps even its Copenhagen interpretation."[32] From the start, he has taken the uncertainty principle to be valid only as a constraint on a special kind of measurement, even though quantum physics refers to properties independent of measurement.[33]

Bohr, Heisenberg, Pauli and like-minded pioneers of quantum physics thought that a realist interpretation would require violations of secure theoretical principles and reliable empirical findings. Though Popper thinks that they were kept from realism by an elementary muddle about probability, his realist interpretation is a Copenhagen dream (more precisely, a nightmare) of what a realist quantum physics would be.[34]

Popper's interpretation turns out to be very different from the one that I have sketched because of a very different view of the causal primacy and the reality of quantum states and of their relation to classical states. Though he takes propensities to be real physical properties of whole systems, he also counts remote correlations dictated by physical laws to constitute the causation of one event within the system by another. Hence, the openness, reluctant though it is, to action-at-a-distance. As for the reality of superpositions, it is a subject on which Popper is uncharacteristically vague. Still, it is hard to see what the pressure toward hidden-variable theories could be, if explanations of statistical patterns at one stage of a process could, in the final analysis, appeal to superpositions at an earlier stage. In one passage, Popper says that "these probabilities (propensities) whose amplitudes can interfere should be conjectured to be *physical and real, and not merely a mathematical device.*"[35] The reference to probabilities whose amplitudes interfere is strange, though perhaps just a turn of phrase. Probabilities do not have amplitudes, one would have thought; probability amplitudes

[32] *Quantum Theory and the Schism in Physics*, p. 25.

[33] See *The Logic of Scientific Discovery* (New York, 1968), pp. 223–36; *Quantum Theory and the Schism in Physics*, p. 54.

[34] "The great quantum muddle" is described in *Quantum Theory and the Schism in Physics*, pp. 50–52. Although I will emphasize what I take to be shortcomings in Popper's "propensity interpretation," his arguments for the physical reality of propensities of whole systems are extremely illuminating. I confess to having written all the rest of this chapter largely in ignorance of the substantial developments in Popper's view of quantum physics since *The Logic of Scientific Discovery*. If I had studied his more recent work earlier, some of my arguments might be different and better.

[35] *The Logic of Scientific Discovery*, p. 84; italics in original.

are not probabilities, and are used to describe states that produce the interference patterns in probabilities. More significantly, Popper is discussing an attempt by Landé, generally judged a failure, to derive the interference effects using non-quantum-physical principles of symmetry imposed on classical probabilities. Evidently, superpositions are not ultimate and independent causal factors for Popper. Rather, facts stated in the language of superpositions must be made true by ordinary propensities. But ordinary propensities of dynamical magnitudes so far discovered cannot account for the interference effects in superpositions, unless action-at-a-distance takes place. Hence, Popper's preference for hidden-variables theory appealing to as yet discovered magnitudes governed by ordinary propensities, and hence his conclusion that action-at-a-distance must exist if such theories are all false.

Not only are the fundamental causal factors in Popper's realist interpretation ordinary propensities, they are, it would seem, propensities for ordinary, i.e., classical, dynamical values to be possessed. Throughout his discussions of the uncertainty principle, he takes the momentum in question to be the same as classical momentum. He does discuss spin, which obviously is not a classical magnitude, and declares, "[W]e have no realistic theory of spin. . . . Spin is really something very queer and is *in a sense* non-classical."[36] Popper's conceptual conservatism, here, helps to account for the devaluing of the uncertainty principle. Given the independence of position and classical momentum, the uncertainty principle could only be a constraint on certain kinds of measurements. Also, one can understand why admitting the defeat of hidden-variable theories might, in Popper's view, force surrender to the Copenhagen interpretation after fifty years of the most intense combat. If physics is not ultimately about ordinary propensities for the occurrence of classical dynamical values (and others with similar structural properties), then its very intelligibility is in doubt. The Copenhagen interpretation would at least preserve meaningfulness, by restricting the subject-matter to propensities for classical measurement outcomes to occur.

Why does the one established realist interpretation come into conflict with standard physical findings at so many points? It will, I hope, become clear that the conflicts are not due to a muddle, but to a deep philosophical commitment. The commitment is to the positivist conceptions of causality, justification and meaning of which

[36] Ibid., p. 24. I have no idea what qualification is suggested by his italicized hedge.

Popper is a distinguished and pioneering advocate. Ironically, this explanation of Popper's views will be an implicit moral of descriptions of the crucial role of the same commitments in the thinking of Bohr, Heisenberg and the other leading Copenhagen instrumentalists.[37]

I have begun the case for a realist interpretation by showing how it naturally emerges from uncontroversial uses of the mathematical theory and from the riddle about the two holes, a basic motivation for anti-realist interpretations. In the rest of my case for this interpretation, I will largely be concerned to criticize standard assumptions, technical and philosophical, that have made this banal realism unavailable.

### Eigenvalues without Eigenstates

It is a standard assumption in interpretations of quantum physics that what has an eigenvalue must be in an eigenstate. More colloquially, what has a definite value of a dynamical magnitude must be in a state that is 100 percent certain to have that value. Historically, it is easy to understand the currency of this assumption. Von Neumann was guided by it in constructing the first and most influential axiomatization of quantum mechanics. However, the assumption has to be dispensable, if the present realist interpretation is right. On this interpretation, the electron has a definite position at the bar-

---

[37] Similar commitments have an important impact on the other interpretation that is close to my own, Margenau's "latency interpretation." For Margenau, the state description characterizes a property of individual systems, governing propensities for events to occur. But in his view, the relevant events are, exclusively, measurement outcomes. His rationales for this restriction are uncharacteristically casual, and usually depend on undefended epistemological assumptions of a positivist or neo-Kantian kind. The restriction to measurement outcomes creates many problems and avoidable burdens. Thus, though superpositions are supposed to exist before measurement has taken place, they do not correspond, at those times, to anything's happening. Also, as in the two-process interpretation, measurement produces a unique, qualitative change. This creates the same problems of boundary setting and anomaly. Though Margenau began by emphasizing the reality of quantum states and the arbitrariness of standard assumptions in the two-process view, he ended up offering self-mocking descriptions of those states as "ghostlike things to which no primary interest attaches" and endorsing wholesale von Neumann's account of measurement (see "Einstein's Conception of Reality" in Schilpp, ed., *Albert Einstein: Philosopher-Scientist*, pp. 263–66). Two concise and illuminating statements of Margenau's general interpretation are "Probability and Causality in Quantum Physics" (1932) in his *Physics and Philosophy* (Dordrecht, 1978), ch. 2, and *The Nature of Physical Reality* (New York, 1950), ch. 18.

rier. But there is no 100 percent propensity for it to be where it actually is. If there were, then uncontroversial uses of quantum physics would dictate that the ultimate pattern at the barrier is the classical, non-interference pattern, pattern B.[38]

In fact, the distinction between actually having a definite value and a 100 percent propensity to have that value is natural, indeed compulsory, in the situations that quantum physics describes, situations in which properties of systems govern events within the systems, in a probabilistic way. Consider the following partial but relevant analogues to quantum systems. Suppose there are sealed automata for tossing coins, each entirely governed by a random internal process. Except for being a closed system, such a device might be useful in casinos. Suppose two identical versions of the fair sort of coin tosser, with fifty-fifty heads/tails propensities, are prepared. They start shaking and, at a given time, the coin in one has come up heads while the coin in the other has come up tails. Still, the real properties of the two systems, the two devices are the same. They are closed systems with identical propensities to affect the phenomena they can affect. Neither system is in an eigenstate, for that would require a 100 percent propensity to come up heads, or to come up tails, and these tossers are fair.[39]

Being in an eigenstate is a property that a system has, a 100 percent propensity for a dynamical magnitude of the system to take on a definite value. Having a definite value is a property of a magnitude in the system, at a given time. It characterizes an event in the system. Also, in the usual manner of speaking, which I follow here, having a definite value is a property of an electron, a photon or something else in the system. Because being in an eigenstate and having a definite value are properties with these different subjects, definiteness, i.e., having an eigenvalue, does not require being in an eigenstate.

This location of the distinctive properties to which state descriptions occur at the level of systems, not events, is needed to solve the riddle of the two holes. As an added benefit, it neatly evades the cat

[38] Two of the rare instances of dissent from the standard assumption are Margenau, "Quantum Mechanical Descriptions," *Physical Review* (1936), pp. 240–42, and Fine, "The Two Problems of Quantum Measurement."

[39] The analogy with quantum systems is not perfect because we usually think of random automata semi-classically, analyzing them into separable parts ultimately governed by simple and conditional probabilities. Such an automaton cannot mimic the behavior of certain superpositions. Feynman presents the Aspect experiments in this light in "Simulating Physics with Computers," *International Journal of Theoretical Physics* (1982), pp. 467–88.

paradox, which is otherwise the most recalcitrant of quantum riddles, for all its simplicity. Just as an electron is in one hole or another when the transmitter-barrier-wall system is characterized by a superposition, the cat in the sealed chamber is either alive or dead.

## REAL SYSTEM PROPERTIES

The state description and the Hamiltonian completely characterize the real internal properties of a dynamical system. This appraisal is based on our normal standard for an alleged property's being a real property of a thing itself, not an external property or an artificial property concocted through fanciful logical devices. As Shoemaker has pointed out, the real internal properties of something are its potentials to contribute causally to the situations it is in.[40] That is why we can conceive of two beds that have the same properties, i.e., the same internal, real ones, even though Washington only slept in one, and they happen to be in different bedrooms. Located in the same bedroom, each would play the same causal role. By the same token, we do not take a bed's being a bed or a goat to be a property of the bed, in addition to its others. The artificial property describes no additional potential causal capacity of the bed. The state description and the Hamiltonian completely determine the potential causal contributions of a quantum system, i.e., all potential influences on the evolution of dynamical events. So by the usual criteria, they fully describe the real properties of the system itself.

In spite of these considerations, it might seem wrong to distinguish two states of affairs as having different properties at a given time when the same dynamical events occur at that time, and the allegedly distinguishing properties solely involve propensities for dynamical events to occur. In any case, this might seem wrong when the propensities have not yet been shown to be due to concurrent nondispositional properties, i.e., properties that are not mere propensities. For example, the realist interpretation distinguishes a system in superposition in which an electron is passing through hole 1 from a system in an eigenstate in which an electron generated at hole 1 is passing through the hole. If there is no difference at the level of current events that could account for the different propensities in subsequent, arrival events, it might seem that current differences in propensities are too "ghostlike," in Margenau's phrase,

---

[40] See "Causality and Properties" in his *Identity, Cause and Mind* (Cambridge, 1984).

to be the distinguishing factor that accounts for the difference in future probabilities.

Certainly, when situations are described without the aid of technical science, differences at a given time are often differences in propensities. In the dusk, all birds look gray. They look gray and, short of relying on relatively technical findings, we cannot specify any property distinguishing them that has a bearing on color, without specifying propensities with a bearing on color phenomena in other, non-dusky situations. The male cardinal and the male bluejay both look gray now, at dusk. The only difference we can identify (non-technically) is that they would look red and blue respectively if the light were substantially brighter. But this difference in propensities would still constitute a difference in properties at dusk. At dusk, it is still true that male cardinals are red. Gray, after all, is how red things look at dusk if they do not glow in the dark. So, if technical science had not supplemented our repertoire of relevant present properties, the cardinal and the bluejay at dusk would be analogous to the two situations in which an electron passes through hole 1: propensities make the difference and are real physical properties.

It might seem, though, that a physical science worthy of the name refuses to accept any difference between states of affairs that is wholly a matter of propensities for events to occur. After all, the colors of feathers can be explained in terms of energy properties of molecules constituting the feathers. Doesn't this mean dispensing with purely dispositional differences in the final analysis? No. Even classical physics made much reference to the purely dispositional, and unavoidably so.

Classical electrodynamics was always open to ultimately dispositional characterizations of systems. A description of what charges there are at a given time, where they are and how fast they are moving does not fully describe an electrodynamic system at a given time. Depending on what charges have done in the past, there may be different behavior on the part of the charges in the future. Field theories ascribe properties to the present system that determine all future events in the system. Some people thought, and many hoped, that distinctions in properties of fields were distinctions among non-dispositional properties of the ether. But not everyone thought this was so. And the view that field properties are dispositional in the final analysis is the one that best survives the Michelson-Morley experiment, the finding that ether drift does not occur, and related observations.

Indeed, not even classical mechanics specifies the present state of a system in a way that requires no reference to its propensities with respect to other times. A complete classical description specifies the positions and momenta within the system, together with any potentials in the system. Classical momenta are masses multiplied by propensities to move at a certain rate during an arbitrarily short amount of time—or rather, such propensities as they would be in the absence of potentials. The classical picture, in other words, requires that velocity be an actual internal physical property, and such a velocity is a propensity. In addition, potentials are, classically, space derivatives of forces, i.e., of propensities for momenta to change in arbitrarily short time-intervals. A non-dispositional mechanical description would be a Cartesian description, in which velocity only figures as a mathematical construction from the ultimately causal, real physical properties. Galileo knew better and, by the end of the seventeenth century, sophisticated physicists knew that Galileo was right.

Finally, causation by quantum properties might seem mysterious, not because the causally relevant state is specified using propensities, but because the effects of that state are specified using propensities. The frequencies of arrival at the detector in the two-hole experiment are the result of individual runs of the apparatus. How can the state of the set-up produce a long-run pattern of cumulative frequencies if electrons do not have mysterious awareness of the cumulative frequencies so far and a mysterious commitment to take part in an electron project of producing a long-run pattern close to the derived propensity?

The quantum physical answer is analogous to classical answers to similar questions about classical patterns. The answer describes how the pattern is produced, i.e., how the causal factors influence individual links in relevant chains of events so as to produce the total patterns among the various final links. The Hamiltonian assigns amplitudes to arbitrarily small transitions, for example, to the possibility that an electron will be in one volume unit given that it was at another an arbitrarily brief instant before. At every instant the tendencies for alternatives to happen are determined by the combination of this transition tendency, roughly analogous to the classical potential, and the amplitudes assigned to alternative possibilities for events within the system at the previous instant, i.e., the quantum state, roughly analogous to a classical state of a dynamical system. Such causation would be mysterious if quantum physical particles were classical particles, with an enduring identity from instant to instant so long as nothing intervenes to destroy them. Because of the role of the state description, an electron would be pushed from the course it would have taken by unactualized possibilities—and without the expenditure of energy. But, notoriously, quantum particles, e.g., real elementary particles, lack such an identity. Events are the ultimate individuals in microphysics. The system has a tendency to give rise to events that are quantized and roughly (not precisely) continuous, in ways that roughly mimic the behavior of classical particles. In Tomonaga's nice analogy, an electron is like a dot moving as flashes come and go on a visual newscasting board.[41] (Though Tomonaga's experience is Tokyo-based, visitors to Times Square will find his example familiar.) While we naturally speak of the movement of a period at the end of a sentence on the board, we know that the corresponding physical process is a series of events in which no physical object that is the period endures from moment to moment. The system produces each event and any final pattern of probabilities is based on propensities for light bulb lightings to arise, not on capacities to push periods, or a commitment on the part of periods to contribute to the patterns. Of course, in the classical way of thinking, the ultimate propensities of a news board at a given time are the separable causal tendencies of individual components of the circuit. Elsewhere, however, where our initial upbringing is not dominated by classical physics, our initial assumptions are more systems-oriented. We do find it easy to say that someone's grouchiness on a certain morning is what produces an increased likelihood of testy response to interruption—i.e., we find it easier to ignore atomistic assumptions that separable parts of the person must be the ultimate subjects of the causal powers. The fact to which Tomonaga's analogy points is no mystery, just a surprise: the ordinary logic of psychological temperament and conduct is a better guide to real physical causation than the logic of causation in classical physics.[42]

These arguments show that the state description could describe an actual property of a situation, capable of influencing its future

---

[41] S. Tomonaga, *Quantum Mechanics* (Amsterdam, 1966), vol, 2, p. 296.

[42] Both Heisenberg and Schroedinger based quantum physics on the denial that there are such things as electron trajectories—and Schroedinger was renowned for his realist inclinations. See Heisenberg, "The Physical Content of Quantum Kinematics and Mechanics," pp. 62–64; Schroedinger, "Quantization as a Problem of Proper Values (Part II)" (1926) in *Collected Papers on Wave Mechanics* (London, 1928), p. 25. I will soon present some of the reasons why particles cannot have indentities of the classical type in the course of sketching the quantum principles for many-particle systems, laws which have the Pauli Exclusion Principle as their most dramatic consequence.

characteristics. Nothing, that is, in the logic of properties and propensities excludes this. Of course it is another matter to show that the system properties described really do exist and help to give rise to future propensities. This argument is, primarily, the theoretical and empirical argument with which good textbooks in quantum physics begin. One outcome of these arguments is that the many observed phenomena of superposition cannot be explained as due to characteristics of individual events in a dynamical system, but can be explained as due to the quantum state of the system as a whole. In recent years, this argument has gained added force. "Cannot be explained as due to characteristics of individual events" used to mean, primarily "cannot be explained as due to any characteristics so far discovered." Recent experimental findings, that will be discussed later in this chapter, provide a new, powerful argument that there is no as-yet-undiscovered characteristic of individual events capable of yielding such an explanation.

A superposition, on the present construal, is, irreducibly, a property of a system. Its characterization refers, in part, to amplitudes of possibilities afforded by the system but not actualized in any event (for example, the possibility of an electron in an actually empty hole). In spite of the analogy with psychological causation, it might seem strange that an irreducible property of a physical system should have a causal influence on the propensities for individual events to occur, so strange that this type of causation should not be posited just as a means of explaining electron diffraction and other phenomena of superposition. Despite its cost in lost explanatory powers, instrumentalism might be preferred. It is worth noting, then, that another, uncontroversial part of quantum theory, with utterly pervasive consequences, directly and obviously entails causation by system properties.

In the same year that Heisenberg developed the general means for describing quantum systems, Pauli presented the work that led to basic principles governing systems of particles of a single kind. According to those principles, systems of electrons or of other kinds of particles with so-called half-integral sins are of one type, "anti-symmetrical," while systems of particles of each of the other kinds, i.e., photons and other integral spin particles, are of another type, "symmetrical." I will concentrate on the anti-symmetry of systems of electrons. In a sense, it is the basis of all observable differences in kind. For it is the basis of valence, without which there would be no relatively stable kinds of observable material stuff.

The principle of anti-symmetry relates the wave function describing a system of electrons to the wave functions that would represent the situation of each electron if it were alone. Since the wave functions are interpreted in terms of probabilities, one might think the rule of construction would equate the wave function of the system to the product of the wave functions that each part would have if isolated. Instead, the principle of anti-symmetry constructs the system description out of the various terms resulting from switching arguments in that product term among pairs of factor functions. For a two-electron system, the rule is to subtract from the product of the wave functions the same product with its arguments interchanged. If the wave functions for the respective isolated subsystems were the same, the result would be zero. So there are no systems of two electrons with the same individual state descriptions (the Pauli Exclusion Principle). The principle entails, more generally, that the difference in the electrons' velocities, for a system of two electrons with the same spin, is inversely proportional to the difference in position. It is as if there were a repulsive force between the electrons, causing them to move away from each other all the faster, the closer they are. *But there is no separable force.* This effect of repulsion would occur in a system of free electrons. It is not the product of an independent potential, entailing the existence of no other entity, and similarly independent characteristics of the component electrons. Commenting on the Hamiltonian for a system governed, in part, by anti-symmetry, Gottfried writes, "The meaning of I is clear; it is the electrostatic interaction energy . . . J, on the other hand, . . . has no analogue whatsoever in classical physics . . . J comes about because of the symmetry requirement put on the wave function. . . . [The difference between this requirement and classical rules of construction] shows that there are correlations in the system's distribution function in spite of the fact that the wave-function is an eigenfunction of a Hamiltonian . . . that neglects the interaction between the particles."[43]

If this isn't causation by an irreducible property of a system, what is? If this kind of causation is entailed by a nearly elementary part of quantum physics, why not use it in interpreting the most elementary part, the description of states using the apparatus of amplitudes?[44]

[43] *Quantum Mechanics*, 1: 377f.

[44] See Dirac, *Principles of Quantum Mechanics*, pp. 207–11 for a precise description of symmetry and anti-symmetry. Margenau, *The Nature of Physical Reality*, ch. 20, is an exceptionally clear elementary presentation of the meaning and consequences of the theory of systems of similar particles. Anti-symmetry is sometimes presented as a triumph of instrumentalism: particles that no measurement could distinguish must

## Quantum Causation and Positivism

The original argument for premise II of the superposition riddle depended on certain beliefs about the impossibility of causation across certain gaps; an electron at hole 1 is not influenced from afar by emptiness (as against a plug) at hole 2. By the same token, the ultimate arguments against premise II were attempts to evade those beliefs; the causal factor is not a property of one part influencing a remote part in a forbidden way, because it is a property of a system and causation by such a property is different from causation by a property of a part of the system. Though the state description describes a cause of electron events and the state description would be different if there were a plug in the actually empty hole, the presence or absence of a plug in the region is not a cause of electron events at the other hole, in the final analysis.

All such efforts to evade prohibitions against remote causation are nonsense, if the covering-law model is an appropriate guide to the nature of causation. Positivism plus physics, that is, the phenomena of superposition and the usual prohibitions against remote causation, equals instrumentalism.

There are a variety of ways in which the deductive-nomological pattern has been altered to allow probabilistic causes. Several were considered in Chapter One. In all the varieties, the fact that one hole is empty would be a cause of sequels to an electron's passing through the other hole. If instrumentalism is abandoned, and the proposition that there is an electron in one hole but not the other is admitted, this proposition has distinctive entailments concerning arrival frequencies, as a matter of quantum-physical laws. In positivism, causation is, entirely, a matter of entailment via physical laws. The denial that hole properties as against system properties are causal would not correspond to the rejection of any entailment depending on separable characterizations of remote holes. So, on a positivist reading of prohibitions against remote causation, they

---

be the same particle. But this would not account for the pseudo-force arising from the general rule of construction. And, in any case, the other rule, for photons and so forth, does admit systems of numerically different indistinguishable particles. As Dirac makes clear, the existence of construction rules of the two kinds can, up to a point, be justified by considerations of indistinguishability. But these considerations concern systems, and require that systems be physically the same if their descriptions only differ in the labelling of particles. When fully developed, this argument would imply that systems and their properties, not separable particles and potentials and their respective properties, are the subject-matter of quantum physics.

must rule out the appeals to system properties in the quantum realist explanation, if they rule out anything.

A covering-law account of causation might still be reconciled with
quantum realism by changing the usual prohibitions against remote
causation. Such tailoring would be especially tempting in response
to recent experimental descendents of the Einstein-Podolsky-Rosen
thought-experiment. If causation is understood in a positivist way,
these findings can only be reconciled with full-fledged prohibitions
against remote causation if Bohr's strict instrumentalist view of the
nature of properties is embraced and the same properties are never
ascribed within different total measurement set-ups. To avoid extreme doctrines such as Bohr's, one might take advantage of the statistical nature of quantum-physical entailments. Because of its statistical nature, causation of quantum phenomena by remote events
would not violate a prohibition against controllable remote causation. More precisely, it would not violate a prohibition against causation that is sufficiently controllable, in principle, to be the basis for
conveying information more swiftly than light travels in a vacuum.
Since current uses of relativity theory require nothing more than a
prohibition against processes that could be used in faster-than-light
signaling, this might seem to be a way to reconcile quantum theory
with relativistic restrictions, without rejecting the positivist analyses
of causation.

The basic tactic of reconciling the two theories through the hedge
about controllability and signaling is as old as Heisenberg's Chicago
lectures of 1929.[45] Jarrett has developed it in rigorous detail, showing that the recent findings only exclude controllable remote causation.[46]

Hedging the prohibition against action-at-a-distance to allow for
non-controllable remote causation would remove a risk of conflict
with the data that support quantum physics—but at an enormous
cost to physics as a whole. For one thing, there is the usual cost of
such hedging. Ad hoc tailoring produces a loss in the degree of justification of the tailored principle. Much more important, the basic

[45] See *The Physical Principles of the Quantum Theory*, p. 39.

[46] See J. Jarrett, "On the Physical Significance of the Locality Conditions in the Bell
Arguments," *Nous* (1984), and A. Shimony, "Controllable and Uncontrollable Non-
Locality" in S. Kamefuchi, ed., *Foundations of Quantum Mechanics* (Tokyo, 1983). I am
not suggesting that Shimony or Jarrett proposes an ad hoc hedge in the interests of
a positivist analysis of causation. They are simply making an important distinction
between a kind of correlation that quantum physics itself entails and another, related
kind, which it does not.

arguments from invariance that justify relativity theory are good reasons to suppose there is no action-at-a-distance, controllable or not. The basic principles of invariance, together with the truth of Maxwellian electrodynamics, show that "[t]here is no such thing as simultaneity of distant events; consequently there is also no such thing as immediate action at a distance in the sense of Newtonian mechanics." The further arguments for the relativistic treatment of mass and energy justify the exclusion of "actions at a distance . . . which propagate with the speed of light," as well.[47] Similarly, the arguments about invariance and force, gravity and acceleration, weight and inertial mass that support general relativity justify a physics of field equations in which action-at-a-distance has no place. Of course, these arguments would be no more than pedagogy and the record of inspired guesswork if deductivism were right and the entailment of observational sequels were all that matters for confirmation. But deductivism has turned out to give a bad account of confirmation.

In addition, robust and general assumptions of locality are standard in quantum physics itself. Quantum physicists constantly rely on the assumption that the underlying cause of a change is a continuous process observing the basic principles of conservation at all times. This standard assumption is often used to justify the assignment of a specific Hamiltonian to a physical system. It is fundamental to most methods of approximation in quantum physics. In these uses, the standard assumption has been eminently successful. Finally, as Shimony notes, no one has succeeded in sketching an explanation of quantum-physical correlations actually observed that postulates uncontrollable violations of locality while excluding the possibility of controllable processes that could convey information faster than the speed of light.[48]

In sum, the hedge that would reconcile the realist interpretation with a positivist view of causes would undermine a standard and well-supported principle, which leads to a variety of successful explanations, in favor of a form of causation that has no specific explanatory use. Such a hedge is only reasonable if the arguments in favor of the covering-law model are good. They turned out to be bad.

Still, the abandonment of the covering-law model cuts in two directions, where causation in quantum physics is concerned. There is

[47] Einstein, "Autobiographical Notes," p. 61. See also ibid., p. 29; "Reply to Critics," pp. 673–75; "The Fundaments of Theoretical Physics" in *Essays in Physics* (New York, 1950), p. 59.
[48] See "Controllable and Uncontrollable Non-Locality," pp. 228f.

no need to suppose that individual dynamical events have causal power, just because of their entailments for correlations. But just the same can be said of the system property characterized by a quantum state description. That physicists derive propensities using these formulas, concerning systems, and could not derive observed propensities using classical means of description, does not show that the former are descriptions of causes. The positivist justification for speaking of causation by quantum system properties is now unavailable.

In Chapter Two, I proposed that the possibility of a new kind of causation is established, not by appealing to a general, a priori analysis of causation, but by a fair, empirical topic-specific argument, that is, an argument for changing the repertoire of causes that is fair to the framework in which the old repertoire is employed. When good textbooks justify quantum-physical principles, the justification has just this form. The textbooks show both that classical physics could not account for relevant phenomena, and that the quantum-physical changes in the classical means of description are justifiable in the framework of a reasonable, informed, initially classical physicist. The classical means of description had to be changed and the changes adopted were the ones most likely to yield truth, given framework principles common to the new physics and the old. The argument itself cannot be stated briefly—for the most part because of the complexity of the version of classical mechanics that demarcates the area of best-justified change. The general strategy is evoked by a slogan of Schroedinger's: quantum mechanics stands to classical mechanics as wave optics stood to geometrical optics, i.e., to the false but extremely useful optics in which light is assumed to travel in straight rays.[49]

Before turning to the main technical objection to the realistic interpretation I have proposed, one more source of, as it were, metaphysical revulsion ought to be considered. All causal power has been given to system properties. Yet individual events in the system, the occurrence of definite values of dynamical magnitudes, are taken to be real, and so are propensities for such events to occur. It might seem wrong to interpret a physical theory as attributing existence where it denies all causal power. In a recent book, Cartwright sometimes seems to appeal to such considerations as showing

[49] See "Quantization as a Problem of Proper Values (Part II)" pp. 13–18. The slogan fits the Heisenberg version of quantum mechanics, too, though somewhat different aspects of classical mechanics are, initially, singled out for nonclassical transformation. See Goldstein, *Classical Mechanics* (Reading, Mass., 1981), p. 416; Dirac, *Principles of Quantum Mechanics*, pp. 84–94, 108–16.

that probabilities to have a position or a momentum are only useful fictions in quantum physics since they do not "play a causal role in the stories the theory tells about the world."[50]

Though dynamical events are not causes, on the interpretation I have proposed, they are relevant to causation, so much so that it would be unreasonable to deny that they and their propensities exist, while accepting the reality of the causal factors, quantum system properties. To begin with, the rationale for a specific state description or Hamiltonian almost always includes, as an essential part, appeals to spatial symmetries in propensities for dynamical events to take place. If the positional symmetry requirements were just aesthetic, so too would be virtually all directly causal claims. In the second place, no one has ever succeeded in assigning a meaning to the descriptions of the causal factors, i.e., the state descriptions and Hamiltonians, that did not take them as governing propensities for location, among other dynamical propensities. Finally, the bare possession of a dynamical value does have a potential impact on causation, even if it is not itself a cause. The state description and the Hamiltonian govern the evolution of a system so long as it is closed. However, in quantum physics as in classical physics, the same factors do not determine the development of the system once it is opened up. Just what the state and Hamiltonian of the new, expanded system are may be determined, in part, by actual dynamical values at the moment closure is broken.[51]

## MOMENTUM AND MEANING

The most important challenge to this interpretation from technical physics is that it violates the uncertainty principle. A quantum state

[50] N. Cartwright, *How the Laws of Physics Lie* (New York, 1983), p. 181.

[51] In the final analysis, Cartwright does accept that the process governed by the time-dependent Schroedinger equation is one real process in nature. So I am not sure that she does mean to deny the reality of the positional probabilities without which such a process seems to become unintelligible. She also proposes that there is a second real process, discontinuous and indeterministic, of which the measurement process is one variety. Though it would be difficult ⌐ mentally, that the Schroedinger evolution spontaneously and indeterministically shifts to the other process, she points out that such findings are not unattainable in principle. And she demonstrates in detail that physicists have been rash to suppose that the statistics of superposition rule out experimental vindication of her version of quantum physics. My intention has been to offer a banal interpretation, to show that established findings and standard empirical expectations do not rule out realism, though they are often supposed to. Of course, new tests might uncover more real processes than the banal interpretation assumes. In short, Cartwright's work might point the way to an important liberalization of realist quantum physics.

description can be expressed in terms of position eigenfunctions or momentum eigenfunctions. The uncertainty principle, as everyone uses it, sets a minimum to the product of two intervals, the interval within which the position eigenvalues have non-zero amplitude and the interval within which the momentum eigenvalues do. As usually interpreted, this limitation entails that nothing can have, simultaneously, a precise and definite position and a precise and definite linear momentum. But on the present interpretation of quantum state descriptions, each representation of the state of a system at a given time will dictate the possibility of dynamical events within the system in which the corresponding dynamical magnitude takes on precise and definite values (or better: values in intervals as small as you please). And it is fundamental to quantum physics that both representations of a state, i.e., in terms of position and in terms of momentum, are always valid. No wonder that Tomonaga, in an illuminating textbook, could base the case for instrumentalism on the uncertainty principle.[52]

There is a short answer to this objection that is perfectly adequate so far as it goes. When one looks at arguments for the uncertainty principle, they are of two kinds.[53] First, there are the arguments about limits to sensitivity in detection that Heisenberg and Bohr developed when Heisenberg originated the principle. According to these arguments, the sensitivity of a detector for position in a system and the sensitivity of a simultaneously operating momentum detector must, in their ultimate limits, be inversely proportional, in the way described by the uncertainty formula. These arguments depend on the fact that transfers of dynamical magnitudes that are crucial to the relevant detection processes cannot be controlled more finely than a threshold of coarseness on the order of Planck's constant. The other sort of argument concerns the relationship between the two ways of describing a system. These arguments establish the same inverse mathematical relation between the narrowness of the interval in which the wave functions in the position representation have a non-zero amplitude and the narrowness of the interval in which the wave functions in the momentum representation have non-zero amplitude (i.e., the narrowness of the interval of eigenval-

[52] Tomonaga, *Quantum Mechanics*, 2: 256–58. The pairs of magnitudes governed by the uncertainty principle can be described more generally and more precisely than by "position and momentum." But nothing of substance would be changed in the basic objection or my subsequent response.

[53] See Fock's parallel distinction between two kinds of uncertainty principles in "Criticism of an Attempt to Disprove the Uncertainty Relation between Time and Energy," *Soviet Physics JETP* (1962), pp. 784–86.

ues in "momentum space," when the same system is being represented). These arguments depend on the so-called de Broglie relation. The positional wave function describing an eigenstate to have
a momentum p always has a wave number k in a fixed ratio to the
momentum. p/k is $\hbar$. (A wave number is the rate at which phase varies with position, the spatial analogue of frequency, the rate at which
phase changes with time. $\hbar$ is Planck's constant, h, divided by $2\pi$.)
Qualitatively, the inference to the uncertainty principle uses the de
Broglie relation to impose limits on the construction of any "wave
packet," a superposition of positional wave functions with zero amplitude outside of a small area. The zero amplitudes result from de-
structive interference between amplitude waves that are out of
phase. The smaller the area of non-zero amplitude, the more interference. More interference requires more waves with different
phases and, hence, according to the de Broglie relation, the superposition of more momentum eigenstates.

Both arguments are valid in any defensible version of quantum
physics. In instrumentalist versions, the two arguments and their
conclusions will be different ways of saying the same thing. This is
not the case in a non-instrumentalist interpretation. Still, both the
constraint on sensitivity in detection and the constraint on intervals
of non-zero-amplitude eigenvalues will exist. But neither constraint
is obviously incompatible with the simultaneous occurrence, for the
same system, of the dynamical event, the momentum's happening
to have a definite value, and the dynamical event, the position's happening to have a definite value. To identify this simultaneous occurrence with simultaneous perfect sensitivity of a momentum detector
and a position detector is to presuppose the instrumentalist interpretation. To identify it with the simultaneous validity of a momentum representation consisting of just one eigenstate and a position
representation consisting of just one eigenstate is to identify eigenstates, propensities for occurrence characterizing a system, with dynamical events, the happenings governed by propensities of systems.

Nonetheless, *if "momentum" is used with its old meaning in classical
physics*, this realist response is open to lethal objections, when further aspects of quantum physics are brought into play. As Bohr and
Heisenberg often emphasized, Copenhagen instrumentalism uses
the old repertoire of dynamical magnitudes, merely restricting
meaningful talk of them to the context of measurement reports. It
is conceptually conservative. By contrast, the realist interpretation
requires conceptual novelty. The old repertoire of indispensable

dynamical magnitudes must be changed. In other words, what counted as a complete description in classical physics must be changed, and not just by replacing determinate and objective assertions by talk of corresponding probabilities or probabilities of corresponding measurements.

For one thing, if "momentum" retains its old meaning, then the general realist uncertainty principle, the one that makes no reference to measurement, lacks a convincing physical justification. Bohr and Heisenberg, identifying the general principle with the principle about measurement, were able to justify the former because they had an argument of sorts for the latter. Analyzing familiar paradigms of measurement, for example, the use of a microscope to determine location, they were able to show that spontaneous, indeterministic and discontinuous changes required by quantum physics force a trade-off, in which processes powerful enough to increase fineness in the measurement of one magnitude increase uncontrollable disruption and, hence, coarseness in the other. Admittedly, the extrapolation from the analysis of a few thought-experiments to the general constraint on measurement required an appeal to "the wave-particle duality" or a general "principle of complementarity," which many physicists came to regard as a metaphorical statement of a problem, not a solution. Still, since the cases analyzed were paradigmatic, the Bohr-Heisenberg analyses gave some support, on their own, to the measurement principle.

On the other hand, if the uncertainty principle is detached from questions of measurement, its justification rests, directly and almost entirely, on the de Broglie relation. And if momentum, in this relation, is classical momentum, the de Broglie relation is at best an extrapolation from observed phenomena, crying out for explanation and receiving none. There is no theoretical reason whatever (putting instrumentalist arguments to one side) why there should be any general correlation between position and momentum at a given time. Mere empirical regularities and their consequences have an honorable role to play in science. But their proper role seems very different from the actual use of the uncertainty principle. For the general uncertainty principle is often used in theoretical explanations of enormously important facts about matter, for example, the fact that the electrons in an atom do not collapse into the nucleus. In any case, the present version of quantum realism, depending as it does on the rejection of the covering-law model, makes a mere empirical regularity ill-suited to this explanatory task. (De Broglie, admittedly, based his case for the basic relation on considerations of relativistic invariance. But he relied on underlying claims about the nature of energy that would raise the same problems, if one insisted on giving classical meanings to quantum terms.)

Worse yet, if "momentum" is classical momentum, then the realist interpretation would produce an intolerable determinism at the level of dynamical events. If, in a system of free particles, each particle has a precise position and classical momentum, future dynamical events are precisely determined, forevermore. If the system contains forces, then, when the potentials are supplied, precise locations and classical momenta dictate determinism for dynamical events. But quantum physics, with its distinctive apparatus of state descriptions, does not dictate future events with such precision. So, at a minimum this conceptually classical realist interpretation would make quantum physics incomplete. Actually, matters are much worse. For reasons that I will soon discuss, precise determination by events is inconsistent with consequences of quantum physics, consequences borne out in experiments. So a realist quantum physics employing classical means of description would be false.

My proposal will be that quantum physics, even in its most elementary part, nonrelativistic mechanics without "spin," requires a non-classical repertoire of dynamical magnitudes. It would be impossible to vindicate this physics in a fair argument if a certain common opinion were correct. According to this view, classical physics made clear, fully comprehensible statements which, unfortunately, proved to be false; a main task of the interpretation of quantum formulas is to preserve as much of this clarity as possible, by interpreting quantum formulas by classical means. This was, explicitly, Bohr's and Heisenberg's project. Most modern textbooks are faithful to it as well. They interpret quantum physics in an instrumentalist way, as a theory of position and (classical) momentum measurement, until the topic of "spin" is reached and classical interpretations become physically implausible. In fact, classical physics was no conceptual Eden.

Classical physics has certain characteristic ways of describing dynamical systems. That anything ever corresponds to a classical description depends on certain assumptions about causality and composition (see 1 and 2 below). That every physical system can be described by one or another classical description depends on further assumptions (see 3 and 4). All of these assumptions were always arbitrary, in 1860 quite as much as 1925. By the end of the nineteenth century, a variety of data contradicted the always arbitrary assumptions. For a reasonable physicist employing an initially classical framework, the changes justified by the mounting anti-classical data were not mere changes in laws—the limited revision in the grossly inconsistent "old quantum theory"—but changes in the basic means of description. As Heisenberg put it, in the first statement of the new physics, there was a need not just for a new theory of dynamics, i.e., of the causes of change in systems, but for a new kinetics, the basic means of describing the state of a system.[54]

1. According to classical physics, spatio-temporal processes evolve deterministically. At least by the middle of the eighteenth century, when attempts to create a unified physics based on gravitation alone had failed, this was an utterly arbitrary assumption. No other successful field lays down all-embracing deterministic laws. Since collisions among elastic particles were supposed to be the epitome of deterministic processes, the establishment of indeterminism there, in the twentieth century, was especially devastating. But what was devastated had never been plausible. Despite the arbitrariness of the assumption of determinism, the basic framework for describing the state of a dynamical system had depended on it. A state was to be described by specifying positions and momenta of particles and by specifying potentials, defined in terms of forces. Classical physics has no way of specifying potentials that does not presuppose determinism. It has no way of ascribing a magnitude to a force that only probably causes a change of momentum in a particle that would only probably maintain its momentum in the absence of force. Indeed, the positing of classical momenta presupposes determinism. The existence of momenta requires that limits converge where only determinism would motivate an assumption of convergence. (Why shouldn't average velocities change in disorderly ways when smaller and smaller time intervals are considered?)

2. In classical physics, a strictly accurate description of a dynamical system must attribute positions and momenta to particles in which no internal processes are taking place, while locating the sources of change in potentials in the environment of the particles. This distinction between passive particles and active environments is essential. Classical physics applied directly to what we ordinarily think of as the basic moving massy bodies always fails miserably.

---

[54] See "Quantum-Theoretical Reinterpretation of Kinematic and Mechanical Relations," p. 262. For the next year, Born and Jordan collaborated with Heisenberg in developing the new ideas. These sequels begin, as well, by noting that a change in the basic means of description is called for. See Born and Jordan, "On Quantum Mechanics," p. 277, and Born, Heisenberg and Jordan, "On Quantum Mechanics II," p. 322, both in van der Waerden, *Sources of Quantum Mechanics*.

The constant excuse is that the analysis of the situation has not been carried far enough. Within the bodies, energy is being dissipated or transmuted, for example, mechanical energy is turned into heat. The observed gross error reflects the fact that classical physics only literally applies to bodies without moving parts. But of course, it is wholly arbitrary to suppose that bodies so lifeless exist.[55] To avoid this assumption by declaring that point masses are the ultimate units of analysis was to embrace the absurdity that something volumeless can contain significant mass. As previously noted, Boltzmann and Maxwell were well aware that the entities they treated as atomic were not literally atoms, and they expected this fact to be reflected in an eventual new mechanics.

3. According to classical physics, whatever exists and has causal properties relevant to space-time events is either a definitely localized particle with definite mass (or a collection of them) or an all-pervasive massless field consisting of energy fluctuations that vary continuously in space and time (or part of such a field). No other bearers of properties are part of a classical description. Probably since the time of Huyghens, certainly since the nineteenth-century beginnings of the modern physiology of perception, this was an arbitrary assumption. One can't imagine a particle without imagining the impression that a classical "wave packet" would make, and vice versa. So it is arbitrary to deny that the selfsame entity can display the interference properties characteristic of waves, while, like a classical particle, it would lose its identity if a certain magnitude were to change. If the arbitrary assumption is lifted, the possible systems of classical physics include such entities. Yet they cannot be described in the classical terms for state descriptions.

4. Classical physics assumes that one can describe any dynamical situation by presenting separate descriptions of phenomena, none of which refers to any one of the other phenomena described, and then asserting that all the descriptions are true of the situation at hand. Such separability is presupposed in procedures as routine as the description of forces using vectors. But the assumption was always arbitrary. Indeed, the thought-experiments that make it tempting were always suspect. In those thought-experiments, one imagines creating any state of affairs bit by bit, creating particles, putting the particles in place, giving them momenta, turning on the fields of force. In Newtonian physics it is, however, impossible to create particles without creating forces, i.e., gravitational forces. In

[55] See Dirac, *Principles of Quantum Mechanics*, p. 3.

classical electron theory, there are no possible electrons lacking the electron charge. In classical electrodynamics, the way the changes are put in place permanently limits the possibilities for creating fields. Classical physics had no grounds for excluding non-separable situations. Yet it had no means of describing them.

How delightful to leave the conceptual mists of classical physics for the clear bright land of quantum physics. Here, descriptions presuppose no more determination of future events than is required by specific features of the system described. While there is a certain distinction between active system and passive occurrences within the system, this distinction depends on a commitment to a way of explaining events, not on a characterization of components that is false on the face of it. (The new mechanics does require that components lack an enduring identity of a classical kind. This new assumption is empirical and contingent—and has abundant empirical support.) What displays wave-like behavior can also display corpuscular behavior, and there is no need for an arbitrary decision as to whether the properties in question are really possessed by particles or by waves. Through the construction of appropriate state descriptions, situations can be made as separable or non-separable as the facts of the case require.

Like most cheap travelogues, this sketch is just a promise. It is fulfilled by developing the mathematical theory and interpreting it in appropriate ways. To suggest how the promise of greater conceptual clarity is kept, I will briefly discuss two magnitudes that are not classical: spin, which is presented as non-classical in standard textbook accounts, and momentum, whose standard classical construal now seems an important obstacle to quantum realism.

## QUANTUM MEANINGS

The first half of an introductory textbook in quantum physics is concerned with position and (linear) momentum and with energy relations constructed by analogy with the classical mechanics of position and momentum. The student is permitted to think of "momentum" as ordinary classical momentum in this first half, but is often reminded that the quantum-physical laws governing momentum are utterly new, suggesting novel relations between description and measurement. Then, the student is introduced to a new magnitude, spin, with an explicit warning that it is not, as the term might suggest, intrinsic angular momentum or any other magnitude in classical physics. "The spin," Dirac warns, "does not correspond very closely to anything in classical mechanics, so the method of classical analogy is not suitable for studying it."[56]

As often happens, a nearly elementary part of quantum physics sheds much light on the most elementary parts. Seeing how physicists were led to accept, unanimously and self-consciously, that "spin" refers to a dynamical magnitude that does not exist in classical physics will make it easier to accept that "linear momentum," as the phrase is used in quantum physics, has a non-classical meaning.

Spin is the fundamental magnitude that someone with a passion for classical analogies would compare to the intrinsic angular momentum of a top turning on its axis. In a famous experiment in 1922, Stern and Gerlach began the development of the modern quantum-physical notion of spin by showing that there is a property of objects of atomic dimensions that resembles classical intrinsic angular momentum but violates classical statements about it, by being quantized—i.e., by only assuming certain values, with uniform gaps in between. Stern and Gerlach vaporized silver in an oven and sent a stream of vapor through a horizontal slit and then through a magnetic field, sharply varying in strength but not in direction. After passing through the field, a silver atom would strike an emulsion, making a dark spot. According to electromagnetic theory, the field that Stern and Gerlach created would deflect a silver atom vertically, the deflection depending on its angular momentum with respect to the vertical axis. Since the atoms in the vapor in the oven ought to be thoroughly randomized by their collisions, one would expect the dark spots to accumulate to a uniform smear along the vertical. Instead, there is darkening at just two discrete areas.

The Stern-Gerlach experiment might seem to reveal nothing more than that electromagnetic interactions can regiment angular momenta in a previously unsuspected way. This was not predicted by any physical theory of the time, but it would not be deeply surprising, given the quantization that pervades the periodic table. Einstein immediately saw that the surprise was more profound. As he pointed out in a paper with Ehrenfest, written in the same year, there is no way that the Stern-Gerlach result can be attributed to a process before collision with the emulsion that does not conflict with important constraints on physical possibilities. More precisely, there is no way in which this can be done if the process depends on classical angular momentum. The atoms in the vapor must have highly random angular momenta, on account of their randomizing colli-

[56] Ibid., p. 143.

sions. And, as Einstein and Ehrenfest show, it would be physically impossible for atoms whose momenta are initially random to be regimented into the final states in the time allowed by the Stern-Gerlach set-up. Short of the instrumentalism that Einstein could never accept, the state of the system before arrival at the emulsion must be responsible for the pattern of spots. But classical magnitudes do not describe a possible state that could be responsible for the observed pattern.[57]

The paper with Ehrenfest is an early example, perhaps the earliest, of Einstein's worries about anti-realist implications of quantum physics. By the same token, the Einstein-Ehrenfest argument is compatible with an instrumentalist physics in which the Stern-Gerlach phenomenon is a quantization of outcomes of the measurement of classical intrinsic angular momenta, measurement outcomes that are not to be attributed to any preceding causal process. So far, the conceptual shifts are of the sort Bohr welcomed. Phenomena of quantization turn out to preclude causation by individual classical events not subjected to measurement, i.e., the momenta of individual atoms as they leave the oven.

Spin is specially revealing because further experiments and theorizing made it clear that a further step had to be taken away from classical physics. The magnitude concerned in spin phenomena is not an outcome of measurements of a classical magnitude, or a set of propensities for such outcomes to occur. A variety of considerations, some of which resembled the Stern-Gerlach experiment, soon showed that electrons have a property involved in electromagnetic phenomena in the same ways as the spin of the silver atoms. If it is classic intrinsic angular momentum, spin must be a property of a rigid body. (Spin is not the analogue of orbital angular momentum; it is fundamental to the quantum theory of the atom that the analogue of the latter, what might have been called "swing," is not spin.) No rigid body hypothesis fit experimental findings. The best such model, Goudsmit and Ulenbeck's, required arbitrary and implausible assumptions and still did not fit the most precise results.[58] In Pauli's theory of spin, the basis of the modern theory of the electron, an eigenstate for a spin with respect to one axis is a superposition of eigenstates for spin along the other axes. The certainty of a value for spin with respect to the z-axis precludes the certainty of any def-

[57] See Einstein and Ehrenfest, "Quantentheoretische Bemerkungen zum Experiment von Stern und Gerlach" (1922) in P. Ehrenfest, *Collected Scientific Papers* (Amsterdam, 1959).

[58] See H. A. Kramers, *Quantum Mechanics* (Amsterdam, 1957), p. 233.

inite value for spin with respect to x or spin with respect to y. This is nonsense if spin is intrinsic angular momentum. If spin is the outcome of a classical measurement, the Pauli rules are a mystery that is not at all removed by reflections on the nature of the measurement process.

The acceptance of spin as a fundamental and utterly non-classical magnitude took place in less than a decade, changing a three-centuries-old consensus about the fundamental terms of dynamical description. The shift was motivated, not by a general theory of meaningful description, but by arguments that were fair to the theoretical framework of physicists who initially did not accept the existence of nonclassical spin. Especially after the triumphs of relativity theory, electrodynamics was basic to the framework of physics. At the core of electrodynamics is the principle that the changes in the location of charges that are due to the presence of fields are due to the interaction of the dynamical properties of charges and the structure of the fields. The Stern-Gerlach experiment and the later experiments on intra-atomic processes showed that the laws of those interactions that were suitable for large-scale objects were unsuitable for objects of atomic dimensions. The former laws turned out to be only approximate truths about large random aggregates of atomic processes. The core principles of the old framework required a new way of describing dynamical systems that would combine with the unaltered parts of physical theory to explain the new phenomena together with the approximate truth of the old laws. Spin, as described by Pauli, Dirac and Heisenberg, fulfilled this role, and, among the alternatives, was the one best sustained by further experiment and theorizing. In sum, electrodynamics circa 1922 combined with the Stern-Gerlach experiment to set the task of identifying a new dynamical property, missing from the classical repertoire. Combined with subsequent experiments and the new quantum mechanics, it ultimately singled out spin as the missing ingredient. Spin is not classical intrinsic angular momentum, but an analogue, i.e., a causal analogue: quite unlike the classical property for the most part, it plays the causal role that the classical property was supposed to play in processes that are the ones that reveal atomic properties in both pre-spin and post-spin physics. In addition to sorting out by means of inhomogeneous magnetic fields, à la Stern and Gerlach, these processes include spectroscopy and collision experiments.

"According to the old framework, certain phenomena stand in need of explanation, and the old repertoire of causes cannot provide one; in light of the deepest principles of that framework, and new phenomena, a change in the old repertoire is justified." This is a familiar story, by now. In Chapter Two, I described the justification of universal gravitation in just this way. The spin version of the familiar story shows that a similar change took place in the twentieth century, and transformed the terms for describing bare states, quite apart from any further novelties in the description of how states are changed. That such a transformation occurred in one corner of the quantum revolution, where what seemed a new role for intrinsic angular momentum turned out to require its replacement, suggests that a similar transformation might have occurred elsewhere, say, in the treatment of ordinary linear momentum. This is my proposal. Quantum mechanics replaces linear momentum with a partial, causal analogue. The replacement is les visible because Copenhagen instrumentalism obscures it. In the case of spin, the classical magnitude cannot be salvaged at all by the restriction to reports of measurement-outcomes. In the case of the quantum analogue of momentum (i.e., ordinary, linear momentum), instrumentalism salvages the classical magnitude for purposes of explaining the outcomes of particular experiments. Of course, the instrumentalist restrictions need to be forgotten when physicists describe processes inside stars, or explain the whole periodic table. Alternatively, if the two-process alternative is preferred, questions about the boundaries between the measured process and the measurement intervention had better not be raised. However, such selective inattention is compatible with superb physics. A classical conception of spin measurements is not.

Just as the introduction of spin was the best-justified response to the need for a new account of the interaction between charges and fields, a replacement for momentum was the best justified response to the failures of the old mechanics of position and momentum. Though I have not sketched the experimental basis for the indictment of the old mechanics, the discussion of superposition indicates one important class of findings. Among the alternative formulations of modern, quantum mechanics, Feynman's path-integral approach makes the theoretical basis for the change clearest, and makes it easiest to say what it is that replaces talk of momentum.

In an especially abstract and sophisticated formulation, the classical laws of motion can be summed up as a least action principle. Suppose a particle is at one location at a certain time, at another at some later time. If the path integral of a certain function, the Lagrangian, is taken over every possible trajectory between the departure and the arrival, the actual trajectory is the one that minimizes the path integral. Here, a trajectory is a space-time history, such as a movie portrays. Classically, the Lagrangian is the classical kinetic energy minus the classical potential energy, for the various space-time points in the possible trajectories. It follows from the least-action principle that trajectories are deterministic, essentially because each intermediate, "partially completed" journey must be determined by the earlier stages if only one trajectory can actually occur.

Because true physics is non-deterministic, definite departures only make definite arrivals more or less probable, within a system. Because phenomena of superposition occur, the probability of an arrival must depend on values attaching to all possible trajectories. Given the framework that reflective classical physicists employed, these are the modifications most likely to create a true theory in response to the anti-classical data available by 1925. In effect, these modifications suspend requirements of determinism, separability and wave-particle distinctness that were always arbitrary. At the same time, classical physics is not all wrong. If one poses questions within limits of precision much coarser than Planck's constant and if the questions are posed of systems in which interactions on the scale of Planck's constant are not magnified so that they coarsely effect the answer, then the answers fit the classical laws. Feynman shows, in effect, that the new version of the classical principle that adequately responds to the falsehood of the classical assumptions while acknowledging their limited and approximate truth equates the probability amplitude for an arrival given a departure to a sum of amplitudes associated with each possible trajectory. Each amplitude is a wave function with phase determined by the integral of the classical Lagrangian for that path. When only coarse-grained questions and situations are at issue, Feynman's principle yields correct, classical answers. The path integrals vary so rapidly in phase, outside a tiny region around the classically possible trajectory, that they cancel each other out and make no net contribution. Although the classical formula for the Lagrangian is used, it receives a neutral formulation in terms of ratios characterizing intermediate subtrajectories. No classical division into active environments and passive particles is required.

Feynman's argument for quantum mechanics is an especially general and elegant development of Schroedinger's idea that classical mechanics needs to be developed into a new one that stands to the old as geometric optics, with straight-line rays, stands to wave optics, with interference. It is hardly surprising, then, that Schroedinger's wave functions reappear as ways of answering the question of what the state of a system is at a given time. The positional wave functions describe Feynman amplitudes to be at a certain location at a certain time having come from anywhere whatever.

The new definition of momentum is motivated by considering the amplitude for a free particle of mass m, starting at a given location and time, to arrive at various other locations along a single dimension at a given subsequent time. A graph of amplitude against distance is a wave. (More precisely, since the amplitude is a complex number the real part yields a wave, and the imaginary part does, too. Ignoring this complication will do no harm.) Putting the start at the origin, the wave has a nearly constant wavelength and, hence, a fairly definite wave number, in regions around points that are reasonably far from the origin. "Reasonably far" means enormously far on the scale of Planck's constant. The basic equation for the distance amplitudes entails that for these arrival regions, the product of m times x/t (x being the distance, t the time interval for arrivals) equals ħ times k, the wave number of the amplitude function in the region. This is de Broglie's equation.

Feynmann and Hibbs summarize this result in a statement which, quite uncharacteristically for them, tangles the classical and quantum-physical perspectives. "From the quantum-mechanical point of view, when the motion can be adequately described by assigning a classical momentum to the particle of p = mx/t, then the amplitude varies in space [according to the de Broglie equation."[59] The quantum/classical tangle is appropriate because it would be absurd to claim, literally, that classical momentum has been shown to have the indicated relation to amplitudes for arrival. The oscillations of amplitude against distance are irregular for the graph as a whole, highly irregular near the origin. The state of motion of the particle itself, at the initial time, would be represented by the whole wave function, which lacks a wave number. Yet a particle cannot lack clas-

[59] Feynman and Hibbs, *Quantum Mechanics and Path-Integrals*, p. 45. Though the equation they give links momentum, wave number and Planck's constant in de Broglie's way, the wave number refers to a wave function for arrivals after a given interval following departure from a given origin. It does not refer to the location at a given time given any previous history whatever. So it is a bit misleading of me to call this the de Broglie equation. However, Feynman and Hibbs immediately show that the original de Broglie relation does follow, as a result of the role of the classical Lagrangian in determining amplitudes. Since the wave numbers are the same, I will treat the two equations as if they were the same relation. Because transition amplitudes are primary in Feynman's formulation, reflection on arrivals is the more natural way of motivating the extension of the term "momentum."

sical momentum, if there is such a dynamical magnitude. If one takes momentum to be a property of a particle event, the particle's having traversed a certain distance in a certain time, the de Broglie relation, classically interpreted, would dictate that the "slow" events, close to the origin, are, absurdly, without momentum (even zero momentum). Near the origin, oscillations are too irregular for any assignment of a wave number, even as an approximation. In the further development of the theory, it is extremely important that phase changes near the origin do not literally correspond to classical momentum and do not as a consequence entail instantaneous velocities. Otherwise, all free electrons would have to be assigned the speed of light, and photons would have to be allowed to travel faster than light.[60]

In contrast to their tangled statement of the relation between classical momentum and quantum physics, Feynman and Hibbs have a straightforward, unhedged formulation of the "way the [concept] of momentum . . . [is] extended to quantum mechanics. . . . If the amplitude varies as $e^{ikx}$, we say that the particle has momentum $\hbar k$."[61] In the mathematical development of the theory, this statement of the non-classical, quantum mechanical concept of momentum has the following consequences. If a system is described by a single positional wave function with a wave number $k$, then the system is in an eigenstate for the (quantum-mechanical) momentum $\hbar k$. Such a system turns out to have equal amplitudes for location anywhere, as required by the uncertainty principle. More localized systems are characterized by superpositions of such wave functions, and, hence, are in superpositions of momentum states. These are not laws governing classical momentum at the quantum level, but statements of what a certain dynamical magnitude in quantum physics is. This entity governs the statistics of distance over time. At the "classical limit," the answers to coarse-grained questions about arrival are the same as would result from the pretense that the de Broglie relation describes classical momentum. For these reasons, the new quantity is named after the old one. But it is genuinely new. The classical concept of momentum turns out to play no role in literally true characterizations of dynamical properties.

From the perspective of Feynman's formulation, one can appreciate both what an enormous achievement the uncertainty principle is and how easily it can mislead in the assessment of the realist inter-

---

[60] See Dirac, *Principles of Quantum Mechanics*, p. 262, Feynman, *QED*, pp. 89f.
[61] *Quantum Mechanics and Path Integrals*, p. 47.

pretation. There are two questions, among others, which one can ask about the situation of a free particle of mass m at a given time. One can ask about propensities to be at various locations at that time. And one can ask about propensities to be at various distances after a subsequent time interval. In classical mechanics, these are quite independent questions, about position and momentum, respectively. In quantum physics, as the work of Heisenberg and de Broglie showed, the answer to one question entails the answer to the other, and vice versa. The state description that directly yields answers to the first question must, as a mathematical consequence of the quantum physics of spatio-temporal location, be equal to another wave function whose eigenfunctions and amplitudes directly yield answers to the second question. This is an enormous change from classical assumptions. Because the second kind of eigenfunction would, by itself, represent an eigenstate causally analogous to classical momentum, it is natural to speak of the second kind of representation as a momentum representation. It is a further consequence of the mathematics of quantum physics that an eigenstate in the one representation cannot be an eigenstate in the other. The amount of superposition in one representation is inversely proportionate to that in the other, in the way described by the uncertainty principle.

Does the uncertainty principle, so understood, conflict with the realist statement that there are definite spatio-temporal events in superpositions? Any appearance that it does is based on a confusion between the analogy motivating talk of "momentum" as a characteristic of states and the analogy motivating a different usage, talk of "momentum" as a characteristic of events.

If the event, the occurrence of mass m at location $x_1$ at time $t_1$ is succeeded by the event, the occurrence of m at $x_2$ at $t_2$, one can divide $x_2 - x_1$ by $t_2 - t_1$ and multiply by m. If classical mechanics were correct then this number would be the average momentum of the particle during the interval between $t_1$ and $t_2$. If the particle were a free particle, one not subject to forces, then the number would be its instantaneous momentum at all times; otherwise it would be an average of instantaneous momenta. On account of these analogies, one might name the number "the momentum for the interval." The actual analogy is only partial. Because classical assumptions of enduring particle identity, continuous trajectory and determinism are incorrect, the quantum momentum number does not correspond to any property of a particle at an instant. The necessary convergence on a definite instantaneous value does not occur, even for a free particle—unless the particle happens to be in a momentum eigenstate.

It is easy to forget how incomplete the analogy is. At any given instant there is a definite momentum state, i.e., a particular momentum representation is correct, even though there is no definite momentum number at that time. If one forgets the difference between the causal momentum state and the purely retrospective momentum number, then the existence of a definite momentum number for every interval of actual history (which the realist interpretation does require) will seem to require the evolution of definite instantaneous properties, whose nonrelativistic characterization is the mass times the instantaneous rate of change of position at that time. The realist interpretation does not require this magnitude. But it might seem to. And if realism did require a definite instantaneous momentum number, it would produce the determinism at the level of events that quantum physics forbids.

The resolution of questions about the meanings of quantum terminology has depended on the strategy of justifying realist quantum physics as the most reasonable modification of classical physics in light of non-classical findings. Quite apart from questions about meaning, this strategy has the enormous benefit of dissolving the so-called "measurement problem," which many see as the central difficulty posed by quantum physics. More precisely, the measurement problem turns out to have been solved already, through widely accepted developments of uncontroversial parts of quantum theory.

Though many difficulties have been placed under the heading, "the measurement problem," the most important has been the effort to reconcile the following three propositions, all assumed to be true, with uncontroversial quantum-physical laws.

(a.) It is possible, in principle, to measure with absolute accuracy any single definite value that something in a quantum system definitely possesses.

(b.) A quantum state description is a complete description of the causally relevant features of a quantum system, and every physical system is truly described by such a description, throughout its history. For a given dynamical magnitude, typical quantum states are superpositions of the corresponding eigenstates.

(c.) When measurement takes place, and the object subsystem interacts with the measuring subsystem, the event in the measuring subsystem that marks the end of the measurement definitely has a definite value relevant to measurement. For example, the pointer does point to a particular position on the dial.

The result of attempts to reconcile these three propositions is always negative. The typical conclusion is that the second proposition must be tampered with. One kind of tampering results in Bohr's instrumentalism. The "state description" is taken to be just a device for predicting the frequency with which given preparation procedures are followed by certain sequels in other, measuring apparatus. Apart from these measurement phenomena, there is no such thing as the possession of a definite value in quantum physics. Another kind of tampering results in the two-process view, in which the laws governing the history of a system are abruptly suspended when measurement takes place. Superpositions "collapse" into an eigenstate. Other tamperings have been urged, but they seem at least as bizarre, in ways evoked by the labels "the many-worlds interpretation" and "quantum logic." Since all three propositions seem basically right, it is utterly frustrating that adjustment in the interest of consistency leads to such strange consequences.

In the realist quantum physics for which I have been arguing, the second proposition is true. And so is the third. The ultimate event in measurement involves the possession of a definite value. However, neither conclusion is the outcome of any argument specifically concerned with measurement. Rather, the rational modification of classical physics in light of non-classical findings (the rationale traced in all good textbooks) establishes that the causal factors in microphysics are irreducible system properties governing the statistics for the occurrence of definite dynamical events; final events in measuring subsystems are definite, so are events in object subsystems, and so are events in systems having nothing to do with measurement. I have also tried to show that the intelligibility of the new forms of causation is established by the arguments for modifying classical physics, without any special role for reflections on measurement. This relative independence of justification and meaning from reflections on measurement makes it possible to reject the first principle.

Why must it be possible to measure, with absolute accuracy, any definite value that is definitely possessed? This demand might result from a general principle that the meaning of any ascription is identical with its test implications. But this general view of meaning turned out to be an avoidable disaster, in previous chapters. Within quantum physics, the first proposition might also be based on Copenhagen instrumentalism. But the latter view is at least as avoidable, and has consequences that are just as bad. Finally, and most plausibly by far, one might think that the belief that magnitudes such as quantum physics describes are definitely possessed could only be justified by showing that it is possible for an absolutely accurate measurement to reveal the presence of the magnitudes in question. After all, the existence of the quantum events is hardly a banal truism taken over from everyday inquiry. Some justification is needed. However, the justification has turned out to consist of arguments at the level of general physical theory that do not depend on the possibility of absolutely accurate measurement.

The pervasive commitment to the first principle is due, I think, to the continued influence of positivist views about meaning, even among people who would not explicitly accept them. The influence of the identification of meaning with test implications leads people to give the most plausible argument, "What could justify the claim of definite values if not the possibility of accurate measurements of them?" more credence than it deserves.

Of course, the rejection of principle a is very, very far from constituting an adequate account of measurement. And realist quantum physics, embracing b and c, had better be compatible with an adequate account of measurement—not least because quantum physics had better be empirically justifiable and measurement will be vital for the justification, even if it is not all-important. Fortunately, the needed account has been present in the literature for decades. (The basic literature, whose bearing I will now describe, is cited in footnote 28.)

Actually, there are two different kinds of discussions of measurement that are revealing, for present purposes, and compatible with the realist interpretation. They correspond to different specifications of our pre-theoretical ideas as to what constitutes measurement. That the different specifications lead to assertions that are verbally quite different (i.e., different until one realizes that "measurement" is specified in different ways) is an important discovery of quantum physics. It is like discoveries of unsuspected ambiguity in spatio-temporal attribution, in relativity theory.

One thing that might be meant by saying that a system is, strictly and literally, a measurement system is this: an object event has a definite property of the kind in question just in case there is an indicator event with a certain definite property. If all systems are quantum systems, this specification has a restatement in the language of amplitudes. If the object property occurs, the system will be in an eigenstate for the associated indicator property at the appropriate time; and conversely, if the indicator property occurs, the system was in the eigenstate for the associated object property at the appropriate time. There is no amplitude for non-registration and no amplitude for misindication. These consequences for the system are not the results of associating measurement with any physical process, mysterious or ordinary. They are logical consequences of saying that the system in question is a measurement system, once measurement has been defined in a certain way.

In realist quantum physics, it is easy to show that in such a system, the object subsystem must be in an eigenstate at the time for which values are ascertained. At that time, the object event will happen to have a definite value, as events always do. So the measuring subsystem will be certain to have the associated value. But if the measuring subsystem has the associated value, the object subsystem was certain to have had that object value. There is no amplitude for misindication. This fact about the object subsystem has important consequences for its future. Since the object subsystem was in an eigenstate, its future development does not involve the interference of probabilities characteristic of superposition. In terms of the two-hole experiment with Heisenberg's microscope: if passage through hole 1 is certain to be associated with a microscope image of an electron emerging from hole 1, and similarly for passage through hole 2, then at the barrier, in each run of the experiment, there is one or the other eigenstate. If equal probabilities for passage are revealed by the microscope, the classical, non-interference pattern B must develop at the detector wall.

These eigenstates and classical statistics are not the consequence of something that the microscope did to a subsystem that was a superposition. They are entailments of the assumption that the total system is a measurement system, when "measurement system" is meant in the indicated way. In fact, if proposition b is maintained and all systems are taken to be quantum systems, it can be shown that a superposition—for example, the superposition that is involved in electron emission from a filament—never develops into an eigenstate. So if "measurement" is defined in the first way, measurement of a property of an event in a superposed system is physically impossible.

Still, we must be able to measure definite properties of quantum events in some sense that is relevant to the claim that quantum physics is empirically justifiable. After all, state-descriptions are supposed to dictate the probabilities with which such properties are possessed. Fortunately, the other sense of "measurement" is easy to find, and connected with another kind of well-established argument. Something else that we mean by "measurement" is the reliable indication of the actual properties of the object subsystem. "Reliability," here, does not mean absolute reliability, the perfect accuracy assumed in the first sort of account. We all know that nothing we call a measuring process is absolutely reliable. However, if a theory is empirically justified, we do insist that this second kind of account tell us how actual measuring processes can be reliable enough to produce the empirical justification we have. We also want such an account to reveal any interesting general principles concerning the actual consequences of improving reliability.

The cited work by Bohm and Gottfried and subsequent developments give the general physics of measurement in this second sense. Applied to the real world, in which measurement systems, object subsystems and measuring subsystems all involve superpositions, the main results are these. It is possible, in principle, to construct a measurement system indicating the value of an individual dynamical magnitude with any finite degree of reliability, i.e., any degree short of perfection. In each run of an experiment involving measurement, the object subsystem continues to be a superposition after measurement. However, from run to run of an experiment, there are random variations in the phase relations characterizing the interference of measuring subsystem amplitudes with object subsystem amplitudes once measurement has taken place. The effect of these variations is to make the subsequent cumulative frequencies more closely resemble the classical, pattern B type. As the reliability of a measuring process is increased, more and more interference is cancelled out in subsequent cumulative frequencies. Some interference effects always remain. Superpositions never become eigenstates and their effects are never precisely the same as those of probabilistic "mixtures" in which eigenstates are produced with certain probabilities in the runs of an experiment. Still, with readily attainable degrees of reliability, subsequent evolution becomes so close to the behavior of a mixture that it is impossible in practice to detect the difference. As the gamma-ray microscope is made more and more reliable, the pattern at the detector wall become indistinguishable from pattern B—which is just what happens in realistic versions of Heisenberg's thought-experiment.

For justifying quantum-physical statements, measurement in the second sense is all we need and all we can have. So far as mere measurements can serve to justify any theory at all, these measurements do provide us with empirical justifications for realist quantum-physical assertions about the evolution of quantum-systems. The mere occurrence of indicator events together with assertions of their reliability would not justify us in saying that events in superposed systems definitely possess definite values. If the indications were absolutely reliable, the object events would not be in superpositions. Indications that need not reflect an actual value could, in principle, correspond to the absence of any actual definite value. This gap in the justification of realist quantum physics only reflects the fact that there are tasks that mere measurement cannot accomplish. These tasks are accomplished by interpreting the actual measurement results by appropriately justified theoretical means.

## POSITIVISM AND QUANTUM MEANINGS

Bohr always insisted that his instrumentalism had "its roots in the indispensable use of classical concepts in the interpretation of all proper measurements."[62] One path from such conceptual conservatism to instrumentalism is now clear. If one insists that the classical magnitudes be the magnitudes ascribed in quantum state descriptions, the ascriptions must be not just probabilistic but instrumental, i.e., ascriptions of measurement outcomes alone. Otherwise, the uncertainty principle is undermined and quantum indeterminism is circumvented.

The insistence that *all* classical concepts be preserved might seem dogmatic and shallow, given the uncontroversial partial overlap between the new physics and the old. Even if quantum state descriptions do not really refer to classical momentum, they do refer to spatio-temporal location, the same spatio-temporal location described in classical (i.e., non-quantum) physics. Though the "path-integral" label better evokes the use of Lagrangian techniques, Feynman's original label for his formulation was "the space-time approach." This accurately suggests the primacy of familiar space-time questions. The basic idea that state descriptions govern propensities for spatio-temporal location was quite familiar from Schroedinger's and Dirac's fundamental work, as Feynman has always acknowledged. So it might seem that the state descriptions, on a non-instrumentalist construal, can be analyzed in terms of some classical magnitudes, even if others, for example, momentum, play no role in this analysis. It might seem dense to ignore this possibility and reactionary to insist on the full range of classical magnitudes, once the possibility was noted. Yet Bohr's notion that instrumentalism is justified

[62] "Can Quantum-Mechanical Description of Physical Reality Be Considered Complete?" p. 150.

by the need to use classical concepts was shared by most of the pioneers of quantum physics. Bohr, Heisenberg, Pauli and Landau were not stupid or reactionary.[63]

The conceptual conservatism that Bohr's instrumentalism requires is not glib, but deeply principled. It is the outcome of the deductivist view of justification, applied to quantum physics. From the deductivist standpoint, a hypothesis is tested by comparing test implications that are part of its content with the actual course of observations. More precisely, this is the basic position from which deductivists depart at great peril: deviations open the floodgates to nonsense. If the basic position is accepted, then the meaning of a hypothesis, so far as it is testable, consists of its observable test implications. That Bohr was guided by this view of testability and meaning is suggested by his descriptions of the ways in which classical concepts are indispensable. They are indispensable for communication among physicists.[64] And they are indispensable in the statement of experimental findings.[65] It is far from clear that any plausible general account of the difference between the observational and the theoretical would put classical assertions on the observational side of the divide. But Bohr's claim of indispensability in the statement of observations does suggest a reasonable constraint on tests of quantum physics. Where quantum physics posits a property that does not occur in classical physics, a test of the quantum statement involving the property should involve observations that can be described in the vocabulary that is common to classical physics and quantum physics. If the observation reports transgress the conceptual limits of classical physics, it would be question-begging to use them to confirm the novel hypothesis. According to the basic deductivist view, this limit on the content of test implications is a limit on meaning, i.e., on the content of the tested hypotheses themselves, assuming they are testable.

So far, there might seem to be room for a realist interpretation of quantum physics. In the space-time approaches of Feynman,

[63] See Heisenberg, "The Development of the Interpretation of the Quantum Theory," p. 26; Pauli, *General Principles of Quantum Mechanics*, pp. 7f.; Landau and Lifshitz, *Quantum Mechanics*, pp. 2f.

[64] *Atomic Physics and Human Knowledge* (New York, 1958), p. 89.

[65] "The Quantum Postulate and the Recent Development of Atomic Theory," p. 88; "Can Quantum-Mechanical Description of Physical Reality Be Considered Complete?" p. 150. In "Discussion with Einstein on Epistemological Problems in Atomic Physics," Bohr puts in italics the principle, "*[H]owever far the phenomena transcend the scope of classical physical explanation, the account of all evidence must be expressed in classical terms*" (p. 209).

Schroedinger and Dirac, the state description makes a distinctive contribution to the evolution of propensities for events to happen in space and time. The spatio-temporal characterizations of events are in the common vocabulary, even if they do not include all of the characteristic descriptive devices of classical physics.

Bohr would have regarded this answer as a failed attempt to give meaning to quantum statements, on account of a combination of physical insights with the deductivist view of meaning. *What* propensities for location does the state description entail? It won't do simply to derive propensities concerning location at the time in question, using the absolute square rule. If the content of the state description were exhausted by these present propensities, there would be no such thing as superposition. The distinctively quantum-physical nature of a state description is brought out by considering its bearing on propensities for future location. But what are these consequences? By itself, the state description has none. It only has consequences for other times when combined with a Hamiltonian—just as a classical description in terms of position and momenta needs to be combined with a description of potentials to have a bearing on other times. For example, the consequences Feynman and Hibbs extract to motivate a new usage for "momentum" only follow for a free particle.

This limitation might seem to require a mere increase in complexity: the content of the state description is determined, in the old vocabulary, by entailments for future propensities given the various possible Hamiltonians. None of the pioneers of quantum physics took this option seriously, and rightly so. It does not reflect the relation between state descriptions and Hamiltonians. In space-time approaches to quantum physics, the relation of the Hamiltonian to the basic spatio-temporal vocabulary is specified indirectly, in terms of the state description. For example, in Schroedinger's format, the Hamiltonian is (roughly) the magnitude whose values are instantaneous rates of change of the state description. This interdependence is essential to the argument that Schroedinger-format statements and Heisenberg-format states are different ways of saying the same thing, a crucial argument for any quantum realist. For a deductivist, the state-description is not given a meaning by a scheme that depends on an already established meaning for the Hamiltonian. Unless the state description is already meaningful, the Hamiltonian isn't.

A certain holism at the level of meanings, a claim that only a conjunction of state description and Hamiltonian are meaningful, would also be unfaithful to quantum physics. For example, in quantum physics good arguments constantly presuppose the meaningfulness of principles solely referring to relations among state descriptions or to relations among Hamiltonians. The principles prescribing symmetrical or anti-symmetrical statistics are of the former sort. The sort that independently refer to Hamiltonians are, if anything, more common. Virtually all quantum-physical arguments appeal to the plausibility of certain principles for modifying a Hamiltonian in light of a perturbation or a physical constraint. These considerations would rarely have independent plausibility if the Hamiltonian did not refer to a distinctive, independent magnitude.

Copenhagen instrumentalism evades these difficulties at the cost of its enormous sacrifice of explanatory power and underlying justifications. The only meaningful statements are assertions of propensities for classical measurement outcomes when various total measurement processes are operating. Once this limitation is made, the meaninglessness of the state description can be conceded without further pain. The state description is, as Bohr came to regard it, just part of a way of calculating the measurement probabilities that are all that true physics describes.[66] This is no loss if one has already given up the goal of describing states as they exist in the absence of measurement. Sometimes a rationale for calculations can still be constructed, by reflection on the process of measuring classical magnitudes. Often, however, what seemed plausible premises will turn out to be no more than rules of calculation, with a pleasantly classical sound, that have turned out to succeed, so far. But such arbitrariness is not surprising if physics cannot describe the prior processes causing the patterns in measurement when devices are put to work.

The only alternative is to abandon the deductivist view of meaning in favor of another, in which the argument that a formula is a meaningful description of a state of affairs can be the argument that an old means of description must be altered, on topic-specific grounds, both theoretical and empirical. In arguments that I have partially reproduced, in rough fragments, the textbooks show that the classical state descriptions had to be changed, to produce quantum state descriptions, while the classical descriptions of force and energy had to be changed to produce Hamiltonians. This is all that

---

[66] "[T]he quantum-mechanical formalism . . . represents a purely symbolic scheme permitting only predictions . . . as to results obtainable under conditions specified by classical concepts" ("Discussion with Einstein," p. 210).

there is and all that is needed, to show that the two kinds of formulas meaningfully describe distinct but interdependent aspects of reality. (More precisely, this is all that is needed if one presupposes, as Bohr does, that the classical formulas would have been meaningful descriptions if classical assumptions had been correct.) Suppose, by way of contrast, that the calculus had been developed in the fourteenth century as a way of solving abstract geometrical problems and a fourteenth-century scientist with Schroedinger's mathematical talent had cooked up Schroedinger's formulas, and discovered that they yielded observed patterns in measurement outcomes. The rootless formulas really would be meaningless tools for successful calculation.

Before, the covering-law model made it impossible to reconcile realist quantum physics with the prohibition against action-at-a-distance. It has turned out that the deductivist view of meaning makes it impossible to reconcile realist quantum physics with the uncertainty principle. Indeed, the achievements in justification and explanation that realism seeks to preserve are incompatible with the practice of quantum physics, if the deductivist view of meaning is right. Positivism would make the realist interpretation into bad physics. However, once the present anti-positivist view of explanation and justification is adopted, the explanatory power and justification of quantum physics are as great as they seem to be when instrumentalist constraints are ignored. Positivism should be abandoned in the interests of microphysics, which has often seemed its main scientific ally.

## BELL'S SPINS AND EINSTEIN'S MOON

These days, realist interpretations of quantum physics are often said to conflict with recent experimental findings. These experiments are direct descendents of the Einstein-Podolsky-Rosen thought-experiment—an irony, since Einstein meant to show that an instrumentalist physics was bound to be defective (in his view, incomplete). The actual experiments are often thought to produce findings that can only be explained by supposing that the spin properties of a photon depend on the orientation of the polarizer with which its spin is measured. Since the findings in these experiments are just what quantum physics dictate, it would seem that the existence of the moon might depend, in quantum physics, on whether someone is looking at it.

In fact, these experiments show that the realist quantum physics that I have sketched, in which probabilities for events are determined, not by prior events, but by properties of systems, is the only way to avoid strict instrumentalism. As usual, avoiding instrumentalism will require accepting concepts that are irreducibly non-classical.

In these experiments (the best have been performed in a laboratory near Marseilles), atoms are prepared in a total spin zero state, under conditions in which they descend to their state of lowest energy. The "cascade" requires the release of two photons. Photons can have only two values for spin with respect to a given axis, often called "up" and "down." Conservation principles dictate that the photons are in a total spin zero state, which entails that they move in opposite directions, with opposite spins with respect to any identically directed axes.

Swivelled polarizers are set up on opposite sides of the photon-generating cascades, and reasonably far apart (12 meters apart at the French laboratory). A polarizer treats photons differently depending on their spin with respect to the polarizer's axis. When the polarizers are aligned vertically (Figure 2a), then, if one of them lets an up photon through, the other, simultaneously, lets a down photon through, and vice versa. There is perfect anti-correlation, reflecting the opposite spins with respect to identical axes required by the quantum physics of the situation. Each opposed pair of spins appears half of the time on the average, as the quantum description of the total spin zero state for two photons requires. This state is a superposition of a $\sqrt{1/2}$ amplitude for left up, right down and a $-\sqrt{1/2}$ amplitude for left down, right up. Whenever the two polarizers are both pointed in a single direction, perfect anti-correlation is observed, as the quantum physics dictates. (See Figure 2b.) When the axes are at a tilt with respect to one another, the probability of a pair of photons having the same spin is non-zero. In general, this probability is a function of the angle between the two polarizers. In quantum physics, arguments from symmetry and invariance dictate that the probabilities be $P_{++} = P_{--} = \frac{1}{2}\sin^2(A_{12}/2)$, where $A_{12}$ is the angle between directions 1 and 2, the respective directions of the axes. (See Figure 2c.) The parallel axis cases are the extremes of this general formula. Observations are as the formula requires, with the usual problems of experimental error. (The photons are hard to filter for spin. I will ignore problems of instrumental reliability at the polarizers from now on.)

No matter how careful one is to produce indistinguishable predecessors to photon production, different runs of the experiment

(a)

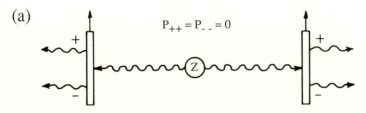

$$P_{++} = P_{--} = 0$$

(b)

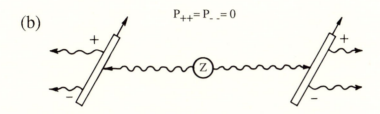

$$P_{++} = P_{--} = 0$$

(c)

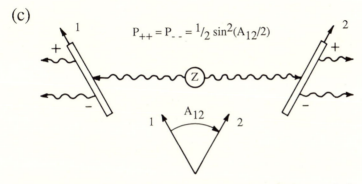

$$P_{++} = P_{--} = \frac{1}{2}\sin^2(A_{12}/2)$$

FIGURE 2. Within device Z, atoms with total spin zero drop to their state of lowest energy. Swivelled polarizers are set up on either side. Each registers the spin of an arriving photon with respect to the direction of the polarizer axis. The spin of a photon is either up (+) or down (−). If the axes are both vertical, then, whenever one polarizer registers a spin, the other registers the opposite spin, (a). There is the same perfect anti-correlation whenever the axes point in the same direction, (b). In general, the amount of correlation is related to the angle, $A_{12}$, between the axes, according to the formula $P_{++} = P_{--} = \frac{1}{2}\sin^2(A_{12}/2)$, (c).

produce different spin outcomes. Still, at each run with axes parallel, if one photon is up at one polarizer, the other is absolutely certain to be down at the other, and vice versa. Suppose that the guaranteed upness of the left hand photon when the right hand one is down is caused by some property of an event, affecting spin. Here, as elsewhere, I mean a property that does not entail anything about another part of the system, a property characterizing an event that can be identified without reference to more than one location in the system. The properties and events are local, as all values of dynamical events are in the realist interpretation. The experiment can be set up so that such a property, if it affects spins at the polarizers, must characterize the creation of the photons; otherwise action at a distance would be taking place. Since the anti-correlation is perfect, the creation events must necessitate definite spins for the respective particles. Some necessitate left up, right down, others the reverse. Since no one has discovered any such difference in predecessors to photon emission, these are hidden event properties, so-called local hidden variables. I will sometimes call them "flavors"—as good a description as any other since their nature is quite unknown. The observed perfect anti-correlations (and perfect correlations at perpendicular) require, as just noted, that every flavor be deterministic for spin with respect to parallel axes. Presumably each is deterministic for spin with respect to all axes. After all, the creation event does not depend on the position of the polarizers, which might be changed after creation takes place. (Actually, there is a version of the argument that follows which allows for local properties with definite but indeterministic propensities to create spins. The argument is along the same lines as the one I will discuss but a bit more complicated.)

Suppose that someone takes these various emission-event properties to have probabilities of occurrence. These will then determine the probabilities of correlation and anti-correlation for various polarizer alignments. Conversely, he might suppose that the probabilities of correlation and anti-correlation for various alignments can be explained in terms of causal events and their properties; this would require those flavors to have probabilities of occurrence. Either of these equivalent starting points might be summed up as the hypothesis that the correlations in the end results are a result of probabilities with which initial events have causally relevant local properties. If a scientist says this and nothing more, it might seem that his very sparse hypothesis could be scorned as overly speculative, but could not be disproved, until the speculation is made more precise. This was the attitude toward hidden variables theories of most quantum physicists, until Bell developed the Einstein-Podolsky-Rosen thought-experiment into the abstract blueprint for the real experiments at Marseilles and elsewhere. It turns out, thanks to Bell's argument, that the sparse hypothesis can be tested. It is incompatible with the squared sine formula.

Suppose the polarizers are set up so that each can take one of three directions, the same three available for each. For any two directions, we can compute the probability that there will be spin up at both polarizers, when the left polarizer is pointed in one direction, the right in another. We can compute the probability using the squared sine formula, taken over from quantum physics. We can also state, if we accept the hidden property proposal, that these probabilities will be the sums of the probabilities of occurrence of flavors that: (a) create destinies for each photon to be up at its axis; (b) are permitted by the observed fact that spins with respect to parallel axes are always opposite. Flavors incompatible with b do not exist, and make no contribution to the total probabilities. The only relevant differences in kind between flavors are differences producing different spin destinies for some relevant alignment of axes. We can use a virtually transparent notation of Wigner's to label these kinds. To read $(+ - +; - + -)$ note that "$+$" means up, "$-$" down, to the left of the semi-colon means at the axis of a polarizer to the left, similarly for the right, and nth position after punctuation means nth direction. The formula just given describes a possible flavor. Most do not, since at some point there are destinies for identical polarization with respect to parallel axes.

The following equations identify two ways of determining the probability that spin is up at both polarizers, in the indicated alignment. In each case, the expression to the left of the equal sign sums probabilities for all permitted kinds of flavors producing spin up at both polarizers at the settings in question, while the right hand expression is the empirically correct formula, the one derived from the quantum theory of the spin zero state. If the prior event hypothesis is true, then all these equations are correct.

Left polarizer at 1, right at 2:
$$P(+ - +; - + -) + P(+ - -; - + +) = \tfrac{1}{2}\sin^2(A_{12}/2)$$
Left polarizer at 2, right at 3:
$$P(+ + -; - - +) + P(- + -; + - +) = \tfrac{1}{2}\sin^2(A_{23}/2)$$
Left polarizer at 1, right at 3:
$$P(+ + -; - - +) + P(+ - -; - + +) = \tfrac{1}{2}\sin^2(A_{13}/2)$$

Adding and subtracting in accordance with the equations, we get:

$$\tfrac{1}{2}\sin^2(A_{12}/2) + \tfrac{1}{2}\sin^2(A_{23}/2) - \tfrac{1}{2}\sin^2(A_{13}/2) =$$
$$P(+ - +; - + +) + P(- + -; + - +)$$

Since probabilities are not negative:

$$\tfrac{1}{2}\sin^2(A_{12}/2) + \tfrac{1}{2}\sin^2(A_{23}/2) \geqq \tfrac{1}{2}\sin^2(A_{13}/2)$$

This is a so-called "Bell inequality." If it is false, the prior events hypothesis (the flavors exist and have probabilities or, alternatively, the flavors explain correlations) is false. And the inequality certainly is false. Rely on the fact that $\sin 60° = \sqrt{3/4}$, $\sin 30° = 1/2$, to derive $1/2 \geqq 3/4$ from the inequality, for angles of $60°$, $60°$, and $120°$.

As Bell emphasized in his original article, the argument for the inequality requires the assumption that the spin-determining properties have probabilities that do not depend on the relative orientations of the polarizers.[67] Since the emission event precedes contact with the polarizers as actually oriented (they might even be aligned after photon departure), an event theorist must certainly say this. If he were not stuck with this invariance of probabilities, the above argument would not work, since the same Wigner probability term for different polarizer alignments would not have to stand for the same number in each equation. There would be no basis for the crucial subtraction. An instrumentalist would seize on the role of this invariance as indicating that the bad statistics depend on the false assumption that facts about spin can be asserted other than facts that a measurement set-up of a certain kind will produce spin measurements with certain probabilities. Independent of the existence of polarizers in specific alignments, there are no spin properties that photons have.

In the realist quantum physics that I have described, real properties of systems, described using distinctively quantum-physical means, are all that influences events within the systems. The mistake in the events hypothesis is the assumption that events and their separable properties are the causes of events; rather, properties of systems, typically superpositions irreducible to separable properties of parts, govern the course of events.

On this realist conception of the evolution of the system, there is a possibility for left up right down, and an equally probable possibility of left down right up, as dictated by the state description. Photons have no amplitude to change spin. So, if the photons happen to have certain spins at certain times, they always do, unless some relevant intervention changes a spin.

If a perfect polarizer is operating, then the amplitude for the transition, departure through the "up" channel given arrival with spin up, squares to 1. And spin up or spin down are exhaustive, mu-

[67] J. S. Bell, "On the Einstein-Podolsky-Rosen Paradox" (1964) in Wheeler and Zurek, eds., *Quantum Theory and Measurement*, pp. 404f., 407. Wigner's simplification of Bell's argument is in his "Interpretation of Quantum Mechanics" in ibid., pp. 291–94.

tually exclusive possibilities for arrival. So, if there is departure through the "up" channel at the right hand polarizer, the right hand photon was spin up. It follows that the left-hand photon is spin down with reflect to a parallel axis, since in that case there is no amplitude for right up, left up. This looks like influence that observation at the right exerts on polarization at the left. Really, though, it has nothing to do with observation. Since up and down with respect to an axis are always exhaustive and exclusive possibilities for a photon, the existence of the spin to the right entails the existence of the spin to the left, regardless of whether polarizers have been set up. Indeed, our knowledge of how polarizers operate dictates the irrelevance of observation. Variations in other laboratories of the Marseilles experiment use calcite crystals, naturally occurring polarizers. The observed processes are, then, the same as would occur if appropriately placed calcite crystals developed spontaneously, crystals so tiny that the human eye could not see them.[68]

It might seem that the entailment of a spin at the left by a spin at the right must be a case of action-at-a-distance. Whether this is true will, in fact, depend on which terms in the derivation of "left down" from "right up" correspond to causal agents. In the realist interpretation that I have proposed, only the state description does. The prohibition against action-at-a-distance was only meant to prohibit a particular kind of causal process, a process in which a change in properties of one part of a system instantaneously affects separable properties of a distant part. Properties are separable if a change in one does not, in itself, entail a change in the other. My jumping three inches off the ground does not, in itself, entail a change in the forces to which Venus is subject. My change of position can be specified completely and explicitly without reference to the forces on Venus. In classical gravitation theory, however, my position helps to determine the gravitational forces on Venus, instantaneously changing the forces when the position changes. So the prohibition against action-at-a-distance is violated. But the change in the center-

---

[68] If we are analyzing real polarizers, which are never perfectly reliable, Bohm's and Gottfried's analyses, emphasizing random interference of amplitudes, could be applied. They might be preferred, since they answer the question, "What happens inside the polarizers?" If such an analysis is adopted, there is a change in the state of the system when the right-hand photon passes through the right-hand polarizer, which entails a change in system properties involving the remote left-hand photon. However, as on the view that postulates perfect measurement, the process is in no way confined to measurements. And the subsequent arguments against the charge of action-at-a-distance are the same.

of-mass of the Earth-Miller system when I jump from the Earth's surface is a matter of direct entailment. A complete description of my change in location entails a change in the center of mass of the Earth-Miller system. So the prohibition is not violated. Similarly, if the laws of New York State are such that the failure of a bank on Long Island instantaneously produces a loss of value of a check in Montreal, there is no violation. A complete description of what the value of the check consists in would describe legally recognized means to redeem claims for the amount inscribed.

In the quantum realist analysis of the derivation of one spin from another, the only causal agent is a state that is only a state of the whole system. The system state gives rise to spin pairs, and can only give rise to some, not others. The corresponding probabilities are not caused by separable properties of events in parts of the system. So the prohibition against action-at-a-distance is not violated. Being spin up is a separable property of a photon, but causes nothing. Being a superposition of opposite spin possibilities with equal amplitudes of opposite sign is a causal property of the system, but not a conjunction of separable properties of parts of the system.

It has always been clear that the causal factors to which quantum physics refers must be characteristics of whole systems, and not conjunctions of separable properties of parts, if the state description is complete. For the state description assigns amplitudes to all possibilities in the system, and superposition prevents us from reducing those amplitudes to independent propensities of parts. In the zero total spin situation, assigning independent propensities for spin to each photon results in the falsehood that identical spins with respect to the same axis occur one-fourth of the time.

Outside of classical physics, there are many parallels to this state of affairs, one physical event's making the other more likely as a result of the physical situation in which they occur, but not as a result of a physical process connecting them. For example, relations between psychological events in a person's life often require no intervening psychological process. I hear your words and understand them, because I can understand spoken English, not because of a psychological process triggered by the hearing and leading to the understanding. In any case, this is an open possibility until special findings and theoretical arguments foreclose it. The inseparability of quantum causation, i.e., the impossibility of analyzing causal processes as due to a conjunction of independent facts about separate parts of a system, is non-classical, but not conceptually strange.

Indeed, it is a way of removing incoherence and arbitrariness in the descriptive scheme of classical physics.

Most people, perhaps all, who encounter Bell's argument wonder why a hypothesis as sparse as the bare speculation about prior events can only supply false statistics. This question can be meant in a number of ways, and it is important at least to sketch an answer to each. After all, it might turn out that the only falsehood in the false prior events hypothesis that can necessitate false statistics is the assumption that quantum physics refers to properties independent of the presence of a definite measurement arrangement.

The question of why false statistics must result could be just a matter of mathematics: taking the squared sine laws as given empirical relations, why can't mixtures of patterns of destinies be described that would produce these relations? Bell's general answer develops an idea from calculus. The empirically correct relation between the angle of the polarizers and the degree of correlation is a squared-sine curve. At the tops and bottoms, where a tangent would be horizontal, the effect on correlation of a small change in angle tends toward nothing. This is not true anywhere else. The pattern cannot be mimicked, even to an arbitrarily small approximation, by mixing patterns of destiny subject to the constraints of anti-correlation for parallels, equiprobability of each spin for a vertical polarizer. It is a nice exercise in instructive frustration to try to approximate the correct correlations, assigning probabilities to patterns of destiny while observing these rules. Three directions defining two sixty-degree angles are a relevant and simple case. As when a person who is too big struggles with clothes that are too small, improvements in the fit with the correct correlation at one alignment eventually produce a worsened fit elsewhere.

There is another, much more important version of the question, "Why can't event theory yield the quantum physical results?" It concerns the physics of the experiment, rather than the mathematics, the sine formulas as laws entailed by a theory, rather than as formulas that observations confirm. Why is it that quantum physics must give rise to different correlation laws from any event theory? This question singles out the most interesting stage in the argument for physicists, very few of whom doubted that quantum physics would be vindicated experimentally, once Bell established the conflict in entailments. It is also the important question for the argument about realism, the question as to where quantum physics disagrees in its basic view of physical processes from any events theory.

After all, the squared-sine laws are consequences, not basic principles of quantum physics.

The arguments producing the squared-sine laws begin by deriving transformation rules from considerations of symmetry and invariance that only apply to causation by system properties, and conclude by applying the transformation rules to superpositions. So the moral of Bell's argument ought to be that causation by the system properties described using state descriptions is not reducible to causation by properties of events, however hidden. While the standard arguments for the squared-sine law are too complex and presuppose too much to be reproduced here, a bare sketch of a few crucial steps should make it clear that the argument is unavoidably biased toward holism, but not toward instrumentalism.[69]

Much of the standard argument concerns the rule for changing the correct description of properties of a one-particle system when the coordinate axes are rotated. Suppose the system is spherically symmetrical, i.e., the propensities to which it gives rise, if not interfered with, are the same in all directions. Therefore, the argument begins, the absolute square of an amplitude of an eigenfunction cannot be changed by a rotation of axes. But suppose the system were to be opened up. Its effects on a larger system are to be considered, or another system interferes with it. A rotation of the spherically symmetrical system will not affect its internal propensities, but it will affect its orientation with respect to another, fixed system. As a consequence, the interference relations between the amplitude waves will be different, leading to different propensities for the joint system. A true description of the physical properties of a system should reflect such distinctions in causal potential. So the rotation of coordinate axes should make some difference to the description, even if the difference does not affect the absolute squares. For these constraints to be respected, the effect of the rotation must be to multiply the amplitude of each eigenfunction by a phase factor, $e^{id}$, which can be different for each eigenfunction. Applied to spin, such reasoning ultimately leads to principles such as this: a single photon, if certain to be spin up with respect to an axis, has an amplitude of $\cos(A/2)$ to be spin up with respect to an axis rotated

[69] It is reassuring that the leaders of the Marseilles team summarize their findings in ways that suggest such holistic morals, but have no suggestion of instrumentalism. See A. Aspect and P. Grangier, "Experiments on Einstein-Podolsky-Rosen-Type Correlations with Pairs of Visible Photons" in S. Kamefuchi, *Foundations of Quantum Mechanics in the Light of New Technology* (Tokyo, 1984), p. 217.

through angle A. (The transition to trigonometry is due to the marvel that $e^{ix} = \cos(x) + i \sin(x)$.)[70]

This argument would be nonsensical if applied to the task of transforming descriptions of events producing spherically symmetrical states. If a single event and the sequels it determines are spherically symmetrical, for example, are a nested series of spherical waves starting at the origin, then a rotation of coordinates should not affect the description at all. Of course, such an event could not be the pair-creation event postulated in the hidden-event theory. As particles in a zero-spin system, a photon pair propelled by a creation event must travel in a single straight line. Any spherical symmetry would be a matter of cumulative frequency, governed by propensities of occurrence of the creation events. Still, the latter propensities are supposed to be basic, not the result of squaring amplitudes whose evolution really governs future events; there will be no superposition if the system is opened up. So there is no reason to introduce phase factors into the transformation rule.

If events theory is correct, the empirical validity of the quantum-physical transformation rules is a kind of fluke. In their non-hidden properties, systems behave as if they were governed by the system properties that figure in the transformation argument, when really their behavior is the result of correlation-producing events. Could there be such a fluke? For a one-particle system, there could. The correlations for spin at various axes required by the quantum transformation rules can always be mimicked by assigning appropriate hidden flavors to the photon emissions in question.

Bell's argument concerns a two-particle system, and would not work, otherwise. However, not just any two-particle system will do. By assigning appropriate frequencies to flavors, one can mimic the consequences of combining the rotation rules for a single photon with the quantum-physical analysis of a system in which one photon is in an eigenstate for spin up along a given axis, the other is in an eigenstate for spin down along that axis. Similarly, there is a hidden-events approximation to the statistics that result from applying the transformation rules to a system that sometimes creates left eigenstate up, right eigenstate down, sometimes left eigenstate down, right eigenstate up (all with respect to a given axis), randomly going into some state or other that is bound to produce one or another kind of pair. Such a system would be a kind of random double catapult. In principle, a system of this kind could be created that pro-

---

[70] See *The Feynman Lectures, vol. 3*, chs. 6, 17, 18 for the real argument.

duces double catapultings that are always anti-correlated with respect to an axis vertical to the line of flight, with spin up and spin down occurring half the time with respect to the axis, in each half of the system. The right mixture of flavors in catapulting events could produce these statistics. Given the description of how the system works it would be a mystery if this were not so. Perhaps instrumentalism, even with its loss of explanatory power, would be worth the gain of avoiding such a mystery.

None of these two-particle systems obeys the squared-sine rule for correlation. None of them figures in Bell's argument. None of them is prepared in the laboratory at Marseilles. The only two-photon system with zero total spin is a superposition, with an amplitude of $\sqrt{1/2}$ for left up, right down and an amplitude of $-\sqrt{1/2}$ for left down, right up. The random double catapulter described at the end of the last paragraph would not be perfectly anti-correlated if the axes in question were swiveled but kept parallel. It would not be as a matter of empirical fact, and could not be as a matter of quantum theory. The quantum-physical laws of rotation transformation require that there be some left up, right up and left down, right down outcomes in these cases. Far from leading to the mysterious denial that deterministic properties of the catapultings cannot correspond to statistics for spin outcomes produced by the catapultings, quantum physics precludes the statistics for which this would be true. Nor would a superposition of $\sqrt{1/2}\,L_+R_- + \sqrt{1/2}\,L_-R_+$ give rise to statistics that no set of propensities of flavors could approximate. According to the quantum theory of spin, this state is not a total spin zero state. It does not lead to Bell's pattern of anti-correlations. That pattern depends on the minus sign between the terms in the relevant superposition, a sign whose presence only has physical significance if superpositions describe real properties. Events theories are inadequate because the relevant propensities are governed by system properties that are irreducible to separable properties—irreducible because they can only be described using superpositions. In the words of Bell's original article, there is no "separable predetermination."[71] As Aspect and Grangier, the leaders of the Marseilles team, put it, "[T]he conflict only arises when the quantum-mechanical calculations involve an interference between terms where each subsystem has a definite state."[72]

[71] "On the Einstein-Podolsky-Rosen Paradox," p. 407.

[72] "Experiments on Einstein-Podolsky-Rosen-Type Correlations with Pairs of Visible Photons," p. 217.

Everyone learns quantum physics after learning classical physics. Such is the power of this upbringing, that one is apt to be guided by the classical assumption of separability in imagining any physical process. One imagines how the process might be constructed, part by part, through the occurrence of separable events. Seen in this way, the apparatus that cascades calcium atoms at Marseilles is a random double catapult. More precisely, one might think that Aspect, Grangier and their co-workers used knowledge of calcium to produce devices governing spin in the same way as a more artificial device, a device giving an up spin (with respect to a given axis) to a photon at the right and giving a down spin to a photon at the left, or vice versa, and giving the photons opposite and equal impulses. However, a thought-experiment along these lines cannot create an analogue to the cascader at Marseilles. The cascader would be irrelevant to the experimenters' purposes, if it had such an analogue. And there is nothing mysterious about the device that prepares the cascades. It is constructed on the basis of knowledge of the distinctive energy properties of the total zero spin state, properties that lead, for instance, to distinctive spectroscopic lines. What happens in nature cannot always be constructed part by separable part. The classical assumption to the contrary was always a tenuous pretense, for all its power to influence our imaginings.

## QUANTUM PHYSICS AND MODERN ANTI-REALISM

I have been arguing that quantum physics really does refer to unobservables, for example, to electrons, photons and superpositions of their states. The argument is needed because the strict form of anti-realism associated with classical positivism is still alive in interpretations of quantum physics. People with no strong inclination to accept classical positivist arguments that theories in general can only refer to tendencies among observables think quantum physics must be so interpreted, or paradox will result. I have tried to show that quantum physics adds nothing new to the case for such anti-realism. The attraction to the anti-realist interpretation depends on the continuing influence of classical positivism—even among those who would like to reject it, indeed, even among those who have never heard of it.

There is also a milder, more modern anti-realism, according to which quantum physical descriptions refer to unobservables, but reason and evidence cannot dictate belief in the truth of those descriptions. The practice of inference and discovery in quantum physics makes this milder claim attractive. Quantum physics is a good example of a field in which the piecemeal and topic-specific image of reason is needed for a defense of realism, in the sense of the modern debate.

There have been many discoveries in the short history of modern quantum physics. Many arise in the following ways. The current repertoire of eigenstates is shown to permit the description of a kind of phenomenon that no one has taken to exist. Or certain phenomena are shown to be derivable if descriptions are extended, in a mathematically elegant way, to include objects that would seem impossible, on physical grounds (electrons with negative kinetic energy, for example). Or, as in much current nuclear physics, an aesthetically appealing descriptive scheme is set up, and a gap is perceived when known phenomena are fit into the scheme. In all of these cases, experimentalists look for evidence supporting the existence of the undiscovered component described in the more complete, more mathematically perspicuous or more aesthetic repertoire of means of description. Often, they have found what they are looking for.

Of course, this is just the story of some successes. In physics as in everyday life, it is one thing to have elegant dreams, another thing to bring them to fruition. The strategy of filling gaps in a formally appealing extension of current physics does not always succeed. Moreover, considerations of physical plausibility and the effort to maintain consistency with relativity theory have led to successes, too. Still, a preference for pretty formalisms has contributed as much to successful prediction and control as any other method.

As for the inferences depending on belief in theories as opposed to mere acceptance of them—for example, appeals to intra-theoretical plausibility or to requirements of inter-theoretic consistency—these theory-dependent methods have blocked progress about as often as they have contributed to it. Indeed, inferences of this kind have favored virtually all the hypotheses that were, for a time, barriers to instrumental reliability and control, for example: quantum wave-equations describe effects of fluctuations in fields; spin is intrinsic angular momentum; the representability of electrons with negative kinetic energy is a mere notational possibility in the formalism; quantum electrodynamics must be deeply misguided since renormalization cannot be a correction for a real physical process. In all of these cases, a preference for pretty mathematics led to a more reliable theory than a commitment to the truth of current basic theories. So quantum physics is quite unpromising territory for the realist strategy that appeals to the enormous contribution of theory-dependent methods.

Perhaps no entities first posited in the era of modern quantum physics, dating it from Heisenberg's presentation of quantum mechanics, has the special status demanded by modern realism. Still, quantum physicists have distinctive things to say about entities from an earlier era. Much of what they say concerns molecules and atoms. Stern and Gerlach put silver atoms, not pions, through the magnet. Most of the rest of what physicists say with confidence concerns electrons. And such phenomena as Millikan's oil-drop experiment have a similar status here to the Brownian motion studies. The arguments for molecules, atoms, probably electrons and, possibly, photons (but not so-called virtual photons) occur against a background of topic-specific truisms, creating a need for explanation that it would be unreasonable to deny and making in unreasonable not to accept the standard explanation as likely to be true. By way of contrast, physicists also have a quantum theory of sound whose unit is a phonon and a quantum theory of radiation making much use of so-called virtual photons. The universal belief in phonons may simply reflect a universal preference for the employment of field theories in the study of periodicity, a preference which is not unreasonable, which leads to success after success, but which a reasonable person might take to be no more than a matter of convenience in representation.[73] Similarly "virtual" photon exchanges are sometimes posited in schemes for deriving amplitudes for transitions, even though a photon with the properties required could not be part of an event with non-zero probability, according to current theory. This tactic creates enormous simplifications. But, again, there is as yet no non-pragmatic argument for altering current theory to admit such photons. That is why they are labelled "virtual," as opposed to "real."[74] In sum, when all physicists refer to a kind of micro-entity, agnosticism about actual existence sometimes is, and sometimes is not, a reasonable option.

It might seem that cloud chambers are, epistemologically, extensions of Leeuwenhoek's microscope, permitting secure inferences from the visible to the invisibly small. This is true, in a way. Physicists can use cloud chambers to establish that something that ionizes is behaving in ways that are unexpected unless some new proposal

---

[73] See Feynman and Hibbs, *Quantum Mechanics and Path Integrals*, pp. 229–31.
[74] See Feynman, *QED*, pp. 95, 120.

is adopted. But the positing of a new fundamental particle says much more than that an ionization sequence is taking an unexpected course. This something more does not seem supported, beyond reasonable dissent, by current arguments for most quantum posits.

Of course, the distinctive claim of modern quantum physics is not that electrons exist, which was known before, but that superpositions of electron states exist. The reality of such superpositions is established, in part, by showing that phenomena of interference cannot be accepted without generating paradoxes, unless superpositions are real. Indeed, despite Heisenberg's positivist prejudices, the role of quantum mechanics from the start was to remove paradoxes in causal explanations, not, primarily, to predict. Quantum mechanics for many years added little in the way of predictions, and gave rise to many false predictions. It was justified, and widely accepted from the start, because it removed the notorious paradoxes of the old quantum theory. For example, the electron in the Saturnine atom of that theory should have radiated energy as it revolved, very quickly dropping into the nucleus. If he had been instrumentalist in practice, Heisenberg would never have developed quantum physics. He would have remained loyal to the old theory as a wonderfully useful way of summarizing diverse empirical regularities and predicting new ones. The cumbersome, artificial mathematics of the new theory, and the false empirical expectations to which it often gave rise, would have filled him with revulsion, and reasonably so, if, by chance, he had thought of this strange scheme.

## FAREWELL

This account of quantum reality is incomplete, even given the qualitative character of most of the physics. For example, I have said nothing in any detail about the relation of truths about ordinary middle-sized objects to truths about micro-events framed in the distinctive language of quantum physics. These gaps cannot be filled by any straightforward extrapolation from the general principles of this book. The general principles are a guide, but the details of the physics matter.

I apologize for the gaps, though this book is long enough with them. But the need for novel insights based on the details of the field is, I think, a virtue. Though the classical positivists admired science, sometimes even made it their shrine, they thought that general lessons extracted from any science could, in principle, yield enough philosophical insight to answer basic questions of what explains, what is justified and what exists, posed about any other science, given its hypotheses and the data. Once the initial lessons were extracted, often in brilliant discussions of theoretical physics, the discussions of problems of particular sciences became more and more predictable. In fact, one science cannot provide a methodology for all. Yet there is such a thing as a methodological problem. Discovery and debate in every field give rise to obstacles, confusions and tempting false inferences that philosophical reflection can remove. There are even valid inferences to positive conclusions that philosophical reflection can reveal, by shedding extra light on field-specific achievements. There will be a need for philosophical creativity about science so long as there are new scientific discoveries.

LIBRARY OF CONGRESS CATALOGING-IN-PUBLICATION DATA

Miller, Richard W., 1945–
  Fact and method.

  Includes index.
  1. Science—Philosophy. 2. Causation. 3. Realism.
4. Positivism. I. Title.
B67.M53 1987    121     87–45527
ISBN 0–691–07318–X (alk. paper)
ISBN 0–691–02045–0 (alk. paper : pbk.)